HR

DENISI | GRIFFIN

CENGAGE
Learning™

Australia • Brazil • Japan • Korea • Mexico • Singapore • Spain • United Kingdom • United States

HR

HR, 1st Edition
DeNisi | Griffin

Executive Editors:
Maureen Staudt
Michael Stranz

Senior Project Development Manager:
Linda deStefano

Marketing Specialist:
Courtney Sheldon

Senior Production/Manufacturing Manager:
Donna M. Brown

PreMedia Manager:
Joel Brennecke

Sr. Rights Acquisition Account Manager:
Todd Osborne

Cover Image:
Getty Images*

*Unless otherwise noted, all cover images used by Custom
Solutions, a part of Cengage Learning, have been supplied
courtesy of Getty Images with the exception of the Earthview
cover image, which has been supplied by the National
Aeronautics and Space Administration (NASA).

For product information and technology assistance, contact us at
Cengage Learning Customer & Sales Support, 1-800-354-9706

For permission to use material from this text or product,
submit all requests online at **cengage.com/permissions**
Further permissions questions can be emailed to
permissionrequest@cengage.com

This book contains select works from existing Cengage Learning resources and
was produced by Cengage Learning Custom Solutions for collegiate use. As such,
those adopting and/or contributing to this work are responsible for editorial
content accuracy, continuity and completeness.

Compilation © 2011 Cengage Learning
ISBN-13: 978-1-133-22899-8

ISBN-10: 1-133-22899-2

Cengage Learning
5191 Natorp Boulevard
Mason, Ohio 45040
USA
Cengage Learning is a leading provider of customized learning solutions with
office locations around the globe, including Singapore, the United Kingdom,
Australia, Mexico, Brazil, and Japan. Locate your local office at:
international.cengage.com/region.

Cengage Learning products are represented in Canada by Nelson Education, Ltd.

For your lifelong learning solutions, visit **www.cengage.com/custom.**
Visit our corporate website at **www.cengage.com.**

Printed in the United States of America

BRIEF Contents

© Andresr/Shutterstock

Contents

© Lukiyanova Natalia/frenta/Shutterstock

THE Nature OF Human RESOURCE Management

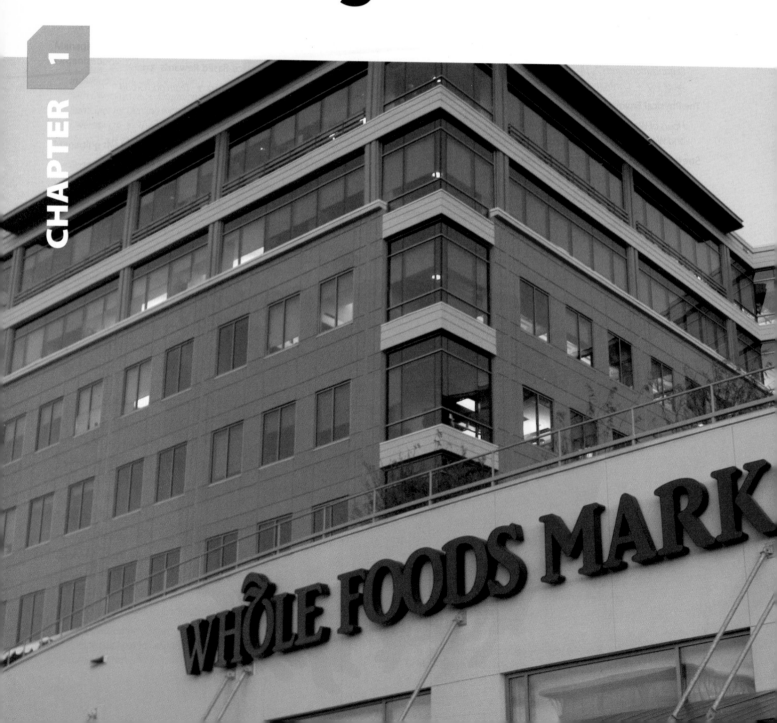

THEIR MOST PRECIOUS RESOURCE . . .

Southwest Airlines, Whole Foods, The Container Store, and Google compete in different industries, and in unrelated markets, use different resources, provide different products, and have different organization structures from one another. But they also have a few key things in common: They are consistently successful in virtually everything they do; they are consistently profitable, regardless of economic forces; and they are almost universally admired for how they conduct business.

Underlying all of these achievements is a common theme: Each company invests heavily in attracting the best employees and then works diligently to make those employees feel valued and appreciated. As a result, these firms have become employers of choice in their respective industries, and each has a dedicated and highly motivated workforce. Each one has developed a unique

relationship with its employees that provide it with a rare and valuable set of resources that its competitors cannot easily duplicate or sustain.

This doesn't mean that these and other successful companies all do the same thing. Indeed, each firm has developed a unique culture in which employees feel valued and reciprocate by doing whatever it takes for the firm to be successful. This is not something that can be purchased or easily replicated, and it is the reason why Southwest was the only U.S. airline to consistently show a profit in the aftermath of September 11 and during the surge in fuel costs in 2005 and 2006. It's also why Whole Foods continues to grow at a rate exceeding 10 percent annually, even in the midst of a global financial crisis, why The Container Store consistently posts above industry-average

" We hit upon the philosophy that I think will be the dominant philosophy in business in the twenty-first century. It's this principle that the purpose of business is not primarily to maximize shareholder value. "

—John Mackey, founder and chief executive officer (CEO) of Whole Foods[1]

LEARNING OBJECTIVES
After studying this chapter, you should be able to:

LO1 *Describe contemporary human resource perspectives*

LO2 *Trace the evolution of the human resource function in organizations*

LO3 *Identify and discuss the goals of human resource management*

LO4 *Discuss the setting for human resource management*

LO5 *Describe the job of human resource managers from the perspectives of professionalism and careers*

that other strategic decisions significantly affect the firm's human resources as well.

It was only natural, therefore, that human resource management would eventually be elevated to the same level of importance and status as other major functional areas of the firm.[8] The top HR executive at most companies today has the status of vice president or executive vice president and is a fully contributing member of the firm's executive committee, the body composed of key top managers that makes major policy decisions and sets corporate strategy. Today, most firms use a term such as *human resource management* to reflect more accurately the sophistication and maturity of the function. But some people argue that even this term is outdated and does not do justice to the role the HR manager plays. Instead, some organizations have moved toward using more specialized terminology that fits their corporate culture more closely. The top human resource executive at Southwest Airlines, for example, has the title of Vice President for People, while other firms, recognizing the importance of human resources as knowledge resources, have started using titles such as chief knowledge officer. To keep things simple, though, we will use the human resource management terminology throughout this book.

Many aspects of the modern HRM function actually date back to the 1980s and 1990s. It became apparent to many firms then that they were not able to compete effectively in the global marketplace. Some of these firms went out of business, and employees lost their jobs. Some firms were acquired by other, more successful companies, and in the aftermath many employees of the acquired firm were seen as redundant and let go. Still other firms sought mergers with former or potential competitors in the hope of forming a new joint enterprise that could compete successfully. But again, in most cases, merged companies often did not find the same need for as many employees, and many workers lost their jobs.

Instead of simply managing the layoffs following a merger or acquisition, HR executives were part of the team deciding which firms to merge with or to acquire outright. HR managers could help identify the critical human resources that the firm would need in the future, and they could also help identify other firms that might already have those

resources and thus be prime targets for takeovers or mergers. As knowledge became more critical in gaining competitive advantage, HR managers helped define strategies to acquire or develop knowledge resources. They also developed strategies for ensuring that any knowledge acquired was fully dispersed throughout the organization. As firms compete more broadly on a global basis, these factors become even more critical as firms try to integrate work processes and employees from diverse cultures around the world.

At the same time, though, that human resource managers were taking on a more strategic role, many organizations began shrinking the more traditional roles played by HR managers. As these organizations looked for new ways to be competitive by reducing costs, they often looked for activities within the company that could be done more efficiently by outsiders. For example, it became common for a company to eliminate cleaning and maintenance units and contract with an outside cleaning firm that could perform the tasks more efficiently.

This trend has spread to other areas as well. Today, many large organizations hire outside firms to handle payroll, insurance and benefits, and even recruitment and selection in some cases.[9] This practice, commonly known as **outsourcing**, has resulted in smaller HR staffs within companies and more reliance on outside consultants to provide the services once provided by those staffs. Thus, although the importance of HRM activities is growing, the importance of HR departments may be shrinking, and the kind of work performed by human resource managers is certainly changing as the size of the human resource function is shrinking.

Outsourcing can indeed be an important competitive weapon for organizations. If done properly, outsourcing results in more efficient operations. Outside are hired benefit from the fact firms that they perform the same tasks for many companies. Also, outsourcing tends to eliminate jobs that tend to be more repetitious and perhaps dull. As a result, the employees who work on these jobs are more likely to be dissatisfied at work, which can have tremendous cost for the firms. But not all functions can be outsourced for competitive advantage. Thus, it is critical that a firm retain any function that is either of strategic importance in its own right (i.e., strategic

MODERN BRICK–LAYING IN CHICAGO.

This cartoon, more than 100 years old, depicts how some critics of scientific management thought that labor might use Taylor's time-and-motion study ideas against management.

planning) or can lead to some advantage because the firm is especially expert at this function (e.g., selection or training). Therefore, the issue for most firms today is not whether to outsource but what to outsource and what to keep in-house.

In addition, the legal imperatives that in large part elevated the importance of the HRM function are changing and becoming more complex. In what has been termed a post–affirmative action world, issues regarding differential test performance of members of different ethnic and racial groups, especially in high-stakes situations (where jobs or entrance into academic institutions are involved), are becoming more rather than less complex. How do we address differences in test scores in a society where credentialing and accountability are becoming more important, and when we still haven't figured out how to deal with the diversity our society presents us?[10]

Furthermore, since September 11, 2001, employers and employees need to deal with entirely new challenges.[11] Questions of security have become more important. For example, issues related to how to select, train, and motivate airport security personnel, who are the first line of defense against terrorism, fall squarely under the purview of human resource management. Following Hurricanes Katrina and Rita and the devastating effects they had on the Gulf Coast of the United States, firms are becoming much more concerned about the security of their data (such as employee records), as well as their buildings and equipment, and how to protect them from natural disasters. Those hurricanes also demonstrated how important it is to have evacuation plans for employees and contingency plans for how to conduct business if a firm's buildings are destroyed or inaccessible. Yet, at the same time, organizations must find a balance between these different types of security needs and recognizing the rights and privileges of

all employees and not engaging in stereotyping or illegal profiling.

Before moving on to a more detailed discussion of the tasks and functions of modern human resource management, it is useful to consider how we arrived where we are today. The struggle of human resource management for legitimacy within the organization, and how that legitimacy came about, is due in large part to the history of how human resource management developed.

EVOLUTION OF THE HUMAN RESOURCE FUNCTION

Even though businesses have existed for thousands of years, the practice of management itself has only been of special interest and concern for about 100 years.[12] Many early businesses were small enterprises and farms run by families interested only in supporting themselves and providing security for family members. The Industrial Revolution of the eighteenth century, however, sparked a greater interest in business growth and expansion, and large-scale business operations began to emerge throughout Europe and the United States. As these businesses grew and became increasingly complex, owners began to step aside and turn the operation of their firms over to full-time professional managers. Owners who remained in control of their businesses still needed to rely on managers to oversee a portion of their operations. This transition, in turn, resulted in greater awareness of the various functions of management that were necessary for long-term organizational success.[13]

A few early management pioneers and writers such as Robert Owen, Mary Parker Follette, and Hugo Munsterberg recognized the importance of people in organizations, but the

the military and its major suppliers became interested in better matching people with jobs. They wanted to optimize the fit between the demands and requirements of the jobs that needed to be performed and the skills and interests of people available to perform them. Psychologists were consulted to help develop selection tests, for example, to assess individual skills, interests, and abilities more accurately. During the 1950s, the lessons learned during the war were adapted for use in private industry. New and more sophisticated techniques were developed, especially in the area of testing, and companies also began to experiment with more sophisticated reward and incentive systems. Labor unions became more powerful and demanded a broader array of benefits for their members. In addition, government legislation expanded and continued to add complexity to the job of the personnel manager.

Still, from the first days of its inception until the 1970s, personnel management was not seen as a particularly important or critical function in most business organizations. Although other managers accepted personnel as a necessary vehicle for hiring new operating employees, personnel management was also seen primarily as a routine clerical and bookkeeping function. For example, personnel was responsible for placing newspaper ads to recruit new employees, filling out paperwork for those employees after they were hired, and seeing that everyone was paid on time.

While other organizational units like marketing, finance, and operations grew in status and importance, the personnel department of most organizations was generally relegated to the status of necessary evil that had to be tolerated but that presumably contributed little to the success of the organization. Its offices were often drab and poorly equipped and were often located away from the central activity areas of the organization. And personnel managers themselves were often stereotyped as individuals who could not succeed in other functional areas and were assigned to personnel either because the organization had nothing else for them to do or as a signal that the individual was not deemed to be a candidate for promotion to a higher-ranking position.

1964 act, combined with several subsequent amendments, executive orders, and legal decisions, made the processes of hiring and promoting employees within the organization far more complex. Thus, it quickly became critically important to organizations that those responsible for hiring and promoting employees fully understand the legal context within which they functioned. For example, ethical and moral issues aside, improper or inappropriate hiring practices left the organization open to lawsuits and other legal sanctions, accompanied by large fines, judgments, and new expenses. (We discuss the 1964 Civil Rights Act and related regulation more fully in the next chapter.)

But, as we noted earlier, the HR manager's role as a compliance officer has grown into the role of strategic partner, and this is the role we stress in this book. As firms continue to recognize the importance of human resources, they must do more than just obey the laws. Firms are increasingly competing to attract and retain the best talent they can and then to develop strategies or tactics that leverage those talented people into a competitive advantage. At the same time, however, HR management is changing in response to new technological innovations, so we must consider how the electronic age has affected the HRM function.

HUMAN RESOURCE MANAGEMENT IN THE ELECTRONIC AGE

Through the years, as social and market dynamics changed, dramatic changes in technology also affected how we manage human resources. Some of these changes were related to the technologies available for measurement, although new technologies such as television, videotaping, and facsimile machines were also important in the development of the HRM function. In recent years, however, the popularity of the Internet has profoundly affected the HRM function, and those effects are still developing and growing.

The widespread use of electronic technology and the Internet has had a major effect on the delivery of HRM systems.

As noted earlier, the first real impetus for the increased importance for the role of human resource management came with the passage in 1964 of the Civil Rights Act. This law made it illegal for employers to consider factors such as gender, religion, race, skin color, or national origin when making employment-related decisions. The

The widespread use of electronic technology and the Internet has not drastically affected the basic approach to how we manage human resources, but it has certainly had a major effect on how HRM systems are delivered. For example, in Chapter 5 we discuss methods for conducting job analysis, but we also note that the new O*NET system may allow many organizations to obtain the job-analysis information they need from an online database. Chapter 7 discusses issues of recruiting, but one of the more popular ways for job seekers to search for jobs is by accessing one of the many job-search Web sites (such as Monster.com). As a result, most organizations now realize they must post job openings online in addition to using more traditional methods. Our examination of selection techniques in Chapter 7 also includes discussion of online testing and other ways in which the Internet has changed how organizations select employees. Training programs can now be purchased from vendors and provided to employees online, allowing them to take classes and training programs on their own schedule. Information systems, including information on benefits, make it easier for employees to check their benefit coverage and change it if desired.

Have these new applications of technology made human resource management easier? Clearly, management can now easily deliver information and communicate with employees, but the openness of communication also means that employees can communicate with management, and this presents new challenges to managers. Electronic systems for communication and monitoring also bring up new challenges for the legal system (discussed in Chapter 2) and have led to new discussions about ethics and privacy. Thus, the new technology has made human resource management easier in some ways but more complicated in others. Have these new applications of technology made the management of human

KNOWLEDGE

resources more effective? This question is important, but little data has addressed it. Nonetheless, we will discuss the opportunities and challenges presented by new technology and the Internet throughout the book.

One other way in which technology has affected the HRM function needs to be mentioned. As organizations introduced new technologies for manufacturing, communication, and human resource management, they also increased their need for more specialized employees. **Knowledge workers** are employees whose jobs are to acquire and apply knowledge, and they contribute to the organization by the nature of what they know and how well they can apply what they know. Although knowledge workers include more than workers who deal with computer technology (scientists and lawyers, for example, are usually considered knowledge workers), the explosion of technology at work has led to a huge increase in the need for workers who can learn and apply the management of this technology. These employees present special problems for recruitment, retention, and compensation, as well as for motivation; we will discuss these challenges throughout the book.

EMERGING HUMAN RESOURCE CHALLENGES

Like all managers, human resource executives continue to face an array of new challenges on a regular basis. For instance, the economic recession that swept the world in 2008–09, created havoc in most businesses. Major financial institutions around the world learned that they held "toxic assets" such as "subprime mortgages" that had little actual value in the market. As these firms were forced to "mark to market" (i.e., state the true market value of these assets), they discovered that they were in serious financial straits. Major banks and financial institutions around the world failed. In the government tions such billions Motors In vir- United States, the federal took control of corpora- as Citicorp and provided of dollars to help General regain financial solvency. tually every case, many more people lost their jobs through cost-cutting procedures or as the result of mergers or takeovers.

All of these developments have profoundly affected the HRM function. In most case, it is the job of the HRM department to determine how and when layoffs take place. This is not a pleasant part of anyone's job, and considerable pain was inflicted on families as a result of these decisions (we will discuss these issues in more detail in Chapter 5). When firms go out of business, the HRM department is usually charged with making sure that applications for unemployment were filed and that employees received due notice of closings. When a merger or acquisition takes place, the HR manager plays a critical role in integrating the two workforces and workplace cultures, and it will be HR managers who will take the lead in addressing a projected future shortage of workers.

Stress is becoming a major factor in people's lives.

Stress is also becoming a major factor in people's lives. There is stress over the economy, keeping one's job, and making mortgage payments, as well as the stress of terrorist threats to our military abroad (as well as to individual travelers). Stress at work is simply one more factor that adds to our growing overall discomfort. Unfortunately, overall stress affects the ways in which people

Knowledge workers *are employees whose jobs are primarily concerned with the acquisition and application of knowledge, and they contribute to an organization through what they know and how they can apply what they know.*

behave at work, so the management of stress—both on the job and outside of work as it manifests itself on the job—has become an important part of the HR manager's role.

These stressors, combined with general uncertainty from the impact of the recent financial crisis, have also resulted in declines in employee morale. Job security is threatened as corporate profits shrink and yet, at the same time, many employees not only see huge bonuses paid to bankers whose banks failed but also see crooked investors such as Bernie Madoff stealing people's retirement funds. There is a lot going on to demoralize an employee, and yet the HR manager must find ways to actually motivate that employee to work harder and exert even more effort on the behalf of the firm.

In addition, all of this is taking place in an atmosphere of repeated calls for greater corporate oversight. We will

within offices to designing buildings that blend in with the environment and designing workplaces and buildings that can offset the carbon emissions of doing business. Some of the electronic innovations for managing human resources are integral to these efforts, but they extend to videoconferencing to replace face-to-face meetings and setting up work schedules so that employees use less fuel commuting to and from work.

This trend differs from the corporate social responsibility trend because it is seen as a way to enhance profitability rather than as a competing goal. Evidence suggests that employees in so-called green workspaces tend to be more satisfied and are healthier and more productive. Thus, green management is becoming yet another element of challenge for modern human resource managers.

Going green can mean anything from paperless offices to videoconferencing.

touch on some issues relating to corporate governance in the next chapter, but it is conceivable that, under the Obama administration, we may see strong pushes to increase corporate accountability in ways that may affect the entire corporate governance model. Recent court cases also have raised serious questions about the selection methods typically used (discussed in more detail in Chapter 7), while President Obama has already begun to make his mark on the Supreme Court with the nomination and elevation of federal Judge Sonia Sotomayor. It is likely that as the president makes other appointments, the nature of the Court will change and there may be an increased concern over civil rights issues. Finally, as the full implications of the new health-care legislation become clear, organizations will have to rethink their benefits programs in the coming years.

Many organizations are also concerned about the effects their business has on the environment. "Going Green" can range from anything such as paperless communications

All of these changes mean that the job of the HR manager will continue to evolve. The role of these managers will continue to expand, and they will have to gain expertise in wider and wider sets of skills than ever before. We will discuss the effects of some of these changes throughout the book, but in a few years we will certainly have to revise our view of the human resource manager as the job continues to evolve to deal with other changes in the world.

GOALS OF HUMAN RESOURCE MANAGEMENT

This modern view of human resource management has also meant that these departments have taken on increasingly important goals. Understanding the goals of HRM not

EXHIBIT 1.1 Goals of Human Resource Management

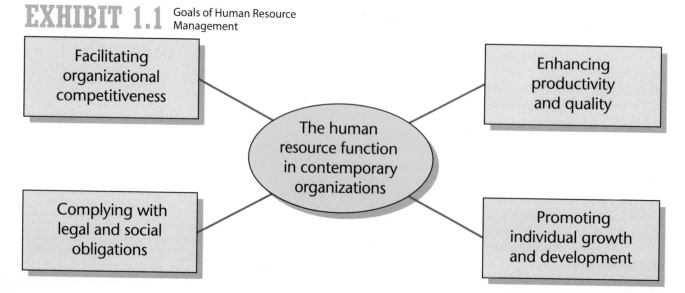

only helps us put human resource management in proper perspective but also provides a framework for evaluating any activities carried out by this area.[22] Exhibit 1.1 illustrates the four basic goals of the human resource management function in most organizations today.

FACILITATING ORGANIZATIONAL COMPETITIVENESS

All organizations have a general set of goals and objectives that they try to accomplish. Regardless of the time horizon or the level of specificity involved in these goals, they are generally intended to promote the organization's ability to be competitive in fulfilling its purpose or mission. For example, business organizations such as Microsoft, Walmart, Nestlé, and Toyota exist primarily to make profits for their owners. Thus, their goals and objectives usually deal with sales or revenue growth, market share, profitability, return on investment, and so forth. Other organizations exist for different purposes and thus have goals other than increased profitability. Educational organizations such as Ohio State University, Houston Community College, and the St. Louis Independent School District have their unique purposes. The same can be said for health-care organizations such as the Mayo Clinic, governmental organizations such as the U.S. Federal Bureau of Investigation (FBI) and the state of Missouri's revenue department, and charitable organizations such as the United Way.

People often associate competitiveness only with businesses, but each of these other types of organizations also must be managed effectively and compete for the right to continue to work

toward fulfillment of its purpose. For example, a state university that misuses its resources and does not provide an adequate education for its students will not be held in high regard. As a result, the university will have difficulty competing for high-quality faculty and students, which are needed to enhance the university's reputation and thus make it more competitive. Similarly, a hospital that does not provide technical support for its doctors or adequate health care for its patients will find it more difficult to compete for the doctors and patients who might use and pay for its services.

Given the central role that human resources play in organizational effectiveness, it is clear that the organization needs to employ those individuals most able to help it accomplish its goals and remain competitive. The HRM function in any organization must therefore have as one of its basic goals a clear understanding of how the organization competes, the kinds of human resources necessary to promote its ability to compete, and the most appropriate methods for attracting and developing those human resources.[23] This goal relates clearly to the strategic perspective developed more fully in Chapter 4.

Facilitating organizational competitiveness must be the most important goal for modern human resource management. This is the goal that sets the modern function apart even from the HRM function of 20 years ago. It is also the way in which the HRM function provides the most value to the organization. Of course, the second goal we will discuss also contributes to this goal of competitiveness.

> **"Quality in a product or service is not what the supplier puts in. It is what the customer gets out and is willing to pay for. A product is not quality because it is hard to make and costs a lot of money, as manufacturers typically believe. This is incompetence. Customers pay only for what is of use to them and gives them value. Nothing else constitutes quality."**
>
> —HENRY FORD
> American educator and writer (1909–2005)

ENHANCING PRODUCTIVITY AND QUALITY

A related but somewhat narrower concern for most organizations in the world today involves the issues, hurdles, and opportunities posed by productivity and quality. **Productivity** is an economic measure of efficiency that summarizes and reflects the value of the outputs created by an individual, organization, industry, or economic system relative to the value of the inputs used to create them.[24] **Quality** is the total set of features and characteristics of a product or service that bears on its ability to satisfy stated or implied needs.[25] In earlier times, many managers saw productivity and quality as being inversely related; the best way to be more productive was to lower quality and therefore costs. Most managers today realize that productivity and quality usually go hand in hand—that is, improving quality almost always increases productivity.

Organizations around the world have come to recognize the importance of productivity and quality for their ability not only to compete but also to survive. Actually improving productivity and quality, however, takes a major and comprehensive approach that relies heavily on human resource management. Among other things, an organization that is serious about productivity and quality may need to alter its selection system to hire different kinds of workers. It will definitely need to invest more in training and development to give workers the necessary skills and abilities to create high-quality products and services, and it will need to use new and different types of rewards to help maintain motivation and effort among its employees. Thus, in most organizations, HRM also has the goal of helping to enhance productivity and quality through different activities and tasks.

Complying with Legal and Social Obligations

A third fundamental goal of the human resource management function today is to ensure that the organization is complying with and meeting its legal and social obligations. We noted earlier the impact of the 1964 Civil Rights Act and other regulations on hiring and other related human resource management practices and activities. More recently, the Americans with Disabilities Act has also had a major impact on HRM. Clearly, organizations must stay within the relevant legal boundaries whenever they deal with their employees.

> ## "Take our twenty best people away, and I will tell you that Microsoft would become an unimportant company."
> —BILL GATES, CEO of Microsoft, *Fortune*

An organization that does not comply with government regulations and various legal constraints risks huge financial penalties as well as considerable negative publicity and damage to its own internal corporate culture.

The near financial collapse of 2008, however, added a new wrinkle to the relationship between the government and the human resource function. As Barack Obama assumed the presidency of the United States, major U.S. businesses such as General Motors, Chrysler, AIG, and Citicorp were clearly at risk of total collapse and bankruptcy. Major investment firms such as Lehman Brothers ceased to exist, and there was a real concern that major banks such as J.P. Morgan Stanley and financial firms such as Merrill-Lynch would soon disappear as well if the federal government did not act. The government thus intervened with a financial support package worth hundreds of billions of dollars. As part of this support, the government became a major stockholder in many of these firms. Thus, the government was no longer just an interested third party observing and regulating some aspects of business, it was also now a real owner of major corporations. As a result, the government exercised

> ## Increasing numbers of organizations today are assuming some degree of social obligation and being good contributing citizens.

its influence over companies that accepted federal dollars by limiting salaries and bonuses paid to top executives.[26] It is not clear how long the U.S. government will play this role or to what extent it will exercise the power it has, but it will be interesting to see exactly how important this becomes for the HRM function.

Beyond the strict legal parameters of compliance, however, more and more organizations today are also assuming at least some degree of social obligation to the society in which they operate. This obligation extends beyond the minimum activities necessary to comply with legal regulations and calls for the organization to serve as a contributing "citizen." Such efforts might include outreach programs

Productivity *is an economic measure of efficiency that summarizes and reflects the value of the outputs created by an individual, organization, industry, or economic system relative to the value of the inputs used to create them.*

Quality *is the total set of features and characteristics of a product or service that bears on its ability to satisfy stated or implied needs.*

to help attract individuals—often from minority populations—who may lack the basic skills necessary to perform meaningful jobs, or it might even mean the divestiture of holdings in countries with poor records on human rights. These activities are becoming increasingly important as financial-management firms offer investment funds that specialize in socially responsible organizations, and corporate social performance (CSP) is often considered another dimension of organizational performance.

Whole Foods Markets views CSP as an old-fashioned way of discussing these issues. The argument is that usually some department is set up to deal with social responsibility and that this is always weighed against profitability. Whole Foods' goal is to make the world a better place. Under such a banner, doing good around the world is not just a function of some manager but the imperative for the entire organization. This includes establishing a charitable foundation for helping countries where Whole Foods does business, as well as initiatives established by the managers and employees at each market. As a result, Whole Foods attracts like-minded employees, and this has led to a rather unique corporate culture.

Promoting Individual Growth and Development

Finally, a fourth goal for human resource management in most contemporary organizations is promoting the personal growth and development of its employees.[27] As a starting point, this goal usually includes basic job-related training and development activities. But in more and more organizations, it is increasingly going far beyond basic skills training. Some firms, for example, now offer basic educational courses in English, math, and science for their employees. Many organizations also include some provision

> **Some organizations are providing employees with programs that help them cope with the anxieties and tensions of modern life.**

for career development—helping people understand what career opportunities are available to them and how to pursue those opportunities. Formal mentoring programs are also commonly being used to help prepare women and minorities for advancement in the organization.[28]

Individual growth and development may also focus on areas that do not relate directly to job responsibilities. For example, some organizations provide stress-management programs to help their employees better cope with the anxieties and tensions of modern life. Wellness and fitness programs are also becoming more common as organizations seek new and different ways to help their employees remain physically, mentally, and emotionally fit and better prepared to manage their lives and careers. Still another common area for continuing education is personal financial planning, which may even include assistance in writing a will or retirement planning.

Organizations, however, are viewing this goal much more broadly. For many, it means that the firm should do everything it can to ensure that employees are personally fulfilled on the job. This may involve designing jobs that are more challenging and provide more personal satisfaction (see more in Chapter 14), or it may involve providing employees opportunities to be more creative at work (see Chapter 13). In general, more firms are seeing human resource management as part of the psychological contract that they have with employees: Provide a personally rewarding work experience in return for the employees' working toward the firm's strategic goals. A **psychological contract** is the overall set of expectancies held by the employee with regard to what he or she will contribute to the organization and held by the organization with regard to what it will provide to the individual in return. These firms know that they will get the most out of employees as sources of competitive advantage when the employees feel that their work experience is meaningful and helps them meet their potential. It is worth noting that this has largely come full circle to the early days of human resource management and the human relations movement.

THE SETTING FOR HUMAN RESOURCE MANAGEMENT

Another important factor to consider in the modern view of human resource management is the setting in which the human resource manager operates. Traditionally, all HR activities resided in a separate department, but this model is becoming rare. Instead, HR activities are carried out by both line and staff managers. Furthermore, we are seeing differences in the way human resource management operates in larger versus smaller companies. We will explore some of these different settings.

Human Resource Management as a Staff Versus Line Function

Organizations historically divided their managers into two groups: line management and staff management. Human resource management was traditionally considered to be a staff function. **Line managers** were those

*A **psychological contract** is the overall set of expectations held by the employee with regard to what he or she will contribute to the organization and that are held by the organization with regard to what it will provide to the individual in return.*

***Line managers** are those directly responsible for creating goods and services.*

directly responsible for creating goods and services; that is, their contributions to the organization were generally assessed in terms of their actual contributions and costs to the organization's bottom line. The performance of a sales manager whose unit costs $500,000 per year to support (for salaries, administration, and so forth) and that generates $3.5 million per year in revenue can be evaluated this way. Operations managers, financial managers, and marketing managers were generally considered to have line functions.

Staff managers, on the other hand, were those responsible for an indirect or support function that would have costs but whose bottom-line contributions were less direct. Legal, accounting, and HR departments were usually thought of as staff functions. Their role was to support line management's efforts to achieve organizational goals and objectives.

Today, however, many organizations have blurred this distinction. New forms of organizational design (such as teams and an emphasis on flatter and more decentralized organization) have made it more likely that many HRM activities are actually carried out by line managers. For example, it is fairly common today for line managers to be involved in recruiting new employees for a work group and sometimes to actually make the selection decision (although a staff member might help collect information needed to make that decision). Line managers are intimately involved in most of the interventions designed to enhance performance, and they often make decisions about pay raises and promotions.

In some organizations, the HRM function is structured in a completely different way. In these firms, the human resource management department is structured around "centers of excellence." In these cases, the HR department is responsible for providing services only in those cases where it can provide higher-quality services than can be purchased on the outside (i.e., through the outsourcing discussed earlier). When they cannot provide higher-quality services, they are often asked to identify and then manage the outside consultants who are brought in to perform the services. In still other cases, the HR department itself functions as a consulting operation within the organization. These departments are expected to be responsive to the needs of the other functional areas, but they have to be able to demonstrate their added value, and they must actually "sell" their services to the line managers. In these arrangements, the HRM department budget is small, and the only way to hire and retain employees in that area is to provide services that other managers are willing to pay for. Thus, the HRM department becomes a self-funding operation, or it could even become somewhat of a profit center.

THE HUMAN RESOURCE DEPARTMENT IN SMALLER VERSUS LARGER ORGANIZATIONS

There are also noteworthy differences in the way human resource management operations are carried out in larger versus smaller organizations. As noted, responsibilities for carrying out HR functions may reside in a separate HR department, but many smaller organizations do not have such departments and must deliver the required services in different ways.[29] Most small organizations require line managers to handle their basic HR functions. In the case of a franchised operation such as a single McDonald's or Pizza Hut restaurant or an individual retail outlet such as a Gap or The Limited clothing store, the store manager generally hires new employees, schedules and tracks working hours for all employees, and disciplines problem employees. The franchiser or home office, in turn, generally suggests or mandates hourly wages, provides performance appraisal forms for local use, and may handle payroll services.

A small independent business is generally operated in the same way, with the owner or general manager handling human resource duties. Payroll and other basic administrative activities may be subcontracted to businesses in the local community that specialize in providing such services for other local organizations. Relatively little training is provided in these small organizations, and other HR issues are relatively straightforward. Very small organizations are exempt from many legal regulations (again, we cover this

Staff managers are those responsible for an indirect or support function that would have costs but whose bottom-line contributions were less direct.

© tkemot/Shutterstock

EXHIBIT 1.2 The Human Resource Management Function at Texas Instruments

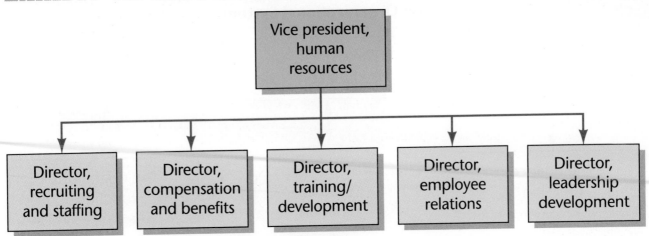

topic more fully in Chapter 2). Thus, a single manager can usually handle the HR function in smaller firms without too much difficulty.

As a firm grows beyond a certain size (usually around 250 employees), however, a separate HR unit becomes a necessity, and the issues involved become much more complicated. No standard approach exists, but a firm of this size might have one full-time manager and a single secretary or assistant to function as its HR department. These individuals handle all of the firm's human resource administration.

As the firm continues to grow, however, more assistance is needed to staff the HR department, and so that department also grows. Indeed, in the largest organizations, HR functions are themselves likely to have specialized subunits. For example, large firms might have separate departments to handle recruiting and selection, wages and salaries, training and development, and labor relations. Exhibit 1.2 shows how Texas Instruments has organized its HR function.

The Human Resource Management System

The modern view of human resource management is also a systems-oriented view. By its very nature, a strategic perspective requires the coordination of the various HRM activities to ensure that they are consistent with corporate strategy. If those services are provided primarily internally by the HRM department, this coordination can be fairly simple. As those activities move outside the organization, perhaps by contracting with outside vendors, the coordination problem becomes much more complex. But, in any case, a strategic perspective means understanding that a decision made in any one area of human resource management will affect what happens in every other area. If an organization needs highly skilled, knowledgeable workers to carry out its strategy, then all staffing activities must

be coordinated toward identifying and attracting such employees. Once these employees join the firm, however, performance appraisals, compensation, and performance management systems must all be changed to reflect the nature of the new employee.

Thus, although we will often discuss various tasks and functions of HRM from the perspective of discrete, self-contained activities, this is not the case in practice. In fact, these tasks and functions are highly interrelated and do not unfold neatly and systematically. Each of the various tasks and functions can affect or be affected by any of the other tasks and functions. And most basic human resource functions are practiced on an ongoing and continuous basis.

Indeed, it is truly appropriate to think of human resource management as a system. A system is an interrelated set of elements functioning as a whole. A **human resource management system**, then, is an integrated and interrelated approach to managing human resources that fully recognizes the interdependence among the various tasks and functions that must be performed. This viewpoint is illustrated in Exhibit 1.3. The basic premise of this perspective is that every element of the HRM system must be designed and implemented with full knowledge and understanding of, and integration with, the various other elements. For example, poor recruiting practices will result in a weak pool of applicants. Even if the organization has sophisticated selection techniques available, it will not make much difference without a pool of truly qualified applicants to choose from. As a result, there will be a greater need for training before a new employee starts work to provide him or her with the necessary skills. Subsequent performance appraisals will also be more

> A **human resource management system** *is an integrated and interrelated approach to managing human resources that fully recognizes the interdependence among the various tasks and functions that must be performed.*

EXHIBIT 1.3 A Systems View of Human Resource Management

The Organizational System

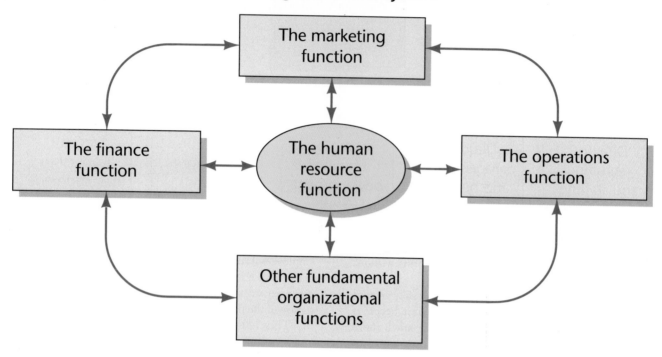

difficult because it may take longer for these employees to become truly proficient in their jobs, affecting how much they are paid.

Exhibit 1.3 also illustrates another useful systems-based perspective on human resource management. Many systems are themselves composed of subsystems—systems within a broader and more general system. By viewing the overall organization as a system, HRM then can be conceptualized as a subsystem within that more general organizational system. As the figure shows, the HRM subsystem both affects and is affected by the other functional subsystems throughout the organization. This perspective can help reinforce the idea that human resource management must be approached from the same strategic vantage point afforded the other areas within the organization. Failure to do so can result in unanticipated consequences, poor coordination, and less-effective performance.

To illustrate, if the organization makes a strategic decision to compete on the basis of high-quality service, then it will almost certainly need to use several mechanisms to do so. For example, the organization will need to recruit and subsequently hire more-qualified new workers and provide more training to both new and current workers. Similarly, if the financial function of an organization dictates that major cost cutting be undertaken, some portion of those costs may come from the human resource area. Thus, HR managers may need to reduce the size of the workforce, attempt to renegotiate labor contracts for a lower pay rate, defer payment of some benefits, and so forth.

The increasing globalization of business also reinforces the need to view the HRM function from a systems perspective; that is, human resource managers must take a global perspective in managing people. Within the borders of their own country, HR managers must consider the social norms, individual expectations, and so forth that shape worker behaviors. Cross-national assignments for managers are also an important consideration for many businesses today.

Thus, the global perspective on HRM includes the need to understand domestic similarities and differences in managing human resources in different countries and the role of international assignments and experiences in the development of human resource skills and abilities.

This systems approach has also led to organizations becoming increasingly interested in ways to evaluate the effectiveness of HRM

EXHIBIT 1.4 Human Resource Management as a Center for Expertise

The Organizational System

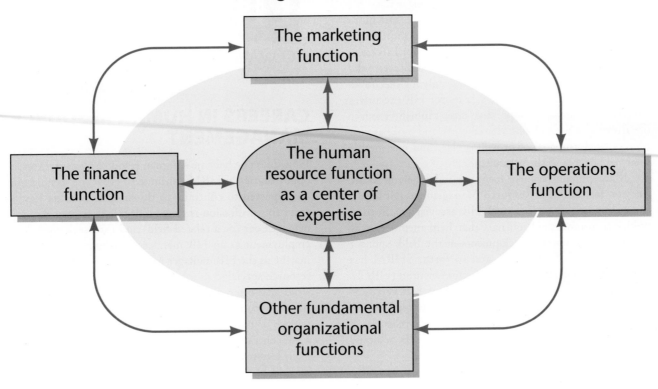

activities relative to the firm's strategic goals. Traditionally, many experts believed that HRM practices could not be assessed with anywhere near the objectivity that we could evaluate the effectiveness of a sales campaign, for instance. But the 1980s and 1990s saw further developments in utility analysis that made it possible to determine exactly how much human resource management activities contributed to a company's bottom line.[30] **Utility analysis** is the attempt to measure, in more objective terms, the impact and effectiveness of HRM practices in terms of metrics such as a firm's financial performance. The advent of high-performance work systems resulted in broader metrics for evaluating human resource management activities.[31] As a result, it is now possible to develop fairly objective measures of the effects or effectiveness of HRM practices. It remains the role of the HRM department, however, to develop these metrics and apply them to all HRM activities undertaken on behalf of the organization.

HUMAN RESOURCE MANAGERS

Who are today's human resource managers? Given the rapid and dynamic changes that have characterized this field, it should come as no surprise that HR managers represent a diverse set of professionals with a variety of backgrounds, experiences, and career objectives. An HR

executive today needs to understand different specialized areas such as the legal environment, the process of change management, labor relations, and so forth. In addition, contemporary HR executives must also possess general management abilities that reflect conceptual, diagnostic, and analytical skills. It is important that they fully understand the role and importance of the HR function for their organization.[32] Thus, both a solid educational background and a foundation of experience are necessary prerequisites for success.[33]

Consistent with these changes, it is often more useful to conceptualize human resources as a center of expertise within the organization. In other words, everyone in the organization should recognize human resource managers as the firm's most critical source of information about employment practices, employee behavior, labor relations, and the effective management of all aspects of people at work. This view of HRM is illustrated in Exhibit 1.4, which builds on the systems view of human resource management presented earlier in Exhibit 1.3.

Professionalism and Human Resource Management

Accompanying the shifts and changes in human

Utility analysis *is the attempt to measure, in more objective terms, the impact and effectiveness of HRM practices in terms of such metrics as a firm's financial performance.*

resource functions and importance is a greater emphasis on professionalism, which is reflected by a clear and recognized knowledge base and a generally understood way of doing business.[34] HR managers are no longer regarded as second-class corporate citizens, and more and more organizations are including a stint in human resources as a normal step on a person's way to the top. Senior HR executives in large firms earn six-figure salaries and receive the same sorts of perquisites once reserved only for executives of operating units. Indeed, the salaries for HR executives continue to rise at an impressive rate. Human resource departments are also being viewed more and more as cost centers, with the goal of providing clear and measurable financial benefits to the organization.[35]

Many human resource managers today belong to the Society for Human Resource Management (SHRM), the field's largest professional HR association. SHRM publishes professional journals that help members stay abreast of the newest developments in the field, sponsor workshops and conferences, and so forth. SHRM has created the Human Resource Certification Institute (HRCI). The HRCI is the recognized symbol of HR certification in much the same way that the accounting profession uses the certified public accountant exam and credential to designate those individuals who have formally achieved basic minimal competencies in prescribed areas.

The HRCI currently offers three core certifications: the Professional in Human Resources (PHR), Senior Professional in Human Resources (SPHR), and Global Professional in Human Resources (GPHR). In addition, HRCI also offers a state-specific certification for California. To be eligible to take the PHR, SPHR, or GPHR exam, an HR professional must have a minimum of two years of professional (exempt-level) experience and pass a rigorous examination covering the body of human resource knowledge as it relates to the particular certification. Beginning in 2011, the exam eligibility requirements will be changing to become more stringent. The HRCI Web site (www.hrci.org) has detailed information on the changes to the eligibility requirements.

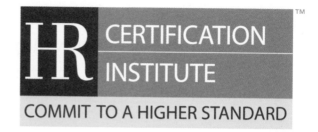

CAREERS IN HUMAN RESOURCE MANAGEMENT

How does one become a human resource manager? Career opportunities in HRM continue to grow and expand and are expected to continue to do so. One obvious way to enter this profession is to get a degree in human resource management (or a related field) and then seek entry-level employment as an HR manager. Alternative job options may be as the HR manager for a small firm or as a human resource specialist in a larger organization. Some universities also offer specialized graduate degree programs in human resource management. For example, a master of science or master of business administration degree with a concentration in human resource management would likely lead to a higher-level position in an organization than would a bachelor's degree alone.

Another route to HRM would be through line management. As described earlier, more and more firms are beginning to rotate managers through the HR function as part of their own personal career-development program. Thus, people who go to work in marketing or finance may well have an opportunity at some point to sample central HRM responsibilities. Regardless of the path taken, however, those interested in human resource management are likely to have a fascinating, demanding, and rewarding experience as they help their organization compete more effectively through the power of the people who make up every organization in every industry in every marketplace in the world today.

Courtesy of the HR Certification Institute

CLOSING CASE

ENTERPRISE BUILDS ON PEOPLE

When most people think of car-rental firms, the names Hertz and Avis usually come to mind. But in the last few years, Enterprise Rent-A-Car has overtaken both of these industry giants, and today it stands as the largest and most profitable business in the car-rental industry. In 2009, for instance, the firm had sales in excess of $10 billion, a fleet of more than 700,000 vehicles, and more than 70,000 employees.

Jack Taylor started Enterprise in St. Louis in 1957. Taylor had a unique strategy in mind for Enterprise, and that strategy played a key role in the firm's initial success. Most car-rental firms such as

Hertz and Avis base most of their locations in or near airports, train stations, and other transportation hubs. These firms see their customers as business travelers and people who fly for vacation and then need transportation at the end of their flight. But Enterprise went after a different customer. It sought to rent cars to individuals whose own cars are being repaired or who are taking a driving vacation.

The firm got its start by working with insurance companies. A standard feature in many automobile insurance polices is the provision of a rental car when one's personal car has been in an accident or stolen. Hertz, Avis, and others charge relatively high daily rates because their customers need the convenience of being near an airport or their expenses are being paid by their employers. These rates are often higher than insurance companies are willing to pay, so customers who use these firms end up paying part of the rental bill themselves. In addition, their locations are also often inconvenient for people seeking a replacement car while theirs is in the shop.

But Enterprise located stores in downtown and suburban areas, where local residents actually live. The firm also provides local pickup and delivery service in most areas. It also negotiates exclusive contract arrangements with local insurance agents. They get the agent's referral business while guaranteeing lower rates that are more in line with what insurance covers.

In recent years, Enterprise has started to expand its market base by pursuing a two-pronged growth strategy. First, the firm has started opening airport locations to compete with Hertz and Avis more directly. But its target is still the occasional renter rather than the frequent business traveler. Second, the firm also began to expand into international markets and today has rental offices in the United Kingdom, Ireland, and Germany.

Another key to Enterprise's success has been its HR strategy. Many employers seek only the top students, but Enterprise targets a certain kind of individual: Its preferred new employee is a college graduate from the middle to bottom half of the graduating class, and preferably one who was an athlete or who was otherwise actively involved in campus social activities. The rationale for this unusual academic standard is actually quite simple. Enterprise managers do not believe that especially high levels of academic prowess are necessary to perform well in the car-rental industry, but having a college degree nevertheless

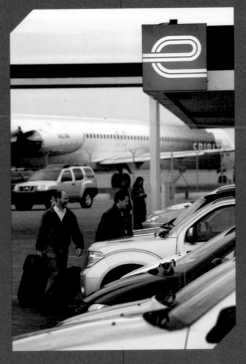

© AP Photo/Carlos Osorio

demonstrates intelligence and motivation. In addition, because interpersonal relations are important to its business, Enterprise wants people who were social directors or high-ranking officers of social organizations such as fraternities or sororities. Athletes are also desirable because of their competitiveness.

Once hired, new employees at Enterprise are often shocked at the performance expectations placed on them by the firm. They generally work long, grueling hours for relatively low pay. And all Enterprise managers are expected to jump in and help wash or vacuum cars when business at a rental agency gets backed up. All Enterprise managers must adhere to a stringent set of dress and grooming requirements. For instance, men must wear coordinated dress shirts and ties and can have facial hair only when "medically necessary." And women must wear creased pants or skirts no shorter than 2 inches above their knees.

So what are the incentives for working at Enterprise? For one thing, it's an unfortunate fact of life that college graduates with lower grades often struggle to find work. Thus, a job at Enterprise is better than no job at all. The firm also does not hire outsiders for anything other than entry-level positions; every vacancy is filled by promoting someone already inside the company. Thus, Enterprise employees know that if they work hard and do their best, they may well succeed in moving higher up the corporate ladder at a growing and successful firm.[36]

THINK IT OVER

1. Would Enterprise's approach to human resource management work in other industries?
2. Does Enterprise face any risks from its HR strategy?
3. Would you want to work for Enterprise? Why or why not?

CLOSING CASE

STUDY TOOLS

CHAPTER 1

- Rip out the chapter review card located at the end of the book.
- Review the valuable study tools located online at www.cengagebrain.com
    - Review the Key Terms flashcards.
    - Download audio and visual summaries to review on the go.
    - Complete practice quizzes to prepare for the test.
    - Play "Beat the Clock" and "QuizBowl" to master chapter concepts.
    - Complete "Crossword Puzzle" to review key terms.
    - Watch the chapter video for a real-life example of key concepts.

The LEGAL ENVIRONMENT

MANAGERS IN NAME ONLY?

For years, former RadioShack store manager Omar Belazi enthusiastically logged 65-hour workweeks, stayed late to clean the store's restrooms and vacuum the floor, and worked all weekend just to help meet the store's sales goals. Regardless of the hours he worked, however, he received the same monthly salary. Belazi gradually grew tired of the long hours, extra work, and stress and left RadioShack.

He eventually became part of a class-action lawsuit against RadioShack that included 1,300 current and former California store managers. Their contention was that they were managers in title only. More specifically, the lawsuit argued that all true management decisions were made at higher levels in the organization, leaving those with the title of store manager little more than sales workers. But because they had a managerial title and were paid

salaries, the company did not have to pay them overtime. The lawsuit was settled when RadioShack agreed to pay $29.9 million to the plaintiffs.

At the heart of the argument was a decades-old law that mandates overtime payments for hourly operating workers who work more than 40 hours a week but which allows firms to pay salaries to professionals regardless of how many hours they work. The Fair Labor Standards Act specifically exempts those in executive, administrative, or professional jobs from overtime payments. But because so many jobs have shifted from manufacturing settings to service settings, and because the nature of so many jobs has changed, the lines between different kinds of work have blurred.

And whether intentional or not, many firms now routinely use general titles such as *manager*, *administrator*, and *analyst*

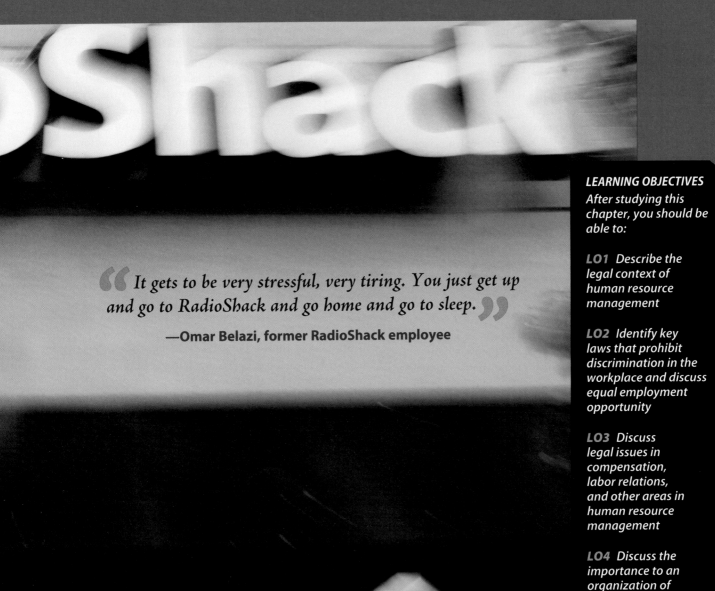

> " *It gets to be very stressful, very tiring. You just get up and go to RadioShack and go home and go to sleep.* "
>
> —Omar Belazi, former RadioShack employee

LEARNING OBJECTIVES

After studying this chapter, you should be able to:

LO1 *Describe the legal context of human resource management*

LO2 *Identify key laws that prohibit discrimination in the workplace and discuss equal employment opportunity*

LO3 *Discuss legal issues in compensation, labor relations, and other areas in human resource management*

LO4 *Discuss the importance to an organization of evaluating its legal compliance* but assign employees with those titles tasks that do not always fit the title. For instance, Mr. Belazi was not specifically directed to work extra on weekends or to clean the restrooms. But if an hourly worker had been hired, that person's time would have been charged against the store's weekly labor budget. If he didn't maximize the labor hours he and his employees devoted to selling, then his store's sales would drop and he would be reprimanded.[1]

THINK IT OVER

1. From a management perspective, what are the key issues in this case?
2. How might you respond if your employer (current or future) directly or indirectly required you to work extra hours with no additional compensation?

Like every other organization today, RadioShack must adhere to the laws and regulations that govern its employment practices. In general, organizations try to follow such laws and regulations for several reasons. One is an inherent commitment in most organizations to ethical and socially responsible behavior. Another is to avoid the direct costs and bad publicity that might result from lawsuits brought against the organization if those laws and regulations are broken. But as the opening case illustrates, these laws and regulations are sometimes ambiguous and open to different interpretations. As we will see, failure to follow the law, even because of a well-intentioned misunderstanding, can be enormously costly to an organization.

As we noted in Chapter 1, the proliferation of laws and regulations affecting employment practices in the 1960s and 1970s was a key reason for the emergence of human resource management (HRM) as a vital organizational function. Managing within the complex legal environment that affects human resource (HR) practices requires a full understanding of that legal environment and the ability to ensure that others within the organization also understand it.[2] This chapter is devoted to helping you understand the legal environment of human resource management. First, we establish the legal context of HRM and then focus on perhaps the most important area of this legal context—equal employment opportunity—and review several key court cases that have established the law in this area. Subsequent sections introduce legal issues in compensation and labor relations. Various emerging legal issues are also introduced and discussed. Finally, we summarize how many of today's organizations evaluate their legal compliance.

THE LEGAL CONTEXT OF HUMAN RESOURCE MANAGEMENT

The legal context of human resource management is shaped by different forces. The catalyst for modifying or enhancing the legal context may be legislative initiative, social change, or judicial rulings. Governmental bodies pass laws that affect human resource practices, for example, and the courts interpret those laws as they apply to specific circumstances and situations. Thus, the regulatory environment itself is quite complex and affects different areas within the HRM process.[3]

The Regulatory Environment of Human Resource Management

The legal and regulatory environment of human resource management in the United States emerges as a result of a three-step process. First is the actual creation of new regulation. This regulation can come in the form of new laws or statutes passed by national, state, or local government bodies; however, most start at the national level. State and local regulations are more likely to extend or modify national regulations than create new ones. In addition, as we will see later, the president of the United States can also create regulations that apply to specific situations. Finally, court decisions, especially decisions by the Supreme Court of the United States, set precedence and so also play a major role in establishing the regulatory environment.

There are also numerous instances where court decisions have narrowed definitions of some laws and have reduced the ability of plaintiffs to bring charges under other laws. As a result, in some cases, activists have called for new laws to reestablish the original intent of a law that has been altered by various court decisions. Indeed, for instance, the Civil Rights Act of 1991 was passed to reestablish certain provisions of the original Civil Rights Act passed in 1964 (we discuss these laws later).

The second step in the regulation process is the enforcement of these regulations. Occasionally, the laws themselves provide for enforcement through the creation of special agencies or other forms of regulatory groups. (We will discuss one important agency, the Equal Employment Opportunity Commission, later in the chapter.) In other situations, enforcement might be assigned to an existing

Shanahan

"I've been speaking to my attorneys, Larson, and this time we think we've got you fired."

© Danny Shanahan/Riley Illustration

agency such as the Department of Labor. The court system also interprets laws that the government passes and provides another vehicle for enforcement. To be effective, an enforcing agency must have an appropriate degree of power. The ability to levy fines or bring lawsuits against firms that violate the law are among the most powerful tools provided to the various agencies charged with enforcing HR regulations.

The third step in the regulation process is the actual practice and implementation of those regulations in organizations. In other words, organizations and managers must implement and follow the guidelines that the government has passed and that the courts and regulatory agencies attempt to enforce. In many cases, following regulations is a logical and straightforward process. In some cases, however, a regulation may be unintentionally ambiguous or be interpreted by the courts in different ways over time. Regardless of the clarity of the regulation, the actual

process of implementing and demonstrating adherence to it may take an extended period of time. Thus, organizations are sometimes put in the difficult position of figuring out how to follow a particular regulation or needing an extended period to fully comply.

EQUAL EMPLOYMENT OPPORTUNITY

Regulations exist in almost every aspect of the employment relationship. As illustrated in Exhibit 2.1, equal employment opportunity intended to protect individuals from illegal discrimination is the most fundamental and far-reaching area of the legal regulation of human resource management. Indeed, in one way or another, almost every law and statute governing employment relationships is essentially

EXHIBIT 2.1 Legal Regulation of Human Resource Management

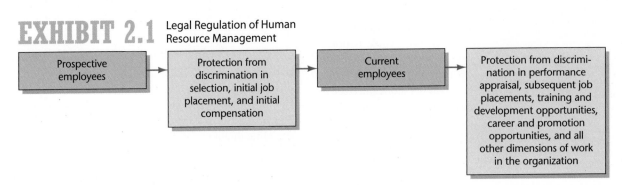

Prospective employees → Protection from discrimination in selection, initial job placement, and initial compensation → Current employees → Protection from discrimination in performance appraisal, subsequent job placements, training and development opportunities, career and promotion opportunities, and all other dimensions of work in the organization attempting to ensure equal employment opportunity. Such opportunity, however, has been interpreted to include protection that goes beyond ensuring that a person has a fair chance at being hired for a job for which the person is qualified. As also illustrated in Exhibit 2.1, this protection extends to preventing illegal discrimination against current employees with regard to performance appraisal, pay, promotion opportunities, and various other dimensions of the employment relationship. In addition, several related legal issues warrant separate discussion as well.

Some managers assume that the legal regulation of HRM is a relatively recent phenomenon. In reality, however, concerns about equal opportunity can be traced back to the Thirteenth Amendment passed in 1865 to abolish slavery and the Fourteenth Amendment passed in 1868 to provide equal protection for all citizens of the United States. The Reconstruction Civil Rights Acts of 1866 and 1871 further extended protection offered to people under the Thirteenth and Fourteenth Amendments, and together with those amendments, these laws still form the basis for present-day federal court actions that involve the payment of compensatory and punitive damages.[4]

or managers within an organization that cause members of a protected class to be unfairly differentiated from others. (We discuss protected classes later in this chapter.)

Although numerous laws deal with different aspects of equal employment opportunity, the Civil Rights Act of 1964 clearly signaled the beginning of a new legislative era in American business. The act grew out of the growing atmosphere of protest for equal rights in the early 1960s and contains several sections called *titles* that deal with different areas of application of the Civil Rights Act. Our discussion will focus on Title VII, which deals with work settings under the heading of Equal Employment Opportunity.

Title VII of the Civil Rights Act of 1964 The most significant single piece of legislation specifically affecting the legal context for human resource management to date has been **Title VII of the Civil Rights Act of 1964**. Congress passed the Civil Rights Act and President Lyndon Johnson signed it into law in 1964 as a way to ensure that equal opportunities would be available to everyone. Title VII of the act states that it is illegal for an employer to fail or refuse to hire,

> ## The Reconstruction Civil Rights Acts of 1866 and 1871 further extended protection offered to people under the Thirteenth and Fourteenth Amendments.

Discrimination and Equal Employment Opportunity

The basic goal of all equal employment opportunity regulation is to protect people from unfair or inappropriate discrimination in the workplace.[5] However, most laws passed to eliminate discrimination do not explicitly define the term itself. It is also instructive to note that discrimination per se is not illegal. Organizations routinely "discriminate" between effective and ineffective employees in how they are treated. As long as the basis for this discrimination is purely job-related, however, such an action is legal

and appropriate when based on performance or seniority and applied objectively and consistently. Problems arise, though, when differentiation between people is not job related; the resulting discrimination is illegal. Various court decisions and basic inferences about the language of various laws suggest that **illegal discrimination** is the result of behaviors or actions by an organization

to discharge any individual, or to discriminate in any other way against any individual with respect to any aspect of the employment relationship on the basis of that individual's race, color, religious beliefs, sex, or national origin.

The law applies to all components of the employment relationship, including compensation, employment terms, working conditions, and various other privileges of employment. Title VII applies to all organizations with fifteen or more employees working 20 or more weeks a year and that are involved in interstate commerce. In addition, it also applies to state and local governments, employment agencies, and labor organizations. Title VII also created the Equal Employment Opportunity Commission (EEOC) to enforce the various provisions of the law (we discuss the EEOC later in this chapter). Under Title VII, as interpreted by the courts, several types of illegal discrimination are outlawed. These types are discussed next and are illustrated in Exhibit 2.2.

Disparate Treatment **Disparate treatment** discrimination exists when individuals in similar situations are treated differently *and* when the differential treatment is based on the individual's race, color, religion, sex, national origin, age, or disability status. For example, if two people with the same qualifications for the job apply for a promotion and the organization uses one individual's religious beliefs or gender to decide which employee to promote, then the

Illegal discrimination *results from behaviors or actions by an organization or managers within an organization that cause members of a protected class to be unfairly differentiated from others.*

Disparate treatment *discrimination exists when individuals in similar situations are treated differently based on the individual's race, color, religion, sex, national origin, age, or disability status.*

individual not promoted is a victim of disparate treatment discrimination. To prove discrimination in this situation, an individual filing a charge must demonstrate that there was a discriminatory motive; that is, the individual must

people as servers based on the argument that their customers prefer young and attractive servers. In fact, customer or client preference can never be the basis of a BFOQ. As we shall see, this situation can become quite complex.

> **Under Title VII of the Civil Rights Act, it is illegal for an employer to fail or refuse to hire or to discharge any individual or to in any other way discriminate against any individual with respect to any aspect of the employment relationship on the basis of that individual's race, color, religious beliefs, sex, or national origin.**

prove that the organization considered the individual's protected class status when making the decision.

One circumstance in which organizations can legitimately treat members of different groups differently is when there exists a **bona fide occupational qualification (BFOQ)** for performing a particular job. This means that some personal characteristic such as age legitimately affects a person's ability to perform the job. For example, a producer casting a new play or movie can legally refuse to hire an older person to play a role that is expressly written for a young person. Few legitimate BFOQs exist, however. For example, a restaurant cannot hire only young and attractive

President Lyndon Johnson signed the Civil Rights Act into law on July 2, 1964.

To claim a BFOQ exception, the organization must be able to demonstrate that hiring on the basis of the characteristic in question (e.g., age) is a **business necessity**; that is, the organization must be able to prove that the practice is important for the safe and efficient operation of the business. But what if customers at a casino would prefer female card dealers or if customers at an automobile dealership prefer male salespeople? These customers might go elsewhere if these preferences were not satisfied, and those decisions could surely hurt the business involved. In general, neither case would qualify as a BFOQ, but reality is rarely this simple.

The case of *Diaz* v. *Pan American World Airways*, for example, was filed after Celio Diaz (a male) applied for the job of flight attendant with Pan American Airlines (Pan Am).[6] He was rejected because Pan Am had a policy of hiring only women for this position (as did many airlines in 1971). Diaz filed suit for discrimination, but Pan Am argued that gender was a BFOQ for the job of flight attendant. This argument was based on Pan Am's own experience with male and female flight attendants and on the fact that Pan Am's customers overwhelmingly preferred to be served by female attendants. A lower court accepted the airlines' argument that "an airline cabin represents a unique [and stressful] environment in which an air carrier is required to take account of the special psychological needs of its passengers. Those needs are better attended to by females."[7] The appeals court reversed that decision, however, citing that Pan Am's data on the relative effectiveness of male and female flight attendants was not compelling and that customer preference was not relevant because no evidence existed that hiring male flight attendants would substantially affect the business performance of

A **bona fide occupational qualification (BFOQ)** states that a condition like race, sex, or other personal characteristic legitimately affects a person's ability to perform the job, and therefore can be used as a legal requirement for selection.

A **business necessity** is a practice that is important for the safe and efficient operation of the business.

EXHIBIT 2.2 Forms of Illegal Discrimination

```
Disparate                              Disparate
impact                                 treatment
              Forms of
              illegal
              discrimination
Retaliation                            Pattern or
                                       practice
```

the airlines. But while this ruling may seem clear, Asian restaurants are routinely allowed to hire only Asian American waiters because they add to the authenticity of the dining experience and are therefore deemed a business necessity.

Disparate Impact

A second form of discrimination is **disparate impact** discrimination that occurs when an apparently neutral employment practice disproportionately excludes a protected group from employment opportunities. This argument is the most common for charges of discrimination brought under the Civil Rights Act. For example, suppose a restaurant determined that, for health reasons, no one who had hair long enough to cover his or her ears would be hired to handle food. Although this practice would be applied to all applicants and would certainly result in some long-haired males not being hired, it would have a much greater impact on female applicants because they are more likely to have longer hair. As a result, even though all applicants would be treated the same, this practice would result in the rejection of many more female applicants. This situation would be an example of disparate impact discrimination because the organization, even with no direct intention of discriminating against women, is using a particular employment practice that results in discrimination against women. In this situation, intent to discriminate is irrelevant (and the proper solution is to have all employees wear hairnets).

One of the first instances in which disparate impact was defined involved a landmark legal case, *Griggs* v. *Duke Power*. Following passage of Title VII, Duke Power initiated a new selection system that required new employees to have either a high school education or a minimum cutoff score on two specific personality tests. Griggs, a black male, filed a lawsuit against Duke Power after he was denied employment based on these criteria. His argument was that neither criterion was a necessary qualification for performing the work he was seeking. After his attorneys demonstrated that those criteria disproportionately affected blacks and that the company had no documentation to support the validity of the criteria, the courts ruled that the firm had to change its selection criteria on the basis of disparate impact.[8]

The important criterion in this situation is that the consequences of the employment practice are discriminatory, and thus the practice in question has disparate (sometimes referred to as *adverse*) impact. In fact, if a plaintiff can establish what is called a *prima facie case* of discrimination, the company is considered to be at fault unless it can demonstrate another legal basis for the decision.[9] This finding doesn't mean that the company automatically loses the case, but it does mean that the burden of proof rests with the company to defend itself rather than with the plaintiff trying to prove discrimination. Therefore, it is extremely important to understand how one establishes a prima facie case.

Several avenues can be used to establish a prima facie case, but the most common approach relies on the so-called **four-fifths rule.** Specifically, the courts have ruled that disparate impact exists if a selection criterion (such as a test score) results in a selection rate for a protected class that is less than four-fifths (80 percent) than that for the majority group. For example, assume that an organization is considering 100 white applicants and 100 Hispanic applicants for the same job. If an employment test used to select among these applicants results in 60 white applicants (60 percent) being hired, but only 30 Hispanic applicants (30 percent) being hired, then disparate impact is likely to be ruled because Hispanics are being hired at a rate that is less than four-fifths than that of whites. At this point, the organization using the test would be required to prove that its differential selection rate of whites versus Hispanics could be justified (the basis for this justification will be explained below).

But demonstrating that an organization's policies have violated the four-fifths rule can sometimes be complicated. In the case of *Ward's Cove Packing* v. *Antonio*, the defendant, a salmon cannery in Alaska, had two distinct types of jobs for which people were hired.[10] Cannery jobs

Disparate impact discrimination occurs when an apparently neutral employment practice disproportionately excludes a protected group from employment opportunities.

The **four-fifths rule** suggests that disparate impact exists if a selection criterion (such as a test score) results in a selection rate for a protected class that is less than four-fifths (80 percent) of that for the majority group.

were seen as skilled (administrative and engineering) while noncannery jobs were viewed as unskilled. The plaintiff's attorneys argued that because the noncannery jobs were predominantly filled by Filipino and Native Alaskans and the cannery jobs were held predominantly by whites, the company had violated the four-fifths rule and had therefore established a prima facie case for disparate impact. The defendant did not dispute the statistics but argued that the policies in place did not lead to apparent disparate impact and therefore there was no prima facie case. The Supreme Court agreed with the defendant, ruling that the statistical proof alone was not sufficient for establishing a prima facie case. Therefore, the burden of proof did not shift to the defendant but rested with the employee involved. Ward's Cove won the case. In addition to illustrating the problems with establishing a violation of the four-fifths rule, the Ward's Cove case was also widely seen as dealing a major blow to the enforcement of the Civil Rights Act of 1964—a topic to which we will return shortly.

A plaintiff might be able to demonstrate disparate impact by relying on so-called **geographical comparisons**. These involve comparing the characteristics of the potential pool of qualified applicants for a job (focusing on characteristics such as race, ethnicity, and gender) with those same characteristics of current employees in the job. Thus, if the potential pool of qualified applicants in the labor market for the job of bank teller is 50 percent African American, then a bank hiring from that market should have approximately 50 percent African American tellers. Failure to achieve this degree of representation is considered a basis for a prima facie case of disparate impact discrimination. This comparison requires a clear understanding of the labor market from which the organization typically recruits employees for this job because different jobs within the same organization might draw on different "relevant" labor markets with different characteristics. For instance, a university might rely on a national labor market for new faculty members, a regional labor market for professional staff employees, and a local labor market for custodial and food-service employees. It is also important to note that the definition of the "potential pool of qualified applicants" draws heavily on census data for the area.

Finally, the **McDonnell-Douglas test**, named for a Supreme Court ruling in *McDonnell-Douglas v. Green*, is another basis for establishing a prima facie case.[11] Four steps are part of the McDonnell-Douglas test:

1. The applicant is a member of a protected class (see below).
2. The applicant was qualified for the job for which he or she applied.
3. The individual was turned down for the job.
4. The company continued to seek other applicants with the same qualifications.

Pattern or Practice Discrimination

The third kind of discrimination that can be identified is **pattern or practice discrimination**. This form of disparate treatment occurs on a classwide or systemic basis. Although an individual can bring charges of practice discrimination, the question is whether the organization engages in a pattern or practice of discrimination against all members of a protected class instead of against one particular member. Title VII of the 1964 Civil Rights Act gives the attorney general of the United States express powers to bring lawsuits against organizations thought to be guilty of pattern or practice discrimination. Specifically, Section 707 of Title VII states that such a lawsuit can be brought if there is reasonable cause to believe that an employer is engaging in pattern or practice discrimination. A good example of pattern or practice discrimination allegedly occurred several years ago at Shoney's, a popular family-oriented restaurant chain with operations and locations throughout the South. A former assistant manager at the firm alleged that she was told by her supervisor to use a pencil to color in the "o" in the Shoney's logo printed on its employment application blanks for all African American applicants. The presumed intent of this coding scheme was to eliminate all those applicants from further consideration.[12]

To demonstrate pattern or practice discrimination, the plaintiff must prove that the organization intended to discriminate against a particular class of individuals. A critical issue in practice or pattern discrimination lawsuits is the definition of a statistical comparison group or a definition of the relevant labor market. A labor market consists of workers who have the skills needed to perform the work and who are within a reasonable commuting distance from the organization. The definition of labor market is a major issue in resolving lawsuits brought under pattern or practice discrimination suits.

Geographical comparisons *involve comparing the characteristics of the potential pool of qualified applicants for a job (focusing on characteristics such as race, ethnicity, and gender) with those same characteristics of the present employees in the job.*

The McDonnell-Douglas test *is used as the basis for establishing a prima facie case of disparate impact discrimination.*

Pattern or practice discrimination *is similar to disparate treatment but occurs on a classwide basis.*

Retaliation A final form of illegal discrimination that has been occasionally identified in some reorganizations is retaliation for "participation and opposition." Title VII states that it is illegal for employers to retaliate against employees for either opposing a perceived illegal employment practice or participating in a proceeding that is related to an alleged illegal employment practice. If an employee's behavior fits the legal definition of participation or opposition and the organization takes some measure against that particular employee—such as a reprimand, demotion, or termination—then the employee can file a lawsuit against the organization under Title VII.

Employer Defense Our discussion so far has focused on the types of illegal discrimination and the ways in which a plaintiff can establish a case of discrimination. As noted earlier, however, once a prima facie case has been established, the burden of proof shifts to the defendant; that is, the defendant has to provide evidence for nondiscriminatory bases for the decisions made. Therefore, it is critical to understand that just because a prima facie case has been established, the defendant (typically the company) will not necessarily be found liable. The company can defend itself by providing evidence that the selection decision (or employment decision of any type) was based on criteria that are job related. In other words, the defendant (usually an organization) must be able to prove that decisions were made so that the persons most likely to be selected (or promoted or to receive a pay raise) are those who are most likely to perform best on the job (or who have already performed best on the job). This situation is also referred to as *validation* of the practice in question. In Chapter 7, we will discuss how one validates a selection technique and therefore establishes that it is job related. Many of these issues are also based on the court ruling in the *Albermarle Paper Company* case, which is also discussed in Chapter 7.

Protected Classes in the Workforce

Now we turn our attention to what the term *protected classes* means in practice. Many of the discriminatory practices described earlier stemmed from stereotypes, beliefs, or prejudice about classes of individuals. For example, common stereotypes at one time were that African American employees were less dependable than white employees, that women were less suited to certain types of work than were men, and that disabled individuals could not be productive employees. Based on these stereotypes, many organizations routinely discriminated against African Americans, women, and disabled people. Although such blatant discrimination is rare today, that does not mean that discrimination at work has disappeared. Instead, as we shall see, it has found new targets and, in many cases, a much more subtle approach.

To combat this past discrimination, various laws have been passed to protect different classes or categories of individuals. Although it varies from law to law, a **protected class** consists of all individuals who share one or more common characteristics as indicated by that law. The most common characteristics used to define protected classes include race, color, religion, gender, age, national origin, disability status, and status as a military veteran. As we will see, some laws pertain to several protected classes, while others pertain to a single protected class. Class definition generally involves first specifying the basis of distinction and then specifying which degree or category of that distinction is protected. For example, a law may prohibit discrimination on the basis of gender—a basis of distinction—and then define the protected class as females. This distinction does not mean that an organization can discriminate against men, of course, and in some cases men could even be considered members of a protected class. But the law was almost certainly passed on the assumption that most gender-based discrimination has been directed against women and thus it is women who need to be protected in the future.

At the same time, an important issue is to what extent an organization can give preferential treatment to members of a protected class. Although exceptions can be made in certain circumstances, by and large the intent of most equal employment opportunity legislation is to provide fair and equitable treatment for everyone, as opposed to stipulating preferential treatment for members of a protected class.[13] This interpretation becomes a bit complicated, though, and can result in charges of reverse discrimination, our next topic.

Affirmative Action and Reverse Discrimination

When charges of illegal discrimination have been supported, courts sometimes impose remedies that try to reverse the effects of past discrimination. Most frequently,

A **protected class** consists of all individuals who share one or more common characteristic as indicated by that law.

these remedies have taken the form of some type of affirmative action. (As we shall see below, some organizations are also required to file affirmative action plans even without charges of illegal discrimination.) **Affirmative action** refers to positive steps taken by an organization to seek qualified employees from underrepresented groups in the workforce. When affirmative action is part of a remedy in a discrimination case, the plan takes on additional urgency and the steps are somewhat clearer. Three elements make up any affirmative action program.

The first element is called the **utilization analysis** and is a comparison of the racial, sex, and ethnic composition of the employer's workforce compared to that of the available labor supply. For each group of jobs, the organization needs to identify the percentage of its workforce with that characteristic (i.e., African American, female, etc.) and identify the percentage of workers in the relevant labor market with that characteristic. If the percentage in the employer's workforce is considerably less than the percentage in the external labor supply, then that minority group is characterized as being underutilized. Much of this analysis takes place as part of the discrimination case, if one is involved, and the affected groups are defined by the specifics of the case.

The second part of an affirmative action plan is the development of goals and timetables for achieving balance in the workforce concerning those characteristics, especially where underutilization exists. Goals and timetables generally specify the percentage of protected classes of employees that the organization seeks to have in each group and the targeted date by which that percentage should be attained, but these are much more flexible than quotas, which are illegal (except in rare cases when these have been imposed by courts). The idea underlying goals and timetables is that if no discriminatory hiring practices exist, then underutilization should be eliminated over time.

The third part of the affirmative action program is the development of a list of action steps. These steps specify what the organization will do to work toward attaining its goals to reduce underutilization. Common action steps include increased communication of job openings to underrepresented groups, recruiting at schools that predominantly cater to a particular protected class, participating in programs designed to improve employment opportunities for underemployed groups, and taking all steps to remove inappropriate barriers to employment. In some cases, this third part might also include preferential hiring; that is, given two equally qualified applicants for a job, the organization would be required to hire the member of the underrepresented group in every case until its goals and targets are met.

In the late 1990s, the courts began to impose many more restrictions on what was acceptable (or required) in the way of preferential hiring and quotas. We will discuss representative relevant court decisions shortly, but the impetus for some of these decisions was the concern that affirmative action *could* in some cases appear to be a form of *reverse discrimination*, or a practice that has a disparate impact on members of *nonprotected* classes. Thus, charges of reverse discrimination typically stem from the belief by white males that they have suffered because of preferential treatment given to other groups.

The two most famous court cases in this area help

> "Affirmative action is an effort to develop a systematic approach to open the doors of education, employment, and business development opportunities to qualified individuals who happen to be members of groups that have experienced long-standing and persistent discrimination."
>
> —BILL CLINTON,
> Forty-second U.S. president, 1993–2001

Affirmative action *represents a set of steps, taken by an organization, to actively seek qualified applicants from groups underrepresented in the workforce.*

A **utilization analysis** *is a comparison of the racial, sex, and ethnic composition of the employer's workforce compared to that of the available labor supply.*

to illustrate how complicated this issue can be. In one case, Allan Bakke, a white male, applied to medical school at the University of California Davis but was denied admission.[14] At issue was the fact that the university had set aside 16 of its 100 seats for an incoming class for minority students to promote diversity and affirmative action at the school. Bakke's attorneys argued that he was not necessarily more qualified than those admitted for the 84 "white" openings, but that he was more qualified than those admitted to the 16 openings set aside for minorities. Because the school had imposed this system on its own (to correct past injustice), the Court ruled that this "set-aside" program constituted reverse discrimination because it clearly favored one race over another and ruled in favor of Bakke.

In another case, Brian Weber, also a white male, applied for a temporary training program that would lead to a higher-paying skilled job at a Kaiser Aluminum facility.[15] He was not admitted into the program; he then sued because he claimed that African American applicants with less seniority were admitted into the program strictly because of their race. In fact, Kaiser and United Steelworkers had agreed to a contract whereby 50 percent of the openings for these programs would be reserved for African Americans in an attempt to address the fact that African Americans had been systematically excluded from these programs in the past. The Supreme Court found in favor of Kaiser and the union, acknowledging that a collective-bargaining agreement such as this one was binding and was a reasonable means of addressing past discrimination.

Given these two legal decisions, one might question the current status of reverse-discrimination cases. In fact, it is by no means clear. Within the space of a few years, the Supreme Court:

- ruled against an organization giving preferential treatment to minority workers during a layoff;[16]
- ruled in support of temporary preferential hiring and promotion practices as part of a settlement of a lawsuit;[17]
- ruled in support of the establishment of quotas as a remedy for past discrimination;[18] and
- ruled that any form of affirmative action is inherently discriminatory and could be used only as a temporary measure.[19]

It would appear that the future of affirmative action is unclear, suggesting that the courts will be leaning more toward interpretations in line with reverse discrimination in the future.

Indeed, the concept of affirmative action is increasingly being called into question. In 1996, for instance, a circuit court judge ruled that a goal of increasing student diversity at the University of Texas was not sufficient grounds for giving preference to racial minorities in terms of admission or financial aid.[20] In 1998, California voters ratified a proposition called the California Civil Rights Initiative, which outlawed any preferential treatment on the basis of race, gender, color, ethnicity, or national origin for all public employment, education, and contracting activities. However, in 2003 the Supreme Court ruled that the University of Michigan could use diversity as one of several factors in making its admissions decisions, although it disallowed explicit rules that awarded extra points to underrepresented groups in the student population.

In a more recent case (*Ricci v. Stefano*, 2009), the Supreme Court ruled that the city of New Haven, Connecticut, violated the rights of a group of white firefighters when they decided to discard the results of a recent promotion exam that was shown to have disparate impact. The city developed and validated this test and administered it to group of candidates. Based on the test scores and corresponding job openings, no non-white firefighters would be promoted. This caused the city to throw out the results of the test and to order a new exam. The white firefighters subsequently sued the city for reverse discrimination. The city of New Haven argued that the test did not really measure what was needed to be successful as a lieutenant, but the Supreme Court, in a 5–4 decision, ruled that if the city did not believe the test measured the right thing it should not have been used and that the decision to throw out the results was simply a reaction to "racial statistics."

Sexual Harassment at Work

One final area of coverage for the Civil Rights Act that is critical to the human resource manager is sexual harassment. This area is particularly important in this context because much of the litigation and the organization's liability in these cases depend on the initial responses to charges of sexual harassment, and these responses are typically the responsibility of someone in human resources. Sexual harassment is defined by the EEOC as unwelcome sexual advances in the work environment. If the conduct is indeed unwelcome and occurs with sufficient frequency to create an abusive work environment, the employer is responsible for changing the environment by warning, reprimanding, or perhaps firing the harasser.[21]

© Anatoli Styf/Shutterstock

HR in the 21st Century

In July 2005, Justice Sandra Day O'Connor (most of whose decisions would be considered moderate) announced her retirement. President George W. Bush announced that his choice to replace O'Connor was John Roberts, a conservative judge with a great deal of judicial experience. But then Chief Justice William Rehnquist died after a long battle with cancer in early September 2005. President Bush subsequently switched his nomination of John Roberts to replace Rehnquist as chief justice, and Roberts was confirmed as chief justice in late September 2005. President Bush next announced his choice of Samuel Alito, another conservative judge, to fill the remaining opening; Alito was subsequently confirmed in early 2006. These appointments resulted in a clear shift to the political right in the nature of Supreme Court decisions. More recently, though, President Barack Obama had the opportunity to make his first appointment to the Supreme Court. His choice was Sonia Sotomayor, a judge with a relatively liberal track record. She promises to bring a new perspective to the court, and it will be interesting to see how much influence she has in upcoming decisions.

Regardless, discussions of affirmative action have also become linked to a discussion of a "new racism" by both sides of the debate. Many conservatives, for instance, were arguing that

affirmative action was itself a form of racism in which people were classified according to their race and stereotyped because of that classification. Individuals opposed to affirmative action argued that it made more sense for organizations to deal with everyone on the basis of individual ability and potential. They also claimed that affirmative action condemned African Americans to second-class status because of the assumption that they could not get ahead on their own.

Advocates of affirmative action also started to invoke charges of racism in arguing their case. These individuals suggested that the conservatives arguing against affirmative action were guilty of a new form of racism. Specifically, they argued that opponents of affirmative action were calling for decisions based on merit—and that those decisions would open the door to the same types of discrimination that had occurred in the past. These arguments are certain to continue with no clear answer likely to emerge.

THINK IT OVER

1. What is your position on reverse discrimination?
2. Do you think it appropriate that Supreme Court appointments have substantial influence on policy?

The courts have ruled that there are two types of sexual harassment and have defined both types. One type of sexual harassment is **quid pro quo harassment**. In this case, the harasser offers to exchange something of value for sexual favors. For example, a male supervisor might tell or imply to a female subordinate that he will recommend her for promotion or provide her with a salary increase, but only if she sleeps with him. Although this type of situation definitely occurs, organizations generally have no problem in understanding that it is illegal and in knowing how to respond.

But a more subtle (and probably more common) type of sexual harassment is the creation of a **hostile work environment**, and this situation is not always so easy to define. For example, a group of

male employees who continually make off-color jokes and lewd comments and perhaps decorate the work environment with inappropriate photographs may create a hostile work environment for a female colleague to the point where she is uncomfortable working in that job setting. Most experts would agree that this situation constitutes sexual harassment. But what if an employee has an inappropriate magazine in a desk drawer and a co-worker sees it

> **"Welcome sexual harassment is an oxymoron."**
>
> —RICHARD POSNER,
> Judge on the U.S. Seventh Circuit
> Court of Appeals, Chicago

Quid pro quo harassment *is sexual harassment in which the harasser offers to exchange something of value for sexual favors.*

A **hostile work environment** *is one that produces sexual harassment because of a climate or culture that is punitive toward people of a different gender.*

only when she (or he) happens to walk by when the drawer is open?

In *Meritor Savings Bank* v. *Vinson*, the Supreme Court noted that a hostile work environment constitutes sexual harassment, even if the employee did not suffer any economic penalties or was not threatened with any such penalties.[22] In *Harris* v. *Forklift Systems*, the Court ruled that the plaintiff did not have to suffer substantial mental distress to receive a jury settlement.[23] Hence, it is critical that organizations monitor the situation and be alert for these instances because, as noted, it is the organization's responsibility for dealing with this sort of problem.[24]

Therefore, the human resource manager must play a major role in investigating any hint of sexual harassment in the organization. The manager cannot simply wait for an employee to complain. Although the Court had ruled in the case of *Scott* v. *Sears Roebuck*[25] that the employer was not liable for the sexual harassment because the plaintiff did not complain to supervisors, the ruling in the *Meritor* case makes it much more difficult for the organization to avoid liability by claiming ignorance (although this liability is not automatic). This responsibility is further complicated by the fact that, although most sexual harassment cases involve men harassing women, there are, of course, many other situations of sexual harassment that can be identified. Females can harass men, and in the case of *Oncale* v. *Sundowner* the Supreme Court ruled unanimously that a male oil rigger who claimed to be harassed by his coworkers and supervisor on an offshore oil rig was indeed the victim of sexual harassment.[26] Several recent cases involving same-sex harassment have focused new attention on this form of sexual harassment.[27] Regardless of the pattern, however, the same rules apply: Sexual harassment is illegal, and it is the organization's responsibility to control it.

Other Equal Employment Opportunity Legislation

In addition to the Civil Rights Act of 1964, a large body of supporting legal regulation has also been created in an effort to provide equal employment opportunity for various protected classes of individuals. Although the 1964 act is probably the best known and most influential piece of legislation in this area, a new civil rights act was passed in 1991 and numerous other laws deal with different aspects of equal employment or are concerned with specific areas of work; these are discussed in this section. Some of them apply only to federal contractors, and these are discussed separately, while others apply more widely. We will discuss each one briefly here and again in the chapters where they are most relevant.

The Equal Pay Act of 1963 The **Equal Pay Act of 1963** requires that organizations provide the same pay to men and women who are doing equal work. The law defines equality in terms of skill, responsibility, effort, and working conditions. Thus, an organization cannot pay a man more than it pays a woman for the same job on the grounds that, say, the male employee needs the money more because he has a bigger family to support. Similarly, organizations cannot circumvent the law by using different job titles for essentially the same work: If the work is essentially the same, then the pay should be the same as well. The law does allow for pay differences when there are legitimate, job-related reasons for pay differences such as difference in seniority or merit.[28]

© Michael Iedray/Shutterstock

The Age Discrimination and Employment Act The **Age Discrimination and Employment Act (ADEA)** was passed in 1967 and amended in 1986. The ADEA prohibits discrimination against employees 40 years of age and older. The ADEA is similar to Title VII of the 1964 Civil Rights Act in terms of both its major provisions and the procedures that are followed in pursuing a case of discrimination. Like Title VII, enforcement of the ADEA is the responsibility of the Equal Employment Opportunity Commission.

The ADEA was felt to be necessary because of a disquieting trend in some organizations in the early 1960s. Specifically, these firms were beginning to discriminate against older employees when they had to lay people off or otherwise scale back their workforce. By targeting older workers—who tended to have higher pay because of their

> **The Equal Pay Act of 1963 requires that organizations provide men and women who are doing equal work the same pay.**

seniority and experience with the firm—companies were substantially cutting their labor costs. In addition, there was some feeling that organizations were also discriminating against older workers in their hiring decisions. The specific concern here was that organizations would not hire people in their forties or fifties because (1) they would have

The Pregnancy Discrimination Act of 1979

As its name suggests, the **Pregnancy Discrimination Act of 1979** was passed to protect pregnant women from discrimination in the workplace. The law requires that the pregnant woman be treated like any other employee in the workplace. Therefore, the act specifies that a woman

> **The Age Discrimination and Employment Act (or ADEA) prohibits discrimination against employees age forty and older.**

to pay those individuals more based on their experience and salary history and (2) they would have a shorter potential career with the organization. Consequently, some organizations were found guilty of giving preferential treatment to younger workers over older workers. These concerns have been raised again as firms deal with the economic downturn by reducing the size of their workforce. It is vital that firms that are downsizing be aware of the implications of this legislation and ensure that their efforts are not differentially affecting older workers.

Mandatory retirement ages is the other area in which the ADEA has generated a fair amount of controversy. The Supreme Court has indicated that an agency or an organization may require mandatory retirement at a given age only if an organization could demonstrate the inability of persons beyond a certain age to perform a given job safely. But, in several decisions, the Court has indicated that it will interpret this BFOQ exception very narrowly. In fact, in *Johnson v. Mayor and City of Baltimore*, the Court ruled that not even a federal statute requiring firefighters to retire at age 55 would qualify as an exception to the law.[29]

As the workforce continues to age, the number of age-discrimination complaints seems to be growing rapidly.[30] Statistics released by the EEOC, for instance, indicate that age-discrimination complaints increased from 19,000 in 2007 to more than 24,000 in 2008; they are now almost as common as race-discrimination complaints (the most common type of complaint filed with the EEOC). Thus, it is interesting to note that the Supreme Court recently ruled that in age-discrimination cases it is up to the worker to prove that age was the decisive factor in a decision made by the employer—even if there is evidence that age played some role in the decision (*Gross v. FBL Financial Services 08-441*, in June 2009). By making it more difficult to file these so-called mixed motive cases in ADEA charges, the Court has essentially made it much more difficult to demonstrate age discrimination. Leaders in Congress soon began working on a revised ADEA to deal with this issue, but that new legislation is a long way from becoming law.

cannot be refused a job or promotion, fired, or otherwise discriminated against simply because she is pregnant (or has had an abortion). She also cannot be forced to leave employment with the organization as long as she is physically able to work. Finally, the Pregnancy Discrimination Act also specifies that if other employees have the right to return to their jobs after a leave, then this benefit must also be accorded to pregnant women. Several years ago, actress Hunter Tylo won a $5 million judgment against the producers of her television show, *Melrose Place*, after they used her pregnancy as a basis for writing her out of the show.[31]

The Civil Rights Act of 1991

The **Civil Rights Act of 1991** was passed as a direct amendment of Title VII of the Civil Rights Act of 1964. During the 25 years following the passage of the original act, the U.S. Supreme Court handed down several rulings that helped define how the Civil Rights Act would be administered. But in the course of its 1989 Supreme Court session, several decisions

> **The Civil Rights Act of 1991 makes it easier for individuals who feel they have been discriminated against to take legal action against organizations and provides for the payment of compensatory and punitive damages in cases of discrimination under Title VII.**

were handed down that many people felt seriously limited the viability of the Civil Rights Act of 1964.[32] In response to this development, the Civil Rights Act of 1991 was passed essentially to restore the force of the original act. Although some new aspects of the law were introduced as part of the Civil Rights Act of 1991, the primary purpose of this new law was to make it easier for individuals who feel they have been discriminated against to take legal action against organizations. As a result, this law also reinforced the idea that a firm must remain within the limits of the law when engaging in various human resource management practices.

Specifically, the Civil Rights Act of 1991 prohibits discrimination on the job and makes it easier for the burden of proof to shift to employers (to demonstrate that they did not discriminate). It also reinforces the illegality of making hiring, firing, or promotion decisions on the basis of race, gender, color, religion, or national origin; it also includes the Glass Ceiling Act, which established a commission to investigate practices that limited the access of protected class members (especially women) to the top levels of management in organizations. For the first time, the act provides the potential payment of compensatory and punitive damages in cases of discrimination under Title VII. Although the law limited the amount of punitive damages that could be paid to no more than nine times the amount

completed, her career opportunities would not have been compromised in any way.[33]

The Americans with Disabilities Act of 1990

The **Americans with Disabilities Act of 1990 (ADA)** is another piece of equal employment legislation that has greatly affected human resource management. The ADA was passed in response to growing criticisms and concerns about employment opportunities denied to people with various disabilities. For example, one survey found that of 12.2 million Americans not working because of disabilities, 8.2 million would have preferred to work. Similarly, another survey found that almost 80 percent of all managers surveyed found the overall performance of their disabled workers to be good to excellent. In response to these trends and pressures, the ADA was passed to protect individuals with disabilities from being discriminated against in the workplace.[34]

Specifically, the ADA prohibits discrimination based on disability in all aspects of the employment relationship such as job application procedures, hiring, firing, promotion, compensation, and training, as well as other employment activities such as advertising, recruiting, tenure, layoffs, leave, and benefits. In addition, the ADA also requires that organizations make reasonable accommoda-

> The Americans with Disabilities Act of 1990 (or ADA) prohibits discrimination based on disability and all aspects of the employment relationship such as job application procedures, hiring, firing, promotion, compensation, and training, as well as other employment activities such as advertising, recruiting, tenure, layoffs, and leave and fringe benefits.

of compensatory damages, it also allowed juries rather than federal judges to hear these cases.

This law also makes it possible for employees of U.S. companies working in foreign countries to bring suit against those companies for violation of the Civil Rights Act. The only exception to this provision is the situation in which a country has laws that specifically contradict some aspect of the Civil Rights Act. For example, Muslim countries often have laws limiting the rights of women. Foreign companies with operations in such countries would almost certainly be required to abide by local laws. As a result, a female employee of a U.S. company working in such a setting would not be directly protected under the Civil Rights Act. However, her employer would still need to inform her fully of the kinds of discriminatory practices she might face as a result of transferring to the foreign site and then ensure that when this particular foreign assignment was

tions for disabled employees as long as they do not pose an undue burden on the organization. The act initially went into effect in 1992 and covered employers with twenty-five or more employees. It was expanded in July 1994 to cover employers with fifteen or more employees.

The ADA defines a *disability* as (1) a mental or physical impairment that limits one or more major life activities, (2) a record of having such an impairment, or (3) being regarded as having such an impairment. Clearly included within the domain of the ADA are individuals with disabilities such as blindness, deafness, paralysis, and similar disabilities. In addition, the ADA covers employees with cancer, a history of mental illness, or a history of heart disease. Finally, the act also covers employees regarded as having a disability, such as individuals who are disfigured or who for some other reason an employer feels will prompt a negative reaction from others. In addition, the ADA covers mental and psychological disorders such as mental retardation, emotional or mental illness (including depression), and learning disabilities.

On the other hand, individuals with substance-abuse problems, obesity, and similar non–work-related characteristics may not be covered by the ADA.[35] But because

human resource manager and other executives in organizations. Clearly, for example, organizations must provide ramps and wide hallways to accommodate individuals confined to a wheelchair.

At the same time, however, providing accommodations for other disabilities may be more complex. If

> **The ADA Amendments Act (or ADAAA) of 2008 broadens the protection offered to persons with disabilities at work by defining certain disabilities as "presumptive," thus negating several court cases that had ruled certain persons having disabilities as not qualifying for coverage under the ADA.**

the ADA defines disabilities in terms of limitations on life activities, myriad cases continue to be filed. For example, in recent years workers have attempted to claim protection under the ADA on the basis of ailments ranging from alcoholism to dental problems! These activities have led some critics to question whether the ADA is being abused by workers rather than protecting their rights.[36]

In fact, the definition of a disability and what constitutes a "reasonable accommodation" pose the greatest potential problems for the HR manager. Individuals who are confined to wheelchairs, visually impaired, or have similar physical disabilities are usually quite easy to identify, but many employees may suffer from "invisible" disabilities that might include physical problems (e.g., someone needing dialysis) as well as psychological problems (e.g., acute anxiety) and learning disabilities (e.g., dyslexia). It is not always obvious who among a group of employees is actually eligible for protection under the ADA.[37]

One area of coverage where the courts and the EEOC (the agency charged with the administration of the ADA) have taken a fairly clear position deals with AIDS and HIV in the workplace. Both AIDS and HIV are considered disabilities under the ADA, and employers cannot legally require an HIV test or any other medical examination as a condition for making an offer of employment. In addition, organizations must maintain confidentiality of all medical records, they should strive to educate co-workers about AIDS, and they must accommodate or try to accommodate AIDS victims.

In addition, the reasonable accommodation stipulation adds considerable complexity to the job of

an applicant for a job takes an employment test, fails the test (and so is not offered employment), and *then* indicates that he or she has a learning disability (for example) that makes it difficult to take paper-and-pencil tests, the applicant probably can demand an accommodation. Specifically, the organization would likely be required either to find a different way to administer the test or provide the applicant with additional time to take the test a second time before making a final decision. Likewise, an existing employee diagnosed with a psychological disorder may be able to request on-site psychological support.

Recently, another issue involved with granting accommodations has been identified.[38] The nature of many accommodations granted to employees is such that other employees who are not disabled and not requesting an accommodation are unlikely to be envious or resentful about the accommodation. But this is not the case for all requested accommodations. For example, a woman claimed that having every Friday off was the only accommodation that would help to reduce her stress at work.[39] What if the organization granted her that accommodation? Surely other employees would wonder why they could not have Fridays off, especially since stress is not typically a visible disability. This situation would lead to resentment and potentially to other problems. Therefore, although the ADA does not consider co-worker reactions as relevant to determining whether or not an accommodation is reasonable, the knowledgeable human resource manager will at least think about how others might react to an accommodation when trying to deal with the legal requests of employees with disabilities.

But a series of court decisions have worked to actually narrow the protection

© Christophe Testi/Shutterstock

offered by the ADA.[40] For example, in 1999 the U.S. Supreme Court ruled that individuals who can correct or overcome their disabilities through medication or other means are not protected by the ADA. Similarly, in 1999 (*Sutton v. United Airlines*), the Court ruled that a person suffering from heart disease who was taking medication to control that heart disease was not covered by the ADA. In 2002, in *Toyota Motor Manufacturing Company, Kentucky Inc, v. Williams*, the Court ruled that, for persons to be disabled, they had to have conditions that precluded

provide the employee with the same or comparable job on the employee's return.[41]

The law also requires the organization to pay the health-care coverage of the employee during the leave. However, the employer can require the employee to reimburse these health-care premiums if the employee fails to return to work after the absence. Organizations are also allowed to exclude certain key employees from coverage (specifically defined as the highest paid 10 percent), on the grounds that granting leave to these individuals

> **The Family and Medical Leave Act of 1993 requires employers having more than fifty employees to provide as many as 12 weeks unpaid leave for employees after the birth or adoption of a child; to care for a seriously ill child, spouse, or parent; or if the employee is seriously ill.**

them from doing activities central to one's daily life. Thus, they ruled that Ella Williams was not disabled, even though her carpal tunnel syndrome and tendinitis prevented her from performing the assembly-line job she was transferred to because she was able to attend to her personal hygiene.

In an attempt to return to the original intent of the ADA, in September 2008, President Bush signed into law the new **Americans with Disabilities Amendments Act (ADAAA)**. In June 2009, the EEOC finally voted on a set of guidelines to be used with the new law. The new guidelines broaden the definition of disability for the ADA, countering recent court decisions that have tended to narrow the definition of disability for cases brought forward (which was the original impetus for the law). For example, the changes would include specifying major life activities to include walking, seeing, bending, reading, and concentrating. The new guidelines also include a list of presumptive disabilities that will always meet the definition of disability under the AADA, including blindness, deafness, cancer, multiple sclerosis, limb loss, and HIV and AIDS. Also, under the new guidelines, persons will be "regarded as having a disability" if they can show that they have been discriminated against because of real or perceived disabilities.

The Family and Medical Leave Act of 1993
The **Family and Medical Leave Act of 1993** was passed in part to remedy weaknesses in the Pregnancy Discrimination Act of 1979. The law requires employers with more than fifty employees to provide as many as 12 weeks of unpaid leave for employees (1) after the birth or adoption of a child; (2) to care for a seriously ill child, spouse, or parent; or (3) if the employee is seriously ill. The organization must also

would grant serious economic harm to the organization. The law also does not apply to employees who have not worked an average of 25 hours a week in the previous 12 months.[42] The FMLA was also amended in 2009 with the passage of the Supporting Military Families Act, which mandates emergency leave for all covered active-duty members.

Regulations for Federal Contractors In addition to the various laws described above, numerous other regulations apply only to federal contractors. Note, however, that the definition of a federal contractor is quite broad. For instance, all banks (that participate in the U.S. Federal Reserve system) and most universities (that have federal research grants or that accept federal loans for their students) would qualify as federal contractors.

Executive Order 11246 was issued by President Lyndon Johnson, who believed that Title VII of the 1964 Civil Rights Act was not comprehensive enough. This order prohibits discrimination based on race, color, religion, sex, or national origin for organizations that are federal contractors and subcontractors, and it requires written affirmative action plans from those organizations with contracts greater than $50,000.

Executive Order 11478 was issued by President Richard Nixon and required the federal government to base all of its own employment policies on merit and fitness and specifies that race, color, sex, religion, and national origin should not be considered. The executive order also extends to all contractors and subcontractors doing $10,000 or more worth of business with the federal government. These executive orders are enforced by the Office of Federal Contract Compliance Procedures (OFCCP), which is discussed later.

The **Vocational Rehabilitation Act of 1973** requires that executive agencies and subcontractors and contractors of the federal government receiving more than $2,500 a year from the government engage in affirmative action for disabled individuals. This act is administered by the Department of Labor. Finally, the **Vietnam Era Veterans' Readjustment Act of 1974** requires that federal contractors and subcontractors take affirmative action toward employing Vietnam-era veterans. Vietnam-era veterans are specifically defined as those serving as members of the U.S. armed forces between August 5, 1964, and May 7, 1975. This act is enforced through the OFCCP.

Enforcing Equal Employment Opportunity

The enforcement of equal opportunity legislation generally is handled by two agencies. As noted earlier, one agency is the Equal Employment Opportunity Commission, and the other is the Office of Federal Contract Compliance Procedures. The EEOC is a division of the Department of Justice. It was created by Title VII of the 1964 Civil Rights Act and today is given specific responsibility for enforcing Title VII, the Equal Pay Act, and the Americans with Disabilities Act. The EEOC has three major functions: (1) investigating and resolving complaints about alleged discrimination, (2) gathering information regarding employment patterns and trends in U.S. businesses, and (3) issuing information about new employment guidelines as they become relevant.

The first function is illustrated in Exhibit 2.3, which depicts the basic steps that an individual who thinks she has been discriminated against in a promotion decision

> **Executive Order 11478 requires the federal government to base all of its own employment policies on merit and fitness and specifies that race, color, sex, religion, and national origin should not be considered.**

60-day period, then the individual has the right to sue in a federal court.

If the EEOC believes that discrimination has occurred, then its representative will first try to negotiate a reconciliation between the two parties without taking the case to court. Occasionally, the EEOC may enter into a consent decree with the discriminating organization. This consent decree is essentially an agreement between the EEOC and the organization stipulating that the organization will cease certain discriminatory practices and perhaps implement new affirmative action procedures to rectify its history of discrimination.

On the other hand, if the EEOC cannot reach an agreement with the organization, then two courses of action may be pursued. First, the EEOC can issue a

> **The Vocational Rehabilitation Act of 1973 requires that executive agencies and subcontractors and contractors of the federal government receiving more than $2,500 a year from the government engage in affirmative action for disabled individuals.**

might follow to get her complaint addressed. In general, if an individual believes that she or he has been discriminated against, the first step in reaching a resolution is to file a complaint with the EEOC or a corresponding state agency. The individual has 180 days from the date of the incident to file the complaint. The EEOC will dismiss out of hand almost all complaints that exceed the 180-day time frame for filing. After the complaint has been filed, the EEOC assumes responsibility for investigating the claim itself. The EEOC can take as many as 60 days to investigate a complaint. If the EEOC either finds that the complaint is not valid or does not complete the investigation within a

right-to-sue letter to the victim; the letter simply certifies that the agency has investigated the complaint and found potential validity in the victim's allegations. Essentially, that course of action involves the EEOC giving its blessings to the individual to file suit on his or her own behalf. Alternatively, in certain limited cases, the EEOC itself may assist the victim in bringing suit in federal court. In either event, however, the lawsuit must be filed in federal court within 300 days of the alleged discriminatory act. The courts strictly follow this guideline, and many valid complaints have lost standing in court because lawsuits were not filed on time. As already noted, the EEOC

EXHIBIT 2.3 Investigating and Resolving a Discrimination Complaint

MARY SMITH believes she has been discriminated against at work. She was passed over for a promotion to supervisor, and believes it was because she was a woman, rather than because she was unqualified. Specifically, all candidates for promotion must be approved by their immediate supervisor, and most of these supervisors are older white men who have been heard to say that women should not be promoted. In fact, almost no women have been promoted to supervisor in this organization. What can Mary do?

STEP 1: Mary files a complaint with her local or state EEO agency.

STEP 2: Local/state EEO agency agrees to investigate Mary's claim on behalf of EEOC, and the agency contacts Mary's employer to determine whether the claim has any merit.

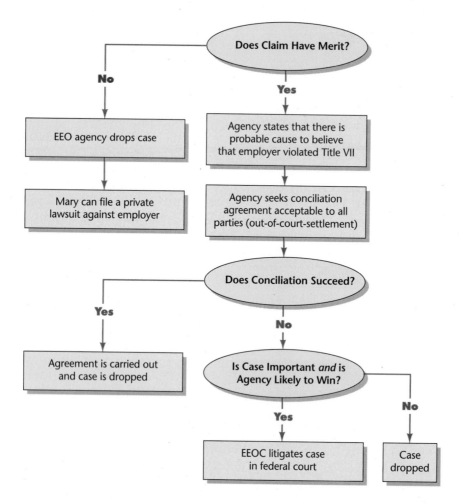

has recently become backlogged with complaints stemming primarily from the passage of the newer civil rights act. One recent court case that involved the implementation of a discriminatory seniority system was settled in such a way that it helped provide the grounds for amending Title VII to provide exceptions to the 300-day deadline for filing a lawsuit. In recent years, the EEOC has been working to better prioritize its caseload, giving the highest priority to cases that appear to have the potential for widespread or classwide effects.[43]

The second important function of the EEOC is to monitor the hiring practices of organizations. Every year, all organizations that employ 100 or more individuals must file a report with the EEOC that summarizes the number of women and minorities that the organization employs in nine different job categories. The EEOC tracks these reports to identify potential patterns of discrimination that it can then potentially address through class-action lawsuits.

The third function of the EEOC is to develop and issue guidelines that help organizations determine whether their decisions are violations of the law enforced by the EEOC. These guidelines themselves are not laws, but the courts have generally given them great weight when hearing employment-discrimination cases. One of the most important set of guidelines is the uniform guidelines on employee-selection procedures developed jointly by the EEOC, U.S. Department of Labor, U.S. Department of Justice, and U.S. Civil Service Commission. These

EXHIBIT 2.3 (Continued)

Once the case goes to court, and assuming that Mary and EEOC believe they have a case of disparate impact, the process goes through several more crucial steps.

STEP 1: Mary tries to establish a *prima facie* case of discrimination.

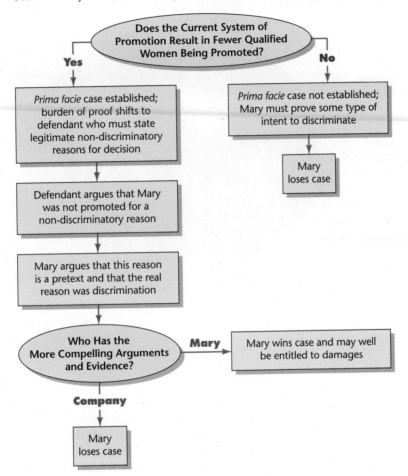

guidelines summarize how organizations should develop and administer selection systems to avoid violating Title VII. The EEOC also frequently uses the *Federal Register* to issue new guidelines and opinions regarding employment practices that result from newly passed laws.[44] This was the case discussed earlier relating to the new ADAAA.[45]

The other agency primarily charged with monitoring equal employment opportunity legislation is the Office of Federal Contract Compliance Procedures. The OFCCP is responsible for enforcing the executive orders that cover companies doing business with the federal government. Recall from our earlier discussion that businesses with contracts of more than $50,000 cannot discriminate based on race, color, religious beliefs, national origin, or gender, and they must have a written affirmative action plan on file.[46]

The OFCCP conducts yearly audits of government contractors to ensure that they have been actively pursuing their affirmative action goals. These audits involve examining a company's affirmative action plan and conducting

on-site visits to determine how individual employees perceive the company's affirmative action policies. If the OFCCP finds that its contractors or subcontractors are not complying with the relevant executive orders, then it may notify the EEOC, advise the Department of Justice to institute criminal proceedings, or request that the labor secretary cancel or suspend contracts with that organization. This latter step is the OFCCP's most important weapon because it has a clear and immediate effect on an organization's revenue stream.

The EEOC and the OFCCP are the two primary regulatory agencies for enforcing equal employment legislation, but it is important to recognize that other agencies and components of our government system also come into play. The Departments of Labor and Justice, for example, are both heavily involved in the enforcement of equal employment opportunity legislation. The U.S. Civil Service Commission is also actively involved for government organizations where civil-service jobs exist. The

U.S. judicial systems reflected by our courts also play an important role in enforcing all human resource management legislation.

OTHER AREAS OF HUMAN RESOURCE REGULATION

As noted earlier, most employment regulations are designed to provide equal employment opportunity, but some legislation goes beyond that and really deals more substantively with other issues. We will only touch on these different areas of legislation here and then discuss them in more detail when we discuss the content area involved. So, for example, we begin with a discussion of legislation dealing with compensation and benefits and then discuss these laws in more detail in Chapter 9.

Legal Perspectives on Compensation and Benefits

The most basic and yet far-reaching law dealing with compensation at work is the Fair Labor Standards Act. The **Fair Labor Standards Act (FLSA)**, passed in 1938, established a minimum hourly wage for jobs. The rationale for this legislation was to ensure that everyone who works would receive an income sufficient to meet basic needs. The first minimum wage was $0.25 an hour but, as shown in Table 2.1, the minimum wage has been raised many times in the decades since as the law has been amended. The most recent change came in 2007, when then President Bush signed into a law a staged increase that brought the minimum wage to $7.25 an hour as of July 2009.[47] States are also allowed to pass laws that provide a minimum wage rate higher than the federal level. For example, in 2010, both Connecticut and Illinois set minimum wages of $8.25.

The FSLA also established, for the first time, the workweek in the United States as 40 hours per week. It further specified that all full-time employees must be paid

> **The Fair Labor Standards Act (FLSA) established a minimum hourly wage for jobs.**

at a rate of one and a half times their normal hourly rate for each hour of work beyond 40 hours in a week. Note,

however, that the law makes no provision for daily work time. Thus, a normal workday might be considered 8 hours, but an employer is actually free to schedule, say, 10 or 12 hours in a single day without paying overtime as long as the weekly total does not exceed 40 hours. The FLSA also includes child labor provisions, which provide protection for persons 18 years of age and younger. These protections include keeping minors from working on extremely dangerous jobs and limiting the number of hours that persons younger than sixteen can work.

Another important piece of legislation that affects compensation is the **Employee Retirement Income Security Act of 1974 (ERISA)**. This law was passed to protect employee investments in their pensions and to ensure that employees would be able to receive at least some pension benefits at the time of retirement or even termination. ERISA does not mean that an employee *must* receive a pension; it is meant only to protect any pension benefits to which the employee is entitled. (This topic will be discussed in somewhat more detail in Chapter 9.) ERISA was passed in part because some organizations had abused their pension plans in their efforts to control costs or to channel money inappropriately to other uses within the organization and in part because of corruption.

Two other emerging legal perspectives on compensation and benefits involve minimum benefits coverage and executive compensation. Recent publicity about the poor benefits Walmart provides some of its employees, for example, led the Maryland General Assembly to pass a bill requiring employers with more than 10,000 workers to spend at least 8 percent of their payroll on benefits or else pay into a fund for the uninsured. At the time the bill was passed (in early 2006) Walmart was the only company to be affected. Moreover, several other states are exploring similar legislation. On another front, the Securities and Exchange Commission (SEC) is also developing new guidelines that will require companies to divulge more complete and detailed information about their executive-compensation packages.[48]

One of the major agenda items first tackled by President Obama was health care. Congress worked throughout 2009 in an attempt to pass legislation that would call for major reforms of health care in the United States.

TABLE 2.1 — Minimum Wage Histroy

Effective Date	Minimum Wage ($)
1938	0.25
1939	0.30
1945	0.40
1950	0.75
1956	1.00
1961	1.15
1963	1.25
1967	1.40
1968	1.60
1974	2.00
1975	2.10
1976	2.30
1978	2.65
1979	2.90
1980	3.10
1981	3.35
1990	3.80
1991	4.25
1996	4.75
1997	5.15
2007	5.85
2008	6.55
2009	7.25

The Health Care reform Bill passed in 2010 focused on benefits for employees who were not already covered by employer programs. The notion that employers who did not provide health care coverage would be required to pay a fine was part of the "Affordable Care for America Act"[49] proposed by the Democrats in 2009. The final Bill did not include the much-debated "public option" and both parties agree that there will continue to be modifications to and challenges to the new health care bill in the coming years, and it may take quite some time before all the implications of this legislation are clear. We will discuss these regulations again in Chapter 9.

Legal Perspectives on Labor Relations

The **National Labor Relations Act**, or **Wagner Act**, was passed in 1935 in an effort to control and legislate collective bargaining between organizations and labor unions. Before 1935, the legal system in the United States was generally considered hostile to labor unions. The Wagner Act was passed in an effort to provide some sense of balance in the power relationship between organizations and unions. The Wagner Act describes the process through which labor unions can be formed and the requirements faced by organizations in dealing with those labor unions. The Wagner Act served to triple union membership in the United States and granted labor unions significant power in their relationships with organizations.

Following a series of crippling strikes, however, the U.S. government concluded that the Wagner Act had actually shifted too much power to labor unions. As a result, businesses had been placed at a significant disadvantage. To correct this imbalance, Congress subsequently passed the **Labor Management Relations Act (Taft-Hartley Act)** in 1947 and the **Landrum-Griffin Act** in 1959. Both of these acts regulate union actions and their internal affairs in a way that puts them on an equal footing with management and organizations. The Taft-Hartley Act also created the National Labor Relations Board (NLRB), which was charged with enforcement of the act.

Although the basic issues of unionization and collective bargaining have become pretty well established, some legal issues have emerged in this area. The Taft-Hartley Act guarantees these rights but also guarantees that these unions should be independent. This issue has come up in two fairly recent cases. More important for the future, in both these cases, the company involved was setting up autonomous work teams that were empowered to make certain decisions about employees. In *Electromation* v. *NLRB*,[50] the NLRB ruled that the company's "action committees," which were formed to deal with employee working conditions and were staffed by employees, actually

> **The Employee Retirement Income Security Act of 1974 (ERISA) guarantees a basic minimum benefit that employees could expect to be paid at retirement.**

President Barrack Obama achieved his goal of health care reform with the passage of new health care legislation in 2010.

constituted a threat to the union already in place in the company. These action committees, which the NLRB ruled were dominated by management, were seen as an alternative way to deal with problems concerning working conditions and could allow the company to circumvent the union and the collective-bargaining process. As such, the company was found in violation of the Taft Hartley Act. In a similar case, *E.I. Du Pont de Nemours v. NLRB*,[51] the board ruled that Du Pont's safety committees were

vote that now exists. Although the law has not yet been passed, it has generated considerable support as well as opposition. President Obama is said to support the new law.[52]

Employee Safety and Health

Employees also have the right to work in safe and healthy environments, and these rights continue to be important in

> **The Labor Management Relations Act (or Taft-Hartley Act) curtailed and limited union powers and regulates union actions and their internal affairs in a way that puts them on equal footing with management and organizations.**

essentially employer-dominated labor organizations and thus were in violation of the Taft Hartley Act.

Recently, a new amendment was proposed for the Taft-Hartley Act. We will discuss this proposed change, along with these other labor relations laws, in Chapter 11. It is worth noting that the **Employee Free Choice Act,** also known as the Union Relief Act of 2009, would change the way in which unions become certified as bargaining agents in companies, eliminating the secret ballot

organizations. The **Occupational Safety and Health Act of 1970 (OSHA)** is the single most comprehensive piece of legislation regarding worker safety and health in organizations. OSHA granted the federal government the power to establish and enforce occupational safety and health standards for all places of employment directly affecting interstate commerce. The Department of Labor was given power to apply OSHA standards and enforce its provisions. The Department of Health was given responsibility for conducting research to determine the criteria for specific operations or occupations and for training employers to comply with the act itself. OSHA also makes provisions through which individual states can substitute their own

users). As a result, several alternatives have begun to appear in organizations, including testing an employee's individual hairs.[54] Perhaps these new technologies will reduce some of the concerns over drug testing while providing

> **The Landrum-Griffin Act focused on eliminating various unethical, illegal, and undemocratic practices within unions themselves**

safety and health standards for those suggested by the federal government.

The basic premise of OSHA (also known as the *general duty clause*) is that each employer has an obligation to furnish each employee with a place of employment that is free from hazards that can cause death or physical harm. OSHA is generally enforced through inspections of the workplace by OSHA inspectors, and fines can be imposed on violators. We will deal with these issues in more detail in Chapter 12.

Drugs in the Workplace

The **Drug-Free Workplace Act of 1988** was passed to reduce the use of illegal drugs in the workplace. This law applies primarily to government employees and federal contractors, but it also extends to organizations regulated by the Department of Transportation and the Nuclear Regulatory Commission. Thus, long-haul truck drivers and workers at most nuclear reactors are subject to these regulations. The actual regulations themselves are aimed at establishing a drug-free workplace and include the requirement, in some cases, for regular drug testing.

Concerns over the problems of drug use at work have also led many other companies not covered by this law to establish drug-testing programs of their own. In fact, drug testing is becoming quite widespread, even though there is little hard evidence addressing the effectiveness of these programs.[53] The issue for the current discussion is whether these testing programs constitute an invasion of employee privacy. Many opponents of drug-testing programs argue that drug testing is clearly appropriate in cases in which there is some "reasonable" basis for suspected drug use, but not otherwise. Others argue that organizations that test for drug use often do not test for alcohol use which, although not illegal, can cause problems on the job. Of course, what makes the privacy issues here even more salient is the method generally used to test for drugs on the job. Urinalysis (by far the most common method) is extremely invasive and has been known to result in a fair number of false-positive tests (i.e., employees are incorrectly identified as drug

employers the protection they deserve from drug use on the job.

Plant Closings and Employee Rights

The **Worker Adjustment and Retraining Notification (WARN) Act of 1988** stipulates that an organization with at least 100 employees must provide notice at least 60 days in advance of plans to close a facility or lay off 50 or more employees. The penalty for failing to comply is equal to 1 day's pay (plus benefits) for each employee for each day that notice should have been given. An organization that closes a plant without any warning and lays off 1,000 employees would be liable for 60 days of pay and

> **The Occupational Safety and Health Act of 1970 (or OSHA) grants the federal government the power to establish and enforce occupational safety and health standards for all places of employment directly affecting interstate commerce.**

benefits for those 1,000 employees, which could translate into a substantial amount of money. The act also provides for warnings about pending reductions in work hours but generally applies only to private employers. There are exceptions to the WARN requirements; those exceptions are related to unforeseeable business circumstances such as a strike at a major employer or a government-enforced

OSHA provides detailed specifications for the safety equipment this steel worker is wearing (the gloves, goggles, and helmet), the distance he should maintain from the vat, and the procedures he should use to carry out the key elements of this job.

shutdown.[55] The events of September 11, 2001, represent one such exception to this law.

Privacy Issues at Work

In recent years, issues of privacy have become more important to Americans, so it is not surprising that privacy at

But the larger concerns with privacy these days relate to potential invasions of employee privacy by organizations. For example, organizations generally reserve the right to monitor the e-mail correspondence of employees. Presumably, employees should be using company e-mail only for company business, so this practice may not be a problem, but it does mean that employees who receive

> **The Worker Adjustment and Retraining Notification (WARN) Act of 1988 stipulates that an organization employing at least 100 employees must provide notice at least 60 days in advance of plans to close a facility or lay off 50 or more employees.**

work has also become more important. The history of legislation dealing with privacy at work, however, actually goes back several years. The **Privacy Act of 1974** applies directly to federal employees only, but it has served as the impetus for several state laws. Basically, this legislation allows employees to review their personnel files periodically to ensure that the information contained in them is accurate. Before this privacy legislation, managers could place almost any information they pleased in a personnel file, certain that only other managers could see those files.

unsolicited e-mails from suspect vendors (such as pornographic Web sites) may also have that information shared with their employers.

Late in 2009, Congress passed a law dealing with a different type of privacy. The **Genetic Information Non-discrimination Act (GINA)** prohibits employers from collecting any genetic information about their employees, including information about family history of disease. This would mean that such information could not be obtained even during a medical examination, although there is some recognition that such information could be obtained "inadvertently" in some cases. One of the more interesting challenges posed by this new legislation is that some information about family medical history is often collected

human resource management, it is critically important that organizations comply with the laws and regulations that govern human resource management practices to the best of their ability. The assurance of compli-

The Genetic Information Nondiscrimination Act (GINA) of 2009 prohibits employers from obtaining genetic information about employees.

as part of determining whether or not a person requires an accommodation under the ADA. Such practices are now illegal, and it is not clear what effect this will have on the enforcement of the ADA.

The **PATRIOT Act** was passed shortly after the terrorist attacks on September 11, 2001, to help the United States more effectively battle terrorism worldwide. Many of the act's provisions expand the rights of the government or law enforcement agencies to collect information about and pursue potential terrorists. Some major provisions include those that allow law enforcement agencies to use surveillance to gather information related to a full range of terrorist crimes; those that allow law enforcement agencies to carry out investigations of potential terrorists without having to inform the targets of those investigations; and those that allow law enforcement agencies to obtain search warrants any place a terrorist activity might occur.

EVALUATING LEGAL COMPLIANCE

Given the clear and obvious importance as well as the complexities associated with the legal environment of

ance can best be done through a three-step process. The first step is to ensure that managers clearly understand the laws that govern every aspect of human resource management. In other words, all managers must understand and be intimately familiar with the various laws that restrict and govern their behavior vis-à-vis their employees.

Second, managers should rely on their own legal and human resource staff to answer questions and review procedures periodically. Almost all larger organizations have a legal staff consisting of professionals trained in various areas of the legal environment of business. A human resource manager or other manager with a legal question regarding a particular employment issue or practice is well advised to consult the firm's attorney about the legality of that particular action.

And third, organizations may also find it useful to engage occasionally in external legal audits of their human resource management procedures. This audit might involve contracting with an outside law firm to review the organization's HRM systems and practices to ensure that they comply with all appropriate laws and regulations. Such an external audit will, of course, be expensive and somewhat intrusive into the organization's daily routine. When properly conducted, however, external audits can keep an organization out of trouble.

CLOSING CASE

SEINFELD AND SEXUAL HARASSMENT

What role can a popular television show possibly play in a major sexual harassment lawsuit? As it turns out, a pretty big one! The show in question is *Seinfeld*, one of the most popular sit-coms in television history. The event that sparked the lawsuit took place in the corporate headquarters of Miller Brewing Company and involved Jerold MacKenzie, a 55-year-old executive with 19 years at Miller, and Patricia Best, his secretary.

The incident occurred several years ago. The *Seinfeld* episode in question involved a story in which the show's main character, Jerry

Seinfeld, meets and starts dating a woman whose first name he cannot recall. But he does recall that it rhymes with a part of the female anatomy. He subsequently spends the rest of the episode mentally running through different possible names for the woman. She dumps him when she realizes that he doesn't know her name. After she leaves, he finally remembers that her name is Delores.

Mr. MacKenzie apparently found the show to be especially funny. On the day after the show aired, he made a point of bringing it up for discussion with his secretary. Ms. Best indicated that she had not seen the show. As he began to describe the show for her, she indicated to him that she didn't want to discuss it. Mr. MacKenzie persisted, however, and continued to push her into discussing it with him. When he couldn't bring himself to say the name of the female body part, however, he made a photocopy of a dictionary page containing the word and gave it to Ms. Best.

Ms. Best became quite upset and reported to Miller Brewing Company's HR department that Mr. MacKenzie had sexually harassed her. She also indicated that he had harassed her on earlier occasions. A few days later, Mr. MacKenzie was summoned to a meeting with a group of Miller attorneys and a senior HR manager. He was asked about the *Seinfeld* incident, and he acknowledged that it had happened as Ms. Best had reported. He also indicated that he saw their discussion simply as office conversation and that Ms. Best had not seemed to be bothered or upset at the time of the conversation.

The next day, Mr. MacKenzie was visited by another senior corporate executive; this executive indicated that he (MacKenzie) was being terminated for unacceptable management performance. The incident with Ms. Best was identified as a major part of the final decision to terminate MacKenzie's employment with Miller, but he was also told that it was part of a pattern of poor decisions that had already attracted the attention of senior managers. Mr. MacKenzie indicated surprise but left with little argument or discussion.

As time passed, however, Mr. MacKenzie gradually began to feel that he had been mistreated. He eventually reached the point where he felt compelled to take some action. After consulting with his attorney, he filed a lawsuit against Miller Brewing Company, the executive who had made the decision to terminate him, and Ms. Best. Among his charges were wrongful discharge and libel. After hearing both sides of the case, a jury of ten women and two men decided that he was right. Indeed, they so strongly believed that Mr. MacKenzie was a victim rather than a sexual harasser that they awarded unusually large judgments, including punitive damages, of $24.5 million against Miller Brewing Company, $1.5 million against Ms. Best (this amount was later dropped due to a legal technicality), and slightly more than $600,000 against the executive who had terminated him.[56]

THINK IT OVER

1. Do you think Mr. MacKenzie's actions constituted sexual harassment? Why or why not?
2. Do you think Miller Brewing Company's termination of Mr. MacKenzie was justified? Why or why not?
3. What is your opinion of the jury's decision?

© Bruce T. Brown/Getty Images

STUDY TOOLS

- ■ **Rip out the chapter review card located at the end of the book.**
- ■ **Review the valuable study tools located online at www.cengagebrain.com**
  - ■ **Review the Key Terms flashcards.**
  - ■ **Download audio and visual summaries to review on the go.**
  - ■ **Complete practice quizzes to prepare for the test.**
  - ■ **Play "Beat the Clock" and "QuizBowl" to master chapter concepts.**
  - ■ **Complete "Crossword Puzzle" to review key terms.**
  - ■ **Watch the chapter video for a real-life example of key concepts.**

LEARN YOUR WAY!

SHE DID

We know that no two students are alike. You come from different walks of life and with many different preferences. You need to study just about anytime and anywhere. **HR** was developed to help you learn Human Resource Management in a way that works for you.

Not only is the format fresh and contemporary, it's also concise and focused. And, **HR** is loaded with a variety of study tools, like in-text review cards, printable flash cards, and more.

Go to CourseMate for HR to find plenty of resources to help you study—no matter what learning style you like best! Access at login.cengagebrain.com.

THE GLOBAL ENVIRONMENT

THE GLOBAL TALENT SEARCH

When international businesses from the United States and Europe first began to aggressively move into China and India, they generally transferred expatriate managers from their home companies to run these new operations. Among other reasons, the firms believed they needed to export their corporate cultures and work procedures to the emerging markets they were entering; they also felt there was a lack of local managerial talent.

As recently as the mid-1990s, for example, virtually every U.S. company doing business in China filled most of its middle- and upper-management positions there with Americans. The few positions not held by Americans were often filled with managers groomed in Singapore and Hong Kong, markets where these firms had operated for several years.

In the 1990s, things began to change. In China, for instance, many locals sharpened their English-language skills, developed more leadership and decision-making skills, and became increasingly familiar and comfortable with the international business world. As a result, more and more locals are now entering the ranks of middle- and upper-level managers. An estimated 70 percent of foreign firms' top management positions in China are today filled by Chinese managers. This trend is not restricted to China; the same pattern is also occurring in India.

This pattern is found among other national firms in China. The German company Siemens, for instance, has Chinese nationals holding seven of its nine regional management positions there. And Ericsson, a Swedish telecommunications giant, currently fills

" You're not just moving people from the U.S. to the rest of the world anymore. You're sending people from all continents to all continents. "

—Robin Lissak, Deloitte principal[1]

© Mika/Corbis

LEARNING OBJECTIVES
After studying this chapter, you should be able to:

LO1 Describe the growth of international business

LO2 Identify and discuss global issues in international human resource management

LO3 Discuss the human resource management function in international business

LO4 Identify and discuss domestic issues in international human resource management

LO5 Describe the issues involved in managing international transfers and assignments

LO6 Summarize the issues in international labor relations

90 percent of its middle-management positions and half of its top management positions in China with local managers.

Why are firms moving in this direction? There are actually several reasons. For one thing, hiring local managers is much cheaper. The company avoids costly relocation expenses and does not risk expatriate failure. Further, the compensation package for a local Chinese manager is only around 20 percent to 25 percent of that of a comparable manager transferred from a Western country. Local managers have a strong understanding of local market conditions, competitive behaviors, and government regulations. In addition, hiring locally can boost employee morale and motivation.

The local manager has a strong understanding of cultural issues in the workplace and also serves as a symbol of advancement and success for other rising local managers.[2]

Despite the 2009 economic recession that hit most of the world's major marketplaces and business centers, international business remains a central component of the global economy. Almost every large firm located anywhere in the world remains on the alert for new business opportunities anywhere else in the world. Such opportunities include new markets where products and services can be sold, new locations where products and services can be created for lower costs, and areas where new information, financing, and other resources may be obtained. To manage international expansion effectively, firms need skilled and experienced managers and employees who understand both specific individual foreign markets (such as Japan or Germany) and general international issues (including areas such as exchange rate fluctuations, political risk, and the cost of labor). One of the fastest-growing and most important concerns for human resource managers in many companies today is preparing other managers for international assignments. In reality, however, this is only one part of international human resource management (HRM).

This chapter will explore international human resource management in detail. We begin with a general overview of the growth of international business and then discuss global issues in international HRM. Next we examine the HR function in international business. Domestic issues in international HRM are identified and described, and then we describe the management of international transfers and assignments. Finally, we summarize the basic issues in international labor relations.

LEARNING OBJECTIVE 1

THE GROWTH OF INTERNATIONAL BUSINESS

International business is not a new phenomenon. Indeed, its origins can be traced back literally thousands of years to merchants plying their wares along ancient trade routes linking southern Europe, northern Africa, the Middle East, and Asia. Silks, spices, grains, jade, ivory, and textiles were among the most popular goods forming the basis for early trade. Even in more recent times, Columbus's voyages to the so-called New World were motivated by the economic goal of discovering new trade routes to the Far East. Wars have been fought over issues arising from international commerce, and the British empire was built around

> *International business is not a new phenomenon: It can be traced back thousands of years to merchants plying their wares along ancient trade routes linking Europe to Asia.*

the financial and business interests of the British nobility. In more recent years, however, several specific trends have emerged in international business that provide a meaningful context for the study of human resource management.

The forces that shaped today's competitive international business environment began to emerge in the years following World War II. As a result of that global conflict, Japan and most of Europe were devastated. Roads and highways were destroyed, and factories were bombed. The United States was the only major industrial power that emerged from World War II with its infrastructure relatively intact. Places not devastated by the war, such as South and Central America and Africa, were not major players in the global economy even before the war, and Canada had yet to become a major global economic power.

Businesses in war-torn countries had little choice but to rebuild from scratch. They were in the unfortunate position of having to rethink every facet of their business, including technology, productions, operations, finance, and marketing. Ultimately, however, this position worked to their advantage. During the 1950s, the United States was by far the dominant economic power in the world. Its businesses controlled most major marketplaces and most major industries. At the same time, however, Japan, Germany, and other countries were rebuilding their own infrastructures and developing new industrial clout.

During the 1960s, this newly formed Japanese and German industrial clout began to exert itself in the world marketplace. Such German firms as Siemens, Daimler-Benz, and Bayer and Japanese companies such as Toyota, NEC, and Mitsubishi began to take on new industrial strength and slowly but surely began to challenge the dominance of U.S. firms in markets ranging from automobiles to electronics. Firms from other parts of Europe had also fully recovered and were asserting themselves in areas ranging from petroleum and energy (e.g., Shell and British Petroleum) to food (e.g., Nestlé and Cadbury) and luxury goods (e.g., LVMH and Gucci).

By the late 1970s, businesses from other countries emerged as major players in the world economy, and by the 1980s many of them had established dominant positions in their industries. At the same time, many U.S. firms had grown complacent, their products and services were not of high quality, and their manufacturing and production methods were outdated and outmoded.

Eventually, U.S. firms decided that they had little choice but to start over as well, so many of them practically rebuilt themselves in the late 1980s and early 1990s. They shut down or renovated old factories, developed new manufacturing techniques, and began to renew their emphasis on quality. By the mid-1990s, global competitiveness seemed to have become the norm rather than the exception. The United States, Japan, and Germany remained the three leading industrial powers in the world. However, other western European countries such as France, England, the Netherlands, Spain, and Belgium were also becoming increasingly important. In Asia, Taiwan, Singapore, and Malaysia were also emerging as global economic powers. Of course, China and India are clearly emerging as global powers. Few events illustrate this fact better than the acquisition by Lenovo (a Beijing-based personal computer company) of IBM's personal computing division a few years ago and the growth of call-center operations in India.

Substantial developments in Europe (which we will discuss below) have strengthened the position of countries there. In North America, Canada and Mexico also began to show promise of achieving economic preeminence in the global marketplaces, and many countries in South America have also begun to globalize their operations. Exhibit 3.1 illustrates the regions of the world that are especially significant in today's global economy. It is also worth noting that of the 100 largest firms in the world in 2009 (based on sales), two-thirds are headquartered outside the United States, a total of 18 different countries have businesses on the list, and international business operations are a vital part of each firm's success.

Several other developments in the world also have affected the new global economy. First, many developed countries such as the United States, Japan, and the countries of Western Europe have experienced slowing rates of growth in their populations. This trend has implications for the demand for certain types of consumer goods as well as for the availability of individuals to work producing

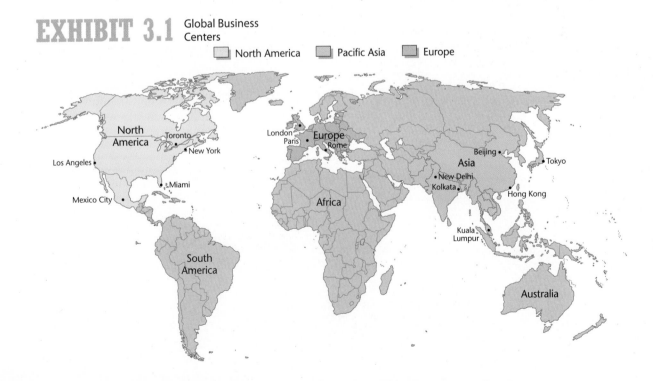

EXHIBIT 3.1 Global Business Centers

North America   Pacific Asia   Europe

those goods. On the other hand, countries such as Mexico, India, Indonesia, and China (despite its one-child-per-couple policy) continue to experience rapid population growth. This growth is fueling a demand for international goods and also makes these locations attractive sites for new businesses or joint ventures. Furthermore, the collapse of the Japanese markets in the late 1990s and downturns in the U.S. stock market in 2002 (especially the high-tech sector) and in 2008–09, and the effects these events had on world markets, made it clear exactly how interdependent global economies really are.

Perhaps the clearest evidence of the interrelatedness of global markets came in late 2008 and early 2009. Many people believed that at that point the U.S. stock market was overvalued. Also, government policies designed to make housing more available to many Americans had produced a large number of so-called subprime mortgages. These mortgages were offered at more affordable rates and required little security. Eventually, these loans were packaged, securitized, and sold all over the world. When it

became clear that many people could not afford their new homes and default rates began to accelerate, these factors combined with an overpriced stock exchange to trigger a major economic downturn, first in the United States and then in most of the rest of the world.

Today, no global organization can ignore elections in Iraq, the developments in the Gaza Strip, or the valuation of the Chinese renminbi. All of these events, once seen as far removed from the concerns of American businesses, now strongly and immediately affect how firms in this country and other countries around the world do business. Finally, as we discuss later, the growth of regional economic alliances has also had substantial effects on the global business community.

GLOBAL ISSUES IN INTERNATIONAL HUMAN RESOURCE MANAGEMENT

Various global issues in international HRM must be addressed by any international firm. As shown in Exhibit 3.2, one issue is the development of an international HRM strategy.[3] Another is developing an understanding of the cultural environment of human resource management. A third is developing an understanding of the political and legal environment of international business.

International Human Resource Management Strategy

The overall strategy of a business has to be logical and well conceived. The effective management of a firm's international human resources also must be approached with a cohesive and coherent strategy. As a starting point, most international businesses today begin by developing

EXHIBIT 3.2 Global Issues in International Human Resource Management a systematic strategy for choosing among home-country nationals, parent-country nationals, and third-country nationals for various positions in their organization.[4]

Some firms adopt what is called an **ethnocentric staffing model.** Firms that use this model primarily use parent-country nationals to staff higher-level foreign positions. This strategy is based on the assumption that home-office perspectives and issues should take precedence over local perspectives and issues and that parent-country nationals will be more effective in representing the views of the home office in the foreign operation.[5] The corporate HR function in organizations that adopt this mentality is primarily concerned with selecting and training managers for foreign assignments, developing appropriate compensation packages for those managers, and handling adjustment issues when the manager is reassigned back home. Local HR officials handle staffing and related human resource issues for local employees hired to fill lower-level positions in the firm. Sony Corporation's operations in the United States follow this model. Sony Corporation of America, a wholly owned subsidiary of Sony Corporation, handles local HR issues, but top executives at the firm's operations around the United States are Japanese managers from the firm's Japanese home office.

Other international businesses adopt what is called a **polycentric staffing model** that calls for a much heavier use of host-country nationals (HCNs) from top to bottom throughout the organization. Thus, polycentric staffing is used with the assumption that such individuals (that is, host-country nationals) are better equipped to deal with local market conditions. Organizations using this approach usually have a fully functioning HR department in each foreign subsidiary that is responsible for managing all local HR issues for lower- and upper-level employees alike. The corporate human resource function in such companies focuses primarily on coordinating relevant activities with their counterparts in each foreign operation. U.S. energy companies operating in Asia often adopt this model, especially because these operations are often joint ventures between the U.S. company and one or more local companies.

Still other firms adopt what is called a **geocentric staffing model.** The geocentric staffing model puts parent-country nationals, host-country nationals, and third-country nationals in the same category. The firm then attempts to hire the best person available for a position, regardless of where that individual comes from. The geocentric staffing model is most likely to be adopted and used by fully internationalized firms such as Nestlé and Unilever.[6] In many ways, the corporate HR function in geocentric companies is the most complicated of all. Every aspect of the HRM process—planning, recruiting, selection, compensation, and training—must be undertaken from an international perspective. Each foreign subsidiary or operation still needs its own self-contained HR unit to handle ongoing employment issues.

UNDERSTANDING THE CULTURAL ENVIRONMENT

The cultural environment of international business also poses a variety of more applied challenges and opportunities for human resource managers. A country's **culture** can be defined as the set of values, symbols, beliefs, and languages that guide the behavior of people within that culture. A culture does not necessarily coincide precisely with national boundaries, but these two different constructs are sometimes similar in terms of geographic area and domain. All managers in an international business need to be aware of cultural nuances (by definition, HR managers are concerned with people), but they must be especially cognizant of the role and importance of cultural differences and similarities in workers from different cultures.

Cultural beliefs and values are often unspoken and may even be taken for granted by those who live in a particular country. When cultures are similar, relatively few problems or difficulties may be encountered. Human resource managers can extrapolate from their own experiences to understand their function in the other culture. Thus, U.S. managers often have relatively little difficulty doing business in England. Managers in both countries speak the same language, and a common framework exists for understanding both commercial and personal relationships.

More significant issues can arise, however, when considerable differences

The **ethnocentric staffing model** primarily uses parent-country nationals to staff higher-level foreign positions.

The **polycentric staffing model** calls for the dominant use of host-country nationals throughout the organization.

The **geocentric staffing model** puts parent-country, host-country, and third-country nationals all in the same category, with the firm attempting to always hire the best person available for a position.

Culture refers to the set of values that helps an organization's members understand what it stands for, how it does things, and what it considers important.

exist between the home culture of a manager and the culture of the country in which business is to be conducted. Thus, there is a higher likelihood of culturally related problems and difficulties between managers from, say, Canada and India. Differences in language, customs, and business and personal norms increase the potential for misunderstandings, miscommunication, and similar problems. In these instances, HR managers must be careful to avoid overgeneralizing from their own experiences or perspectives.

Cultural differences can also directly affect business practices in international situations. For example, the religion of Islam teaches that people should not make a living by exploiting the problems of others and that making interest payments is immoral. As a result, no outplacement consulting firms exist in Saudi Arabia and the Sudan (because outplacement involves charging a fee to help terminated workers cope with their misfortunes). As a result of these and myriad other cultural differences, then, managers may encounter unexpected complexities when doing business in countries where these sorts of cultural differences exist.

Language is another important cultural dimension that affects international HRM practices. Most obviously, differences in specific languages such as English, Japanese, Chinese, and Spanish dramatically complicate the issues involved in dealing with international business. Unfortunately, U.S. managers who are fluent in different languages still tend to be relatively rare. When a U.S. organization does find such an employee, that individual usually becomes a valuable asset. On the other hand, it is fairly common for Asian managers to learn English in school, and most European managers are multilingual. It is interesting to note that several years ago, many U.S. colleges and universities (and especially business schools) began dropping foreign-language requirements. As it turns out, those decisions may result in some competitive disadvantage for managers educated in the United States.

Another cultural factor that is most directly related to HRM practices is the roles that exist in different cultures. The United States has seen considerable change over the last few decades regarding the role of women in our society. Women have made considerable strides in pursuing and achieving career opportunities previously closed to them. In some parts of the world, however, the situation is quite different. In Japan, for example, women may still find it fairly difficult to launch a successful

career. Similar situations exist in some European countries, as well as in almost all the countries in the Middle East. Some role differences are related to status and hierarchy. In the United States, for example, relatively little psychological distance exists between managers and subordinates, resulting in a certain degree of familiarity and informality. But in many Asian countries, this psychological distance is much greater, resulting in more formalized roles and less informal communication across levels in the organization.

Perhaps the most systematic study of national values was undertaken by Dutch scholar Geert Hofstede, who studied cultural differences among managers in fifty-three countries.[7] He defined five dimensions of culture:

1. power distance (or status and authority differences between a superior and a subordinate),
2. individualism versus collectivism (or the extent to which persons define themselves as individuals rather than as members of groups),
3. masculinity versus femininity (assertive, competitive, success-driven values versus quality of life, relationship-oriented values in society),
4. uncertainty avoidance (or preferences for structured rather than unstructured situations), and
5. time orientation (or emphasizing long-term values such as thrift and persistence versus short-term values such as fulfilling social obligations).

Hofstede's work has been influential in the field of international management and provides useful general guidelines for what to expect when dealing with managers or employees from different countries.

Hofstede's work has some limitations as well. The initial sample, although quite large (100,000), was drawn from a single organization (IBM). Thus, it is difficult to tell if some of the effects found in the study resulted from country cultures or from one or more elements of the corporate culture that all respondents shared. Even though the sample was large, it is still difficult to make generalizations across the entire populations of countries. For example, the United States was described as being the highest on individualism, in the middle on masculinity versus femininity and on time orientation, and quite low on power distance and uncertainty avoidance. But is this description true of all Americans? Surely not. It is not even clear that they describe the "typical" American (whoever that might be). Even within countries, for instance, regional and ethnic differences account for large differences in values. Thus, one must be careful not to overgeneralize from these results.

Nonetheless, Hofstede's work provides some interesting and useful ideas about differences across cultures that are relevant to HR managers.

Yet another significant cultural factor has to do with children. In the United States, child labor is closely regulated, and children traditionally attend school until they become young adults. In other countries, however, this practice may be quite different. In Bangladesh, it is quite common for children to be a major source of income for their families. Many children do not attend school at all and begin seeking jobs at very young ages. A business operating in such an environment thus faces a significant dilemma. On the one hand, local cultural factors suggest that it is acceptable to hire young children to work for low wages because other businesses do the same. On the other hand, this practice would be illegal or unethical by the standards that exist in most industrialized countries.

The HR manager dealing with international issues thus faces two fundamental cultural challenges. The first challenge is simply understanding and appreciating differences that exist in different cultures. The value of work, attitudes, orientation toward work, and common work-related attitudes and practices vary significantly from culture to culture, and the HR manager needs to develop an understanding of these differences if she or he is to function effectively.[8]

The second challenge is more ethical in nature. On the one hand, many businesses relocate manufacturing facilities to other countries to capitalize on lower labor costs. Indeed, it is quite possible for a business from a country such as Japan or the United States to set up a factory in Bangladesh, Pakistan, or other regions of the world and have minimal labor costs there. The ethical issue, however, is the extent to which this situation becomes exploitation. Many people, for instance, would agree that it is reasonable for a company to take advantage of low prevailing wages and benefit costs to achieve low-cost production. But if a company goes too far and truly begins to exploit foreign workers, then problems may arise.

These protestors are symbolizing the "faceless" exploited workers some manufacturers used to make the clothing and athletic gear used in the 2004 Olympic Games in Athens, Greece.

Understanding the Political and Legal Environment

It is also important for HR managers in international businesses to understand the political and legal environment of the countries in which they do business. Exhibit 3.3 illustrates four fundamental aspects of the political and legal environment of international business that are of primary concern for HR managers: government stability, potential incentives for international trade, controls on international trade, and the influence of economic communities on international trade. In addition, laws that affect the management of human resources are basic issues, but we will say more about those issues later.[9]

Government stability can be thought of as either the ability of a given government to stay in power against opposing factions or as the permanence of government policies toward business. In general, companies prefer to do business in countries that are stable in both respects because managers have a higher probability of understanding how those governments affect their business. In recent years, several governments in the Middle East have

EXHIBIT 3.3 Political and Legal Issues of International Business

Government stability

Trade incentives

Political and legal issues

Trade controls

Economic communities

been facing mounting pressure from Islamic radicals to establish governments more in line with fundamentalist interpretations of the Koran; it is not clear, for example, how stable or effective the Iraqi government will be over time or how much longer the Israelis and Palestinians will continue to struggle. These events have made the Middle East a less attractive region for doing business. On the other hand, the easing of tensions between the Chinese and the government on Taiwan has made that entire region more attractive.

A major HR issue relating to the topic of government stability is the extent to which expatriate managers, or any other representatives of a U.S. firm, may be put at risk as a result of political instability. For years, extremist groups have targeted U.S. executives for terrorist activities. But since September 11, 2001, these fears have grown considerably. The kidnapping and murder of journalist Daniel Pearl, for example, provided graphic evidence that U.S. employees assigned overseas can face considerable danger. In the post–September 11 world, many U.S.-based managers are more uncomfortable about traveling to parts of the world where they fear they may be threatened. Heightened security measures on planes and in airports have made these dangers salient to anyone traveling abroad.

In addition, some firms continue to face situations in which their managers are closely watched or even harassed by local government officials on the grounds that they are alleged illegal informants or spies for the U.S. government. Still another risk is the extent to which a business itself might become nationalized, or seized by a foreign government, which claims the company's facilities. Nationalization has occasionally occurred in the Middle East and in certain countries in South America.

Another aspect of the political and legal environment involves the incentives for international trade that are sometimes offered to attract foreign business. Occasionally, municipal governments offer foreign companies tax breaks and other incentives to build facilities in their area. Over the last few years, for example, BMW, Mercedes, and Toyota have built new assembly factories in the United States. In each instance, various state and local governments started what essentially became bidding wars to see who could attract the manufacturing facilities. Examples of incentives include reduced interest rates on loans, construction subsidies and tax incentives, and the relaxation of various controls on international trade. Some countries have also offered guaranteed labor contracts with local unions as a form of incentive designed to reduce the uncertainties that an entering foreign business faces in negotiating its own initial labor contract.

A third dimension of the political and legal environment of international business consists of those very controls that some countries place on international trade. Several different controls exist. One is a *tariff*, essentially a tax collected on goods shipped across national boundaries.

Tariffs may be levied by the exporting country, countries through which goods pass, or the importing country. The most common form of trade control, however, is the *quota*, a limit on the number or value of goods that can be traded. The quota amount is typically designed to ensure that domestic competitors will be able to maintain a predetermined market share. Honda Motors in Japan, for example, is allowed to export exactly 425,000 automobiles each year to the United States. Sometimes, however, companies can circumvent quotas. Honda has built assembly factories in the United States for this purpose because the automobiles they produce within the United States do not count against the 425,000-unit quota.

> ## Economic communities can help reduce or eliminate international trade barriers among their member nations.

For the international HR manager, an important set of international controls involves the control of human resources. Some countries require that a foreign business setting up shop within its borders hire a minimum percentage of local employees to work there. For example, a country might require that 80 percent of the production employees and 50 percent of the managers of a foreign-owned business be local citizens. A less common but still salient factor is the control of international travel. Some countries, for instance, limit the number of trips that foreign managers can make in and out of their country in a given period of time. HR in the 21st Century discusses a variation on this issue related to child labor in other countries.

A final aspect of the political and legal environment is the growing importance of the influence of economic communities. Economic communities consist of sets of countries that agree to reduce or eliminate trade barriers among their member nations. One of the most commonly cited economic communities is the European Union (EU). The original EU members were Belgium, France, Luxembourg, Germany, Italy, and the Netherlands. Denmark, Ireland, the United Kingdom, Greece, Portugal, and Spain joined later. Austria, Finland, and Sweden have also been admitted, and several nations have also recently joined, including Cyprus, Malta, and many former Soviet-bloc countries (Bulgaria, the Czech Republic, Estonia, Hungary, Latvia, Lithuania, Poland, Romania, Slovakia, and Slovenia). For the past several years, these countries have been systematically working toward a unified market in which trade barriers and controls are gradually eliminated.

HR in the 21st Century

> "You can't take juice companies seriously about trying to eradicate child labor when they are promoting a system that clouds accountability in the workplace." [10]
>
> —Raimundo Limao de Mello, Brazilian attorney

For years, large U.S. juice distributors such as Minute Maid, Tropicana, and Nestlé have bought fruit juices from suppliers in South America. But a few years ago, it was learned that many of these suppliers relied heavily on child labor to harvest oranges, lemons, and other fruit. Children as young as nine were commonly taken out of school by their impoverished parents and put to work in the citrus groves. The parents often saw no problem with this action because they themselves had also picked fruit when they were children.

In the last few years, though, the situation has begun to change. For example, the U.S. Congress recently amended a 1930 trade law to ban the importation of products made with child labor. Similarly, the International Brotherhood of Teamsters has also taken on a watchdog role to ensure that Brazilian exporters are held accountable for adhering to the law. Of course, critics claim that the Teamsters' motivation is self-interest, but regardless of its reasons, the union is having a positive effect.

Many South American countries are themselves trying to stamp out child labor. For example, child advocacy groups in Brazil helped pass a labor code that banned child labor. Another measure paid $45 per month for each child who stayed in school and maintained good attendance records; the sum was about the same that the child might earn picking fruit. The juice companies themselves also have claimed to be imposing more stringent controls on their suppliers, although watchdog groups question their real commitment to eradicating child labor.

It is difficult to trace accurately the activities of child fruit pickers, but most experts do agree that, slowly but surely, conditions are improving. For example, Brazilian government statistics suggest that child labor in general is down about 20 percent over the past 10 years. And more adults in Brazil also seem to be more aware of the importance of education and are actively discouraging fruit picking by children. But as the global economy floundered in 2009, there seemed to another jump in the use of child labor. And even though the overall percentage is down, thousands of children are still being used to pick fruit. Clearly, then, there is still a long way to go.

THINK IT OVER

1. When and under what conditions is child labor most likely to proliferate?
2. What measures can you as a consumer take to help eradicate child labor?

Sources: "Alarming Trends in Child Labor," *U.S. New & World Report* (Jan. 4, 2010): 34; "U.S. Child-Labor Law Sparks a Trade Debate Over Brazilian Oranges," *Wall Street Journal* (Sept. 9, 1998): A1, A9; "Chile's Labor Law Hobbles Its Workers and Troubles the U.S.," *Wall Street Journal* (Oct. 15, 1997): A1, A14; "Sweatshop Police," *Business Week* (Oct. 20, 1997): 39.

This European Union became much more formidable with the introduction of the euro, a common currency designed to eliminate exchange-rate fluctuations and make cross-national transactions easier. Twelve early members of the EU (all except Denmark, Sweden, and the United Kingdom) officially converted their domestic currencies to the euro on January 1, 2002. These twelve countries now make up what is called the *eurozone*. From a human resource management perspective, the advent of the euro brings up two issues: (1) Individuals and employers in the eurozone can more readily compare their compensation packages to those of their peers in other countries because they are all paid in the same currency, and (2) it is easier for firms in the eurozone to transfer managers to other countries.

Nonetheless, the rejection by French and Dutch voters of the new EU constitution in 2004 raised questions about the long-term viability of the union. Furthermore, with the admission of countries such as Romania and Hungary, subsidies long enjoyed by Spain and Ireland rapidly disappeared and were transferred to these newer, and economically poorer, members. These shifts are also putting new strains on the EU.

Another less-comprehensive economic community was created by the North American Free

Trade Agreement (NAFTA). NAFTA attempts to reduce the trade barriers that exist among Canada, the United States, and Mexico, making it easier for companies to do business in each of the three countries. Extending NAFTA to other countries

> **The North American Free Trade Agreement (NAFTA) reduced trade barriers between Canada, the United States, and Mexico. NAFTA also includes separate labor agreements among the three countries.**

in Latin America, especially Chile, has been discussed, but for now at least it remains a three-country union. No plans for a single currency have been seriously discussed, and human resource management practices and laws remain independent. But NAFTA also includes separate labor agreements, which have the potential to affect HRM practices dramatically. The Commission on Labor Cooperation, for example, was established to hear cases dealing with these labor agreements in areas such as child labor, occupational safety and health, and union–management relations. Some of these standards are more stringent than those imposed by U.S.-based legislation (see Chapter 2). Although it is not clear how much enforcement power the Commission on Labor Cooperation will have, it is possible that HR managers will have to deal with an even more complex set of regulations in the future. It is interesting

to note that these standards would apply not only to U.S. companies doing business in Mexico or Canada but also to U.S. companies doing business solely in this country.

THE HUMAN RESOURCE FUNCTION IN INTERNATIONAL BUSINESS

All basic international functions—marketing, operations, finance, and human resources—play a vital role in international business. The HR function, for example, must deal with several general, fundamental management challenges in international business.[11] These challenges are illustrated in Exhibit 3.4. In addition, specific HRM implications exist for the different forms of international business activity that firms can pursue.

General Human Resource Issues in International Business

One general set of challenges relates to differences that may exist in culture, levels of economic development, and legal systems that typify the countries where the firm operates. These differences may force an international organization to customize its hiring, firing, training, and compensation programs on a country-by-country basis. A particularly difficult set of issues arises when conflict exists between the laws or cultures of the home country and those of the host country.

The first issue of conflict is discrimination. For example, as described in Chapter 2, it is illegal in the United States to discriminate in an employment relationship on the basis of gender. In Saudi Arabia, on the other hand, such discrimination is not only allowed but also expected. Women are highly restricted in their career

EXHIBIT 3.4 Fundamental Management Challenges in International Business

opportunities, and a firm doing business in that country has to balance its own affirmative action efforts with the legal and cultural restrictions imposed by that country. And overt discrimination is still actively practiced in many other countries as well.[12] As we noted, the Civil Rights Act of 1991 allows employees of U.S. firms working abroad to sue their employers if they violate the Civil Rights Act. But exception to this privilege exists when a country has a law that specifically contradicts the Civil Rights Act. For example, a woman could not sue a U.S. company operating in Saudi Arabia for sex discrimination because some discrimination against women is actually prescribed by law in that country. On the other hand, Japan has no laws institutionalizing such discrimination, so a woman could bring suit against a U.S. firm operating there if it were guilty of discriminatory practices.

The second fundamental HR challenge in international business (a topic introduced earlier) is the determination of the most appropriate source of employees: the host country, the home country, or a third country. The ideal combination of employees differs according to the location of a firm's operations, the nature of its operations, and myriad other factors. A company is more likely to hire local employees, for example, for lower-level jobs with minimal skill requirements and for which there is a reasonable local supply of labor. Again, it is also necessary to consider local laws or customs that may limit or constrain hiring practices. For instance, immigration laws may limit the number of work visas that a firm can grant to foreigners, and employment regulations may mandate the hiring of local citizens as a requirement for doing business in a particular country.

But this situation is changing to some extent. Twenty-five years ago, companies doing business in places such as Singapore would have relied on the local labor market for hourly employees only. Over the years, however, Singapore and other countries have made significant investments in their human capital. As a result, a large pool of well-educated (often at Western universities), highly motivated locals who are qualified for and interested in management positions now exists in these same countries. Some U.S.-based organizations are taking advantage of these relatively new labor pools by hiring local employees and then transferring them to the United States for training before returning them to their home country, where they can play a key role in managing the global enterprise. U.S.-based universities are increasingly opening branches for graduate study in places such as Singapore and China, as are European universities, especially INSEAD.

Third, international businesses must also deal with complex training and development challenges. At one level, for example, HR managers need to provide cross-cultural training for corporate executives who are chosen for overseas assignments. In addition, training programs for production workers in host countries must be tailored to represent the education offered by local school systems. Dramatic differences in the skill and educational levels within a labor force make it necessary for international business to pay close attention to the training and development needs of all its employees in foreign markets.[13] But again, the establishment of institutions of higher education from the United States, the United Kingdom, France, and Australia has changed the face of local training and education in many countries, especially in Asia.

The fourth important international HRM question relates to working conditions, compensation, and the cost of living. It costs more for people to live and work in some countries than in others. A general stance adopted by most international businesses is that an employee should not suffer a loss of compensation or a decrease in his or her standard of living by virtue of accepting an international assignment. Thus, HR managers must determine how to compensate executives who accept overseas assignments and who face higher costs of living, a reduction in their quality of life, or unhappiness or stress because of separation from family or friends. This stance, however, can create some additional complications that we will address later when dealing with issues for expatriate managers.

Specific Human Resource Issues in International Business

Organizations can adopt a wide variety of strategies for competing in the international environment. Each strategy poses its own unique set of challenges for HR managers. One common strategy is **exporting**, which is the process of making a product in the firm's domestic marketplace and then selling it in another country. Exporting can involve both goods and services. U.S. agricultural cooperatives export grain to Russia while major consulting firms sell their services to companies in Europe and Asia. Other businesses ship gas turbines to Saudi Arabia, locomotives to Indonesia, blue jeans to Great Britain, computers to Japan, disposable diapers to Italy, and steel to Brazil; others sell airline service, information-technology support, and various other service products.

Such an approach to international business has many advantages. First, it is

Exporting *is the process of making a product in the firm's domestic marketplace and then selling it in another country. Exporting can involve both goods and services.*

usually the easiest way to enter a new market. In addition, it typically requires only a small outlay of capital. Because the products are usually sold "as is," there is no need to adapt them to local conditions. Finally, relatively little risk is involved. On the other hand, products exported to other countries are often subject to taxes, tariffs, and high transportation expenses. In addition, because the products are seldom adapted to local conditions, they may not actually address the needs of consumers in local markets, and consequently the products may not achieve their full revenue potential. The shipment of some products across national boundaries is also restricted by various government regulations. For example, textile products made in Turkey cannot be exported easily to the United States because of complex regulations developed to protect U.S. cotton producers.

If the firm functions solely as an exporter, the human resource function faces no meaningful differences in responsibilities from those in a domestic business. An exporting company usually has an export manager, and that manager likely has a staff to assist in the various parts of the exporting process. Human resource managers usually play a role in hiring people for these jobs and oversee other aspects of their employment, such as compensation and performance appraisal. But other than perhaps some exporting-specific skills required for workers in this department, these employees are treated the same as employees in the operations, sales, or finance departments. Thus, when a domestic firm begins to export to a foreign market, the human resource function may be extended to include another set of employees, but it does not change in any other meaningful way.

Another popular form of international business strategy is called **licensing**. Under this agreement, a company grants its permission to another company in a foreign country to manufacture or market its products in the foreign country's local market. For example, a clothing manufacturer might allow a manufacturer in another country to use its design, logo, and materials to manufacture clothing under the original firm's name. Under such an agreement, the licensing firm typically pays a royalty or licensing fee to the original firm based on the number of units it actually sells. Microsoft licenses software firms in other countries to produce and distribute software products such as Office and Windows in their local markets.

The major advantage of this strategy is that it allows the firm to enter a foreign market with relatively little risk and to gain some market exposure and develop name recognition that will make it easier for it to enter the market more aggressively in the

Disney's new theme park in Hong Kong is a major direct foreign investment.

future. On the other hand, its profits are limited to those it receives from the royalty payment. Likewise, the firm must also be vigilant to ensure that its quality standards are upheld.

If a firm is involved in international business activities exclusively via licensing, the HR function is approached in the same way as in a pure exporting enterprise. In other words, no meaningful differences in the HR function likely exist, but HR managers need to extend their existing services and responsibilities to employees associated with the licensing activities. The HR function itself does not really change in any meaningful way.

A third international strategy for doing business is **direct foreign investment**. A direct investment occurs when a firm headquartered in one country builds or purchases operating facilities or subsidiaries in a foreign country; that is, the firm actually owns physical assets in the other country. Kodak, for example, constructed a research-and-development laboratory in Japan. This business activity represents a direct investment on the part of Kodak. Other examples of direct investment include the Disney Corporation's construction of a new theme park near Hong Kong, BMW's construction of an assembly plant in South

Licensing *involves one company granting its permission to another company in a foreign country to manufacture or market its products in its local market.*

Direct foreign investment *occurs when a firm headquartered in one country builds or purchases operating facilities or subsidiaries in a foreign country.*

Carolina, and Procter & Gamble's construction of a major new distribution center in Brazil.

As already noted, there are actually two different forms of direct investment. First, the firm can simply acquire an existing business in the foreign country. This has been the primary strategy enacted by WalMart as it entered Germany and the United Kingdom—it bought existing retail chains and then converted them to WalMarts. This approach provides nearly instant access to new markets, but it may require protracted negotiations over the acquisition; afterward, the firm also faces the challenge of how to integrate the new acquisition into its other operations. Alternatively, the firm can create or build a new wholly owned subsidiary, factory, or other unit. This takes much more time, carries much greater risk, and is much more expensive, yet it also represents the path to the greatest potential profits.

In either case, direct investment has the advantage that it provides the firm its own company-owned facilities in the foreign country, and allows it to become truly integrated in a particular foreign market. Considerably more profit potential can be realized in direct investment because the company itself keeps all the profits its investment earns in that country. On the other hand, considerably more risk is attached to this strategy. Just as the investing firm can keep all its profits, so too must it absorb any and all losses and related financial setbacks. In addition, of course, the costs of direct investment are also quite high and borne solely by the investing firm.

At this level of international business activity, the HR function changes substantially from that of a domestic firm or business using a pure exporting or licensing strategy. This difference stems from the fact that in a direct investment, employees of the firm are working in foreign locations. Depending on the nationalities reflected in the foreign workforce (i.e., whether the firm uses a polycentric, geocentric, or ethnocentric approach to hiring), the corporate HR function will need to extend and expand its scope and operations to provide the appropriate contributions to firm performance as determined by the philosophy used for staffing the foreign operations.

A fourth form of international strategy is a **joint venture** or **strategic alliance**. In this case, two or more firms cooperate in the ownership or management of an operation, often on an equity basis. *Joint venture* is the traditional term used for such an arrangement and describes a situation in which actual equity ownership exists. A strategic alliance might not involve ownership but still involves cooperation between firms. Both arrangements are rapidly growing in importance in the international business environment. They represent a way for two or more firms to achieve synergy from working together, they reduce risk, and they provide mutual benefit to both partners. The airline industry has seen several strategic alliances. One of the largest is known as the Star Alliance. This group includes United Airlines, Lufthansa, Swiss Air, Air New

Zealand, South African Airlines, Singapore Airlines, and Air China, among other airlines from all over the world. This alliance makes it easier for travelers to place reservations, purchase tickets, and make connections between any two or more partners in the alliance. This flexibility also makes the group itself more competitive relative to other airlines.

Human resource managers in a firm that uses this strategy face an even more complex set of issues and challenges. If the new operation is a separate legal entity that functions as a semiautonomous enterprise, the corporate human resource staff of each strategic partner needs to determine how to link and coordinate with their counterparts in both the new venture (seen as a separate entity) and their partner. If the new venture is operated within the context of one of the existing partner's organization structures, the HR function becomes more complicated still because of the disparate relationships among the HR staff for the new venture and its counterparts in both the partner within which it operates and the other partner (this latter relationship is somewhat more distant).

DOMESTIC ISSUES IN INTERNATIONAL HUMAN RESOURCE MANAGEMENT

Regardless of their level of internationalization, all firms dealing in foreign markets must confront three sets of domestic issues in the management of their human resources. These domestic issues, shown in Exhibit 3.5, are local recruiting and selection, local training, and local compensation.

Local Recruiting and Selection Issues

Nonmanagerial employees, such as blue-collar production workers and white-collar clerical and office workers, are usually HCNs in international business. Basic and fundamental economic reasons explain this pattern. Simply put, host-country nationals are usually cheaper to employ than parent-country or third-country nationals. Host-country nationals are also frequently used because local laws usually promote the hiring of locals.[14] Immigration laws, for example, may restrict jobs to citizens and legal residents of a country. Thus, an international business must develop and implement a plan for recruiting and selecting its employees in a host-country market. This plan must include assessments of the firm's HR needs, primary sources of labor in that country, labor force skills and talents, and training requirements. In addition, the plan should also account for special circumstances that exist in the

In a joint venture (strategic alliance), two or more firms cooperate in the ownership or management of an operation on an equity basis.

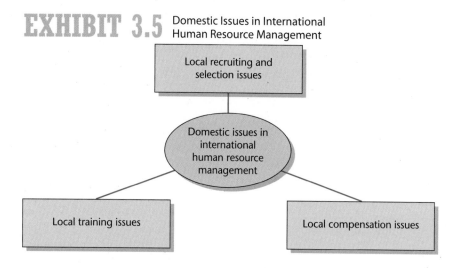

EXHIBIT 3.5 Domestic Issues in International Human Resource Management

Local recruiting and selection issues

Domestic issues in international human resource management

Local training issues

Local compensation issues

local markets. When firms hire parent-country nationals for foreign assignments, they must obviously adhere to their home-country hiring regulations. But when hiring HCNs, they must also be aware of the regulations, laws, and norms that govern employment relationships within the host country. Thus, even though the reliance on parent-country nationals may be less expensive, it adds complexity to the employment relationship.[15]

Local Training Issues

Human resource managers must also understand the training and development needs of the host country's workforce to help host-country nationals perform their jobs most effectively. These needs of a local workforce depend on several factors. One, of course, is the location of the foreign market. In highly industrialized markets such as England and Japan, organizations can usually find a cadre of capable employees who may need only a small amount of firm-specific training. But in a relatively underdeveloped area, training and development needs will be much more extensive.

For example, when Hilton first began opening hotels in Eastern Europe, it found that restaurant waiters, desk clerks, and other customer-service employees lacked the basic skills necessary to provide high-quality service to guests. Because Eastern European employees were accustomed to working in a planned economy in which they did not have to worry about customer satisfaction, they had difficulty recognizing why it was important to shift their focus. As a result, Hilton had to invest considerably more than originally planned in training employees to provide customer service. Training is also important if international business wants to take full advantage of locating production abroad. Many firms move production facilities to areas with low labor costs such as Malaysia and Mexico but then find that the productivity of the labor force is relatively low. Thus, they have to invest additional training and development dollars to bring the workforce up to the performance standards they expect.

> **"Globalization has changed us into a company that searches the world, not just to sell or to source, but to find intellectual capital—the world's best talents and greatest ideas."**
>
> —JACK WELCH, American businessman and author, former chairman and CEO of General Electric, 1981–2001

Local Compensation Issues

Compensation must also be addressed at a local level for international businesses. Some countries, such as the United States, focus compensation on assessing an individual's performance and then compensating that individual accordingly. In other countries, however, such as Japan, the emphasis is based more on group work and less on individual performance. Dramatic differences in lifestyles, standards of living, and regulation also cause a wide variation in the way in which firms compensate their employees in different foreign locations.

Of course, dramatic differences in benefit packages are offered to workers in different countries as well. In countries with socialized medicine such as the United Kingdom, firms do not have to worry as much about paying all or part of employee health-insurance premiums (although they pay higher taxes to help support the government program). In Italy, most workers expect to have several hours off in the afternoon. In Germany, most workers get 6 weeks of paid vacation time a year, and many work only 30 hours a week. German autoworkers earn $39 an hour in wages and benefits, compared to $25 in the United States and $27 in Japan.[16] Italy and Britain legally mandate 4 weeks of vacation time per year, while France mandates 5 weeks. In contrast, U.S. firms are not legally required to provide any vacation leave.[17]

It is also important for international HR managers to look at the total picture of compensation rather than on some simple index such as the hourly wage. For example, as already noted, some firms choose to move production to Mexico to take advantage of lower labor costs. Although labor costs in Mexico are cheaper than they are in the United States (when compared on an hourly basis), Mexican law requires employers to pay maternity leave to their employees, provide a Christmas bonus equal to 15 days' pay, and provide at least 3 months of severance pay for workers who are terminated. Lower labor costs thus may be at least partially lost because of these and other higher costs for other benefits.

MANAGING INTERNATIONAL TRANSFERS AND ASSIGNMENTS

Another extremely important part of international human resource management is the effective management of expatriate employees.[18] **Expatriates** are employees who are sent by a firm to work in another country; they may be either parent-country or third-country nationals. Particularly important areas here include selecting, training, and

compensating expatriates. It is also important to understand how the management of expatriates is related to a firm's international strategy.[19]

Expatriates and Corporate International Strategy

To a large extent, how a firm deals with expatriates should depend on the strategy the firm is pursuing in terms of its international operations. We can best understand this relationship if we think about how expatriates help multinational corporations (MNCs)s compete by playing a role in the knowledge-transfer process. This process involves the acquisition of knowledge as well as the diffusion of knowledge throughout the organization; indeed, some people have argued that MNCs exist primarily because they can transfer and exploit knowledge more efficiently and effectively than by using external market mechanisms.[20]

The expatriate manager is the key player in this knowledge-transfer and diffusion process; unfortunately, this manager may not have a real incentive to share the information he or she has acquired. If the expatriate manager does not share all the information acquired, then he or she will have a monopoly on that information, which can be to the manager's advantage (referred to as "opportunistic behavior"). Furthermore, the organization cannot possibly know all the information the expatriate manager has acquired. This then poses the classic agency problem[21] in which the incentives of the parties are not aligned and there is an asymmetry in terms of who knows what. Furthermore, this problem can become more or less severe, depending on which international strategy the organization uses.

Table 3.1 shows the situation relative to potential agency problems for each of four international strategies proposed by Bartlett and Goshal.[22] Firms carrying out a global strategy rely heavily on direction from the home office, with one global strategy applied to all operations. Expatriate managers are not capable of making important decisions and so have less opportunity to behave opportunistically, and there is a low level of information

Expatriates *are employees who are sent by a firm to work in another country; they may be either parent-country or third-country nationals.*

as we shall see later, a great deal of attention is given to the problem of how to compensate expatriate managers. Most of the policies and practices result in expatriate managers earning considerably more than any host-country counterparts. In the past, this problem was not that serious because few local managers had the background and training of the expatriates. In fact, it was this very lack of local competence that led many organizations to assign expatriate managers. But, as noted earlier, organizations increasingly see expatriate assignments as helpful to the home-country manager. As a result, he or she may be assigned to a foreign post even though other HCNs or local employees are capable of doing the same job. As many countries more routinely send potential managers abroad for training and education, the local employee may well be as qualified in every way as the expatriate. To date, however, most expatriate policies dictate that the expatriate manager would earn more than the local doing the same or a similar job. This situation can lead to resentment on the part of the HCN and can potentially lead the HCN to withhold the help and support the expatriate needs to be successful. Does this mean that expatriates should not be compensated for their overseas assignments? Surely not, but it does mean that organizations may have to take a closer look at their expatriate policies and practices and evaluate them in light of the importance of obtaining HCN support for the expatriate once he or she arrives in the new assignment.[35]

TRAINING EXPATRIATES

Given the potential costs involved in failure, it is not surprising that organizations also spend a great deal of time and money on training expatriate managers. General Motors spends almost $500,000 a year on cross-cultural training for 150 or so U.S. managers and their families heading to international assignments. The firm reports that less than 1 percent of its expatriate assignments fail, and it attributes much of its success to its training program.[36] Training (as we will cover more fully in Chapter 14) is instruction directed at enhancing specific job-related skills and abilities and most often focuses on operating employees and technical specialists. For example, a training program might be designed to help employees learn to use a new software package as part of an international communication network. Development (we will also cover this topic more fully in Chapter 14) is general education devoted to preparing future managers for higher-level positions or new assignments within the organization. For example, a development program might span several months or even years and be targeted to help managers improve their ability to make decisions, motivate subordinates to work harder, and develop more effective strategies for the organization.[37]

Training for expatriate managers may be as "simple" as language training (which is not especially simple if it involves a completely unfamiliar language such as Japanese or Arabic for the English speaker) or it can be rather involved. For example, language-training programs and other forms of language training from CD-ROMs, videos, and similar media are common and fairly inexpensive.[38] In addition, it is common to have some type of classroom training dealing with the history of the country or the area and with daily living conditions (e.g., how to make a phone call or hail a taxicab). It is also typical to have some training component that deals with social manners and issues involved in social exchanges (when one should and should not shake hands, for example, and how deeply to bow).[39]

The Cultural Assimilator is a more complex training program built around short case studies and critical incidents. It asks the manager how he or she would react to different situations, and it provides detailed feedback on the correct responses.[40] In addition, firms are more often sending prospective expatriates to their ultimate foreign destination for short periods of time before their permanent move. This experience allows them to become acculturated on a gradual basis and to obtain a truly realistic picture of what life will be like. But whatever the exact nature of the training, the goals of expatriate training are becoming clearer and more consistent. Increasingly, multinational organizations are recognizing that managers given overseas assignments must be able to communicate with others in the host country and be able to adapt to different lifestyles and values. When we consider all the factors that seem to go into expatriate success, it becomes clearer why some have suggested that a manager given an assignment in a foreign country must possess "the patience of a diplomat, the zeal of a missionary, and the language skills of a U.N. interpreter."[41]

Compensating Expatriates

As noted earlier, compensation is another important issue in international human resource management. To remain competitive, an organization must provide compensation packages for its managers that are comparable to those in a given market. Compensation packages include salary and nonsalary items and are jointly determined by labor-market forces such as the supply and demand of managerial talent, professional licensing requirements, the standard of living, occupational status, and government regulations.[42]

Most international businesses need to provide expatriate managers with differential compensation to make up for differences in currency valuation, standards of living, lifestyle norms, and so on. When managers are on short-term assignments at a foreign location, their salaries are often tied to their domestic currency and home-country living standards. Of course, these managers are reimbursed for short-term living expenses such as the cost of hotel rooms, meals, and local transportation. If the foreign assignment is for a longer time period, however, compensation is usually adjusted to allow the manager to maintain her or his home-country standard of living. This adjustment is particularly important if the manager is transferred from a low-cost location to a high-cost location or from a country with a relatively high standard of living to one with a relatively low standard of living.[43]

Differential compensation usually starts with a cost-of-living allowance. This basic difference in salary is intended to offset the differences in the cost of living between home and host countries. The logic is that if managers accept a foreign assignment, they should enjoy the same standard of living as they would have enjoyed had they remained in their home country. If the cost of living in the foreign country is higher than that at home, then the manager's existing base pay alone will result in a lower standard of living. The firm may therefore need to supplement the base pay to offset the difference. On the other hand, if the cost of living at a foreign location is lower than that at home, no such allowance is needed (few companies would actually lower the manager's salary).

Occasionally, organizations might have to provide an additional salary inducement simply to convince people to accept a foreign assignment. Many employees may be relatively interested in accepting assignments to countries such as England, France, Italy, or Japan, but it may be more difficult to entice people to accept a position in Haiti, Pakistan, or Vietnam. Thus, organizations sometimes find it necessary to provide what is called a **hardship premium** or a **foreign-service premium**. Total Fina Elf S.A. is a large French oil company. The firm has substantial holdings in the African country of Angola. During a recent bloody civil war in the country, however, Total pulled its employees out. When the war ended, Total began to again assign managers to run its Angolan operations. But because of lingering violence and other concerns, the firm had to provide them with a 25-percent salary premium and many other incentives to get the desired mix of managers who would agree to accept their new assignments. Likewise, during the reconstruction efforts in Iraq in 2004–07, U.S. contractors such as KBR (a Halliburton subsidiary) also paid substantial premiums to attract and retain employees willing to work there. This premium (called an *uplift* by the firm) was sometimes more than the individual employee's base salary.

Many international businesses also find that they must set up a tax-equalization system for their managers on foreign assignments. This system ensures that the expatriates' after-tax income in the host country is comparable to what the after-tax income would have been in the person's home country. Every country has its own unique income tax laws that apply to the earnings of its citizens or to earnings within its borders by foreign citizens, and companies must develop plans to make sure that the tax burden for individuals is equalized relative to the amount of salary they earn.

The other part of compensation besides salary is benefits. Most international businesses find that, in addition to salary adjustments, they must also provide benefit adjustments. Special benefits for managers on foreign assignments usually include housing, education, medical treatment, travel to the home country, and club membership. Housing benefits are usually provided as a way to help equalize housing expenses in different areas. Equalizing the type of housing an executive enjoys in her or his home country may be expensive, so housing is usually treated as a separate benefit for expatriate managers. If a manager is going

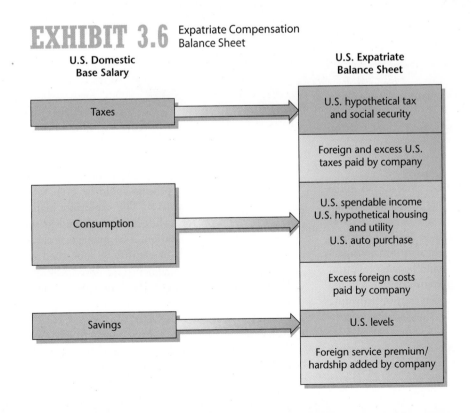

EXHIBIT 3.6 Expatriate Compensation Balance Sheet

U.S. Domestic Base Salary

Taxes

Consumption

Savings

U.S. Expatriate Balance Sheet

U.S. hypothetical tax and social security

Foreign and excess U.S. taxes paid by company

U.S. spendable income
U.S. hypothetical housing and utility
U.S. auto purchase

Excess foreign costs paid by company

U.S. levels

Foreign service premium/hardship added by company

*A **hardship premium** (also called a **foreign service premium**) is an additional financial incentive offered to individuals to entice them to accept a "less than attractive" international assignment.*

on a long-term or permanent foreign assignment, then the organization may buy the manager's existing home and help the manager buy a home in the host country.

Firms also find it increasingly necessary to provide job-location assistance for the spouse of an executive being transferred abroad and to help cover the education costs for their children. Children may need to attend private schools, and the firm would pay the tuition and perhaps other school fees. Medical benefits are also often adjusted for managers on international assignment. For example, some people consider medical facilities in Malaysia to be substandard; as a result, firms that transfer employees to that country often find it necessary to agree that their employees can travel to Singapore whenever they need something other than routine medical attention.

International businesses may also provide expatriates with a travel allowance for trips back to the home country for personal reasons such as visiting other family members or celebrating holidays. Managers and their families may typically be allowed one or two trips home per year for personal reasons at the company's expense. If the assignment is relatively short term and a manager's family remains at home, then the manager may be provided with even more trips home to compensate for the fact that the manager and her or his family are separated.

Finally, it may be necessary to provide certain kinds of club memberships. In some cultures, for example, belonging to a specific club or participating in a particular activity is a necessary part of the business world. The Japanese, for instance, often conduct business during a round of golf. At the same time, golf-club memberships in Japan cost thousands of dollars, and a single round of golf costs many times more what it costs in the rest of the world. As a result, managers assigned to foreign posts in Japan may be given supplemental benefits to cover the costs of memberships and be able to conduct business effectively.[44] When we take all these factors into consideration, it is easy to see how HCNs could become resentful about the salary and perks that expatriates receive. On the other hand, most companies believe that only by providing such inducements can they persuade qualified managers to accept overseas assignments.

Exhibit 3.6 illustrates how one company conceptualizes its compensation package for expatriates. The left side of its "balance sheet" summarizes what an employee currently earns and spends in the United States as broken down into taxes, consumption, and savings. The right side of the sheet provides more detail for these categories, allowing managers to provide comparable income to managers taking international assignments. Although more than 85 percent of North American companies use this approach, it is not without its critics.[45] Furthermore, the high costs associated with this approach have led some critics to call for shorter-term assignments and some forms of cost sharing by the expatriates.[46]

Repatriation

The final step in managing the human resources of global business involves bringing the expatriate manager home. This issue may seem quite simple, but it is much more involved than simply packing belongings and putting the manager and his or her family on a plane. A great deal of adjustment is often required (more or less depending on how long the assignment was) on both the personal and professional levels.[47]

On a personal level, the expatriate manager may have to become accustomed to living on less real income and going without perks such as club membership or an assigned car. In addition, the manager and the manager's family may all have to become reaccustomed to U.S. practices, including driving on the right-hand side of the road, tipping at restaurants, and not bargaining over the price of everything they buy. If the overseas assignment was for a longer period of time, then the returning managers may also need to learn new styles in clothing, food, and music. For some managers who were not living in the United States before the tragedy of September 11, 2001, but who returned home afterward, there may be a need to adjust to a much different way of life.

The repatriation process could be even more difficult on a professional level. The expatriate manager has been out of sight for awhile and may have lost some status within the organization. The manager's old job may no longer exist, and he or she may be concerned about the nature of the new assignment and have questions about how much the company truly values the manager's overseas experience. Perhaps these are some of the reasons why roughly one-half of repatriated managers leave their companies within 2 years of repatriation.[48] In any event, most experts emphasize the importance of explaining the entire expatriation and repatriation process to managers before they are sent overseas. It is also critical to stay in touch with expatriates so that they can maintain their social and network ties within the company. This step includes regular phone calls and visits, and it also means ensuring that expatriated managers are considered when other opportunities present themselves. Finally, most experts agree that some type of career counseling is helpful at the time of repatriation. Note, however, that few companies actually follow the advice of these experts and fail to complete the process successfully. A recent survey indicated that 40 percent of expatriates leave their companies within 2 years of repatriation because of reported poor career opportunities.[49]

INTERNATIONAL LABOR RELATIONS

Labor relations, which we will discuss more fully in Chapter 11, are the processes of dealing with employees who are organized into labor unions. Labor relations are also heavily regulated by law, as we noted briefly in Chapter 2, and the actions of management toward labor and the actions of labor toward management are heavily restricted. Different situations, however, exist in other countries. In many countries throughout the world, labor parties seek to achieve the political goals of unions in those countries, and these parties are often quite powerful. Also, in many countries,

labor unions are much more concerned with social issues than they are in the United States, and so their political activism often extends beyond the wages and conditions of employment. In any case, union membership is quite large in many countries and continues to grow. In fact, more than half the world's workforce outside the United States belongs to labor unions.

Different norms or expectations exist in other countries about the relationships between unions and management. In England, labor "contracts" are not really legal contracts at all but are merely understandings that can be broken at any time by either party with no penalty. And throughout Europe, temporary work stoppages are frequently used by unions in a bid for public backing of their demands. In Paris, for example, 1-day work stoppages by employees who work in the city's buses, subways, and railroads are frequently used for this purpose. And during recent contentious contract negotiations at French operations for Caterpillar, Sony, and 3M, angry labor officials actually took senior managers hostage in efforts to win better employment contracts.[50] In contrast to the situation in Europe, labor relations in Japan tend to be cordial. Unions are created and run by the businesses themselves. Because Japanese culture discourages confrontation and hostility, unions and management tend to work together cooperatively. Disputes are usually dissolved cordially and through mutual agreement, and it is rare that a third-party mediator must be consulted. Strikes are also rare in Japan.

CLOSING CASE

HUMAN RESOURCES AND INTERNATIONAL MERGERS

Mergers and acquisitions are nothing new, of course, but some recent megamergers between international giants may portend a new era in global consolidation. Two of these mergers, in particular, had the potential to reshape international competition, and each also had significant implications for international HR practices. One megamerger involved Chrysler Corporation and Daimler-Benz. The other involved Amoco and British Petroleum.

The news about Chrysler and Daimler-Benz made headlines around the world when the deal was announced in midsummer 1998. Most experts agreed at the time that it was a good match. Chrysler made moderately priced cars and light trucks, was strong in North America but weak in Europe, and had distinctive competencies in design and product development. Daimler-Benz, on the other hand, made luxury cars and heavy trucks, was extremely strong in Europe, and had distinctive competencies in engineering and technology. While billed as a merger, Daimler-Benz actually bought Chrysler for

© AFP/Getty Images

© KRT/Newscom

$38 billion. The new company, called DaimlerChrysler AG, remained headquartered in Germany and became the fifth-largest automobile company in the world.

Myriad strategic, technical, and operational systems had to be integrated before the two firms truly became one, and these problems proved to be dramatically more complex than originally thought. Indeed, integration problems proved to be insurmountable; as a result, the firm never captured the efficiencies and economies of scale and scope that the firm's managers intended. Blending the two firms' human resources also presented a formidable challenge. Before merging, Chrysler and Daimler-Benz had a combined worldwide workforce of 421,000 employees. After the merger was complete, however, not all these workers were needed, so job cuts occurred at the production, technical, operations, and executive levels. But the two firms also had to deal with powerful unions, the United Auto Workers (UAW) for Chrysler in the United States and IG Metall in Germany.

Other issues were associated with employment conditions. Consider, for example, representative conditions at three plants. In Germany before the merger, Daimler-Benz autoworkers had an hourly wage range of from $15 to $20 per hour, got 6 weeks of annual vacation and 12 sick days, and worked an average of 35 hours a week. The Mercedes-Benz plant in Alabama, however, had substantially different conditions. Its workers earned from $14.05 to $19.20 an hour, got 12 days of vacation time and 10 sick days, and worked an average of 40 hours per week. At Chrysler's biggest plant, in Detroit, meanwhile, workers earned between $19.37 and $23.22 an hour, got 4 weeks of vacation time and 5 sick days, and worked an average of 50.5 hours per week (of which 10.5 hours were compensated at a rate of time and a half). Clearly, then, integrating these disparate conditions under a single employment umbrella was a challenge. As a result of all these challenges, managers eventually gave up. In 2008, Chrysler was sold to a private equity firm, and DaimlerChrysler became simply Daimler AG.

A second big international merger was announced later the same year, this one between Amoco and British Petroleum (BP). At the time of the announcement, Amoco was the fourth-largest oil producer in the United States, while BP was the third largest in the world, behind Royal Dutch/Shell and Exxon. Like the Chrysler and Daimler deal, this one was also not a true merger—BP was actually the buyer, with a 60-percent ownership stake in the new company.

The firm remained headquartered in London, but all of its U.S. operations shifted to the Amoco organization and brand name.

Again, the firms had to address significant HR issues with the integration of the two operations. BP's operations in the United States were based in Cleveland, while Amoco operated out of Chicago. BP announced that it would shut down most of its Cleveland operation, with some employees there transferred to Chicago. To make room, Amoco also indicated that several jobs in its own headquarters would be eliminated. All told, the firms cut about 6,000 of their combined 99,000 jobs. Most of these cuts were in marketing and exploration. Unlike the failed marriage between Daimler and Chrysler, however, BP eventually managed to achieve full integration between the two companies. About 5,000 jobs were eliminated during the 2009 recession, but BP has managed to remain profitable and highly competitive.[51]

THINK IT OVER

1. What are the likely advantages and disadvantages that firms in these kinds of mergers can expect?
2. What are the advantages and disadvantages for individual workers at firms that merge with international partners?
3. What basic HR issues, besides those mentioned in the case, must be addressed as a result of these mergers?

STUDY TOOLS

CHAPTER 3

THE COMPETITIVE Environment

CHAPTER 4

FRENCH ROA

TORRÉFACTION FR

For the past two decades Starbucks Corporation has been one of the highest-profile and fastest-growing food and beverage companies in the United States. Howard Schultz bought Starbucks in 1987 when it was still a small mail-order operation. He promptly reoriented the business away from mail-order sales and emphasized retail coffee sales through the firm's coffee bars. Today, Starbucks is not only the largest coffee importer and roaster of specialty beans but also the largest specialty coffee-bean retailer in the United States. Starbucks closed several hundred low-performing stores in 2009 but continues to aggressively expand in high-demand and growth markets, especially overseas. The firm has also broadened its product offerings to include a lower-priced brew (Pike's Roast) and more breakfast items (such as fresh oatmeal). It also launched a line of instant coffees, Via, in 2010.

What are the keys to Starbucks's success? One important ingredient is its well-conceived and implemented strategy. Starbucks has managed to locate its coffee shops in high-traffic areas and continues to adjust its product line to meet consumer tastes. For instance, many of its newer stores offer drive-through service to attract more consumers who don't have time to go inside. Starbucks's growth is planned and coordinated each step of the way through careful site selection. And as noted above, underperforming stores are closed as needed. Through its astute

> " *One reason a lot of youths don't find corporate America so attractive is because of the IBM image: I'll become a blue suit. Starbucks makes you feel like a partner.* "
>
> —**Karen Hunsaker, Starbucks employee**[1]

LEARNING OBJECTIVES

After studying this chapter, you should be able to:

LO1 Describe the competitive environment of human resource management

LO2 Identify three types of strategies and relate each to human resource management

LO3 Discuss human resource strategy formulation and relevant organizational factors

LO4 Discuss the processes through which human resource strategy is implemented

LO5 Discuss how the human resource function in organizations can be evaluated promotional campaigns and commitment to quality, the firm has elevated the coffee-drinking taste of millions of Americans and fueled a significant increase in demand.

Another key to Starbucks's success is its near-fanatical emphasis on quality control and operations efficiencies. For example, milk must be heated to precise temperatures before it is used, and every espresso shot must be pulled within 23 seconds or else it is discarded. And no coffee is allowed to sit on a hot plate for more than 20 minutes. Schultz also refuses to franchise his Starbucks stores, fearing a loss of control and a potential deterioration of quality. (Starbucks does license the operation of its kiosks in airports and shopping malls.)

The people who work for Starbucks have also played a major role in the firm's success. Managers at each store have considerable autonomy over how they run operations, as long as the firm's basic principles are followed. Starbucks also uses a state-of-the-art communication network to keep in contact with its employees. The firm hires relatively young people to work in its restaurants and starts them at hourly wages that are somewhat higher than most entry-level food-service jobs. The company also offers health insurance to all of its employees, including part-timers, and it has a lucrative stock-option plan for everyone in the firm. In addition, a state-of-the-art information system allows every employee to keep abreast of what's happening in the company.

Its rapid growth rate notwithstanding, Starbucks is continually on the alert for new business opportunities, including internationally. It was only a little more than a decade ago that Starbucks opened its first coffee shops outside the United States: two in Japan and another in Singapore. By the end of 2009, there were more than 8,500 company-owned or licensed Starbucks stores in 36 countries.

Another growth area for the company is brand extension with other companies. For instance, the firm collaborates with Dreyer's to distribute five flavors of Starbucks's coffee ice cream to grocery-store freezers across the country. Starbucks also collaborates with Capital Records on Starbucks jazz CDs, which are available in Starbucks stores. Redhook Brewery even uses Starbucks's coffee extract in its double black stout beer. And Jim Beam markets Starbucks Coffee Liqueur.[2]

THINK IT OVER

1. How interested might you be in working for Starbucks? Why?
2. Visit the firm's Web site and navigate through it using the point of view of a prospective employee. What things on the site increase or decrease your interest in applying for a position?

Starbucks has achieved undeniable success through an astute combination of strategy, control, and human resources. Under the leadership of Howard Schultz, the firm has been on a phenomenal growth and expansion pace, with everything dictated by an overarching strategy. Precise operations systems and control standards ensure consistent product quality, and highly motivated people throughout the organization keep everything running according to plan. Take away any of the three elements—strategy, operations, and motivated people—and both the company and its remarkable performance would not be the same. Indeed, more and more managers today are recognizing the important links that exist among strategy, operations, and human resource management. Further, a strategic orientation to human resource management provides a useful and effective perspective on how to create these linkages.

Thus, this chapter is devoted to the strategic human resource (HR) environment. The first section discusses the strategic context of human resource management (HRM) in terms of the organization's purpose, mission, and top management team. The next section focuses on corporate, business, and functional strategies and their relationship to HRM. We then address the increasingly important area of strategic HRM in terms of its formulation and its implementation. Important organizational characteristics that affect and are affected by these processes are also described. Finally, we provide a framework for how organizations evaluate the HR function.

THE COMPETITIVE ENVIRONMENT FOR HUMAN RESOURCE MANAGEMENT

Human resource management does not occur in a vacuum but instead occurs in a complex and dynamic milieu of forces within the organizational context.[3] A significant trend in recent years has been for HR managers to adopt a strategic perspective on their job and to recognize the critical links between organizational and HR strategies. In this way, an organization may be able to gain a competitive advantage through its management of human resources. Exhibit 4.1 illustrates the framework we will use in discussing strategic HRM. As the exhibit shows, this process starts with an understanding of the organization's purpose and mission and the influence of its top management team and culminates with the HR manager serving as a strategic partner to the operating divisions of the organization. Under this new view of HRM, the HR manager's job is to help line managers (at all levels) achieve their strategic goals. In this way, the human resource manager adds value to the organization by providing expertise concerning how to use the firm's human resources to accomplish its objectives and gain competitive advantage.

This view also has important implications for how HR managers are trained and how HRM courses are designed.

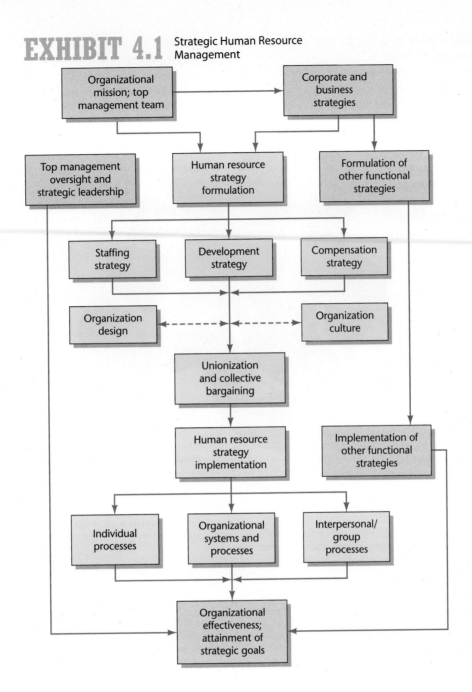

EXHIBIT 4.1 Strategic Human Resource Management

Traditionally, managers, scholars, and textbook authors have discussed the newest—and presumably the best—ways to interview candidates or select employees, as well as the best models for compensation and performance appraisal. But when we begin to consider the role of the human resource department as being that of a strategic partner, does it still make sense to talk about the *single* best way to do anything? Are there truly "best practices" that all firms should adopt, or should the practices adopted by a firm depend exclusively on the firm's specific strategic goals? The "truth" probably lies somewhere between these two extremes, but there have been loud debates within the HR community over whether a best-practices approach or a contingency approach (based on the strategy pursued) is most logical.[4]

Indeed, it seems that some general practices *are* better. If we examine fundamental HRM practices, it seems reasonable to suggest two points:

1. Formal performance appraisals are better than no appraisals (see Chapter 10).
2. Using systematic selection techniques is better than hiring based on intuition or some nonsystematic basis (see Chapter 7).

But, within some constraints, exactly *how* these practices are implemented probably should depend on the firm's strategic goals. In other words, although formal appraisals are better than no appraisals, exactly what is appraised should be consistent not only with a firm's strategic goals and missions but also with the other factors we discuss throughout this chapter.

Therefore, an organization must choose HR practices that fit its strategy and mission, and so the best practices for one firm may not be exactly the best for another. We will remind the reader of this fact throughout the book, but we recognize that this ambiguity can be a source of frustration. Students and managers alike often want to know what will work best in a particular organization. Although we will provide information and suggestions about general practices that should work (usually), the specific best solution or practice will depend on various characteristics of the organization such as strategic goals and top management values. There are few, if any, simple answers once we recognize the strategic role of human resource management.

A Strategic Perspective

We begin by explaining exactly what we mean when we refer to *strategy* and a *strategic* perspective. First, remember that all firms exist in a competitive environment. There are competitors who are trying to attract the same customers or sell the same goods and services, and each firm must fight to be successful; that is, each firm seeks to earn higher returns for its stockholders than do its competitors. Starbucks competes with Dunkin' Donuts and various local coffeehouses for its business. Southwest Airlines competes with Continental, Delta, United, and American Airlines to attract passengers who will fly with them. A basic tenet of capitalism is that there should be competition among different firms because this competition spurs each firm to try harder to provide better services, lower prices, or higher quality, and the public gains as a result.

Sometimes, though, a market is not large enough to support all the firms competing in it. For example, from the 1920s until the 1960s, New York City had two large department store chains competing for retail sales in the city. Macy's and Gimbels were fierce rivals (this rivalry played a role in the original version of the movie *Miracle on 34th Street*), and their flagship stores were located within two blocks of each other. But over time, Macy's was able to establish a more recognizable brand name (the Thanksgiving Day Parade was a big part of that), and Macy's reacted more quickly to changes in the way people liked to shop and the kinds of items they bought. As a result, Macy's established much stronger customer loyalty, which enabled them to spend less on advertising and allowed them to occasionally charge more for a product. Thus, Macy's created a strategy, and that strategy created value for Macy's (lower costs and higher prices meant greater profits) and allowed Macy's to survive until this day, while Gimbels is a name recognizable only to old-time New Yorkers and some film fans.

When a firm implements a strategy that its competitors are unable to implement (for any number of reasons), that firm has gained a sustained competitive advantage. This, then, is the goal of competitive strategy. In the case of Macy's and Gimbels, Gimbels could have copied Macy's initially, but over time, it would have been too costly for Gimbels to shift its focus. This is often the case. If a firm is strategic in its thinking, it develops a strategy that it thinks will be successful and then finds the people and the other resources needed to implement that strategy. Any number of competitors could have decided on the same strategy and made the same attempts to gather the resources needed, but, assuming they made other choices, they could not easily switch strategies later.

Of course, for our discussion, we are most interested in how firms can use their human resources and the human resource practices to gain competitive advantage. If a firm can

1. hire the right people
2. train them to be effective
3. place them in the right jobs
4. motivate them to work hard, and
5. retain them

Then it can gain a sustained competitive advantage over its competitors. These employees will work efficiently and effectively, and, if they are managed so that they also work toward the organization's strategic goals, the firm can reduce costs, increase quality, or develop innovative solutions to business problems. The only way a competitor can copy this would be to hire the employees away from the firm and then manage them and treat them as well as the original firm.

It is not enough to simply hire similar employees or even hire the firm's employees away from it. Employees are important resources that are difficult to copy or replace; therefore, they are potentially an excellent source of competitive advantage. But all of the pieces must fit together for this to work. Let us assume that a baseball team (which surely exists in a competitive environment) decides to make a serious run at winning a championship. The team management believes it has good pitching, reasonable hitting, and solid fielding, but it has no power hitters. The first part of implementing the championship plan is to draft, trade for, or otherwise obtain a few players who can hit home runs instead of singles. But once these players have been acquired, the team must then formulate a strategy that leverages these new resources in order to win. This may include using something like a "designated hitter" to get more of these players into the lineup, but it may also include obtaining other players who can hit and reach base before the power hitters come up in the batting order. The team might also add to its training staff by hiring experts in building muscle and strength to further develop the new hitters. However, to fully leverage these new resources, the baseball team might go even further. Perhaps the team could refurbish the baseball stadium in a way that favors the team's new hitters. So, for example, if there were several right-handed sluggers on the team, the new stadium could have a slightly closer or shorter wall in left field, where these hitters would probably hit most of their long balls. Finally, in a defensive maneuver, the owners might instruct the ground crew to let the infield grass grow a bit longer to slow down opponents' ground balls.

Whether all these moves make sense in the context of a baseball team, they do illustrate the process of gaining a sustained competitive advantage. The organization must do more than acquire critical resources; it must also develop a complete strategy that leverages these resources. Even if the original team loses some of these new sluggers, it will be difficult for other teams to replicate the effects of the new strategy unless they also could rebuild their stadiums, recut their infield grass, and hire the other players and personnel needed to truly leverage the hitters. In general, an organization must acquire the best human resources it can, but it must then develop strategies to use those resources in the most effective manner. Every individual HRM practice and policy, then, must serve this larger goal.[5]

Although the strategy that is developed is the most important part of the strategic context for human resource

owners; the purpose of a university is to discover and disseminate new knowledge; the purpose of a museum is to preserve artifacts and historical relics.

2. An organization's **mission** is how its managers have decided to fulfill its purpose. A mission statement specifies how the organization intends to manage itself so it can pursue the fulfillment of its purpose most effectively. A mission statement attempts to specify the unique characteristics and strengths of an organization and identifies the scope of the business's operations in particular products and markets.[6]

Exhibit 4.2 shows the Starbucks mission statement. Note the prominence given to the firm's employees as the very first "guiding principle." This statement—and its placement—convey clearly the importance that Starbucks places on its employees.

Both its purpose and its mission affect an organization's human resource practices in some obvious ways. A university, for example, must employ highly educated faculty members to teach courses and conduct research in specialized areas. A civil-engineering firm must employ people who understand construction and structural engineering; a natural history museum needs people who understand history and science; a marketing firm needs employees with sales expertise. But even finer gradations can be drawn within each type of organization as defined by their respective missions. For example, an oil-exploration firm like Shell needs more petroleum engineers, while an electronics firm like Intel needs more electrical engineers, and a construction firm like Bechtel needs more civil engineers.

Mission statements often provide subtle cues about the importance that the organization places on its human resources. Many progressive firms today, such as Starbucks, refer to the importance of their human resources in their mission statement. Southwest Airlines and Walmart also

[*Mission statements sometimes explicitly state how important employees are to an organization.*]

management, it is not the only one. Several other factors are important for determining this context, and we turn our attention to some of the more important factors next.

The Influence of Organizational Purpose and Mission

An organization's purpose and mission are among the most fundamental contextual forces that define the strategic context of human resource management.

1. An organization's **purpose** is its basic reason for existence. The purpose of a business is to earn profit for its

stress the value of their employees in their mission statements. But some firms do not explicitly refer to employees in their mission statements. Most of these firms really do value the people who work for them, but the lack of specific reference to those people might be an indication that human resources are somehow not seen as being as important to the organization as other issues and goals. Although mission statements make a public commitment to some course of action (such

*An organization's **purpose** is its basic reason for existence.*

*An organization's **mission** is a statement of how it intends to fulfill its purpose.*

EXHIBIT 4.2 Starbucks Corporate
Mission Statement

STARBUCKS MISSION STATEMENT

Establish Starbucks as the premier purveyor of the finest coffee in the world while maintaining our uncompromising principles while we grow.

The following six guiding principles will help us measure the appropriateness of our decisions:

- Provide a great work environment and treat each other with respect and dignity.
- Embrace diversity as an essential component in the way we do business.
- Apply the highest standards of excellence to the purchasing, roasting and fresh delivery of our coffee.
- Develop enthusiastically satisfied customers all of the time.
- Contribute positively to our communities and our environment.
- Recognize that profitability is essential to our future success.

as valuing human resources), we must recognize that, in some cases, the language of a mission statement is intended to placate a group of stakeholders, such as employees, rather than to signal an organization's true priorities.[7]

THE INFLUENCE OF THE TOP MANAGEMENT TEAM

The **top management team** of an organization is the group of senior executives responsible for the overall strategic operation of the firm. Common organizational positions that are assumed to be part of the top management team include:

1. the chairperson of the board of directors,
2. the chief executive officer (CEO),
3. the chief operating officer (COO), and
4. the president.

Other members of the top management team generally include the senior executive (usually having the title of vice president) responsible for each major functional area within the organization. For example, the senior vice presidents responsible for marketing, finance, and human resource management, respectively, are all likely to be considered part of an organization's top management team.

The top management team sets the tone for the organization and plays a major role in shaping its culture (as discussed later in this chapter). Some top management teams have a clear vision of where the firm should go and how it should get there. They also do a good job of articulating this vision throughout the organization. In this case, middle- and lower-level managers know what is expected

> *How top managers behave reveals far more than what they say about their organizations.*

of them and can direct their own efforts and the efforts of members of their own division, department, or team toward this common goal. Other top management teams, however, present ambiguous, contradictory, or vague visions of where they see the organization headed. As a result, other managers in these organizations may be unsure about how to proceed and be unable to communicate effectively with

The **top management team** of an organization refers to the group of senior executives responsible for the overall strategic operation of the firm.

their own employees.[8] In fact, views of leadership that emphasize the importance of personal charisma in leaders tend to suggest that effective leaders need both a clear vision and a means of communicating that vision. If an organization has top managers who are unable to accomplish both these goals, then the organization is less likely to be successful.[9]

Top managers sometimes use speeches and proclamations to articulate the organization's vision and purpose, but their actual behavior more commonly communicates their true personal values and beliefs—and thus those of the organization. Herb Kelleher, the legendary CEO of Southwest Airlines, knew many of the firm's employees by name and insisted that they call him Herb. Before his death, Sam Walton personally visited every Walmart store at least once a year and spoke with all employees via the firm's satellite telecommunications network almost once a week. Employees who work for leaders like these recognize that they are important and that their effort is valued by senior managers. In contrast, other top managers try to insulate themselves from lower-level members of the organization. They seldom visit work locations and treat their employees with disdain. James Dutt, a former CEO of a major conglomerate called Beatrice Foods, once told a subordinate that if his wife and children got in the way of his working 24 hours a day, 7 days a week, he should get rid of them. In the late 1990s, Enron CEO Kenneth Lay created a culture that promoted internal cutthroat competition and a win-at-all-costs mentality. Although some employees embraced this culture, others felt uncomfortable and many valuable employees left the firm.

But we should not assume from this discussion that the top management team or even the CEO will always have a major influence on what goes on in an organization. In many cases, serious constraints restrict the top management team's power and preclude it from having a great effect. Researchers who have examined this problem suggest that the ability of the top management team to influence the organization is constrained by the nature of the industry (commodity product industries tend to limit the influence of the top management team), the nature of the organization (more powerful boards of directors tend to constrain the influence of the top management team), and the nature of the individuals themselves.[10] This research, using the term *managerial discretion*, has found that the abilities of top management teams to influence their organizations and success can vary widely as a function of these constraints. We turn now to one of the determinants of managerial discretion: the model of corporate governance used by the organization.

THE ROLE OF CORPORATE GOVERNANCE

Stockholders are the true owners of a modern corporation. These people, who often represent institutions such as pension funds, are not typically the same people who actually run the organizations on a day-to-day basis. That task is left to the CEO and the top management team. It is possible (and even likely), however, that the interests of the owners are different from those of the management. This produces a situation known as an *agency problem*. We will discuss agency theory again in Chapter 13, but for now

The top management team in an organization plays a major role in determining its strategies and its culture. For example, employees will almost certainly realize when a top manager is only pretending to be interested in their welfare.

it is sufficient to note that stockholders prefer decisions that will increase the current value of the firm's cash flow. These decisions may carry a certain level of risk, but these owners are not overly concerned about risk because they can diversify their investments across several firms and so have a hedge against any one source of risk.

Managers, however, are much more risk averse because they cannot diversify their investments in people and equipment in the same way investors can diversify their investments. Thus, the best interests of the managers are somewhat different and might be at odds with the interests of the owners, creating an agency problem. This requires the owners to somehow monitor the actions of the managers to make sure they work for the best interests of the owners. One important means to accomplish this is through the operation of the board of directors. In most organizations, all officers and employees technically report to the board.[11]

Boards typically have ten to fifteen members. Some are members of the top management team, while others are major stockholders, and still others might be prominent members of the community. The role of the board is to monitor the actions of the top management team to ensure that stockholders' interests are protected. But boards differ not only in terms of their power but also in terms of their activity. Throughout the 1990s, there was an increase in the level of activism by boards in the United States,[12] but there were still those who believed that there was not enough monitoring of top management, especially in terms of compensation. As a result, when major U.S. banks and investments firms turned to the government for financial assistance, many people blamed the boards for not being vigilant enough. One response to this was for the U.S. government to become an "owner" of some of these institutions and to try to use its power to rein in any abuse.

In March 2009, President Obama said he was outraged by the bonuses paid to AIG executives (after the firm received billions of dollars in funding from the government) but there was not much he could do about it; this suggests that government oversight may not be the answer.[13] In fact, it is increasingly clear that corporate governance mechanisms do not represent a serious constraint to managerial discretion when there are a sufficient number of insider managers on the board. These and related issues are discussed more fully in HR in the 21st Century.

CORPORATE, BUSINESS, AND FUNCTIONAL STRATEGIES

As indicated earlier, top managers are responsible for the strategic operations of their firms. The key to strategic operations, in turn, is developing and implementing effective strategies. These strategies may be at the corporate, business, or functional level, including the human resource function.[14] In addition to strategy formulation (as shown earlier in Exhibit 4.1), the organization's top management team also provides oversight and strategic leadership for the organization on an ongoing basis. It should be clear by now that functional strategies should be consistent with and supportive of corporate strategy.

1. **Corporate strategy** deals with determining what businesses the firm will operate.
2. **Business strategy** deals with how the firm will compete in each market where it conducts business.
3. **Functional strategy** deal with how the firm will manage each of its major functions (such as marketing, finance, and human resources).

Strategies at all three levels, however, affect the human resource management function under the strategic approach to HRM.

Corporate Strategy and Human Resource Management

As noted earlier, the corporate strategy should be closely tied to the HRM practices within the firm, and only through this close relationship can these practices lead to higher corporate performance and competitive advantage.[15] There are several broad strategies that a firm might adopt at the corporate level, and each one has different implications for HRM practices. The first three we will discuss are all relevant for firms that decide to compete in a single market.

Growth Strategy When a business has identified a unique niche and is successfully and aggressively expanding within that particular market niche, it is pursuing what experts call a **growth strategy**. As the term suggests, a growth strategy focuses on the growth and expansion of the corporation. For example, Starbucks has been using a rapid growth strategy as it continues its geographic and brand expansion, opening on average at least one new store somewhere in the world every day.

A key challenge for HR managers with firms using a growth strategy is recruiting and training the large numbers of qualified employees to help operate growing operations. When organizations view the human resource area as a true strategic partner, however, they also use input from human resource managers in their initial formulation of corporate strategy. Thus, before the top management

HR in the 21st Century

Over the last several years, corporate governance has come under growing scrutiny in the United States. Several developments have led to this scrutiny. First, corporate boards of directors have been increasingly linked to major corporate scandals. For instance, the board of directors at WorldCom approved a personal loan of $366 million to the firm's CEO, Bernard Ebbers, even though there was little evidence that he would be able to repay it. Likewise, Enron's board of directors approved a $20-million bonus for one of its own members simply for helping with the acquisition of another company. And the Enron board also infamously once set aside its own corporate board of ethics to approve a transaction that would violate that code. After the transaction was finalized, the code of ethics was reinstated.

Board independence has also become a source of complaint. Traditionally, boards included members who were also officers of the company (such as the CEO). But boards also included several independent members who had little personal stake in the company other than representing the best interests of shareholders. In recent years, the composition of some boards has again been slanted toward insiders or people with vested personal interests. When independent board members are long-time personal friends with the CEO, for example, the potential for conflicts of interest may increase.

Moreover, since the board of directors sets—or at least approves of—the compensation packages for the firm's senior executives, it follows that criticisms of executive compensation are ultimately directed at corporate boards. In 2010, for example, there was a public outcry when it was announced that the CEO of AIG was in line for a bonus exceeding $100 million even though AIG had been the recipient of a U.S. government bailout less than a year earlier. It was AIG's board of directors that had approved the original contract that led to the bonus.

A firm's HR managers are responsible for managing executive compensation, although they seldom have a voice in setting that compensation, at least at the senior level. They can provide a useful role, though, in providing the board with useful comparative data to show what senior executives are paid at similar firms. They can also play an important role in documenting the performance achievements of senior managers to help the board make the best decisions possible regarding executive compensation.

THINK IT OVER

1. Do you think the U.S. government should play a role in setting executive compensation?
2. What are the complications in trying to tie executive compensation directly to firm performance?

---

team of a firm decides to pursue a growth strategy, it would consult with the HRM team to ensure that it had the capability to attract and train the large number of new employees needed to implement the anticipated growth. In other words, a true partnership requires both parties to consult with and support each other.

A growth strategy can also be pursued externally through mergers, joint ventures, and the acquisition of other businesses.[16] When these happen, a major initial challenge for human resource managers is determining how to merge two existing workforces into a single cohesive and integrated unit. In some cases, for example, there will be unnecessary duplication of employees, and choices will have to be made about which overlapping employees to retain, which to transfer, and which to lay off. Similarly, it is likely that the two firms will be using different human resource philosophies for issues such as training practices, promotion policies, and so forth. HR decision makers thus

will have to decide which practices to retain and which to discard. When the Walt Disney Company acquired the ABC television network, among the first questions that had to be answered were:

1. Who would manage various parts of the new enterprise?
2. How would the two firms' human resources departments be integrated into one new operation?

In fact, there is reason to believe that the failure to integrate different strategies and cultures may be an important factor in the failure of some mergers and acquisitions.[17] Furthermore, because there is always a great deal of concern and speculation over what will happen to employees, the entire merger or acquisition process must be managed well relative to its effects on employees. Failure to do so can result in undue stress, the loss of valued employees, and long-lasting morale problems.[18]

Retrenchment or Turnaround Strategy Sometimes, firms are forced to adopt, at least in the short run, a strategy usually referred to as a **retrenchment** or a **turnaround strategy**, which occurs when an organization finds that its current operations are not effective. For example, a firm might find that its dominant products are in declining markets, its technology is rapidly becoming obsolete, or it is in some other way not performing as well as it should. Major changes are usually needed to rectify these kinds of problems. In most of these cases, organizations go through a period of *downsizing* (or *rightsizing*, as some managers prefer to call it) in an effort to get back on the right track (we will discuss this further in Chapter 6). They close operations, shut down factories, terminate employees, and take other actions to scale back current operations and reduce their workforces. Their ultimate goal is to take the resources generated as a result of these steps and reinvest them into other more promising products and markets.

Downsizing has become a common response to competitive problems. As more employees find their jobs at risk, the traditional psychological contract between the organization and the employee is changing. No longer can employees feel certain of keeping their jobs if they perform well, and the increased uncertainty makes it more difficult for employees to commit fully to their organizations. As a result of these problems, HR managers clearly need to be involved when the organization is eliminating jobs or decreasing the size of its workforce. They need to help manage the process so that employees continue to feel attached to and committed to the organization. In addition, human resource managers must help ensure that decisions about who will be let go are made for job-related reasons as opposed to reasons that might reflect or suggest bias or illegal discrimination. Similarly, HR managers can help optimize the transition process for displaced workers through practices such as equitable severance packages and outplacement counseling. International Harvester declared bankruptcy and was reborn as Navistar, a much smaller operation. Human resource managers were involved in all phases of this process and in making decisions about which employees would be most valuable to the new enterprise and how best to retain them.

Stability Strategy A third single-market strategy that might be adopted by some firms is a **stability strategy**. This strategy essentially calls for maintaining the status quo. A company that adopts a stability strategy plans to stay in its current businesses and intends to manage them as they are already being managed. The organization's goal is to protect itself from environmental threats. A stability strategy is frequently used after a period of retrenchment or after a period of rapid growth. When the firm is using a stability strategy, HR managers play a major role in determining how to retain the firm's existing employees when the firm can offer little in the way of advancement opportunities, salary increases, and so forth.

Diversification Strategy In addition to the strategies focusing on one specific market, *diversification* is another widely used approach to corporate strategy.[19] A corporation that uses the **diversification strategy** usually makes the decision to own and operate several different businesses. For example, General Electric, one of the most successful practitioners of this strategy, owns varied businesses that manufacture aircraft engines, industrial products, major appliances, and technical products as well as financial services and insurance businesses.

1. The various businesses owned by a corporation are usually related to one another in some way, a strategy called **related diversification**.[20] The basic underlying assumption for using this strategy is that the corporation can achieve synergy among the various businesses it owns. For example, Limited Brands has an ownership stake in more than a dozen different retail chains, including Express, Victoria's Secret, and Bath & Body Works. A single group of buyers supplies all of the firm's chains, a single development operation seeks new locations for all chains, and so forth. This type of organization often adopts a policy of rotating managers across the various businesses so they develop an overall managerial perspective on the whole firm. A manager might start out with Express, get promoted to a new position at Bath & Body Works, and then move into yet another position with Victoria's Secrets. The related aspects of the businesses presumably make such cross-business transfers easier. Because the markets for each business are similar, the firm can develop relatively uniform procedures for selection, compensation, training, and so forth.

2. Sometimes, however, an organization decides to expand into products or markets that are unrelated to its current products and markets. This approach

---

A retrenchment or turnaround strategy occurs when an organization finds that its current operations are not effective, and major changes are usually needed to rectify the problem. In most cases, this strategy involves rightsizing the organization by closing operations, shutting down factories, and terminating employees in order to get back on the right track.

Stability strategy *essentially calls for maintaining the status quo. A company that adopts a stability strategy plans to stay in its current businesses and intends to manage them as they are already being managed. The organization's goal is to protect itself from environmental threats. A stability strategy is frequently used after a period of retrenchment or after a period of rapid growth.*

A diversification strategy *is used by companies that are adding new products, product lines, or businesses to their existing core products, product lines, or businesses.*

Related diversification *is used when a corporation believes it can achieve synergy among the various businesses that it owns.*

is called **unrelated diversification**. A firm that pursues this strategy attempts to operate several unique businesses in different, unrelated markets. General Electric, as already noted, owns businesses that compete in different unrelated areas. The basic logic behind unrelated diversification is that a company can shield itself from the adverse effects of business cycles, unexpected competition, and other economic fluctuations. Because the various businesses are presumably unrelated, a downturn or setback in one does not necessarily suggest a corresponding downturn or setback in another. Human resource executives in a firm that uses unrelated diversification must approach the HR function in a very different way. In most cases, managers remain within a single business unit as they progress up the corporate ladder. Because each unrelated business is likely to have its own unique hiring, compensation, and training needs—as dictated by its own competitive environment—these functions will likely be customized and decentralized for each business. Thus, even though the career tracks and compensation packages for managers at Express and Victoria's Secret will likely be similar to one another, the career tracks and compensation packages for managers at GE Jet Engines and GE Appliances may be quite different from one another. The GE Jet Engine compensation packages, for instance, will more closely resemble those at Rolls Royce, another large jet engine manufacturer, while the GE Appliance compensation packages may be more like those at Whirlpool and Maytag.

Organizations that use the diversification approach for managing their corporate strategy must also work to ensure close coordination between their corporate human resource functions and the HR functions within each of their businesses or divisions. Essentially, the corporate HR group must interface with three sets of constituents. One set of constituents is the top management team or corporate management. Second, corporate human resources can also be involved in representing the firm in its interactions with external constituents such as the government, labor unions, and benchmark companies (companies to which the organization compares itself). Third, corporate human resources can also be involved with the division management, division human resources, and the employees of each division or business owned by the corporation.[21]

BUSINESS STRATEGY AND HUMAN RESOURCE MANAGEMENT

As noted earlier, decisions must also be made about how to compete in each market where a firm operates. This question determines business strategy. A diversified corporation must therefore develop a business strategy for each operating unit.[22] A variety of approaches can be used to develop a business-level strategy. One of these is the adaptation model.

The Adaptation Model

One approach to business strategy is called the **adaptation model**.[23] This model suggests that managers in an organization should try to match the organization's strategy with the basic conditions of its environment. Different levels of environmental complexity and change are expected to be matched most appropriately with different forms of strategy. The three basic strategic alternatives from which managers should select are the defender strategy, the prospector strategy, and the analyzer strategy.

1. A *defender strategy* is assumed to work best when a business operates in an environment with relatively little uncertainty and risk and a high degree of stability. The goal of the defender is to identify for itself a relatively narrow niche in the market and then to direct a limited set of products or services at that niche. Although defenders may compete with other firms aggressively, their primary approach is to guard and secure their position within an

Unrelated diversification *is used when a firm attempts to operate several unique businesses in different, unrelated markets. The basic logic behind unrelated diversification is that a company can shield itself from the adverse effects of business cycles, unexpected competition, and other economic fluctuations.*

The adaptation model *is one popular approach to business strategy where a business seeks ways to adapt to its environment.*

existing market. Even though they monitor trends and developments outside their chosen domain, they focus primarily on their existing environment. Hershey Foods is a good example of a defender. The firm concentrates almost exclusively on the confectionery market. Another good example of a defender is Wrigley, the venerable chewing gum company founded in 1891. Human resource managers in organizations using this strategy are most likely to recruit and seek to retain stable employees who exhibit high levels of commitment and loyalty to the firm.

2. A second type of strategy used in this approach is the *prospector strategy*. This strategy anchors the other end of the continuum and works best when the environment is dynamic and growing and has considerable uncertainty and risk. Prospectors are advised to be on constant alert to discover and capitalize on new ideas and opportunities. They continually focus on new products and markets and try to avoid a long-term commitment to any single type of technology, using multiple technologies instead. This strategy makes it easier for the organization to shift easily from one product market to another. General Electric is a good example of a prospector. As noted earlier, the firm owns everything from a jet-engine business to a television network. For the right opportunity, the firm will buy any business that might be for sale or sell any business it currently owns. Human resource managers in organizations using this strategy may prefer to recruit and retain entrepreneurial employees who are highly flexible and who are more dedicated to their craft or profession than to the organization itself.

3. The *analyzer strategy* falls between the extremes of the defender and prospector strategies. The analyzer strategy is most appropriate in relatively stable conditions with a moderate degree of uncertainty and risk. An analyzer tries to identify and take advantage of new markets and products while simultaneously maintaining a nucleus of traditional core products and customers. The Walt Disney Company is a good example of an analyzer. The firm cautiously moved into television and video markets a few years ago, has expanded its movie division, and is currently investing in electronic games and virtual reality products, but it takes each step slowly and only after careful deliberation. Human resource managers in firms that pursue this strategy may seek to recruit and retain employees who might be moderately entrepreneurial and flexible but who will also be quite dedicated and loyal to the organization.

4. The adaptation model also identifies a fourth strategic alternative called the *reactor*. The reactor is really seen as a strategic failure, however, and is not held up as a model that any firm should emulate. A reactor is a firm that either improperly ignores its environment or else attempts to react to its environment in inappropriate ways. During the early 1980s, Kmart was guilty of using the reactor strategy. It failed to keep pace with Walmart, for example, and spread itself too thin by investing heavily in specialty retailing. HR managers in organizations functioning as reactors may lack a clear understanding of exactly what qualities they are seeking in their employees. And, indeed, this lack of understanding may contribute to the firm's poor performance.

Other Competitive Strategies

The other dominant approach to business-level strategies identifies three specific competitive strategies—namely, differentiation, cost leadership, and focus. These three are presumed to be appropriate for a wide variety of organizations in diverse industries.[24]

1. A company that uses a **differentiation strategy** attempts to develop an image or reputation for its product or service that sets it apart from its competitors. The differentiating factor may be real or objective, such as product reliability or design, or it may be more perceptual or subjective, such as fashion and appearance. Regardless of its basis, however, a firm that can differentiate its products or services from those of its competitors can charge higher prices for those products or services, thereby earning a larger profit. Rolex and BMW are both examples of firms that have used a differentiation strategy successfully. Human resource managers contribute to the successful use of a differentiation strategy by recruiting and retaining employees who can perform high-quality work or provide exemplary customer service. Likewise, employee training will likely focus on quality improvement, and reward systems may be based on factors such as quality of work and customer satisfaction.[25]

A company that uses a **differentiation strategy** attempts to develop an image or reputation for its product or service that sets the company apart from its competitors.

2. A **cost leadership strategy** is one that focuses on minimizing the costs as much as possible. This strategy allows the firm to charge the lowest possible prices for its products, thereby presumably generating a higher overall level of revenue. Low cost may be achieved through production efficiencies, distribution efficiencies, or product design efficiencies. Timex and Hyundai are examples of businesses that have used a cost leadership strategy successfully. HR contributions here focus on recruiting and retaining employees who can work as efficiently and productively as possible. On the other hand, more experienced employees may demand higher wages, and so it might also be possible to reengineer jobs so that they require minimal skills and then select employees who can perform the jobs but who may not remain with the organization long. Fast-food restaurants often control labor costs using an approach such as this one. In any case, training may emphasize efficient production methods, and reward systems may be based more on quantity than on quality of output. One popular approach to reducing costs today is moving production to other countries where labor costs are lower.

3. Finally, when an organization uses the **focus strategy**, it tries to target a specific segment of the marketplace for its products or services. This focus may be toward a specific geographic area, a specific segment of the consuming population based on ethnicity or gender, or some other factor that segments the market. Within that focus, a firm may attempt to either differentiate or cost lead its products or services. Fiesta Mart is a Houston-based grocery store chain that has prospered by focusing its marketing on the large number of immigrants, especially Hispanics, who live in the Southwest. These stores sell Mexican soft drinks, cornhusks for wrapping tamales, and many other products that are not carried in general-purpose grocery stores. The key HR goal in this instance is recruiting and retaining employees who understand the focal market. For example, Fiesta Mart must recruit, hire, and retain employees who really understand the products they are selling and who speak Spanish, the language of most of its customers.

Functional Strategies and Human Resource Management

The third level of strategy formulation and implementation is at the functional level. Functional strategies address how the organization will manage its basic functional activities, such as marketing, finance, operations, research and development, and human resources. Thus, at this level, HR strategy formulation formally begins to take shape. It is clearly important that an HR functional strategy be closely integrated and coordinated with corporate, business, and other functional strategies. Indeed, without such integration and coordination, organizational competitiveness will clearly suffer.[26]

Much of our discussion throughout the remainder of this text explicitly or implicitly addresses the human resource function from a contextual perspective that includes other fundamental business functions. As you saw in Exhibit 4.1, HR strategy is, of course, our primary concern. Keep in mind, however, that other functional strategies are also developed and (as shown in the exhibit) combine with the HR strategy and top management strategic leadership to determine the firm's overall performance.

HUMAN RESOURCE STRATEGY FORMULATION

Using the organization's overarching corporate and business strategies as context, managers can formally develop the organization's HR strategy, as noted above. As illustrated in Exhibit 4.1, this strategy commonly includes three distinct components—a staffing strategy, a development strategy, and a compensation strategy. These dimensions are shown in more detail in Exhibit 4.3.

1. *Staffing* refers to the set of activities used by the organization to determine its future human resource needs, recruit qualified applicants interested in working for the organization, and select the best of those applicants as new employees. Obviously, however, this process can be undertaken only after a careful and systematic strategy has been developed to ensure that staffing activities mesh appropriately with other strategic elements of the organization. For example, as already noted, if the business employs a growth strategy, then the staffing strategy

> **A cost leadership strategy** is one that focuses on minimizing the costs as much as possible.
>
> **The focus strategy** is undertaken when an organization tries to target a specific segment of the marketplace for its products or services.

© ARTSILENSEcom/Shutterstock

EXHIBIT 4.3 Human Resource Strategies

must be based on the aggressive recruiting and selection of large numbers of qualified employees.[27] But if retrenchment is the expectation, then the staffing strategy will focus instead on determining which employees to retain and how to handle best the process of terminating other employees.

2. Similarly, HR managers must also formulate an employee-development strategy for helping the organization enhance the quality of its human resources. This strategy usually involves performance management, the actual training and development of employees and managers, and career planning and development for appropriate employees. As with staffing, the development strategy must be consistent with corporate and business strategies. For example, if an organization uses a differentiation strategy, the firm needs to invest heavily in training its employees to produce the highest-quality products or provide the highest-quality service. Performance management must also be focused on recognizing and rewarding performance leading to improved quality. But if cost

leadership is the strategy of choice, then the firm may choose to invest less in training (helping to keep overall costs low) and orient the training that is offered toward efficiency and productivity-improvement methods and techniques.

3. Third, the compensation strategy must likewise complement other strategies adopted by the firm. Basic compensation, performance-based incentives, and employee benefits and services—the major components of the compensation strategy—must all be congruent with their relevant strategic contexts to be effective. For example, if a firm uses a strategy of related diversification, its compensation system must be geared to (a) rewarding those employees with

different skills that allow them to transition across businesses and (b) be flexible enough to facilitate those same cross-business transfers. If a manager moves from one division to another, for instance, then that manager's pension plan should be readily portable to the new assignment. If the firm uses unrelated diversification, on the other hand, compensation may instead be focused on depth of knowledge and skills. Hence, the firm may choose to pay a premium salary to a highly talented expert with unusual skills relevant to one of the firm's businesses. The ability of this expert to transition across businesses is less important and thus is not likely to be a factor in compensation.[28]

Of course, these three components cannot be treated independently of each other. Each component must be tied to the overall human resource strategy, and each must consider the factors and constraints produced by the other components. A recently proposed theoretical model attempts to look at the entire array of interrelationships

> ## *Four types of employment modes are possible within an organization: internal development, acquisition, contracting, and alliance.*

with employees from a strategic perspective. The model of HR architecture suggests that not all employees possess capabilities of equal strategic value to a firm, and so they should be treated differently.[29] Specifically, the authors argue that a firm can have at least four types of employment modes—which they refer to as internal development, acquisition, contracting, and alliance—for its employees. The model suggests strategic imperatives for establishing these different relationships.

To help explain the complexities of the interchange among these aspects of HR strategy and corporate strategy, we can consider a situation where an organization is moving into a new line of business or at least changing its emphasis within existing businesses. A good case in point is the major oil companies in the United States. Someone growing up in this country in the 1960s and 1970s would remember gas stations as places where someone stopped to get gas for a car and perhaps was able to buy a cold drink or a snack from a vending machine. Over time, the image of the gas station changed dramatically.

Through the 1980s and 1990s, oil companies expanded the services available at these stations, and many of them became minimarts offering a wider variety of food and beverages. By the beginning of the twenty-first century, many oil companies entered into alliances with fast-food chains (such as McDonald's and Kentucky Fried Chicken) so that patrons could buy a meal as well as gas.

These services were viewed as a means to get potential customers to stop at a given gas station. Although the oil companies made money from products sold at the minimarts, they did not see these products as a primary line of business. At the end of the 1990s and in the early years of the twenty-first century, however, several large mergers occurred between major oil companies (e.g., British Petroleum and AMOCO, Exxon and Mobil). Newly merged companies suddenly discovered they owned a large number of food marts around the country.

When attempting to formulate the HR strategy as well as its three basic components, human resource managers must also account for other key parts of the organization. These components are important because they affect both how strategies are formulated and how they are implemented. Three critical components are organization design, the corporate culture, and unionization.[30] A fourth component, the labor force and how it relates to HR planning, will be discussed in more detail a bit later in the chapter.

The Impact of Organization Design

Organization design refers to the framework of jobs, positions, groups of positions, and reporting relationships among positions that are used to construct an organization.[31]

1. One form of organization design used by many smaller or newer organizations is the *functional design* (also called the *U-form organization*, with *U* representing *unitary*). The organization groups its members into basic functional departments such as marketing, finance, and operations. For this form of organization to operate effectively, considerable coordination across departments must exist. Senior management is usually expected to provide this coordination. A U-form organization typically has a single HR department responsible for organizationwide HR functions and activities, and the HR manager and department work with all other functional areas across the firm.

2. A second form of organization design used in some organizations today is the *conglomerate*, or *H-form design* (the *H* stands for *holding company*). A conglomerate design is used when an organization has implemented a strategy of unrelated diversification. The corporation itself is essentially a holding company that results from this unrelated diversification. Because the various businesses that make up the organization are unrelated to the others, each functions with a high degree of autonomy and independence. A corporate-level staff usually plays a key role in coordinating the activities of the various divisions, and HRM is a common staff function in an H-form organization. But each of the unrelated businesses within the corporation also has its own HR department that functions with relative autonomy within that specific business.

   The corporate-level staff provides broad and general oversight and links business-level and corporate-level issues.

3. A third form of fairly common organization design is the *divisional* or *M form* (the *M* stands for *multidivisional*). The divisional design looks similar to the H-form design except that the businesses are closely related to one another. The M-form design is especially popular because of the presumed synergies that can result from related business groupings. Coordination is usually decentralized down to the various operating companies where the work is actually being performed. Although M-form organizations may have a corporate HR staff, most of the basic human resource functions are handled within each division.[32] The primary function of the corporate-level HR department is to facilitate synergy across businesses. Presumably, the U.S.-based oil companies discussed earlier are moving to this type of form.

Regardless of the specific design, in recent years many firms have been moving toward becoming *flat organizations*. This involves eliminating levels of management, reducing bureaucracy, using wide spans of management, and relying heavily on teamwork and coordination to get work accomplished. Flatter organizations are believed to be more flexible and more easily adaptable to changing conditions. The HR function in these organizations is likely to be diffused so that operating managers take on more of the responsibility for HR activities, with a somewhat smaller human

> **Organization design**
> refers to the framework of jobs, positions, clusters of positions, and reporting relationships among positions that are used to construct an organization.

resource staff providing basic services and playing more of a consultative role.

THE IMPACT OF CORPORATE CULTURE

The culture of the organization also affects how it formulates and implements its human resource strategy. An organization's **culture** refers to the set of values that helps its members understand what the organization stands for, how it does things, and what it considers important.[33] Culture is a complex and amorphous concept that defies objective measurement or evaluation. Nevertheless, it is the foundation of an organization's internal environment and thus plays a major role in shaping managerial behavior and is a strong element in how the organization manages its human resources.

Although there is no such thing as an ideal culture, an organization should have a strong and well-articulated culture. This type of culture enables people within the firm to know what the organization stands for, what it values, and how they should behave with regard to the organization.[34] The HR department often plays a key role in helping new employees learn about the culture through orientation and through the telling and retelling of stories and corporate history. For current organizational employees, culture can be communicated through training, consistent behavior, and other organizational activities. Sometimes something as simple as a slogan can be used to manage culture. For example, when Continental Airlines' current management team took over, it touted the company's turnaround strategy as the "Go Forward Plan"—a signal to look ahead and not back. And when Schwinn, a 100-year-old bicycle company, changed its corporate culture a few years ago, it helped enact the change with a new slogan: "Established 1895. Reestablished 1994."

Although an organization's culture is shaped by several different forces, one important force is the founder of the organization. Organizations with strong-willed and visionary founders often find that the remnants of that founder's vision remain a central part of their culture today. Walt Disney's influence is still found throughout the corporation that bears his name. Even though Sam Walton died almost two decades ago, his values and approach to doing business will likely remain a part of Walmart for decades to come. As an organization grows, its culture is modified, shaped, and refined through other forces. These forces include symbols, stories, slogans, heroes, and ceremonies. Shared experiences also play a role in determining and shaping the culture of an organization. Members of teams who work long hours together to develop a major new product such as the new Ford F150 pickup truck or who jointly experience a major crisis such as the aftermath of September 11, 2001, often develop a common frame of reference and become a more cohesive work group.

Human resource managers may find that, depending on the circumstances, corporate culture may either facilitate or impede their work. If the firm has a strong and well-understood culture that seems attractive to people, then recruiting qualified applicants is often easier. Southwest Airlines and Starbucks fall into this category, with each firm receiving large numbers of applications

> *An organization's culture is the set of values its members understand, including what the organization stands for, how it does things, and what it considers important.*

from prospective employees. But organizations that have strong cultures and that wish to maintain those cultures have a tendency to select people who have values consistent with that culture. We will discuss the role of fit later in Chapter 7, but for now note that some organizations select individuals who are qualified enough to do the job (even if they are not the *most* qualified) but who also share the values and beliefs of the firm's culture. In other words, they select the person who best fits the organization's culture and image.

Finally, managing culture is important for the success of corporate mergers and acquisitions, which we will discuss further in Chapter 6. The ability to integrate two cultures—in fact, to form a new unique corporate culture and identity for the merged organization—is critical for the overall success of any merger or acquisition, and is the role of the human resource management area. Several scholars have noted that the failure to deal with the human resource implications of mergers and acquisitions leads to their failure far more frequently than do problems with finances.[35] An interesting example of these culture problems occurred several years ago when Philip Morris acquired General Foods. The employees of General Foods considered themselves part of a benevolent company that made family-oriented products such as Jell-O and Maxwell House coffee. Imagine their surprise when their new employers (who also owned Miller Brewing Company)

An organization's **culture** refers to the set of values that helps its members understand what the organization stands for, how it accomplishes what it wants to accomplish, and what it considers important.

continued *their* usual practice and distributed cartons of cigarettes to each employee every Friday!

The Impact of Unionization and Collective Bargaining

Other important aspects of the workforce that affect the development and implementation of strategy in the HRM function are unionization and collective bargaining. Labor relations is the process of dealing with employees who are represented by an employee association, usually called a *union*. Union membership in the United States has been declining gradually for the last few decades, but it remains an important force in many industries, as we shall see in Chapter 11. In fact, the AFL-CIO has recently been linking living-wage issues to larger social movements, introducing new sources of pressure on human resource management.[36] In any case, unions can play an important role in formulating and implementing human resource strategy. Unionized firms tend to have more rules and formal procedures that might limit a firm's ability to formulate an ideal strategy and, if management and union leaders do not work together, the union can be a major obstacle in implementing any strategic change. On the other hand, a strong union can actually facilitate these changes, if its leaders and the firm's management are working together productively.

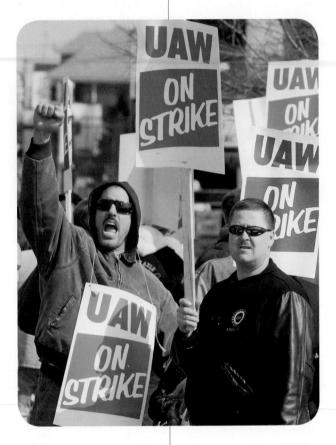

© Rebcca Cook/Reuters/Corbis

INTERPERSONAL PROCESSES AND STRATEGY IMPLEMENTATION

The formulation of an HR strategy is clearly important and can be affected by many factors. Ultimately, the best formulated strategy will not help unless it is properly implemented.[37] We will discuss strategy implementation in more detail in the next chapter, where we will consider strategy as a major source of information for decision making in the arena of human resource management. For now, it is also important to consider the role that interpersonal processes play in the implementation of strategy.

Interpersonal processes are especially important because of the role they play in affecting the performance effectiveness exhibited by each employee in a firm.[38] The starting point for understanding these processes is the psychological contract that an organization has with its employees. A **psychological contract** is the overall set of expectations held by an individual with respect to what he or she will contribute to the organization and what the organization, in turn, will provide to the individual.[39] Individuals see themselves as contributing their time, energy, effort, experience, and talent, and they expect to receive compensation, benefits, security, challenge, opportunities for promotion, and similar forms of rewards. Properly established and maintained psychological contracts are a fundamental starting point in ensuring that employees are committed to working toward organizational goals and contributing to organizational effectiveness by implementing the strategies that managers have developed. Special problems arise when the implementation of a new strategy involves a change in the terms of the psychological contract.[40]

Individual personality traits and attitudes are also important parts of individual processes in an organization. **Personality** is the relatively stable set of psychological attributes or traits that distinguish one person from another. Some organizations believe that one or more particular personality traits may relate to how well an employee can perform a certain job or type of job. Personality traits such as self-esteem and agreeableness may be important traits for someone who will be working in a job that requires regular interaction

> *A **psychological contract** is the overall set of expectations held by an individual with respect to what he or she will contribute to the organization and what the organization will provide the individual in return.*
>
> ***Personality** is the relatively stable set of psychological attributes or traits that distinguish one person from another. Some organizations believe that one or more particular personality traits may relate to how well an employee can perform a certain job or type of job.*

with the public; conscientiousness appears to be important for performance in a wide variety of jobs.[41] Human resource managers are usually responsible for determining the best way to measure relevant personality traits in job applicants and for being able to verify that those measures—as well as the underlying traits themselves—do indeed relate to job performance.

Attitudes also play an important role in implementing strategy in an organization. If people have positive attitudes toward their work and organization, then they will be more committed to making contributions to organizational effectiveness and in helping achieve strategic goals. Workers with negative attitudes, on the other hand, are less likely to make this commitment and may be more inclined to be absent frequently or seek alternative employment. Human resource managers are often called on to help other managers assess the attitudes of their workers by developing attitude surveys, administering those surveys to employees, and then interpreting and evaluating the results.

Perhaps the most important individual process in organizations, however, is **motivation**, or the set of forces that cause people to behave in certain ways. Individual motivation is also a major determinant of individual performance, but motivation is at the heart of what causes an employee to choose to expend the effort that will support any organizational activity. Unfortunately, the process of motivating employees to behave in desired ways is quite complicated, and there is a great deal we do not understand about it. Nonetheless, theories and models of motivation attempt to explain the phenomenon, and we will discuss several in Chapter 13.

Still another important individual process in organizational settings is **stress**, or a person's adaptive response to a stimulus that places excessive psychological or

physical demands on him or her. Important considerations for HR managers include an understanding of the causes of stress, the processes by which stress affects individuals, and how organizations and individuals can cope better with stress in organizational settings. Human resource managers are increasingly being called on to help employees cope with stress, and we will discuss some of the issues involved in these efforts in Chapter 12.

Finally, because little behavior in organizations takes place in isolation, human resource managers also need to consider interpersonal processes that develop from the relationships an employee has with co-workers, supervisors, and subordinates. These processes are becoming even more important as organizations move more and more toward having employees work as part of a team instead of as individuals. HR managers must deal with various issues rising from the emphasis on teams, ranging from deciding who should be part of a team to how to evaluate the performance of team members and reward them. Clearly, in this new work environment, the management of interpersonal processes is important for implementing HR strategy.

Leadership is also an important priority for many organizations. Most experts believe that effective leadership is vitally important to organizational success, yet they cannot agree on how to define, measure, or predict leadership. Human resource managers are expected to help identify potential leadership qualities among existing employees and then to help structure procedures for developing and enhancing those qualities.[42] Obviously, these managers must have a basic understanding of leadership to help the organization achieve its goals.

A final important interpersonal process that is directly related to the implementation of human resource strategy is communication. Communication is the process by which two or more parties exchange information and share meaning. Written communication, oral communication, and nonverbal communication are all pervasive in organizations. Electronic mail has become an especially important area of communication in recent years. In many organizations, the HR department is responsible for coordinating communication among employees through newsletters, bulletin boards, intranets, and so forth. Clearly, human resource managers need to understand how to enhance communication to make sure that their efforts are indeed helping to implement their strategies.

"Ability is what you're capable of doing. Motivation determines what you do. Attitude determines how well you do it."

—LOU HOLTZ, American football coach (b. 1937)

Motivation *is the set of forces that causes people to behave in certain ways. Individual motivation is also a major determinant of individual performance, but motivation is at the heart of what causes an employee to choose to expend the effort that will support any organizational activity.*

Stress *is a person's adaptive response to a stimulus that places excessive psychological or physical demands on that person. It is important for HR managers to include an understanding of the causes of stress, the processes by which stress affects individuals, and how organizations and individuals can cope better with stress in organizational settings.*

Human resource managers must obviously have a keen understanding of the behavioral processes that are critical in determining the relative effectiveness of various HR functions such as compensation, rewards, performance appraisal, and training and development. All managers need to understand and appreciate these behavioral processes to understand the actions of those with whom they work. Finally, human resource managers are often charged with the responsibility of developing and implementing programs aimed at improving various behavioral processes. For example, they may be asked to overhaul the reward system to boost motivation and productivity, develop training programs for workers to cope better with stress, or help identify ways to improve interpersonal communication or resolve interpersonal conflict.

LEARNING OBJECTIVE 5

EVALUATING THE HUMAN RESOURCE FUNCTION IN ORGANIZATIONS

Evaluating the effectiveness of the HR function has become an important trend in recent years. Human resource management was historically seen as an organizational cost or expense; that is, the organization budgeted a certain amount of money to spend on the management of its HR function. As long as the HR manager stayed within this budget and the employees seemed generally happy, everything was assumed to be fine. More recently, however, many organizations have become more concerned with the cost as well as the benefits of human resource management for two seemingly contradictory reasons.

First, as we discussed in Chapter 1, many organizations are now subcontracting or outsourcing some of their HRM functions to external vendors. Whether or not to outsource a function depends on the actual cost of keeping the function in-house.

At the same time, many organizations are coming to view effective HRM as a source of competitive advantage, so they are focusing on its potential benefits and examining the costs and benefits to see which ones actually contribute to competitive advantage and which should be outsourced. Functions that add little value are likely to be outsourced, even if they are not terribly expensive, and functions that add competitive advantage are likely to be retained, even if they are relatively expensive. Of course, the functions themselves may or may not contribute to competitive advantage, but it is the way the organization chooses to allocate its resources to manage those functions that will determine where the firm derives its competitive advantage.

In any event, line managers may even be allowed to decide between the corporation's HR department or an outsider vendor when they need HRM help. Traditionally, organizations relied primarily on indirect measures of the effectiveness of their HRM practices. For example, high turnover or high absenteeism indicated low satisfaction with the job, and this predicament was seen as a problem with human resource management. Low levels of absenteeism and turnover or low costs were associated with positive HRM practices and, as noted above, costs were not seriously considered. Later, as we noted in Chapter 1, more sophisticated methods of utility analysis allowed organizations to put a dollar value on the contributions of various HRM practices and consider costs as well.

In addition to the evaluation of specific human resource functions, there has been a recent trend toward evaluating entire systems of HR activities. Instead of determining if any one HRM practice can produce value, this approach examines the relationship between "bundles" of practices and the overall performance of the organization in terms of factors such as profitability, stock price, and productivity. Although the specific practices that have been investigated differ somewhat from study to study, and despite issues raised about the measurement of effectiveness,[43] the evidence

TABLE 4.1	Human Resource Management Practices That May Lead to Improved Firm Performance
Self-directed work teams	
Total quality management (TQM)	
Contingent pay	
Attitude surveys	
Formal performance appraisals	
Continuous training	

seems to show that organizations that adopt more enlightened HRM practices actually do better than other organizations.[44] Although, as noted, we need to know exactly which practices work, these sets of practices have generally become known as *high-performance work systems*, and they include practices such as those illustrated in Table 4.1.

Of course, several questions must be answered before we can fully understand the importance of these human resource management practices. For example, there is some question about whether these practices are truly universally effective. There are also questions about the mechanisms through which these practices lead to firm performance; clearly the practices listed in Table 4.1 (which are derived from several research studies and are typical of the work in this area) are quite broad and cover several different elements. For example, formal performance appraisals can take many different forms, as we will see later in Chapter 10. Although it may be better to have some formal appraisal than none at all, it is also probably true that different types of appraisal systems will lead to different outcomes. Although it might be preferable to make pay contingent on something, exactly what that is may be important as well. In general, however, there is reason to believe that an organization can be more competitive if it adopts these practices, and this represents a new way of evaluating a firm's HR practices.

CLOSING CASE

WHEN IS A GAME NOT A GAME?

Activision Blizzard is one of the leading players in the computer gaming industry. However, its path to greatness was not easy. Activision was founded in 1979 by a former music industry executive and four disgruntled programmers from Atari, a pioneer in arcade games and home videogame consoles. In part, Activision was founded as a haven for game developers who were unhappy with prevailing industry policy. At the time, systems providers like Atari hired developers to create games only for their own systems; in-house developers were paid straight salaries and denied credit for individual contributions, and there was no channel at all for would-be independents. Positioning itself as the industry's first third-party developer, Activision began promoting creators as well as games. The company went public in 1983 and successfully rode the crest of a booming market until the mid-1980s.

The company struggles began in 1986, when it entered an ill-advised merger with Infocom, a software firm founded to develop interactive fiction games. The relationship was rocky from the first, and Activision closed down Infocom operations in 1989 after 3 years of mismanagement and escalating losses. Meanwhile, Activision had also begun to branch out from videogames into other types of software, and changed its name to Mediagenic to underscore its new commitment to a broader product line. By this time, however, competition in the videogame market had increased substantially, and the decision to expand into areas beyond its distinctive competence turned out to be a major strategic blunder. By 1991, Mediagenic was bankrupt.

This is the point at which Robert Kotick happened upon Activision–Mediagenic, "a company," as *Forbes* magazine put it, "with a sorry balance sheet but a storied history." An entrepreneur with no particular passion for videogames, Kotick bought one-third of the firm for $440,000. He then turned his attention to finding why the firm was underperforming and what he could do to turn the tide.

What he discovered was actually a common condition in businesses based on individual creativity and innovation. The talented creators who developed the firm's products were attracted to their profession to start with by its flexibility, opportunity to work independently, and freedom to experiment and occasionally even fail. They also disliked deadlines and schedules and were deeply distrustful of so-called corporate types. But a growing business almost by necessity tends to take on the very qualities that creative people reject. Schedules and deadlines become the norm, and independence and freedom are tempered.

Kotick concluded that this basic tension existed in all of the firms in the gaming industry. Clearly, the business of making and marketing videogames succeeded when the creative side of the enterprise was supported by financing and distribution muscle, but it was equally true that a steady stream of successful games came from a company's creative people. The key to getting Activision back in the game, Kotick decided, was managing this complex of essential resources better than his competitors.

So, in 1996, Kotick raised $40 million through a stock offering, moved the company (rechristened Activision) to Los Angeles, and began to recruit the people who could furnish the resources that he needed most—creative expertise and a connection with the passion that its customers brought to the videogame industry. Activision, he promised prospective developers, would not manage its human resources the way that other firms did. At Activision, he promised, "we won't commoditize development. We won't absorb you into a big Death Star culture."

Between 1997 and 2003, Kotick proceeded to buy no fewer than nine studios. But he allowed each one to keep its own name, allowing it to stay where it was, and further encouraged autonomy by providing seed money for Activision alumni who wanted to strike out on their own. He has conducted market research out of the company's L.A. headquarters but does not use the results to put pressure on his creative teams; rather, he shares the data with his studios and lets them draw their own conclusions. Each studio draws up its own financial statements and draws on its own bonus pool, and the paychecks of studio heads reflect company-wide profits as well as losses.

Kotick's strategy has paid off big time. In 1999, Activision's Neversoft studio came up with *Tony Hawks' Pro Skater*, which broke through the monotony of sports games by letting players proceed at their own pace through a virtual landscape. Activision's next blockbuster franchise—the World War II game *Call of Duty*—came in 2003 from a group of developers who'd left a competitor to found a studio called Infinity Ward. In 2006, Kotick paid $100 million for a company called Harmonix, which had developed a game revolving around a guitar-shaped peripheral: The *Guitar Hero* franchise has revolutionized not only videogames but also the relationship between videogames and popular music and, as of this writing, has generated more than $2 billion in revenue. The firm, now known as Activision Blizzard, generated combined revenues in excess of $3.5 billion for calendar year 2009—enough to move into the top spot as the best-selling videogame publisher in the world not affiliated with a maker of game consoles (such as Nintendo and Microsoft).[45]

THINK IT OVER

1. Discuss the impact of strategy and culture on Activision Blizzard
2. Describe the operational issues a firm faces in trying to blend individual creativity and freedom with corporate bureaucracy.
3. What role would HR managers play at a business like Activision as opposed to a firm like General Motors and American Airlines?

STUDY TOOLS

- Rip out the chapter review card located at the end of the book.
- Review the valuable study tools located online at www.cengagebrain.com
  - Review the Key Terms flashcards.
  - Download audio and visual summaries to review on the go.
  - Complete practice quizzes to prepare for the test.
  - Play "Beat the Clock" and "QuizBowl" to master chapter concepts.
  - Complete "Crossword Puzzle" to review key terms.
  - Watch the chapter video for a real-life example of key concepts.

CHAPTER 4

Information
Human
RESOURCE
Decisions

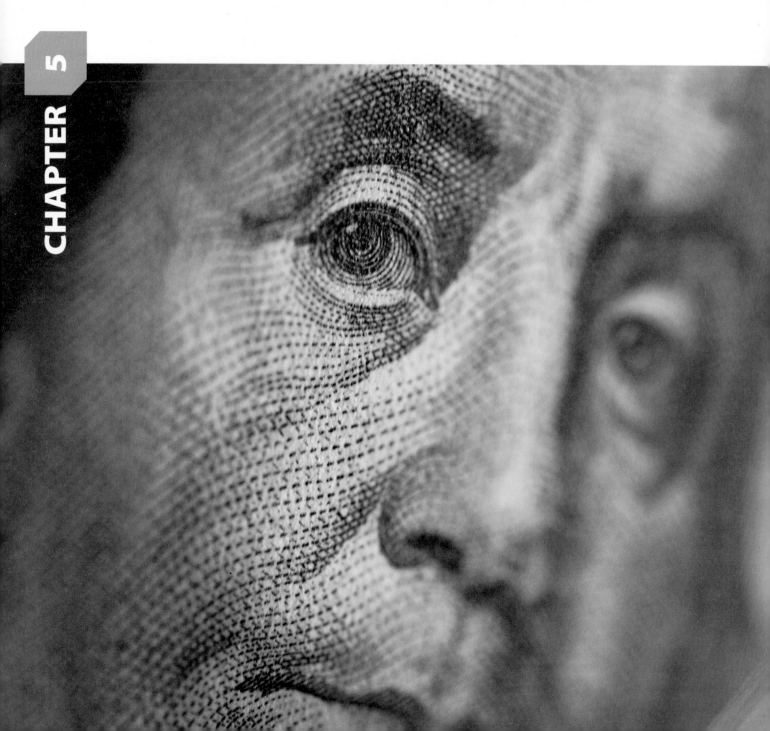

HIRING BY THE THOUSANDS

Walmart faces a daunting challenge. From its humble origins as a small discount operation in1962, Walmart has grown to become one of the world's largest and most profitable businesses. Today, the firm has more than 4,000 retail outlets in the United States and another 2,000 in other countries, most notably Mexico, Canada, Brazil, Japan, and China. Walmart generates almost $400 billion in annual revenues and more than $12 billion in profits.

So, what's the challenge? Well, one of the firm's biggest challenges is its workforce. Because of its low-cost business strategy, the firm has to pay relatively low wages and cannot offer lucrative benefits to its workers. As a result, the firm has a reasonably high level of turnover as its employees look for and find higher-paying jobs elsewhere. In addition, continued growth at Walmart requires hiring more and more new employees all the time—some to fill new jobs created by growth, and others to fill jobs vacated by current employees who take other jobs.

A few years ago, for example, Walmart established a target of hiring 1 million new employees over a 5-year period. About 800,000 of the new hires were targeted to fill new jobs to fuel the firm's expansion. The other 200,000 hires were targeted to replace current employees expected to leave because of natural turnover. As a result of this ambitious hiring plan, Walmart's global workforce now exceeds 2 million people. Indeed, more people work for Walmart than serve in the U.S. armed forces. To add further perspective, Walmart could employ every resident from the states of Alaska and Rhode Island combined and still need more workers.

So what does Walmart have to offer prospective employees? During the economic recession of 2008–09, simply offering a job

"The biggest challenge is the numbers. The numbers are just so large. But the issue is no different than the one [founder] Sam Walton faced. We have to focus on one associate at a time."

—Coleman Peterson, Wal-mart executive[1]

LEARNING OBJECTIVES

After studying this chapter you should be able to:

LO1 *Describe human resource planning as a source of information for decision making*

LO2 *Discuss strategy as a source of information for making human resource decisions*

LO3 *Discuss economic conditions as a source of information for making human resource decisions*

LO4 *Describe job analysis as a source of information for making human resource decisions*

LO5 *Discuss the job-analysis process and identify and summarize common job-analysis methods*

was often enough. But overall, Walmart provides steady employment, hourly pay only slightly more than minimum wage, and basic benefits. It also offers promotion opportunities, and its benefit package does include health-care insurance, an increasingly rare and costly benefit.

Walmart also faces other challenges regarding its workforce. For one thing, the retailer, like many other companies, hires a growing percentage of its workforce into the ranks of part-time jobs. The advantage to the firm in doing this is that it can offer part-timers much smaller benefit packages. And these smaller packages often do not include health care. Although this saves the company money, it attracts criticism from observers who argue that the only reason for using part-timers is to avoid providing them with insurance.

The company has also had some legal setbacks with its workers. The issue concerns the alleged practice of requiring workers to work "off the clock." For example, in some cases, workers claimed that their supervisors told them they had to report to work 30 minutes before they officially started to work in order to stock shelves or clean work areas. Similarly, other workers claimed that they were coerced to remain at work after their official ending time to take care of similar chores. In 2007, Walmart agreed to pay $33.5 million in back wages and interest to settle these claims.[2]

THINK IT OVER
1. How would you describe Walmart's human resource strategy?
2. Have you ever been encouraged to work "off the clock"? How did you handle it? How would you respond if you were told to do so in the future?

Walmart executives face a continuous challenge of hiring and retaining workers in a low-wage environment. But as with most things, Walmart does an outstanding job of forecasting its needs for employees. These forecasts come from a logical and systematic analysis of the firm's current and projected human resource (HR) needs. And as the ongoing hiring process continues, it will be critical that company officials monitor the environment and the firm itself and make any required midcourse adjustments. Both current hiring goals and their implementation have one major thing in common: information. Indeed, it is critical that firms have the information they need to make informed human resource management (HRM) decisions.

With an understanding of the nature of HRM and the HR environment as a foundation (as provided in Chapters 1 through 4), it is now possible to begin a more focused and detailed analysis of the kinds of decisions that HR managers must make and the information they need to make those decisions. This chapter opens this section with a discussion of the critical information needs of the human resource manager. Chapter 6 begins dealing with the decisions themselves and addresses decisions concerning size and structure of the organizational form, including who to let go, who to retain, and how we make sure that the right people are retained and separated. Finally, Chapter 7 deals with staffing by discussing issues involved in recruiting and selecting employees. These are critical decisions for the HR manager because they will determine the nature of the workforce available to try to meet strategic objectives.

We begin, then, with the information that human resource managers need to make the decisions required. The most basic type of information deals with the supply and demand for labor in the marketplace, and so we first look at human resource planning and forecasting as input for decision making.

LEARNING OBJECTIVE 1

HUMAN RESOURCE PLANNING AS A SOURCE OF INFORMATION

Probably the most important factor that affects the human resource management function is the labor force (also referred to as the *workforce*). An organization may pursue a growth strategy, and the HR manager may attempt to recruit and hire new employees, but if there are not enough people in the labor force with the required skills or background, then efforts to recruit and hire will fail and so will the overall growth strategy. Thus, the composition of the labor force is a major limiting factor in pursuing strategic goals. The successful management of this component requires what is called **human resource planning**, and this planning can often make the difference between organizational success and failure.[3] Human resource planning, illustrated in Exhibit 5.1, can be defined as the process of forecasting the supply and demand for human resources within an organization and developing action plans for aligning the two. This section examines that process in more detail.

Forecasting the Supply of Human Resources

An important first step in HR planning is forecasting the future supply of human resources—predicting the availability of current or potential employees with the skills, abilities, and motivation to perform jobs that the organization expects to have available. Several mechanisms can help managers forecast the supply of human resources in regard to current employees. By looking internally at its

Human resource planning *is the process of forecasting the supply and demand for human resources within an organization and developing action plans for aligning the two.*

EXHIBIT 5.1 The Human Resource Planning Process

Forecasting the supply of human resources

↓

Forecasting the demand for human resources

↓

Comparing forecasted supply and forecasted demand

↓

Taking appropriate actions

discuss them, particularly as they pertain to HR planning. A human resource information system is an integrated and increasingly automated system for maintaining a database regarding the employees in an organization. For example, a properly developed HR information system should have details on each and every employee regarding date of hire, job history within the organization, education, performance ratings, compensation history, training and development profile, and various special skills and abilities.[4] Of course, the HR manager also needs to look carefully at impending retirements and the firm's experiences with involuntary turnover. We will discuss these issues more fully in Chapter 6.

Because a firm often expects to need new employees in the future, it is also important to forecast the supply of human resources outside the firm that will be potentially available for it to recruit and hire. Here it is important to consider both general trends in the population and the workforce while simultaneously generating specific data about availability as it relates to the specific firm. Specifically, these trends and issues serve as valuable information related to forecasting the supply of human resources.

Labor Force Trends and Issues

Several changes in the labor force continue to emerge and affect human resource management. Decades ago, the labor force in the United States was primarily male and white. Now, however, the workforce is much more diverse in numerous ways.[5] For example, most people once followed a fairly predictable pattern of entering the workforce at a young age, maintaining a stable employment relationship for the period of their work lives, and then retiring at the fairly predictable age of sixty-five. But today, these patterns and trends have all changed. For example, the average age of the U.S. workforce is gradually increasing and will continue to do so. Several reasons have contributed to this pattern:

1. The baby boom generation continues to age.
2. Declining birthrates for the post–baby boom generation are simultaneously accounting for a smaller percentage of new entrants into the labor force.
3. Improved health and medical care also contribute to an aging workforce. People are now simply able to be productive at work for longer periods of their lives.
4. Mandatory retirement ages have been increased or dropped altogether, allowing people to remain in the labor force for longer periods.

Gender differences in the workforce also play an important role. More and more women have entered the workforce, and their presence is felt in more and more occupational groupings that were traditionally dominated by men. In 2009,

own records, the organization is likely to be able to draw on considerable historical data about its own abilities to hire and retain employees. In addition, the organization can glean information about the extent to which people leave their jobs voluntarily or involuntarily. All of this information is then useful in predicting the internal supply of human resources in the future.

Suppose, for example, that Atlas Industries, a regional manufacturing and supply business serving the plumbing industry, has averaged 15 percent turnover for each of the last 10 years, with little variation from year to year. When Atlas's HR manager attempts to predict the future supply of existing workers, at least initially it seems reasonable to predict a relatively similar level of turnover for the forthcoming year. Thus, the internal supply of the human resources at Atlas will likely decline by about 15 percent during the next year. Assuming the firm plans to maintain its current operations and will need a workforce comparable to what it has today, the organization needs to plan to replace those individuals who will depart by recruiting and hiring new employees.

An increasingly important element in this part of the HR planning process for most organizations is the effective use of the organization's **human resource information system.** We discuss the concepts associated with human resource information systems more completely in Appendix 1, but it is relevant here to introduce and briefly

Black Images/Shutterstock

A human resource information system is an integrated and increasingly automated system for maintaining a database regarding the employees in an organization.

the composition of the workforce in the United States was almost 50 percent female, although some critics claim that a glass ceiling—an invisible barrier that keeps women from progressing to higher levels in a firm—still exists in some organizations.

Changing ethnicity is also reflected in the workforce today. The percentage of whites in the workforce is gradually dropping, while the percentage of Hispanics is climbing at an almost comparable rate. The percentage of African Americans and Asians in the workforce is also growing but at a much smaller rate. In addition to age, gender, and ethnicity, other diversity forces are also affecting the labor force. For example, country of national origin is an important diversity dimension. Physically challenged employees and employees with other disabilities are also an important part of workforce trends. Many other dimensions of diversity, such as single-parent status, dual-career couples, gays and lesbians, people with special dietary preferences, and people with different political ideologies and viewpoints also are each playing an important role in organizations today. We cover diversity more fully in Chapter 8.

In addition, external data can also be used to predict the supply of labor in specific regions. Over the last several years, for example, there has been a gradual population shift away from the northern and northeastern parts of the United States and toward the southern, southeastern, and southwestern parts of the country. Thus, the supply of labor in the north and northeast is gradually declining, and the supply of labor in the southern parts of the United States is gradually increasing. In other parts of the world, wherever immigration rules permit, workers are gradually shifting away from developing parts of the world and toward industrialized and economically prosperous regions. For instance, many workers in eastern regions of Europe continue to move into western areas in anticipation of better employment prospects.[6]

In any case, immigration patterns are important inputs for forecasting the supply of labor. But borders are not as open as they once were, even in the United States. Concerns over homeland security have made it much more difficult for individuals from certain parts of the world to even visit the United States. Young males from predominantly Arab countries have had an especially hard time coming to the United States to work, or

even study, and some business leaders have become concerned about this and argue that security concerns are taking precedence over the need for qualified people to fill jobs. Furthermore, several critics, including Robert Gates (defense secretary during both the Bush and Obama administrations), have warned that these policies can hurt the long-term productivity of the United States and cut the country off from an important pool of talent.

Future labor supplies are typically forecast by developing mathematical trend models using data from the past, with appropriate adjustments for migratory trends and predictions. These models, which essentially assume that

> ## *Economic upheavals such as that seen in 2008–09 often challenge predictive models.*

trends will continue in a linear (i.e., straight-line) fashion, are usually reasonably accurate. But they can be far less accurate when some unforeseen event or trend disrupts expectations. An example was the unexpected increase in the labor force participation rates for women during the 1980s. Although women's participation rates had been climbing for years, statistical predictions based on simple trend lines substantially underestimated the growth rates in the 1980s. In retrospect, observers realized that new (i.e., first-time) entries by women into the labor force were being substantially supplemented by other women already in the labor force but who were previously underemployed.

But major economic upheavals, such as those experienced in the United States and much of the rest of the world in 2009, can present major challenges to predictive models. Many organizations actively cut the size of their workforces, which dramatically increased the supply of labor in the market. Because stock prices initially tumbled, many employees who had planned to retire found that they could no longer afford to do so, further increasing the supply of labor in the market. These forces, of course, also lowered the "price" of labor (i.e., what a firm had to pay), but many firms were too busy dealing with the new financial realities to be able to take advantage of lower labor costs. In any case, events such as this cannot be predicted by any linear model, which makes planning much more difficult.

Finally, we should also note the special forecasting situation generally known as **executive succession**. Executive succession involves systematically planning for future promotions into top management positions. This process is far more complicated because it is often critical that exactly the right type of person is selected for a top position, the development costs to groom this person are very high, and the actual decision may have major effects on the firm's future. Thus, many organizations try to bring as much order and logic to the process as possible. For example, senior executives usually indicate well in advance when they expect to retire—sometimes several years in advance. The firm can then draw on its cadre of up-and-coming managers for replacement candidates. Sometimes a specific set of individuals may be moved into special high-profile jobs, with the expectation that whoever does the best job will receive the promotion when the senior person steps down. In other cases, the most likely successor is moved into the second spot to eliminate all uncertainties and allow this person to concentrate on learning as much as possible about the senior position.[7] For example, a few years ago, Procter & Gamble's board of directors realized that the firm was facing substantially greater competition than in the past and that its performance was beginning to slide. To accelerate the change in strategy, it promoted its new heir apparent to the top spot earlier than originally planned; this was possible because Procter & Gamble had already done succession planning.[8] Unfortunately, planning disruptions at this level are especially prone to upheavals such as the financial crisis of 2008–09.

Forecasting the Demand for Human Resources

In addition to supply, strategic planning requires that HR managers must also develop forecasts about future demand. In other words, they need to ascertain the numbers and types of people the organization will actually need to employ in the future. One important ingredient in this assessment is the organization's own strategic plans regarding anticipated growth, stability, or decline, which are described later in the chapter.

It is also necessary to consider larger, broader trends in the economy when forecasting the demand for human resources. For example, the chart illustrated in HR in the Twenty-First Century shows how some jobs, such as retail sales, have remained in high demand since 1900. But other jobs, such as tailors, masons, tobacco factory workers, and butchers, have dropped sharply. Still others, such as nurses, hotel and restaurant managers, and moving equipment operators, have seen demand increase significantly. These general demand trends influence the availability of human resources for two reasons. First, employees for jobs in high demand will be more difficult to hire and will be more expensive to hire. In addition, students and future employees who track these demand trends often make decisions about what majors to pursue in college based on their anticipated employability. Thus, general trends such as the ones described here must be part of the planning process.

Clearly, the planning process, and the associated forecasting of supply and demand relative to labor, is an important source of information for the HR manager. Information about what kinds of people will generally be in demand, as well as information about what kinds of people will be available, is critical as the HR manager begins thinking about staffing decisions, downsizing or rightsizing decisions, and how to develop a diverse organization. This information not only will serve as a set of constraints on what the manager can accomplish but also help the manager identify ways to meet the organization's strategic goals. A related source of information for the HR manager comes out of the strategic-planning process itself.

STRATEGY AS A SOURCE OF INFORMATION

We discussed the relationship between strategic planning and effective human resource management in Chapter 4, but clearly the need for human resources in an organization depends to a large extent on the organization's overall strategy. As noted in Chapter 4, if an organization intends to grow, then it will most likely need to hire additional human resources in the future.[9] Likewise, if the organization expects to enter a period of stability, its HR demand is also likely to be relatively stable.[10] Finally, if a period of decline or retrenchment is anticipated,

> **Executive succession** *involves systematically planning for future promotions into top management positions.*

© Ilin Sergey/Shutterstock

HR in the 21st Century

Easy Come, Easy Go Managers attempting to forecast the future supply of and demand for jobs and employees face numerous uncertainties. One major uncertainty for long-term planning is the extent to which any given job may become more or less popular in the future. The following graph clearly illustrates this point. The graph rank orders the top thirty jobs (by millions of workers) for the years 1900, 1960, and 1995. Only eight job categories among the most popular in 1900 are still on the list by 1995. Some jobs (e.g., carpenters) have consistently dropped further down the list, whereas others (e.g., police officers and guards) have steadily risen. But most striking is simply the array of jobs on the 1995 list that did not appear previously—jobs such as computer programmers, health technicians, and lawyers and judges.

Over the course of the twentieth century, the structure of U.S. employment changed enormously, and this change continued (and perhaps even accelerated) in the first decade of the new century. Only eight top job categories have survived throughout. And many more top job categories now require substantial education.

THINK IT OVER

1. What are some very new kinds of jobs of which you are aware?
2. What jobs on the 1995 list may be in danger of disappearing in the near future?

TOP 30 JOBS (millions of workers)

#	1900		1960		1995	
1	Farmers and farm laborers	10.1	Retail salespersons	4.4	Retail salespersons	6.6
2	General laborers	2.6	Farmers and farm laborers	3.8	Teachers*	4.5
3	Private household workers[1]	1.6	Teachers*	1.7	Secretaries	3.4
4	Retail salespersons[2]	1.4	Truck drivers	1.7	Truck drivers	2.9
5	Secretaries[3]	0.6	Secretaries	1.5	Farmers and farm laborers	2.3
6	Carpenters	0.6	Private household workers	1.3	Janitors and cleaners	2.1
7	Railroad workers	0.6	Manufacturing laborers	1.0	Cooks	2.0
8	Miners	0.6	Bookkeepers	0.9	Nurses*	2.0
9	Truck drivers[4]	0.5	Carpenters	0.9	Engineers*	1.9
10	Teachers*	0.4	Waiters and waitresses	0.9	Freight and stock handlers	1.9
11	Launderers	0.4	Engineers*	0.9	Policemen and guards	1.8
12	Dressmakers	0.3	Vehicle mechanics and repairers	0.9	Bookkeepers	1.8
13	Iron and steel workers	0.3	Apparel and textile workers	0.8	Nursing aides, orderlies, etc.	1.8
14	Machinists	0.3	Construction workers	0.8	Vehicle mechanics and repairers	1.7
15	Painters	0.3	Assemblers	0.7	Financial salespersons*	1.7
16	Bookkeepers	0.3	Janitors and cleaners	0.6	Health technicians*	1.6
17	Cotton mill workers	0.2	Sewers and stitchers	0.6	Wholesale commodities brokers*	1.5
18	Tailors	0.2	Cooks	0.6	Accountants and auditors*	1.5
19	Blacksmiths	0.2	Typists	0.5	Waiters and waitresses	1.4
20	Firefighters	0.2	Machinists	0.5	Hotel and restaurant managers	1.3
21	Shoemakers	0.2	Mfg. checkers, examiners, etc.	0.5	Carpenters	1.3
22	Sawyers	0.2	Policemen and guards	0.5	Precision production supervisors*	1.2
23	Masons	0.2	Packers and wrappers	0.5	Math and computer scientists*	1.2
24	Printers	0.2	Cashiers	0.5	Moving equipment operators	1.1
25	Seamstresses	0.2	Accountants and auditors*	0.5	Computer programmers*	1.0
26	Physicians*	0.1	Deliverymen and routemen	0.4	Postmen, clerks, messengers	1.0
27	Tobacco factory workers	0.1	Painters	0.4	Receptionists	0.9
28	Barbers and hairdressers	0.1	Launderers[5]	0.4	Lawyers and judges*	0.9
29	Policemen and guards	0.1	Attendants (hospital, etc.)	0.4	Child care workers	0.9
30	Butchers	0.1	Welders and frame cutters	0.4	Professors*	0.8

Over the century, the structure of U.S. employment has changed enormously. Only eight top job categories have survived throughout. And many more top job categories now require substantial education.

* Requires education. [1] Servants and housekeepers in 1900. [2] Merchants and salespeople in 1900. [3] Clerks in 1900. [4] Teamsters and coachmen in 1900. [5] Launderers and dry cleaners in 1960.

Source: "Top 30 Jobs" from *Forbes* (May 6, 1996): 17. Reprinted by permission of Forbes Magazine. ©2003 Forbes, Inc.

then the organization may be confronting a decreased demand for human resources. In each case, it is up to the human resource manager to implement the chosen strategy. Therefore, we will discuss the implications of each strategy for HRM decisions.

Implications of a Growth Strategy

A strategy of growth indicates growing sales, increasing demand, and expanding operations for the organization. When the organization is growing and expanding, it most likely needs to hire new employees in the future.[11] In some cases, the organization may be able to hire employees readily without additional work. For example, if the organization is currently receiving 1,000 qualified applications per year and has been hiring only 50 of those individuals, then it may be able to meet its new target growth rate by simply increasing the number of people that it hires. Instead of 50, the firm may begin hiring 75 or 100 people a year.

In other situations, implementing a growth strategy may be more difficult. Market conditions may be such that qualified employees are hard to find. For example, a firm receiving 100 qualified applications per year and hiring as many as 90 of them is not likely to hire dramatically larger numbers of them without taking additional actions. The organization may have to increase its recruiting efforts to attract more job applicants and even perhaps begin to provide additional support to apprentice or training programs. Support of various college and university programs might also be a way of increasing the future supply of available labor talent.

A related incident recently involved United Parcel Service (UPS), the giant delivery business. UPS is based in Louisville, Kentucky, and maintains a huge operation there. The firm recently wanted to launch a major expansion but was concerned about its ability to attract enough new workers, especially those who might be interested in working the night shift. The firm threatened to build its expansion in another state unless Kentucky would help. Facing the threat of losing such a big employer, the state passed and funded major job-training legislation and programs to help it attract and develop capable workers of the type that UPS needed.[12]

Implications of a Stability Strategy

In many ways, a stability strategy may be the easiest for the HR manager to implement because the organization presumably must do what it has been doing all along. But, even here, specific and subtle planning nuances must be considered. For example, the organization will naturally experience a certain amount of attrition in its employee ranks each year. As noted earlier, some people will leave for better jobs, some people will retire, some will leave because of poor performance, and others will leave for reasons such as career relocation on the part of a spouse or significant other. Thus, even an organization that is projecting a period of stability is likely to need to augment its labor force to replace those individuals who leave the organization for various reasons. In such cases, the organization can implement programs such as training to upgrade the skills of current employees, making them more valuable to the organization. Alternatively, the organization might implement programs that help reduce turnover among current employees, making stability easier to maintain.

Implications of a Reduction Strategy

In some cases, an organization may find itself facing reductions. Perhaps an organization is experiencing cutbacks, such as many organizations in the United States have faced over the last several years. Organizations such as IBM, General Motors, Chrysler, and others reduced their workforce by the thousands. Levi Strauss, Starbucks, and American Airlines have also reduced their workforce. And in the wake of the 2008–09 recession, many Wall Street investment firms have laid off stockbrokers and analysts.[13]

Sometimes these reductions can be handled through normal attrition processes as described earlier. For example, if the organization currently has 1,000 employees and it knows from experience that approximately 100 of those individuals will retire, resign, or be fired next year, and if it forecasts that it will need only 900 employees following next year, then it may need to do little. But if the actual

forecast calls for only 700 employees, the organization must figure out how to eliminate the other 200 jobs in addition to the 100 that will disappear automatically. This sort of situation may call for laying people off, and we will discuss some important issues associated with this downsizing process in Chapter 6.

A popular alternative to terminations and layoffs, especially for managers, is early retirement. The idea is to make offers to employees to enhance their retirement benefits so that people might consider retiring at an earlier age than they would have done otherwise. Of course, this process involves costs to the organization. The organization may be forced to pay additional benefits to those employees above and beyond what they would have ordinarily expected to pay. It is also possible that the organization might lose people that it would have preferred to keep; that is, its highest-performing employees may be those who opt for early retirement. In fact, they may see early retirement as an opportunity for increasing their income by taking retirement benefits from their current employer but using their high-performance credentials to gain new employment with another organization. On the other hand, lower-performing employees are less likely to have this option and thus may be more likely to remain with the current organization.

Clearly, the actual strategy chosen is an important source of information for decision making because it determines what kinds of decisions will need to be made. It will determine whether the HR manager needs to be concerned with recruiting new talent or finding ways to reduce the workforce. Strategy will also determine whether the HR manager needs to worry about reducing turnover or encouraging it. Another source of information operates at this macro level: the general state of the economy. We discussed this briefly earlier, but we now need to consider more seriously how the state of the economy is an important source of information for HR decision making.

ECONOMIC CONDITIONS AS A SOURCE OF INFORMATION

We noted above how the economy influenced the supply of and demand for different types of employees, but the economy also has a more general effect on the workforce that the HR manager must consider. To understand this, think about an employee as having a valued asset (his or her effort at work) and as having to make some decision about how to use that asset. The employee could decide to keep the asset for himself and not work for anyone else. The employee may start her own business or find some other way to support herself. On the other hand, the employee may decide to enter the marketplace and see how much her effort is worth and so decide for whom to go to work. Although this example is oversimplified, it illustrates the importance of economic-based decisions by potential employees and how these might affect HRM decisions. Many factors could affect a person's decision to enter the labor market and seek employment. We will discuss some of these next.

Unemployment Rates

The **rate of unemployment** (or the *rate of employment*) is an important determinant of an individual's employment choices. The national unemployment rate is, of course, relevant, but the local unemployment rate is more closely linked to an individual's choices. Most people who live in, say, Denver cannot just pack up and move to Miami just because there are more jobs available there. This lack of mobility means that people respond more to local labor market conditions. There is considerable evidence that turnover rates are better predicted by unemployment statistics than by any other variable (see Chapter 6 for a discussion of these other variables).[13]

Therefore, if unemployment is relatively high, then individuals are less likely to leave their current jobs to look for alternatives. As a result, firms may be able to find many willing applicants among the unemployed but are unlikely to be able to lure desirable employees from a different company. Also, during times of high unemployment individuals who are contemplating entering the labor market would be less likely to do so because they would see their chances of finding a job lower than they would prefer. Finally, some people might decide to move to a more attractive location (from an employment perspective). But given that unemployment rates in 2010 reached 10 percent nationally in the United States, employee retention was not a major concern in any markets in the country, and there were few places where individuals could go to find better opportunities.

On the other hand, when employment rates are quite high, although there can be a general shortage of workers available for hire, this situation tends to be short-lived. If opportunities are good, some people will migrate to the location, inflating the local labor supply in the longer run. Also, if employment is high, workers are more likely to quit their jobs when they believe they can find a better alternative. This may be good news for the company trying to hire good people, but it is a problem for

The **rate of unemployment** *is calculated by the Bureau of Labor Statistics as the percentage of individuals looking for and available for work who are not currently employed.*

© Robert F. Balazik/Shutterstock

EXHIBIT 5.2 Wages and Salaries Across the United States (Hourly Basis)

Accountant: $25.90	Accountant: $25.52
Bank Teller: $11.85	Bank Teller: $ 9.90
Firefighter: $22.83	Firefighter: $16.79
Truckdriver: $15.69	Truckdriver: $13.38

Accountant: $28.41
Bank Teller: $11.29
Firefighter: $25.58
Truckdriver: $16.78

Accountant: $23.65
Bank Teller: $10.81
Firefighter: $15.89
Truckdriver: $15.14

Accountant: $26.13
Bank Teller: $10.46
Firefighter: $16.33
Truckdriver: $14.47

the company trying to retain good employees because problems at work are more likely to lead to turnover decisions during these times. Thus, employment rates can affect not only the size of the labor pool, but also its makeup, and so it is an important factor to consider in the planning process.

Market Wage Rates

A related factor that will influence decisions about joining the labor force is the **market wage rate**. Most people are aware that wages are generally higher in a place such as New York City than in a place such as Houston (although this did not necessarily hold in late 2009 because the financial sector was hardest hit and the energy sector of the economy was more

An individual is more likely to decide to enter the labor force when the higher relative wage rate is available to him or her. Again, limited mobility makes it difficult for individuals to find the optimal wage rate for their skills, but some movement is possible. Thus, it is important to understand some determinants of local wage rates.

The simplest explanation relies on supply and demand. Given a fixed demand for veterinarians, for example, the average wage paid for vets will be higher if the supply is lower; likewise, given a fixed supply, the wage rate will go up as the demand for the services of a veterinarian increases. But some firms try to attract the best employees they can. These organizations seek to be

Where a company locates is often determined by the local availability of relevant skilled or potentially skilled workers.

insulated). The differences in salaries and wage rates partly result from differences in the cost of living, but they also are caused by different levels of competitiveness for talent in the market. Thus, teachers in university towns are often paid poorly because there is a surplus of qualified teachers looking for jobs in those locations. On the other hand, civil service jobs pay almost no premium for cost of living, so a mail carrier in New York City makes almost exactly what a mail carrier makes in Houston or in West Lafayette, Indiana. Exhibit 5.2 illustrates the range of salaries paid for different jobs in different parts of the United States.

"the employer of choice" in their market and will pay more than the going market rate to attract the best employees. These "efficiency wages" are believed to be justified by the fact that the best employees are assumed to be more productive and that the higher wages will bind the employee more tightly to the firm, thus reducing turnover. Of course, these benefits will need to offset the higher labor costs associated with the higher wages in order for the firm to

The **market wage rate** is the prevailing wage rate for a given job in a given labor market.

remain competitive. Thus, although local wage rates can affect an individual's decision to enter the labor market, efficiency wages can influence which firm the individual decides to join.

Human Capital Investments

Just as a firm can differentiate itself by paying higher wages, individuals can differentiate themselves as well by making **human capital investments**. In other words, individuals can invest in themselves, through training and education, to increase their value to employers.[14] These investments must be made in areas that an employer considers valuable enough to pay more for, but general education is usually a worthwhile investment and will yield a higher wage. Not surprisingly, then, as unemployment began to rise to

national) is an important source of information for the HR manager. Economic variables will influence how many potential employees will be available and what kinds of employees those will be. Such variables will also influence the wages that will need to be paid to attract employees to the labor force or to a specific firm. Decisions about what kinds of activities should be conducted in an area should depend on what kinds of people will be willing to enter the labor force and what kinds of people a given firm will be able to attract. Only by understanding the economic forces operating can the human resource manager make the decisions that need to be made.

The types of information we have discussed thus far operate at the level of the organization, or even the region of the country. Each type of information is important for the

> **The Americans with Disabilities Act prohibits discrimination based on disability and all aspects of the employment relationship such as job-application procedures, hiring, firing, promotion, compensation, and training, as well as other employment activities such as advertising, recruiting, tenure, layoffs, and leave and fringe benefits.**

historic levels in 2009 and 2010, many universities saw a marked increase in the number of applications, especially for graduate programs.

In fact, employers often make decisions about where to locate a facility based on the human capital available in a market. For example, in the 1960s the Boston area was suffering through a minor regional recession as traditional employers shifted operations elsewhere or went out of business. But the population of the Boston area was highly educated and considered to have a strong work ethic. As a result, it made sense for the early computer and technology firms to locate in the area and take advantage of the availability of a highly educated workforce, and so Boston enjoyed a real boom in the early 1970s as it became the hub of the new computer industry. Thus, human capital investments can increase wages for an individual and so influence decisions to enter the labor market, and the availability of persons who have already made human capital investments can affect a firm's location strategies.

Thus, the state of the economy (both local and

HR manager who will need to make critical decisions. But the HR manager also needs information at a much more basic level—information about what is required on each of the jobs that will be staffed, evaluated, compensated, and so on. That information comes from job analysis.

JOB ANALYSIS AS A SOURCE OF INFORMATION

Job analysis is the process of gathering and organizing detailed information about various jobs within the organization so that managers can better understand the processes through which the jobs are performed most effectively.[15] Generally, job analysis is an effort to study and understand specific jobs in the organization so that managers can have a full sense of the nature of those jobs and the kinds of skills and abilities needed to perform them. As we already noted, job analysis is a fundamental input and building block of the planning process, but, as illustrated in Exhibit 5.3, it also relates to other HRM processes.

As shown in the exhibit, job analysis affects selection or hiring decisions because the job-analysis process indicates the tasks to be performed by the person to be hired. Job analysis results in assessments about the underlying skills and abilities needed to perform the job,

Human capital investments *are investments people make in themselves to increase their value in the workplace. These investments might take the form of additional education or training.*

Job analysis *is the process of gathering and organizing detailed information about various jobs within an organization so that managers can better understand the processes through which they are performed most effectively.*

EXHIBIT 5.3 Job Analysis and Other Human Resource Functions

Human resource planning		Selection process
Job analysis		Performance appraisal
Basic line management functions		Training and development
		Compensation

and it leads to logical and appropriate plans to recruit individuals who are most likely to have these skills and abilities. Selection techniques, for instance, can be designed and administered to determine which of the applicants recruited have the necessary skill and ability levels.

Under the Americans with Disabilities Act (ADA), job analysis has taken on an even more important role in the selection of new employees in many companies. As we noted in Chapter 2, the ADA outlaws discrimination based on disabilities. The ADA does not require an organization to hire someone who cannot perform the job in question, of course, but it does require an organization to hire a "qualified individual with a disability," specified as "an individual with a disability who, with or without a reasonable accommodation, can perform the essential functions of the employment position that such an individual holds or desires" (Americans with Disabilities Act, Title I, section 101).

Further, imagine the implications of an organization refusing to hire a disabled applicant because a manager assumes that the individual cannot perform the job. The individual might have grounds for a discrimination claim if ambiguity exists about exactly which job elements are essential to the organization and which are less essential or optional and if the applicant can demonstrate a capacity for performing the job. Thus, it becomes more important than ever for managers to determine the essential functions of the jobs within the organization because they must identify those parts of jobs (e.g., tasks, duties) that must be carried out effectively for the person to be successful in performing the job. This information can best be obtained through job analysis.

Exhibit 5.3 also indicates that job analysis relates to performance appraisal. This relationship stems from the understanding of what an employee should be capable of doing in a job before one can assess how well that employee is actually performing. Job analysis similarly affects training and development because it provides information that helps managers better understand the kind of training and development programs that are necessary to enhance employee competencies and capabilities so the employees can achieve ideal levels of performance. Job-analysis information is also important for compensation (job-analysis methods used for establishing compensation rates are often referred to as *job evaluation*) because work behaviors have traditionally been a primary basis for compensation. (As we will see later, however, compensation based on knowledge or competencies, rather than behaviors, is becoming more common.)

In addition to its fundamental role in HR planning and other aspects of the HR function, job analysis is also important to line managers for various general reasons. First, they must thoroughly understand the work-flow processes that characterize their particular work units. They must understand how work flows from employee to employee, from job station to job station, and from work group to work group. To develop this understanding, of course, they must also have a fundamental insight into the basic mechanics, character, and nature of each job. Job analysis provides this. Also, because line managers are often involved in hiring and appraisal decisions, they must rely on the information provided by job analysis to help determine who should be hired and how well employees are doing their jobs.

> ## Job families may allow an employee to chart a career course within a company.

Job analysis provides fundamental input to the human resource manager by defining the kinds of both general work and specific jobs that the organization currently relies on and will be relying on in the future.[16] Whereas the focus of job analysis is typically an individual job, in many organizations the tasks and responsibilities on some jobs may be similar to those on other jobs. Likewise, the **knowledge, skills, and abilities (KSA)** requirements may be similar for a set of jobs. As a result, for planning purposes, organizations often try to form *job families*—groups of jobs that have task and KSA requirements that are quite similar.

These job families can be quite useful in several ways. First, if the jobs within a job family have similar KSA requirements, then it might be possible to train employees so that they can apply what they have learned to the entire family of jobs, making them much more flexible resources for the organization. In addition, this training for job families rather than for specific jobs can help employees remain useful to the organization even if their current jobs become obsolete.[17]

Well-conceived job families can also be used to help organizations in career planning. The jobs within a family represent jobs that have similar patterns of requirements. If they occur at different levels within an organization, then those jobs can represent a typical career path for an employee.

Thus, managers can plan where an employee might go as his or her career builds, and they might also discover where to find replacements when a job opening occurs.

Knowledge, skills, and abilities (KSA) *are the fundamental requirements necessary to perform a job.*

Finally, job families can be used in selection decisions. For instance, once an organization has established the selection requirements for one job within a family, managers may be able to use this information to predict requirements in other jobs within the family.[18] In fact, if it is reasonable to believe that an employee will progress through all the jobs in a job family, then the organization might well choose to select individuals based on the needs of the *highest-level* job within the family rather than on those of the specific job for which an individual is applying. For example, suppose Texas Instruments needs to hire technicians to support engineering work teams. The HR manager in charge of this hiring might determine that each technician will rotate across several groups over a 4-year period, performing different functions for each. The astute manager might therefore set as the performance requirements for all such support roles as the hiring standard for all technicians, even though some technicians may start out in less-demanding roles.

THE JOB-ANALYSIS PROCESS

The job-analysis process itself is generally clear and straightforward. As a starting point in this process, it is helpful to understand the steps involved, including who is responsible for job analysis. As illustrated in Exhibit 5.4, the job-analysis process generally follows three steps: (1) determining information needs, (2) determining methods for obtaining information, and (3) determining who will collect information.[19]

The first step is determining the organization's precise information needs. A wide range of information on various jobs may be obtained during the course of job analysis. The exact type and nature of the information obtained, however, depend on both the intended purposes of the job-analysis information and various constraints imposed by the organization such as time and budget limitations. Regardless of constraints, the job analysis must provide enough information about what someone does on a job to allow a determination of the knowledge, skills, and abilities

EXHIBIT 5.4 Steps in Job Analysis

Determining information needs

↓

Determining methods for obtaining information

↓

Determining who will collect information

necessary to perform the job. Job-analysis information might include general work activities (such as a description of the specific tasks that are carried out, how the job interfaces with other jobs and equipment, the procedures used in the job, behaviors required on the job, and the physical movements and demands of the job) and the machines, tools, equipment, and work aids used to perform the job.

Other useful information that may be collected includes details regarding the job context (physical working conditions such as exposure to dust, heat, and toxic substances; the indoor environment versus outdoor environment; and so forth). Information may also be collected regarding the organizational context and social context of the job. In addition, details regarding work schedule, various financial and nonfinancial incentives, and personal requirements (job-related attributes such as specific skills, education, and training; work experience and related jobs; physical characteristics and aptitudes) are usually desirable pieces of information.[20]

The next step in the job-analysis process is to determine how that information will be collected. The most common methods of collecting job-analysis information include the observations of task and job behaviors, interviews with job incumbents, and the use of questionnaires and checklists. For example, the individuals who perform the job analysis—**job analysts**—can sometimes gather the desired information on jobs simply by observing people performing them. This method is especially useful for unskilled manual jobs but is less relevant for jobs involving creative thought and analytic skills. In many cases, it is also beneficial to interview individuals who are performing the jobs being analyzed.[21] These individuals are in a position to explain both the nature of the work they are performing and the qualifications and credentials they believe are necessary for the successful performance of those jobs. Of course, these individuals may overstate the skills and qualifications needed to perform the job and the complexities and sophistication of the job, especially if the employee believes (correctly or not) that the job analysis is being conducted to determine compensation rates.

Someone other than the incumbent who is also knowledgeable about the job can also be interviewed. Any such person, whether the incumbent or someone like the supervisor, is referred to as a **subject matter expert (SME)**. SMEs are the individuals from whom job analysts obtain data for the job analysis; they may be existing job incumbents, supervisors, or other knowledgeable employees such as

higher-level managers, or industrial engineers. For the job analysis to be successful, the employees selected to provide the job-analysis information must be intimately familiar with the nature of the jobs themselves. Thus, participants in job analysis tend to be experienced and high-performing individuals who thoroughly understand the job.[22] Of course, if critical job-analysis information must be collected through the interview process, then it is best to interview multiple individuals who have different perspectives on the actual job and then integrate or average the information collected.

The job analyst could be a specialist within the human resource management function or a consultant hired from the outside. Many times, however, firms (especially smaller ones) do not actually collect their own job-analysis information at all. Instead, when they need to obtain information about jobs, they may instead refer to available reference materials. The major source of such information is a system known as the **Occupational Information Network (O*NET)**, a computerized job classification system that contains continually updated information regarding the KSAs required for virtually every job in the U.S. economy. O*NET is technically not a job-analysis procedure; it is a database that provides both basic and advanced job-analysis information. As such, it can be viewed as an alternative to conducting job analysis.[23] O*NET currently has information for more than 1,000 occupations and is organized according to a system known as the *standard occupational classification*.

For each occupation, information is provided about the relative importance of worker characteristics, including fifty-two separate abilities for effective job performance. These abilities are classified as representing (1) cognitive abilities such as oral comprehension, deductive reasoning, and spatial orientation; (2) psychometric abilities such as manual dexterity and reaction time; (3) physical abilities

Job analysts *are individuals who perform job analysis in an organization.*

A **subject matter expert (SME)** *is an individual presumed to be highly knowledgeable about a particular job and who provides data for job analysis. An SME may be an existing job incumbent, a supervisor, or another knowledgeable employee.*

Occupational Information Network (O*NET) *is technically not a job-analysis procedure but a database that provides both basic and advanced job-analysis information; as such, IT can be viewed as an alternative to conducting job analysis.*

such as explosive and static strength and stamina; and (4) sensory abilities such as peripheral vision, heat sensitivity, and speech clarity. Also classified are occupational interests (such as interests in artistic occupations, realistic occupations, and social occupations), values (such as achievement, status, and comfort), and work styles (such as achievement orientation, conscientiousness, and practical intelligence). Information is also included regarding general occupational characteristics and occupation-specific requirements.

In addition, information is provided about appropriate worker requirements such as knowledge (fifty-two cross-occupation knowledge areas), skills (including ten basic skills such as writing and speaking, and thirty-six cross-functional skills such as negotiating, persuading, and time management), and education. There is also information about the experience requirements (including requirements regarding training and licensure), as well as occupational requirements, including general work activities (such as getting information needed to do the job and thinking creatively), work context (such as environmental conditions), and organizational context (such as type of industry, organizational structure, and organizational culture). Links to other resources are provided, and they yield information about legal requirements, job hazards, and environmental conditions.

Although this is quite an array of information, and, in fact, new information is being added all the time, it is still possible that the O*NET does not have information that an organization needs about a specific job. Also, the match between the job as it exists in a given firm and the job as it is classified in the O*NET may not be perfect. Nonetheless, the O*NET provides a valuable resource for anyone interested in doing job analysis, and it is likely to become even more important as various branches of the U.S. government move toward implementing the system. But there are still many cases where more traditional job-analysis methods are needed because more detailed information is desired. Many such methods are available.

Job-Analysis Techniques

Several job-analysis techniques are used in organizations, although the trend is away from these more traditional methods and toward competency modeling, which we will discuss later. The most commonly used methods are the straight narrative, the Fleishman job-analysis system, task-analysis inventory, functional job

analysis, the Position Analysis Questionnaire, the Managerial Position Description Questionnaire, and the critical incidents approach.[24]

1. **Narrative Job Analysis.** The most common approach to job analysis is simply to have one or more SMEs prepare a written narrative or text description of the job. These narratives can vary in terms of length and detail. To some extent, the quality of the information depends on the writing skills of the job analyst. Although it is possible to specify the format and structure of these narratives, they are typically individualistic, making it difficult to compare the tasks on one job with the tasks on another. They are relatively inexpensive, however, and it generally does not require a great deal of training for someone to complete a narrative job analysis.

2. **Fleishman Job-Analysis System.** Another popular method of job analysis is the Fleishman job-analysis system.[25] This approach defines abilities as enduring attributes of individuals that account for differences in performance. The system itself relies on the taxonomy of abilities that presumably represents all the dimensions relevant to work. The taxonomy includes a total of fifty-two abilities. In general, these fifty-two specific abilities are presumed to reflect cognitive, psychomotor, and sensory abilities. Examples of the specific abilities included in the Fleishman system include oral comprehension, written comprehension, oral expression, written expression, fluency of ideas, night vision, depth perception, auditory attention, and speech clarity. The actual Fleishman scales consist of descriptions of each ability followed by a behavioral benchmark example of the different levels of the ability along a seven-point scale. An organization using this job-analysis technique relies on a panel of SMEs (again, incumbent workers or supervisors are most commonly used) to indicate how important the ability is for the job, and the actual level of ability required for a particular job. Because of its complexity, job analysts who use this method require training, but it is also much closer in operation to the notion of competency modeling, which we will discuss below.

3. **Task-Analysis Inventory.** Another method of job analysis is the task-analysis inventory. The task-analysis inventory method actually refers to a family of job-analysis methods, each with unique characteristics. However, each one focuses on analyzing all the tasks performed in the focal job. Any given job may have dozens of tasks, for example. Again relying on SMEs, this method requires the generation of a list of tasks performed in a job. Once the list has been developed, a job analyst—frequently the job incumbent—evaluates each task on dimensions such as the relative amount of time spent on the task, the frequency with which the task is performed, the relative importance of the task, the relative difficulty of the task, and the time necessary to

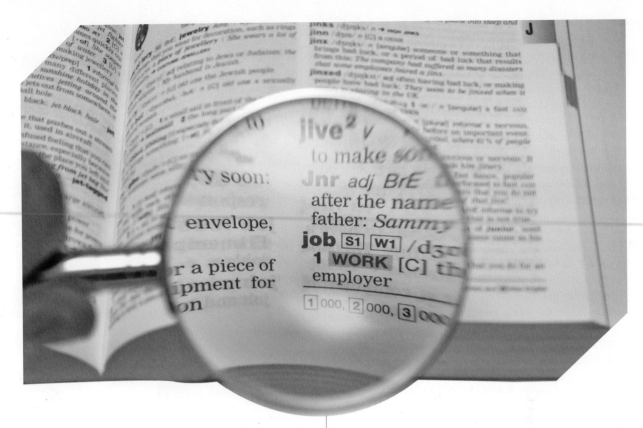

© Maciej Oleksy/Shutterstock

learn the task. Task inventories require a fair amount of effort to develop. Once they are developed, however, they are relatively easy to use. This approach to job analysis is often used in municipal and county governments and is also the most common form of job analysis used in the U.S. military. The information generated by this approach to job analysis is often detailed, and it is useful for establishing KSAs and training needs. The military has used these inventories to establish career paths and job families where the jobs clustered together have a large amount of overlap in terms of the important tasks.[26] Managers then use a single task inventory to analyze all the jobs in the family. It is more difficult, though, to make comparisons across job families, and this drawback reduces the usefulness of task inventories to some degree.

4. **Functional Job Analysis.** One attempt to have a single job-analysis instrument that can be used with a wide variety of jobs resulted in the development of functional job analysis.[27] According to this approach, all jobs can be described in terms of the level of involvement with *people*, *data*, and *things*. For example, employees on a job at a Halliburton manufacturing site might be said to *set up* machines (things), *mentor* people, and *synthesize* data. All are high levels of involvement and would indicate a complex job. The exact definition of each term is provided to the job analyst. The U.S. Department of Labor relies on functional job analysis for some of its classifications of jobs, but it is not used widely in private industry. Nonetheless, this approach is important because it represents the first attempt to develop a single instrument that can describe all jobs in common terms.

5. **Position Analysis Questionnaire.** One of the most popular and widely used job-analysis methods is the **Position Analysis Questionnaire (PAQ).** The PAQ was developed by Ernest McCormick and his associates, and it is a standardized job-analysis instrument consisting of 194 items. These items reflect work behavior, working conditions, and job characteristics that are assumed to be generalizable across a wide variety of jobs.[28] The items that make up the PAQ are organized into six sections. *Information inputs* include where and how a worker gets information needed to perform his or her job. *Mental processes* represent the reasoning, decision-making, planning, and information-processing activities involved in performing the job. *Work output* refers to the physical activities, tools, and devices used by the worker to perform the job. *Relationships with other people* include the relationships with other people that are required in performing the job. *Job context* represents the physical and social contacts where the work is performed. Finally, *other characteristics* include the activities, conditions, and

*The **Position Analysis Questionnaire (PAQ)** is a standardized job-analysis instrument consisting of 194 items that reflect work behavior, working conditions, and job characteristics that are assumed to be generalizable across a wide variety of jobs.*

characteristics other than those previously described that pertain to the job.

Job analysts are asked to determine whether each scale applies to the specific job being analyzed. The analyst rates the item on six scales: extent of use, amount of time, importance of the job, possibility of occurrence, applicability, and special code. *Special code* refers to unique and special rating scales that are used with a particular item. These ratings are then submitted to a centralized location indicated on the questionnaire where computer software compiles a report regarding the job scores on the job dimensions.

A major advantage of the PAQ is that, like functional job analysis, its dimensions are believed to underlie all jobs. This feature allows a wide variety (although probably not all) jobs to be described in common terms. In the case of the PAQ, this feature results from the items and dimensions of the PAQ that describe what a worker does on the job rather than what gets done. For example, a baker bakes bread and a pilot flies an airplane, but when we examine how these workers get the information they need to do their jobs, we find that they both rely heavily on dials and instruments for critical information. We do not mean to suggest that the two jobs are related, just that workers perform similar functions even on diverse jobs.

Unlike functional job analysis, the PAQ can provide information on 187 separate items, allowing a much richer picture of what happens on a job (the PAQ actually includes 194 items, but the remaining items deal with methods of pay). Finally, another strength of the PAQ is the fact that, because it has been widely used for many years, a considerable database of information exists that attests to its validity and reliability.

In general, research supports the validity and reliability of the instrument. Research also suggests that the PAQ measures thirty-two dimensions and thirteen overall job dimensions. A given job score on these dimensions can be useful in job analysis.[29] Because the instrument has been so widely used, it has also been statistically related to other measures, including the scores of job applicants on standardized selection tests, compensation rates on various jobs, and even the importance of various abilities.[30]

Even though it is widely used, however, the PAQ also has some noteworthy shortcomings. The PAQ instrument itself is relatively complex, and an employee must have the

reading level of a college graduate to be able to complete it. Although the PAQ is supposed to be applicable to most jobs, there is reason to believe that it is less useful for higher-level managerial jobs and less useful for describing white-collar jobs.[31] Despite these limitations, the PAQ remains the most popular standardized job-analysis instrument available and is commonly used by firms such as Kodak, Nestlé USA, and Delta Airlines.

6. **Management Position Description Questionnaire.** The **Management Position Description Questionnaire (MPDQ)** is a standardized job-analysis instrument similar in approach to the PAQ and also containing 197 items. The focus here, however, is on managerial jobs, and the analysis is done in terms of 13 essential components of all managerial jobs.[32] These essential components are supervision, staff service, internal business control, complexity and stress, coordination of other units, public and customer relations, HR responsibility, autonomy of action, advanced consulting, advanced financial responsibility, approval of financial commitments, product and service responsibility, and product market and financial planning. The information generated by the MPDQ can be used to classify managerial positions as well as estimate reasonable compensation for them.

Management Position Description Questionnaire (MPDQ) *is a standardized job-analysis instrument, similar in approach to the PAQ, that also contains 197 items. The MPDQ's focus, however, is on managerial jobs, and the analysis is done in terms of 13 essential components of all managerial jobs.*

© Tetra Images/Getty Images

EXHIBIT 5.5   Example Job Description and Job Specification

Job Title: Accounts Payable and Payroll Accountant, Johnson & Johnson Corp.

Job Description: Business partner with Accounts Payable and Payroll Departments to develop expense forecasts and commentary; prepare Accounts Payable and Payroll shared services charge-outs to affiliates; ensure Accounts Payable and Payroll inputs are posted weekly; perform account analysis/reconciliations of Cash, Liability, and Employee Loan accounts related to Accounts Payable and Payroll; submit routine reports to Corporate; identify and implement process improvements relative to all responsibilities listed above.

Job Specification: BS degree in accounting or finance; 2+ years of accounting/finance experience; sound knowledge of Integral Accounts Payable and General Ledger Systems; working knowledge of Hyperion Software, PACT; good communication skills; able to work independently at off-site location.

7. **Critical Incidents Approach.** Critical incidents are examples of particularly effective or ineffective performance.[33] When used for job analysis, the **critical incidents approach** focuses on the critical behaviors that distinguish effective from ineffective performers. Although this approach to job analysis is most widely used in connection with the development of appraisal instruments, it is generally useful because it focuses the organization's attention on aspects of the job that lead to more or less effective performance.

Although these techniques are the most commonly used in industry, we should note that, in many cases, the organization simply develops its own job-analysis technique or instrument. This is especially true for managerial jobs and for jobs performed by teams rather than by individuals. In both cases, no widely accepted standardized job-analysis instruments are available. Regardless of which job-analysis technique an organization employs, however, at some point a narrative description of the job will probably be needed. Therefore, it is important to draw a distinction between a job description and a job specification, which we discuss in the next section.

Job Descriptions and Job Specifications

A **job description** lists the tasks, duties, and responsibilities that a particular job entails. Observable actions are necessary for the effective performance of the job. The job description specifies the major job elements, provides examples of job tasks, and provides some indication of their relative importance in the effective conduct of the job.[34] A **job specification** focuses more on the individual who will perform the job. Specifically, a job specification indicates the knowledge, abilities, skills, and other characteristics that an individual must have to perform the job. Factual or procedural capabilities and levels of proficiency refer more to skills. In general, enduring capabilities that an individual possesses can be thought of as abilities. Job specifications may include general educational requirements (such as

having a high school degree or a college degree) as well as the specifications of job-related skills (such as the ability to keyboard seventy words a minute, or the requirement that an individual be fluent in Japanese or Spanish).

Taken together then, the job description and the job specification should provide a parallel and mutually consistent set of information and details that focuses on the job itself and the individual most likely to be successful performing that job. This information should then inform all subsequent recruiting and selection decisions. Exhibit 5.5 illustrates an actual job description and job specification for a particular kind of accountant at Johnson & Johnson. This description and specification were created as part of a job analysis and are used to communicate to job applicants and managers what skills and abilities are necessary to perform the job.

Modeling Competencies and the End of the "Job"

Given the rate of change in work, some scholars and other HR experts have argued that the nature of work is changing so much that the concept of a "job" is becoming obsolete. Although many people will continue to have "jobs" for some time to come, in some work settings it may well be true that the traditional view of jobs and work is no longer applicable. In these settings, people usually work on teams where the focus is on getting tasks accomplished rather than on specific task requirements. Thus, there is reason to suggest that we should think

> The **critical incidents approach** to job analysis focuses on critical behaviors that distinguish effective from ineffective performers.

> A **job description** lists the tasks, duties, and responsibilities for a particular job. It specifies the major job elements, provides examples of job tasks, and provides some indication of their relative importance in the effective conduct of the job.

> A **job specification** focuses on the individual who will perform the job and indicates the knowledge, abilities, skills, and other characteristics that an individual must have to be able to perform the job.

about roles that have to be filled within the organization and how employees will need to emphasize flexibility, teamwork, and accomplishing tasks, rather than job descriptions and sets of duties. In light of these developments, then, some critics have argued that traditional methods of job analysis (including the O*NET) have little place in the modern organization, and that the information needed by human resource managers can be better provided by modeling competencies instead of by describing jobs.

In fact, data from a survey conducted in 1998 indicated that 75 percent of the companies surveyed were using some type of competency modeling.[35] Nonetheless, there is little agreement about what exactly is meant by the term *competency*. Some view competencies as being broader than abilities, and others suggest that competencies exist at a deeper level and really underlie abilities. Generally, however, experts view competencies as characteristics of employees (or teams of employees) that lead to success on the job. Thus, abilities such as decisiveness and adaptability are seen as competencies that might underlie more specific abilities such as decision making or coping with change.[36]

Clearly, this approach has the potential for providing critical information to the human resource manager in a more useful form because it emphasizes what a person needs to be successful. Thus, it may not be important to know whether an employee will type letters or run a lathe, but it may be critical to know that an employee needs to be adaptable.

Competencies are determined in several ways, but typically teams of top managers, working with consultants, identify the competencies necessary to compete in the future. These competencies are then described in clear behavioral terms, measures are designed, and each is rated according to its relative importance for future success. Employees who have these competencies are then sought through the recruiting and selection process, or current employees are provided training opportunities to acquire these competencies and are then rewarded when they do acquire them. (See the discussion of skill-based pay and knowledge-based pay in Chapter 9.) The critical difference is that the HR manager no longer focuses on what is needed to be successful at one job but instead focuses on what is needed to be successful at any and all jobs within the organization. There are also some applications of competency modeling to selection, which we will discuss in Chapter 7.[37]

> ## "A wise man adapts himself to circumstances as water shapes itself to the vessel that contains it."
> —Anonymous

Legal Issues in Job Analysis

Because job analysis is a critical building block for much of the HRM process, it should not be surprising that numerous legal issues have been raised with regard to job analysis. In fact, federal guidelines on selection include discussion of the appropriate ways to conduct job analysis and the statement that any attempt to establish the job relatedness of a selection instrument must begin with a careful analysis of the jobs in question. Most of the specific cases, in fact, have been concerned more with the *failure* of an organization to perform a job analysis. For example, in *Albermarle* v. *Moody* the Albermarle Paper Company argued that tests found to be job related for one set of jobs could be used to select employees for another set of jobs that they argued were similar.[38] The Court found that, in the absence of clear job-analysis information to support such a claim (and there was no job-analysis information), it was unacceptable to assume that the jobs in question were the same.

The Americans with Disabilities Act of 1990 (ADA), and its recent modification (the American with Disabilities Amendment Act of 2009) raise additional legal issues associated with job analysis. As noted in Chapter 2, the ADA states that an employer must offer a reasonable accommodation to any employee who has a disability and who can perform the "essential functions" of the job. Basically, essential functions are those that take up a significant part of the employee's time, are performed regularly, and have consequences for other parts of the job. Organizations need to rely on careful job analysis to determine exactly what those essential functions are and thus determine if the employee is entitled to an accommodation under the law.

Several issues regarding the accuracy of job-analysis information have potential legal implications.[39] Perhaps the most troubling of these issues relates to potential gender discrimination in job analysis. Specifically, evidence suggests that jobs occupied primarily by male incumbents are more likely to be rated as more complex and of a higher level than similar jobs occupied primarily by female incumbents.[40] One striking result that has been published relates to different job-analysis information generated for the jobs

Board ruled that the autonomous work teams and action committees created at the company were illegal labor organizations.[41] In other words, they were labor organizations because they scheduled work, determined wages, and made selection and promotion decisions—and they were illegal because they were created and controlled by management.

In summary, job analysis can provide extremely important information for the HR manager because it reveals what a person does on the job. This information can be used for a

> ## Gender discrimination is one possible problem in job analysis, with males seen as holding jobs that are more complex than comparable jobs held by females.

of prison guard and prison matron, which are simply the traditional titles for persons of different gender doing the same job (these different titles are no longer used, incidentally). Because the information from job analysis can be used for determining appraisal systems as well as compensation rates, this problem is potentially serious.

Finally, as discussed in Chapter 2, the creation of autonomous work teams has presented a new legal challenge. In the *Electromation* decision, the National Labor Relations

variety of applications, and it can be collected using different types of job analysts using a variety of job analysis techniques. Recently, many organizations have moved toward competency modeling to replace traditional job analysis, and this approach has the potential to provide even more useful information about what is required for someone to be successful on the job. Finally, because job-analysis information is a basic building block for HRM decisions, several legal issues have been raised relative to the applications of job-analysis information.

CLOSING CASE

DOING THE DIRTY WORK

Business magazines and newspapers regularly publish articles about the changing nature of work in the United States and about how many jobs are being changed. Indeed, because so much has been made of the shift toward service-sector and professional jobs, many people assume that the number of unpleasant and undesirable jobs has declined.

In fact, nothing could be further from the truth. Millions of Americans work in gleaming, air-conditioned facilities, but many others work in dirty, grimy, and unsafe settings. For example, many jobs in the recycling industry require workers to sort through moving conveyors of trash, pulling out those items that can be recycled. Other relatively unattractive jobs include cleaning hospital restrooms, washing dishes in a restaurant, and handling toxic waste.

Consider the jobs in a chicken-processing facility. Much like a manufacturing assembly line, a chicken-processing facility is organized around a moving conveyor system. Workers call it the *chain*. In reality, it's a steel cable with large clips that carries freshly killed chickens down what might be called a "disassembly line." Standing along this line are dozens of workers who do, in fact, take the birds apart as they pass.

Even the titles of the jobs are unsavory. Among the first set of jobs along the chain is the skinner. *Skinners* use sharp instruments to cut and pull the skin off the dead chicken. Toward the middle of the line are the *gut pullers*. These workers reach inside the chicken carcasses and remove the intestines and other organs. At the end of the line are the *gizzard cutters*, who tackle the more difficult organs attached to the inside of the chicken's carcass. These organs have to be individually cut and removed for disposal.

The work is obviously distasteful, and the pace of the work is unrelenting. On a good day, the chain moves an average of ninety chickens a minute for 9 hours. And the workers are essentially held captive by the moving chain. For example, no one can vacate a post to use the bathroom or for any other reason without the supervisor's permission. In some plants, taking an unauthorized bathroom break can result in suspension without pay. But the noise in a typical chicken-processing plant is so loud that the supervisor cannot hear someone calling for relief unless the person happens to be standing close by.

Jobs such as these on the chicken-processing line are actually becoming increasingly common. Fueled by Americans' growing

© Selena/Shutterstock

Human Resource Decision MAKING in Organizations

> " *You have to be really efficient with your resources in times like these.* "
> —Joe Poulin, CEO of Nucor

CUT JOBS . . . OR CUT HOURS?

For decades, most U.S. businesses have followed the same pattern: When times are good, they hire new employees. But when times are bad, they cut jobs to reduce payroll. But during the prolonged recession that started in late 2008 and continued into 2010, many businesses took different approaches. But at their most basic level, these various approaches had the same basic theme: Let's keep as many employees as possible but pay them less through salary reductions or reductions in working hours. These approaches could help businesses reduce their labor costs while avoiding the payment of severance packages.

Some companies took their cuts from the top. FedEx, for example, cut the pay of its most senior executives between 5 percent and 10 percent, with CEO Frederick Smith taking a self-imposed reduction of 20 percent. Unionized employees, hourly workers, and

FedEx pilots, meanwhile, were exempted from the cuts. Hewlett-Packard also cut salaries for many of its salaried employees, but spared its highest performers from any cuts and tied other cuts to performance: Higher performers got smaller cuts, and lower performers got bigger cuts.

Other firms focused their reductions on lower-level employees. In general, these workers were also given commensurate time off. For instance, Steve Wynn, a Las Vegas casino mogul, mandated that all of his employees would keep their jobs but that hourly employees would work 32 hours per week rather than 40. Although this amounted to a 20 percent cut in pay, employees also had an extra day of time they could spend with their families, devote to part-time work with another employer, take training classes to develop new job skills, and so forth.

LEARNING OBJECTIVES

After studying this chapter you should be able to:

LO1 *Discuss the role of ethics in human resource decision making*

LO2 *Describe the concept of rightsizing and identify organizational strategies for rightsizing*

LO3 *Describe how to manage termination and retention*

LO4 *Describe the elements of voluntary turnover*

LO5 *Discuss the key human resource issues during mergers and acquisitions*

A few especially creative companies even rented their workers to other employers. Vermont's Rhino Foods makes the cookie dough used in Ben & Jerry's ice cream. As demand for the cookie dough dropped, a nearby company, lip balm maker Autumn Harp, needed extra help, so Rhino sent fifteen factory workers to work for Autumn Harp for a month. Rhino continued to pay the workers but invoiced Autumn Harp for the expense.

Other firms also came up with unique and creative options. Steelmaker Nucor paid its employees a below-market base wage but offered attractive bonuses tied to performance. When it needed to cut its workforce, the company cut the employee work-week from 40 to 32 hours per week. But workers who chose to do so could work on lower-skills jobs such as maintenance on their temporary free days. Alternatively, they could attend company-sponsored training seminars. For either option, they were paid their base wage but no bonus.

Computer maker Dell even made work-hour reductions voluntary. During December 2009, it offered all employees the option of taking as many as 5 extra free days off without pay. Enough of its employees chose this option to have a meaningful effect on the firm's bottom line, but those who really needed the money were also allowed to earn their full pay simply by not taking off any extra time.[1]

THINK IT OVER

1. Which do you think is more fair—cutting work hours for everyone or eliminating the jobs of some while retaining most employees on a full-time schedule?
2. What factors would most likely affect a person's willingness to accept a salary reduction accompanied by extra time off work?

In Chapter 5, we discussed some of the sources of information for making human resource management (HRM) decisions. In this chapter and the next, we will discuss the details of some of those decisions that are made on a regular basis. Chapter 7 will describe the details of how organizations recruit and select employees for organizations. This chapter looks at decisions about the size of an organization; that is, our focus here is the decisions about how many employees should be on the payroll at any time. This is often referred to as the *headcount*. We will discuss both temporary and more permanent decisions that can be made about headcounts, and we will also discuss some special problems about the size of an organization's workforce after a merger or acquisition. Before dealing with any of these decisions, we begin by discussing the importance of ethics in decision making.

ETHICS AND HUMAN RESOURCE MANAGEMENT

In Chapter 2, we discussed how the legal framework provided a set of parameters for human resource management decisions, and, as noted above, we discussed various sources of information for these decisions in the previous chapter. But ethics is another important aspect of decision making for all managers, not just human resource (HR) managers.[2] Ethics is a separate concept from the law but is closely intertwined. **Ethics** refers to an individual's beliefs about what is right and wrong and what is good and bad. Ethics are formed by the societal context in which people and organizations function. In recent years, ethical behavior and ethical conduct

on the part of managers and organizations have received considerable attention, usually fueled by scandals at firms such as Enron, WorldCom, Imclone, and Tyco International and unscrupulous managers such as Kenneth Lay, Jeffrey Skilling, and Barnard Madoff. The basic premise is that laws are passed by governments to control and dictate appropriate behavior and conduct in a society. The concept of ethics serves much the same purpose because of its premise about what is right and what is wrong.

> ## Ethical behavior and legal behavior are not always the same.

But ethics and law do not always coincide precisely. For example, it may be perfectly legal for a manager to take a certain action, but some observers might find his or her action to be unethical. For example, an organization undergoing a major cutback might be legally able to terminate a specific employee who is nearing retirement age, but if that employee has a long history of dedicated service to the organization, then many people could consider termination to be ethically questionable. Managers from every part of the organization must take steps to ensure that their behavior is both ethical and legal. Some organizations develop codes of conduct or ethical statements in an attempt to communicate publicly their stance on ethics and ethical conduct.

The various scandals of the 1990s raised many public questions about the ethical training and orientation of managers. A survey published in *USA Today* created even more questions. In that survey of 443 master's of business administration (MBA) students, more than 50 percent responded that they would buy stock based on insider information, more than 25 percent said they would allow

Ethics *refers to an individual's beliefs about what is right and wrong and what is good and bad. Ethics are formed by the societal context in which people and organizations function.*

a gift to influence a company purchasing decision, and more than 10 percent said they make a payoff to help close a deal.[3] Even more serious questions of business ethics emerged in the aftermath of the financial meltdown of 2009.

Following the near collapse of several major banks and financial institutions, the U.S. government instituted its Troubled Asset Relief Program (TARP) to provide billions of dollars in loans to institutions such as Bank of America and JPMorgan Chase. Many of these institutions had paid back those loans by the end of 2009, or were in the process of doing so, but it seemed clear that these institutions would have never survived without the federal funds. The problems really arose, however, over the year-end bonuses the companies were paying to their executives. We will discuss executive compensation more fully in Chapter 9, but suffice it to say that Wall Street firms paid multimillion dollar bonuses to top executives in early 2010. There was no question that these bonuses were perfectly legal, but questions were raised about the ethics of paying out huge bonuses to executives while many Americans were unemployed or struggling financially—especially when the firms were in a position to pay those bonuses only because of government bailout dollars. In fact, in early 2010, Andrew Cuomo, New York's attorney general, sent a letter to eight of the nation's largest banks demanding to know how they structured those bonus payouts.[4]

One interesting ethical challenge facing an organization became apparent when Internet search provider Google announced that it was going to close its operations in China.[5] The huge company had formally entered China in 2005 (although it had provided a Chinese-language version of Google since 2000). As the company saw its market share shrink, however, Google's executives realized they must formally enter the Chinese market. The problem was that Google considered itself a company that was socially responsible; to enter the Chinese market, the company

> ## "There is no playbook for responding to turmoil we have never faced. We adjusted our strategy to reflect the facts of a severe market crisis."
> —HENRY M. PAULSON, JR.,
> Secretary of Treasury

had to agree to a certain level of censorship required by the government. Not only was information that was critical of government policies censored but also there was evidence that the Chinese government used Internet access to track down and prosecute dissidents within China.

To access the hundreds of millions of Chinese Internet users, Google agreed to this censorship, even though it was clearly at odds with Google's corporate philosophy and what most Americans would consider ethical behavior.[6] As a result, in January 2010 Google announced that it had uncovered a Chinese government plot to use e-mail attachments to get access to sensitive information and to identify political dissidents, and this was seen as going too far. The source of the attacks has been speculated to be students at Chinese universities. In March 2010, Google transplanted its Chinese operations to Hong Kong. This case illustrates how some companies must balance ethics with profits, and how complicated it is to maintain a real balance.

This case also helps illustrate how the scope of business ethics can be even more complicated when one thinks about the global environment of modern business. Different countries and different cultures have different values and norms, and this translates into different ideas about what kinds of behaviors are ethical and what kinds are unethical. Specifically, nations and cultures differ in what they see as acceptable behaviors relative to corruption, exploitation of labor, and environmental impact. For example, a recent survey indicated that Iceland, Finland, and New Zealand were the least corrupt countries and Chad, Bangladesh, and Haiti were the most corrupt. The United States was ranked as the seventeenth least corrupt nation.[7] Thus, it is important to recognize that one's sense of ethics is always part of any decision made, but that individuals as well as countries can differ in terms of their sense of what constitutes ethical behavior. We will refer back to questions of ethics throughout these next two chapters.

RIGHTSIZING THE ORGANIZATIONS

One of the more basic decisions an organization must make concerning human resources is the size of the workforce. Whether a company is forecasting revenue growth or decline, the number of its employees must be adjusted to fit the changing needs of the business. In all cases, therefore, it is essential that the organization, through the HRM function, manage the size of its workforce effectively. This process is called **rightsizing**, and it is the process of monitoring and adjusting the organization's workforce to its optimal size and composition.

Managing the size of the workforce may, in turn, involve layoffs or early-retirement programs to reduce the size of the workforce, retention programs to maintain the size of the workforce, and using temporary workers as a bridge between the current state of affairs and either growth or reduction. In any case, the organization must ensure that it has the "right" people. Reduction, retention, or any other

however, most organizations took a more strategic approach than they had in the 1980s; as a result, many were in a good position to capitalize when markets rebounded again in 2006. In late 2008 and early 2009, however, things took a turn for the worse. Problems with bad mortgages led to foreclosures, and banks that had invested in mortgage-backed securities began to have serious problems, and there were massive layoffs. In fact, as noted earlier in the chapter, if it not been for the intervention of the U.S. government, many large banks and financial institutions would have failed during 2009. As 2010 began, many of these institutions were doing much better, but unemployment still hovered around 10 percent as the new decade began—a level that was alarmingly high. There are hopes for better times in the coming years, but there is also a great deal of uncertainty.

How, then, do organizations manage the size of their workforces to deal with their current needs and potential future economic realities? One important, short-term solution is the use of temporary or contingent workers, who provide a buffer for the organization. When facing declining needs for employees, the organization can simply decide

> ## Nations and cultures often differ in what they see as acceptable behaviors involving corruption, exploitation of labor, and environmental impact.

strategy affecting the size and composition of the workforce must target the specific types of employees the organization would like to eliminate or keep. For the most part, organizations choose to retain highly committed, highly motivated, and productive employees and would prefer to lose less committed and less productive employees. How an organization achieves this goal while staying within the limits of the law is one major focus of this chapter.

Over the past three decades, people in the United States have witnessed firsthand the cyclical nature of economic forces. In the 1980s, numerous layoffs and workforce reductions occurred at U.S. firms, primarily as the firms adjusted to increased global competition. Both academic researchers and the popular press discussed at length the best ways to manage layoffs and the challenges of dealing with their survivors. Then the economy began to grow at an unprecedented rate in the 1990s, and expert opinion began to focus more on recommendations for recruiting and retaining valuable employees. Then came September 11, 2001, and its aftermath: The economy slowed, and workforce reductions began again. By the middle of 2002, the Dow Jones Industrial Average had its sharpest decline since the Great Depression, and layoffs and reductions were again the order of the day. This time,

not to renew the contracts of temporary workers or end their relationship with contingent workers in other ways. When facing increasing demand for employees, the organization can increase overtime or hire contingent workers until it determines if it will need more permanent workers. Once the need for permanent employees is established, companies must deal with the recruitment and selection issues discussed in the next chapter. This chapter is more concerned with temporary fixes for increased demand and the special issues that face an organization with declining demands for employees: These are the true focus of any discussion of rightsizing. We begin with an examination of the increased demands for employees.

Dealing with Increased Demand for Employees

When an organization anticipates an increased need for employees, the traditional approach has been to recruit and hire new permanent employees. In recent years, that model has changed. Specifically, if the demand for new employees is not expected to last, or if it would take a long time to find the needed permanent employees, then a firm may try a more temporary solution—at least for awhile. This is the case, for example, when the increased need for employees is part of a normal and well-understood cycle such as the practice of retailers hiring temporary help during November and December.

The easiest way to deal with a temporary increase in the demand for employees is to offer **overtime**

Rightsizing *is the process of monitoring and adjusting the composition of the organization's workforce to its optimal size.*

Overtime *refers to hours worked above the normal 40-hour workweek, for which there is usually a pay premium.*

opportunities, which simply means asking current workers to put in longer hours for extra pay. As noted, this alternative is especially beneficial when the increased need for human resources is short term. For example, a manufacturing plant facing a production crunch might ask some of its production workers to work an extra half-day, perhaps on Saturday, for 2 or 3 weeks to get the work done. An advantage to this approach is that it gives employees the opportunity to earn extra income. Some employees welcome this opportunity and are thankful to the organization for making it available. In addition, it keeps the organization from having to hire and train new employees because the existing employees already know how to do their work.

On the other hand, labor costs per hour are likely to increase. The Fair Labor Standards Act (described earlier in Chapter 2 and discussed further in Chapter 9) stipulates that employees who work more than 40 hours a week must be compensated at a rate of one and a half times their normal hourly rate. Furthermore, if the organization doesn't really need all the members of a work group for overtime, then it may face a complicated situation in deciding who gets to work the overtime. Unionized organizations often have contracts that specify the decision rules that must be followed when offering overtime. Finally, there is the problem of poten-

Young's Dairy, a Midwestern restaurant and ice cream company, employs about 300 high school and college students as part-time workers.

temporary employees tend not to understand the organization's culture as well as permanent employees. In addition, they are not as likely to be as productive as permanent full-time employees of the organization.

Employee leasing is yet another alternative. An organization can pay a fee to a leasing company that provides a pool of employees to the client firm. This pool of employees usually constitutes a group or crew intended to handle all or most of the organization's work needs in a particular area. For example, an organization might lease a crew of custo-

> ## The Fair Labor Standards Act stipulates that hourly workers must be compensated at a rate of one and a half times their normal hourly rate for work in excess hours of 40 hours per week.

tial increased fatigue and anxiety on the part of employees, particularly if the overtime is not particularly welcome and if they have to work the overtime for an extended period of time.

Another increasingly popular alternative to hiring permanent employees is a growing reliance on temporary employees. The idea behind temporary employment is that an organization can hire someone for only a specific period of time, and a major advantage to the organization is that such workers can usually be paid a lower rate, although they are now more likely to be entitled to the same benefits as full-time workers.[8] Considerable flexibility comes from the fact that employees themselves realize their jobs are not permanent, so the organization can terminate their relationship as work demands mandate.[9] On the other hand,

dial and other maintenance workers from an outside firm specializing in such services. These workers appear in the organization every day at a predetermined time and perform all maintenance and custodial work. To the general public, they may even appear to be employees of the firm occupying the building. In reality, however, they work for a leasing company.

The basic advantage to the organization is that it essentially outsources to the leasing firm the HR elements of recruiting, hiring, training,

Employee leasing *involves an organization paying a fee to a leasing company that provides a pool of employees who are available on a temporary basis. This pool of employees usually constitutes a group or crew intended to handle all or most of the organization's work needs in a particular area.*

compensating, and evaluating those employees. On the other hand, because the individuals are not employees of the firm, they are likely to have less commitment and attachment to it. In addition, the cost of the leasing arrangement might be a bit higher than if the employees have been hired directly by the firm itself.

Our final alternative to hiring permanent workers is to rely on **part-time workers**, or individuals who routinely expect to work fewer than 40 hours a week. Among the major advantages of part-time employment is the fact that these employees are usually not covered by benefits, thus lowering labor costs, and the organization can achieve considerable flexibility. The part-time workers are routinely called on to work different schedules from week to week, thereby allowing the organization to cluster its labor force around peak demand times and have a smaller staff on hand during downtimes. Part-time workers are common in organizations such as restaurants. Wait staff, bus persons, kitchen help, and other employees might be college students who want to work only 15 or 20 hours a week to earn spending money. Their part-time interest provides considerable scheduling flexibility to the organization that hires them.

Each group of employees described in the preceding can be considered part of the *contingent workforce*, which includes (1) all temporary employees, (2) all part-time employees, and (3) all part-time employees who are employed by organizations to fill in for permanent employees during peak demand. Thus, these contingent workers are considered alternatives to recruiting, but usually as alternatives that are less desirable. Some recent views of staffing take a more strategic perspective, however, and suggest that there may be situations when it would be preferable to hire temporary or contingent workers instead of permanent employees.[10]

In this view, whenever a firm requires additional human resources unrelated to its core competencies or required to have skills or knowledge that is generally available in the marketplace, then it may be to the firm's competitive advantage to add resources through some other arrangement besides permanent hires. Eventually, though, it may become clear that the firm needs to hire more permanent employees, and that is the focus of the next chapter. For now, we turn instead to the situation in which rightsizing requires the firm to reduce the number of employees.

Part-time workers *refers to individuals who are regularly expected to work less than 40 hours a week. They typically do not receive benefits and afford the organization a great deal of flexibility in staffing.*

Dealing with a Declining Need for Employees

There are also cases in which an organization needs fewer employees. If the organization employs a large contingent workforce, then the easiest solution is to cut those workers and simply retain its core of permanent employees. This approach works best in cyclical industries in which demand increases and decreases with the time of year, such as farming and its use of migrant farmworkers. But dealing with more permanent decreases in the demand for employees is more problematic, although there are some approaches we can discus for this possibility as well.

Early retirements and natural attrition can be used when it is possible to plan systematically for a gradual decrease in the workforce. In some cases, organizations can even conduct planning exercises that may suggest the need to reduce the workforce over the next few years. This reduction may result from anticipated changes in technology or customer bases or even to anticipated changes in corporate or business strategies. The organization can attempt to manage the reduction by simply not replacing workers who leave voluntarily, or by providing incentives for other employees to retire early, or both.

Clearly, a certain number of employees will retire every year in any mature organization, which can reduce the size of the workforce by simply not replacing those retired employees. But what if normal retirement rates are not expected to be enough to produce the necessary reductions? In those cases, the organization can offer certain types of incentives to convince some employees to retire earlier than they had planned.

For example, in an organization that has a defined benefit retirement plan (see Chapter 9), the pension that an employee earns at retirement is a function of (among other things) the number of years that person has worked and her or his salary. An organization could simply announce that those who are thinking about retiring will automatically have, say, 3 years added to their years of service if they make a decision to retire by a certain date. As a result, employees could feel comfortable about retiring 3 years earlier than they had planned. An organization could also increase the rate at which it matches employee contributions to 401(k) plans (also discussed in Chapter 9) or in some other way make it financially more attractive for employees to retire early. Some firms actually provide employees with opportunities to learn more about wealth management so they are better able to take advantage of early retirement opportunities. But, in all cases, these plans must truly be voluntary or the organization may encounter legal problems. By definition, early-retirement plans target older workers, so any attempt—real or perceived—to coerce them into leaving can be construed as age discrimination. As noted in Chapter 2, age discrimination toward older workers is illegal.

Strategies for Layoffs

In many cases, there is not enough warning to rely on early retirements, or the early retirement strategy simply does not result in enough decrease in employee numbers. In these cases, it is usually necessary to reduce the workforce through layoffs. Layoffs are not popular for obvious reasons. When notified of a layoff, some employees decide to sue the organization for wrongful termination. In these cases, the former employee alleges that the organization violated a contract or a law in deciding who to terminate. Even if an employee does not pursue legal remedies, many employees who have lost their jobs develop negative feelings toward their former employer. These feelings usually manifest themselves through negative comments made to other people or refusing to conduct personal business with their former employer. In some extreme cases, they may even result in aggressive or

low distributive justice and when someone loses his or her job but someone else does not, then it is difficult to see how this difference in outcome can be linked to differences in contribution.[13]

2. Nonetheless, those who lose their jobs may still react reasonably as long as they feel that the organization has not also violated another type of justice—**procedural justice**—or perceptions that the process used to determine the outcomes was fair. Thus, an employee who loses his or her job may be less angry if everyone in a department also lost their jobs or if layoffs were based on objective and accepted criteria. Several models of procedural justice have been proposed, and these models have yielded the dimensions of procedural justice presented in Table 6.1.

   It is also clear, however, that an employee (or any other observer) will judge a process to be fair when it leads to an outcome that is favorable.[14] This perspective explains why most students generally consider fair tests to be the ones they perform best on. It is also why employees who do not lose their jobs are more likely to view the basis for layoff decisions as being more just (see, however, the discussion on the survivor syndrome).

3. Finally, a third dimension of justice, **interactional justice**, refers to the quality of the interpersonal treatment

> ## The HR manager who deals with layoffs should consider distributive, procedural, and interactional justice issues.

violent responses directed at those perceived to be responsible. Hundreds of such attacks occur each year, and several dozen result in the loss of life. For these reasons, it is critical that layoffs be carried out humanely and carefully.

A critical determinant of an employee's reaction to being laid off is his or her perceptions of the justice involved in the layoff process. Three types of justice—distributive, procedural, and interactional—seem to be related to reactions to layoffs.[11]

1. **Distributive justice** refers to perceptions that the outcomes a person faces are fair when compared to the outcomes faced by others. This type of justice is often important in determining an employee's reactions to pay decisions, for example. Most experts believe that these perceptions are based on both the actual outcomes faced (e.g., how much I am paid, whether or not I lose my job) and the perceptions of what others have contributed.[12] For example, a person may be paid less than his co-worker, but if he can see that she contributes more to the company than he does and that the difference in the pay is proportional to the difference in contributions each makes, then he can still view the outcome as fair. Others argue, however, that unequal outcomes alone lead to perceptions of

people receive when a decision is implemented.[15] Thus, employees losing their jobs will feel that the decision was more just if it is communicated to them in a considerate, respectful, and polite manner. In fact, scholars have proposed more recently that there are two separate dimensions to interactional justice. The first dimension deals with the extent to which the person was treated with respect and dignity when he or she was told about the decision, while the second dimension refers to the extent to which the decision maker provides information about the decision rules used and how they were applied. These two dimensions have been called *interpersonal justice* and *informational justice*, respectively.[16]

The human resource manager who has to deal with layoffs should consider these justice issues. Basically, they suggest that

Distributive justice *refers to perceptions that the outcomes a person faces are fair when compared to the outcomes faced by others.*

Procedural justice *refers to perceptions that the process used to determine the outcomes were fair.*

Interactional justice *refers to the quality of the interpersonal treatment people receive when a decision is implemented.*

TABLE 6.1 Critical Dimensions of Procedural Justice

Voice: The perception that the person had some control over the outcome or some voice in the decision.

Consistency: The perception that the rules were applied the same way to everyone involved.

Free from bias: The perception that the person applying the rules had no vested interest in the outcome of the decision.

Information accuracy: The perception that the information used to make the decision was accurate and complete.

Possibility of correction: The perception that some mechanism exists to correct flawed or inaccurate decisions.

Ethicality: The perception that the decision rules conform to personal or prevailing standards of ethics and morality.

Representativeness: The perception that the opinions of the various groups affected by the decision have been considered in the decision.

Source: Adapted from Jason Colquitt, Donald Conlon, Michael Wesson, Christopher Porter, and K. Yee Ng, "Justice at the Millennium: A Meta-Analytic Review of 25 Years of Organizational Justice Research," *Journal of Applied Psychology* (2001), 86: 425–445.

necessary layoffs should be implemented using a well-formulated strategy that can be communicated to and understood by the employees and follows the rules implied by the dimensions of procedural justice in Table 6.1. Finally, the decisions should be communicated in a way that conveys respect and caring for the people involved.

Of course, the actual strategy used for determining who will be laid off must also be reasonable. As noted above, a layoff strategy that targets older workers is probably illegal and would rarely be considered as fair. Sometimes, layoff decisions are made on the basis of performance; that is, the organization decides to lay off its poorest performers. But how does an organization decide who these employees are? Typically, this decision is based on past performance appraisals, but, as we shall see in

need to demonstrate that the performance ratings are job related or valid. This process is not always simple, as we shall see in the next chapter. In addition, the layoff strategy must also include some plan for callbacks if the demand for labor increases again. For example, a strategy that states the first to be laid off will also be the first to be called back will often be perceived as a fair strategy.

Finally, as noted in Chapter 2, when an organization is about to undertake a large-scale layoff or site closure, it is necessary to announce this step far enough in advance to allow employees (and others) to take some action to adjust to the coming changes. The Worker Adjustment and Retraining Notification (WARN) Act requires at least 60 days' notice for a facility closure or a mass layoff. Failure to provide this notification can result in serious financial penalties, especially for a firm facing pressure to reduce costs. From the organization's perspective, however, some potential costs come with announcing planned layoffs. Once this plan is made known, many employees will seek alternative employment to avoid being out of work (which is the intention of the law). The employees most likely to find alternative employment are the best employees, however, and the firm is most likely to want to retain these employees. It is difficult to balance the requirements of the law (and of the individual employees) with the needs of the organization that desires to retain its top talent. Additional legal issues may arise in the future if the current trend toward exporting jobs to foreign countries continues to expand. HR in the Twenty-First Century presents additional information about exporting jobs.

Is Downsizing Effective?

Given the prevalence of downsizing as a way to reduce labor costs and make a firm more efficient, it would seem that the effectiveness of downsizing as a strategy would get a lot of support. Why else would so many firms turn to this strategy as a means of becoming more competitive?

> **The Worker Adjustment and Retraining Notification (WARN) Act requires at least 60 days' notice for a facility closure or a mass layoff.**

Chapter 10, performance appraisals are far from perfect and prone to various biases. When layoff decisions are based on performance ratings, those ratings take on the role of employment tests. In other words, because the organization is making a decision based on the performance ratings, the courts consider the performance ratings to be employment tests. Thus, if there is evidence of disparate impact in the layoffs, the organization will

The data on the effectiveness of downsizing is rather mixed, however, and most of the data suggests that downsizing is *not* an effective strategy.

A major study of the effects of downsizing was conducted in the 1990s.[18] The authors compared several groups of companies that were tracked from 1980 through 1994, but we will focus on only three for the current discussion. "Stable employers" were defined as those firms

HR in the 21st Century

Exporting Jobs? American workers have become used to the fact that large organizations will occasionally downsize their workforce and some people will lose their jobs. In recent years, though, U.S. workers in have seen some jobs exported to other countries where workers expect and are paid much less than their American counterparts. Quite recently, however, this problem has

> ## "By the year 2015, it is expected that the U.S. will export 3.3 million white-collar jobs and $136 billion in wages abroad."[17]

spread to groups of workers that have not been affected by the exportation of jobs in the past.

A person who earns an MBA from a reasonable program can earn a great deal of money. In fact, a typical MBA with 3 years of experience will earn about $100,000 per year. That, of course, is for someone who earns an MBA from a U.S. school and who works in the United States. In India, an MBA with 3 years of work experience earns an average of $12,000 a year. Although this may sound like a good reason to pursue an MBA in the United States, many American workers are finding that this salary differential is turning into a serious disadvantage for them.

For a quite a few years, U.S.- and European-based companies have been exporting low-level manufacturing jobs to Latin America and Asia. Everything from designer polo shirts to cars are often manufactured for U.S. (or European) companies at offshore locations and then shipped back here for sale. Now U.S. companies not only are continuing to export low-paying, semiskilled jobs overseas but also are beginning to export white-collar jobs overseas. In 2000, it was estimated that the United States exported white-collar jobs that generated $4 billion in payroll. By 2015, it is expected that the United States will export 3.3 million white-collar jobs and $136 billion in wages abroad.

Large U.S. companies are leading this trend, with companies such as IBM, Microsoft, and Procter & Gamble exporting thousands of white-collar jobs to lower-wage markets. The types of jobs that are being exported cover a wide range. As already noted, for instance, manufacturing jobs have been exported for many years; in recent years, many call-center jobs have also been exported overseas. Now jobs such as financial analysts, architectural drafters, and accountants are being exported as well. For example, data from the Department of Labor indicate that in the year 2000, essentially no management jobs were sent overseas but by 2005

almost 40,000 such jobs had been lost to foreign workers. This is in addition to more than 100,000 computer jobs and almost 300,000 office jobs exported by 2005. This is outsourcing on a huge global scale; it is not surprising that many people are upset about it.

Workers themselves are worried. Halfway through fiscal year 2006, the unemployment rate in the United States was about 6 percent; by late 2009, this figure had ballooned to 10 percent. These numbers, of course, fuel worker concerns about losing their jobs and can actually lead to higher unemployment rates. Even when companies are growing and can assure workers that exporting some jobs will not affect them in any way, workers still worry about the future. Organized labor is also concerned about this trend, which they argue is a threat to the American middle-class workforce. As a result, unions such as the Communications Workers of America have actually called for a congressional investigation into the large-scale exporting of these jobs. It will be interesting to see how this trend and the labor movement's reactions to it might translate to gains in unionization among white-collar workers in the future.

The reason for exporting these jobs is actually quite simple. The wage differentials between workers in the United States and workers in countries such as India are huge. Yet Indian workers are highly educated and motivated and, with a little training, can speak colloquial American English quite well. The combination is one that is difficult for many firms to resist. Clearly, if organizations can provide quality goods and services at a lower cost, then they can increase sales and profits as they increase their competitive stance relative to other firms in this country and abroad.

Although some experts claim that the real threat to American jobs is not great and that it will become more apparent as the economy improves, others see it as a real problem and have actually refused to send jobs overseas even though they can save money. This trend is unlikely to slow down in the future unless there is much more pressure from legislative bodies and groups of workers (organized labor and others). Without such pressure, the problem will become more serious and we will have to see exactly how it affects the American workforce and economy.

THINK IT OVER

1. Do you think the exportation of jobs should be regulated by the government? Why or why not?
2. What kinds of jobs are more and less likely be exportable?

Sources: "USA's New Money-Saving Export: White-Collar Jobs," *USA Today* (Aug. 5, 2003): 1B–2B; *Hoover's Handbook of World Business 2009* (Austin: Hoover's Business Press, 2010); Thomas Friedman, *The World Is Flat* (New York: Farrar, Strauss & Giroux, 2005).

© sextoacto/Shutterstock

where changes in employment throughout these years fell between plus and minus 5 percent (this was the largest group in the study). "Employment down-sizers" were firms where the decline in employment was more than 5 percent during this time *and* the decline in plant and equipment was less than 5 percent during the same period. "Asset down-sizers" were defined as firms where the decline in employment was less than 5 percent during this time, but the decline in plant and assets was at least 5 percent

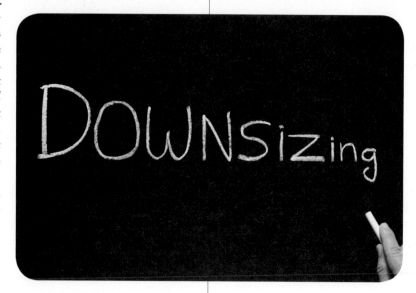

greater than the decline in employment. The authors examined the impact of these strategies over time on two indexes of performance: return on assets (a financial index of profitability) and common stock prices.

The results clearly showed that employment down-sizers had the lowest levels of return on assets over time and also did quite poorly on stock price. In both cases, the asset downsizers produced the greatest performance over the period. Most of the pressure on management to downsize the workforce comes from stockholders, who believe that this method is a good way to cut costs and increase

> ## Data shows that downsizing rarely benefits a company facing economic problems.

profitability. But the results of this study suggest that firms facing increased competition or some other need to downsize should consider reducing plants and assets rather than their workforce.

Other studies have also reported negative effects on stock prices and other financial indexes as a result of downsizing.[19] Given these findings, why do firms continue to downsize as a reaction to the need to cut costs? Some evidence suggests that, in the short run, the stock market reacts positively to these cuts, and so managers are reinforced for their decisions. But other potential costs, not only potential direct financial costs, are also associated with downsizing.

Earlier in this chapter, we emphasized issues that can occur in conjunction with those employees who lose their jobs in a layoff, but issues related to those who avoid losing their jobs in the layoff also crop up. A phenomenon known as *survivor syndrome* can counteract many of the presumed cost savings that led to the layoffs in the first place.[20] This syndrome describes employees who feel guilty over keeping their jobs (that is, they survived) when others lost their jobs. Their morale and commitment to the organization drop dramatically. In fact, according to a study of firms implementing layoffs through the 1990s, almost 70 percent of the HR managers surveyed reported declines in employee morale, more than 40 percent reported increased voluntary turnover, and more than 10 percent reported an increase in disability claims—all within the first year of the layoff.[21] This data may underestimate the total costs of increased layoffs. Evidence suggests that the increasing rates of layoffs and the resulting joblessness are causing serious emotional problems for employees—both those actually affected by layoffs and those who think they *might* be affected by layoffs.

Given this data, we must close with a discussion of alternatives to layoffs as ways of reducing costs. Downsizing the number of employees is a tangible way of demonstrating that a firm is serious about cutting costs, but it may not be the most effective. Reducing assets is an alternative. This could include reducing investments in new machinery, stretching out maintenance schedules for equipment, or actually getting out of some lines of business. Although closing plants will also result in job loss, a firm might be able to sell some of its less productive assets. Thus, some alternatives to layoffs may also result in job loss, but that outcome isn't a foregone conclusion. Some firms find even more productive ways to reduce costs. Some years ago, one of the authors of this textbook learned about a DuPont plant that was facing layoffs or closure because of high labor costs. The plant manager (subsequently promoted several times) asked the employees to get involved in the decision about reducing costs. The employees suggested a combination of job sharing, salary reductions (the plant was nonunion), early-retirement plans, and part-time work, which resulted in almost no employees losing their jobs. At the same time, the plant became extremely profitable and the employees developed a loyalty to the company that was the envy of the manufacturing sector.

MANAGING TERMINATIONS AND RETENTION

Not all decisions regarding who remains with a firm result from changes in the demand for human resources. There are times when an organization wants to sever the employment relationship, not with a large number of employees but with specific employees. There are also times when an organization is concerned over the loss of critical employees (or group of employees) and must instead focus on ways to retain them. We begin this discussion by turning our attention now to the various issues involved in terminating employees whose services are no longer desired—also known as **involuntary turnover**.

Managing Involuntary Turnover

Effective human resource practices are supposed to ensure that employees perform their job satisfactorily. But even the most sophisticated recruitment and staffing practices can still result in hiring an employee who is simply not

(EAP) designed to either help such employees directly or refer them to competent professionals who can provide that help. Originally, many EAPs focused on alcoholism, but more recently they have expanded to deal with drugs and more general problems of mental health.[22] Considerable evidence suggests that effective EAPs can help employees and reduce the costs associated with lost workdays and poor productivity.[23] These plans can also save costs by serving as gatekeepers for employee health plans because they determine what types of services are best suited for each employee.[24] But, more important, these programs make it possible for potentially valuable employees to be brought back to productive levels, thus ensuring their continued employment and yielding savings for the organization.

In many cases, the reason for an employee failing to perform up to standard is that he or she simply does not know how or cannot perform at that level. It may be a lack of ability or a lack of fit between the person's abilities and the job requirements. In these cases, it is in everyone's best interests for the employee to leave the company or be reassigned to another job, and this is what most termination decisions deal with. But, in other cases, poor performance is a motivational problem, not a personal or ability problem. For whatever reason, the employee chooses not to perform at expected levels, even though he or she is capable of doing so. This may the result of poorly designed incentives for performance, which we will discuss in Chapters 13 and 14, but sometimes

> ## Any time an employee is terminated it represents a failure of some part of the human resource system.

capable of or is not willing to perform up to acceptable standards or who presents enough of a disciplinary problem that he or she must be terminated. We should note, first, however, that any time an employee is terminated, it represents a failure of some part of the HR system. It can also be costly because the firm must then seek to recruit, hire, and train a replacement. Therefore, in all the situations we describe in this section, termination should be as the last resort. Before terminating an employee, managers should always start with an effort to rectify the problem. These attempts begin with trying to ascertain the reasons for poor performance.

For example, in some cases, the poorly performing employee might have the potential to perform effectively but he or she was never properly trained or is not properly supervised. In such cases, the employee's performance may be brought up to standard by retraining or reassignment to a supervisor who is better at developing employees. In other cases, the employee may be suffering from various physical or psychological problems such as excessive stress or problems associated with alcohol or drug abuse. Most organizations have some type of employee assistance program

it is possible to convince the employee to exert greater effort by taking some type of disciplinary action.

Progressive Discipline

Disciplinary programs in organizations are designed to try to improve performance through the use of punishment.

1. **Punishment** simply refers to following unacceptable behavior with some type of negative consequences.
2. **Discipline** refers to the system of rules and procedures for how and when punishment is administered and how severe it should be.

In all cases, the goal of the disciplinary program is to convince the employee to stop the ineffective or undesired behavior and engage

Involuntary turnover is *terminating employees whose services are no longer desired.*

Punishment *simply refers to following unacceptable behavior with some type of negative consequences.*

Discipline *refers to the system of rules and procedures for how and when punishment is administered and how severe the punishment should be.*

in more accepted or desired behavior. The goal is not to terminate the employee unless that becomes the only viable alternative.

We refer to these programs as **progressive disciplinary plans** because, almost invariably, the severity of the punishment increases over time or across the seriousness of the problem. A list of typical steps in the progressive disciplinary program is provided in Table 6.2. Each infraction, as well as the schedule of penalties, should be spelled out clearly to employees, both in the form of an employee handbook and orally at employee orientation. Whatever the infractions, the steps in the disciplinary process are almost always the same. It is also true, however, that some types of problems might incur more severe penalties from the outset. For example, it is common in manufacturing facilities to have rules about sleeping on the job. The penalty for an infraction is always severe, but in many organizations, if an employee simply falls asleep at his or her workstation, the penalty might be 2 weeks' suspension without pay for the first infraction. On the other hand, if the employee "makes a bed"—that is, the employee leaves the workstation and lies down to sleep somewhere else—the penalty is immediate dismissal for the first infraction.

Progressive disciplinary plans *are organizational disciplinary programs where the severity of the punishment increases over time or across the problem.*

Verbal warnings—*the first step in most progressive disciplinary programs—are cautions conveyed orally to the employee.*

Written warnings—*the second step in most progressive disciplinary programs—are more formal warnings. They are given to the employee in writing and become part of the employee's permanent record.*

As part of a progressive disciplinary program, a **suspension** *is a temporary layoff, usually with pay, when there is an ongoing investigation.*

As part of a progressive disciplinary program, **termination** *is an act by the organization to end the employment relationship.*

Employment at will *states that an employer can terminate any employee, at any time, for any reason (good or bad), or for no reason at all.*

TABLE 6.2 Typical Disciplinary Problems

Problems with performance	■ Failure to complete work on time ■ Errors in work products ■ Work products that do not meet established tolerances
Problems with attendance	■ Repeated unexcused absences ■ Tardiness ■ Leaving work early
Problems with ethics or honesty	■ Taking credit for the work of others ■ Falsifying records ■ Soliciting or accepting bribes or kickbacks
Other behavior problems	■ Gambling ■ Vandalism ■ Use of drugs or alcohol on the job ■ Sexual harassment
Problems that could lead to immediate termination	■ Major theft ■ Sleeping on the job ■ Selling narcotics on the job

1. Typically, the first step in a progressive disciplinary program is a **verbal warning**, or a caution conveyed to the employee orally rather than in writing. The supervisor or manager should keep a written record of the fact that a verbal warning was given to document the fact that all required steps were taken in dealing with an employee.

2. **Written warnings** are more formal and are the second step in the process. Here the supervisor gives the warning to the employee in writing and provides a copy to the HR department. As a result, a written warning becomes part of the employee's permanent record.

3. **Suspension**, or a temporary layoff, is the next step in the process. The suspension could last a day or a few weeks; it may be with or without pay. At each step, the supervisor should discuss the performance problems with the employee and seek ways for the employee to improve.

4. If all else fails, the final step in the process is **termination**. At this point, the organization faces potential legal problems as well as potentially violent reactions by the employee. This final step should be taken only after serious consideration and the decision that the employee cannot be salvaged.

Employment at Will

It is not always easy to terminate an employee, no matter how problematic he or she may be. Considerable publicity has surrounded the issue of employees suing organizations for wrongful termination, so we might suspect that the formal law dealing with this issue is quite complicated. It might be surprising, therefore, to learn that the only real legal perspective on employee termination is a nineteenth-century common-law rule known as **employment at will**. Basically, this view asserts that, because an employee can terminate an employment relationship at any time (i.e., quit a job), the employer should have similar rights. Therefore, employment at will states that an employer can terminate any employee at any time for any reason (good or bad)—or for no reason at all. This view differs dramatically from the situation in many European countries, where employees can be terminated for criminal behavior only.[25]

In the United States, companies are relatively free to terminate employees anytime they wish, so in most cases an employee has no legal recourse if he or she is terminated. Several important exceptions to the employment-at-will doctrine exist. These exceptions define situations in which an employee who is discharged can sue for wrongful termination and thus get his or her job back. These exceptions are important to keep in mind and are presented in Table 6.3.

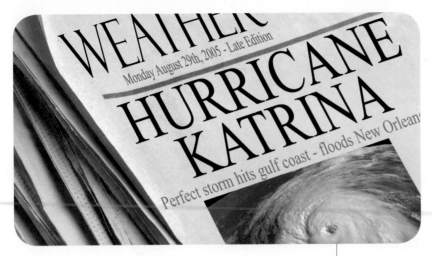

of counseling and problem solving are integral to the process. The employee is given as much help as is reasonable to help him or her identify the behaviors desired by the organization and to eliminate undesirable behaviors.

Employee Retention

Sometimes the focus of human resource decisions is on ways to retain valued employees instead of on ways to terminate undesired employees. In fact, the two work together: Organizations must seek ways to eliminate poorly performing employees while at the same time find ways to retain highly performing employees. Thus, termination is about ways to ensure the involuntary turnover of undesired employees, and retention is about ways of reducing the voluntary turnover of desired employees.

One of the authors of this book works at a university in New Orleans where this problem was played out in dramatic fashion following Hurricane Katrina and the breaching of the New Orleans levee system in August 2005. As a result, the university had to close for a semester, and it lost a great deal of money. When the university was ready to reopen, it became clear that it would be necessary to reduce the size of the staff (and the faculty) to survive. Deans and

Even with these exceptions, employers can still usually terminate employees *for cause*; that is, if the employee violates a written company rule or policy or is an objectively documented poor performer, then he or she can be terminated in virtually every case. The key to successful termination of an employee is documentation. An organization can terminate any employee at any time, but if the employee claims that the termination was wrong, the employer may have to prove otherwise. If an employee is dismissed for poor performance, then it may be necessary to document that most (if not all) of the employee's recent performance appraisals were poor or below standard. If the employee has received generally acceptable evaluations, then it will be extremely difficult to terminate the employee for poor performance. In any case, if a company has a progressive disciplinary program, it must show that each step was followed before the employee was terminated.

If an employer does not follow the proper steps and document each one, the employee may well get his or her job back. This situation may be annoying to the employer, but it is actually far more serious than annoyance. Progressive discipline can work only if the employee truly believes that he or she will be fired without improved performance. If the threat of termination is not credible because procedures were not followed correctly or because of some other reason (perhaps the employee is a civil-service employee), it is extremely difficult to correct a problem employee. The credible threat of termination is actually an important part of the process by which an organization can turn a poorly performing employee into a productive one.

Some organizations have begun to adopt an approach referred to as *positive discipline*, which has a somewhat different orientation.[26] This approach integrates discipline with performance management. (We will discuss this more fully in Chapter 14.) Positive discipline emphasizes positive changes rather than punishment. Typically, the process is still somewhat progressive in nature, with warnings leading to eventual termination if the problem is not corrected. The major difference, however, is that a great deal

TABLE 6.3 Exceptions to the Doctrine of Employment-at-Will

1. **The termination would violate a specific law.** Various laws forbid termination for a specific reason. Some of the most common reasons are termination based on gender or race (violates the Civil Rights Act) or termination because of union activity (violates the Taft-Hartley Act).

2. **The employee has a contractual right to his or her job.** The contract might be a formal contract or an implied contract guaranteeing or implying a guarantee of employment.

3. **The employee's rights of due process have been violated.** For example, if an employee is accused of theft, the employee has the right to know of the charges and to refute those charges—in a court of law if necessary.

4. **Public–policy exception.** This exception has been less common but involves cases in which an employee is discharged for refusing to commit a crime or for reporting a crime or unethical or unsafe behavior on the part of the organization. Thus, whistle-blowers are protected under this exception.

5. **Breach-of-good-faith exception.** This is the most difficult exception to establish because it involves a breach of promise. In one of the best-known cases, an employee claimed that he was terminated after 25 years of employment so that the company could avoid paying him his sales commission.

Note: These exceptions have been cited in various court cases, but there is no guarantee that any specific state will recognize any one of these exceptions in its jurisdiction.

Source: *Fortune* v. *National Cash Register*, 364 Massachusetts 91, 36 N.E. 2d 1251 (1977).

heads of programs were therefore asked to determine which staff positions were critical for the future of the university and to prioritize layoffs among the remainder of the staff. Lists of potential layoffs were thus generated across the university, and hundreds of staff members were scheduled to lose their jobs. But no one really understood the situation from the perspective of the staff employees. Many of them had been forced to evacuate New Orleans, and they had to enroll their children in schools in other cities. Many of them had lived in areas that had been flooded and could not be rebuilt in time to return to work in January 2006.

manage this turnover as much as possible. High rates of turnover cost the organization a great deal in terms of the expense associated with employee replacement, and such turnover can hurt the organization's reputation as a good place to work.

To manage turnover, it is important to understand why people leave. A major cause for turnover is **job dissatisfaction**, or being unhappy with one's job.[28] We will discuss some causes for job dissatisfaction later in the chapter (as well as some additional consequences of dissatisfaction later in the chapter), but for now it is enough to say that the

> *A high turnover rate not only can cost an organization the expense of replacing employees but also hurt the organization's reputation as a good place to work.*

Still others had found jobs elsewhere or had spouses who had found jobs elsewhere and were not planning to return to New Orleans. As a result, hundreds of staff employees voluntarily left their jobs. Unfortunately, these were often not the same people the university had planned to lay off. Instead, these were valued employees whose jobs were critical to the future of the organization. As a result, all the planned layoffs had to be canceled (with a few exceptions), and the university had to scramble to make sure that all critical positions were filled.

This experience illustrates quite graphically that there are two sides to every rightsizing exercise: the termination of employees who are no longer needed, and the retention of those employees who are still needed and who may become even more critical in the light of planned layoffs. Therefore, we turn our attention now to the problems of retaining valued employees. These strategies are always important if the firm hopes to gain competitive advantage through its human resources, but they are especially critical as part of any rightsizing.

MANAGING VOLUNTARY TURNOVER

Managers cannot always control who leaves the organization or why they leave, but they should not assume that all turnover is negative even in the case of voluntary turnover. In fact, although the organization does not want to force someone out, management may not be totally disappointed that the person left, and a certain amount of voluntary turnover is probably healthy for the organization.[27] Yet it is important to

Job dissatisfaction *is the feeling of being unhappy with one's job. It is a major cause of voluntary turnover.*

HR manager plays a major role in ensuring that employees remain reasonably satisfied with their jobs. It is also the role of human resources to help reduce turnover and retain valued employees. As we shall see, job dissatisfaction is often the key to turnover. Different views explain why dissatisfied workers decide to leave.

Models of the Turnover Process

The basic reason people leave their jobs is because they are unhappy with them. Thus, the simplest view of the employee turnover process would suggest that if we increase job satisfaction, then we will decrease turnover. Although this basic view is essentially correct, the processes involved are somewhat more complex.

First, the economy and the labor market play a role. It has been noted that the prevailing unemployment rate is as big a factor in whether a person leaves a job as the level of dissatisfaction.[29] Clearly, this explanation makes a great deal of sense. Even if an employee is extremely dissatisfied, he or she is not likely to quit without real prospects of finding another job.

Recognizing this fact, several turnover models emphasize the role of dissatisfaction in the decision to look for alternatives, and it is seen as a necessary (but not sufficient) first step in the decision to quit. At least two major streams of research have proposed models that incorporate these ideas, and the basic concepts of these models are present in Exhibit 6.1.[30] As you can see in the figure, the process begins with factors leading to job dissatisfaction (which will be discussed below). Job dissatisfaction causes the employee to begin thinking about quitting, which leads to a search for alternatives. Only if those alternatives look better does the employee decide that he or she will quit, a decision first manifested by an intention to quit.

Of course, the implication of this type of model is that managers should reduce the sources of job dissatisfaction.

It is best to stop the turnover before the employee begins searching for alternatives because he or she might find a more attractive alternative. Even if an employee begins searching for alternatives, it may still be possible to retain the employee by convincing him or her that the current job really is better than the alternatives. In fact, the search for alternatives sometimes leads to increased satisfaction on the current job after the employee discovers that the alternatives were not as positive as once believed.

Other models have proposed similar mechanisms but have also suggested that job dissatisfaction must reach a critical level before anything happens and, at that point, it may be too late to do anything. In other words, this approach suggests that increasing job dissatisfaction does little to change the employee's intentions to leave. Those levels of job dissatisfaction finally reach a critical level, however, and the intention to leave becomes so strong that the employee is almost guaranteed to leave.[31]

Another interesting model that deviates a bit from the basic model in Exhibit 6.1 focuses on "shocks" to the individual.[32] First, this model proposes that several paths can lead to turnover, and they do not all require shocks. Nonetheless, the major focus is on a shock—an event that can be either positive or negative but is so profound that it causes the employee to think about the organization, the job, and how he or she fits with both. This model begins with shock and not with job dissatisfaction. In fact, the dissatisfaction occurs only because the employee started thinking about the job in response to the shock. The decision to leave is largely based on the perception that the employee does not really fit with the company—that is, the current job in the current company is not consistent with the image the employee has of him- or herself. In some cases, the employee will leave without even considering alternatives, but in all cases the decision to leave takes place over time.

The model includes other aspects of cognitive processing, but the shocks include events such as winning the lottery or losing a loved one, as well as job-related events such as missing a promotion or receiving an offer from another company. This model has interesting implications for understanding how difficult it is to manage the turnover process, but recently the authors of the model have added one more wrinkle. Although the model was originally proposed as a way of understanding why people leave their jobs, it can also help understand why others stay. The notion of **job embeddedness** has been proposed as an explanation for why some people stay on their jobs, even when they decide they are unhappy and should leave.[33] Some employees are simply tied too strongly to their jobs to leave. Perhaps they are deeply involved in the neighborhood, or perhaps they cannot sell their houses. Whatever the reason, they feel that they cannot

© picamaniac/Shutterstock

EXHIBIT 6.1 A Model of the Turnover Process

quit. These employees may be quite unhappy, which can cause other problems. This state is not always desirable. Nonetheless, the notion of job embeddedness adds a great deal to our potential understanding of the turnover process.

The Causes of Job Dissatisfaction

A common thread in these models of the turnover process is job dissatisfaction. Wherever and however in the process job dissatisfaction occurs, reducing it is likely to reduce turnover. Therefore, it is important to understand the causes of job dissatisfaction. Although most sources of job dissatisfaction that have been studied are related to the job, some of the more creative approaches have focused on factors that have little or nothing to do with the job. For example, one line of research, using identical twins, has (cautiously) suggested that a certain component of job satisfaction may be genetic.[34]

A related line of research has suggested that some individuals are simply disposed toward being satisfied, while others are disposed toward being dissatisfied, and that, although conditions on the job play a role, these tendencies are as important in determining levels of job dissatisfaction.[35] More typical approaches to job dissatisfaction, however, tend to focus on the following job-related factors.

> **Job embeddedness** *refers to the fact that some people stay on their jobs, even when they decide they are unhappy and should leave. Other ties in the community or obligations keep the employee on the job.*

1. **Nature of the Work.** One of the most important sources of dissatisfaction on the job is the nature of the work that a person does.[36] For example, a consistent relationship exists between job complexity (and job challenge) and job satisfaction such that employees with more complex and challenging jobs are more satisfied. We will discuss how jobs can be redesigned to make them more motivating and satisfying in Chapter 14.

   In addition, job satisfaction tends to be higher when the job is less physically demanding. We don't want to suggest that a boring job is preferred—quite the contrary—but a job that requires constant physical exertion and strain tends to lower levels of job satisfaction. Also, jobs that help employees achieve something of value tend to result in higher levels of job satisfaction; that is, if an employee feels that he or she is accomplishing some good on the job, satisfaction tends to be higher. In addition, if an employee values status and a job provides him or her with more of it, then levels of satisfaction are also likely to be higher.[37]

and can work together as a team.[38] Clearly, the impression that co-workers do not share values and attitudes can lead to dissatisfaction. In addition, co-workers can be seen as sources of social support, which can also lead to increased job satisfaction. Employees can be satisfied with supervisors for many of the same reasons. In other words, shared values and social support can be important determinants of satisfaction with a supervisor as well as with a co-worker. In addition, an employee can be satisfied (or dissatisfied) with a supervisor's leadership ability. How a supervisor leads (i.e., his or her leadership style) and the effectiveness of the work group are important determinants of satisfaction with the supervisor.[39]

Each source of job dissatisfaction can be measured and thought of independently or as part of a whole; that is, studying and considering satisfaction with pay in its own right has some value, whereas others consider it simply as one source of overall satisfaction with the job. We will

> ## Happier workers are healthier workers. Dissatisfied employees are more likely to be absent for health reasons.

2. **Pay and Benefits.** It may not be a surprise that an employee's level of satisfaction on the job is affected by the extent to which he or she is satisfied with pay and benefits. In general, higher levels of pay and more attractive benefits tend to result in greater satisfaction, and we will discuss issues of both compensation and benefits in Chapter 9. But another important factor in determining satisfaction with pay is what other people make. Basically, we compare ourselves with similar others, and we gauge what we contribute to an organization versus what a comparison person contributes. We then compare how much we are paid and, if the ratio of rewards to contributions is better for the other person, we tend to be dissatisfied. Note that these calculations are all based on perceptions, which may be incorrect, and note also that this comparison person could be working in the same organization or in another organization.

3. **Supervisors and Co-Workers.** Supervisors and co-workers represent two additional potential sources of job dissatisfaction. An employee may be satisfied (or dissatisfied) with co-workers for several reasons. An important factor for job satisfaction is that the employee believes he or she shares certain values and attitudes with co-workers—that everyone has some shared vision of the world

Organizational commitment *is the degree to which an employee identifies with an organization and is willing to exert effort on behalf of the organization.*

return to this issue later when we discuss methods of measuring satisfaction. Before turning to that topic, however, we turn our attention to some of the outcomes of dissatisfaction on the job.

The Effects of Job Dissatisfaction

We began our discussion of job satisfaction by noting that it is a major determinant of voluntary turnover and thus our major reason for discussing job satisfaction, but job dissatisfaction can have other negative effects, and some of these effects are related to topics we discuss later in the text.

For now, our primary concern with job dissatisfaction is that it leads to increased voluntary turnover. As noted earlier, job dissatisfaction is a major determinant of turnover, but it is also predictive of other types of withdrawal behavior. For example, a strong relationship exists between job dissatisfaction and absenteeism,[40] partly because employees who are dissatisfied may not always be able to leave their jobs (because of a lack of alternatives); thus, they choose to withdraw partially by being absent. In addition, it is possible to withdraw even more gradually (or partially) by simply being late.

A more subtle form of withdrawal that does not involve being away from the job is a reduction of commitment to the organization. **Organizational commitment** is the degree to which an employee identifies with an organization and is willing to exert effort on behalf of the organization.[41] Employees who lack organizational commitment are excellent candidates for turnover when a workable alternative presents itself. They are also unlikely to exert extra effort or even to encourage others to join the organization.

Dissatisfied employees are also more likely to join unions. Several studies support this relationship and, although the process of joining a union is fairly complex, job dissatisfaction has consistently been found to be a good predictor of who joins unions.[42] We will discuss the implications of this relationship in more detail in Chapter 11.

Finally, dissatisfied employees are less likely to engage in behaviors on the job known broadly as *organizational citizenship behaviors*,[43] or sometimes as *contextual performance*.[44] **Organizational citizenship behaviors (OCBs)** include those behaviors that are beneficial to the organization but are not formally required as part of an employee's job. These behaviors include activities such as volunteering to carry out extra tasks, helping and cooperating with others, following rules even when such behavior is inconvenient, and endorsing and supporting organizational goals. We discuss contextual performance further in the next chapter, but clearly the organization benefits when employees engage in these types of behavior, and dissatisfied employees are simply less likely to do so.

In addition, considerable evidence suggests that job dissatisfaction imposes a different type of cost on an organization. Job dissatisfaction has been found to be strongly linked to stress (discussed more fully in Chapter 12), job burnout (the condition of physical, emotional, and mental exhaustion on the job[45]), and (through the first two processes) employee health.[46] Thus, happier workers are healthier workers. Dissatisfied employees are more likely to be absent for health reasons.

The most intriguing possibility, however, is the link between job satisfaction and productivity. The notion that happy workers may be productive workers has attracted scholars for almost 100 years. Although there are cases in which performance and satisfaction have common determinants, and even some in which the most productive employees are also the most satisfied, no consistent causal relationship between job satisfaction and performance has been found. Thus, higher levels of job satisfaction do not necessarily lead to higher levels of performance, and an organization should not target increases in job satisfaction in the hope of raising productivity.

Measuring and Monitoring Job Satisfaction

As should be clear by now, job satisfaction is extremely important for managing workforce size and effectiveness.

As a result, organizations spend a fair amount of time and effort monitoring the levels of their employees' job satisfaction, primarily through the use of attitude surveys that are distributed to employees once or more a year. The responses from these surveys are used to track changes in employees' attitudes—such as job satisfaction—so that the organization can respond to them before they become problematic.

Although many organizations design their own attitude surveys (or hire consulting firms to design them), some widely used measures of job satisfaction often show up as part of these surveys. By using standard measures of job satisfaction, an organization not only tracks changes in its employees' levels of satisfaction but also is able to compare satisfaction levels with other organizations that use the same measures.

The job descriptive index (JDI) is the most commonly used measure of job satisfaction.[47] It assesses satisfaction with specific job aspects such as pay, the work itself, and supervision, but it does not have a single overall measure of job satisfaction (although it is easy to assess overall satisfaction using the JDI). For each aspect of the job, a series of descriptors might apply. For example, for the work itself, adjectives such as *routine* and *satisfying* are listed, among others. Employees are asked to indicate if each adjective "describes your work," "does not describe your work," or if the employee "can't decide." The employee indicates the level of agreement by placing a Y, N, or ? next to each item, with the question mark (?) assumed to indicate a moderate level of dissatisfaction.

Other instruments do include direct measures of job satisfaction, and some include questions about the levels desired versus what is experienced. One instrument, the *faces scale*, presents a series of faces that are either happy or sad, and the employee is instructed to check the face that best reflects his or her feelings about the job.[48]

Whatever the measure, most organizations are interested in changes in the levels of job satisfaction over time. Before leaving this discussion, it is important to make a final note. The primary reason to measure job satisfaction is because dissatisfied employees tend to quit their jobs; over time, those employees who are the most dissatisfied will quit the soonest. The next time the organization surveys its employees, the survey will not include those employees who have already quit. As a result, it is quite likely that the overall levels of job satisfaction will

> **Organizational citizenship behaviors (OCBs)** *include employee behaviors that are beneficial to the organization but are not formally required as part of an employee's job.*

go up, even if the organization does nothing to improve job satisfaction, because only the more satisfied employees are still on the job. The others have already left, indicating a serious problem that the organization could overlook if managers are not paying attention.

Retention Strategies

The purpose of discussing job satisfaction is to provide insights into how to manage voluntary turnover. At the simplest level, one could say that the way to manage turnover is to increase the levels of satisfaction among employees. But the key is in understanding exactly how to do that. When an organization learns of a potential problem, most likely through a survey, it is important that *something* be done. Employees are less likely to respond honestly to survey questions if they feel that no one will respond to their concerns. More specifically, two other types of interventions (both discussed previously in different contexts) have been found to increase levels of job satisfaction.

Job enrichment, discussed in Chapter 14 as a strategy for enhancing performance, has been consistently linked with higher levels of job satisfaction. By making employees' work more challenging and meaningful and by granting them more autonomy and more opportunity to use their skills, the work itself becomes both motivating and satisfying (and more satisfied employees are also more productive). This in turn reduces turnover rates.

Realistic job previews (RJPs) are pre-employment previews that provide accurate and realistic information to the job applicant. They are often used with new employees as a means of socializing them in their new job roles (and they will be discussed further in this context in the next chapter), but they are also effective in reducing turnover. The link to turnover reduction is the result of several aspects of RJPs. First, because potential employees who receive RJPs have more complete information about the job (including the nature of the work, supervision, and pay), those who are more likely to be dissatisfied with the job characteristics are less likely to accept the jobs. Therefore, RJPs help ensure that the people on the job are those most

likely to be satisfied and thus remain. In addition, when new employees are made aware of potential sources of dissatisfaction before encountering them, the employees can prepare themselves (psychologically or even physically) so that, when they encounter the problem, they are ready to deal with it. In fact, when employees learn that they can cope with various problems on the job by preparing for them beforehand, this knowledge alone can be a source of job satisfaction and promote retention.

Another retention strategy involves issuing stock options to new employees at all levels of the organization (these options have typically been given to executives only). **Stock options** are rights, given to employees, to purchase a certain number of shares of stock at a given price. That stock-option price is often just slightly lower than the selling price of the stock when the option is issued.

If the stock appreciates in value, then these options can become very valuable. The employee can exercise the option, buy the stock at an option price that is lower than the current selling price, and then sell the stock for an immediate profit (some firms do not even require the employee to purchase the stock at that point but simply pay out the profit). By the end of the 1990s, however, some firms added a new wrinkle aimed specifically at employee retention. Although an employee was issued stock options early in the employment relationship, the options were restricted so that the employee could not exercise the options for 5 or so years. If the stock was climbing, then the employee who left before he or she had completed 5 years of employment would forgo potentially large profits because he or she would not be able to exercise the stock options. Thus, there was a real incentive for the employee to remain with the firm (at least long enough to exercise her or his stock options). Of course, if the stock price falls below the option price (and the option is said to be "underwater"), there is no reason to exercise the option, and the incentive to remain with the company is lost.

MANAGING HUMAN RESOURCES DURING MERGERS AND ACQUISITIONS

Managing human resources during mergers or acquisitions is the last issue we address concerning decisions regarding the size and nature of the workforce. Every few years, we seem to experience another wave of mergers and

Realistic job previews (RJPs) *are pre-employment previews that provide accurate and realistic information to the job applicant. They can also be used with new employees as a means of socializing them in their new job roles, and they are effective in reducing turnover.*

Stock options *are rights given to employees to purchase a certain number of shares of stock at a given price.*

© Norebbo/Shutterstock

acquisitions. During the 1990s, for instance, many mergers and acquisitions occurred in the oil industry, leading to the creation of four "megafirms"—BP-AMOCO, Exxon/Mobil, Shell, and Chevron/Texaco—that control a large portion of that industry. We have also seen many acquisitions in the casino industry so that now two companies, MGM and Harrah's, control almost 60 percent of all the casino business in the United States. More recently, following the financial crisis of 2009 and the so-called subprime crisis, several banks and financial firms acquired large but financially less viable firms. These included Wells Fargo acquiring Wachovia, Chase buying Washington Mutual, and Merrill Lynch taking over what was left of Bear Stearns.

Although a lot of attention is paid to big mergers and acquisitions, the public is less aware that many of these mergers and acquisitions actually fail. Failure (or success) can be assessed by looking at stock prices, accounting measures, or indicators such as research-and-development (R&D) expenditures. For each of these measures, data usually has shown that mergers and acquisitions typically fail; that is, they result in lower stock prices, lower returns, and lower levels of R&D expenditures.[49]

There is considerable speculation and some limited research on why mergers and acquisitions fail, but much of the attention has been paid to a deal's financial elements (e.g., the acquiring firm paid too much) or to strategic elements (e.g., the new business was too far from the firm's areas of expertise). Although these issues are certainly important, it is also becoming increasingly clear that the successful management of human resources during the merger and acquisition process is also quite important for the overall success of

the project.[50] In fact, several HRM aspects may be critical for successful mergers and acquisitions.

When a merger or acquisition is announced, several interesting processes begin. The most obvious is that employees in the firms involved become concerned about their jobs, especially employees of the firm that is being acquired by another company. In many cases, for example, a merger or acquisition results in a certain amount of redundant human resources, so it is not unusual for layoffs to occur following the merger or acquisition. This awareness causes employees to become more stressed and to worry about their security, and it leads some employees to seek other employment before they become victims of a layoff. Unfortunately, in these cases, it is often the more valued employees who have the market value that makes such a job change easy.

Mergers and acquisition also threaten the way employees think about themselves. This core belief is known as a person's *self-identity*, and a great deal of our self-identity is tied up with what we do and for whom we work. For example, there has been a lot of recent discussion about the merger between Internet giant AOL and media titan Time Warner. When it was announced in 2000, it was valued at $350 billion, and it remains today the largest merger in U.S. business history. By the time that Time Warner spun off AOL in April 2009, billions of dollars had been lost (Ted Turner personally lost a reported $8 billion), and everyone declared the merger a disaster. What went wrong? Clearly, the nature of the Internet business changed, and the bursting of the dot-com bubble was a factor. But most analysts see the real issue as having been that the cultures of the two companies never joined to form one new entity.[51] Few people were involved in doing the deal, so almost no one felt they had a stake in making it work, and no one

> "For whatever reason, right or wrong, I had become kind of a magnet for a lot of anger and frustration, particularly with the Time Warner employees and also with shareholders and if we really were going to get the company on the right track and really capitalize on the promise of the merger, probably the best thing I could do was step aside and get out of the way."
>
> —STEPHEN M. CASE,
> A cofounder of AOL[53]

at the top of the new company really tried to persuade the people in charge of their brands that they needed to try to make this deal work. The fact that the two cultures were never blended was clearly a critical, if not *the* critical issue in explaining the failure of this giant merger.

The problems at AOL and Time Warner are not unique. Employees involved in mergers and acquisitions must abandon one self-identity and then develop a new one: an employee of the acquiring firm or an employee of the new, merged firm. This is not a trivial manner. When people perceive threats to their self-identity, they actually work to reinforce that self-identity. In this case, an employee in a firm about to be acquired would feel his or her identity threatened and, as a reaction, would develop even stronger feelings of identity with the firm about to be acquired. Then, when employees of the acquiring firm were there, they would be seen as the "enemy"—as the people responsible for threatening the employee's self-identity. Intergroup research shows that these feelings are associated with an "us versus them" mentality that results in competition between groups and even dislike for the other group members.[52]

Of course, this is exactly what the organizations want to avoid. They must move to integrate the two firms into one and create a new self-identity for all employees: employees of the newly merged firm. In other words, for a merger or acquisition to be successful, all the employees should identify with the new firm and therefore work with one another and cooperate to help make the new firm the best it can be—especially because it is even more rewarding to be associated with a really successful firm.

The situation thus far does not sound promising. It would seem as if all mergers and acquisitions are doomed to fail because of identity issues, yet we know that many mergers and acquisitions are successful. Moreover, we believe that in successful cases HR managers functioned in such a way as to increase the likelihood that the mergers or acquisitions were successful. One critical role the HR manager can play during this process is to serve as the center of communications. As noted above, there is a great deal of uncertainty for everyone during a merger or acquisition, and the HR manager can work to communicate openly, honestly, and frequently with the employees. Research has shown that realistic information during the merger or acquisition process can reduce stress, increase job satisfaction and commitment, and even reduce turnover, so this communication process can be extremely useful.[54]

In addition, it is important to build employee identification with the new corporate identity. This can be accomplished with simple measures such as distributing shorts or caps with the new corporate logo, or it might involve orientation sessions in which all of the reasons and details of the merger or acquisition are explained. It is easier to do this when the policies and procedures in the new firm are not based solely on the policies and procedures of one party in the merger or acquisition. If some policies are based on one firm's policies, some on the other firm's policies, and still other policies are blends of the two, then it is easier for employees from both firms to retain good feelings about their former employers and also feel good about the newly created firm.[55]

Through programs such as these, the HR manager can be an important player in the merger and acquisition process and thus can add value to the organization in yet another way. Perhaps the human resource manager should never become the final arbiter of which mergers or acquisitions should be pursued, but input from that manager might be useful. For example, input from human resources might help decide how much should be paid for an acquisition or what terms should be agreed to for a merger—with an eye toward how easy it would be to implement the merger or acquisition from the perspective of dealing with the problems identified in this chapter. In any event, once a merger or acquisition begins, the close involvement of the HR manager is obviously critical for the ultimate success of the endeavor.

CLOSING CASE

RETAINING THE BEST EMPLOYEES

Discussions and articles about employee retention usually focus on relatively glamorous high-tech employees such as programmers, engineers, and scientists. But many employers face similar challenges at the other end of the spectrum. Restaurant workers, retail clerks, and clerical workers, for instance, are often in low supply. And employers face a double bind when competing for such workers—market conditions necessitate relatively low wages because most job skills are relatively easy to teach, but the large number of jobs makes worker mobility fairly easy. The hotel industry provides a good case in point.

Annual turnover in the lodging industry generally runs as high as 160 percent. Complicating this situation, wages are often low, job mobility is high, and people who do this work must possess strong interpersonal skills. Little wonder, then, that hotels are working aggressively to figure out new ways to hire and retain the best people.

The Four Seasons chain is considered one of the best in the industry at employee retention. When the chain opened a new hotel in Scottsdale, Arizona a few years ago, it discovered that the public bus system took 45 minutes to transport people from nearby Phoenix, where many of its employees lived, and then dropped them two miles from the hotel. As a result, many Four Seasons workers were always on the alert for jobs closer to home. The firm's response? It launched its own bus service for employees without cars. The Four Seasons also aggressively promotes from within. As a result, its annual turnover rate is only about 25 percent.

Other chains are also creatively engaged in employee-retention programs. Orient-Express Hotels enables any employee to train for a job in another department for 3 weeks at full pay, even if no jobs are open in that department. The program allows employees to learn new skills and experience new job settings. It also enables the firm to be more flexible because it often already has employees trained in the area where new jobs are opening.

Classic Hospitality, a consortium of five boutique hotels in Washington, D.C., works hard to attract motivated and personable employees, but the firm also encourages those

© Dr. Heinz Linke/iStockphoto.com

employees to alert their manager when they are interested in new opportunities.

This approach allows the firm to tailor new opportunities for those employees deemed to be most valuable. Of course, not every employee moves to a new job on request, but many of those employees are less effective and do not particularly create problems if they leave.

Other chains offer incentives that range from bonuses to innovative reward programs to extra paid time off to their very best employees. Programs such as these one, human resource managers argue, go a long way toward helping them keep their most valuable employees.[56]

THINK IT OVER

1. How are low-wage jobs unique with respect to turnover and retention issues?
2. What role might job satisfaction and dissatisfaction play in the hotel industry?
3. When can a hotel chain not worry too much about retention?

STUDY TOOLS

- Rip out the chapter review card located at the end of the book.
- Review the valuable study tools located online at www.cengagebrain.com
  - Review the Key Terms flashcards.
  - Download audio and visual summaries to review on the go.
  - Complete practice quizzes to prepare for the test.
  - Play "Beat the Clock" and "QuizBowl" to master chapter concepts.
  - Complete "Crossword Puzzle" to review key terms.
  - Watch the chapter video for a real-life example of key concepts.

CHAPTER 6

Recruitment & SELECTION

Initial difficulties in hiring and training the passenger screener workforce made it a challenge for TSA to meet the deadline for federalizing this workforce.

—**Gerald Dillingham, director of civil aviation issues, Government Accountability Office**[1]

One of the many consequences of the terrorist attacks of September 11, 2001, was the U.S. government decision to take over passenger security screening at most of the nation's commercial airports. Screening had previously been handled by various private firms hired by individual airports (at larger airports) or by airline employees themselves (primarily at smaller airports). The purpose behind the change was to bring greater control and a higher level of competence and consistency to the screening process and thus boost security and airline safety.

The Transportation Security Administration (TSA), created in response to the September 11 attacks, was assigned responsibility for hiring and maintaining a workforce of screeners at the nation's 429 commercial airports. Five airports continued to have privately employed screeners under a pilot program approved by Congress,

but the other 424 were mandated to have an all-federal workforce by November 19, 2002.

When the government first tried to recruit screeners, officials found that a surprisingly high percentage of the applicants were unqualified. There were also far fewer female candidates than expected. The TSA had initially set a goal of filling half of all the screening positions with women, but because so few qualified women could be recruited, the agency eventually had to reduce this goal to one-third. "Initial difficulties in hiring and training the passenger screener workforce made it a challenge for TSA to meet the deadline for federalizing this workforce," said Gerald Dillingham, the GAO's director of civil aviation issues.

Officials also had to step up advertising and recruitment campaigns—job fairs were launched in various cities, for example. The

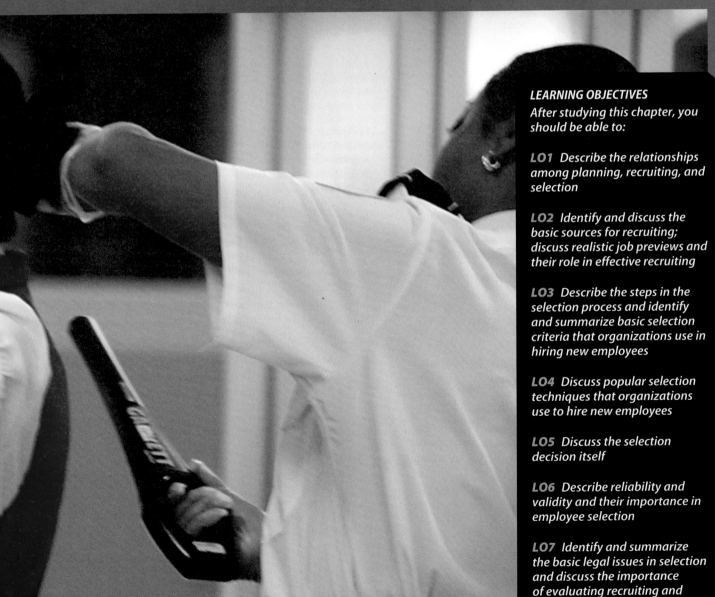

© Ramin Talaie/Corbis

LEARNING OBJECTIVES

After studying this chapter, you should be able to:

LO1 *Describe the relationships among planning, recruiting, and selection*

LO2 *Identify and discuss the basic sources for recruiting; discuss realistic job previews and their role in effective recruiting*

LO3 *Describe the steps in the selection process and identify and summarize basic selection criteria that organizations use in hiring new employees*

LO4 *Discuss popular selection techniques that organizations use to hire new employees*

LO5 *Discuss the selection decision itself*

LO6 *Describe reliability and validity and their importance in employee selection*

LO7 *Identify and summarize the basic legal issues in selection and discuss the importance of evaluating recruiting and selection activities*

TSA also began trying to attract more qualified applicants—and women in particular—by offering part-time positions or seasonal work. In addition, the TSA increased its online advertising and increased listings with both private and public employment agencies. These measures gradually paid dividends, and the TSA was fully staffed at the end of 2007.

However, the TSA has faced continuing challenges in keeping its positions filled. For one thing, the pay is relatively low, starting at $11 an hour. For another, the job is somewhat stressful: Screeners have a lot of responsibility and must deal with many harried travelers in a polite but firm manner. Moreover, the screening requirements change frequently, making it difficult to keep track of the most current FAA guidelines for carry-on items.

During the worst of the economic recession in 2009, the TSA was actually able to cut back on its recruiting efforts, as its applicant pool was larger than normal and managers had little difficulty in hiring new screeners. However, as the economy began to turn the corner in early 2010 the trends began to drift back to pre-2007 conditions. Turnover began to creep up, and fewer applicants were applying for positions.[2]

THINK IT OVER
1. What might TSA managers do to make the screening jobs more attractive?
2. What elements of the position of screening would be least appealing to you?

Managers at the TSA face a real dilemma because they are charged with attracting qualified applicants to fill important jobs but have had difficulties in doing so. In one way or another, all organizations must address the problems and opportunities faced by the TSA: the need to recruit new people who are both interested and capable of working for them.

In this chapter, we examine the recruiting process in more detail. We start by assessing the goals of recruiting. We then look at the sources and methods of recruiting. After describing the importance of realistic job previews in effective recruiting, we discuss the recruitment of part-time and temporary workers, as well as alternatives to recruiting. Finally, we briefly note how organizations evaluate the effectiveness of their recruiting efforts.

LEARNING OBJECTIVE 1

PLANNING, RECRUITMENT, AND SELECTION

In Chapter 6, we discussed how organizations reduce the size of their workforces to optimize their form and structure. We also noted that we would focus on how organizations go about increasing their workforces. Indeed, if an organization is growing, it almost certainly needs to hire new employees. But even when it is stable, it will still likely need to hire new employees to replace those who leave voluntarily and involuntarily. The processes of recruitment and selection are the means by which organizations acquire new human resources. The two processes work together, and if they are carried out effectively, the organization will have not only the number but also the type of human resources it needs to carry out its overall strategy. These two processes are the focus of this chapter, and we begin with the recruitment process.

Recruiting is the process of developing a pool of qualified applicants who are interested in working for the organization and from which the organization might reasonably select the best individual or individuals to hire for employment.[3] As we will see, however, and as illustrated in Exhibit 7.1, recruiting is a two-way street; that is, just as the organization is looking for qualified job applicants, those applicants are also likely to be looking at various potential employment opportunities. Thus, both organizations and individuals have recruiting goals.[4] The best hiring opportunities for organizations and employment opportunities for job seekers emerge when these different goals match.

Both parties in the recruiting process—the organization and the prospective employee—have goals they are trying to accomplish in the recruiting process. The most basic and fundamental goal of an organization's recruiting effort is essentially to fulfill the definition of recruiting: to develop a pool of qualified applicants. This overriding goal, however, also suggests three specific related goals that are important to the recruiting process.

1. The organization wants to optimize the size of the pool of qualified applicants—that is, have enough candidates to be able to have choices but not so many that processing would become overwhelming.

> **Recruiting** is the process of developing a pool of qualified applicants who are interested in working for the organization and from which the organization might reasonably select the best individual or individuals to hire for employment.

EXHIBIT 7.1 Organizational and Individual Goals in Recruiting

Organizational Goals

- Attract a pool of qualified applicants
- Keep pool at a manageable size
- Provide realistic job previews

?

Individual Goals

- Meet work-related goals
- Meet personal goals
- Address personal needs

2. The recruiting process should generate a pool of applicants that is both qualified and interested in working for the organization.

3. The process should give prospective applicants an honest and candid assessment of the kinds of jobs and opportunities that the organization can potentially make available to them. (We examine this issue in more detail later when we discuss realistic job previews.)

Of course, it is also important for the organization to remember that the prospective employee in the recruiting pool also has goals that affect the process. Indeed, human resource (HR) managers must never forget that recruiting is a two-way process. Just as the organization is seeking qualified applicants who are interested in employment with the firm, so too are individuals likely to be approaching several organizations and trying to entice as many of them as possible to offer employment.[5]

In many cases, a prospective employee's goals are relatively straightforward. Individuals choose to work at specific jobs for several reasons, but the most common are:

1. financial income,
2. job security,
3. promotion opportunities,
4. benefits, and
5. challenging work assignments.

In addition to these goals, however, individuals can also have idiosyncratic goals. For example, some people put extra emphasis on the location of a particular job opportunity. They may want to work close to their hometown, close to where they went to school, in a big city, in a small city, near family, near the ocean, or near recreational opportunities.[6]

© Andresr/Shutterstock

SOURCES FOR RECRUITS

One fundamental decision that an organization must make as part of its recruiting strategy is whether to focus recruiting efforts internally or externally. As summarized in Table 7.1 and discussed below, both internal and external recruiting have unique advantages and disadvantages.

Internal Recruiting

Internal recruiting is the process of looking inside the organization for existing qualified employees who might be promoted to higher-level positions. This situation may not seem particularly useful for increasing the size of the workforce, but internal recruiting can play a role even in growth strategies. If an organization can fill higher-level openings with current employees who are ready to move up, it will have to fill lower-level positions from the outside later. These lower-level positions would presumably be easier and less costly to fill. Using this approach in an ideal situation, the organization could fill all of its needs, except those for entry-level jobs, from the inside and then recruit externally for entry-level job openings.

In any event, it is generally important that an organization use internal recruiting as part of its overall planning process because, as noted in Table 7.1, internal recruiting has several advantages over external recruiting. Perhaps the most important of these advantages is employees can see that there is really an opportunity for advancement when a firm relies on internal recruiting. This is likely to serve as a major source of motivation for those employees to perform their jobs as best they can. Employees recruited internally also bring the advantage of familiarity with the company—its heritage, culture, policies and procedures, strategies, and ways of doing business, making transitions to new positions easier. Yet, as shown in Table 7.1, there are also disadvantages to internal recruiting when it is the only type of recruiting a firm uses. This can result in stagnation and stifle creativity. It is unlikely

> **Internal recruiting** *is the process of looking inside the organization for existing qualified employees who might be promoted to higher-level positions.*

that new ideas will be proposed for how to deal with challenges if everyone in the firm has only been familiar with one way of doing things. Finally, internal recruiting creates a ripple effect in the organization. Every time a person is promoted, a new opening must be filled, and a relatively few promotions can sometimes result in a large-scale set of transfers and movements from position to position within the organization.

Methods for Internal Recruiting

The two most common methods used for internal recruiting are job posting and supervisory recommendations.

Job Posting. Perhaps the most common method that organizations use for internal recruiting is a process called **job posting**. This is a relatively simple procedure. Vacancies in the organization are publicized through various media such as company newsletters, bulletin boards, internal memos, or the firm's intranet. Interested individuals simply file an application with the HR department. Some organizations that rely heavily on internal recruiting go so far as to require that jobs be posted internally before any external recruiting is undertaken. Note that a candidate hired through a job posting could be applying for a promotion or merely for a lateral transfer.

Supervisory Recommendations. Another method of internal recruiting is through **supervisory recommendations**. In this case, when a new position needs to be filled, a manager simply solicits nominations or recommendations for the position from supervisors in the organization. These supervisors look at the employees for whom they are responsible, and if any are particularly well suited for the new job opening the supervisors recommend those individuals to the higher-level manager. It is important, however, that supervisors give equal consideration to all potential candidates in these cases. In a landmark decision, *Rowe v. General Motors*, the Supreme Court found General Motors (GM) guilty of discrimination because, under a system in which supervisory recommendations were needed for promotions, supervisors failed to recommend qualified African American candidates as frequently as they recommended white candidates. As a result, almost no African American supervisors were working at most GM facilities at the time of the suit.

We should also point out that, given the large numbers of layoffs and workforce reductions (from downsizing) in recent years, some potential applicants are somewhere between the classifications of internal and external candidates. Individuals who have been laid off (as opposed to terminated) are usually considered first when openings occur in the organization (and indeed this procedure may be mandated by certain union contracts). These individuals may not be active employees at the time, but they would still be considered internal candidates. On the other hand, individuals who actually lost their jobs during downsizing—that is, were officially terminated—are technically no longer employees of the organization and so would be considered external candidates. Because they had worked for the organization previously, however, they would share more characteristics in common with internal candidates and might constitute a good source of potential applicants.

External Recruiting

External recruiting involves looking to sources outside the organization for prospective employees. As noted in Table 7.1, external recruiting has advantages and disadvantages that are directly counter to those of internal recruiting. For example, external recruiting has the advantage of bringing in new ideas, new perspectives, and new ways of doing things. Hence, the organization can enhance its vitality, creativity, and potential ability to innovate by routinely bringing in people from the outside. External recruiting also avoids the ripple effect. In some cases, no internal employees may be able to fill new positions, thereby making external recruiting the only option.

Several years ago, the managers and owners of a small software computer company in Iowa were frustrated because they could not make the major breakthroughs necessary to fuel growth for their firm. After considerable discussion, they decided that it was simply the case that no one inside the firm had the managerial skills to take the company to the next stage in its growth. All current managers were professional engineers, and none really had much managerial experience. Consequently, the firm decided to hire an outsider to come in and run the business. Within a couple of years, he had increased the firm's sales from $750,000 a year to more than $11 million.[7]

TABLE 7.1 Advantages and Disadvantages of Internal and External Recruiting

	Advantages	Disadvantages
Internal recruiting	■ Increases motivation ■ Sustains knowledge and culture	■ May foster stagnation ■ May cause a ripple effect
External recruiting	■ Brings in new ideas ■ Avoids the ripple effect	■ May hurt motivation ■ Costs more

Job posting *is a mechanism for internal recruiting in which vacancies in the organization are publicized through various media such as company newsletters, bulletin boards, internal memos, and the firm's intranet.*

Using **supervisory recommendations,** *a mechanism for internal recruiting, a manager simply solicits nominations or recommendations for a position that needs to be filled from supervisors in the organization.*

External recruiting *is the process of looking to sources outside the organization for prospective employees.*

On the other hand, external recruiting may result in motivational problems in the organization. Current employees may feel that they have been denied opportunities and that outsiders who are brought into the organization at higher levels may be less qualified than the current employees themselves. External recruiting also tends to be a bit more expensive than internal recruiting because of the advertising and other search processes that must be undertaken.

Many organizations prefer to rely on both internal and external recruiting strategies. This combined approach allows an organization to match the advantages and disadvantages of each particular recruiting effort to its own unique context. For example, during a dramatic growth period a few years ago, Compaq Computer (now a part of Hewlett-Packard) recruited both internally and externally. The firm wanted to ensure that current employees had ample promotion opportunities, but it also felt that it needed to hire people at a faster rate than could be accommodated by internal recruitment alone. Thus, each major hiring phase was carefully assessed, and decisions were made in advance about the sources to be used. In some instances, almost all recruiting was done internally, whereas only external recruiting was used in others. In still other cases, the firm looked both inside and outside at the same time for new recruits.

Methods for External Recruiting

Somewhat different methods are likely to be used by an organization engaged in external recruiting because the organization needs to reach potential applicants from outside the company.

Word-of-Mouth Recruiting.
Referrals come to an organization via **word-of-mouth recruiting**. In most cases, the organization simply informs current employees that positions are available and encourages them to refer friends, family members, or neighbors for those jobs.[8] From the organization's perspective, this method is an inexpensive way to generate a large number of applicants. In addition, if we assume that the current employees are satisfactory and

Some job seekers resort to extreme measures to find work.

© Kim Kulish/Corbis

that people generally associate with people who are similar to them, then the organization should have a reasonable chance of generating high-quality applicants with this method, and some portion of the applicants for any job come through word-of-mouth recruiting. If an organization relies on this recruiting technique exclusively, however, problems may arise. If the current workforce is almost completely white and male, for example, the individuals referred will most likely be primarily white males as well, and this situation might represent discrimination in recruitment.

Advertisements.
Advertisements in newspapers and related publications are also popular methods for external recruiting. Any local newspaper is likely to have help-wanted sections ranging from perhaps a few listings to as many as several pages, sometimes organized by different kinds of job openings such as sales, health care, professional, nonprofessional, technical, and so forth. Depending on the job, these advertisements might be placed in local newspapers or national newspapers such as the *Wall Street Journal*. Some professional periodicals and publications also have similar kinds of spaces set aside for help-wanted recruiting ads. This form of advertising tends to be relatively expensive and, perhaps surprisingly, attracts somewhat fewer qualified applicants than some of the other methods of recruiting. It does enable the organization to cast a wide net, how- ever, in its efforts to publicize its affirmative action programs and to reach every sector of the labor market. By targeting specialized publications that might appeal primarily to members of groups that are underrepresented in the workforce, the organization might also advance its affirmative action goals. On the other hand, restricting advertisements to publications that are not widely available could be considered discriminatory.

Employment Agencies.
Reliance on employment agencies is another common method for

In word-of-mouth recruiting, *the organization simply informs current employees that positions are available and encourages them to refer friends, family members, or neighbors for those jobs.*

external recruiting, but there are different types of employment agencies that serve different purposes. *Public employment agencies* became a formal part of the recruiting process with the passage of the Social Security Act of 1935. This law requires that anyone who is paid unemployment compensation must register that fact with a local state employment office. These state agencies work closely with the U.S. Employment Service to get unemployed individuals off state aid as quickly as possible and back in permanent jobs.

Employers register their job openings with the local state employment agency. At the same time, the employment agency collects data (mostly regarding skills, experience, and abilities) from unemployed persons and uses this data to match qualified individuals with available jobs. Two significant advantages of public employment agencies are (1) they are free and (2) they are a particularly useful source of job applicants for minorities, handicapped individuals, and other protected classes. Because they are state agencies, they are fully cognizant of the requirements that organizations must face, and they work hard to maintain an adequate labor pool of all classes of employees.

Private employment agencies are more likely to serve the white-collar labor market (although some serve specialized niches such as office workers), and they charge a fee for their services. Sometimes this fee is paid by the individual; sometimes it is paid by the organization if it hires an individual referred to it. In a public employment agency, all potential employee job applicants are currently unemployed, but many employed individuals use the services of private employment agencies in an effort to find federal work while maintaining their current jobs. Because private employment agencies are supported by the firms and individuals that use their services, however, they may be able to devote more resources to performing their function.

Finally, *executive search firms* specialize in finding applicants for high-level positions. An individual working for an executive search firm is also known as a **headhunter**. An organization that wants to hire a top-level manager can go to an executive search firm and explain exactly what kind of individuals it is looking for. This explanation, for example, might specify the kind of work experience the organization wants the individual to have, the degree that is necessary, the number of years of experience, and perhaps a salary profile as well. The executive search firm then attempts to locate individuals who fit this profile for the organization. Typically, the search firm

screens potential candidates and then presents the organization with a small number of candidates, all of whom are highly qualified and interested.

Executive search firms can perform rather exhaustive searches for qualified candidates, and they allow both parties in the process to maintain confidentiality. Yet they tend to be among the most expensive methods for external recruiting. In addition, one caveat that applies to any type of agency relates to potential discrimination. Many stories have been published in the popular press about employment agencies (both public and private) that referred individuals of one race, ethnicity, or gender for some jobs but not for others. If an organization engages the services of an employment agency that discriminates, then the organization almost certainly will be held liable for the discrimination.

College Placement Offices. Another method of external recruiting is to use the placement offices that most colleges and universities sponsor. Most large organizations visit college campuses every year to interview graduates for jobs within the organization. Large firms may visit many different colleges and universities scattered across the country, or they may choose to visit only regional or local colleges and universities.

An advantage of this method for the organization is that it can specify qualifications such as major, grade point average, work experience, and so forth. It is also a relatively inexpensive method of recruiting because the colleges and universities typically provide the facilities, schedule the appointments, and so forth. The organization sends the interviewer to the campus, and that individual sits in the interview room during the course of the day and meets prospective applicants. For students, this job search method is also quite efficient. The student can visit his or her local placement office on a regular basis, be apprised of which companies are coming to interview, and sign up for interviews using whatever methods and protocols the college or university has established.

Microsoft relies heavily on college recruiting in its efforts to bring in new talent every year. The firm has a staff of twenty-two full-time campus recruiters who visit schools each year. These recruiters conduct half-hour interviews with thousands of prospective employees, selecting about 450 for follow-up visits to company headquarters.[9]

Electronic Recruiting. The Internet has affected many human resource management (HRM) activities, but there are few areas where it has had greater impact than on the recruiting function. In fact, many of the techniques discussed above

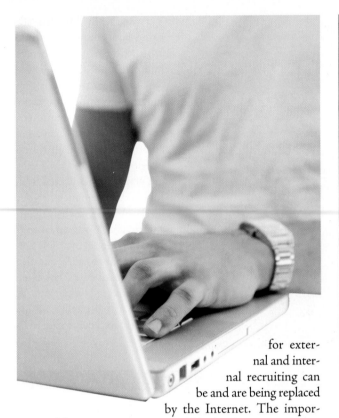
© Yuri Arcurs/Shutterstock

for external and internal recruiting can be and are being replaced by the Internet. The importance of electronic recruiting would be hard to overestimate. In 1998, 29 percent of the Fortune 500 companies generated applicants through their Web sites, but that rate rose to 88 percent in less than 3 years, and 34 percent of these companies accepted applications only through their Web sites.[10]

Perhaps the most important reason for the growing reliance on electronic recruiting is that it is cost-effective. It does not cost much to post a job opening on a job board like those available at monster.com and hotjob.com, and these Web sites are visited by literally millions of people a year. In addition, many organizations who are starting their own Web sites for recruiting find that they can reach potential applicants more easily and that they can use these sites as marketing tools.[11] Thus, exposure is another important reason for the growth of electronic recruiting. Not long ago, the effectiveness of electronic recruiting was somewhat limited by the numbers of potential job applicants who had easy access to the Internet, but data now suggests that there are 200 million Internet users in the United States and 1.8 billion Internet users worldwide. In the United States, approximately 74 percent of those with access to the Internet use it to search for jobs.[12] In other countries, this percentage is even greater because applicants do not have access to other sources of information about available job. Thus, it is not surprising that many organizations have reported that Internet advertising has resulted in a more diverse group of applicants and job seekers than they had reached using more traditional methods.[13] Finally, electronic recruiting saves time. A potential applicant who sees an interesting opening can e-mail questions and answers as well as electronically submit résumés—all in a matter of minutes.

Of course, there are some potential problems associated with electronic recruiting as well. The ease of access by applicants also means that many people may apply for a job when they are not really qualified, and this means more time spent sifting through the résumés of unqualified applicants. Also, although electronic recruiting has the potential to generate a more diverse group of applicants, differences in access to computers and the Internet still exist in the United States. For example, a study by the Department of Labor notes that fewer Hispanic-American and African-American applicants have regular access to computers; as a result, members of both groups are more likely to rely on more traditional sources of job information.[14] Finally, although electronic recruiting can offer a company many advantages, it seems that potential job seekers who visit company Web sites do not always come away happy. Many users report that company Web sites are difficult to navigate or are sloppy, while others complain that it is difficult to apply for a job at the site.[15] It is important for organizations to recognize that, in this electronic age, a company Web site may actually be the first point of contact for an applicant, and it is important for the firm to make a good impression on applicants.

Internships: A Mixed Model

Although it is easier to think about recruiting having either an internal or external focus, it is possible to take an approach that really combines elements of the two. Many students try to obtain internships that will provide real-world experience, but internships are also quite useful from the organization's perspective. Of course, an internship is a type of temporary employment (discussed in Chapter 6) who can help respond to work demands in the short term. More important, internships can be an important recruiting tool.

The intern is hired, in essence, on approval. In other words, if the organization does not think that the person is someone who will be able to contribute to the organization or that the person is a good fit, then the organization simply allows the internship to end. The intern is not really rejected because he or she has never really applied. On the other hand, if the intern is someone the organization is interested in, then it can offer the person permanent employment. Even if the intern is a student who must complete his or her studies, the organization might want to offer a contract to the person that would become effective on graduation.

In fact, using internships to bring people into the organization and then hiring them allows the organization to obtain the best of both internal and external recruiting. The interns bring in a fresh perspective, the organization knows a lot about the intern, and the intern is somewhat familiar with the organization. Many financial firms will not recruit new business school graduates for anything except internships. Permanent offers only come after a student proves her- or himself to the company during the internship. As these companies begin to recover from the crisis in 2009, this practice is becoming even more common because some uncertainty remains about the speed of recovery for anyone in the financial industry.

Realistic Job Previews

A final topic for discussion concerning external recruiting is the use of the **realistic job preview (RJP)**. In the past, many recruiters were guilty of painting a glowing picture of what a particular job might entail. They made the job sound glamorous, exciting, fun, challenging, and rewarding in different ways. Once employees accepted the job, however, they found just the opposite: The job they were hired to fill proved to be boring, tedious, monotonous, and routine. Because their expectations were set so high, and because the reality they faced proved to be so different, they were extremely dissatisfied with their work and consequently were prone to high turnover. These problems can be partly minimized, however, if recruiters paint a more realistic picture of the job.[17] Thus, RJPs were first discussed in the previous chapter as method of retaining valued employees.

Realistic information about the job can be presented using video or film, or it can be presented using brochures and printed materials. An applicant can also get realistic information by observing people at work on the job in question. Disney, for one, has found that using realistic job previews has greatly improved its recruiting and selection processes. At its vast Disney World complex, the firm has an employment office it calls its *casting center*. Before being interviewed or asked to complete a job application, people who visit the center seeking employment are instructed to watch a short video. The video informs job seekers about the firm's strict appearance guidelines and the difficult and rigorous working conditions. The goal is to provide a candid and realistic introduction to the working conditions at Disney.[18]

How RJPs seem to work is interesting. If applicants are given realistic previews before they make a decision, some potential applicants will be discouraged and withdraw from consideration.[19] But these potential applicants would likely have become dissatisfied if they joined the firm and later learned what the job was really like. At the same time, however, those who know what to expect and still choose to join the organization generally are more successful and more likely to remain with the company. A meta-analysis of several studies of realistic job previews reported that they are generally associated with higher performance, higher levels of trust in the organization, and lower turnover.[20] Not only do realistic job previews seem to work but also their effectiveness has been demonstrated with jobs as diverse as bank teller,[21] army recruit,[22] and prison guard![23]

> "Not only does an internship allow you to work hard and gain experience, but it also allows an employer to experience how hard of a worker you are."
>
> R. J. Calvo,
> Health Educator, City of Lubbock
> Health Department[16]

THE SELECTION PROCESS

Once the recruitment process has identified a pool of qualified applicants, it is time to begin the selection process. **Selection** is concerned with identifying the best candidate or candidates for jobs from among the pool of qualified applicants developed during the recruiting process.

Steps in Selection

At a general level, the selection process involves three distinct steps (see Exhibit 7.2).[24]

1. The first step is gathering information about the members of the pool of qualified recruits (as created by the recruiting process described earlier) regarding the levels of requisite knowledge, skills, and abilities (KSAs) possessed by each applicant. In addition, information about factors such as education and experience, as well as attitudes of the individuals toward work and the impressions of current managers about the individuals' likelihood of success are collected.

2. The second step is evaluating the qualifications of each applicant from among the recruiting pool. This evaluation process occurs through the application of explicit or implicit standards to the information gathered in step 1. For example, if the standard for hiring is that the person must be able to keyboard seventy words per minute, then a manager can give each applicant a keyboarding test and compare his or her score to that standard. Similarly, if the standard calls for a certain personality type, then a manager can give personality tests, interpret test scores based on test norms, and then assess how closely each the individual fits the desired profile.

A realistic job preview (RJP) is an effective technique for ensuring that job seekers understand the actual nature of the jobs available to them.

Selection is concerned with identifying the best candidate or candidates for jobs from among the pool of qualified applicants developed during the recruiting process.

EXHIBIT 7.2 Steps in the Selection Process

| The recruiting process | ⇢ | Gather information about pool of qualified applicants | → | Evaluate qualifications of each applicant | → | Make decisions about employment offers |

But sometimes applying standards is not so straightforward. For example, if the standard is 10 years of relevant work experience, someone must make the decision about whether people who exceed that standard are more qualified than individuals who simply meet it. For example, is an applicant with 15 years of experience a more desirable candidate than another applicant with 10 years and 1 month experience, or are these two candidates to be treated as equal on this dimension because they each meet the standard? We will discuss important implications of decisions such as this one later in the chapter.

3. The third step is making the actual decision about which candidate or candidates will be offered employment with the organization. This decision involves careful assessment of the individuals' qualifications relative to the standards of the job and the extent to which those qualifications best prepare and give an individual the requisite skills and abilities for the position. In some cases, an organization may need to select large numbers of people to hire simultaneously. For example, a firm opening a new factory may be hiring hundreds of operating employees from a pool of thousands of applicants, or a rapidly growing restaurant chain may need to hire dozens of management trainees to assume management positions in new restaurants in a year or two. In both cases, the manager does not necessarily have to make fine gradations between, say, candidates numbers 11 and 12. The only decision is determining the extent to which a candidate is in the set of desirable people to hire or is outside that set because of job-relevant characteristics.

But if the selection decision involves hiring a specific single individual for a specific position in the organization, such as a new director of marketing or a vice president of human resources, then one individual must be selected. It is sometimes helpful at this point to rank-order the candidates who are being considered for the job. If the organization does not succeed in hiring its top choice for the job, then decisions will have already been made regarding the relative acceptability of candidate number 2, candidate number 3, and so on. In some cases, for example, if the recruiting process has been handled effectively, the organization may want to hire more than one qualified applicant in the pool. Thus, it may be helpful to develop a backup plan in case the top choice cannot be employed.

Basic Selection Criteria

What exactly are the bases for evaluating the applicants during the selection process? Several possible criteria can be used in the selection decision, and these often differ in terms of how objectively they can be assessed.

Education and Experience.

Education and experience are criteria that are relatively straightforward to assess. In a selection context, **education** refers to the formal classroom training an individual has received in public or private schools and in a college, university, or technical school. Some jobs require high school diplomas; others might require advanced degrees. For some jobs, the educational fields (a person's major) are open; in other cases, they must be within a specified area such as mechanical engineering, French, or human resource management.

Experience refers to the amount of time the individual may have spent working in either a general capacity or a particular field. Experience is presumably an indicator of an individual's familiarity with work and his or her ability to work and a surrogate measure of a person's competencies as an employee. In some cases, it may be necessary that the individual have a predetermined level of experience in a certain field of study. For example, if a large organization is looking to hire someone to be director of advertising, it will quite likely expect applicants to have substantial experience in the advertising field. In other cases, however, the experience requirement may be more general. Simply having a certain number of years of

Education refers to the formal classroom training an individual has received in public or private schools and in a college, university, or technical school.

Experience is the amount of time the individual has spent working in either a general capacity or a particular field of study.

© Tatiana Popova/Shutterstock

experience in full-time work activities might be sufficient evidence of an individual's employability. And some entry-level jobs may require no experience at all.

Skills and Abilities.

The assessment of skills and abilities, on the other hand, is rather mixed in terms of objectivity. It is relatively straightforward to assess someone's typing ability, and it is even possible to measure an ability such as spatial relations (the ability to manipulate three-dimensional objects in one's mind) objectively. But as organizations move toward teamwork and team-based operating systems, many of them are also putting more emphasis on hiring individuals with the skills necessary to function effectively in a group situation.[25] These skills are much more subjective and therefore more difficult to assess accurately.

Personal Characteristics.

Some personal characteristics, which are believed to reflect the applicant's personality, are also difficult to assess objectively. Assessments of characteristics such as friendliness, the ability to deal with others, and perseverance are usually quite subjective and are obtained as part of the interview process (discussed later). More recently, however, a great deal of attention has been paid to assessing applicants in terms of the **big five personality traits**. These traits tend to be more behavioral than cognitive or emotional and so can be assessed in a fairly objective manner. Furthermore, recent research has suggested that they are likely to be more important for job performance than more traditional personality traits.[26] The big five traits are *neuroticism* (disposition to experience states such as anxiety and guilt rather than being better adjusted emotionally), *extraversion* (tendency to be outgoing, sociable, and upbeat), *openness to experience* (tendency to be imaginative and intellectually curious), *agreeableness* (tendency to be altruistic and cooperative), and *conscientiousness* (tendency to be purposeful and dependable and to pay attention to detail).

The big five personality traits—neuroticism, extraversion, openness to experience, agreeableness, and conscientiousness—tend to be more behavioral than cognitive or emotional and are likely to be more important for job performance than more traditional personality traits.

Hiring for "Fit."

A rather unique and interesting criterion for selection is referred to as "fit." When a firm decides to hire someone on the basis of fit, it is choosing not to hire someone because he or she is the most qualified for a specific job, but because she or he is a good fit for the larger organization. Thus, rather than hire someone for a programming position because of his or her computer skills alone, the firm might consider hiring a person whose personal values or personality fit with the rest of the organization. Note that the firm likely would not hire an unqualified person simply because of fit, but it would select the person who it thought would fit in best from among a group of reasonably qualified persons. But fit for a specific job is likely to be based on KSAs, and it can probably be assessed rather objectively, whereas organizational fit is likely to be based on values and personality, which are more difficult to assess objectively.[27] In some cases, the organization might assume that the requisite KSAs can actually be learned after the person has been hired, resulting in even more reliance on selection based on fit. This trend has developed into a growing controversy in selection today. HR managers traditionally believed that they should hire the person with the best set of job-specific skills relative to the work that needed to be performed, but today many argue that the best hires are those who fit into the overall organization based on personal characteristics, values, and so forth.[28]

POPULAR SELECTION TECHNIQUES

Organizations use different techniques for gathering information that reflects an individual's education and experience, skills and abilities, and personal characteristics. Indeed, most organizations rely on a comprehensive system of multiple selection techniques to ensure that they gather all the relevant data and that they assess this data rigorously, objectively, and without discrimination. A fundamental requirement of any technique is that it be reliable and valid. Indeed, reliability and validity are of sufficient importance that we devote an entire section to these properties later in this chapter. In this section, we identify and discuss some of the more popular and commonly used selection techniques. Logic may underlie the sequence in which organizations use these techniques, but at the same time many organizations vary the order to fit their own

EXHIBIT 7.3 A Sample Selection System

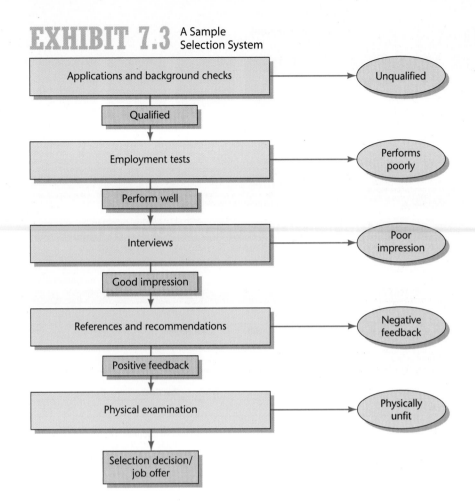

particular needs, circumstances, and beliefs. Exhibit 7.3 illustrates one example selection sequence that an organization might use.

Applications and Background Checks

A first step in most selection systems is to ask applicants to complete an employment application or an application blank. An **employment application** asks individuals for various facts and information pertaining to their personal background. Commonly asked questions include details such as name, educational background, personal career goals, and experience.

Of course, all questions on an employment application must relate to an individual's ability to perform the job. An employment application cannot ask for a person's gender, age, or marital status because these questions have no bearing on that person's ability to perform specific jobs. Such questions could even serve as a basis for an applicant's claims of discrimination on the basis of age or gender. An organization may need this information after someone is hired, but it is illegal to make selection decisions based on these variables, and they should be avoided on application blanks. Exhibit 7.4 presents an example of an application blank.

Application blanks provide a quick and inexpensive mechanism for gathering several kinds of objective information about an individual and information of a type that can be easily verified. Even on a traditional paper application, however, if an individual states that she has a bachelor's degree in electrical engineering from a given university, then the organization can verify this information with a simple call to that university's registrar's office. Organizations can also use application blanks to quickly determine if an applicant meets minimum selection criteria (e.g., years of experience).

Many innovations also have extended the usefulness of application blanks, including the following.

1. The so-called **weighted application blank**[29] relies on statistical techniques to determine the relative importance of various personal factors for predicting a person's ability to perform a job effectively.

*An **employment application** asks individuals for various bits of information pertaining to their personal background.*

*A **weighted application blank** relies on the determination of numerical indexes to indicate the relative importance of various personal factors for predicting a person's ability to perform a job effectively.*

EXHIBIT 7.4 A Sample Employment Application

Notes to Applicants: This application will be considered active for 60 days. If you have not been hired within 60 days of submitting this application and you wish to be considered for employment, you must complete a new application. Applicants' right to privacy will be observed in accordance with applicable law.

Company associates may not work for more than one SHC Company. Self-employed contractors and employees of a licensed business of any SHC Company may not also work as an associate of any SHC Company.

The Sears Holdings Corporation (hereinafter "SHC") company to which you have applied ("Company") is an Equal Employment Opportunity Employer. The Company prohibits discrimination against, or harassment of, any applicant or employee on the basis of race, color, religion, gender, gender identity, sexual orientation, age, national origin, disability, citizenship status, veteran status, marital status, ancestry, pregnancy, ethnicity, genetic information or any other status protected by federal, state, or local law. The Company will provide reasonable accommodations (such as a qualified sign language interpreter or other personal assistance) to individuals with disabilities who need such and accommodation to fully participate in the application process upon request, consistent with applicable laws. Please contact a human resources representative or manager on duty.

APPLICATION FOR EMPLOYMENT
PLEASE PRINT REQUESTED INFORMATION – USE ONLY BLACK OR BLUE INK

Date Of Application _____   Date Available _____   Location # (Company Use Only) _____

PERSONAL INFORMATION

First Name _____   MI ___   Last Name _____

___ - ___ - ___
Social Security Number (Utah Applicants: Do not provide social security number on this application.)

Current Address

	Street & Apt#	City	ST	Zip Code	County	Telephone No.
1						

Previous Address
If you have not lived at your current address for 7 years, please list all prior residential addresses (most recent first) for the 7 years before the date this application is submitted. (Note: if more space is needed, use page 3 of this application.)

	Street & Apt#	City	ST	Zip Code	County	Dates From: mm/yy To: mm/yy
2						
3						
4						
5						

EMPLOYMENT DESIRED

Position Applying for: _____

Number of hours you would prefer to work each week: _____   Maximum number of hours you can work each week: _____

Number of evenings you can work each week: _____   Number of weekends you can work each month: _____

Are you able to work national holidays: Yes ☐   No ☐

Please list the earliest time and the latest time you are available to work each day:

	Sunday	Monday	Tuesday	Wednesday	Thursday	Friday	Saturday
Earliest Time							
Latest Time							

EDUCATION

School Attended	No. of Years	Name of School	City/State	Graduate? (Yes/No)	Course or College Major
High School					
College					
Other (Name and Type)					

Using information gathered from current high and low performers in the organization, it is often possible to determine whether specific levels of education, experience, and so on gathered on the application blank are related to a person's ability to perform a job effectively.

2. The **biodata application blank** focuses on the same type of information found in a regular application, but it also goes into more complex and detailed assessments

EXHIBIT 7.4 (Continued)

PRIOR EXPERIENCE

Have you ever been employed by Sears Holdings Corporation or any of its subsidiaries, including Sears, Kmart, or any of their subsidiaries?

Yes ☐ No ☐

If yes, list when and where were you last employed:	List termination date and reason for leaving:	List job position worked:

Do you have any relatives in the employment of Sears Holdings Corporation or any of its subsidiaries, including Sears, Kmart, or any of their subsidiaries?

Yes ☐ No ☐

If Yes:

Provide name:_____ Relationship: _____ Job: _____ Job Location: _____

RECENT EMPLOYERS

List your three most recent employers, beginning with the most recent one. If you have had less than three employers, use the remaining space for personal references. Also list any periods of unemployment in the boxes below.

Name and address of former employers, beginning with the most recent

NOTE: State reasons for and length of inactivity between present application date and last employer		Your Job Title	Employment Dates		Reason for leaving
1 Employer's Name			From	To	
Address	Telephone No.	Supervisor	Rate of Pay		
			Start	Final	
City	State Zip Code				

NOTE: State reasons for and length of inactivity between employers		Your Job Title	Employment Dates		Reason for leaving
2 Employer's Name			From	To	
Address	Telephone No.	Supervisor	Rate of Pay		
			Start	Final	
City	State Zip Code				

NOTE: State reasons for and length of inactivity between employers		Your Job Title	Employment Dates		Reason for leaving
3 Employer's Name			From	To	
Address	Telephone No.	Supervisor	Rate of Pay		
			Start	Final	
City	State Zip Code				

I authorize the employers listed above to give our company any and all information (except information that cannot be obtained as a matter of law) concerning my previous employment and release all parties from all liability that may result from furnishing the same.

If you were employed under or have otherwise used another name, please provide name(s) _____

ADDITIONAL INQUIRIES

To assist the Company in properly placing you if hired, please list any special skills, ability to speak/read a foreign language, training, licenses, certifications, or degrees that qualify you for the position for which you are applying. (Exclude all information that indicates your membership in any of the protected groups listed at the top of page 1 of this application.) Check the applicable response:

_____

If hired, can you furnish proof that you meet your state's minimum work age requirement?   Yes ☐ No ☐

If hired, can you furnish proof that you are legally entitled to work in the United States?   Yes ☐ No ☐

Answer the following, only if the position for which you are applying requires driving:

  Are you licensed to drive a car?   Yes ☐ No ☐

  If yes, which state(s)? _____

BEFORE answering the following questions, please refer to the instructions at the top of the next page if you are applying for a position in California, Connecticut, Georgia, Hawaii, Massachusetts, Nevada, or New York.

Have you been convicted of a crime within the last seven (7) years (answer "no" for expunged and sealed records, arrests, and minor traffic offenses)?   Yes ☐ No ☐

If yes, provide details: _____

(This information will be kept confidential. A conviction will not automatically bar employment, but will be considered as it relates to the applicant's suitability for the job in question.)

about that background.[30] For example, in addition to asking about an applicant's college major, a biodata application might ask questions about which courses the applicant enjoyed most and why a particular field of study was chosen. As with weighted application blanks, responses to these questions are then studied to see if they differentiate between employees who have done well and those who have done poorly on the job. This information is then used to predict the performance of new applicants from their application blanks. Thus, in both cases, the organization is interested in determining if any of the information collected on application blanks can be used to provide direct predictions of performance on the job.

Employment Tests

Another popular selection technique used by many organizations is an **employment test**,[31] or a device for measuring the characteristics of an individual. These characteristics may include personality, intelligence, or aptitude. Although employment tests are generally traditional question-and-answer exercises that applicants complete on paper or online, the courts consider any device used to make an employment decision, including interviews, to be a test. Typically, though, employment tests per se are either on paper or computer administered. For a paper test, the organization scores the employment test itself or sends it to the agency from which it acquired the test for scoring. For a computer-administered test, the applicant sits at a computer and enters answers to questions using the keyboard or mouse. Exhibit 7.5 shows samples from several popular employment tests.

Different types of employment tests are commonly used. Before identifying them, however, we want to distinguish aptitude tests from achievement tests. These terms often refer to how the test is used rather than the nature of the test. Aptitude tests focus on predicting future performance, and achievement tests focus on the mastery of some set of learned skills. For example, keyboarding tests are usually seen as achievement tests because they focus on whether an applicant has basic proficiency or mastery in using a keyboard. Cognitive ability tests are

is used reflects a cognitive ability, and being able to use the tool is a psychomotor ability (which we discuss later). Intelligence is an extremely important cognitive ability. General intelligence, or g, refers to reasoning, or problem-solving skills, but it is typically measured in terms of the information one learns in school. The Scholastic Aptitude Test (SAT) is a test of general intelligence. Scores on these tests can be expressed in terms of intelligence quotient (IQ). The way these quotients are computed is beyond the scope of this discussion, but it reflects performance on a test relative to other people of the same age.

Two important facts make the use of intelligence tests in selection controversial. First, IQ is related to performance on a wide variety of jobs because more intelligent people perform better.[32] This feature makes the use of intelligence tests in selection procedures popular and is consistent with the ideas discussed earlier about the value of a more educated workforce. The second fact is that, on average, African Americans tend to score lower on these tests than do white Americans. Therefore, using intelligence tests as selection criteria will likely result in disparate impact. Many explanations have been offered about why these differences exist and what they should mean for selection.[33] Among the most common explanations are bias in test construction and fundamental cultural differences that result in different frames of reference. The key point vis-à-vis our discussion is simply that intelligence tests are potentially useful but controversial tests of a special cognitive ability.

> ## Using intelligence tests as selection criteria will likely result in disparate impact.

seen as aptitude tests because they focus on the question of whether the person will be able to perform some specific task in the future.

Cognitive ability tests measure mental skills. The applicant is not required to do anything physical, only to demonstrate some type of knowledge. Therefore, knowing how a specific tool

Other cognitive abilities include vocabulary and reading comprehension (verbal ability) and mathematics (quantitative ability), clerical ability (such as the ability to put names in alphabetical order and to recognize when two names are alike or different from each other), and spatial relations (defined earlier). These cognitive abilities are important for performance on a wide variety of jobs, and they are widely used in selection settings. As noted earlier, auto manufacturers are seeking to improve the general intelligence of their workers. Ford and Chrysler both now

An employment test is a device for measuring the characteristics of an individual such as personality, intelligence, and aptitude.

Cognitive ability tests measure mental skills.

EXHIBIT 7.5 Sample Items from an Employment Test

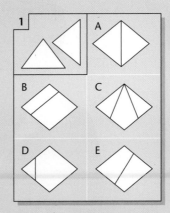

For each item, the subject must choose the figure that would result if the pieces in the first section were assembled.

Sample Items from the Revised Minnesota Paper Form Board.

When the two numbers or names in a pair are <u>exactly the same</u>, make a check mark on the line between them.

66273894	_____	66273984
527384578	_____	527384578
New York World	_____	New York World
Cargill Grain Co.	_____	Cargil Grain Co.

Sample Items from the Minnesota Clerical Test.

A   **B**

X Which room has more of an echo?

A   **B**

Y Which would be the better shears for cutting metal?

Sample Items from the Bennet Mechanical Comprehension Test.

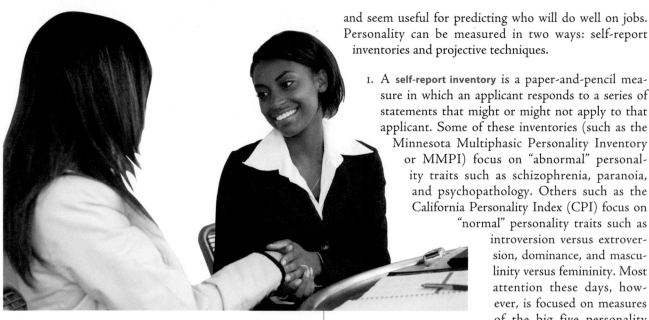

and seem useful for predicting who will do well on jobs. Personality can be measured in two ways: self-report inventories and projective techniques.

1. A **self-report inventory** is a paper-and-pencil measure in which an applicant responds to a series of statements that might or might not apply to that applicant. Some of these inventories (such as the Minnesota Multiphasic Personality Inventory or MMPI) focus on "abnormal" personality traits such as schizophrenia, paranoia, and psychopathology. Others such as the California Personality Index (CPI) focus on "normal" personality traits such as introversion versus extroversion, dominance, and masculinity versus femininity. Most attention these days, however, is focused on measures of the big five personality variables so that instruments such as the Personnel Characteristics Inventory[34] are becoming very popular.

2. The other type of personality measure is known as a **projective technique.** This approach involves showing an individual an ambiguous stimulus such as an inkblot or a fuzzy picture and then asking what he or she "sees." Because nothing is actually represented, whatever the applicant reports is presumed to reflect his or her personality. The best-known projective technique is the Rorschach Inkblot Test, which requires trained clinicians to interpret the results.

rely on cognitive ability tests to assess basic reading and mathematical abilities.

Psychomotor ability tests measure physical abilities such as strength, eye–hand coordination, and manual dexterity. These abilities can be practiced and perfected, and the tests to measure them are usually some type of performance test. For example, the O'Connor Tweezer Dexterity Test requires an applicant to pick up and move small parts with a pair of tweezers (eye–finger coordination). (The popular children's game Operation requires the same essential skills as those tapped by this test.) Psychomotor tests are popular because they apparently measure what is important for performance on the job (human resource experts say that these tests have high "face validity"). In addition, they often measure skills that are important for jobs (e.g., eye–hand coordination is important for any job requiring someone to drive a vehicle), and little evidence of disparate impact occurs when they are used.

Personality tests measure traits, or tendencies to act, that are relatively unchanging in a person. Some tests are designed to measure a wide spectrum of personality traits or dimensions; as noted earlier, however, measures of the big five personality dimensions have become extremely popular in recent years

Personality tests are somewhat controversial. Some critics believe they can lead to legal problems,[35] whereas others disagree whether cognitive ability tests (especially intelligence tests) or personality tests provide the most useful information for selection decisions.[36] Regardless of the merits of these arguments, however, both personality and cognitive ability remain popular criteria in selection techniques, as do all employment tests in general.[37]

A somewhat different but related approach to testing prospective employees is the use of an integrity test. **Integrity tests** attempt to assess an applicant's moral character and honesty. Most of these tests are fairly straightforward and include questions such as "Do you think most people would cheat if they thought they could get away with it?" and "Have you ever taken anything that didn't belong to you at work?" Other tests are less obvious and are based more on personality measures. The use of integrity tests is growing dramatically, with several million administered annually in the United States.[38] The likelihood is that the number will continue to increase as the cost of employee theft rises.[39] Despite their popularity, however, there are important issues involved with their use in selection settings. First, most of the evidence about their accuracy has been supplied by the publishers of the tests, which

Psychomotor ability tests *measure physical abilities such as strength, eye–hand coordination, and manual dexterity.*

Personality tests *measure traits, or tendencies to act, that are relatively unchanging in a person.*

A **self-report inventory** *is a paper-and-pencil measure in which an applicant responds to a series of statements that might or might not apply to him or her.*

The **projective technique** *involves showing an individual an ambiguous stimulus, such as an ink blot or a fuzzy picture, and then asking what he or she "sees."*

Integrity tests *attempt to assess an applicant's moral character and honesty.*

raises the possibility of conflict of interests. Second, these tests may do a good job of identifying potential "thieves," but many other individuals not identified by the tests steal and simply do not get caught. Finally, some applicants find these tests invasive and respond negatively to them.[40]

Work Simulations

Work simulations (sometimes referred to as **work samples**) require an applicant to perform tasks or job-related activities that simulate or represent the actual work for which the person is being considered. For example, suppose an organization needs to hire a new data-entry specialist. The organization has determined that the data-entry specialist must be proficient with Microsoft Office software and be capable of keyboarding seventy-five words a minute. A relatively easy method for assessing a candidate's qualifications, then, is to seat the individual at a computer, ask him or her to perform various data-entry tasks and activities using Microsoft Office software, and then keyboard a letter or document to measure how quickly the person can keyboard. Other jobs for which work simulations are appropriate might be machinist jobs in which an individual can work on a machine under close supervision, a driving test for taxi drivers or school-bus drivers, and an audition for a performing-arts organization such as a musical group. **In-basket exercises**, which consist of collections of hypothetical memos, letters, and notes that require prioritization and responses, are sometimes used as part of management simulations.

Personal Interviews

Although tests are popular, the most widely used selection technique in most organizations is the employment interview. *Interviews* are face-to-face conversations between prospective job applicants and representatives of the organization.[41]

Types of Interviews.
Not all interviews are the same, and we can think about three types of interviews that are commonly encountered: structured, semistructured, and unstructured interviews.

1. In a **structured employment interview**, the interviewer either prepares or is given a list of standard questions by others to be asked during the interview. All interviewers ask the same questions of each candidate to achieve consistency across interviews. Also, because the questions are presumably prepared based on a careful study of the job, they are more pertinent than those that many interviewers would generate on their own. In some cases, after the questions are determined, potential answers are also devised and given scores so that the interviewer can assign overall grades based on a scoring key.
2. The **semistructured employment interview** involves advance preparation of major or key questions to be asked. This method provides a common frame of reference for all people who are interviewed for a job and

requires that they all answer a predetermined set of specific questions. However, the interviewer is also given the prerogative to ask additional follow-up questions to probe specific answers that the interviewee provides, and so forth. For example, a popular strategy used in some firms today, especially high-tech firms, is to ask challenging and unusual questions designed to assess creativity and insight. For example, Microsoft interviewers sometimes ask applicants "Why are manhole covers round?" This question has four different, relatively correct answers, each of which allows the interviewer to probe more in different areas.[42]

3. The **unstructured employment interview** involves relatively little advance preparation. The interviewer may have a general idea about what she or he wants to learn about the job applicant but has few or no advance questions that are formally constructed and ready to be asked. Thus, the interview is likely to be more spontaneous, to be more wide ranging in its focus, and to cover a wide variety of topics.

In addition to these basic types, another form of interview has been gaining popularity. A **situational interview** asks the applicant questions about a specific situation to see how he or she would react. For example, an interviewer might ask the applicant something like:

■ Think back to a situation when a personal conflict between a supervisor and a subordinate was interfering with the work of both parties. How did you deal with this conflict? Was the problem resolved?

In other cases, rather than ask about something that has already happened, the interviewer might ask the applicant to imagine a situation that has not yet occurred. In such cases, the interviewer might ask something like:

- Suppose you had a subordinate who you knew had the abilities to perform his or her job but who simply chose not to exert any effort on the job. How would you approach this problem? What kinds of approaches might you try?

Research results indicate that situational interviews are better predictors of future job performance than are more traditional interviews.[43] They also change the focus of the interview more explicitly from a KSA approach to a job-fit approach.

Interviewers generally prefer unstructured interviews because they believe these interviews allow them to gather richer information and provide the freedom to make employment decisions on their own. But evidence suggests that structured interviews are much better predictors of subsequent job performance (i.e., they are more valid or job related) than are unstructured interviews, and situational interviews are even better at predicting future job performance.[44] None of them do as well predicting future performance as some paper-and-pencil tests, but only interviews are effective at assessing KSAs such as interpersonal skills, and interviews are generally effective at allowing organizations to decide who fits best in the organization.

For these and other reasons, interviews will continue to be a popular means for making selection decisions. Note, however, that the Supreme Court, in *Watson* v. *Forth Worth Bank*, ruled that interviews used for making selection decisions had the same requirements concerning demonstrating job relatedness as did any other selection technique.[45] As we noted earlier, however, it is more difficult to establish the job relatedness of interviews, partly because of the prevalence of interview errors.

1. Interviewers who make the **first-impression error** tend to make a decision early in the interview process.[46] For example, the candidate being interviewed might arrive a minute or two late or might have a few awkward moments at the beginning of the interview. Such events, in turn, may cause the interviewer to make a negative judgment about that individual, even though later evidence in the interview may have been more positive.

2. The **contrast error** occurs when the interviewer is unduly influenced by other people who have been interviewed. For example, suppose an interviewer meets with one candidate who is extremely good or extremely bad. The next person interviewed may suffer or benefit by the contrast with this person.

3. **Similarity errors**, on the other hand, occur when the interviewer is unduly influenced by the fact that the interviewee is similar to the interviewer in one or more important ways. For example, an interviewer might be biased in favor of someone because he or she is from the same hometown or attended the same university.

4. Another type of error interviewers can make is that of **nonrelevancy**. For example, the interviewer may be inappropriately influenced by an individual's posture, dress, or appearance.

5. A final type of error that is common in interview situations has to do with the interviewer's knowledge of the job. Some organizations do not pay adequate attention to selecting appropriate interviewers. They may select employees to interview candidates for a particular job even though the interviewers know little or nothing about that job. Thus, the interviewer may base her or his assessment of the individual's abilities to perform the job on incomplete or inaccurate assessments of the nature of that job.

These problems exist in all interviews to a greater or lesser extent. Their effects can be minimized, however, with proper training of interviewers. Experience itself is not a good substitute for training, and this training should focus on the occurrence of the problems outlined above, making the interviewer aware of what he or she says and does. In addition, the training should provide interviewers with the means to replace behaviors that lead to errors with behaviors more likely to lead to their deciding on the best person for the job.

Other Selection Techniques

Application blanks, tests, and interviews are part of most selection systems, but these techniques are often enhanced by several other techniques that are part of the selection process.

References and Recommendations. One of these other techniques is the use of references and recommendations. The job applicant is usually asked to provide either letters of recommendation or the names and addresses of individuals who may be contacted to write such letters. Presumably, the organization can use this information as a basis for knowing about a person's past experiences and work history. References and recommendations, however, are often of little real value. If a job applicant selects the people to write recommendations, then she is likely to pick people who will write positive letters of recommendation. For example, a student is more likely to ask a professor who gave him an A for a recommendation than a professor who gave him a D. Likewise, a former boss who gave the individual high performance evaluations is a more likely reference than a former boss who gave the individual average or below-average recommendations. Thus, the organization must be somewhat skeptical about a set of glowing recommendation letters that a job applicant submits for consideration.

There is also a growing concern about legal liability in the preparation of recommendation letters. Job applicants have sued people who wrote negative letters of recommendation that were, in turn, the bases for the individuals not then being offered employment. Organizations themselves have sued people who wrote favorable recommendations

based on measuring and evaluating their ability to perform critical work behaviors. Individuals participating in an assessment center are likely to be either current managers who are being considered for promotion to higher levels or a pool of external recruits such as upcoming college graduates whom the firm is considering hiring for management positions.

The individuals to be assessed are brought together in a single place such as the company's training headquarters or perhaps a conference facility at a hotel. While there, they undergo a series of tests, exercises, and feedback sessions. A normal assessment-center schedule lasts 2 to 3 days and involves 10 to 15 individuals at any one time. During the assessment-center schedule, these individuals may undergo experiential exercises; group decision-making tasks; case analyses; individual employment tests, such as personality inventories and so forth; role-playing exercises; and other methods for assessing their potential skills and abilities. Current managers oversee the assessment and serve as evaluators. At the conclusion of the assessment center, each evaluator provides an in-depth evaluation of each person attending the assessment center and makes an overall evaluation about the person's suitability for promotion.

AT&T was one of the first companies in the United States to use the assessment-center concept, and since 1956 more than 200,000 of its employees have attended various assessment centers. AT&T's evaluation of its assessment centers indicates that this method for selecting managers is a fairly effective technique for differentiating between those who are more and those who are less likely to be successful in the organization. This suggests that assessment centers

> *Almost all of the 100 best companies to work for in America (as determined by Fortune magazine), ranging from Southwest Airlines to The Container Store, rely heavily on multiple predictors when making hiring decisions.*

for job candidates who were then found to be highly unsuitable. As a result of these legal concerns, many individuals have begun to take the position that they will provide only objective information about a job candidate as part of a reference letter. Thus, they might be willing to verify dates of employment, salary, history, job title, and so forth, but they may be unwilling to provide any assessment regarding the person's performance, capabilities, or the likelihood for success in a new setting.[47]

Assessment Centers. Another selection technique that is used widely, but only for the selection of managers, is the assessment center.[48] An assessment center is not a physical location but is instead an approach to selecting managers

may be quite useful, but there are some disadvantages as well. The most critical is that assessment centers are rather expensive to run, especially when we consider the lost productivity of both the candidates and the assessors.[49]

THE SELECTION DECISION

The final step in the process is to make the actual decision about whom to hire. If there is only one position to fill, the decision is relatively easy: The organization can simply hire the highest-ranked candidate. Likewise, if there is a need to hire dozens of employees for similar kinds of positions, the selection decision may simply consist of choosing where to draw the line between those who qualify for employment and those who do not.

Multiple Indicators

Because every selection technique has its limitations, most organizations actually rely on several selection techniques and, in fact, may use all or most of the selection techniques discussed earlier. Hence, a person who applies for a job may be subjected to a preliminary screening interview to make sure that she meets the minimum qualifications necessary for the job. Then she may have to complete an application and be subjected to background checks, followed by employment tests, or work simulations, or both. For example, almost all of the 100 best companies to work for in the United States (as determined by *Fortune* magazine), ranging from Southwest Airlines to The Container Store, rely heavily on multiple predictors when making hiring decisions.[50]

By using multiple approaches, the organization is able to counterbalance the measurement error in one selection technique against another, and it is also able to base decisions on the basis of more complete information. This fact can complicate matters, however. The organization must decide if a candidate must pass some minimum requirement on every selection technique (i.e., "multiple hurdles") or if a high score in one area can compensate for a lower score somewhere else (i.e., a compensatory model). Thus, when an organization uses multiple approaches, it is not always clear who the "best" candidate really is.

The hiring decision may also be complicated by the fact that the person hired may not be the one who is ranked first on the selection criteria. As noted earlier, an organization might select a person who has "acceptable" levels of the requisite KSAs but who is a better "fit" with the culture and style of the organization. Furthermore, it is fairly common for organizations to cluster applicants who may differ somewhat in terms of KSAs but who do not differ enough from one another to be critical. Thus, the organization could use any decision rules it wished to select among the people in such a cluster without sacrificing performance on the job. This procedure, known as *banding*, allows an organization to select an applicant, for example, from some underrepresented group in the organization while still ensuring high performance standards. A variation on this approach can also be used to ensure that candidates selected because they fit can also perform the jobs in question. Finally, as discussed in HR in the Twenty-First Century, even when the preferred candidate has been selected some organizations may use even more procedures to verify the person's job worthiness before a final offer is made.

False positives *are applicants who are predicted to be successful and are hired but who ultimately fail.*

False negatives *are applicants who are predicted to fail and are not hired, but if they had been hired, they would have been successful.*

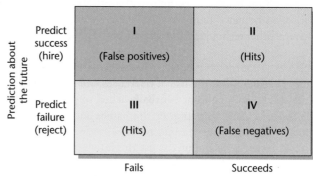

EXHIBIT 7.6 Selection Errors

Prediction about the future

Predict success (hire): I (False positives) | II (Hits)

Predict failure (reject): III (Hits) | IV (False negatives)

Actual future performance: Fails | Succeeds

Selection Errors

No selection system is perfect, and an organization will always make at least an occasional selection error and hire the wrong person. Actually, two basic types of selection errors can be made: **false positives** and **false negatives**. In each case, the decision maker examines the information available, predicts whether the applicant will ultimately succeed or fail on the job, and then decides to hire or reject (not hire) the person on that basis. In each case, some of the predictions are correct and others are incorrect; these situations are illustrated in Exhibit 7.6.

The exhibit shows that some of the people who are predicted to be successful and hired will in fact succeed. These are "hits" (shown in quadrant II) because the right decision was made. The bottom left quadrant (quadrant III) also shows hits. These people are rejected; if they were hired, they would fail. But the other two quadrants illustrate the two types of selection errors. Quadrant I represents the false positives: the applicants who are predicted to be successful and who are therefore hired, but who ultimately fail. Quadrant IV represents the false negatives: the applicants who are predicted to fail and so are not hired. If they had been hired, however, they would have been successful.

It would seem obvious that selection systems that minimize selection errors will be more effective for the organization, but it is not possible to minimize both types of errors at the same time, and so decisions must be made concerning which type of decision is more costly for the organization. Specifically, it is possible to minimize the number of poor performers that are hired by using more rigorous tests or more challenging interviews to make selection decisions. Indeed, the organization may set its standards for selection so high that it might rarely hire anyone who fails. But if decisions are based on more and more stringent criteria, then there will also be fewer people hired overall, and the organization will miss opportunities by rejecting people who could have done the job and been successful. Again, it depends on which error the organization sees as more costly. The information in Exhibit 7.6 also provides some insight into the issue of *test validity*, discussed more fully in the next section. If a test is valid, then there should be many more "hits"

When an organization has effectively used its choice of selection techniques to identify the best candidate for the job, it might still elect to use additional procedures before extending a final job offer to the individual. And as the world of business grows more and more complex, so too does the array of postselection procedures grow. For the most part, once a person has been selected, the formal offer might include language such as "This offer is contingent upon . . ." one or more of the following.

Physical Exam. If a job requires heavy lifting, for example, the firm may want to ensure that the prospective employee does not have any preexisting conditions or unacceptable weaknesses that might result in an injury. For instance, prospective employees for a Home Depot distribution center are checked to make sure they can safely lift heavy boxes and can spend much of their workday walking on hard surfaces.

Background Check. Some organizations want to ensure that a prospective employee does not have a criminal record or a history of unsafe driving. Zales, a jewelry store chain, does not want to have someone who has been convicted of theft handling its diamonds and expensive watches. Likewise, UPS does not want to employ delivery truck drivers who have been guilty of multiple traffic accidents.

Emotional Stability. In some cases, a job may put an employee in a situation that creates unusual stress and strain. As a result, the organization may subject a prospective employee to a battery of psychology tests to ensure that the person can handle those elements of the job. U.S. research labs in the Arctic test prospective employees to make sure they can handle long periods of isolation and extreme weather conditions before deploying them. KBR, a large military contractor that runs U.S. military installations in foreign countries, uses tests to assess its potential new employees' readiness for long working hours in high-risk locations such as Iraq and Afghanistan.

For the most part, these and other new techniques are not used as part of the original selection process because of the time and expense required. Moreover, these techniques relate more to indirect rather than direct performance indicators, so firms typically use various traditional techniques such as tests and interviews to make a preliminary decision on who they want to hire. They then use these techniques as a final set of "checks" to ensure they have identified the person best suited for the job.

THINK IT OVER

1. Can you think of other postselection techniques that an organization might use?
2. How might reliability and validity issues differ between a preselection technique such as a test and a postselection such as a physical exam?

---

than errors. As noted, there are trade-offs between the types of errors we can make, but a test cannot be valid unless it predicts subsequent success more often than it misses.

RELIABILITY AND VALIDITY

Reliability and validity are concepts that are important for any psychological type of measurement and are especially important for establishing the "job relatedness" of a selection technique. Any organization that does not have information about the reliability and validity of its selection techniques is exposed to charges of discrimination, as described in Chapter 2. Specifically, if there is evidence of disparate impact, the organization must prove it is not discriminating by demonstrating that the selection technique is job related. In practice, this means demonstrating that the selection technique is a valid predictor of performance on the job. But even outside the United States, in countries where there might not be any civil rights legislation, it is important for firms to pay attention to issues of reliability and validity. As we discussed and illustrated in Exhibit 7.6, if the selection techniques result in too many errors, then it is not helping the organization and is probably not worth the cost, regardless of any legal requirements.

Reliability refers to the consistency of a particular selection device. Specifically, it means that the selection device measures whatever it is supposed to measure, without random error. Systematic error may be present, though, so reliability is not the same

> **Reliability** is the consistency of a particular selection device—that is, it measures whatever it is supposed to measure without random error; not the same as accuracy.

© AP Photo/Philip Scott Andrews

as accuracy. For example, if your true weight remained constant across 3 days at precisely 135 pounds but your bathroom scale indicated you weighed 137 pounds one day, 134 the next day, and 135 pounds the third day, you would have an unreliable scale. It is unreliable not because the scale is usually not accurate, but because the amount and direction of error are random—on the first day the error is +2 pounds, on the second day it is –1 pound, and on the third day the error is zero. If the scale indicated your weight was 2 pounds more than it actually was every single day, your scale would still be inaccurate, but now it would be reliable—it is always off by 2 pounds in the same direction. In fact, you could always learn your true weight by simply subtracting 2 pounds from the weight indicated on your scale.

No selection technique used today is perfectly reliable. Every one of them is prone to some degree of random error, but most professionally developed tests and selection devices have sufficient reliability to make any results obtained with their use interpretable. In other words, in the selection context, most measures are reliable enough that we can be sure that if Mary scores higher on an arithmetic test than John, Mary is better at arithmetic than John. We would be in a better position to determine how much better Mary is, the more reliable the test. Logically, if most of the differences in scores on a test resulted from random error (i.e., the test is not reliable), it cannot be valid because it obviously does not measure what it is supposed to measure—unless it was designed to measure random error!

The fact that a test is relatively free of random error should also indicate that the test can produce consistent scores. There are different ways of assessing reliability, depending on whether we are concerned with scores that are consistent over time (test–retest reliability); across different forms of the same test (alternate-forms reliability), such as the case with different forms of the SAT or Graduate Management Admission Test; or consistent across all the different items of the same test (internal consistency reliability—i.e., all the items on the test are measuring the same thing). We

discuss test reliability because reliability is a necessary but not sufficient condition for test validity.

Validity refers to the extent to which a measure or indicator is in fact a real reflection of what it is assumed to be. There are actually different forms of test validity, although one is far more important than the others in a selection setting. Therefore, we will focus on what is known as *criterion-related validity*. The other two—*content validity* and *construct validity*—are less relevant, although they can be helpful at times in selection settings.

Criterion-related validity refers to the extent to which a particular selection technique can accurately predict one or more elements of performance. Criterion-related validity is most typically demonstrated by establishing a correlation between a test or measured performance in a simulated work environment with measures of actual on-the-job performance. In this approach, the test or performance measure represents a predictor value variable, and the actual performance score itself is the criterion (there can be other criteria of interest in selection settings such as retention rates, but performance is the most commonly used). If this correlation is meaningful (i.e., statistically significant), then a relationship exists between test scores and performance, and the test is job related.

Different relationships, or correlations, are illustrated in Exhibit 7.7. The first diagram in the exhibit, labeled (a), illustrates a perfect positive correlation (+1.00), which means perfect prediction. If we were to superimpose the four quadrants from Exhibit 7.6 on this exhibit, we would see that we make *no* errors; that is, everyone whom we predict will succeed will be successful and everyone whom we predict will fail will fail. Exhibit 7.7 (b) also illustrates a perfect correlation, but this one is negative (–1.00). In this case, higher predictor scores predict lower performance and vice versa. Exhibit 7.7 (c) shows no correlation (0); in this case, there is no relationship whatsoever between the predictor and performance. Exhibits 7.7 (d) and (e) present positive correlations of different strength, with (d) being a better predictor than (e).

Because selection decisions are most closely related to criterion-related validity, it is worth noting factors that can influence the strength of the relationship between scores on a test and performance on the job—factors other than the idea that the test is simply not related to job performance.

1. As noted above, it is important that both the test and other selection device be reliable and that the measure of performance or success be reliable. Unfortunately,

Validity refers to whether an assessment tool measures what it is supposed to measure. Usually, in selection settings, this is determined empirically by means of criterion-related validity, and it is critical to defending against charges of discrimination in hiring.

Criterion-related validity is the extent to which a selection technique accurately predicts elements of performance. It is most typically demonstrated by establishing a correlation between a test or measured performance in a simulated work environment and measures of actual on-the-job performance.

EXHIBIT 7.7 Scatter Plots for Five Correlation Coefficients

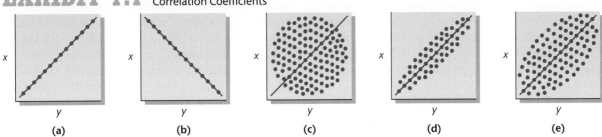

These diagrams illustrate correlations of 1.00 (a), −1.00 (b), zero (c), .80 (d), and .10 (e).

as we discussed earlier in this chapter, some commonly used selection techniques such as the interview are often not reliable; and, as we will discuss in Chapter 10, many measures of performance are also not reliable. Even in the case where a selection technique should be able to predict performance perfectly, if the technique does not use a reliable measure or if the measure of performance is not reliable, then the correlation we obtain will be much less than perfect (exactly how much less depends on how unreliable each measure actually is). If both measures are unreliable, then the resulting correlation will be quite low. As a result, HRM researchers are always looking for better potential predictors of job performance, as well as better measures of job performance itself.

2. Correlations between predictor scores and job performance will also be maximized if we have the complete range of both, scores on the predictor (selection technique), and scores on the criterion (job performance). But this requires hiring people, regardless of their scores on the predictor, and then keeping them employed long enough to collect performance data.

Although this is exactly what some firms do (by making selection decisions on the basis of something other than the predictors to be validated), this is a costly way to go about the validation process. Instead, many organizations attempt to validate selection techniques with their current employees (this is referred to as *concurrent validation*), giving the test or other selection technique to current employees, and then simply using their most recent performance appraisal as a measure of performance. Although cost-effective, this practice does have the effect of restricting the range of scores on both sides of the equation, and thus reducing the size of the obtained correlations.

LEGAL AND EFFECTIVENESS ISSUES IN RECRUITING AND SELECTION

Two final issues of importance for recruiting and selection are an awareness of legal issues and the importance of evaluating the effectiveness of these activities.

Legal Issues in Recruiting and Selection

The Civil Rights Act (and other nondiscrimination legislation) applies to all employment decisions, but this legislation is clearly most critical for selection decisions. We noted in Chapter 2 that an organization faced with a prima facie case of discrimination must prove that the basis for the selection decision was job related, and this is demonstrated by establishing the validity of a selection instrument as described above.[51] But as far back as the *Griggs* decision, the courts have become more insistent that validation studies should be conducted in order to be acceptable.[52] More recently, in *Ricci* v. *Stefano*, the Supreme Court reversed a lower court decisions and ruled that the City of New Haven could not throw out a test just because it would lead to decisions that would promote no minority firefighters. Thus, the Court has moved from imposing guidelines about how to validate

© Monti26/Shutterstock

tests to guidelines about how tests should be used. Even though the Ricci decision would seem to make it easier for companies to defend selection practices in some ways, it also indicates a willingness on the part of the court system to get quite involved in how tests are used in practice. This trend suggests that it will become even more important for HR managers to be familiar with the law and recent court decisions in guiding organizations in ways to select the best employees without violating the law.[53]

Evaluating Recruiting and Selection

Because recruiting and selection are such vital parts of the HRM process for most organizations, it stands to reason that the organization will periodically evaluate their effectiveness. As far as recruiting is concerned, an effective process is one that results in a reasonable pool of qualified employees who are available to the organization and from which the organization can hire people it wants to perform various jobs at a reasonable cost. Therefore, if the organization is having problems attracting qualified candidates or filling jobs, this would suggest that the recruiting process is not working. In addition, it is possible to assess the effectiveness of different recruiting sources the organization might be using in terms of providing successful employees who remain with the firm.[54]

There are also formal methods available for evaluating the success of the selection system, beyond detraining if the selection technique is job related. Most of these represent some variation on what is known as *utility analysis*. **Utility analysis** is an attempt to determine the extent to which a selection system provides real benefit to the organization. This method assesses the practical payoff for any selection system in terms of the percentage of selection decisions that are correct (or the "hit rate"; see earlier discussion about selection errors). The actual formulas for assessing utility are beyond the scope of the current discussion, but it is worth noting that an assessment of utility requires calculating the cost involved in improving the hit rate, and the benefit of that improved hit rate, as well as the costs of making selection errors. This allows an HR manager to show exactly how an improved selection system contributes to the bottom line.

> **Utility analysis** *is an attempt to determine the extent to which a selection system provides real benefit to the organization.*

CLOSING CASE

HIRING HIGH-RISK EMPLOYEES CAN PAY OFF FOR BUSINESS

When most people think of new employees starting to work for an organization, they probably imagine only the brightest, most highly motivated, and most upstanding and respectable applicants being chosen for employment. With surprising frequency, however, new employees may be former drug addicts, alcohol abusers, welfare recipients, and homeless people. What could prompt a business to hire from these ranks as it expands its workforce? The reasons run the gamut from absolute necessity to social conscience. Regardless of the organization's motive, however, many managers report that with a little extra attention and caution, new employees chosen from what might be considered high-risk labor pools can actually pay big dividends.

One example is Candleworks, a small candle-making company based in Iowa City, Iowa. The firm's owners, Lynette and Mike Richards, did not want to hire high-risk employees at first. Instead, they tried to follow the conventional wisdom of hiring only the best and the brightest. The problem, however, was that they simply could not find enough "qualified" workers from this pool who were interested in working long hours for relatively low wages. Unfilled jobs and high turnover eventually forced the owners to look elsewhere for employees; in near desperation, they took a big chance on hiring one applicant who was undergoing treatment for alcohol abuse.

As it turned out, because this employee had few other opportunities, he greatly valued his job and appreciated the trust placed in him by the couple. He eventually became a highly committed and valuable employee. Because of this positive experience, the Richardses subsequently began to recruit and hire high-risk employees systematically and routinely, and these individuals are now the foundation of the workforce at Candleworks.

Ken Legler, owner of Houston Wire Works, a Texas-based enterprise, has also experienced a major labor shortage. Legler's solution has been to tap into a works program sponsored by the Texas Department of Corrections. Depending on the situation, convicts may be bused to and from a work site, or work may instead be shipped to and from a prison. Convicts receive training in how to perform the necessary work and are paid (usually at the minimum wage rate) for their work.

Not all employers use high-risk employees purely out of necessity. For example, Microboard Processing, Inc. (MPI), a small New England electronics firm, makes giving troubled people a second chance a basic part of its business philosophy. MPI is owned and managed by Craig Hoekenga, who has always had a strong sense of social responsibility and believes that his best way of making a contribution to society is by offering second chances to high-risk employees.

Indeed, almost one-third of MPI's employees today might be classified as high-risk. They include former welfare recipients, people who have never held steady jobs, convicted felons, and former drug addicts. Hoekenga insists that at least 10 percent of the firm's new hires each year be from one of these high-risk categories. Although the firm also hires plenty of "conventional" employees—those with respectable backgrounds and solid work histories—Hoekenga considers his high-risk workers to be the backbone of the company.

For example, Ruth Tinney recently applied for employment at MPI. At the time of her application, she had not worked for several years and had spent the three previous years on welfare. Hoekenga gave her a 2-week trial, and now she has a regular position as an assembly-line worker. He can also point to numerous other success stories throughout his business, and he can describe many former employees who were essentially rehabilitated while working at MPI but who then left for other jobs—for advancement opportunities, relocation to other parts of the country, and so forth.

But not all of his new hires succeed, of course. He estimates that about two or three employees out of every ten he hires eventually fail. For example, one former drug addict who had worked at the firm for more than a year returned to drug abuse and went back to jail. Hoekenga points out that he has to give newly hired, high-risk employees time to learn the ropes. Many, for example, have never held a steady job and do not understand or appreciate the need for regular and prompt attendance. Consequently, they may come in late for work or not show up regularly. MPI thus allows them considerable latitude in absenteeism and tardiness during the first few weeks. Each instance of tardiness or absenteeism is followed by a conversation with Hoekenga or a supervisor. In these conversations, Hoekenga and his supervisors stress the need for punctual and regular work schedules and focus on the need for improvement. Their goal is to teach their high-risk employees proper work habits during the first 6 months of employment. After that time, the firm takes a much harder line and cuts people less and less slack. But the ones who make it feel an especially strong sense of loyalty to and appreciation for Hoekenga and his company and make enormous contributions to the firm's continuing profitability and growth.[55]

THINK IT OVER

1. What do you see as the major advantages and disadvantages of hiring high-risk employees?
2. What differences in employment strategies exist between firms such as Candleworks and MPI?
3. The examples cited in this case involve smaller businesses. How might a big corporation like IBM or Ford try to hire high-risk employees?

STUDY TOOLS

■ **Rip out the chapter review card located at the end of the book.**

■ **Review the valuable study tools located online at www.cengagebrain.com**

　■ **Review the Key Terms flashcards.**

　■ **Download audio and visual summaries to review on the go.**

　■ **Complete practice quizzes to prepare for the test.**

　■ **Play "Beat the Clock" and "QuizBowl" to master chapter concepts.**

　■ **Complete "Crossword Puzzle" to review key terms.**

　■ **Watch the chapter video for a real-life example of key concepts.**

CHAPTER 7

Managing A New

AND Diverse

WORKFORCE

THE MARQUIS MELTING POT

Diversity is a fact of life in organizations today. And even though diversity has many benefits, the potential it creates for conflict increases significantly. Different backgrounds, perspectives, customs, and values combine to make it ever more likely that people will disagree and see situations differently.

For example, take the Marriott Marquis Hotel in New York City's Times Square. The hotel employs approximately 1,700 people from more than 70 countries who speak at least 47 languages. One major reason for the hotel's diversity is its labor pool—the area is populated by a diverse set of immigrants, and these residents often apply for these kinds of jobs. But the hotel managers also strongly believe that the diverse workforce is an asset in part because it fits the multicultural clientele that frequents the hotel.

But managing the diversity at Marriott can be a challenge. For example, consider the case of Jessica Brown, an African American quality-assurance manager responsible for housekeeping. Brown says that when she rewards other African Americans, some of her Hispanic employees criticize her for playing favorites. But when she rewards the Hispanic employees, some African Americans accuse her of ignoring them.

Balancing religious preferences is also complicated. One manager, Victor Aragona, recently sought out a room attendant to fix an overflowing bathtub. The attendant was found prostrate on a towel in the housekeeper's closet bowing to Mecca and saying his daily Islamic prayers. Rather than disturb him, Aragona fixed the bathtub himself.

" [A]ll you can really do is hope [the resentment] goes away eventually. And it usually does."

—Cynthia Keating, Marriott manager[1]

LEARNING OBJECTIVES
After studying this chapter you should be able to:

LO1 Discuss the nature of diversity and distinguish between diversity management and equal employment opportunity

LO2 Identify and describe the major dimensions of diversity in organizations

LO3 Discuss the primary impact of diversity on organizations

LO4 Describe individual and organizational strategies and approaches to coping with diversity and discuss the multicultural organization

LO5 Discuss the basic issues in managing the knowledge function in organizations

LO6 Relate human resource management to social issues

To help cope with these challenges, Marriott offers frequent training programs in multiculturalism and conflict management. These courses are required for all managers and are open to most nonmanagers as well. Even so, the hotel still finds it necessary to offer periodic and regular refresher courses to help people work together with a minimum of conflict.[2]

THINK IT OVER

1. Do you agree or disagree with the argument that diversity at the Marriott Marquis in New York gives the hotel a competitive advantage?
2. Besides hotels, what other service businesses are likely to have an especially diverse workforce? Why?

Managers at the Marriott Marquis Hotel face a complex set of challenges and opportunities. On the one hand, the diverse workforce they oversee poses far more complications and complexities than a more homogeneous one would present. On the other hand, the diverse workforce employed at the hotel also provides competitive advantages and opportunities to cater more effectively to the multinational clientele that frequents the area. Balancing the complications and the benefits of diversity is among the most important workplace issues facing most managers and their organizations today.

This chapter is primarily about workforce diversity in organizations. Other new challenges also face organizations today, and some of these will be addressed here as well. We begin by exploring the meaning and nature of diversity. We distinguish between diversity management and equal employment opportunity. Next we identify and discuss several common dimensions of diversity. The impact of diversity on the organization is explored. We address how diversity can be managed for the betterment of both individuals and organizations, and we describe the fully multicultural organization. We then turn to some other types of challenges. One of these is managing knowledge in organizations, so we will discuss issues involving managing knowledge workers. Finally, we will turn to concerns over social issues in today's organizations. We will discuss challenges involved with managing human resources while trying to address social concerns, including some discussion of human resource management and social entrepreneurship,

THE NATURE OF WORKFORCE DIVERSITY

Workforce diversity has become an important issue in many organizations in the United States and abroad. A logical starting point in better understanding this phenomenon is establishing the meaning of the word *diversity* and then examining why such diversity is increasing today.

Diversity exists in a group or organization when its members differ from one another along one or more important dimensions.

The Meaning of Workforce Diversity

Diversity exists in a group or organization when its members differ from one another along one or more important dimensions.[3] If everyone in the group or organization is exactly like everyone else, no diversity exists. But if everyone is different along every imaginable dimension, then total diversity exists. In reality, of course, these extremes are more hypothetical than real; most settings are characterized by a level of diversity somewhere between. Thus, diversity is not an absolute phenomenon wherein a group or organization is or is not diverse. Instead, diversity should be conceptualized as a continuum and thought of in terms of degree or level of diversity along relevant dimensions.[4]

These dimensions of diversity might include gender, age, and ethnic origin, among many others. A group composed of five middle-aged white male U.S. executives has relatively little diversity. If one member leaves and is replaced by a young white female executive, then the group becomes a bit more diverse. If another member is replaced by an older African American executive, then diversity increases a bit more. And when a third member is replaced by a Japanese executive, the group becomes even more diverse.

Trends in Workforce Diversity

As we noted earlier, organizations today are becoming increasingly diverse along many different dimensions. Several different factors have accounted for these trends and changes. Changing demographics in the labor force is one such factor. As more women and minorities have entered the labor force, for example, the available pool of talent from which organizations hire employees has changed in both size and composition. If talent within each segment of the labor pool is evenly distributed (for example, if the number of talented men in the workforce as a percentage of all men in the workforce is the same as the number of talented women in the labor force as a percentage of all women in the workforce), then it follows logically that proportionately more women and fewer men will be hired over time by an organization compared to the employees who were hired in the past.

A related factor that has contributed to diversity has been the increased awareness by organizations that they can improve the overall quality of their workforce by hiring and promoting the most talented people available regardless of gender, race, or any other characteristics. By casting a broader net in recruiting and looking beyond traditional sources for new employees, organizations are

published by the Department of Immigration (part of the Department of Homeland Security), in 2005 (the last year for which complete data were available) more than 1 million Mexican nationals were in the United States illegally, followed by almost 30,000 people from Central America and slightly more than 3,000 from Asia (out of a total of 1.1 million illegal immigrants total). In May 2006, then-President Bush proposed a "guest worker" program along with guidelines for how immigrants living illegally in the United States could gain legal immigrant status. Debate continues over what to do about this problem, but it is clear that managing diversity will become even more important to

> **Diversity can provide an organization with a competitive advantage because it hires and promotes the most talented people available regardless of gender, race, or any other characteristic.**

finding more broadly qualified and better qualified employees from many different segments of society. Thus, these organizations are finding that diversity can be a source of competitive advantage.

Another reason for the increase in diversity has been legislation and legal actions that have forced organizations to hire more broadly. Organizations in the United States were once free to discriminate against women, African Americans, and other minorities. Thus, most organizations were dominated by white males. Over the last 30 years or so, however, various laws have outlawed discrimination against these and other groups. As we detailed in Chapter 2, organizations must hire and promote people today solely on the basis of their qualifications.

A final contributing factor to increased diversity in organizations has been the globalization movement. Organizations that have opened offices and related facilities in other countries have had to learn to deal with different customs, social norms, and mores. Strategic alliances and foreign ownership have also contributed because managers today are more likely to have job assignments in other countries or to work with foreign managers within their own countries. As employees and managers move from assignment to assignment across national boundaries, organizations and their subsidiaries within each country become more diverse. Closely related to this pattern is a recent increase in immigration into the United States. As illustrated in Exhibit 8.1, for example, immigration declined steadily from 1900 until around 1930 but has been increasing since that time, except for a slight dip in the last decade.

As a result of recent trends, immigration has become a hot issue in the United States. According to statistics

organizations in the coming years regardless of what legislation the U.S. government eventually passes.

Diversity Management Versus Equal Employment Opportunity

Many managers assume that diversity and equal employment opportunity are the same. In fact, they have completely different meanings. **Equal employment opportunity** means treating people fairly and equitably and taking actions that do not discriminate against people in protected classes on the basis of some illegal criterion. But **diversity management** places a much heavier emphasis on recognizing and appreciating differences among people at work and attempting to provide accommodations for those differences to the extent that is feasible and possible.

Similarities Among People at Work. Regardless of how different people appear to be, almost all employees share some fundamental similarities.[5] For example, most people work to satisfy some set of needs that almost always have financial bases. Most people have a basic desire to be treated with respect and dignity by their employer. And most people have a capacity for being reasonable and understanding when confronted with reasonable behavior by others.

Equal employment opportunity *means treating people fairly and equitably and taking actions that do not discriminate against people in protected classes on the basis of some illegal criterion.*

Diversity management *places a much heavier emphasis on recognizing and appreciating differences among people at work and attempting to provide accommodations for those differences to the extent that is feasible and possible.*

EXHIBIT 8.1 Immigration Trends into the United States

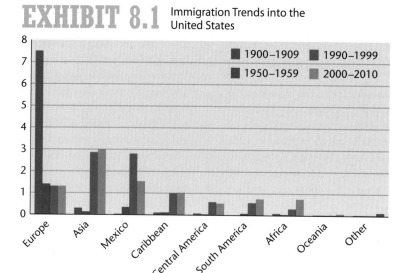

Legend: 1900–1909, 1990–1999, 1950–1959, 2000–2010

Categories: Europe, Asia, Mexico, Caribbean, Central America, South America, Africa, Oceania, Other

Series1

Categories: 1820–1829, 1840–1849, 1860–1869, 1880–1889, 1990–1909, 1920–1929, 1940–1949, 1960–1969, 1980–1989, 2000–2008

Sources: Office of Immigration Statistics, 2008 Yearbook of Immigration Statistics, August 2009; Modified from www.dhs.gov/xlibrary/assets/statistics/yearbook/2008/ois_yb_2008.pdf; Bureau of Labor Statistics, Census of Fatal Occupational Injuries, 2008.

Differences Among People at Work. Although many people share some basic set of similar characteristics, they also display various fundamental differences, a topic that will be discussed more fully in the next major section of the chapter. Common differences include gender, ethnicity, and age. But the list of differences among individuals is much longer and ranges from religious beliefs to dietary preferences to political philosophies.

Identical Treatment Versus Equitable Treatment. In the years immediately after Title VII of the 1964 Civil Rights Act was passed, many human resource (HR) managers operated under the assumption that they were required by law to treat everyone equally. In reality, that assumption is neither the intent of the law nor even truly possible. The real essence not only of Title VII but also of the more contemporary perspective on workforce diversity is that it is appropriate to acknowledge differences among people as long as people are treated fairly.

Consider religion, for example. A typical company in the United States routinely gives days off to employees for basic Christian holidays such as Christmas. But people who have different religious beliefs may not acknowledge the sanctity of these religious holidays and instead have different sets of days that they associate with strong religious beliefs. Thus, an employer who provides Christian holidays off should also be sensitive to the need to provide important religious holidays off for various employees of different beliefs and faiths. The Whirlpool appliance factory near Nashville, Tennessee, for example, employs about 200 Muslims (about 10 percent of its workforce). The factory found it necessary to adjust its work schedules, cafeteria menus, and dress codes to accommodate workers who pray several times a day, do not eat pork, and wear loose-fitting clothing, head coverings, and sandals.[6]

Men and women are also fundamentally different in various ways that cannot be ignored. On average, men have greater muscle mass than do women and can therefore lift heavier weight. And women have the biological capacity to bear children. Consequently, men and women may need fundamentally different treatment in work organizations. For example, women may need to be given longer periods of time off during the time immediately preceding and after the birth of a child. When a woman chooses to return to work after birth, the organization may need to provide a transitional period during which her work-related demands are lessened at first but then gradually increased over time.

The Americans with Disabilities Act (ADA) presents a serious challenge to managers who try to balance treating everyone the same with treating everyone equitably. The ADA specifically states that an organization cannot discriminate against a person with a disability as long as he or she can perform the essential functions of the job *with* or *without a reasonable accommodation*. Therefore, requested employee accommodations must be addressed. At first glance, this situation may not appear problematic because the employee presumably needs this accommodation to perform his or her job. Many of the accommodations requested and granted such as large-print computer screens, allowances for guide dogs, wheelchair ramps, and amplified phones do not present a problem.

But what about an accommodation requested by a person with a disability that would be desirable or useful to other employees who do not have a disability? An interesting example of this dilemma occurred about 10 years ago when the Professional Golf Association ruled that Casey Martin, whose serious leg problems made walking a golf course dangerous, would be allowed to use a golf cart in tournament play. Although there was disagreement over exactly how much of a difference this accommodation would make, many other golfers claimed that if they too were allowed to ride around the course, they would be less tired and so would play better. In this case, other golfers not only wanted the same accommodation that had been granted to Martin but also felt that it gave him an unfair competitive advantage.

Although Martin's case may be a particularly dramatic example of the problem, we can easily imagine other accommodations requested by a person with a disability that also would be valued by other employees or that other employees might perceive the accommodation as providing an unfair advantage. Even in classroom settings, students often perceive it as unfair when a student with a disability is granted extra time for a test. Co-worker resentment over the granting of accommodations can be a problem for all concerned. For the able-bodied employee, these accommodations may be perceived as unjust, leading to dissatisfaction on the job. For the disabled employee, the anticipated

resentment may discourage him or her from asking for the accommodation needed to perform the job effectively. The manager's perspective, of course, focuses on the problem of balancing the concerns of the different parties.[7]

Again, the important message is for managers to recognize that differences among people exist. It is important first to acknowledge the differences and then to make reasonable accommodation to deal with these differences. The key issue, however, is to make sure that the acknowledgment and the accommodation are equitable: Everyone needs to have an equal opportunity to contribute to and advance within the organization.

DIMENSIONS OF DIVERSITY

As indicated earlier, many different dimensions of diversity can be used to characterize an organization. In this section, we discuss age, gender, ethnicity, disability, and other dimensions of diversity.

Age Distributions

One key dimension of diversity in any organization is the age distribution of its workers.[8] The average age of U.S. workers is gradually increasing and will continue doing so for the next several years. Several factors contribute to this pattern. The baby boom generation (the unusually large number of people who were born in the 20-year period following World War II) continues to age. Declining birthrates among the post–baby boom generations simultaneously account for smaller percentages of new entrants into the labor force. Another factor that contributes to workforce aging is improved health and medical care: As a result, people can remain productive and active for longer periods of time. Combined with higher legal limits for mandatory retirement, more and more people are working beyond the age at which they might have retired just a few years ago.

How does this trend affect human resource management? Older workers tend to have more experience, may be more stable, and can make greater contributions to productivity. On the other hand, despite improvements in health and medical care, older workers are nevertheless likely to require higher levels of insurance coverage and medical benefits. As shown in Exhibit 8.2, accident rates are substantially higher for older workers workers up to age 54. In most years, accident rates continue to increase; however, for the year shown (2005) accident rates actually dropped a bit for workers 55 and older. Further, the overall number of retirees combined with fewer younger

© Torian/Shutterstock

EXHIBIT 8.2 Age and Accident Rates

Source: Bureau of Labor Statistics, Household Data Annual Averages, January 2010.

members of the workforce may lead to future labor shortages, even though some workers are staying in the workforce longer.

Gender

As more and more females have entered the workforce, organizations have subsequently experienced changes in the relative proportions of male to female employees. Exhibit 8.3 highlights these trends in gender composition (as well as ethnicity) in the workplace. Census data indicate that in 2010 women constituted 47.9 percent of the workforce, up from 45.2 percent in 1990 and 46.6 percent in 2000.

These trends aside, a significant gender-related problem that many organizations face today is the so-called **glass ceiling**, which was introduced in Chapter 5. The term describes a real and subtle but nonphysical barrier that keeps many females from advancing to top management positions in many organizations. Although women make up almost 50 percent of all managers, female chief executive officers (CEOs) head only 10 of the 500 largest businesses in the United States. Similarly, the average pay of females in organizations is lower than that of males. Although the pay gap is gradually shrinking, inequalities are still present.

Why does the glass ceiling exist? One reason is that some male managers are still reluctant to promote female managers. Another is that many talented women choose to leave their jobs in larger organizations and start their own businesses. And some women choose to suspend or slow their career progression to have children.

Ethnicity

A third major dimension of cultural diversity in organizations is **ethnicity**, or the ethnic composition of a group or organization. Within the United States, most organizations reflect varying degrees of ethnicity and are composed of whites, African Americans, Hispanics, and Asian Americans. Exhibit 8.3 also shows the current ethnic composition of the U.S. workforce.

The biggest changes, over the years, have involved whites and Hispanics. In particular, the percentage of whites in the workforce dropped to 69.2 percent in 2010, down from 73.1 percent in 2000 and 77.7 percent in 1990. Also, the percentage of Hispanics has climbed to 13.3 percent in 2010, up from 10.9 percent in 2000 and 8.5 percent in 1990. The percentage of African Americans has remained relatively stable (10.9 percent in 1990, 11.8 percent in 2000, and 12.7 percent in 2010), while Asian Americans and others represent 6.1 percent of the U.S. workforce in 2010, up from 4.7 percent in 2000 and 3.7 percent in 1990.

As with women, members of the African American, Hispanic, and Asian American groups are generally underrepresented in the executive ranks of most organizations today, as well as in several different occupational groups. Their pay also is lower than might be expected. As is the case for women, however, the differences are gradually disappearing as organizations fully embrace equal employment opportunity and recognize the higher overall level of talent available to them. Table 8.1 shows trends in different occupations for African Americans and Hispanics. For example, the percentage of African Americans and Hispanics comprises several different kinds of business roles plus various professional specialties and increased substantially from 1983 to 2002.

Disability

Disability is another significant dimension of diversity. Disabilities can range from hearing impairments to missing fingers or limbs, blindness, and paralysis. The presence of

The glass ceiling *describes a barrier that keeps many females from advancing to top management positions in many organizations.*

Ethnicity *refers to the ethnic composition of a group or organization.*

a disability represents another aspect of diversity in organizations, but among persons who have disabilities, some differences are important as well. Unlike other dimensions of diversity, reactions to persons with disabilities vary dramatically as a function of several dimensions of the disability. One of these dimensions is termed "origin"; that is, if the disability is perceived as being avoidable (for example, someone who has been injured while driving drunk), co-workers are likely to react more negatively to the disability than when the problem was unavoidable (for example, a person who was born blind).

A second dimension is the aesthetic aspect of the disability, with disabilities that are more disfiguring being perceived more negatively. A third and critical dimension refers to the nature of the disability itself. For example, although mental disabilities might be easier to conceal, they are also more frightening to co-workers. Disabilities related to stress or to back injuries are not as physically obvious and so, when individuals with these disabilities request and are granted an accommodation, resentment by co-workers is more likely.[9]

Other Dimensions of Diversity

In addition to age, gender, ethnicity, and disability status, organizations are also confronting other dimensions of diversity. One of these is sexual orientation. Only twenty of fifty U.S. states (and the District of Columbia) have laws protecting against discrimination on the basis of sexual orientation and sexual identity. In June 2009, Rep. Barney Frank (D-Massachusetts) introduced the Employment Non-Discrimination Act (ENDA) of 2009, which would have prohibited discrimination based on sexual orientation and gender identity at a federal level. The bill would have prohibited employers from making decisions about hiring, firing, promoting, or compensating an employee based on sexual orientation or gender identity. Regardless of the fate of that legislation (the bill did not pass but other, similar bills, will probably be proposed in

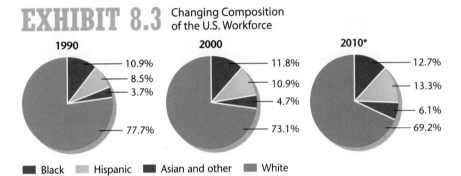

EXHIBIT 8.3 Changing Composition of the U.S. Workforce

1990 — 10.9% / 8.5% / 3.7% / 77.7%
2000 — 11.8% / 10.9% / 4.7% / 73.1%
2010* — 12.7% / 13.3% / 6.1% / 69.2%

■ Black   ■ Hispanic   ■ Asian and other   ■ White

The shifting racial and ethnic makeup of the U.S. workforce: number of workers by race and ethnic origin and their share of the total civilian labor force.

Numbers (thousands)	1990	2000	2010*	Percent	1990	2000	2010*
Total	125,840	140,863	157,721	Total	100.0	100.0	100.0
Men	69,011	75,247	82,221	Men	54.8	53.4	52.1
Women	56,829	65,616	75,500	Women	45.2	46.6	47.9
White, non-Hispanic	97,818	102,963	109,118	White, non-Hispanic	77.7	73.1	69.2
Men	53,731	55,359	57,538	Men	42.7	39.3	36.5
Women	44,087	47,604	51,580	Women	35.0	33.8	32.7
Black, non-Hispanic	13,740	16,603	20,041	Black, non-Hispanic	10.9	11.8	12.7
Men	6,802	7,816	8,991	Men	5.4	5.5	5.7
Women	6,938	8,787	11,050	Women	5.5	6.2	7.0
Hispanic origin	10,720	15,368	20,947	Hispanic origin	8.5	10.9	13.3
Men	6,546	8,919	11,723	Men	5.2	6.3	7.4
Women	4,174	6,449	9,224	Women	3.3	4.6	5.8
Asian and other, non-Hispanic	4,653	6,687	9,636	Asian and other, non-Hispanic	3.7	4.7	6.1
Men	2,572	3,570	5,070	Men	2.0	2.5	3.2
Women	2,081	3,116	4,566	Women	1.7	2.2	2.9

*Projection

Source: U.S. Department of Labor, Bureau of Labor Statistics, *Monthly Labor Review*, November 2001, http://www.bls.gov.

TABLE 8.1 Employment of African Americans and Hispanics in Selected Occupations, 1983, 2002, and 2008

	African Americans			Hispanics		
	1983	2002	2008	1983	2002	2008
Total workforce, ages 16 and older	9.3	10.9	11	5.3	12.2	14
Occupation						
Executive, administrative, and managerial	4.7	7.6	8.3	2.8	6.3	7.1
Officials and administrators in public administration	8.3	13	NA	3.8	7.6	NA
Financial managers	3.5	8.4	7.9	3.1	6.8	8.6
Personnel and labor-relations managers	4.9	8	NA	2.6	5.1	NA
Purchasing managers	5.1	6.6	12.9	1.4	4.7	3.7
Managers in marketing, advertising, and public relations	2.7	3.7	4.9	1.7	4.9	6.2
Managers in medicine and health care	5	9.5	10.1	2	6.2	7.3
Accountants and auditors	5.5	9	8.3	3.3	6	7.6
Management analysts	5.3	6.2	6.2	1.7	2.5	4.6
Professional specialty	6.4	8.3	9	2.5	5.3	6.7
Architects	1.6	2.3	3.3	1.5	5.2	8.2
Engineers	2.7	4.5	4.7	2.2	4	4.5
Mathematical and computer scientists	5.4	7.3	7.2	2.6	5.1	5.1
Natural scientists	2.6	4.1	7.1	2.1	2.9	4.7
Physicians	3.2	5	6.2	4.5	5.8	5.8
Dentists	2.4	4	3.3	1	3.3	5.2
College and university teachers	4.4	5.4	NA	1.8	5.4	NA
Economists	6.3	6.2	NA	2.7	4.6	NA
Psychologists	8.6	9.5	7.2	1.1	3.8	6.6
Lawyers	2.6	4.6	4.6	0.9	3.1	3.8
Authors	2.1	2.3	4.1	0.9	3.8	3.3
Musicians and composers	7.9	12.9	9.7	4.4	5.8	10.8
Editors and reporters	2.9	4.7	5.6	2.1	3.3	6.2

NA, not available.

Source: Modified from (www.bls.gov/cps/cpsaat11.pdf).

the future), diversity concerning sexual orientation and identity is an issue in the American workplace, and one that will become even more important as more Americans are willing to "come out of the closet" concerning their sexual orientations.

Most of the dimensions of diversity we have been discussing are of particular interest to Americans, but they may not be as critical to employers and employees around the world. Religious diversity is, of course, a more universal concern and, in recent years, one religious group has been the target of considerable discrimination

in many parts of the world, and so religion presents a special challenge for diversity. Ever since September 11, 2001, Americans and Europeans have become much more sensitized to religious differences, with special attention paid to Muslims. Estimates of the total number of Muslims in the world vary greatly, but at approximately 1.2 billion they represent about 22 percent of the world's population, second in number to Christians, who are 33 percent of the world's inhabitants.[10] Furthermore, Islam is growing about 2.9 percent per year, which is actually faster than the total world population, which increases about 2.3

percent annually. Clearly, Islam is attracting a progressively larger percentage of the world's population. Within the United States, estimates of the number of Muslims also vary, but there are probably close to 2 million Muslims in the United States, about 0.5 percent of the total population.

Unfortunately, much of the attention paid to and concern over the number of Muslims stems from fears about terrorism. All around the world, there are regular reports about extremist Muslim groups who plot and carry out terrorist attacks, and this leads to a concern that "all" Muslims are potential terrorists. Such a concern, of course, is baseless, but the fact remains that many people are becoming more guarded about interactions with Muslims and are more willing to discriminate against them. Of course, this is illegal in the United States, but recent attitudes about Muslims present new challenges for developing truly diverse workforces.

In addition to sexual orientation and religion, other dimensions of diversity are also relevant. For instance, single parents, people with special dietary preferences (e.g., vegetarians), and people with different political ideologies and viewpoints also represent meaningful dimensions of diversity in today's organizations.

THE IMPACT OF DIVERSITY ON ORGANIZATIONS

No doubt organizations are becoming ever more diverse. But what is the impact of this diversity on organizations? As we will see, diversity provides both opportunities and challenges and plays several important roles in organizations today.

Diversity and Social Change

Diversity can significantly affect an organization as a force for social change. This change generally occurs as the composition of an organization's workforce gradually begins to mirror the composition of the surrounding labor market. For example, if a manager in an organization learns to interact effectively with a diverse set of people at work, then she or he will be better equipped to deal with a diverse set of people in other settings. Conversely, an individual who is comfortable interacting in diverse settings should have little problem dealing with diversity at work. Thus, diversity in organizations both facilitates and is facilitated by social change in the environment.

Another way in which organizations affect social change is through the images they use to promote themselves and their products. An organization that runs print ads showing nothing but white male executives in its workplace conveys a certain image of itself. In contrast, an organization that uses diverse groups as representatives conveys a different image.

Diversity and Competitiveness

Many organizations are also finding that diversity can be a source of competitive advantage in the marketplace. In general, six arguments have been proposed for how diversity contributes to competitiveness.[11] These six arguments are illustrated in Exhibit 8.4.

1. The *cost argument* suggests that organizations that learn to cope with diversity will generally have higher levels of productivity and lower levels of turnover and absenteeism. Organizations that do a poor job of managing diversity, on the other hand, will suffer from problems of lower productivity and higher levels of turnover and absenteeism. Ortho Pharmaceuticals estimates that it has saved $500,000 by lowering turnover among women and ethnic minorities.

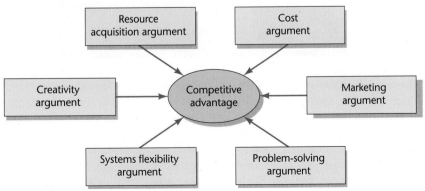

EXHIBIT 8.4 Diversity and Competitiveness

Source: Ricky W. Griffin, *Management*, 10th ed. (Cincinnati: Cengage, 2011), p. 180.

*(vertical text)* © Michael D Brown/Shutterstock

2. The *resource acquisition argument* for diversity suggests that organizations that manage diversity effectively will become known among women and minorities as good places to work. These organizations will thus be in a better position to attract qualified employees from among these groups. Given the increased importance of these groups in the overall labor force, organizations that can attract talented employees from all segments of society are likely to be more competitive.

3. The *marketing argument* suggests that organizations with diverse workforces will be able to understand different market segments better than will less diverse organizations. For example, a cosmetics firm such as Avon that wants to sell its products to women and African Americans can better understand how to create such products and market them effectively if women and African American managers are available to provide input into product development, design, packaging, advertising, and so forth.

4. The *creativity argument* for diversity suggests that organizations with diverse workforces will generally be more creative and innovative than will less diverse organizations. If an organization is dominated by one population segment, then its members will generally adhere to norms and ways of thinking that reflect that population segment. They will have little insight or few stimuli for new ideas that might be derived from different perspectives. The diverse organization, in contrast, will be characterized by multiple perspectives and ways of thinking and is therefore more likely to generate new ideas and ways of doing things.

5. Related to the creativity argument is the *problem-solving argument*. Diversity carries with it an increased pool of information. In almost any organization, there is some information that everyone has, and other information is unique to each individual. In an organization with little diversity, the larger pool of information is common, and the smaller pool is unique. But in a more diverse organization, the unique information is larger. Thus, if more information can be brought to bear on a problem, there is a higher probability that better solutions will be identified.[12]

6. Finally, the *systems flexibility argument* for diversity suggests that organizations must become more flexible as a way of managing a diverse workforce. As a direct consequence, the overall organizational system will also become more flexible. Organizational flexibility enables the organization to respond better to changes in its environment. Thus, by effectively managing diversity within its workforce, an organization simultaneously becomes better equipped to address its environment.[13] As we shall see below, however, the truth is a bit more complex than these arguments suggest.

Diversity and Conflict

Diversity in an organization can also become a major source of conflict for various reasons.[14] One potential avenue for conflict is when an individual thinks that someone has been hired, promoted, or fired because of her or his diversity status.[15] For example, suppose a male executive loses a promotion to a female executive. If he believes she was promoted because the organization simply wanted to have more female managers rather than because she was the better candidate for the job, then he will likely feel resentful toward her and the organization.

Conflict among whites and African Americans within the ranks of the Federal Aviation Administration (FAA) has been a recurring problem. Some blacks have charged that their white supervisors are prejudiced and that African Americans are subject to various subtle forms of discrimination. Some whites, however, believe that the government agency has hired some blacks who are not really qualified for the job of air traffic controller because the agency cannot attract a significant number of qualified employees.[16]

Another source of conflict stemming from diversity is through misunderstood, misinterpreted, or inappropriate interactions between or among people of different groups. For example, suppose a male executive tells a sexually explicit joke to a new female executive. He may

BLAST AREA STAND CLEAR

BLAST AREA STAND CLEAR

BLAST AREA STAND CLEAR

Diversity conflict has been a lingering problem in the Federal Aviation Administration (FAA).

intentionally be trying to embarrass her, he may be trying clumsily to show her that he treats everyone the same, or he may think he is making her feel like part of the team. Regardless of his intent, however, if she finds the joke offensive, she will justifiably feel anger and hostility. These feelings may be directed only at the offending individual or more generally toward the entire organization if she believes that its culture facilitates such behavior. Of course, sexual harassment itself is both unethical and illegal.

Firms that have resisted efforts to diversify their workforce often argue that a diverse workforce can hurt a strong corporate culture. Critics of such firms have argued that maintaining a culture is merely an excuse to discriminate. The clash between diversity and culture has become quite clear at Walmart. A company that likes to think of employees as family and vows to treat everyone with respect, Walmart is facing a huge discrimination suit on behalf of the firm's female employees. Stephanie Odle, a former assistant manager for Walmart who discovered that she was being paid $10,000 less per year than a male assistant manager, was the catalyst for what will be the largest sex discrimination case (*Dukes v. Wal-Mart*) in history, covering some 1.5 million current and former Walmart employees. Part of the problem is that the Walmart culture is built on the Walmart way of doing things. For example, the company does not post openings for management training positions because it believes that would be too bureaucratic; store managers are absolutely trusted to promote the most qualified people. Also, there are no companywide statistics on diversity because, again, managers are trusted to do what is right. However, it is alleged that these practices have been partly responsible for the fact that only 14.5 percent of Walmart managers are women whereas 66 percent of the total workforce is female, and female managers earn an average of $89,000 annually versus almost $106,000 for male managers.

Some evidence suggests that conflict may be especially pronounced between older and younger women in the workplace. Older women may be more likely to have sacrificed family for career and to have overcome higher obstacles to get ahead: They were, in a sense, trailblazers. Younger women, on the other hand, may find that organizational accommodations make it relatively easy for them to balance multiple roles and also may have a less-pronounced sense of having to fight to get ahead.[18]

Conflict can also result from other elements of diversity. For example, suppose a U.S. manager publicly praises a Japanese employee for his outstanding work. The manager's action stems from the dominant cultural belief in the

> ## "[Walmart] has a blatant disregard. They can't continue to treat people that way."
> —STEPHANIE ODLE, a former assistant manager for Walmart[17]

United States that such recognition is important and rewarding. But because the Japanese culture places a much higher premium on group loyalty and identity than on individual accomplishment, the employee will likely feel ashamed and embarrassed. A well-intentioned action thus may backfire and result in unhappiness.

Conflict can arise as a result of fear, distrust, or individual prejudice. Members of the dominant group in an organization may worry that newcomers from other groups pose a personal threat to their own position in the organization. For example, when U.S. firms have been taken over by Japanese firms, U.S. managers have sometimes been resentful or hostile to Japanese managers assigned to work with them. People may also be unwilling to accept people who are different from themselves. And personal bias and prejudices are still very real among some people today and can lead to potentially harmful conflict.

The Bottom Line on Diversity

Despite the arguments, the data supporting the positive effects of diversity on organizational outcomes is not as clear as one might believe. In fact, several studies have found that diversity leads to positive outcomes such as better firm performance and (the absence of) harmful conflict. Other studies have found that diversity results in poorer performance and more conflict, and still others find no relationship between diversity and outcomes such as these.[19] This has led some scholars to propose a nonlinear relationship between diversity and such outcomes as conflict and firm performance.[20]

The arguments all follow lines similar to the following: When diversity is low (i.e., most employees are similar to each other), organizations obtain no benefits from diversity (e.g., creativity), but also suffer no penalties (e.g., greater conflict). As diversity increases, positive gains increase, but the problems increase at a greater rate so that the most problematic situation occurs when there is a moderate amount of diversity. However, when a firm becomes truly diverse, to such an extent that there really are no identifiable "minority groups" within the workforce, the positive results of diversity can be truly maximized while most of the problems disappear. The key here is that when a firm reaches true diversity, the conflicts and subgroup dynamics disappear as everyone begins to view themselves as members of the same organization rather than members of a subgroup within the organization. Thus, firms experiencing problems because of workforce diversity would be advised to further increase diversity to make the firm truly diverse. A growing body of research supports exactly this recommendation.[21]

MANAGING DIVERSITY IN ORGANIZATIONS

Because of the tremendous potential that diversity holds for competitive advantage, as well as the possible consequences of diversity-related conflict, much attention has been focused in recent years on how individuals and organizations can manage diversity better. In the following sections, we first discuss individual strategies for dealing with diversity and then summarize organizational approaches to managing diversity.

Individual Strategies for Dealing with Diversity

One key element of managing diversity in an organization consists of four actions that individuals themselves can take. Individuals can strive for understanding, empathy, tolerance, and communication.

1. The first element in the strategy is *understanding* the nature and meaning of diversity. Some managers have taken the basic concepts of equal employment opportunity to an unnecessary extreme. They know that, by law, they cannot discriminate against people on the basis of gender, race, and so forth. Thus, in following this mandate, they come to believe they must treat everyone the same. But this belief can cause problems when it is translated into workplace behaviors among people after they have been hired. As noted earlier, people are not the same. Although people need to be treated fairly and equitably, managers must understand that differences do exist among people. Thus, any effort to treat everyone the same, without regard to their fundamental human differences, only leads to problems. It is important, then, for managers to understand that cultural factors cause people to behave in different ways and that these differences should be accepted.

2. Related to understanding is *empathy*. People in an organization should try to understand the perspective of others. For example, suppose a group that has traditionally been composed of white males is joined by a female member. Each male may be a little self-conscious about how to act toward the group's new member and may be interested in making her feel comfortable and welcome. But each one may be able to do this even more effectively by empathizing with how she may feel. For example, she may feel disappointed or elated about her new assignment or confident or nervous about her position in the group, and she may be experienced or inexperienced in working with male colleagues. By learning more about these and similar circumstances, the existing group members can facilitate their ability to work together effectively.

3. A third related individual approach to dealing with diversity is *tolerance*. Even though managers learn to understand diversity, and even though they may try to empathize with others, the fact remains that they may still not accept or enjoy some aspect or behavior on the part of others. For example, one organization recently reported that it was experiencing considerable conflict among its U.S. and Israeli employees. The Israeli employees always seemed to want to argue about every issue that arose. The U.S. managers preferred a more harmonious way of conducting business and became uncomfortable with the conflict. Finally, after considerable discussion, it was learned that many Israeli employees simply enjoy arguing and see it as part of getting work done. The firm's U.S. employees still do not enjoy the arguing but are more willing to tolerate it as a fundamental cultural difference between themselves and their Israeli colleagues.

4. A final individual approach to dealing with diversity is *communication*. Problems often become magnified over diversity issues because people are afraid or otherwise unwilling to discuss issues that relate to diversity. For example, suppose a younger employee has a habit of making jokes about the age of an elderly colleague. Perhaps the younger colleague means no harm and is just engaging in what she sees as good-natured kidding. But the older employee may find the jokes offensive. If the two do not communicate, then the jokes will continue and the resentment will grow. Eventually, what started as a minor problem may erupt into a much

bigger one. For communication to work, it must be two-way. If a person wonders if a certain behavior on her or his part is offensive to someone else, the curious individual should probably just ask. Similarly, if someone is offended by the behavior of another person, then he or she should explain to the offending individual how the behavior is perceived and request that it stop. As long as such exchanges are handled in a friendly, low-key, and nonthreatening fashion, they will generally have a positive outcome. Of course, if the same message is presented in an overly combative manner or if a person continues to engage in offensive behavior after having been asked to stop, then the problem will escalate. At this point, third parties within the organization may have to intervene. In fact, most organizations today have one or more systems in place to address questions and problems that arise as a result of diversity.

We now turn our attention to the various ways that organizations can indeed manage diversity better.

Organizational Strategies for Dealing with Diversity

Individuals can play an important role in managing diversity, but the organization itself must also play a fundamental role. Through its various policies and practices, people in the organization come to understand which behaviors are and are not appropriate. Diversity training is an even more direct method for managing diversity. The organization's culture is the ultimate context that diversity must address.

Organizational Policies. Managing diversity starts with the policies that an organization adopts because they directly or indirectly affect how people are treated. Obviously, the extent to which an organization embraces the premise of equal employment opportunity determines to a large extent the potential diversity within an organization. But differences exist between the organization that follows the law to the letter and practices passive discrimination and the organization that actively seeks a diverse and varied workforce.

Another aspect of organizational policies that affects diversity is how the organization addresses and responds to problems that arise from diversity. Consider the example of a manager charged with sexual harassment. If the organization's policies put an excessive burden

of proof on the individual being harassed and invoke only minor sanctions against the guilty party, then the organization is sending a clear signal about the importance of such matters. But the organization that has a balanced set of policies for addressing questions such as sexual harassment sends its employees a different message about the importance of diversity and individual rights and privileges.

Indeed, perhaps the major policy through which an organization can reflect its stance on diversity is its mission statement. If the organization's mission statement articulates a clear and direct commitment to diversity, everyone who reads that mission statement will grow to understand and accept the importance of diversity, at least to that particular organization.

As a result of some of the issues raised here, people have argued that increased diversity should not be a major goal of most organizations. These individuals are not necessarily arguing that diversity is not worth achieving but simply that so many problems are associated with increased diversity that it should not be a major focus of organizations.

Organizational Practices. Organizations can also help manage diversity through various ongoing practices and procedures. Avon's creation of networks for various groups represents one example of an organizational practice that fosters diversity. In general, the idea is that diversity is characterized by differences among people, so organizations can manage that diversity more effectively by following practices and procedures based on flexibility rather than rigidity.

Benefits packages, for example, can be structured to accommodate individual situations. An employee who is part of a dual-career couple and has no children may require relatively little insurance (perhaps because his spouse's employer provides more complete coverage) and would like to be able to schedule vacations to coincide with those of his spouse. Another employee who is a single parent may need a wide variety of insurance coverage and prefer to schedule his vacation time to coincide with school holidays.

Flexible working hours can help an organization accommodate diversity. Differences in family arrangements, religious holidays, cultural events, and so forth may each require that employees have some degree of flexibility in their work schedules. For example, a single parent may need to leave the office every day at 4:30 to pick up the children from their day-care center. An organization that truly values diversity will make every reasonable attempt to accommodate such a need.

© Feliks Gurevich/Shutterstock

HR in the 21st Century

Debating the Merits of Diversity Training

Texaco executives made headlines a few years ago when a tape-recorded conversation was made public in which they were heard making racially insulting remarks. About the same time, AT&T came under fire when a company newsletter used images of monkeys to represent

> **"The objective is to help managers and supervisors to understand how unconscious behavior can impact employees, how differences can get in the way of productivity in the workplace, and how to leverage diversity as a competitive advantage."**
>
> —Edward N. Gadsden, Jr.,
> Texaco's diversity director[23]

people in Africa. And Denny's, the popular restaurant chain, attracted national attention over charges that it discriminated against minority customers and employees.

In each case, company officials made public apologies and offered restitution to those who were most directly offended. Another response from each company was an announcement that key managers throughout the firm must participate in *diversity training*. As the term suggests, diversity training is designed to help individuals better understand people who are different from themselves.

This training is supposed to help people understand the beliefs, values, and lifestyles of others and to make them more tolerant and accepting of diverse points of view. Many experts believe that a well-planned and well-delivered diversity training program can indeed help people become more tolerant of others. On the other hand, some critics believe that such training addresses only surface-level issues. For example, some of the terms that the Texaco executives used disparagingly had been learned in a diversity program!

THINK IT OVER

1. Do you think diversity training can be effective? Why or why not?
2. Do you think a time will come when diversity training is not seen as necessary?

Sources: "Does Diversity Training Work?" *USA Today* (Mar. 2, 2006): 1B; "Companies Try New Tactics in Diversity Training," *Wall Street Journal* (Nov. 10, 2005): B6; "A 3Com Factory Hires a Lot of Immigrants, Gets Mix of Languages," *Wall Street Journal* (Mar. 30, 1998): A1, A12; "Do Diversity Programs Make a Difference?" *Wall Street Journal* (Dec. 4, 1996): B1.

Organizations can also facilitate diversity by making sure that diversity exists in its key committees and executive teams. Even if diversity exists within the broader organizational context, an organization that does not reflect diversity in groups like committees and teams implies that diversity is not a fully ingrained element of its culture. In contrast, when all major groups and related work assignments reflect diversity, the message is quite different.

Diversity Training.

Many organizations are finding that diversity training is an effective means for managing diversity and minimizing its associated conflict. **Diversity training** is specifically designed to enable members of an organization to function better in a diverse workplace. This training can take various forms.[22] As discussed in the HR in the Twenty-First Century feature, diversity training has to be undertaken all too often to remedy specific problems or crises that have erupted. But many organizations find it useful to help people learn more about their similarities and differences for other reasons.

Men and women can be taught to work together more effectively and can gain insights into how their own behaviors affect and are interpreted by others. In one organization, a diversity training program helped male managers gain insights into how various remarks they made to one another could be interpreted by others as being sexist. In the same organization, female managers learned how to point out their discomfort with those remarks without appearing overly hostile.

> **Diversity training** is specifically designed to enable members of an organization to function better in a diverse workplace.

© Radius Images/Photolibrary

Similarly, white and black managers may need training to understand each other better. Managers at Mobil noticed that African American colleagues never seemed to eat lunch together. After a diversity training program, they realized that the black managers felt that if they ate together, their white colleagues would be overly curious about what they were talking about. Thus, they avoided close associations with one another because they feared calling attention to themselves.

Some organizations go so far as to provide language training for their employees as a vehicle for managing diversity. Motorola, for example, provides English-language training for its foreign employees on assignment in the United States. At Pace Foods in San Antonio, Texas, staff meetings and employee handbooks are translated into Spanish for the benefit of the company's 100 Hispanic employees (out of a total payroll of 350 employees).

Organizational Culture. The ultimate test of an organization's commitment to managing diversity is its culture. Unless there is a basic and fundamental belief that diversity is valued, it cannot become a truly integral part of an organization, regardless of what managers say or put in writing. An organization that really wants to promote diversity must shape its culture so that it clearly underscores top management commitment to and support of diversity in all of its forms throughout every part of the organization. With top management support, and reinforced with a clear and consistent set of organizational policies and practices, diversity can become a basic and fundamental part of an organization.

The Multicultural Organization

Many organizations today are grappling with cultural diversity, others are succeeding admirably. For instance, some people think of UPS as a somewhat old-fashioned company, and it certainly isn't as splashy as some of its competitors in the shipping industry. But that doesn't mean that UPS is behind the curve in multiculturalism. Jovita Carranza, the company's highest-ranking Hispanic female executive, began working at UPS 30 years ago. She says she never asked for a promotion, but more responsibility came as a result of doing a good job. She now oversees the daily loading and unloading of 1.5 million packages and the 20,000 employees who handle them as they come through UPS Worldport, a 4-million-square-foot facility, in Louisville. She notes that there is no diversity officer or diversity committee at UPS. Instead, she notes that diversity and multiculturalism are just part of the way UPS does business.

Even though organizations like UPS are becoming more diverse, there are few truly multicultural organizations. The **multicultural organization** is one that has achieved high levels of diversity, one that can capitalize fully on the advantages of the diversity, and one that has few diversity-related problems.[24] Indeed, a multicultural organization is one in which diversity and the appreciation of all cultures is simply the way business is done. One recent article described the six basic characteristics of such an organization.[25] This perspective is shown in Exhibit 8.5.

1. The multicultural organization is characterized by pluralism. Every group represented in an organization works to understand every other group better. Thus, African American employees try to understand white employees, and white employees try just as hard to understand their black colleagues. In addition, every group represented within an organization has the potential to influence the organization's culture and its fundamental norms.

2. The multicultural organization achieves full structural integration. Full structural integration suggests that the diversity within an organization is a complete and accurate reflection of the organization's external labor

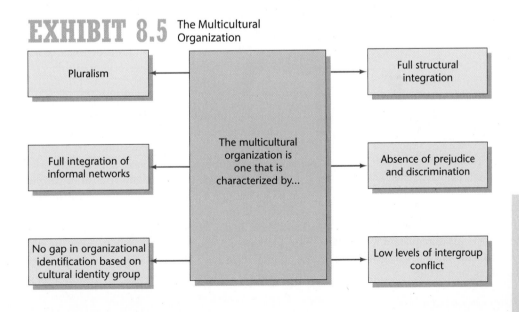

EXHIBIT 8.5 The Multicultural Organization

- Pluralism
- Full integration of informal networks
- No gap in organizational identification based on cultural identity group

The multicultural organization is one that is characterized by...

- Full structural integration
- Absence of prejudice and discrimination
- Low levels of intergroup conflict

*The **multicultural organization** is one that has achieved high levels of diversity, can capitalize fully on the advantages of the diversity, and has few diversity-related problems.*

market. If about half of the labor market is female, then about half of the employees are female. This same proportion is reflected at all levels of the organization. No glass ceilings or other subtle forms of discrimination exist in the organization.

3. The multicultural organization achieves full integration of its informal networks. This characteristic suggests that no barriers to entry and participation in any organizational activity exist. For example, people enter and exit lunch groups, social networks, communication grapevines, and other informal aspects of organizational activity without regard to age, gender, ethnicity, or other dimension of diversity.

4. The multicultural organization is characterized by an absence of prejudice and discrimination. No traces of bias exist and prejudice is eliminated. Discrimination is not practiced in any shape, form, or fashion. Discrimination is nonexistent not because it is illegal but because of the lack of prejudice and bias. People are valued, accepted, and rewarded purely on the basis of their skills and what they contribute to the organization.

5. In the multicultural organization, no gap in organizational identification is based on a cultural identity group. Many organizations tend to make presumptions about organizational roles based on group identity. For example, many people walking into an office and seeing a male and female conversing tend to assume that the female is the secretary and the male is the manager. No such tendencies exist in the multicultural organization. People recognize that males and females are equally likely to be managers and secretaries.

6. The multicultural organization experiences low levels of intergroup conflict. We noted earlier that conflict is a likely outcome of increased diversity. The multicultural organization has evolved beyond this point to a state of almost no conflict among different people. People within the organization fully understand, empathize with, have tolerance for, and openly communicate with, everyone else. Values, premises, motives, attitudes, and perceptions are so well understood by everyone that any conflict that does arise involves meaningful and work-related issues as opposed to differences in age, gender, ethnicity, or other dimensions of diversity.

We began this chapter by discussing how population and immigration patterns in the United States have made the management of diversity such a critical issue. We have also noted recent arguments that suggest moving to a truly multicultural organization might help firms enjoy all the potential benefits of a diverse workforce while avoiding most of the potential problems that can come with increased diversity. But can these same arguments be used to address the issues of diversity in the larger society? The history of the United States has not been characterized by multiculturalism relative to any group. Traditionally, the United States has characterized itself as a "melting pot" in which immigrants from many countries (who have always fueled the growth of the United States) gradually abandoned their identities as Italians or Hondurans or Vietnamese and developed identities as Americans. Perhaps they began by developing a "hyphenated identity" such as Italian-Americans, but the ultimate goal was to become an American. In fact, one of the authors regrets never learning Italian at home—because his parents were raised to be Americans by their immigrant parents.

Thus, foreigners were told that they would be accepted as "Americans" if they simply abandoned their old identities. But until they developed this American identity, immigrants were often pressured to live among others like themselves. Because of this, many cities in the United States developed neighborhoods in which different cultures thrived; many of these became tourist attractions and colorful places to visit such as Little Italy in New York City and Chinatown in San Francisco. But these did not begin as tourist attractions. In fact, these were the only places where the Italians of New York or the Chinese of San Francisco were allowed to live—that is, they were really ghettos. It is instructive to realize that so-called ghettoization has often been the first reaction to dealing with diverse populations until they could become part of the melting pot. Even gay populations, in many cities, tend to be concentrated in certain neighborhoods.

But perhaps our studies of diversity in organizations lead us to an alternative way of dealing with immigrant groups. Is a model of pluralism better in the long run than a melting pot model? Although the traditional model seems to have worked well in the past, perhaps the reasons for immigration have changed and, with them, the effectiveness of the melting pot model.

MANAGING THE KNOWLEDGE FUNCTION

As should be clear, managing an increasingly diverse workforce is one of the major challenges facing human resource managers today. But the workplace also has changed in other ways. One important change has been in the very nature of the organizations we have and the kinds of services they provide. Traditionally, most organizations thought of their products as tangible types of goods; that is, steel companies produced steel, and auto companies produced autos. Over time, however, the economies in many countries, including the United States, shifted from manufacturing to services, and so the orientation shifted to the production of goods *and* services. In today's economy, many organizations are now really trading in knowledge, and this presents a special set of challenges for the HR manager. Investment firms are selling their special knowledge about how to manage a portfolio and plan for retirement or some other goal, consulting firms are selling expertise in dealing with the many management problems that face organizations, and many other types of businesses are actually dealing primarily in knowledge rather than goods or services.

With these shifts also came the recognition that knowledge was also a commodity within an organization that needed to be managed and leveraged. Furthermore, as the nature of work and business changed, many organizations found that that they were employing larger numbers of "knowledge workers" who required special handling. In this section, we focus on the notion of organizational learning, which is an important part of the internal knowledge management function, as well as some issues associated with the management of knowledge workers.

Organizational Learning

Organizational learning refers to the process by which an organization "learns" from past mistakes and adapts to its environment. Over time, rules and procedures change based on experience, but this change is still based on individual learning; that is, individuals learn how to adapt and change and then interact with one another so that the new information gained can be shared and distributed throughout the organization. As a result, a shared vision and interpretation of the information is developed throughout the organization, and the change permeates the entire organization. At this point, the organization can be said to have "learned" how to be more effective.

A few points are important to remember. First, the process begins with individual learning and change. If there is no individual learning, then there can be no

organizational learning. Second, whereas the individual learning process is cognitive, organizational learning depends more on social processes and sharing of information. Thus, individual learning is a necessary but not sufficient condition for organizational learning to occur.[26]

The process of organizational learning, then, involves the acquisition of new knowledge by the organization. Again, it is not enough that individuals acquire

this knowledge: They must then communicate with other organizational members to ensure that this knowledge is available throughout the organization. The organization must then use this information to adapt. There is a strong belief that organizations that can manage this change—that is, organizations that can acquire information and adapt—can gain significant competitive advantage over their competitors.[27]

For example, large conglomerates such as General Electric or Viacom typically grow by acquiring other firms. Each time these firms make an acquisition, they must figure out how to best integrate the new employees into the firm and marry the cultures of the acquired and parent firms. Presumably, these large conglomerates made mistakes over the years in both the targets of their acquisitions and how they managed the acquisitions after they were completed. But they also probably learned from their experiences and got better at it over time. This is a case of organizational learning, and learning how to better target and manage acquisitions would clearly give a conglomerate an advantage over its competitors.

Furthermore, a firm can gain important new knowledge as a result of a merger or acquisition. Thus, for example, a large firm may be contemplating entering a new market in China, but

> **Organizational learning** is the process by which an organization "learns" from past mistakes and adapts to its environment.

the firm lacks the expertise (or knowledge) on how to enter that difficult market successfully. The large firm (company A) could acquire the needed information by sending key employees to some source where they can learn the needed skills, or it can acquire those skills directly by acquiring individuals who already possess the needed skills. In other words, the large firm can look for another firm (company B) that has already mastered the China market. Then company A can either try to hire the experts away from company B or, if the expert knowledge is widely held throughout company B, access the expertise throughout the firm via a merger, a joint venture, or a complete acquisition of company B.

Finally, we should note the concept of organizational memory and the role it plays in organizational learning. **Organizational memory** refers to the collective, institutional record of past events. For an organization to "learn" from past events, it must be possible to "recall" those events in some way. Some of these events and processes are written down or stored electronically so that a physical record exists for a merger, a change caused by legislation, or any other event from which someone might have learned a lesson. These physical records then serve as the organizational memory. In many cases, however, such information is not formally recorded. Instead, one or more people who were there when the event happened become the organizational memory. These individuals are the repository for information that can help the organization learn from experience and avoid repeating mistakes.

An organization thus can gain access to new information through a variety of ways. Once this information is shared and distributed throughout the organization so that all employees now share a view of what this information means and how it can be used to change, organizational learning is said to have occurred. When this information and its interpretation also become part of the organizational memory, change and adaptation can continue for some time. This type of learning and the adaptation involved will clearly be critical to firms as they try to compete effectively in the twenty-first century.

Monitoring the behavior of banks and other financial firms in the United States in the coming years will be interesting. After the financial crisis of 2009, there was a great deal of criticism about the way banks handled mortgage-backed securities and how these securities were rated and monetized.* Early in 2010, many of these same institutions were criticized because of planned bonus payments. As noted earlier, there is growing sentiment to have the government limit bonuses or at least monitor executive pay policies (which will be discussed in more detail in the next chapter). The question is, will these firms "learn" from their experience? Will they be able to avoid similar financial meltdowns in the future, and will they be able to modify their compensation policies to avoid closer government scrutiny?[28]

Knowledge Workers

Traditionally, employees were seen as adding value to organizations because of what they did or because of their experience. As we enter the information age in the workplace, however, many employees add value simply because of what they know.[29] This new reality creates new problems and challenges for managing work relationships. Employees who add value simply because of what they know are usually referred to as **knowledge workers**, and how well these employees are managed is seen as a major factor in determining which firms will be successful in the future.[30] Knowledge workers include computer scientists, engineers, and physical scientists, and they provide special challenges for the HR manager. They tend to work in high-technology firms and are usually experts in some abstract knowledge base. They often believe they have the right to work autonomously, and they identify more strongly with their profession than they do with any organization—even to the extent of defining performance in terms recognized by other members of their profession.[31]

Organizational memory *is the collective, institutional record of past events.*

Knowledge workers *are employees who add value simply because of what they know.*

*In the midst of these discussions about bailouts and bonuses, it was revealed that several G-S employees were short-selling investments they were recommending to their clients. Nothing concrete came of this, but it fueled the arguments that the government should do more to regulate the financial sector

© charles taylor/Shutterstock

As the importance of information-driven jobs grows, so will the need for knowledge workers. But these employees require extensive and specialized training, and not everyone is willing to make the human capital investments necessary to move into these jobs. In fact, even after knowledge workers are on the job, retraining and training updates are critical so that their skills do not become obsolete. It has been suggested, for example, that the "half-life" for a technical education in engineering is about 3 years. Failure to update the required skills by the end of that time not only results in the organization losing competitive advantage but also increases the likelihood that the knowledge worker will go to another firm that is more committed to updating these skills.[32]

Compensation and career-development policies for knowledge workers must also be specially tailored. For example, in many high-tech organizations, engi-

despite overall economic conditions, they need to retain their best employees because these are the people responsible for the profits that were made even when economic times were bad. Without such adjustments or bonuses, once an employee accepts a job with a firm, he or she is more subject to the internal labor market, which is not likely to grow as quickly as the external market for knowledge workers. As a result, the longer an employee remains with a firm, the further behind the market rate his or her pay falls—unless it is regularly adjusted.

Of course, the growing demand for these workers also results in organizations going to rather extreme measures to attract them in the first place.[35] When the boom for knowledge workers really began in the 1990s, high starting salaries and signing bonuses were common. At one point, British Petroleum Exploration paid petroleum engineers with undersea-platform-drilling knowledge (not experi-

> ## More and more organizations are coming to believe they can be successful by addressing the needs of both their employees and society.

neers and scientists have the option of entering a technical career path that parallels a management career path. This option allows the knowledge worker to continue to carry out specialized work without taking on management responsibilities; at the same time, the organization offers the knowledge worker compensation that is equivalent to the compensation available to management. Also, in many high-tech organizations, salary adjustments within various classifications for management workers are most frequently based on maturity curves rather than on performance; that is, because performance is difficult to quantify for these employees, and because a great deal of research-and-development activity may not have an immediate payoff, salary is based on the employee's years of work experience. The assumption is that, in a technical area, more experience makes the employee more valuable to the organization.[33]

In other high-tech firms, though, the emphasis is on pay for performance, with profit sharing based on projects or products developed by the knowledge workers. In addition, the tendency in most firms employing these workers is to reduce the number of levels of the organization to allow the knowledge workers to react more quickly to the external environment and reduce the need for bureaucratic approval.[34]

Perhaps the biggest challenge facing firms that employ knowledge workers is figuring out how to attract and retain them. The growing demand for knowledge workers has resulted in firms introducing regular market adjustments to pay in order to retain those employees. Financial firms have used exactly the same argument in defense of the high bonuses paid to employees in 2010. They argue that,

ence, just knowledge) salaries in the six-figure range with signing bonuses of more than $50,000 and immediate profit sharing. The market for knowledge workers is not as hot as it once was, and these bidding wars are a thing of the past. Furthermore, recent high unemployment rates have further depressed salaries in many industries. As the U.S. economy comes out of the recent recession, however, some of these issues may be with us again. In early 2010, the problems Wall Street had experienced produced a soaring demand for a new type of knowledge worker, one who knew how to assess and manage risk for financial institutions. Clearly, the need to better manage knowledge workers is not going away, and organizations can build competitive advantage if they can learn how to better use and manage the knowledge resources they have.[36]

HUMAN RESOURCE MANAGEMENT AND SOCIAL ISSUES

We turn now to yet another way in which the world of work has changed. Employees, especially younger employees in the twenty-first century, are more interested in social issues than employees have been for quite some time. These interests affect how potential employees decide where to work and what issues they will get involved in once they are working. Thus, they are extremely important for

EXHIBIT 8.6 Social Issues and Human Resource Management

Prison labor

Living wage

Key Social Issues

Immigration

Social responsibility/ Social entrepreneurship

managing a new generation of human resources. Furthermore, around the world, many organizations are becoming more concerned with the effects of their practices on the larger world around them, and these concerns also have implications for the HR manager. In fact, one study conducted a few years ago found that HR executives in the United States (as well as in Australia, China, and India) are more likely to be in charge of implementing and monitoring issues associated with social issues and social responsibility than any other functional executive.[37]

There is an increasing awareness that the needs of the organization can be met even while addressing the needs of the employees or of society as a whole,[38] and there is also an increasing concern with social issues in general. In fact, this is one area in which management and organized labor can often come together, and furthermore, labor unions in the United States have been especially successful at using these issues to change their image as that of a group of people concerned about conditions around the world, and we will discuss that further in Chapter 11. For now, however, we will discuss several social issues that have begun playing a role in the lives of HR managers. These key social issues are shown in Exhibit 8.6.

Prison Labor

Most of us do not spend a lot of time thinking about what prison inmates do with their time, but in most cases they work at jobs inside the prisons. Traditionally, these jobs included manufacturing automobile license plates, repairing roads, or doing the laundry for other state institutions, but that situation has been changing. As we note in Chapter 11, this is a source of concern for the U.S. labor movement, but it is increasingly a source of concern for human resource managers as well.

First, the number of prisoners involved has been changing. In 1990, there were approximately 66,000 federal prisoners and 708,000 state and local prisoners. By 2009, those numbers had risen to 162,000 federal inmates and 1.98 million state and local inmates. Many of these inmates work at paid jobs, but they earn somewhat less than workers on the outside. In fact, in 1991, prison wages ranged from $0.23 to $1.15 per hour on a federal pay scale, although more than half these workers earned $0.40 per hour or less.[39] Second, the laws regulating where and how the goods produced by inmate labor can be sold have been

changing, thus making it easier to sell products produced by inmates on the open market.

The fact that goods produced at such a low cost can compete openly with goods produced by workers who are paid a minimum wage is potentially a serious threat to the jobs of low-paid, unskilled workers in the general population.[40] In fact, some critics argue that prison labor contributes little to the gross domestic product but substantially affects the employment opportunities and wages of high school dropouts in this country.[41] These same critics also argue that these jobs do not prepare prison inmates for outside jobs once they are released and so do not lessen the rates of subsequent arrest and incarceration.

What should we do? Clearly, several different issues are involved. One relates to the problem of allowing products produced by prisoners (who are paid less) to compete with products that are produced by employees who earn a legal wage. Although companies may need incentives to hire prison workers, allowing these goods to compete more freely in the open market may actually be a problem. Other organizations can see this as a way to gain some advantage, and eventually, we can see a very heavy reliance on prison labor. Also, we must think about what we would like to have inmates do while they are in prison. For those who will never be released, this may not be a problem, but for others it may be important that the work they do in prison will help them get and keep jobs on the outside. Furthermore, the employees should probably be paid what their work is really worth.

A Living Wage

In Chapter 2, we discussed the minimum wage noting that there is some controversy over whether the minimum wage should be raised (we discuss this again in Chapter 9). But how does a person earning the national minimum wage of $7.25 actually live? That person will earn less than $300 per week or slightly more than $15,000 per year. It is difficult to imagine how someone would support a family on that much money. Instead, there are proponents in our country who suggest that we should work instead toward paying employees a "living wage"—that is enough to allow a family to live above the poverty level. In fact, this is exactly what several states have done. For example, the minimum wage in Connecticut and the District of Columbia is more than $8.00 per hour. These are attempts to ensure that working people can live at some reasonable level, but they may not be enough.

In New Orleans after Hurricane Katrina, there was a shortage of workers for jobs in fast-food restaurants. As a result, Burger King was offering $10 an hour to start and a $5,000 signing bonus if the employee worked for 1 year. But Katrina destroyed much of the lower-middle-class housing that had been available in New Orleans, and the housing that remained was expensive even at these higher wages. Therefore, even these wages could not attract a sufficient number of employees for some time.

The challenge, then, is how we should determine what someone is paid. The traditional human resource management approach would be either to conduct some type of job evaluation (we discuss some of these in Chapter 9) or do a survey to determine the "going rate" in a given market. The living wage movement would suggest that this is not adequate and that organizations owe their employees the ability to live a reasonable life. Of course, opponents argue that if a state (or a firm) pays above market rate, then it will need to either charge more for its goods (making them less competitive) or accept lower profits. Therefore, no rational businessperson would move to these states. Instead, by this argument, states such as Kansas and Ohio (with state minimum wages below the national level) or states such as Mississippi and Louisiana (with no state minimum wage laws) should be the most prosperous—but they are not. Florida continues to grow in terms of both population and business, and Nevada (which has a state law at the level of the national law) is usually ranked as the best state for business in the United States.

But should HR managers be social activists? Should they argue for a living wage as opposed to a more competitive wage? As with all the issues discussed in this section, the answers to these questions depend on the person and his or her values. For some of our readers, it will be difficult not to speak out.

Immigration

During the spring of 2006, there were hundreds of demonstrations involving hundreds of thousands of people dealing with U.S. immigration policy. Congress had been debating how to deal with the large number of illegal immigrants in the United States, and many people were angry. This was also an important issue for HR managers because much of their work touches on issues that are important for immigrants, both legal and illegal.

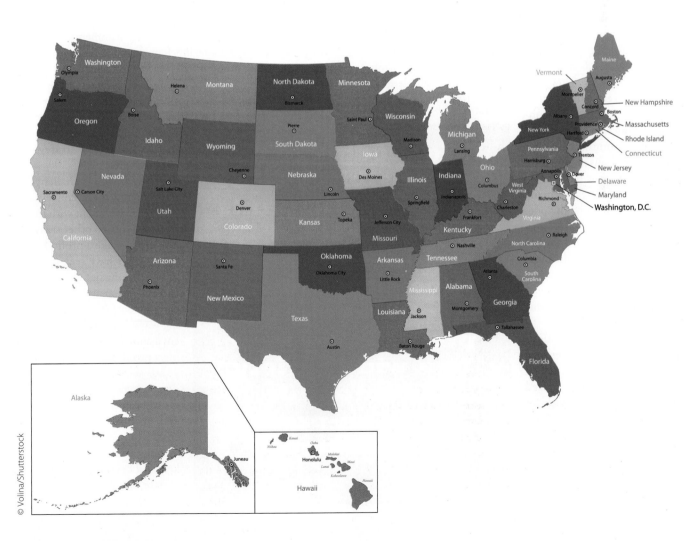

© Volina/Shutterstock

The concerns during 2006 were specifically with illegal immigrants. These are people who have entered the country illegally but who are living (and often working) in this country. These workers are typically willing to accept lower wages, and they are usually in no position to complain about their working conditions, which makes them perfect targets for anyone who wishes to exploit them. Why would someone do that? There are several reasons.

First, as noted, these workers are willing to work for lower wages. This allows organizations and employers to hold down labor costs. These workers are also usually quite willing to work hard, and so they may be especially productive. In some cases, these workers are also willing to perform jobs that other workers are unwilling to do. In addition, even if they are paid exploitative wages, they are probably earning more than they could earn in their home countries. So what is the problem?

As with several of the issues we have been discussing, one problem is that U.S. citizens (or legal immigrants) who need to work to support a family will either not find jobs or will be forced to work for lower wages because an employer can always go to illegal immigrants if necessary, even though these illegal immigrants cannot really support their families on the wages they earn. But the immigration problem is actually even more complex. During the 1960s and 1970s, countries in Europe, especially Germany, found that there was actually a shortage of workers who were willing to perform unskilled jobs. The Germans invited thousands of Turks and Greeks to enter Germany as guest workers. They could remain in Germany legally, and they were paid a fair wage. Over time, this program led to many social problems, however, and after German reunification, the Germans focused more on integrating the citizens of the former East Germany into their economy. In 2006, President Bush recommended a similar solution for this country, although he allowed for a mechanism whereby guest workers could eventually become citizens as well.

How do organizations find employees to perform undesirable and unskilled jobs? Could older, retired workers perform some of them? What do we owe employees, even if they are guests? Do we owe them full benefits? Job security? Education? Is the solution simply to make sure that everyone is paid a living wage so that there would be no advantage to a firm hiring illegal immigrants? Finally, how do all of these issues affect those who have entered the United States legally and are pursuing normal channels to become citizens? In closing, it is interesting to note that as unemployment rates began to rise to 10 percent in the United States in 2010 and as major financial institutions struggled or died, illegal immigration to the United States also seems to have subsided.

Social Responsibility and Social Entrepreneurship

Our discussion about the role of social issues has focused to this point on specific social issues that present challenges for HR managers. But broader social issues also affect the way entire corporations do business and so also affect how they manage their people.

Corporate social responsibility (CSR) is one label that has been frequently used to describe a dedication to build organizations that are accountable, responsible, transparent, and ecologically sustainable.[42] In the United States, much of the impetus for CSR grew out of a series of Supreme Court decisions in the 1950s that allowed corporations to participate in philanthropic enterprises. In the 1960s, much of the attention turned to consumer safety and consumer protection, as well as environmental issues. By the 1980s, CSR became much more concerned with corruption, but beginning in the 1990s the focus broadened to consider every aspect of a company's strategy, business model, and business practices. Today, there is recognition that we must integrate environmental concerns with every aspect of a firm's strategic management.[43]

The ongoing challenge is balancing these concerns for the environment with the responsibility to other stakeholders to make a profit, but recent years have seen much more emphasis on being "green"—that is, reducing carbon footprints and finding ways to actually help the environment while still making a profit. In fact, in recent years, several analysts have demonstrated that it is feasible to be socially responsible and profitable by reducing costs while at the same time gaining access to new markets and being able to differentiate one's products from those of others.[44]

"We recognize our responsibility to be active participants in our local communities. We give a minimum of 5% of our profits every year to a wide variety of community and non-profit organizations."

—Whole Foods core values statement[45]

John Mackey, CEO of Whole Foods, does not like the term *corporate social responsibility*. Instead, he prefers to describe his company's approach as *conscious capitalism*. He believes that a corporation should make a profit, but it should use that profit to further worthwhile social causes around the globe. Mackey and his employees (who make their own commitments) fund projects ranging from microloan programs to schools. Many of these are in Latin America, where Whole Foods buys many of its products.[46] Whole Foods' entire corporate philosophy and corporate culture is guided by Mackey's ideas, so a person who does not share his views probably will not fit comfortably into the Whole Foods organization.

Finally, we should note the concept of *social entrepreneurship*. Many scholars and writers use this term differently (in fact, John Mackey has described Whole Foods as a corporation that follows this concept), but it generally refers to applying business and entrepreneurial skills and tools to deal with social problems. In practice, this might manifest as a business school program designed to train managers for not-for-profit organizations, or it might simply refer to taking a more businesslike approach to dealing with charity. Organizations such as Whole Foods are becoming more active in transferring what they have learned about doing business to deal with social problems, and this is likely to continue as a trend. There is a lot of speculation that the new generation of university students is more socially conscious and so more interested in how to apply business models to social problems. For the HR manager, this may mean recruiting a different breed of employees or at least finding a way to lead and motivate a new generation of employees. It may also mean that business will be run differently, and so human resources will have to be managed differently to support these new strategic directions. In any event, social issues are clearly changing the nature of the workplace and the people working there.

CLOSING CASE

THE AVON WAY

Women have always played an important role at Avon, the largest cosmetics firm in the United States. Starting with the first Avon Lady in 1886, women have long been the foundation of the firm's marketing and sales efforts. Even though Avon has always employed a lot of women throughout its organization, control always remained in the hands of the small group of men who ran the company. A series of disastrous decisions and setbacks in the 1980s, however, caused the firm to rethink its philosophies and to promote its best middle managers, many of them women, into the executive ranks. As a result, Avon has turned itself around. Today the firm is known for both its exemplary financial performance and its acceptance of all people, regardless of their gender, skin color, or age.

Avon's problems started in the 1970s when its top management team tried to change the firm's strategy. This predominantly male group of managers first ignored its own marketing research about women consumers and shifting career patterns that indicated more women were entering the workforce and seeking professional careers. In particular, these managers failed to recognize that the personal-care products preferred by women were also changing. Then, in the 1980s, they tried to buck emerging trends and diversify with several ill-conceived acquisitions.

Finally, as the firm was on the brink of bankruptcy, a new top management team was brought in. Led by CEO Jim Preston, Avon refocused itself on its roots and began to market cosmetics again to a largely female market, albeit a very different market.

This time, the firm adopted new approaches. It decided to recognize and reward individuals' managerial talents rather than gender. As a result, more women were promoted into higher-level positions. In addition, Preston shifted the firm's organization culture to be more accommodating to all its employees—to value differences among people rather than imposing a rigid and controlling model for accomplishing goals. For example, the firm dropped its season-ticket purchases of Knicks and Yankees games and replaced them with season tickets for the New York City Ballet and the New York Philharmonic. The company also eliminated its annual hunting retreat, a male bastion of drinking and card playing.

Avon is also moving aggressively into foreign markets. Avon products are now sold in mature markets such as those in Western Europe and Japan. In addition, the firm sells its products throughout China, Russia, and Eastern Europe. All told, Avon manufactures its products in 18 countries and sells them in 125. Preston credits several key female executives for championing the international push and for making sure that it was done right. And many new

Text on image: 明天更美好 雅芳 AVON 直销咨询热线：400-887 88

managers at the firm have come from international contacts, organizations, and networks that the firm did not previously see as valuable sources of executive talent.

Perhaps the biggest testament to the "new" Avon is its current top management team. In 1999, after Preston's departure, Andrea Jung was named chair and CEO; at the same time Susan Kropf was appointed president and chief operating officer (COO). All told, more than half of the firm's top officers and more than 40 percent of its global managers are women. Almost half of the members of

the board of directors are female. Clearly, Avon is a firm that has changed its own culture and appreciates the power of diversity and multiculturalism.[47]

THINK IT OVER
1. What underlies Avon's commitment to diversity?
2. Why are more companies not following Avon's lead?
3. Can any of the dimensions of diversity derail Avon's success?

STUDY TOOLS

- ■ Rip out the chapter review card located at the end of the book.
- ■ Review the valuable study tools located online at www.cengagebrain.com
  - ■ Review the Key Terms flashcards.
  - ■ Download audio and visual summaries to review on the go.
  - ■ Complete practice quizzes to prepare for the test.
  - ■ Play "Beat the Clock" and "QuizBowl" to master chapter concepts.
  - ■ Complete "Crossword Puzzle" to review key terms.
  - ■ Watch the chapter video for a real-life example of key concepts.

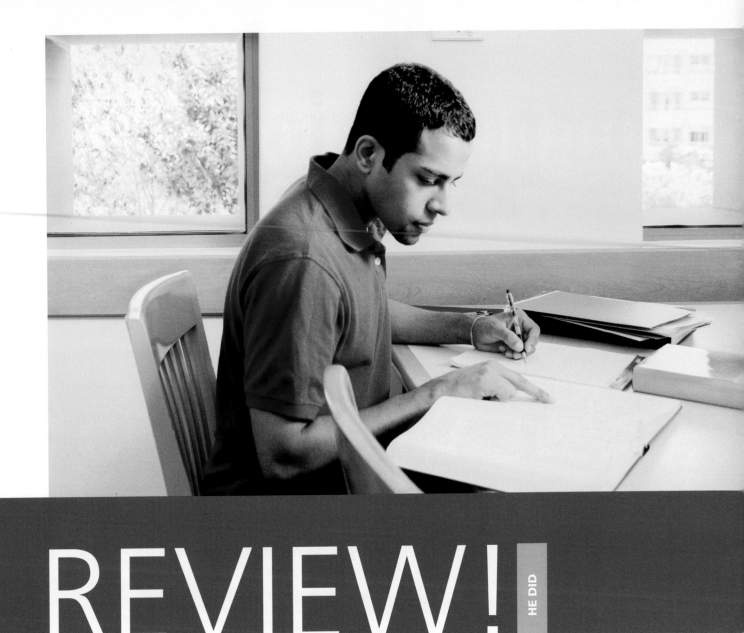

REVIEW!

HE DID

HR puts a multitude of study aids at your fingertips. After reading the chapters, check out these resources for further help:

- **Review Cards,** found in the back of your book, include all learning outcomes, key terms and definitions, and visual summaries for each chapter.

- **Online Printable Flash Cards** give you additional ways to check your comprehension of key Human Resource Management concepts.

- Other great tools to help you review include **interactive games, videos, and auto-graded quizzes.**

Go to CourseMate for HR to find plenty of resources to help you *Review!* Access at login.cengagebrain.com.

Compensation & BENEFITS

"In average-to-bad years, we earn less than our peers in other companies. That's supposed to teach us that we don't want to be average or bad. We want to be good.
—James Coblin, human resources vice president, Nucor"

INNOVATIVE COMPENSATION AT NUCOR

Nucor is a pioneer in the steelmaking industry, one of the first to make new steel from scrap metal. From a tiny upstart in the 1960s, the company today is the largest producer in the United States, shipping 24 million tons in 2009. The Nucor success story is all about the effective use of human resources.

In the 1960s, then–chief executive officer (CEO) Ken Iverson transformed the struggling firm with a unique management perspective. His philosophy required that employee earnings be based on productivity and that workers enjoy job security and be treated fairly. These principles created an organization culture that is egalitarian, participative, and decentralized.

Iverson also designed a simple management structure with few layers and a small staff. General managers supervise department managers, line supervisors, and hourly personnel. There are just four layers and four job titles between a janitor and the current CEO, Daniel DiMicco. Nucor's headquarters staff consists of a mere 65 employees overseeing 12,000 workers, the smallest support staff of any multibillion-dollar firm.

Nucor has the best labor relations of any domestic steelmaker. None of the firm's plants are unionized, and employees do not feel they need a union for protection. For its part, Nucor has never engaged in union-busting tactics. Workers' contributions are recognized. In a gesture of appreciation, every single worker's name is printed on the cover of Nucor's annual reports.

Nucor also has an innovative compensation plan. Hourly workers at other mills earn $16 to $21 per hour, yet Nucor's make just $10. However, Nucor gives generous bonuses that are tied to the quality and productivity of the entire shift. Profit sharing

© AP Photo/The Decatur Daily, John Godbey

LEARNING OBJECTIVES

After studying this chapter, you should be able to:

LO1 Describe the basic issues involved in developing a compensation strategy

LO2 Discuss how organizations develop a wage and salary structure

LO3 Identify and describe the basic issues involved in wage and salary administration

LO4 Discuss the basic considerations in understanding benefit programs

LO5 Identify and describe mandated benefits

LO6 Identify and describe nonmandated benefits

LO7 Discuss contemporary issues in compensation and benefits adds an extra $18,000 annually. Bonuses and profit sharing in 2009 exceeded $190 million, in some cases, almost tripling take-home pay.

Compensation for managers is 75 percent to 90 percent of market average, but performance bonuses can double that amount. However, the hourly workers' bonuses and profit sharing are not offered to managers, creating greater pay equality. Even CEO DiMicco's pay is limited to 23 times the average hourly workers' pay compared to the typical CEO who makes 400 times the pay of a low-level worker. Executives have no perks: no company cars, extra holidays, enhanced insurance benefits, or reserved parking spaces.

Employment at Nucor can be lucrative, but high pay is not guaranteed. If a bad batch of steel is identified before leaving the factory, the workers get no bonus. If the bad steel gets to the customer, they give up three times that amount. Bonuses are also dependent on the cyclical steel market. In 2005, when sales were strong, the average hourly worker made $91,000. In 2009, with steel sales down, the average was $54,000. "In average-to-bad years, we earn less than our peers in other companies," says James Coblin, Nucor's human resources vice president. "That's supposed to teach us that we don't want to be average or bad. We want to be good."

The nonunion workforce is flexible and participative. Workers take the initiative to improve operations in their areas. In fact, worker suggestions are the most important source of new ideas for the firm. Management has pushed decision making down to the lowest possible level. DiMicco refers to his executive vice presidents as "mini CEOs." Workers voluntarily assume responsibility

because their pay is tied to overall performance. Trust is so high that divisions regularly compete for high performance while still maintaining cooperation.

Nucor has grown through more than a dozen acquisitions over the last decade, yet the culture and practices have spread to each newly acquired plant. Leaders are promoted from within, which further strengthens the culture. Nucor takes care to persuade new workers of the advantages of its system. At one newly acquired plant, Nucor based pay on the old system but posted what employees would have earned under the new system. After 6 months, employees realized the benefits and asked to switch to Nucor's formula.

Workers are passionate about Nucor. One vice president describes himself as "an apostle" for Iverson's methods and says, "Our culture is a living thing. It will not die because we will not let it die, ever." That passion has translated into profitability. Nucor has one of the highest returns to shareholders of almost all Standard & Poor's 500 Stock Index, at 387 percent over the past 5 years. Nucor managers routinely credit the workers for Nucor's high performance. General manager Ladd Hall says, "The people in the mills, that's what makes it Nucor."[2]

THINK IT OVER

1. Would you want to work under a compensation system like Nucor's?
2. Why don't more firms use approaches such as the one used by Nucor?

The amount of value people create for an organization and what the organization gives them as compensation for that value are important determinants of organizational competitiveness. If employers pay too much for the value created by workers, then profits (and hence competitiveness) will suffer. But if they pay too little or demand too much from their workers for what they are paying, they will suffer in different ways: lower-quality workers, higher turnover, or employee fatigue and stress. Clearly, then, managing compensation and benefits are important activities for any organization. And just as clearly, Nucor managers have a keen understanding of the relationship between worker compensation and company performance.

Compensation and benefits refer to the various types of outcomes employees receive for their time at work. **Compensation** is the set of rewards that organizations provide to individuals in return for their willingness to perform various jobs and tasks within the organization. **Benefits** are the various rewards, incentives, and other items of value that an organization provides to its employees beyond wages,

salaries, and other forms of financial compensation. The term *total compensation* is sometimes used to refer to the overall value of financial compensation plus the value of additional benefits that the organization provides.

In this chapter, we cover the basic concepts of compensation and benefits. We start by examining how compensation strategies are developed, and then we turn to the administration of compensation programs and how organizations evaluate their compensation programs. We look at benefits, discussing the basic reasons for benefit plans and describing different types of benefit plans typically found in organizations. Next we consider the often controversial topic of executive compensation, discussing the basic components of executive-compensation packages and why they are so controversial. We conclude with a discussion of legal issues associated with compensation and benefits and the ways in which organizations can evaluate their compensation and benefit programs.

LEARNING OBJECTIVE 1

DEVELOPING A COMPENSATION STRATEGY

Compensation should never be a result of random decisions but instead the result of a careful and systematic

Compensation *is the set of rewards that organizations provide to individuals in return for their willingness to perform various jobs and tasks within the organization.*

Benefits *generally refer to various rewards, incentives, and other things of value that an organization provides to its employees beyond their wages, salaries, and other forms of direct financial compensation.*

strategic process.[3] Embedded in the process is an understanding of the basic purposes of compensation, an assessment of strategic options for compensation, knowledge of the determinants of compensation strategy, and the use of pay surveys.

Basic Purposes of Compensation

Compensation has several fundamental purposes and objectives. First, the organization must provide appropriate and equitable rewards to employees. Individuals who work for organizations want to feel valued and be rewarded at a level commensurate with their skills, abilities, and contributions to the organization. In this regard, an organization must consider two different kinds of equity. In addition, compensation serves a "signaling" function. Organizations signal to employees what they feel is important (and less important) for an employee to focus on by paying for certain kinds of activities or behaviors (and not for others). As we discuss in more detail in the next chapter, compensation can serve as an incentive to employees to increase their efforts along desired lines. We turn first to the issues of fairness and equity.

Internal equity in compensation refers to comparisons made by employees to other employees within the same organization. In making these comparisons, the employee is concerned that he is equitably paid for his contributions to the organization relative to the way other employees are paid in the firm. For example, suppose a department manager learns that all the other department managers in the firm are paid more than he is. He subsequently looks more closely at the situation and finds that they all have similar experience and responsibilities. As a result, he becomes unhappy with his compensation and likely requests a salary increase. On the other hand, he might discover that he has much less work experience and fewer responsibilities than the other managers and thus concludes that there is no equity problem. Problems with internal equity can result in conflict among employees, feelings of mistrust, low morale, anger, and perhaps even legal action if the basis for inequity is perceived to result from illegal discrimination.

External equity in compensation refers to comparisons made by employees with similar employees at other firms performing similar jobs. For example, an engineer may experience internal equity relative to her engineering colleagues in her work group because she knows they are all paid the same salary. But if she finds out that another major employer in the same community is paying its engineers

Internal equity in compensation refers to comparisons made by employees to other employees within the same organization.

External equity in compensation refers to comparisons made by employees to others employed by different organizations performing similar jobs.

EXHIBIT 9.1 Example of a Pay Survey

Organization: ABC Trucking
Location: Dallas, TX

Benchmark Jobs	No. of workers (this title)	No. of workers (total)	Average weekly hours	Base Pay			Median total compensation (base pay + benefits)	Industry			
				25th %-tile	50th %-tile	75th %-tile		Mfg.	Trans.	Utilities	Trade
File clerk	10	300	40	$15,000	$20,000	$25,000	$28,000		✓		
Order clerk											
Accounting clerk											

A survey such as this one is sent to other organizations in a given region. In this case, the survey would go to organizations in various industries, but other surveys might be targeted to a specific industry. The jobs that are the focus of the survey should be benchmark jobs, where everyone understands the nature of the job, the content is fairly stable, and the job is likely to be found in a wide variety of organizations. In some surveys, specific benchmark jobs are coded to ensure that everyone reacts to the same job. Also, some surveys ask more specific questions about other areas of compensation. Data from surveys such as this one are then summarized for each job.

HR in the 21st Century

Negotiating Salaries on the Web

Back in the "old days" (probably up to the final years of the twentieth century, in fact) negotiating wages and salaries was typically handled in a meeting between the employee and his or her manager. The same approach was used both for individuals who were being offered their first job with the company and existing employees who felt they deserved a raise. In both cases, the manager and the

> **"The Internet has become the big level playing field for everyone [by exposing businesses that] are way below everyone else as far as pay is concerned."**
>
> —Brian Krueger, consultant[5]

organization usually had the upper hand because both prospective and current employees generally had relatively little knowledge about prevailing wage and salary levels. They usually did not know what others in the firm were being paid, for example, or what similar companies were paying for similar jobs in different parts of the region or country.

The Internet is rapidly changing all that. Several large Web sites now provide salary information for interested parties. Among other information, these sites include salary survey data, job listings with specified pay levels, and even customized compensation analyses. Armed with such detailed information, more and more people today are negotiating better deals for themselves with their employers.

Sometimes the Web can provide even more insights, especially for crafty negotiators. For example, some people have been known to use Internet bulletin boards to track down other individuals who have recently been offered employment with a particular firm, find out how much they were offered, and then use that information as leverage in their own negotiations.

In another unforeseen development, the big-time recruiting firm of Korn/Ferry recently set up its own salary site called Futurestep. But the firm faced internal negotiations when some of its own employees used the site to determine that they themselves were being underpaid! On balance, then, it seems like the Internet will be playing a major role from now on in the kinds of wages and salaries that employees expect and that companies pay.

THINK IT OVER

1. How do you foresee using the Internet in your initial job search after you finish school?
2. Are there drawbacks to using the Internet to search for salary information?

---

higher salaries for comparable work, then she might be concerned about external equity. Problems with external equity may result in higher turnover (because employees will leave for better opportunities elsewhere), dissatisfied and unhappy workers, and difficulties in attracting new employees.

How does an employer learn about compensation rates at other firms? In some cases, a human resource manager might simply ask a colleague for such information, but there are potential charges of "price-fixing" if such discussions are too detailed. More commonly, much of the information concerning external equity comes from a **pay survey**, or a survey of compensation paid to employees by other employers in a particular geographic area, industry, or occupational group. Some such surveys, especially for executive and managerial jobs, are conducted by professional associations such as the Society for Human Resource Management, and the results are then made available to all members. Individual employees may have access to this

> **Pay surveys** *are surveys of compensation paid to employees by other employers in a particular geographic area, industry, or occupational group.*

information, or they may seek their own comparative data on the Internet. Indeed, as discussed more fully in the HR in the Twenty-First Century feature "Negotiating Salaries on the Web," the Internet is making this practice increasingly common and easy today.

Other organizations also routinely conduct wage surveys. Business publications such as *Business Week*, *Fortune*, and *Nation's Business* routinely publish compensation levels for various kinds of professional and executive positions. In addition, the Bureau of National Affairs and the Bureau of Labor Statistics also are important sources of government-controlled wage and salary survey information. To obtain the *exact* data they need, however, many larger firms design their own pay surveys, which allows the firm to take advantage of the expertise available in such firms and minimize their own risk and the prospects of making a significant error or mistake in the conduct of the survey.[4] Exhibit 9.1 presents a sample section from a pay survey.

A survey such as this one is sent to other organizations in a given region. In this case, the survey would go to organizations in various industries, but other surveys might be targeted to a specific industry. The jobs that are the focus of the survey should be benchmark jobs—that is, everyone understands the nature of the job, the content is fairly stable, and the job is likely to be found in a wide variety of organizations. In some surveys, specific benchmark jobs are coded to ensure that everyone reacts to the same job.

it is also important for organizations to control costs and not overpay individuals for the value of their contributions (which could lead to problems with internal equity) or provide excess or superfluous benefits or rewards.[7] Thus, the ideal compensation system would be one that reflects

> ## Under the Equal Pay Act 1962, men and women who perform essentially the same job must be paid the same.

Also, some surveys ask more specific questions about other areas of compensation. Data from surveys such as this are then summarized for each job.

Both internal and external equity are clearly important for an organization's compensation strategy. Perceptions of external inequity can lead to the type of job search that results in the voluntary turnover problems discussed in Chapter 6. But when a female employee, for example, perceives internal inequity vis-à-vis a male employee, this can also lead to a lawsuit. Recall from Chapter 2 that the Equal Pay Act of 1963 stipulates that men and women who perform essentially the same job must be paid the same. If there are differences in the compensation paid to men and

an appropriate balance of organizational constraints, costs, budgets, income, and cash flow relative to employee needs, expectations, demands, and market forces. We will discuss specific models of motivation in Chapter 13 and incentive pay plans in Chapter 14.

The fundamental purpose of compensation, then, is to provide an adequate and appropriate reward system for employees so that they feel valued and worthwhile as organizational members and representatives. Compensation represents more than the number of dollars a person takes home in her or his pay envelope. It also provides a measure of the employee's value to the organization and functions indirectly as an indicator of his or her self-worth.[8]

> ## The Fair Labor Standards Act established a minimum hourly wage for jobs and further stipulated that wages for hourly workers must be paid at a rate of one and a half times the normal rate for work in excess of 40 hours per week.

women, then such differences may be defensible if they are based on factors such as performance differentials. In any case, the organization may well find itself in court defending these decisions when there are perceptions of internal inequity.

Compensation can also serve a *motivational purpose*— that is, individuals should perceive that their efforts and contributions to the organization are recognized and rewarded. Individuals who work hard and perform at a high level should be compensated at a level higher than individuals who do just enough to get by and who perform at only an average or below average rate.[6] If everyone perceives this situation to be true, then employees will believe that the reward system is fair and just and that internal equity exists, and they will be more motivated to perform at their highest level. Clearly, then, organizations must adequately and effectively manage compensation. Underpayment can cause the problems discussed above, although

Wages Versus Salaries

An important distinction in the field of compensation is the difference between wages and salaries. **Wages** generally refer to hourly compensation paid to operating employees. Time is the basis for wages—that is, the organization pays individuals for specific blocks of their time such as payment by the hour. Most jobs that are paid on an hourly wage basis are lower-level or operational jobs within the organization. These employees are also eligible for the overtime provisions of the Fair Labor Standards Act (discussed in Chapter 2), which means they are eligible for extra pay if they work more than 40 hours a week. These employees are typically paid every 1 or 2 weeks. **Salary**, on

Wages *generally refer to hourly compensation paid to operating employees; the basis for wages is time.*

Salary *is income paid to an individual on the basis of performance, not on the basis of time.*

EXHIBIT 9.2 Strategic Options for Compensation

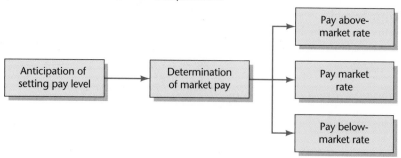

the other hand, describes compensation on a monthly or annual basis and compensates employees not for how much time they spend in the organization but for their overall contributions to the organization's performance. In general, salaries are paid to professional and managerial employees within an organization. Plant managers, product managers, and professional managers in areas such as marketing and finance and accounting, for example, are all likely to be paid on an annual basis; most of these employees are exempt from the overtime provisions of the Fair Labor Standards Act.

Strategic Options for Compensation

Most organizations establish a formal compensation strategy that dictates how they will pay individuals. Several decisions are embedded within such a strategy. The first relates to the basis for pay. Traditionally, most organizations based pay on the functions performed on the job, but more recently they have begun to rely on skill-based pay and pay-for-knowledge programs. In this way, organizations signal to their employees the relative importance of what someone does on the job versus what they bring to the job.

The second decision in developing a compensation strategy focuses on the bases for differential pay within a specific job. In some organizations, especially those with a strong union presence, differences in actual pay rates are based on seniority: With each year of service in a particular job, wages go up by a specified amount, so the longer one works on the job, the more that person makes, regardless of the level of performance on the job. Most public school systems use a seniority system to pay teachers: They get a base salary increase for each year of service they accumulate. As already noted, unions have historically preferred pay based at least in part on seniority.

Sometimes the relationship between seniority and pay is expressed as something called a **maturity curve**, a schedule specifying the amount of annual increase a person receives. This curve

> *A maturity curve is a schedule specifying the amount of annual increase a person will receive.*

is used when the annual increase varies based on the actual number of years of service the person has accumulated. Organizations that use maturity curves might argue that a new person tends to learn more (in part because there is more to learn) than more experienced employees and thus may deserve a larger increase. Meanwhile, more senior people may already be earning considerably higher income anyway and also have fewer new tasks to learn. In any event, the assumption under a seniority-based pay system is that employees with more experience can make a more valuable contribution to the organization and should be rewarded for that contribution. These systems also encourage employees to remain with the organization.

In other organizations, differences in pay are based on differences in performance, regardless of time on the job. These systems are generally seen as rewarding employees who are good performers rather than those who simply remain longer with the organization. For such systems to succeed, however, the organization has to be certain that it has an effective system for measuring performance (as will be discussed in Chapter 10). Most major companies base at least a portion of individual pay on performance, especially for managerial and professional employees. Performance-based incentives will be discussed in more detail in Chapter 14.

A third decision in developing a compensation strategy deals with the organization's pay rates relative to going rates in the market. As shown in Exhibit 9.2, the three basic strategic options are to pay above-market compensation rates, market compensation rates, or below-market compensation rates.[9] This decision is important because of the costs it represents to the organization.[10]

A firm that chooses to pay above-market compensation, for example, will incur additional costs as a result. This strategic option essentially indicates that the organization pays its employees a level of compensation that is higher than that paid by other employers competing for the same kind of employees. Of course, it also anticipates achieving various benefits. Some organizations believe that they attract better employees if they pay wages and salaries that are higher than those paid by other organizations; that is, they view compensation as a competitive issue. They recognize that high-quality employees may select from among several different potential employers and that they have a better chance of attracting the best employees if they're willing to pay them an above-market rate. Above-market pay policies are most likely to be used in larger companies, particularly those that have been performing well.

In addition to attracting high-quality employees, an above-market strategy has other benefits. Above-market rates tend to minimize voluntary turnover among employees. By definition, above-market rates mean that an employee who leaves a company paying such wages may have to take a pay cut to find employment elsewhere. Paying above-market rates also might be beneficial by creating and fostering a culture of elitism and competitive superiority. Cisco Systems, a Silicon Valley computer company, pays higher-than-average salaries specifically as a way of retaining its valued employees in an industry where turnover and mobility are high.

The downside to above-market compensation levels, of course, is cost. The organization simply has higher labor costs because of its decision to pay higher salaries to its employees. Once these higher labor costs become institutionalized, employees may begin to adopt a sense of entitlement, coming to believe that they deserve the higher compensation, making it difficult for the organization to be able to adjust its compensation levels downward.

Another strategic option is to pay below-market rates. The organization that adopts this strategy is essentially deciding to pay workers less than the compensation levels offered by other organizations competing for the same kinds of employees. Thus, it is gambling that the lower-quality employees it is able to attract will more than offset the labor savings it achieves. Organizations most likely to pursue a below-market rate are those in areas with high unemployment. If lots of people are seeking employment and relatively few jobs are available, then many people are probably willing to work for lower wages. Thus, the organization may be able to pay lower than the market rate and still attract reasonable and qualified employees. In other situations, employers may be able to pay below-market rates because of various offsetting factors. For instance, some employers in Hawaii find that the state's beautiful setting and mild weather allow them to pay below-market salaries—some people are willing to work for less money just to be able to live in Hawaii. Again, the benefit to this strategy is lower labor costs for the organization.

On the other hand, the organization will also experience several negative side effects. Morale and job satisfaction might not be as high as the organization would prefer. Individuals are almost certain to recognize that they are being relatively underpaid, and this situation can result in feelings of job dissatisfaction and potential resentment against the organization. In addition, turnover may also be higher because employees will be continually vigilant about finding better-paying jobs. Compounding the problem even further is the fact that the higher-performing employees are among the most likely to leave, and the lower-performing employees are among the most likely to stay.

Finally, a third strategic option for compensation is to pay market rates for employees—that is, the organization may elect to pay salaries and wages that are comparable to those available in other organizations, no more and no less. Clearly, the organization that adopts this strategy is taking a midrange perspective. The organization assumes that it will get higher-quality human resources than a firm that takes a below-market strategy. At the same time, it is willing to forgo the ability to attract as many high-quality employees as the organization that takes an above-market strategy.

The advantages and disadvantages of this strategy are also likely to reflect midrange comparisons with the other strategies. The organization will have higher turnover than a firm paying above-market rates but lower turnover than an organization paying below-market rates. An organization that adopts a market-rate strategy is likely to believe it can provide other intangible or more subjective benefits to employees in return for their accepting a wage rate that is perhaps lower than they might be paid elsewhere. For example, job security is one important subjective benefit that some organizations provide.

Employees who perceive that they are being offered an unusually high level of job security may therefore be willing to take a somewhat lower wage rate and accept employment at a market rate. Universities frequently adopt this strategy because they believe that the ambience of a university environment is such that employees do not necessarily expect higher salaries or higher wages. Microsoft also uses this approach. It offsets average wages with lucrative stock options and an exceptionally pleasant physical work environment.

Determinants of Compensation Strategy

Several different factors contribute to the compensation strategy that a firm develops. One general set of factors has to do with the overall strategy of the organization itself. As detailed in Chapter 4, a clear and carefully developed relationship should exist between a firm's corporate and business strategies and its human resource strategy.[11] This connection, in turn, should also tie into the firm's compensation strategy. Thus, a firm in a high-growth mode is constantly striving to attract new employees and may find itself in a position of having to pay above-market rates to do so. On the other hand, a stable firm may be more likely to pay market rates given the relatively predictable and stable nature of its operations. Finally, an organization in a retrenchment or decline mode may decide to pay below-market rates because it wants to reduce the size of its workforce anyway.[12]

to its employees, it may be necessary to pay higher wages simply as a way of attracting and retaining employees.

Union influences are another important determinant of an organization's compensation strategy. If an organization competes in an environment that is heavily unionized, such as the automobile industry, then the strength and bargaining capabilities of the union influence what the organization pays its employees. On the other hand, if the organization does not hire employees represented by unions or if the strength of a particular union is relatively low, then the organization may be able to pay somewhat lower wages and the union influence is minimal or nonexistent.

> *A firm in a high-growth mode is constantly striving to attract new employees and may find itself in a position of having to pay above-market rates to do so.*

In addition to these general strategic considerations, several other specific factors determine an organization's compensation strategy. One obvious factor is simply the organization's ability to pay. An organization with a healthy cash flow or substantial cash reserves is more likely to be able to pay above-market wages and salaries. On the other hand, if the organization suffers from a cash flow crunch, has few cash reserves, and is operating on a tight budget, it may be necessary to adopt a below-market wage strategy. The organization's ability to pay is thus an important consideration. During the economic stagnation of recent years, many firms have found themselves in this predicament. In response, several major companies reduced the pay increases they granted to their employees.[13]

In addition, the overall ability of the organization to attract and retain employees is a critical factor. For example, if the organization is located in an attractive area, has several noncompensation amenities, and provides a comfortable, pleasant, and secure work environment, it might be able to pay somewhat lower wages. But if the organization is located in, for example, a high-crime area or a relatively unattractive city or region, and if it has few noncompensation amenities that it can provide

Mailbox with MAIL text

© Myotis/Shutterstock

Job evaluation *is a method for determining the relative value or worth of a job to the organization so that individuals who perform that job can be compensated adequately and appropriately.*

The classification system *for job evaluation attempts to group sets of jobs together into clusters, which are often called grades.*

DETERMINING WHAT TO PAY

Once a compensation strategy has been chosen, it is necessary to determine exactly what employees on a given job should be paid. The starting point in this effort has traditionally been job evaluation. We will briefly describe this more traditional method first, but then discuss a more innovative and strategic approach to determining what to pay.

Job-Evaluation Methods

Job evaluation is a method for determining the relative value or worth of a job to the organization so that individuals who perform that job can be compensated adequately and appropriately. In other words, job evaluation is mostly concerned with establishing internal pay equity. Several job-evaluation techniques and methods have been established.[14] Among the most commonly used are classification, point, and factor-comparison systems.

Classification System. An organization that uses a **classification system** attempts to group sets of jobs together into classifications, often called *grades*. After classifying is done, each set of jobs is then ranked at a level of importance to the organization. Importance, in turn, may be defined in terms of relative difficulty, sophistication, or required skills and abilities necessary to perform that job.

EXHIBIT 9.3 Job-Classification System

Grade GS–1

Grade GS–1 includes those classes of positions the duties of which are to perform, under immediate supervision, with little or no latitude for the exercise of independent judgment:

    A. the simplest routine work in office, business, or fiscal operations; or

    B. elementary work of a subordinate technical character in a professional, scientific, or technical field.

Grade GS–6

Grade GS–6 includes those classes of positions the duties of which are:

    A. to perform, under general supervision, difficult and responsible work in office, business, or fiscal administration, or comparable subordinate technical work in a professional, scientific, or technical field, requiring in either case–
        1. considerable training and supervisory or other experience;
        2. broad working knowledge of a special and complex subject matter, procedure, or practice, or of the principles of the profession, art, or science involved; and
        3. to a considerable extent the exercise of independent judgment; or

    B. to perform other work of equal importance, difficulty, and responsibility, and requiring comparable qualifications.

Grade GS–10

Grade GS–10 includes those classes of positions the duties of which are:

    A. to perform, under general supervision, highly difficult and responsible work along special technical, supervisory, or adminstrative lines in office, business, or fiscal administration, requiring–
        1. somewhat extended specialized, supervisory, or administrative training and experience which has demonstrated capacity for sound independent work;
        2. thorough and fundamental knowledge of a specialized and complex subject matter, or of the profession, art, or science involved; and
        3. considerable latitude for the exercise of independent judgment; or

    B. to perform other work of equal importance, difficulty, and responsibility, and requiring comparable qualifications.

Source: U.S. Office of Personnel Management

A third step is to determine how many categories or classifications to use for grouping jobs. The most common number of grades is anywhere from eight to ten, although some organizations use the system with as few as four grades and some with as many as eighteen.

The U.S. postal system is a good example of an organization that uses the classification system. The U.S. postal system has sixteen job grades, with nine pay steps within each grade. Once the grades have been determined, the job evaluator must write definitions and descriptions of each job class. These definitions and descriptions serve as the standard around which the compensation system is built. Once the classes of jobs are defined and described, jobs that are being evaluated can be compared with the definitions and descriptions and placed into the appropriate classification.

A major advantage of the job-classification system is that it can be constructed relatively simply and quickly. It is easy to understand and easy to communicate to employees. It also provides specific standards for compensation and can easily accommodate changes in the value of various individual jobs in the organization. On the other hand, the job classification assumes that a constant and inflexible relationship exists between the job factors and their value to the organization, which sometimes results in jobs within a grade not fitting together very well. Exhibit 9.3 presents an example of a job-classification system.

Job-classification systems require clear definitions of classes and benchmark jobs for each class. The most widely known example of a job-classification system is the General Schedule (GS) system used by the federal government. This system has eighteen grades (or classes). Most federal employees fall into one of fifteen grades; the top three grades have been combined into a single "supergrade" that covers senior executives.

Exhibit 9.3 describes three grades from the GS system. An example of a job classified as a GS-1 would be a janitor; a GS-6 job would be a light truck driver; and an example of a GS-10 job would be an auto mechanic. Within each grade are ten pay steps based on seniority so that the range of salaries for a GS-6 job starts at just under $20,000 a year and goes up to more than $25,000 a year.

Point System. The most commonly used method of job evaluation is the point system.[15] The point system is more sophisticated than the classification system and is also relatively easy to use. The **point system** requires managers to quantify, in objective terms, the value of the various elements of specific jobs. Using job descriptions as a starting point, managers assign points to the degree of various *compensable factors* that are required to perform each job—that is, any aspect of a job for which an organization is willing to provide compensation. For instance, managers might assign points based on the amount of skill required to perform a particular job, the amount of physical effort needed, the nature of the working conditions involved, and the responsibility and authority involved in the performance of the job. Job evaluation simply represents the sum of the points allocated to each of the compensable factors for each job.

Point systems typically evaluate eight to ten compensable factors for each job. The factors chosen must not overlap one another, and they must immediately distinguish between substantive characteristics of the jobs, be objective and verifiable in nature, and be well understood and accepted by both managers and employees. Not all aspects of a particular job may be of equal importance, so managers can allocate different weights to reflect the relative importance of these aspects to a job. These weights are usually determined by summing the judgments of various independent but informed evaluators. Thus, an administrative job within an organization might result in weightings of required education, 40 percent; experience required, 30 percent; predictability and complexity of the job, 15 percent; responsibility and authority for making decisions, 10 percent; and working conditions and physical requirements for the job, 5 percent.

Because the point system is used to evaluate jobs, most organizations also develop a point manual. The **point manual** carefully and specifically defines the degrees of points from first to fifth. For example, education might be defined as follows: (1) first degree, up to and including a high school diploma, 25 points; (2) second degree, high school diploma and 1 year of college education, 50 points; (3) third degree, high school diploma and 2 years of college, 75 points; (4) fourth degree, high school education and 3 years of college, 100 points; and (5) fifth degree, a college degree, 125 points. These point manuals are then used for all subsequent job evaluation.

Factor-Comparison Method.

A third method of job evaluation is the factor-comparison method. Like the point system, the factor-comparison method allows the job evaluator to assess jobs on a factor-by-factor basis. At the same time, it differs from the point system because jobs are evaluated or compared against a standard of key points; instead of using points, a factor-comparison scale is used as a benchmark. Although an organization can choose to identify any number of compensable factors, commonly used systems include five job factors for comparing jobs: responsibilities, skills, physical effort, mental effort, and working conditions. Managers performing a job evaluation in a factor-comparison system are typically advised to follow six specific steps.

1. The comparison factors to be used are selected and defined. The five universal factors are used as starting points, but any given organization may need to add factors to this set.
2. Benchmark or key jobs in the organization are identified. These jobs are typically representative of and common in the labor market for a particular firm. Usually, ten to twenty benchmark jobs are selected.
3. The benchmark jobs are ranked on each compensation factor. The ranking itself is usually based on job descriptions and job specifications determined by a job analysis.
4. Part of each benchmark's job wage rate is allocated to each job factor based on the relative importance of the job factor. Each manager participating in the job evaluation might be asked to make an independent allocation first, without consulting with other managers. Then the managers would meet as a group to develop a consensus about the assignment of monetary values to the various factors.
5. The two sets of ratings are prepared based on the ranking and the assigned wages to determine the consistency demonstrated by the evaluators.
6. A job-comparison chart is developed to display the benchmark jobs and the monetary values that each job received for each factor. This chart can then be used to rate other jobs in the organization as compared to the benchmark jobs.

The factor-comparison system is a detailed and meticulous method for formally evaluating jobs. Thus, it provides a rigorous assessment of the true value of various jobs, which is one of its advantages. It also allows managers to recognize fully

The point system for job evaluation requires managers to quantify, in objective terms, the value of the various elements of specific jobs.

The point manual, used to implement the point system of job evaluation, carefully and specifically defines the degrees of points from first to fifth.

The factor-comparison method for job evaluation assesses jobs, on a factor-by-factor basis, using a factor-comparison scale as a benchmark.

© xy/Shutterstock

how the differences in factor rankings affect the compensation that the organization allocates to various jobs. On the other hand, the factor-comparison method is also extremely complex, difficult to use, time consuming, and expensive for an organization that chooses to adopt it. A fair amount of subjectivity is involved, and it is possible that people whose jobs are evaluated with this system may feel that inequities have crept into the system through either managerial error or politically motivated oversight.

Hay and Associates is a well-known compensation consulting firm that often does job evaluations for large organizations. It uses a factor-comparison system based on three factors: know-how, problem solving, and accountability.

Pay for Knowledge and Skill-Based Pay

The steps, decisions, and processes outlined above still apply in many organizations, but recent proposals have suggested a whole different approach to compensation: Employees should be rewarded for what they know rather than what they are specifically required to do on the job.

Pay for knowledge involves compensating employees (usually managerial, service, or professional employees) for learning specific material. This approach might include paying programmers for learning a new programming language or rewarding managers who master a new manufacturing system. These systems can also be designed to pay for learning supervisory skills or for developing more in-depth knowledge about a topic relevant to the organization. Pay-for-knowledge systems reward employees for mastering material that allows them to be more useful to the organization in the future and are based on mastering new technology or mastering information that relates to global issues. These systems tend to be fairly expensive to start because the organization needs to develop methods for testing whether the employee has mastered the information in question, but once in place, the costs are usually not excessive. These plans also have the potential to clash with more traditional incentive systems

(see Chapter 14) because employees might choose to perfect and apply knowledge they already have rather than learn new material.[16]

Skill-based pay operates in much the same way as a pay-for-knowledge system, but these plans are more likely to be associated with hourly workers. Instead of rewarding employees who master new material, employees are rewarded for acquiring new skills. Under such a plan, for example, an administrative assistant would be paid for learning how to use spreadsheets. The skills involved can be either for the same job (or in the same job family) or relevant for other jobs in the organization. For example, in manufacturing plants, it is often useful for employees to be cross-trained so that they have the skills to do several different jobs in the plant. This approach affords management a great deal of flexibility in scheduling, and it benefits employees because they can rotate through different jobs (providing some variety) and acquire skills that may increase their market value if they choose to seek another job.

WAGE AND SALARY ADMINISTRATION

Once wages and salaries have been determined, the resulting compensation system must be administered on an ongoing basis. Most organizations call this process **wage and salary administration** or *compensation administration*. Much of this administration involves making adjustments to wages and salaries as the result of pay raises or changes in job responsibilities. In addition, in organizations where jobs are arranged in a more hierarchical structure, programs should be implemented to maintain progression to a higher-level job within a job class. In addition, certain issues related to compensation must also be addressed as part of this administration process. Two of the most important involve pay secrecy and pay compression.

Pay for knowledge *involves compensating employees for learning specific information.*

Skill-based pay *rewards employees for acquiring new skills.*

Wage and salary administration *is the ongoing process of managing a wage and salary structure.*

PAY SECRECY

Pay secrecy refers to the extent to which the compensation of any individual in an organization is secret or the extent to which it is formally made available to other individuals. Each approach has merit.[17] On the one hand, advocates of pay secrecy maintain that what an individual is paid is his or her own business and not for public knowledge. They also argue that if pay levels are made known to everybody else, then jealousy or resentment may result. Indeed, most businesses practice pay secrecy, sometimes to the point of formally forbidding managers from discussing their pay with other people.

On the other hand, some organizations adopt a more open pay system in which everyone knows what everyone else makes. The logic is that this promotes equity and motivation. If high performers are known to make more money than low performers, then it logically follows that people throughout the organization will be motivated to work harder under the assumption that they too will be recognized and rewarded for their contributions. Many publicly funded organizations such as state universities and public schools have open pay systems whereby interested individuals can look at budgets or other information to determine how much any employee is being paid.

Pay Compression

Another problem that some organizations must confront occasionally during wage and salary administration is pay compression. **Pay compression** occurs when individuals with substantially different levels of experience or performance abilities are being paid wages or salaries that are relatively equal. Pay compression is most likely to develop when the market rate for starting salaries increases at a rate faster than an organization can raise pay for individuals who are already on the payroll. As a result, an employee with experience may find him- or herself not making much more than an entry-level employee. In some cases, the external market can change so rapidly that new employees are actually paid more than experienced employees; this is known as **pay inversion**.

Pay secrecy refers to the extent to which the compensation of any individual in an organization is secret or the extent to which information on compensation is formally made available to other individuals.

Pay compression occurs when individuals with substantially different levels of experience, or performance abilities, or both are paid wages or salaries that are relatively equal.

In pay inversion, the external market changes so rapidly that new employees are actually paid more than experienced employees.

LEARNING OBJECTIVE 4

THE NATURE OF BENEFITS PROGRAMS

As noted above, in addition to wages and salaries, most organizations provide their employees with an array of other indirect compensations, or *benefits*. Although these benefits were once called *fringe benefits* (and a few people still use this expression today), once managers began to fully realize that they were spending more than one-third of wages and salaries in additional expenses on benefits they decided that the word *fringe* might have been understating the true value of these benefits.

The Cost of Benefits Programs

Data from the U.S. Chamber of Commerce provides some insights into the composition of the total compensation paid to a typical employee in the United States. According to these figures, the typical employee costs the company almost $50,000 a year in total compensation. Of this amount, roughly $30,000 is paid for time worked, and the remaining $20,000 is pay for other than time worked, including vacation time, mandated benefits, pensions, insurance, and so forth.[18]

Hence, it is quite clear that organizations are spending huge amounts of money on benefits. It also appears that many organizations are trying to hold the tide, or even reverse it, by asking employees to bear more of the costs of these benefits. But surely benefits costs will continue to be a large part of labor costs in the United States. Note that despite these statistics, however, the United States actually ranks rather low in terms of the relative costs of benefits around the world.

These global differences result almost entirely from mandated benefits, which are based on the different social contracts (guarantees made by the government in return for higher taxes) in place in the respective countries, and they are substantial. For example, the German workweek is 38.3 hours (on average). The German worker works 1,685 hours per year, has 42 days off, and has mandated benefit costs alone that equal almost 30 percent of wages. For comparison purposes, the average U.S. worker spends 40 hours a week at work, spends 1,847 hours a year working, has 23 days off a year, and has mandated benefits costs equal to about 10 percent of wages. Indeed, when Ford acquired Swedish automobile maker Volvo, several years ago, Volvo workers immediately started to express their concerns about the potential loss of their relatively lavish benefits. These included an Olympic-size swimming pool, tanning beds, and tennis courts at the main manufacturing plant in Gothenburg, Sweden. Ford's strong U.S. benefits program paled in comparison to the program at Volvo.[19] This clash may well have been part of the reason why Ford finally decided to divest itself of Volvo in late 2009 and brokered a deal to sell the company to Chinese brand Zhejiang Geely Holding Group Co. Ltd.

As you can see, the exact benefits offered differ substantially from one country to the next, but in each case the benefits are designed to meet the specific needs (relative to balancing work and family) in the host country. For example, in Egypt, resorts are quite expensive, so offering short vacations for families to spend together is helpful. Because Muslims are expected to make the pilgrimage to Mecca at least once during their life (if at all possible), vacation time is a valuable benefit. Another example involves a multinational oil company, which operates in countries such as Norway, Trinidad, and the United Kingdom, where drilling operations tend to be off-shore or in rather remote regions of the country. As a result, employees do not see their families every day and do not generally live at home. Under these circumstances, compressed workweeks are extremely important to employees, as are other benefits such as family days, where families are brought to work sites for visits at company expense.

Purposes of Benefit Programs

In general, benefit programs serve several purposes for the organization. First, many experts believe that organizations willing to spend more money on total compensation are able to attract better-qualified people and convince employees to work harder, saving the company money. The general concept underlying this approach is known as *efficiency wage theory*. Little data exists to support or refute this position, but some organizations appear to view wages and benefits as a means of attracting better applicants.

Most experts would also argue that money spent on benefits affects job satisfaction and subsequent turnover. Even if employees do not work harder in response to better benefits, they are more likely to remain with a firm that provides better benefits and are more satisfied with that firm. In part, an employee's reactions to specific benefits programs reflect that individual's

belief about the value of benefits at the current company compared with the value of benefits at other companies. As a result, the need to remain competitive with other firms in an industry is a major force driving up the price of benefits. Just as when one airline in a market lowers fares and all others follow suit, once one visible organization in an industry starts offering a given benefit, it is usually not long until its competitors offer similar benefits.

In addition, various social, cultural, and political forces may promote the introduction of new and broader benefits programs. For example, increases in the number of women in the workforce and the rising costs of health care have each affected benefits programs in recent times. Because of the growth in the numbers of female workers, more and more companies offer on-site day care, dual-parent leave for the birth of a child, and other benefits that make it easier for people to work and have productive careers. Likewise, the health-care environment has prompted growth in benefits programs, including health maintenance organizations, managed health care, and so forth.

Finally, employee expectations are a driving force in determining what benefits a firm must offer. For example, even though an organization is not legally required to offer any vacation time, this benefit is so desirable and has become so common that almost every person who accepts a new job expects that he or she will be given vacation time. Indeed, most people today would be unlikely to accept a permanent full-time job without this basic benefit. A major implication of these issues, then, is the strategic importance of employee benefits. Their costs are high, and their effects are great. Thus, careful planning, monitoring, and communication about benefits are of paramount importance.

MANDATED BENEFITS

Some common benefits are mandated by law. Specifically, in the United States several laws have been passed that require organizations to offer certain types of benefits to their employees or that legislate the way benefit plans are administered. In Chapter 2 we discussed several of these, including the Family and Medical Leave Act of 1993, the Pregnancy Discrimination Act of 1979, and the Employee Retirement Income Security Act of 1974. Another significant law, the Social Security Act of 1935, is discussed later. Each of these laws has resulted in mandated benefits or legally restricted the way organizations treated certain benefits. Protection plans are benefits designed to provide protection to employees when their income is threatened or reduced by illness, disability, death, unemployment, or retirement. Unemployment insurance was created in the United States as part of the Social Security Act of 1935. The rationale for the act was to protect those people who were experiencing the high levels of unemployment that were pervasive in the United States during the 1930s.

Unemployment insurance is intended to provide a basic subsistence payment to employees who are between jobs—that is, for people who have stopped working for one organization but who are assumed to be seeking employment with another organization. Employers pay premiums to the unemployment insurance fund. In addition, in the states of Alabama, Alaska, and

variations in how these laws are administered from state to state.

Social Security

A second mandated benefit created by the same law is **Social Security** itself. What most people think of as Social Security is officially the **Old Age Survivors and Disability Insurance Program**. The initial purpose of this

> **Among other things, the Social Security Act of 1935 provides social welfare and social insurance coverage for retired workers.**

New Jersey, employees also contribute to the fund. The premium payment is increased if more than an average or designated number of employees from the organization are drawing from the fund at any given time. To be covered by unemployment insurance, an individual must have worked a minimum number of weeks, must now be without a job, and must be willing to accept a suitable position if one is found through a state's unemployment compensation commission or department.

Furthermore, if a covered employee is out of work through no fault of his or her own (as in the case of a layoff), then benefits start almost immediately. If the employee quits or is fired for cause (e.g., for poor performance), there is usually a waiting period before the individual can collect unemployment benefits. Regardless of the starting time, however, compensation is available for only a limited period (typically 26 weeks). Extensions beyond this term can also be granted if there is an emergency situation as was the case in 2010 as unemployment soared. Payments are generally about half of what individuals might have been earning on their former jobs, although an upper limit is placed on the benefit paid. As noted above, this program is funded through employer contributions, but there are considerable

program was to provide some limited income to retired individuals to supplement their own personal savings, private pensions, part-time work, and so forth. Unfortunately, many people have come to view Social Security as their primary source of retirement income. Problems associated with this assumption are discussed later in this section.

The Social Security program is funded through employee and employer taxes that are withheld on a payroll basis. Currently, the percentage of payment is 7.65 percent. Individuals are eligible for partial benefits when they reach age 62 or full benefits when they reach age 65. Effective in 2027, however, individuals will not be able to retire with full benefits until they reach age 67. If an employee dies before reaching retirement age, then a family with children under age 18 receives survival benefits, regardless of the employee's age at the time of her or his death. In addition, an employee who becomes totally disabled before age 65 is also eligible to receive insurance benefits; Medicare benefits are also provided under this act.

The amount of money any individual is eligible to be paid from the Social Security system is a function of the average monthly wage that individual earned, weighted toward the latter years of a person's career. In addition, an individual has to have worked a minimum period of time and made a minimum amount of contributions to the system to be eligible to draw full benefits. Actual funding for social security benefits, however, comes from the withholdings of current employees. They do not directly depend on the withholdings assessed against the employee who is retiring. This is a potential problem for the Social Security

Unemployment insurance, *a mandated protection plan, is intended to provide a basic subsistence payment to employees who are between jobs.*

Social security *(officially the* **Old Age Survivors and Disability Insurance Program***), another mandated program, was originally designed to provide limited income to retired individuals to supplement their personal savings, private pensions, part-time work, and so forth.*

system because retirees are living longer and it takes more current employees to fund the benefits of each retiree.

Workers' Compensation

Workers' compensation is also an important legally mandated benefit available to most employees. **Workers' compensation** is insurance that covers individuals who suffer a job-related illness or accident. Employers pay the cost of workers' compensation insurance. The exact premium paid is a function of each employer's past experience with job-related accidents and illnesses. About 100 million workers in the United States are protected under the Workers' Compensation Insurance Program.

In addition to these major forms of mandated benefits, a few others are also mandated by most states. For instance, in most instances organizations must give employees time off to vote and when they have been summoned for jury duty. The organization might or might not choose to pay the employee for the time off, but the employee cannot be penalized or otherwise sanctioned for taking the time.

NONMANDATED BENEFITS

Most organizations today provide other benefits in addition to those mandated by law. Businesses may elect to provide these benefits in order to attract more qualified workers. However, even if offering the benefit is elective, if a business does make the decision to offer that benefit, there are laws or regulations that must be followed.

Private Pension Plans

In addition to the pension benefits guaranteed under the Social Security Act, many companies elect to establish **private pension plans** for their employees. These prearranged plans are administered by the organization that provides income to the employee at her or his retirement. Contributions to the retirement plan may come from either the employer or the employee, but in most cases they are supported by contributions from both parties. Different retirement plans are available, including individual retirement accounts (IRAs) and employee pension IRAs. In addition, a 401(k) plan allows employees to save money on a tax-deferred basis by entering into salary deferral agreements with their employer.

There are two basic types of pension plans: defined benefit plans and defined contribution plans. Under **defined benefit plans**, the size of the benefit is precisely known and is usually based on a simple formula using input such as years of service and salary. This type of plan is often favored by unions and is closely monitored under the Employee Retirement Income Security Act of 1974, or ERISA (as discussed in Chapter 2). Although the employee may contribute to these plans, the amount of the contribution has little or no bearing on the actual pension payments. Under **defined contribution plans**, the size of the benefit depends on how much money is contributed to the plan. This money can be contributed by either the employer alone (noncontributory plans) or the employer and the employee (contributory plans). Most new pension plans are contributory, defined contribution plans, and there are legal restrictions concerning how the money is invested.

> ## The Employee Retirement Income Security Act of 1974 guarantees a basic minimum payment that employees could expect to be paid on retirement.

Paid Time Off

Most organizations also provide their employees with some amount of time off with pay. No U.S. laws mandate this type of benefit, but most employees now expect it. One major type of paid time off is the paid holiday. Most full-time employees receive about ten paid holidays per year. The most common holidays for which workers are paid without having to work include New Year's Day, Memorial Day, Independence Day, Labor Day, Thanksgiving Day, and Christmas. In addition, religious holidays (in addition to Christmas) are also often given. Organizations have to be careful with this practice, however, because growing diversity in the workplace is accompanied by an increasingly diverse set of religions and thus religious holidays, requiring clear policies about religious holidays, which are enforced equitably.[20]

Paid vacations are also common but are likewise not required by law. They are usually periods of 1, 2, or more weeks when an employee can take time off from work and continue to be paid. Most organizations vary the amount of paid vacation according to an individual's seniority with the organization, with newer employees receiving 1 week of paid vacation, and the most senior employees receiving as many as

Workers' compensation, *another mandated protection program, is insurance that covers individuals who suffer a job-related illness or accident.*

Private pension plans *are prearranged plans administered by the organization that provides income to employees at their retirement.*

Defined benefit plans *are private pension plans in which the size of the benefit is precisely known and is usually based on a simple formula using input such as years of service.*

Defined contribution plans *are private pension plans in which the size of the benefit depends on how much money is contributed to the plan.*

TABLE 9.1 Minimum Annual Vacation by Law in Different Countries

Country	Minimum Vacation Time (Days per Year)
Finland	30
France	30
United Kingdom	28
Russia	28
Norway	25
South Africa	21
Australia	20
Belgium	20

Source: Mercer (www.mercer.com/summary.htm), accessed on Feb. 24, 2010.

4 weeks of paid vacation a year. One part of the rationale for such long vacation breaks is that senior management employees need a break to escape from the stress of their jobs.[21] But, as can be seen in Table 9.1, some countries actually mandate extensive vacation benefits for all employees. Moreover, these vacation breaks are in addition to public holiday time. For example, Finnish workers get not only a mandated 30 days of vacation time per year but also an additional 10 public holidays.

Another common paid time-off plan is sick leave. This benefit is provided when an individual is sick or otherwise physically unable to perform his or her job duties. Most organizations allow an individual to accumulate sick time on the basis of some schedule, such as 1 sick day per month worked. Some organizations require that employees submit a doctor's note verifying illness in order to be paid for the day, but others do not. Further, some organizations extend sick day coverage when the employee needs to help with a spouse, child, or parent who is sick. Also, some organizations require the employee to use his or her allocation of sick days within a certain period of time (such as by December 31) or lose them. Under such a system, it would seem illogical for an employee not to take all the sick days allocated during the year. Finally, another form of paid time off is personal leave. Sometimes an organization allows an employee to take a small number of days off for personal business such as funerals and weddings.

Health Insurance Coverage

Perhaps the most common nonmandated benefit for full-time employees in the United States is health insurance coverage. In most cases, the employer and the employee share the cost of health insurance, with the proportion handled by each varying considerably. In many cases, the insurance includes special programs for prescription drugs, vision-care products, mental-health services, and dental care. In the United States, an estimated 85 percent to 90 percent of all health-insurance coverage is purchased by employers as group plans covering their employees.[22]

During much of 2009 and early 2010, the U.S. Congress debated the most sweeping health-care reform bill ever considered in this country. The bill that was finally passed in March 2010 did not have the public option that Democrats wanted so badly. The full impact—both in terms of coverage and cost—will slowly unfold over the next few years.. Why reform health care in the United States? Although there is a serious concern over the rising costs of health care, perhaps the biggest impetus for the proposed new legislation was the fact that many Americans were simply not covered by any type of health-care insurance. In fact, according to AARP, 47 million Americans had no health-care insurance in 2009.[23]

President Obama had argued that we needed a so-called public option in the insurance field—that is, he proposed that the federal government offer health care that would be available at a lower cost. This could help drive down costs for other plans and would also provide a more affordable alternative for those who could not afford private health insurance. This public option was not popular with private insurers, and remains one of the most controversial parts of health-care reform, and the whole idea fell victim to political deals that were needed to gain passage of the legislation. The bill still includes some requirement for all employers to provide some form of health-care insurance for employees or be taxed in order to help pay for the uninsured, and the elimination of preexisting condition exclusions

"Harvard just completed a study that shows 45,000 Americans die every year because they don't have health insurance, almost 1,000 a week in America."

—SENATE MAJORITY LEADER HARRY REID (D-NEVADA), White House health-care summit, February 25, 2010

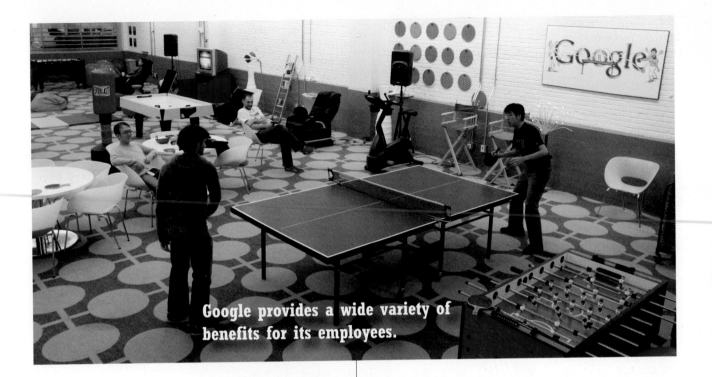

Google provides a wide variety of benefits for its employees.

© William Perlman/Star Ledger/Corbis

used by insurance companies to refuse payment for health care is an important part of the bill as passed. Of course, regardless of your views about health-care reform, one of the more troubling remaining issues for people on all sides of the discussion is how to pay for the estimated $1 trillion that will be required to truly reform health care in the United States.[24]

Other Benefits

Private pensions, pay for time not worked, and health insurance are the most common nonmandated benefits, but many other benefits also are available. For example, disability insurance pays for employees who cannot work because of some injury or disability. Also, in an attempt to reduce health-care costs, some companies have introduced a different type of benefit known as a **wellness program**. Wellness programs concentrate on keeping employees from becoming sick rather than simply paying expenses when they do become sick.[25] In some organizations, these programs may be simple and involve little more than organized jogging or walking during lunch breaks, but some organizations have full-fledged health clubs on site and provide counseling and programs for fitness and weight loss. These plans are either paid for by the company or heavily subsidized because they are attractive to employees who appreciate the ease and low costs; at the same time, they can reduce costs by reducing the number of sick days, cut medical costs, and improve productivity as the organization gains a more physically fit workforce.[26]

An additional group of benefits is often referred to collectively as *life-cycle benefits*, or benefits targeted at different stages in an employee's life. The most common are child-care and elder-care benefits. Child-care benefits are becoming more popular because the changing nature of the workforce and the fact that being considered a family-friendly organization (which must, at a minimum, have some type of child-care benefits) is increasingly viewed as a competitive advantage in attracting talented workers.[27] These plans might include scheduling child-care help, referrals to various types of child-care services, or reimbursement accounts for child-care expenses. Company-paid day care has been found to strongly affect employee attitudes and job performance.[28] Elder-care benefits are also growing in popularity. These typically take the form of referrals for employees with a disabled parent or one who needs constant care. Long-term health-care insurance is also becoming a more common benefit, and these plans provide for nursing homes or at-home care.

A somewhat different type of service is contained in what are referred to as *employee assistance plans*. These programs are designed to assist employees who have chronic problems with alcohol or drugs or who have serious domestic problems. An increase in the number of programs for mental problems and stress, as well as for bereavement, have also been part of a recent trend.[29] These programs are typically voluntary, and referrals are confidential. Yet the needs of the organization (especially when the personal problem is causing performance problems on the job) must be balanced with the needs of

Wellness programs *are special benefits programs that concentrate on keeping employees from becoming sick rather than simply paying expenses when they do become sick.*

the individual to avoid any stigma attached to having the specific problem.[30]

Finally, employee perquisites are sometimes provided. A *perquisite*, or *perk*, as it is more informally known, is an extra benefit that may or may not have any direct financial value but is considered an important reward by employees. A perk might include a bigger office, a company car, membership in a country club, stock-purchase options, premium insurance coverage, and so forth. Perquisites are usually made available only to members of top management or to certain especially valuable professionals within the organization.

Sometimes organizations provide special perquisites that might be available to all employees. For example, Google provides free transportation from many remote locations to its headquarters, and the company also provides free meals for employees in its various cafeterias.

Although most benefits programs are designed for all the employees in an organization, **cafeteria-style benefits plans** allow the employee to choose the benefits that he or she really wants. Under these plans, the organization typically establishes a budget indicating how much it is willing to spend per employee on benefits.[31] The employee is then presented with a list of possible benefits and the cost of each; they are free to choose the benefits in any combination they wish. Such an approach should maximize the effectiveness of the benefits program for achieving the organizational goals discussed at the beginning of the chapter, and some evidence suggests that cafeteria-style benefits programs can lead to increased satisfaction and reduced turnover.[32]

Nonetheless, these programs are not without problems. One challenge is the cost of administering such plans. Because every employee has a potentially unique set of benefits, someone has to keep track of what benefits each employee has chosen, and these choices can usually be changed over time. Another problem is what is known as *adverse selection*. This refers to the fact that the employee most likely to select a benefit, such as children's braces, is also most likely to use the benefit, which tends to drive up benefit costs. Finally, given a choice of benefits, employees are not always rational in their choices. A younger employee may elect to contribute less to his or her retirement because retirement seems like a distant future event and wait until later in life before increasing the contribution. But given the power of compounding interest, a larger contribution early in life, followed by a smaller contribution later, is actually worth much more at retirement age than a smaller contribution made early in life followed by a larger contribution made later. It is thus extremely important for employees to have full information about the available benefits, and in some cases it may be necessary for the organization to mandate minimum benefits levels in some areas.

One of the most controversial issues for benefits programs involves the question of whether to extend benefits to same-sex partners. It has become fairly typical for organizations to extend benefits to spouses of employees, but the move to extend these benefits to life partners or spousal equivalents has been accepted much more slowly.[33] Obviously, objections to such a plan are based on different points of view, but more organizations are coming to believe that it is simply fair to extend benefits to same-sex partners. Chevron's corporate headquarters is located in San Francisco, California, and, in an attempt to be fair and to remain competitive for employees in the local market, the company decided to extend all health and insurance benefits to same-sex partners. Although this move was applauded in San Francisco, employees at headquarters for the firm's production company located in Houston, Texas, were less enthusiastic. The company made it clear, however, that the provision of these benefits is company policy and that it believed that gay and lesbian partners deserved equal treatment on the job—and employees who could not live with this policy were invited to seek employment elsewhere.

CONTEMPORARY ISSUES IN COMPENSATION AND BENEFITS

Three contemporary issues in compensation and benefits include executive compensation, growing legal issues, and how best to evaluate compensation and benefits programs.

Executive Compensation

Quite simply stated, many human resource management practices and techniques do not work well with top executives. Selection and appraisal of these executives cannot be accomplished using the methods used for other employees.

Cafeteria-style benefits plans *allow employees to choose those benefits they really want.*

© L. Barnwell/Shutterstock

But the area of human resource management that is most important for executives deals with their compensation. Therefore, we will concentrate primarily on the issue of executive compensation, discussing techniques and methods as well as some of the issues that arise in this area.

Most senior executives receive their compensation in two forms: base salary and some form of incentive pay. The traditional method of incentive pay for executives is in the form of bonuses, which can exceed their base pay by some multiple. Bonuses are typically a function of the performance of the organization and are less dependent on the perceived performance of the executive. Near the end of a fiscal year, some portion of a corporation's profits are diverted into a bonus pool, and the share received by each executive is determined partially by perceived performance but mostly in advance as part of the executive's employment contract.

For example, in 2009, Goldman Sachs set aside $16.7 billion for compensation, most of which was paid out in year-end bonuses. As a result, the average salary of a Goldman employee was reported to be $595,000 in 2009. This figure may be shockingly high for some readers, but the fact that Goldman also reported record profits for the year suggests that executives may well have earned their huge paychecks.[34] All of these announcements took place, however, against the backdrop of the highest unemployment rate (10%) in living memory in the United States. Furthermore, many financial firms, including Goldman had accepted large amounts of government support to keep the company viable after the financial meltdown in late 2008. Although Goldman had repaid that money, the outcry over the size of the payouts led the firm to actually consider requiring that some portion of the bonus money be donated to charity.[35]

New York's State Attorney General Andrew Cuomo released a report in July 2009 that described how many employees in each of several large financial firms received bonuses of at least $1 million in 2008—before most of the funds had been repaid. Those totals are presented in Table 9.2.[36]

But annual bonuses are not the whole story. In addition to bonuses, many executives also receive stock options. Although in some cases annual bonuses are paid out in the form of stock options (which was what Goldman Sachs reported would be the case for its year-end bonuses in 2010), these options are usually above and beyond year-end bonuses. A stock-option plan is established to give senior managers the option to buy the company stock in the future at a predetermined, fixed price. The basic idea underlying stock-option plans is that if the executives contribute to higher levels of organizational performance, then the company stock should increase. Then the executive can purchase the stock at the predetermined price that, theoretically, should be lower than its future market price. The difference then becomes profit for

TABLE 9.2	Number of Executives Receiving a Bonus of at Least $1 Million in 2008
Institution	**Number of Executives**
Bank of America	172
Bank of New York Mellon	74
Citigroup	738
Goldman Sachs	953
JPMorgan Chase	1,144
Merrill Lynch	696
Morgan Stanley	428
State Street	44
Wells Fargo	62

the individual. These options can be worth huge sums of money, such as the case for Steve Jobs in 2006 when his then fully vested stock options were valued at $646 million (his total compensation was only $14.6 million in 2007).

Of course, in 2009 many of these stock options were not worth as much as they had been as stock prices plummeted. However, by 2010, most of the lost value of the stock market had been recouped, presumably making stock options once again a viable form of compensation. In fact, in a report issued several years ago, KPMG Peat Marwick stated that, for all of top management (managers with annual salaries of more than $750,000), stock options constituted a full 60 percent of their total compensation. The KPMG Peat Marwick report also indicated that even among exempt employees at the $35,000-a-year level, stock options represented 13 percent of total compensation.

Agency theory arguments are often cited as the rationale for stock-option plans. The owners of the firm (typically the stockholders) want to increase firm's profitability, but the CEO does not necessarily have any incentive to work toward maximizing profits. By basing a considerable portion of the CEO's compensation on stock, however, the interests of the CEO are presumably aligned more closely with the interests of the owners, and everyone works toward the same goal. But some critics have noted that CEO and firm interests are not really aligned, however, until the CEO or executive actually exercises the stock option. Up to that point, the executive might actually even have an incentive to lower stock prices in the short run in the hope of being offered more options at the lower price of the stock.[37] Moreover, stock options generally tend to have relatively short timelines, so managers may be motivated to make short-term decisions that are likely to drive up stock prices even though a different decision might have been better for the firm's long-term success.

Aside from stock-option plans, other kinds of executive compensation are also used by some companies. Among the more popular are such perquisites as memberships in private clubs, access to company recreational facilities, and

similar kinds of benefits. Some organizations occasionally make low- or no-interest loans available to senior executives. These loans are often given as incentives to new executives who are being hired away from other companies.

Given the money involved, it is not surprising that executive compensation continues to be a controversial topic. CEO compensation now runs almost 100 times the average wage rate of an hourly employee. In 2010, with the memory of the financial problems of 2009 still fresh in everyone's mind, it was not unusual for people to ask why CEOs should be paid so much when they seemed responsible for much of the country's financial problems.

Furthermore, executive compensation in the United States seems far out of line with that paid to senior executives in other countries. For example, compensation for foreign CEOs has only recently crept into the seven-figure range, their annual bonuses are much smaller, and they seldom participate in lavish stock-option plans like those enjoyed by their U.S. counterparts. Looking at the total package clouds the compensation comparisons a bit. For example, Exhibit 9.4

EXHIBIT 9.4 Senior Executive Perquisites in Different Countries

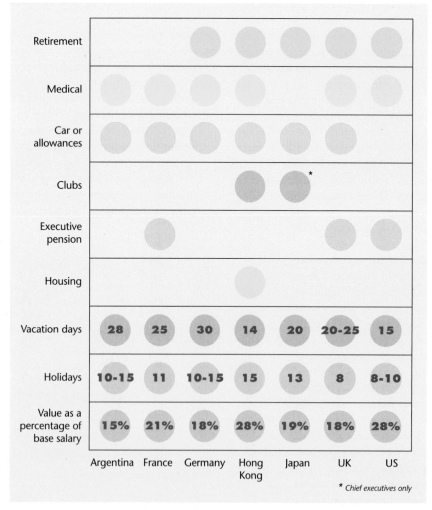

Source: "How Perks Stack Up Worldwide" from *Forbes*, May 19, 1997, p. 162. Reprinted by permission of *Forbes* Magazine © Forbes, Inc., 1997.

shows the complete package of executive perquisites for seven countries. Although U.S. executives clearly top the list, their counterparts tend to receive more vacation and sick time, plus a car or car allowance.

Compounding the problem created by perceptions of executive compensation is the fact that little or no relationship seems to exist between the performance of the organization and the compensation paid to its senior executives.[38] Certainly, if an organization performs at an especially high level and its stock price is increasing consistently, then most observers would agree that the senior executives responsible for this growth should be entitled to attractive rewards.[39] However, it is more difficult to understand situations in which executives are paid huge salaries and other forms of rewards when their companies are performing at only a marginal level or even poorly, yet this is fairly common today. A few years earlier, Oracle's CEO Lawrence Ellison pocketed more than $700 million from the sale of previously granted stock options, but during the same year the value of Oracle stock dropped by 57 percent.

Several highly publicized bankruptcies in 2001–02 further raised concerns over executive pay and especially over stock options. Enron, for example, declared bankruptcy even as CEO Ken Lay enjoyed the gains from the stock options he had recently exercised. Similar tales from other companies led to a strong belief for many people that something should be done about how stock options were treated.

Finally, there is some concern about the effects the huge gap between CEO pay and everyone else's pay might have on those other employees. On the one hand, he or she may not believe that the CEO is making 100 times the contribution made by the typical employee, or at least that no one could be working 100 times as hard. This perception may lead to resentment and other problems on the job, and evidence suggests that such large dispersions result in decreased satisfaction, willingness to collaborate, and overall productivity.[40] On the other hand, the typical employee may view this huge salary as a prize worth aiming for. From this perspective, pay structures are seen as tournaments, and the bigger the prize, the more intense the competition, and so the greater the effort and productivity. In fact, some evidence supports this position, indicating that managers cannot really be sure of the effects of these income gaps.[41]

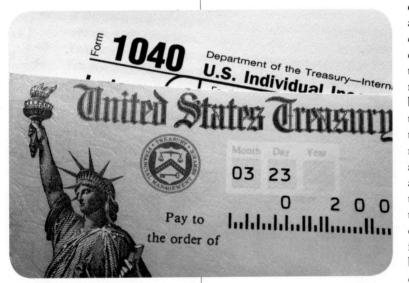

Legal Issues in Compensation and Benefits

The major legal issues involved in compensation and benefits were discussed in Chapter 2, but we will review them briefly here. The Fair Labor Standards Act includes provisions for the minimum wage, overtime, and child labor. It also specifies which employees are covered by the overtime provisions and which are exempt; this usually affects whether an employee is paid wages or a salary. Even nonexempt workers are sometimes asked to work more than 40 hours with no overtime pay; in exchange, they are offered time off, which is usually referred to as *comp time*. Thus, someone who has to work 45 hours one week might be assigned only 35 hours the next week but still receive full pay. Comp time is often not as beneficial to the employee, who would otherwise earn more in total pay, but it is more cost-efficient for the organization. And it does give employees something that many of them value: time away from work.

The legal issues related to benefits are a bit more complicated. Organizations typically seek to ensure that their benefit plans are qualified; that is, where the employer receives an immediate tax deduction for any contributions made, the employee does not incur a tax liability at the time of the employer deduction, and investment returns (such as from stocks and bonds) are accumulated tax-free. Although the requirements for qualification differ for different types of benefits plans, it is critical that the plan be nondiscriminatory: The plan cannot disproportionately favor employees with higher income levels.[42]

Of course, the most important legal issue in this area deals with the Employee Retirement Income Security Act (ERISA) of 1974. We introduced this law in Chapter 2, but it deserves additional attention here. As noted earlier, this law was passed to protect employees who had contributed to their pensions but were unable to collect those benefits later. This situation occurred primarily because of the restrictions that the organizations had placed on employees before they could receive retirement benefits. Specifically, organizations required that employees remain with the company as long as 30 years before they were vested. (**Vesting rights** are guaranteed rights to receive

Vesting rights *are guaranteed rights to receive pension benefits.*

© cabania/Shutterstock

pension benefits.) For example, before 1974 a 60-year-old employee with 29 years of service would not be entitled to pension benefits if he or she left the company—or even if he or she died—before his or her 30-year anniversary. Under ERISA, however, vesting rights become operational after 6 years *at the most*, and employees with less service are still usually eligible to receive some portion of their retirement benefits.

ERISA also provides protection for the funding underlying the pension plan. The Pension Benefit Guaranty Corporation oversees how pension plans are funded, and it can seize corporate assets to support underfunded plans. In addition, ERISA allows an employee to carry a portion of his or her benefits to another job. This notion of portability is especially important when employees change jobs frequently. ERISA also imposes some minimum requirements for how pension plans are communicated to employees. If an organization does not follow ERISA guidelines, its pension plan will not be qualified as just defined.

Evaluating Compensation and Benefit Programs

Given the enormous cost to an organization of compensation and benefit packages, it managers clearly must carefully assess the benefit of these packages for the organization. Although it may not be easy to assess the effectiveness (or even the "right" level) of executive compensation, it is easier to deal with the other aspects of compensation and benefits. Organizations that do not offer competitive pay and benefit packages will find it increasingly difficult to attract employees—especially the best potential employees. Furthermore, because satisfaction with pay and benefits is an important part of overall job satisfaction, noncompetitive packages will lead to higher rates of voluntary turnover as well.

In any case, many organizations may find that their benefit programs do not seem to be as much as they could be simply because the organization has not communicated effectively with employees about those benefits. Indeed, many organizational surveys suggest that many employees are not fully informed about their benefits. For example, some evidence suggests that awareness about benefits could be increased through communication via several media and that, as awareness increased, so would satisfaction with benefits.[43] The reason for this relationship is underscored by the results of another study in which employees were asked to estimate the value of the employer's contribution to their benefits. When asked about family coverage, the average estimate was only 38 percent of the actual cost of those benefits to the employer.[44] It seems clear that an organization can never expect to appreciate the full advantage of its benefits program when employees underestimate the cost of their benefits by such a large amount.

CLOSING CASE

WAGING WAR OVER WAGES

The intent and application of the overtime pay law seems perfectly clear. The Fair Labor Standards Act (FLSA) of 1938 requires workers to be paid time-and-a-half for any hours worked beyond 40 each week. The 70-year-old law should be well understood. Yet over the last 10 to 15 years, the number of employee lawsuits alleging violations of the overtime laws has grown tremendously. American companies pay out more than $1 billion annually to settle the claims. A former defense attorney in wage cases, J. Nelson Thomas, switched to the plaintiff side. "I was amazed at how prevalent the violations were and the size of the settlement," says Thomas.

The FLSA aided the country's recovery from the Great Depression by encouraging workers to work longer hours and for employers to hire additional workers. The modern workforce and business environment have changed so much since the 1930s, however, that the justification for the law is no longer so straightforward. In 1938, there was a clear distinction between white-collar workers (exempt from overtime pay) and blue-collar labor (eligible for overtime). White-collar jobs were seen as easier and less in need of legal protection. By the 1960s however, professionals worked more hours on average than working-class employees. Today, there is blurred distinction between "management" and "workers."

Employers must judge whether an employee is exempt from overtime, based on the uses of "discretion and independent judgment." But as businesses become more standardized and controlled, fewer and fewer workers work independently. If an accountant's work consists primarily of entering data or checking facts, then he or she is not acting independently. Computer programmers "get to pick whatever code they want to write, but [only to] implement someone else's desires," says Mark Thierman, a labor attorney.

Some companies simply cheat their employees. For example, Hollywood Video had to pay $7.2 million in damages to workers who had been required to punch out their time cards before closing the cash register nightly. The "off the clock" time was documented by store surveillance cameras. Walmart settled one suit for $72.5 million because of "off the clock" time and has several other lawsuits pending.

Companies can also make good faith mistakes in classifying employees as exempt or nonexempt because of the complex and changing nature of work. When does the workday begin for utility workers who download their day's schedule from home computers every morning? Do workers who check e-mail remotely deserve overtime? Can an employee claim overtime for working at home or during lunch? What about flight time, on-call time, time spent entertaining, or time spent on continuing education?

Many industries and workers are affected: an $87-million settlement for 23,000 UPS drivers; a $98-million settlement for 20,000 stockbrokers at Citigroup; $65 million paid to IBM customer support staff; pharmaceutical sales representatives for Bristol-Myers winning judgments; thousands of Intel programmers; Starbucks' store managers; pizza delivery workers; tax auditors. Eighty-six percent of the U.S. workforce—115 million workers—is covered by overtime laws. This enormous number of affected workers makes this issue potentially much more damaging than other class-action matters. Thomas says, "I can hit a company with a hundred sexual harassment lawsuits and it will not inflict anywhere near the damage that [a wage and hour suit] will."

White-collar workers often resist the idea of claiming overtime pay. "They associate it with a labor pool that is valued for brawn rather than brains," suggests *Business Week* writer Michael Orey. Yet the FLSA applies to employees paid either wages or salaries, regardless of income, education, or job title. "You don't have to be stupid to get overtime," says Thierman. "In fact you're stupid if you don't get overtime."

As professionals become more aware of and comfortable with their rights to overtime pay, organizations may have to come up with billions more in compensation. One middle manager declares the new attitude toward overtime pay. "If a company wants my knowledge 24/7, they should have to pay for it, whenever they use it. No different from using the muscles of an assembly-line worker."[45]

THINK IT OVER

1. What does this case suggest to you about the differences between salaried managers and hourly employees? What does it suggest to you about equity between workers in the same organization and across different organizations?

2. What types of behavior are encouraged by companies who do not pay overtime to their white-collar workers? What behaviors are encouraged when companies do pay overtime?

3. Some experts are concerned that if American white-collar workers increase their compensation by demanding and receiving overtime pay, then offshore labor will gain an even larger cost advantage, hurting U.S. companies. Do you agree or disagree?

STUDY TOOLS

- ■ Rip out the chapter review card located at the end of the book.
- ■ Review the valuable study tools located online at www.cengagebrain.com
  - ■ Review the Key Terms flashcards.
  - ■ Download audio and visual summaries to review on the go.
  - ■ Complete practice quizzes to prepare for the test.
  - ■ Play "Beat the Clock" and "QuizBowl" to master chapter concepts.
  - ■ Complete "Crossword Puzzle" to review key terms.
  - ■ Watch the chapter video for a real-life example of key concepts.

Performance Appraisal & CAREER Management

"It's pretty blatant that they're trying to get rid of older employees."

—John Van Hoose, 59, Goodyear employee and member of a C group

"WHEN IS ACCEPTABLE UNACCEPTABLE?"

For years, General Electric has used a ruthlessly efficient method for evaluating the performance of its employees. The system is widely known informally as the ABC approach. Each year, managers are required to sort all of their subordinates into one of three categories. The best, as much as 10 percent of the workforce, makes up the A group; the next set, as much as 80 percent, includes those in the middle and is called the B group (this large group subsequently gets broken down into smaller groups).

The lowest 10 percent, though, is called the C group—and these workers lose their jobs even if they are generally seen as exhibiting acceptable performance! GE executives argue that this allows the firm to continuously elevate the quality of the firm's human capital. Moreover, they note, everyone knows the rules when they sign on and no one has ever sued the company over this practice.

It is no surprise, then, that a few other companies have tried to follow in GE's footsteps. Goodyear was one of the first. Its first efforts identified 2,800 employees making up the worst performers in the company. These workers were then given their walking papers. Not too long afterward, though, Goodyear said it was abandoning the ABC method. Why? The tire maker became the target of an age-discrimination lawsuit that claimed that it singled out too many older employees as bad workers.

Another big company that experimented with—but quickly dropped—the ABC method was Ford Motor Company. The firm paid handsomely for its brief experiment when it agreed to pay $10.6 million to settle an age-discrimination suit filed by a group of fired employees. Since then, most other recent adopters of the ABC system have also dropped it.

LEARNING OBJECTIVES

After studying this chapter you should be able to:

LO1 *Describe the purposes of performance appraisal in organizations*

LO2 *Summarize the performance-appraisal process in organizations*

LO3 *Identify and describe the most common methods that managers use for performance appraisal*

LO4 *Discuss other general issues involving performance appraisal in organizations*

LO5 *Describe the nature of careers in organizations*

LO6 *Discuss human resource management and career management*

LO7 *Identify and discuss basic career-development issues and challenges*

© AP Photo/Tony Dejak

OPENING

One catalyst for the quick demise of the ABC system was when AARP, an advocacy group for Americans 50 years of age and older committed itself to provide legal resources to those suing Goodyear company. The lawsuit named eight plaintiffs aged 55 to 59, whose annual salaries ranged from $48,700 to $71,700. The lawsuit claimed that hundreds of workers in more than ten states could join if the case was granted class-action status.

Jim Skykora, 55, the youngest and best-paid plaintiff, said in an interview that he had been designing tires for various Goodyear customers and had had all eleven of his projects approved in the

4 years leading up to his termination. He was graded a B– the first year the system was in place and downgraded to a C the next year. In fact, the first lawsuit ended with the court agreeing with Goodyear that the company's practice was not discriminatory, but the tire maker still decided to retreat from the ABC system and revert to its old methods.[1]

THINK IT OVER
1. Would you like to work under an ABC system?
2. How would you feel about using the ABC for a group of your own subordinates?

Virtually all businesses must focus some degree of attention on performance management. Indeed, the effective management of performance may be the difference between success and failure. Many firms, such as Merrill Lynch, find it necessary to occasionally adjust how they approach performance management. Performance-appraisal systems are designed to provide organizations with the information to manage performance improvement. To develop employees to their full potential, however, organizations also must help employees manage their careers. Career management and career development enable employees to grow both personally and professionally. Further, performance appraisals help provide employees with information on how they can best manage their own careers. This chapter is about performance-appraisal systems and their implications for how individuals manage their careers. We also cover careers from other perspectives.

Performance appraisal is the specific and formal evaluation of an employee to determine the degree to which the employee is performing his or her job effectively. Some organizations use the term *performance appraisal* for this process, and others prefer to use different terms such as *performance evaluation, performance review, annual review, employee appraisal,* or *employee evaluation.* The outcome of this evaluation is some type of score or rating on a scale. These evaluations are typically conducted once or twice a year. A related topic, **performance management**, refers to the more general set of activities carried out by the organization to change (improve) employee performance. Although performance management typically relies heavily on performance appraisals, performance management is a broader and more encompassing process and is the ultimate goal of performance-appraisal activities. We will touch on some concepts of performance management in this chapter but will discuss these ideas much more fully in Chapter 14.

A performance appraisal is the specific and formal evaluation of an employee to determine the degree to which the employee is performing his or her job effectively.

Performance management is the general set of activities carried out by the organization to change (improve) employee performance.

LEARNING OBJECTIVE 1

WHY ORGANIZATIONS CONDUCT PERFORMANCE APPRAISALS

Most people involved in performance appraisals tend to be dissatisfied with them. This is true for both the person being rated and the person doing the rating. We will discuss some of the major reasons for this dissatisfaction in this chapter. But the fact that performance appraisals are so widely used in spite of this dissatisfaction is a strong indicator that managers believe that the performance appraisals are important and that they have a meaningful role to play in organizations. In fact, managers conduct performance appraisals for several different reasons. Organizations also hope to achieve several goals with performance appraisals.[2]

The Importance of Performance Appraisal

Although most managers are dissatisfied with the appraisal process, most would also agree that performance appraisal is an important part of human resource management. The results of performance appraisals serve many important functions in organizations, and this is why they are still prevalent despite their problems.

1. For example, appraisal results provide a benchmark for assessing the extent to which recruiting and selection processes are adequate; that is, appraisal results help managers assess the extent to which they are indeed recruiting and selecting the most appropriate employees. When this information is used in conjunction with performance-management techniques (described in more detail in Chapter 14), it can lead to real improvements in the performance of individual employees and, ultimately, the entire organization.
2. Performance appraisals are also important for legal reasons. Organizations must be able to demonstrate that their promotions, transfers, terminations, and reward allocations are based on merit (or the lack

218   Part 3: Managing the Existing Workforce

thereof), as opposed to discriminatory factors such as gender or race. Performance appraisal, therefore, is the mechanism by which the organization can provide this documentation.

3. Appraisals play a role as part of the larger performance-management process. The goal of performance management is to improve employee performance. Part of this process is letting employees know how well they are currently doing so they can correct their deficiencies, capitalize on their strengths, and improve their overall contributions to their jobs.[3] Performance appraisal should provide this information to employees.

4. Finally, performance-appraisal information should be the basis of incentive pay systems and other performance-management interventions designed to improve motivation and performance.

Goals of Performance Appraisal

The preceding discussion makes the goals of appraisals almost self-evident. A basic goal of any appraisal system is to provide a valid and reliable measure of employee performance along all relevant dimensions. In other words, the appraisal results should reflect the true picture of who is and is not performing well, and they should indicate the areas of specific strengths and weakness for each person being rated. Although it is extremely difficult to assess the extent to which an appraisal system accomplishes these goals, it is probably just as important that employees perceive appraisals to be fair and accurate.[4]

Although documentation, as discussed, is another important goal of the appraisal process, the ultimate goal for any organization using performance appraisals is to improve performance on the job. Accomplishing this goal requires that employees receive useful and accurate feedback about their job performance, as well as guidance on how to improve. The goal also relies on the organization's ability make decisions about things such as raises and promotions on the basis of performance on the job. When these two requirements are met, managers can generally assume that, when employees get feedback about areas that need improvement, they will be motivated to make these improvements if they recognize that improving their performance will improve their chances for a promotion, pay increase, or other important outcome or benefit. At the same time, employees should also gain a clear understanding of where they stand relative to the organization's expectations of them vis-à-vis their performance.

THE PERFORMANCE-APPRAISAL PROCESS

Several tasks are necessary for the performance-appraisal process to be successful. Some should be done by the organization, some by raters (the individuals who will be conducting the performance appraisal), and in many organizations by the ratee (the individual whose performance is evaluated). In addition, follow-up and discussion should accompany the process. Although some of this follow-up and discussion may be more accurately considered performance management rather than performance appraisal per se, it is still an integral part of how organizations manage the entire process. Exhibit 10.1 illustrates the actual performance-management system of one major corporation. Although some firms might make minor modifications to reflect their philosophies more closely, these general steps are almost always followed. The performance-appraisal part of this overall process is highlighted and will be the framework for much of the discussion that follows. In later sections of this chapter, we will address and discuss the remaining parts of the process.

The Role of the Organization

The organization, primarily through the work of its human resource (HR) function, develops the general performance-appraisal process for its managers and employees to use. One of the first considerations relates to how the information gained from performance appraisals is to be used. For example, will it be used for developmental feedback only? Or will decisions about merit pay or other outcomes be based on these ratings as well? It is obviously important that everyone understand exactly what the ratings are to be used for and exactly how they will be used. The organization also generally determines the timing of the performance appraisals. Most organizations conduct formal appraisals only once a year, although some organizations conduct appraisals twice a year or even more frequently for new employees. However frequent the appraisals, the organization and its HR managers must decide when they will be conducted. The most common alternatives are for appraisals to be done on the anniversary date of each individual employee's hiring (which spreads out the need to do appraisals throughout the year but makes budgeting for raises more problematic) or for all appraisals throughout the organization to be conducted during a specified period of time each year (which makes budgeting and

EXHIBIT 10.1

The Performance Management Process in a Typical Organization

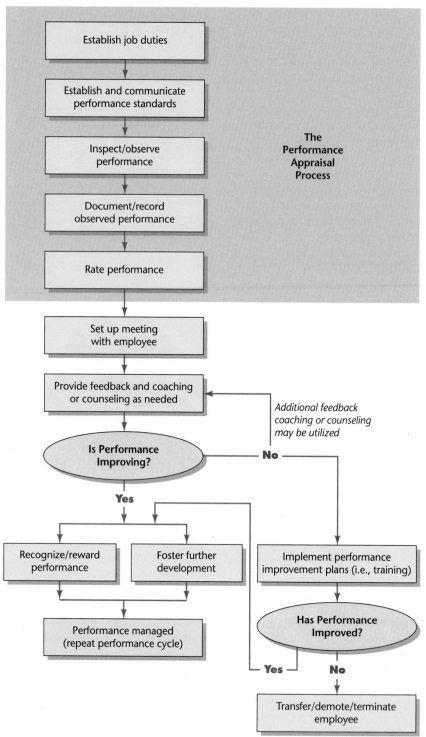

The Performance Appraisal Process

- Establish job duties
- Establish and communicate performance standards
- Inspect/observe performance
- Document/record observed performance
- Rate performance

Set up meeting with employee

Provide feedback and coaching or counseling as needed

Additional feedback coaching or counseling may be utilized

Is Performance Improving?

No →

Yes ↓

Recognize/reward performance | Foster further development

Implement performance improvement plans (i.e., training)

Performance managed (repeat performance cycle)

Has Performance Improved?

Yes | No

Transfer/demote/terminate employee

---

comparisons easier but requires a great deal of work during a short period of time).

The organization is also responsible for ensuring that clear and specific performance standards are available to managers. The organization should also ensure that these standards are communicated carefully to the employees. Although this step involves those individuals performing the ratings as well, the organization must ensure that everyone rates performance using the same set of standards and that employees know what is expected of them. Otherwise, performance appraisal cannot accomplish its goals, and the organization may have serious problems by creating a disgruntled workforce or by exposing itself to legal liabilities.

The Role of the Rater

The rater (traditionally and most typically the supervisor of the employee being appraised) plays the largest role in the appraisal process. As noted earlier, the organization is responsible for making sure that all raters have clear performance standards, but raters have to help develop and learn those standards. As performance information is acquired about a ratee, the rater also has to compare the information acquired with these standards as a way of evaluating the employee's performance. When making these decisions, the rater must consider the context in which performance occurs so that any extenuating conditions can be taken into consideration. In addition, the rater has to communicate those standards to the ratees so that each individual will know what is expected.

The rater has a more critical role to play as well. On a day-to-day basis, an employee behaves, or performs, on the job and exhibits many behaviors that might be relevant to performance on that job. The rater's task is to collect information about those behaviors and translate that information into the ratings themselves. Therefore, the rater truly becomes a decision maker who must observe ratee performance and process the information gleaned from the observations. Because most formal appraisals are conducted only once a year, the rater must also somehow store this information in memory, recall what has been stored at the appropriate time, and use the information to provide a set of ratings. This task is potentially difficult and time consuming.[5]

Once ratings have been completed, it is also usually the rater who must then communicate the results and consequences of the appraisal to the ratee. When the results are somewhat negative, this task may be uncomfortable, and it is often stressful for managers. This communication process should also include goals for the future and a performance plan for helping the employee improve, thus adding a positive element. This set of activities, of course, is really part of the performance-management process. Finally, the rater is ultimately responsible for preparing the employee to perform at desired levels. In other words, the supervisor must be sure that the employee knows what is required on the job, has the needed skills, and is motivated to perform at the level desired.

The Role of the Ratee

Although attempts to improve appraisals often focus on the organization or the rater, the ratee also has responsibilities in the appraisal process. First, for performance appraisals to work most effectively, a ratee should have a clear and unbiased view of his or her performance. Problems can occur during the appraisal process if there is disagreement between the rater and the ratee, so it is essential that both parties have all the information they can collect about the ratee's performance. This approach may require the ratee to acquire information about the performance of co-workers and requires the ratee to gain an understanding about how his or her behavior affects performance. This approach should also allow the ratee to be more receptive to feedback from the rater (especially if it is somewhat negative), which in turn makes it more likely that the ratee will change his or her behavior in response to that feedback.

Who Performs the Performance Appraisal?

Another important aspect of performance appraisal is the determination of who conducts the appraisal and what information will be used. The most common appraisers are shown in Exhibit 10.2.

As noted earlier, the individual's supervisor is the most likely rater. Supervisors are perhaps the most frequently used source of information in performance appraisal. The assumption underlying this approach is that supervisors usually have the most knowledge of the job requirements and the most opportunities to observe employees performing their jobs. In addition, the supervisor is usually responsible for the performance of his or her subordinates and thus is both responsible for employees' high performance and accountable, perhaps, for their low performance.[6]

At the same time, it should also be recognized that supervisors are not necessarily a perfect source of information. A supervisor may have been promoted from another part of the organization and thus may have never performed the jobs that she or he is supervising and, in some job settings (such as outside sales jobs), the supervisor may not really have an adequate opportunity to observe employees

One weakness of annual performance reviews is that managers tend to be biased toward the most recent behaviors of their subordinates.

EXHIBIT 10.2 Sources of Information for Performance Appraisal

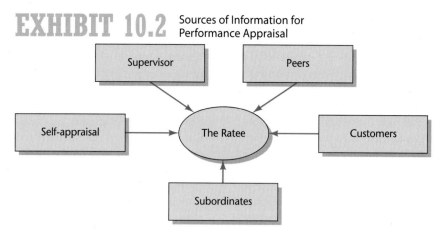

performing their work. But in addition to these potential constraints on the supervisor's *ability* to provide a meaningful appraisal, we must also consider the supervisor's *motivation* to provide such ratings. Stated simply, supervisors are not always motivated to give the most accurate ratings they can. For example, there is always the possibility that the supervisor is biased (either for or against) the person being rated. Only mixed evidence of systematic bias against members of identifiable groups based on race,[7] age,[8] gender,[9] and disability exists.[10] Nonetheless, a supervisor may be negatively or positively biased toward various workers because of personal liking, attitudes, personal relationships, and so forth. As a result favoritism or negative bias may be possible.

Supervisors might also choose to be inaccurate in their ratings because they feel threatened by a particular subordinate and want to prevent him or her from getting ahead, or because the supervisor wants to get rid of a problem subordinate and tries to do so by getting her or him promoted into a different department. In addition, supervisors may be concerned about team member relations and decide to rate all team members the same, regardless of what they deserve, to avoid jealousy or conflict. These and other motivational factors that affect supervisory ratings are beyond the scope of this discussion but are treated in detail in various specialized sources.[11] The main point here is to recognize that supervisors may choose to be inaccurate in their ratings for a wide range of reasons.

Peers, colleagues, and co-workers represent other potential sources of information for performance-appraisal systems. An advantage of using peers in such a process is that, by definition, they have expert knowledge of job content and may also have more opportunities than the supervisor to observe the performance of a given worker on a day-to-day basis. Peers also have a different perspective on the performance of their work: They really understand their own opportunities and limitations regarding performance. Merck and 3M Corporation both use peer evaluations as a major component of their performance-appraisal process.

Of course, friendship, group norms, and other personal factors may intervene in this situation. And individuals may see their own performance as being significantly different than others in the group may see it.[12] In some situations, co-workers might be competing with each other for a promotion (or some other reward), which may affect their motivation to be accurate in their peer evaluations. Because peers or co-workers remain in an ongoing relationship with each other, someone who received poor ratings from his or her co-workers may try to retaliate and rate those co-workers poorly during subsequent evaluations.[13] Nevertheless, peer evaluation is particularly useful in professional organizations such as law firms, architectural firms, academic departments, and so forth. As more and more organizations begin to use work teams for production work, peer evaluations are becoming more widely used in those contexts as well.

A third source of information in the performance-appraisal process is subordinates of the individual being appraised. Subordinates are an especially important source of information when the performance of their own manager is being evaluated, and this information is perhaps most useful when the performance appraisal is focused on the manager's leadership potential. If top-level managers in an organization are appraising the performance of a certain middle manager on the basis of his or her leadership potential, for example, then the subordinates of that manager are perhaps the best source of information for evaluating that person's performance. Of course, a major problem with using subordinates as input to the performance-appraisal process is that this approach may influence the manager's behavior in the sense that she or he may be more focused on making workers happy and satisfied than in making them perform at a high level.[14] Nonetheless, there has been a great deal of recent interest in so-called upward appraisals and in the ways to make them more effective.[15]

Occasionally, appraisal information is obtained from the employees themselves. Although few (if any) organizations rely on self-evaluations for decision making, it is often useful to have the ratee consider his or her own performance as part of the overall appraisal process. Finally, in some service organizations (such as Chili's and Red Lobster), customers are formally brought into the process when they fill out feedback forms or respond to mail surveys after using the services of an organization. In any event, it is important to realize that each source of performance-appraisal information is subject to various weaknesses and shortcomings. As a result, many organizations find it appropriate and effective to rely on different information sources when conducting a performance appraisal. In fact, in a number of companies, ratings are obtained from supervisors, peers, and subordinates; these are then compared with self-ratings. Such systems are known as *360-degree appraisals*.

Organizations that use **360-degree appraisals** gather performance information from people on all sides of the

rely on an imperfect memory to provide ratings. In addition, the diary information can help raters provide detailed feedback to ratees, which should increase the perceptions of procedural fairness. Finally, if an employee is discharged for poor performance and subsequently sues the organization, these diaries can serve as the documentation of performance that the organization needs to defend itself in court.

[*Feedback concerning rating traits is often less instructive and helpful than other types of feedback.*]

manager: above, beside, below, and so forth.[16] By focusing on 360-degree feedback, they obtain information on a person's performance from all perspectives. This approach allows them to match the strengths and weaknesses, the benefits and shortcomings, from each perspective and gain a more realistic, overall view of a person's true performance.[17] Recognize, however, that the feedback from the different sources could be inconsistent. Otherwise, there is no value in obtaining evaluations from different sources. But this approach means that the manager has to reconcile different feedback and that the organization probably needs to use these ratings for feedback and development purposes only. If decisions are to be based on these evaluations, then the organization would have to decide how to weight the ratings from the different sources.[18] Although it is not a panacea (and few studies have evaluated its effectiveness), variations on 360-degree appraisal systems are likely to continue to be popular for some time.

Regardless of who conducts the appraisals, it is important to remember that most organizations do performance appraisals only once a year. As a result, the rater must observe and then remember the relevant performance information that occurred over that entire time,[19] but memories are not perfect. Raters forget what happened, especially if something happened many months earlier. Rater memory is therefore a critical factor and limits the accuracy and effectiveness of performance appraisals. If a rater cannot remember a performance incident, then he or she cannot rate it. Fortunately, there may be a rather simple solution to this problem, such as having raters keep performance diaries (or performance logs).[20] Performance diaries (electronic or otherwise) record the relevant performance information when the behavior actually occurs, so the rater does not have to

© elisa75/Shutterstock

What Gets Rated?

Another important decision to make regarding the design of appraisal systems is what should be rated. The choice of appraisal instruments (discussed below) is related to this issue because some systems are clearly designed to measure some aspects of performance rather than others. But the decision of what to rate should be based more on the needs of the organization than on the choice of rating instrument. Although the decision about what to rate can probably include many factors, three are most commonly encountered.

Many organizations choose to rate traits in conducting appraisals. Traits are abstract properties of individuals that generally cannot be observed directly but can be inferred from behavior. Ratings of attitude, leadership, and initiative are particularly popular traits for appraisals. Rating traits allows an organization to use the same appraisal instrument for all or most employees, and this approach is based on the assumption that similar traits underlie effective performance for all jobs. Note, however, that an analysis of court cases involving performance appraisals suggests that trait-based appraisals are the most difficult to defend because the courts tend to see them as more subjective than other systems.[21] Also, feedback concerning rating traits is often less instructive and helpful than other types of feedback.

In some cases, organizations base their appraisals on behaviors. These appraisals tend to be based on job analysis, and they tend to be tailored for specific jobs. For example, a ratee may be evaluated on how well he or she

*In a **360-degree appraisal**, performance information is gathered from people on all sides of the manager: above, beside, below, and so forth.*

follows up on sales leads. These appraisals are still subjective, but they require the rater to evaluate behaviors that he or she can physically observe, so they seem more objective. Reliance on behaviors can also lead to an emphasis on processes underlying effective performance. In the example above, one might assume that following up sales leads is part of the process of being an effective salesperson. Providing feedback about behaviors and processes can be instructive and useful because it can help employees to understand how to improve their performance.

The final commonly encountered option is to rate performance based on outcomes. For example, rather than evaluating whether the salesperson has a good attitude or follows up on leads, an organization could simply tally actual sales. Focusing on outcomes has the advantage of emphasizing the most objective measures of performance available. Also, these systems are usually tied to specific goals, which have added benefit (discussed below). Feedback can be relatively straightforward and easy to interpret (i.e., you did or did not meet your sales goal), although feedback is even more useful if it includes information on how to improve future performance. Goals can be stated in terms of absolute amounts or in terms of improvement (e.g., increase sales by 10 percent over last year). It is important to set the right goals (goals that help the organization achieve its objectives), and it is important to monitor the means by which employees meet their goals (i.e., to make sure they act ethically and legally). Appraisal systems built around outcome measures are a reasonable alternative for organizations to consider.[22]

Who Should Be Rated?

A final issue to consider is exactly who should be rated in the appraisal process. Specifically, this issue is connected with the use of work teams. With work teams, the organization must decide whether to evaluate individual performance or team performance, and this issue can become quite complicated.

If individuals are rated and rewarded based on their individual performance, they have less reason to cooperate with other team members to accomplish the team's goals. In some cases, this situation might be desirable. For example, although the Ryder Cup in golf is considered to be a team competition, the team's performance is simply the sum of the scores of individual team members, so having team members seek to maximize their own performance helps the team as well. In other team settings that are structured in a similar manner, the team leader or fellow team members can also provide ratings.

In other team settings, though, it is critical that team members work together toward a common goal. In these cases, it is critical that performance be measured and rewarded only at the team level. One person's performance should not be considered except as part of the whole. Some employees are uncomfortable with this kind of system and believe they should be recognized for their individual efforts. Also, in such settings, it is possible for one employee to relax and let the other team members carry the workload. This free-rider problem is a real challenge to work teams. Nonetheless, if the team functions as a team rather than as a set of individuals, it is essential that the team's performance is appraised and rewarded.[23]

METHODS FOR APPRAISING PERFORMANCE

Different performance-appraisal methods and techniques are used in organizations. By their very nature, most appraisals are subjective—that is, we must rely on a rater's judgment of an employee's performance. As a result, performance appraisals are also prone to problems of bias (some of which were discussed earlier) and rating errors (which are discussed later in this chapter). Raters tend to be uncomfortable passing judgment on employees, and employees generally do not care to be judged in this way. The question then becomes, why don't managers simply use objective measures of performance in evaluating employee performance?

The simplest answer is that, for most jobs, and for all managerial jobs, straightforward objective measures of performance do not exist. Moreover, even when such measures do exist, they are usually contaminated by factors such as locations of sales territories. In many other cases where objective measures exist, they are meaningful only at the level

© Andresr/Shutterstock

HR in the 21st Century

Counting Seconds, Measuring Scans

One of the most important jobs in retailing is the person who takes the customer's money, in part because paying for their items is about the last thing customers do before leaving. An efficient and pleasant experience can leave a customer walking out of the store with a smile, and a slow or unpleasant experience can leave a bad taste in the customer's mouth. There is also a lot of variation in how checkout operators work. Some are fast and efficient, and others are plodding and never seem to get in a hurry.

Meijer, a family-owned discounting chain, operates 185 huge megastores in Michigan, Illinois, Indiana, Kentucky, and Ohio. The company has recently installed a new performance-measurement system for its checkout operators that might potentially revolutionize those jobs. Essentially, the system works like this:

1. Meijer has established minimum baseline performance metrics for the job based on the number of units a person should reasonably be able to scan and bag in a specified amount of time.
2. When a checkout operator scans a customer's first item, a timer in the scanning system is activated.
3. This timer runs until a customer's last item is scanned.
4. The operator's "score" is adjusted for the kinds of items being purchased (large, bulky items, for instance, take longer to scan than do small tightly packed ones) and how the customer is paying (checks usually take longer than cash or credit, for instance).
5. Each checkout operator's score is averaged across an entire shift.

6. The minimum performance expectation at Meijer is 95 percent of the standard. If an operator falls below this standard too many times, the person is either demoted to a lower-paying job or fired.

Interviews with Meijer cashiers suggest mixed results. On the one hand, they all agree that the new system causes them to work faster. On the other hand, that feel more stress. Moreover, several suggested that they avoid conversations with their customers because that can detract from their work and slow them down.

Feedback from customers is also mixed. Some think the new system is great. One woman, for instance, said "A lot of the [cashiers] like to stop and chat, and I don't really have the time for it." But another suggested that "elderly people . . . feel so rushed at checkout that they don't want to come here."

But the Meijer system, developed by Accenture, may be the wave of the future. Gap, Office Depot, Limited Brands, and Toys "R" Us are all testing it. On the other hand, other retailers such as Kroger and Abercrombie & Fitch have said "Thanks, but no thanks" because they are afraid the new system will detract from customer service.

THINK IT OVER

1. How would you feel about working under the Meijer system?
2. What other kinds of jobs might be amenable to this sort of performance-measurement technology?

Sources: "Stores Count Seconds to Cut Labor Costs," *Wall Street Journal* (Nov. 28, 2009): A1, A15; *Hoover's Handbook of Private Companies 2009* (Austin: Hoover's Business Press, 2010): 313–314.

---

of the team (or an assembly line) and not at the level of the individual. Of course, objective data that does reflect conditions under the control of the individual employee are sometimes available. These data could be sales figures for outside sales employees. In other cases, a rater could measure outcomes such as reductions in complaints. These examples are best suited for outcome-based appraisal methods. But as shown in HR in the Twenty-First Century, even objective outcome-based methods may not always tell the full story. In many other cases, however, organizations have no choice but to rely on judgments and ratings. Therefore a great deal of effort has been spent in trying to make these subjective evaluations as meaningful and as useful as possible. Some of the methods that have been proposed are based on relative rankings, while others rely more on absolute ratings.

Ranking Methods Versus Rating Methods

Probably the simplest method of performance appraisal is the **simple ranking method**, which involves having the manager simply rank-order, from top to bottom or from best to worst, each member of a particular work group or department. The individual ranked first is presumed to be the top performer, the individual ranked second is presumed to be the second-best performer, and so on. The ranking is generally global or based on overall performance. A variation on the ranking method is the

> The **simple ranking method** involves having the manager rank-order each member of a particular work group or department from top to bottom or from best to worst.

EXHIBIT 10.3 Examples of Graphic Rating Scales

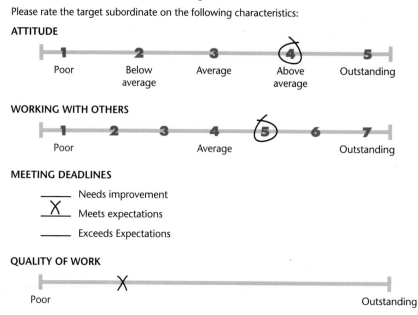

Please rate the target subordinate on the following characteristics:

ATTITUDE

1	2	3	4	5
Poor	Below average	Average	Above average	Outstanding

WORKING WITH OTHERS

1	2	3	4	5	6	7
Poor			Average			Outstanding

MEETING DEADLINES

_____ Needs improvement

___X___ Meets expectations

_____ Exceeds Expectations

QUALITY OF WORK

Poor   X   Outstanding

---

paired-comparison method of performance appraisal, which involves comparing each individual employee with every other individual employee, one at a time. This technique is simply an alternative way to generate rankings, however.

Although ranking techniques are simple and easy to implement, there are some serious shortcomings. It is true that organizations that are seeking to make relatively simple decisions such as which person to promote can obtain clear and useful information about the "most promotable," but even in such cases where an organization must then turn to the "second-most promotable," ranking methods provide no information about the difference between the persons ranked first and second. The absence of such information is even more problematic for the employee who might be told that she or he is the "second best" but is not given any information about how to become the best.

A related technique for performance appraisal is forced distribution, a method that has been in practice for many years.[24] The **forced-distribution method** involves grouping employees into predefined frequencies of performance ratings. Those frequencies are determined by the organization in advance and are imposed on the rater. For example, a decision might be made that 10 percent of the employees in a work group can be grouped as outstanding, 20 percent as very good, 40 percent as average, 20 percent as below average, and the remaining 10 percent as poor. The manager then classifies each employee into one of these five performance classifications based on the percentage allowable. The forced-distribution method is familiar to many students because professors who grade on a so-called bell or normal curve are using this method.

An advantage of this system is that it results in a normal distribution of performance ratings, which many people see as inherently fair. Also, from the organization's perspective, if employees are to receive merit pay increases, a forced distribution ensures control over how much money is spent on merit pay. On the other hand, the distribution that is being imposed may have no relationship to the true distribution of performance in the work group. It is possible, for example, that *all* the employees are performing at acceptable levels, but the forced-distribution methods, as well as the other ranking methods, force the rater to make distinctions that might not really be meaningful. As a result, most organizations rely instead on some type of absolute judgments and employ a system of performance ratings rather than rankings.

Specific Rating Methods

One of the most popular and widely used performance-appraisal methods is the graphic rating scale. A **graphic rating scale** simply consists of a statement or question about some aspect of an individual's job performance. Following that statement or question is a series of answers; the rater must select the one that fits best. For example, one common set of responses to a graphic rating scale is *strongly agree, agree, neither agree nor disagree, disagree,* and *strongly disagree.* These descriptors or possible responses are usually arrayed along a bar, line, or similar visual representation, and this representation is marked with numbers or letters that correspond to each of the descriptors.

Exhibit 10.3 illustrates a graphic rating scale. A wide array of performance dimensions can be efficiently tapped with

---

In the **paired-comparison method** *of performance appraisal, each individual employee is compared with every other individual employee, two at a time.*

The **forced-distribution method** *involves grouping employees into predefined frequencies of performance ratings.*

A **graphic rating scale** *consists of a statement or question about some aspect of an individual's job performance.*

various rating scales on the same form. Each of the descriptors on the rating form is accompanied by a number or a letter for responses. Most graphic rating scales have ranges of 1 to 5 or 1 to 7, although occasionally a scale may use only 1 to 3 or perhaps even 1 to 9. The rater assigns a score for each dimension rated and then can sum these to form a measure of overall performance, or the form might simply add an overall performance scale. The specific dimensions measured by graphic rating scales should be based on job analysis, but this approach is not typically taken. Instead, to have a single instrument that can be used with all or most employees in an organization, graphic rating scales typically measure performance relative to traits or behaviors such as initiative or problem-solving capabilities or even attitudes. In addition, a number of problems have been associated with the use of graphic rating scales, but these will be discussed later when we consider various types of rating errors.

A somewhat different type of rating instrument involves the use of the **critical incident method**. (Recall from Chapter 5 that this method can also be used as a job analysis technique.) A critical incident is simply an example or instance of especially good or poor performance on the part of the employee.[25] Organizations that rely on this method often require raters to recall such instances on the job and then describe what the employee did (or did not do) that led to success or failure. Thus, this technique provides rich information for feedback to the employee and defines performance in fairly clear behavioral terms. In other cases, managers are asked to keep a log or diary in which they record examples or critical incidents that they believe reflect good and bad performance on the part of individual employees.[26]

For example, a critical incident illustrating good performance by a gasoline station attendant might be as follows: "On Monday, January 15, you were observed to have fully restocked certain merchandise counters in the store without being instructed to do so. And you also illustrated very pleasant and service-oriented behavior when dealing with three customers. You handled each quickly and efficiently but gave each customer the prompt and courteous attention that each one wanted." An advantage of the critical incident method is that it allows managers to provide individual employees with precise examples of behaviors that are believed to be both effective and less effective performance. On the other hand, the critical incident method requires considerable time and effort on the part of managers because they must maintain a log or diary of these incidents. In addition, the method may make it difficult to compare one person with another. The sample of behaviors developed from one employee may not be comparable to the sample of behaviors acquired for another.

Another method for appraising performance involves the use of a **behaviorally anchored rating scale (BARS)**.[27] BARS appraisal systems (also known sometimes as *behavioral expectation scales*) represent a combination of the graphic rating scale and the critical incident method. They specify performance dimensions based on behavioral anchors associated with different levels of performance. Exhibit 10.4 presents an example of a BARS developed by one of the authors to measure one dimension of teacher performance: interpersonal skills. As shown in the exhibit, the performance dimension has different behavioral examples that specify different levels of performance along the scale.

EXHIBIT 10.4 Behaviorally Anchored Rating Scales

PERFORMANCE DIMENSION 1.
Interpersonal skills: Instructor's ability to establish rapport with students in and out of the classroom.

7 —

Instructor encourages students to ask questions.

⑥ —

Instructor comes down to the level of the students.
Instructor maintains an informal relationship with the students.

5 —

4 —

Instructor doesn't draw out students who don't ask questions.

3 —

2 —

Instructor "puts down" students who ask questions.
Instructor lowers students' self-esteem.

1

The **critical incident method** *relies on instances of especially good or poor performance on the part of the employee.*

A **behaviorally anchored rating scale (BARS)** *is an appraisal system that represents a combination of the graphic rating scale and the critical incident method.*

Developing a BARS is a complicated and often expensive process. Generally, these scales are developed by the same managers who eventually use them to evaluate employees. First, the managers must develop a pool of critical incidents that represent various effective and ineffective behaviors on the job. These incidents are then classified into performance dimensions, and the dimensions that the managers believe represent a particular level of performance are used as behavioral examples, or anchors, to guide the raters when the scales are used. At each step, an incident is discarded unless the majority of managers can agree on where it belongs or what level of performance the incident illustrates.[28] The manager who then uses the scale has to evaluate an employee's performance on each dimension and determine where on the dimension the employee's performance fits best. The behavioral anchors serve as guides and benchmarks in helping to make this determination.

A BARS system has the significant advantage of dramatically increasing reliability by providing specific behavioral examples to reflect effective and less effective behaviors. Because the managers themselves develop the scales, they tend to be more committed to using them effectively, and the process of developing the scales helps raters develop clearer ideas about what constitutes good performance on the job. The process of developing a truly effective BARS is extremely expensive and time consuming, and so these scales are rarely used in their pure form. Instead, some modified BARS procedures are often adopted in an attempt to reap some of the benefits without incurring the costs.

A related measure of performance is the **behavioral observation scale (BOS)**.[29] Like a BARS, a BOS is developed from critical incidents. Rather than using only a sample of behaviors that reflect effective or ineffective behavior, a BOS uses substantially more of the behaviors to define specifically all the measures necessary for effective performance. A

second difference between a BOS and a BARS is that a BOS allows managers to rate the frequency with which the individual employee has exhibited each behavior during the rating period. The manager then averages these ratings to calculate an overall performance rating for the individual. Although the BOS approach is an improvement over the limitations of the BARS approach, it takes even more time and can be even more expensive to develop.

Earlier in the chapter, we noted that it might be reasonable to evaluate an employee based on outcomes. In fact, another popular method of appraising performance that does focus on outcomes is a **goal-based** or **management-by-objectives (MBO)** system.[30] Management by objectives is the most popular term used for this approach, although many companies develop their own label to describe the system used in their organization. In an MBO system, a subordinate meets with his or her manager, and together they set goals for the subordinate for a coming period of time, often one year. These goals are usually quantifiable, objective, and almost always written down. During the year, the manager and the subordinate meet periodically to review the subordinate's performance relative to attaining the goals. At the end of the year, a more formal meeting is scheduled. During that meeting, the actual degree of goal attainment is assessed. The degree of goal attainment then becomes the individual's performance appraisal. If an individual has attained all the goals that she or he set for her- or himself, then employee performance is deemed to be very good. On the other hand, if not all goals were accomplished and the individual is directly responsible for that performance deficiency, then her or his performance is judged to be less than adequate or acceptable.

Goal-based systems are often seen as the best alternative available for rating performance, but care must be taken when these systems are used. Specifically, the kinds of behaviors specified in the goal-setting process are exactly what the employee will tend to focus on, so it is critical that the organization really wants to encourage these particular behaviors. For example, if a sales representative's goals are stated in terms of dollar volume of sales, then he or she might exert a lot of pressure on customers to increase the dollar volume of merchandise they're ordering in a coming period to boost his or her performance measures. At the same time, however, the sales representative may also hurt the firm's relationship with the customer if too much pressure is applied or if the customer ends up ordering more

A behavioral observation scale (BOS) is developed from critical incidents like a BARS but uses substantially more critical incidents to define specifically all the measures necessary for effective performance.

A goal-based or management-by-objectives (MBO) system is based largely on the extent to which individuals meet their personal performance objectives.

© Cheryl Casey/Shutterstock

Part 3: Managing the Existing Workforce

merchandise than is really needed. Thus, an important long-term goal may be sacrificed for the achievement of a short-term goal. The only solution to this type of potential problem is to emphasize the need for care in setting goals.

One relatively new innovation in performance-appraisal methods is the use of computer monitoring. Employees can now be monitored electronically to see how they spend their time and how productive they are. These systems are now used widely with customer-service representatives and reservations clerks. In fact, you may have heard a telephone recording (after you pressed the right numbers to get the service you wanted) stating, "This call may be monitored for quality purposes." This recording is an indication that electronic monitoring is taking place. For example, it is possible to track how many calls an employee receives, how long each call takes, and (with minimal input) the outcome of those calls. It is also possible to track when an employee is not at his or her phone station, which has caused some people to raise serious questions about invasions of privacy.[31] Although only a limited number of studies have investigated the effectiveness of this method, it seems as though the approach can be effective without triggering negative reactions on the part of employees—at least under certain circumstances.[32] While we need to know a great deal more about the effects of computer monitoring on individuals, the fact remains that this approach is being used with growing frequency in the workplace, and it is likely to become even more popular in the future.[33]

Which System Is Best?

Despite the time and effort that have gone into developing and improving performance-appraisal systems, it is difficult to find much advantage for any one system over the others.[34] We shall discuss issues of rating errors later in the chapter, and much research has focused on the susceptibility of different types of rating instruments to different types of errors. But this research has been inconclusive, and it is somewhat misguided. As noted at the beginning of this chapter, the ultimate reason for conducting performance appraisal is to improve performance. Therefore, it is difficult to suggest which system is best because it is difficult to predict how a set of employees will react to a given system. The HR manager must take what is known about each type of system and decide how well the system fits into the culture and operations of the organization.

OTHER ISSUES IN PERFORMANCE APPRAISAL

We noted earlier that all the participants in the appraisal process tend to be dissatisfied with the process. Several issues that arise when we try to appraise performance contribute to this dissatisfaction, and we will discuss some of these problems below, as well as one additional issue that deals more with exactly what should be appraised.

Rating Errors

Several rating errors have been identified that can affect performance appraisals. Although it is not always clear that these are really "errors," they are nonetheless important to consider as part of our discussion of performance appraisal. One such error is known as **contrast error**; it occurs when we compare people against one another instead of against an objective standard. For example, suppose a particular employee is a good performer but not an outstanding one. If that individual happens to work in a group of people in which everyone else is a relatively weak performer, then the "average" individual may appear to be a better performer than he or she really is. Likewise, if the same person works in a group of exceptionally strong performers, the person may be seen as a poorer performer than might otherwise be the case.

One of the major criticisms that had been leveled against graphic rating scales is that they were especially prone to a series of **distributional errors**. A distributional error occurs when the rater tends to use only one part of the rating scale.

1. Sometimes the distributional error may be *severity*, which occurs when the manager gives low ratings to all employees by holding them to an unreasonably high standard.

2. The opposite error is *leniency*, which occurs when a manager assigns relatively high or lenient ratings to all employees.[35]

3. A *central tendency* distributional error occurs when the manager tends to rate all employees as average, using only the middle part of a rating scale.

Contrast error *occurs when we compare people against one another instead of against an objective standard.*

A distributional error *occurs when the rater tends to use only one part of the rating scale.*

© Darren Whitt/Shutterstock

A different type of error that may occur is what is known as either halos or horns. A **halo error** occurs when one positive performance characteristic causes the manager to rate all other aspects of performance positively. For example, suppose a given employee always comes to work early and is always full of energy and enthusiasm at the beginning of the workday. The manager may so appreciate this behavior that he or she gives the employee a high performance rating on all other aspects of performance, even when those other aspects may be only average or merely adequate.[36] The opposite of a halo error is a **horns error**. In this instance, the manager tends to downgrade other aspects of an employee's performance because of a single performance dimension. For example, the manager may feel that a given employee does not dress appropriately and views that characteristic negatively. As a result, the manager may also give the individual low performance ratings on other performance dimensions when higher ratings are justified.

Except for contrast errors, however, it is not always clear that these other "errors" are really errors. Using the term *error* implies that there is a correct rating and that the observed rating in some cases is incorrect. But when we discuss leniency error as indicating that ratings are "too high," we imply that we know how high the ratings really should be—but we don't. Therefore, what we observe might be leniency or it might simply mean that the employee is really good. Whether or not these are really errors, the presence of these response tendencies can make it difficult to differentiate between different employees or to accurately identify the strengths and weaknesses of a given employee. Furthermore, employees (ratees) might be less likely to perceive a set of lenient ratings as accurately reflecting their performance and so may not be willing to work to improve their performance.

As a result, organizations often do work to reduce rating error. One method for error reduction is to train managers to overcome these weaknesses, even when that means nothing more than pointing out to managers their tendency to commit distributional errors or contrast errors. Rater accuracy training is usually more involved than that, however. Specifically, an approach known as "frame of reference training" attempts to emphasize for managers the fact that performance is multidimensional in nature and to train those managers with the actual content of various performance dimensions.[37] As noted earlier, however, regardless of training or ability, there are cases where a rater simply chooses to be inaccurate. It is critical, therefore, that organizations do whatever they can to reward raters for doing a good job in performance appraisal by reinforcing the fact that these appraisals are important. Perhaps the most important and useful thing an organization can do to improve the quality of performance appraisals is simply to demonstrate to raters how and why it in their own best interests to do the best job they can in appraising employee performance.[38]

Contextual Performance

Formal performance-appraisal systems assess performance on aspects of one's job. Recently, however, interest has focused on what has been termed *contextual performance*, which brings a different dimension to the question of what should be appraised.[39] **Contextual performance** refers to tasks an employee does on the job that are not required as part of the job but that nevertheless benefit the organization in some way (we introduced this topic in the previous chapter). These behaviors might include willingly staying late at work to meet deadlines, helping co-workers get their work done, and performing any other task that benefits the general good of the organization. These behaviors are also often referred to as *organizational citizenship behaviors.*[40] Because these behaviors are never stated as formal requirements of the job, the employee is never formally told that he or she is expected to do these tasks. They might be told informally, however, that such behaviors are valued by the organization in general or the manager in particular. In any event, they do benefit the organization, and raters do consider them when conducting employee evaluations.[41]

How important are contextual performance behaviors in determining the overall ratings an employee receives? A recent study indicates that, although they are important, they are not as important as task behaviors (or even as important as counterproductive behaviors), but they do matter.[42] The next question is, how important are these behaviors for organizational effectiveness? Clearly, the organization benefits if someone engages in these behaviors, so they represent part of an employee's overall contribution to the organization. On the other hand, they are not required of anyone. As a result, some, especially union members, argue that it is inherently unfair to evaluate someone on something that is not part of his or her job. Perhaps that assertion is true, but it seems that, consciously or not, raters do take these behaviors into account in making appraisal decisions.

A **halo error** occurs when one positive performance characteristic causes the manager to rate all other aspects of performance positively.

A **horns error** occurs when the manager downgrades other aspects of an employee's performance because of a single performance dimension.

Contextual performance refers to tasks an employee does on the job that are not required as part of the job but that still benefit the organization in some way.

© gualtiero boffi/Shutterstock

Evaluating the Performance-Appraisal Process

At the beginning of this chapter, we noted the strategic importance of the performance-appraisal system. Clearly, the organization must monitor the extent to which it is conducting its performance appraisals effectively, adequately, and appropriately. As with selection, performance appraisal must be free from bias and discrimination.

Beyond these stipulations, however, the performance-appraisal system must also help the organization identify its strongest performers so that they can be appropriately rewarded and efforts can be made to retain them. It should also identify low performers so that their performance deficiencies can be remedied through training or other measures. Periodic audits of the performance-appraisal system by trained professionals can be an effective method for assessing the effectiveness and appropriateness of the performance-appraisal process used by the organization.

Because performance appraisal feeds into the performance-management process, and because the ultimate goal of this process is to improve performance on the job, managers should be able to see real improvements in organizational performance if the process is working. This improvement may take the form of fewer errors in production, fewer returns in sales, improved performance appraisals, or lower levels of absenteeism or turnover. In the long run, however, these outcomes are not critical to the organization unless they translate into some improvement in overall firm performance. If performance-appraisal and performance-management systems are doing what they were designed to do, the organization as a whole should perform better.

LEGAL ISSUES IN PERFORMANCE APPRAISAL

When performance appraisals are used as the basis for human resource decisions (as in the case of merit pay or promotion decisions), they are considered the same as any other test under the law. This designation includes decisions about layoffs based on performance. Therefore, appraisals that show evidence of disparate impact must be validated the same as any selection technique. This principle was first established in *Brito* v. *Zia Company*[43] and reinforced as part of the decision in the *Albermarle Paper Company* case discussed in Chapter 2.

As noted above, performance-appraisal decisions are known to suffer from various types of biases and problems. Also noted earlier in the chapter was the fact that ratings based on traits tend to have ambiguous standards, and so they are probably more prone to these biases. It is difficult to validate appraisal decisions using the methods described in Chapter 7 (i.e., content validity, construct validity, and criterion-related validity). Therefore, it is critical that the organization can demonstrate that the ratings provided are in areas that are "job related," that raters can observe the behaviors they are rating, and that raters received some

training to help them do a better job with rating performance. If an appraisal system is used for providing feedback only, however, it is not subject to these same legal requirements.

In closing, although there are clearly problems with performance appraisals as they are conducted in most organizations, they provide critical information for the organization and the employee and are not likely to disappear. One way to use this information is by providing the feedback that employees need to work their way through their careers. We turn now to the topic careers and career management.

THE NATURE OF CAREERS

Most people have a general idea of the meaning of *career*. For instance, they generally agree that careers have something to do with the work a person does in an organization, but they also recognize that a career is a broader and more general concept than a single job or task in an organization.

The Meaning of Career

We define a **career** as the set of experiences and activities in which a person engages related to his or her job and livelihood over the course of a working life. This definition, then, suggests that a career includes the various specific jobs that a person performs, the kinds of responsibilities and activities that make up those jobs, movements and transitions between jobs, and an individual's overall assessment of and feelings of satisfaction with these various components of her or his career.

Most people have historically thought of the various components making up a person's career as having some degree of interrelation. This perspective stems from the fact that, in the past at least, people generally wanted to work for a single organization and spent most of their work life within that single organization. Presumably, if they performed effectively and were successful at their work, they advanced up the organizational hierarchy. Even when people changed jobs, they tended to work for other organizations in the same industry. For example, Lee Iacocca is perhaps best remembered for saving Chrysler several years ago, but earlier in his career he worked for both General Motors and Ford.

In recent times, however, conceptualizations of careers have become considerably more general. Because of organizational downsizing efforts and innovations in strategies such as outsourcing and shared services, considerably more change has occurred in the work patterns of individuals than in the past.[44] For instance, people are likely to leave an organization in one industry and go to work for an organization in a totally different industry, and they may also spend

*A **career** is the set of experiences and activities that people engage in related to their job and livelihood over the course of their working life.*

EXHIBIT 10.5 The Traditional Model of Career Stages

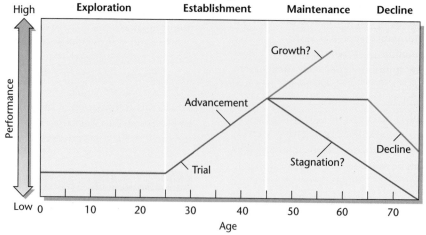

Source: Adapted from *Careers in Organizations*, by Douglas T. Hall. Copyright © 1976 by Scott, Foresman, and Co. Reprinted by permission of Douglas T. Hall and Lyman Porter.

time between jobs and organizations consulting or working in otherwise independent contractor-type positions.

More and more frequently, people are taking breaks from their work. These breaks include sabbaticals, discretionary periods of unemployment, and similar activities that may make a positive contribution to a person's overall work life but do not involve formal employment by an organization. People who return to school to enhance their education now more than ever before are likely to consider that period of their lives as part of their career.

Traditional Career Stages

One traditional view, shown in Exhibit 10.5, suggests that a typical individual progresses through four career stages:

1. The first stage is called **exploration**. During this period in people's lives, they try to identify the kind of work they are interested in doing. This period of a typical person's career starts in the mid- to late teens and lasts through the mid- to late twenties. It generally encompasses the time when he tries to assess his own interests, values, preferences, and career opportunities and to relate them to what he thinks represents a feasible career option. His coursework in school and his first jobs play an important role in the exploration stage of career development. For example, it is not uncommon for someone who anticipates majoring in a certain field of study to change his major once he begins taking courses in that area. Sometimes people take their first jobs in particular fields only to discover they are not

what they expected and so begin to look for alternative options. Of course, sometimes people are perfectly happy with the outcome of the exploration stage. They find that the coursework of their field is indeed of interest to them and their first job assignments are exciting, challenging, and just what they expected them to be.

2. The second stage of a typical career is called the **establishment** stage. During this period, an individual begins to create a meaningful and relevant role for herself and the organization. She may, for example, become a valuable member of a work team, achieve success and recognition by her superior, and be acknowledged by the organization as someone whom the company values and wants to retain. There is considerable range in terms of age and time in this stage, but it generally encompasses an individual's late twenties through mid- to late thirties.

3. The **maintenance** stage is the next stage in a typical career. During this period, the individual begins to reach a level in the organization that optimizes his talents or capabilities. Not everyone can become a chief executive officer, however, and only a small percentage of the total workforce in any organization attains the rank of top executive. For many employees, then, this stage marks a midcareer plateau. Many successful managers, especially in larger companies, may never progress beyond the rank of middle manager and so end their careers on this plateau, but they nevertheless enjoy careers considered to be highly productive and worthwhile. Individuals in the maintenance stage of their career must often devote extra effort to learning new job skills and remaining current in their professional skills and abilities. They are also frequently called on to fill mentoring roles in which they help newcomers to the organization get their feet on the ground and launch their own careers.[45]

Exploration *is the first traditional career stage and involves identifying interests and opportunities.*

The **establishment** *stage of the traditional career model involves creating a meaningful and relevant role in the organization.*

The **maintenance** *stage involves optimizing talents or capabilities.*

4. Finally, the fourth stage of a typical career is the **disengagement** stage. During this period, the individual gradually begins to pull away from her work in the organization, her priorities change, and work may become less important to her. Consequently, she begins thinking more and more about leaving the organization and finding other sources for fulfilling her personal needs and goals. Some employees may evolve toward part-time work status, some retire from the organization, and some simply cut back on their activities and responsibilities.

New Views of Career Stages

Of course, in the contemporary era of downsizing and layoffs, sometimes people go through these four stages of career development in a relatively short period of time. People may find themselves disengaging from the organization at a relatively young age, and they may also anticipate beginning the entire process again by seeking new opportunities, new challenges, and new interests.[46] Many experts agree that even though the traditional model of careers summarized above still has conceptual value, new perspectives on careers are better reflections of today's realities. Some experts, for instance, argue that we should think about career ages (how long someone has been on a job) rather than career stages or even chronological age.[47] Furthermore, they suggest that we must directly incorporate the premise of multiple careers into any modern view of careers. At the beginning of each new career, though, the employee begins a process of exploration, trial, and establishment, followed by another period of exploration. This second level of exploration in turn is likely to take the person away from the current career and into a new one where the process begins again.

This perspective also suggests that employees face different types of challenges at each step.[48] At the beginning of one's career there are issues about making the transition from a student to an employee. This involves questions about one's self-identity, and these questions also influence decisions about exactly what career someone plans to enter. Individuals may choose to enter certain careers because they are considered "hot," or because of general economic trends. They also choose careers because they are more consistent with their own interests, education, and values.

Once a career has been chosen and the person begins to build on that career, the issues that emerge often deal with trying to establish the proper balance between work and family life. It is at this point in one's career when these issues become more salient and the individual must deal with the potential trade-off between working hard to build and advance a career and establishing lasting relationships with others, including building a strong family life. Also, at this stage, decisions are more frequent regarding whether or not the person should remain with a given firm or move to a different organization. The decision as to how best to advance one's career in terms of moving is, of course, also tied to the growing importance of balancing work and family. By the time a person reaches some sort of midcareer point, there are often questions about the worth of continuing to work on one's career, and new questions about self-identity emerge (sometimes leading to a so-called midlife crisis).[49]

Issues Facing Older Workers and the Decision to Retire

As workers continue to age, they have new career issues to deal with, and some of them relate to potential age discrimination. As noted in Chapter 2, persons age forty and older are protected by the Age Discrimination in Employment Act, but the fact remains that many people assume that abilities and job performance decline with age. In fact, the evidence regarding such declines is rather mixed and generally weak. For example, although there is evidence of declines in abilities such as motor coordination and dexterity, these effects can be explained by differences in education and job type, and there is no evidence of age-related declines in intelligence, verbal ability, or numerical ability.[50] Perhaps more critically, there is almost no relationship between age and job performance—in fact, some studies have found a curvilinear relationship between age and performance with performance highest when workers are youngest *and* older.[51]

*The fourth traditional career stage, **disengagement**, involves the individual gradually beginning to pull away from work in the organization. Priorities change, and work may become less important.*

In any event, eventually older workers must confront the decision to retire. In truth, however, the decision to retire is not as simple as it once was. Today, there is really a whole continuum of choices available to a person contemplating retirement. The person can actually retire, take a pension, and begin some other nonwork activities (the traditional view of retirement), but this is becoming less common. More commonly, individuals retire and then take on full-time work at other organizations, or they retire and take on part-time work or work as consultants either at their former employers or elsewhere. Over time, they may reduce the amount of time they spend at work until they gradually move into full retirement, but retirement has become much more of a process than an event.[52]

important for HR managers as the workforce ages and as lives and productive work careers expand.

HUMAN RESOURCE MANAGEMENT AND CAREER MANAGEMENT

Most successful organizations and managers today recognize that careers do not simply happen; they must be planned and managed. Indeed, of the 100 firms on *Fortune's* 2010 list of the best places to work, 98

The Age Discrimination in Employment Act (or ADEA) prohibits discrimination against employees age forty and older.

Nonetheless, many factors are related to the decision to retire (or begin the retirement process). For example, individuals are more likely to retire when they have the financial resources needed to maintain their preretirement lifestyles, and they are more likely to retire when their health makes continuing to work excessively burdensome. Individuals are also more likely to retire when their spouses have retired. In addition, several factors are related to adjustment after retirement. Of course, as noted above, many people tend to continue with some type of "bridge work," and these people generally adjust well to retirement. Also, individuals who have structured leisure activities and those who do volunteer work tend to adjust better to retirement. But one of the most important factors related to adjustment is one's health. Individuals who avoid serious health problems adjust better, partly because they can engage in the kinds of activities outlined above. It is important to realize that these and any other issues relating to the decision to retire are likely to become much more

have formal career-planning systems for their employees.[53] Part of the responsibility for this career planning resides with the organization, and the feedback from the appraisal process is a critical factor in this process. But the individual her- or himself must also play a role in this process.[54] This section examines the organizational and individual perspectives on careers shown in Exhibit 10.6.

Organizational and Individual Perspectives on Careers

Organizations are generally responsible for determining the jobs that people will perform for the organization, the pattern of interrelationships between jobs in an organization, the kinds of people who will be hired for those jobs, the development of those individuals to prepare them for more meaningful jobs, and the decisions regarding the movement of people from one job to another. Clearly, it is in the organization's best interest to take an active role

EXHIBIT 10.6 Individual and Organizational Perspectives on Career Planning

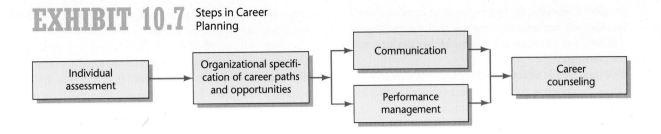

EXHIBIT 10.7 Steps in Career Planning

in career management for people in the firm, and for this reason career management is often part of the larger performance-management process.[55]

The organization can take steps from the outset to facilitate career management. For example, in Chapter 7 we discussed the idea of selecting individuals not because of their match with the requirements of a specific job but because of their fit with the organization. Despite any other problems associated with this selection strategy, it seems helpful for career management because the organization presumably hires individuals who fit different jobs. In fact, even when organizations select individuals for a specific job, it is still possible to do so with subsequent career moves in mind. In other words, if an entry-level position is not particularly demanding, then it is possible for an organization to hire people whose skills and abilities match a higher-level job that they might be expected to move into later. This practice can be defended as long as the employee will likely move up to the higher-level job eventually.

If an organization does indeed help its employees plan and manage their careers more effectively, it can expect to find itself with a larger pool of talented individuals who are generally more satisfied and motivated. On the other hand, if the organization does a poor job with managing the careers of people in the organization, then it will find that the quality of its talent pool might vary in inefficient ways; that is, it might have an abundance or surplus of highly talented and qualified employees in some areas and at some levels of the firm but have a shortage of talented and capable people at other levels or areas of the organization. In addition, the workforce of such an organization might be more dissatisfied and unmotivated because people are not given appropriate promotion opportunities or are not placed in appropriate positions. When the organization needs to transfer people or lay people off, it may be unsure about who can handle the new assignments.

Individuals obviously have an important stake in their own careers. They experience most directly the benefits and rewards of successful careers and incur the costs and frustrations of unsuccessful careers. A person's perceived and experienced career success or failure is also likely to have a major effect on his or her self-esteem and similar indications of self-worth.

People who understand and carefully monitor their careers are likely to understand the reasons behind their successes and failures. These individuals will know why they have or have not been promoted and will have accurate assessments of future promotion prospects and possibilities. In addition, people who accept responsibility for managing their careers will also be better prepared to deal with unanticipated career setbacks such as job losses and demotions. Unfortunately, many people are surprisingly uninformed and uninvolved in their own careers.

The Importance of Career Planning

Career planning is clearly important to both organizations and employees. Furthermore, effective career planning requires careful coordination between individual employees and the organization itself. Usually, HR managers represent the organization in the career-planning process. General Electric and Shell Oil are known to be especially effective with their managers' career planning and development. In general, most career-planning systems involve the steps shown in Exhibit 10.7.

1. In the **individual assessment phase**, individuals need to analyze carefully what they perceive to be their own abilities, competencies, skills, and goals. Many organizations provide employees with forms or questionnaires to help them develop this information.
2. At the same time, the HR manager should be developing a potential career path an employee may take up the corporate ladder.[56] Shell's career-path model, for example, is available to managers on the firm's corporate intranet.
3. Communication is also an important part of this process. For example, the organization may know the paths that are most likely to be followed from one position to another and be able to gauge the probability or likelihood that a specific individual will follow this path or a prescribed path for a promotion to another position. But if this information is not communicated to the individual employee, then it is of little or no value to anyone. At the same time, the organization must also integrate its performance-management system with its career-management system. A person should not expect to

*The **individual assessment phase** of career planning requires that individuals analyze carefully what they perceive to be their own abilities, competencies, skills, and goals.*

progress automatically from one job to another along a certain path but instead recognize that this movement will be determined in part by his or her performance effectiveness.

4. The final step in effective career planning is **career counseling**. As the term suggests, career counseling involves interaction between an individual employee or manager in the organization and either a line manager or a human resource manager. This counseling session typically involves frank and open dialogue with the goal of making sure that the individual's assessment and the organization's assessment of the individual's role and prospects in the organization are congruent. We discuss career-counseling programs in more detail in the next section.

Even though career planning is important to both organizations and individuals, and effective career planning benefits both, everyone should also recognize that career planning has limitations and potential pitfalls. For example, no amount of sophisticated forecasting can predict with absolute certainty the level of talent, expertise, motivation, or interest a given individual will have in the future. People experience changes in interests, for example, and they may redefine their priorities. Even though the organization and the individual may expect that the individual will be capable of performing a certain job in the future, it may turn out that both parties are wrong.

The organization's future human resource needs can also change. For example, it may become more or less successful than originally envisioned, or it may decide on new strategies to pursue. Or new managers may come in and want work done differently than in the past. And new opportunities may present themselves to both the individual and the organization. For instance, an organization may have a certain current member of its workforce who has been tapped to assume an important position in a couple of years. But a substantially stronger individual for that same position may unexpectedly emerge. In this case, the organization may have to alter its

> **"If an institution wants to be adaptive, it has to let go of some control and trust that people will work on the right things in the right way."**
>
> —ROBERT B. SHAPIRO,
> CEO of chemical company Monsanto,
> Harvard Business Review
> (Jan.–Feb., 1997)

original strategy, even at the risk of alienating the individual originally tapped for the job.

Similarly, individuals sometimes find new opportunities at unexpected times. Both an individual and the organization, for instance, may expect that individual to take a certain job in the future. But another organization may appear on the scene to lure the individual away, perhaps at a substantially higher salary. In this instance, the individual is likely to be happy with this turn of events because he or she will have a new position and a higher salary. The organization, on the other hand, may face disruption and may have to alter its existing plans.

Unanticipated mergers and acquisitions can also result in changes in career opportunities. For example, when Amoco was acquired by British Petroleum a few years ago, the new organization found itself with a surplus of qualified managers and had to offer early retirement incentives to some of them. Others were presented with unanticipated opportunities for new assignments that were substantially different from what they expected. For example, a senior Amoco manager based in Houston, Texas, had been on a career path that did not include the possibility of an international assignment. Shortly after the integration of the firms, however, this manager was offered a promotion to a new job in London.

CAREER-DEVELOPMENT ISSUES AND CHALLENGES

Regardless of the career stages for individual employees, many organizations who are sincerely interested in more effective career management for their employees deal with and address various issues and challenges. In this section, we introduce and describe some of these issues and challenges in more detail.

Career-Counseling Programs

As already noted, career-counseling programs are important to an organization interested in career development for its employees. Such programs usually address a wide variety of career-related issues and are readily accessible

Career counseling involves interaction between an individual employee or manager in the organization and either a line manager or a human resource manager.

to people in the organization. Some programs are formal; others are considerably informal.

Formal career-counseling programs usually take the form of workshops, conferences, and career-development centers. In some cases, the organization establishes general-purpose career-counseling programs that are available to all employees. They may also create special programs targeted for certain categories of employees. Among the more popular special programs are counseling programs for fast-track managers, women managers, and minority managers. These special programs serve various purposes in addition to addressing the specific needs of certain categories of employees. They also help to integrate those employees into the mainstream of the overall organization, and they create important networking opportunities for these individuals.

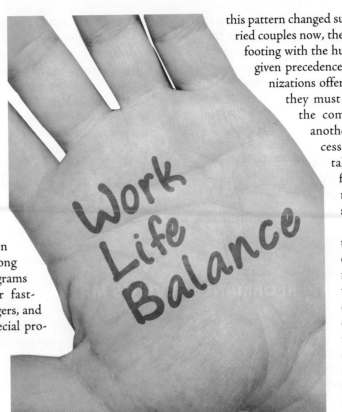

Organizations also have informal counseling programs. Much of this counseling takes the form of one-on-one interactions between an employee and his or her supervisor and typically occurs during the performance-appraisal period. For example, when supervisors appraise and evaluate the performance of a subordinate and then provide performance feedback to that individual, part of the conversation also deals with issues such as promotion prospects, skill development, and so forth. Sometimes employees may simply drop by the HR department for advice on career-related questions and issues. When drop-ins are common, it is important that the HR department fulfill its center of expertise role and provide useful and accurate information.

Dual-Career and Work–Family Issues

Back in the 1950s and into the 1960s, most married couples in the United States were characterized by roles that gave the male partner career precedence over the female partner; that is, the family tended to live where the husband needed to live. When the husband was given a job transfer, his decision to take it was not usually questioned. And if the wife happened to be employed outside the home, it was assumed that she would resign from her job and that the family would move.

But as increasing numbers of women entered the workforce, primarily beginning in the mid- to late 1960s,

this pattern changed substantially. For many married couples now, the wife's career is on an equal footing with the husband's or perhaps may be given precedence over it. Thus, when organizations offer a transfer to an employee, they must be prepared to deal with the complexities associated with another career. The entire process of career planning must take into consideration the fact that another career must often be managed simultaneously.

Perhaps related to this trend is the growing concern over balancing family needs with the demands of work. As noted above, as dual-career and single-parent employment increases, these concerns pose yet another challenge to career management, especially in the midcareer stages.[57] First, concerns over family-friendly work practices (such as child care, elder care, and flexible work schedules) have an influence over the choices that employees make concerning where to work. In fact, many organizations are now advertising their family-friendly practices as a means of competing for employees.[58] It is also increasingly clear that concerns at home and with the family affect an employee's behavior at work. Stress over how to arrange for child care or who will care for an ailing parent can cause the employee problems at work. Relieving these pressures allows the employee to concentrate more on the job and thus better realize his or her career potential.[59]

Finally, evidence shows that work stressors influence family stress, which in turn is related to long-term health.[60] As the workforce becomes more diverse, organizations thus will have to recognize that both dual-career issues and concerns over work–family balance will become increasingly important factors for determining career success and must be considered as part of career management.

Evaluating Career-Management Activities

The ultimate goals of career management are to have employees reach their full potential at work, enjoy productive and satisfying work careers, and then make a successful transition to retirement. Full appreciation of career-management activities on the part of the employee may not come until after retirement. But as employees are increasingly unlikely to spend their entire careers in a single organization, success in retirement is much more likely to be a

Managing Labor RELATIONS

"We want to do a deal that's good for both sides."

—Robert Kraft, owner, New England Patriots football team

ALL SHAPES AND SIZES

Many people associate unions, union members, collective bargaining, and strikes with blue-collar manufacturing jobs in factories and on assembly lines. In reality, of course, unions and their members come in all shapes and sizes. For instance, many airline pilots, teachers, firefighters, hotel employees, police officers, and writers belong to unions. So, too, do some people who work in the broadcasting and music industries and in the federal government. And just like factory workers, union members have gone on strike against television networks, airlines, and public school districts.

One of the more interesting—and public—venues for non-traditional labor relations is the world of professional sports. Labor unions represent players and officials in virtually all sports. And within the last 25 years, professional baseball, basketball,

football, and hockey have all had significant labor crises, ranging from strikes to lockouts led by players, officials, and team owners.

Disharmony may again be rearing its ugly head. In 2010, the collective bargaining agreement between teams of the National Football League (NFL) and their players entered its final year, with the current deal set to expire in March 2011. Opening negotiations between the league and the players' union quickly showed that the two sides were far apart. The owners, not surprisingly, argued that they were spending too much on player costs. The current agreement set a salary spending cap of $123 million per team. The players' union also gets a share of all NFL revenues—television contracts, merchandise licensing fees, and so forth—and the owners want to lower this revenue-sharing commitment by 18 percent.

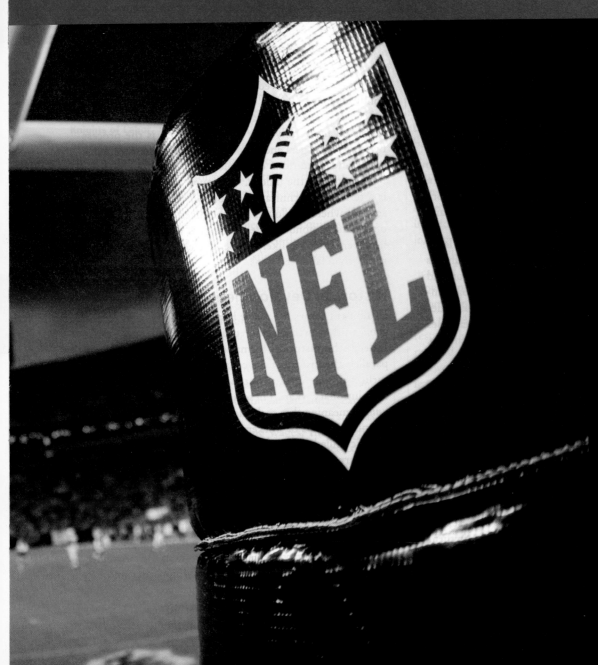

LEARNING OBJECTIVES

After studying this chapter, you should be able to:

LO1 *Describe the role of labor unions in organizations*

LO2 *Identify and summarize trends in unionization*

LO3 *Discuss the unionization process*

LO4 *Describe the collective-bargaining process*

LO5 *Discuss how labor agreements are negotiated*

LO6 *Describe how impasses get resolved and agreements are administered*

LO7 *Discuss emerging labor union issues in the twenty-first century* members were called. The union's opposition to U.S. involvement in World War I led to its prosecution for treason and the jailing of most of its leaders.

For the mainstream organized labor movement, many of these fringe groups were too radical, and workers preferred the businesslike approach of the AF of L. As a result, the federation grew rapidly throughout the early decades of the twentieth century, reaching a peak membership of 5 million by the end of World War I. Its membership declined over the next several years, and by the mid-1930s membership stood at approximately 2.9 million.

One of the AF of L's weaknesses was its continued focus on crafts, accepting only skilled craftspersons for specifically defined jobs. During the 1930s, however, a new kind of unionization began to emerge that focused on industrial unionization. Rather than organizing workers across companies or across industries based on their craft, this new type of union activity focused on organizing employees by industry, regardless of their craft, skills, or occupation.

In the late 1930s, John L. Lewis of the United Mine Workers led a dissenting faction of the AF of L to form a new labor organization called the **Congress of Industrial Organizations (CIO)**. The CIO was the first major representative of the new approach to unionization noted above. The CIO quickly began to organize the automobile, steel, mining, meatpacking, paper, textile, and electrical industries. By the early 1940s, CIO unions had almost 5 million members.

In the years following World War II, union memberships in the AF of L and the CIO, as well as other unions, gradually increased. However, a series of bitter strikes during that same era led to public resentment and calls for union reform. Congress intervened to curtail the power of unions, and

the AF of L and the CIO began to contemplate a merger to consolidate their strength. Eventually, in 1955, the AFL-CIO was formed with a total membership of around 15 million employees. In 2005, however, citing unhappiness with the strategic direction of the AFL-CIO, two of its largest member unions, the Service Employees International Union and the International Brotherhood of Teamsters, withdrew from the parent organization and set out on their own.[3]

Legal Context of Unions

Partly because of the tumultuous history of labor unions in the United States, a great many laws and regulations have been enacted to deal with unions, and this legislative history is critical to understanding the development of the U.S. labor movement. The earliest legislation simply dealt with the question of whether unions were legal. As early as 1806, the local courts in Philadelphia declared the Cordwainers to be, by its very existence, in restraint of trade and thus illegal. This Cordwainer doctrine, as it became known, dominated the law's view of unions until 1843, when the Massachusetts Supreme Court, in *Commonwealth* v. *Hunt*, ruled that unions were not by their very nature in restraint of trade but that this

> ## The National Labor Relations Act (or Wagner Act) was passed in an effort to control and legislate collective bargaining between organizations and labor unions, to grant power to labor unions, and to put unions on a more equal footing with managers in terms of the rights of employees.

issue had to be proven in each individual case. This court decision led to increased union activity, but organizations responded by simply firing union organizers. After the Sherman Antitrust Act was passed in 1890, businesses once again (successfully) sought court injunctions against unions for restraint of trade. By the 1920s, organizations also sought to identify union leaders as communists to reduce public sympathy toward them and to give the government an excuse to control the unions.

By the end of the 1920s, the country was in the grip of the Great Depression, and federal intervention was required to end work stoppages and start the economy on the road to recovery. The first significant piece of legislation was the **National Labor Relations Act**, which was passed in 1935. This act is more commonly referred to as the **Wagner Act** and still

*Another important early union was the **Congress of Industrial Organizations (CIO)**, which focused on organizing employees by industry, regardless of their craft, skills, or occupation.*

*The **National Labor Relations Act** (or **Wagner Act**) administers most labor law in the United States.*

© microstocker/Shutterstock

forms the cornerstone of contemporary labor relations law; it was discussed earlier in Chapter 2. The basic purpose of the Wagner Act was to grant power to labor unions and put them on a more equal footing with managers in terms of the rights of employees. It gives workers the legal right to form unions, to bargain collectively with management, and to engage in group activities such as strikes to accomplish their goals. This act also forces employers to bargain with properly elected union leaders and prohibits employers from engaging in certain unfair labor practices, including discriminating against union members in hiring, firing, and promotion.

The Taft-Hartley Act also established procedures for resolving strikes deemed threatening to the national interest. For example, the president of the United States has the authority under the Taft-Hartley Act to request an injunction to prohibit workers from striking for 60 days, a so-called cooling-off period in which labor and management have a greater chance of resolving their differences. For example, in February 1997 the union representing the pilots at American Airlines announced that its members had voted to strike. Within minutes of this announcement, President Clinton invoked the

> **The Labor Management Relations Act (or Taft-Hartley Act) curtailed and limited union powers and regulates union actions and their internal affairs in a way that puts them on equal footing with management and organizations.**

The Wagner Act also established the **National Labor Relations Board (NLRB)** to administer its provisions. The NLRB still administers most labor law in the United States. For example, it defines the units with which managers must collectively bargain and oversees most elections held by employees that will determine whether they will be represented by a union.

In the previous section, we noted congressional activity in the years after World War II that curtailed the power of the unions. The most important piece of legislation in this era was the **Labor Management Relations Act**, also known as the **Taft-Hartley Act**, which was passed in 1947. This act was a response to public outcries against a wide variety of strikes in the years following World War II. The basic purpose of the Taft-Hartley Act was to curtail and limit union practices. For example, the act specifically prohibits practices such as requiring extra workers solely as a means to provide more jobs and refusing to bargain with management in good faith. It also outlawed an arrangement called the **closed shop**, which refers to a workplace in which only workers who are already union members may be hired by the employer.

Section 7 of the Taft-Hartley Act also allowed states, if they wished, to restrict union security clauses such as closed-shop agreements. Roughly twenty states took advantage of this opportunity and passed laws that also outlawed **union shop agreements** (where a nonunion member can be hired but must join the union within a specified time to keep his or her job) and various other types of union security agreements. These laws are known as *right-to-work laws*, and the states that have adopted them (predominantly in the Southeast) are known as *right-to-work states*.[4]

Taft-Hartley Act and ordered the union to cancel its strike. His argument was that American Airlines is the nation's largest air carrier and a shutdown would be extremely detrimental to national interests. In addition, the Taft-Hartley Act extended the powers of the NLRB. For example, following passage of the act, the NLRB was also given the power to regulate unfair union practices.

A final significant piece of legislation affecting labor relations is the **Landrum-Griffin Act**, which was passed in 1959. Officially called the **Labor Management Reporting and Disclosure Act**, this law focused on eliminating various unethical, illegal, and undemocratic union practices. For instance, the Landrum-Griffin Act requires that (1) national labor unions elect new leaders at least once every 5 years and (2) convicted felons cannot hold national union office (which is why Jimmy Hoffa was removed as president of the Teamsters union).

The National Labor Relations Board (NLRB) administers most labor law in the United States.

The Labor Management Relations Act (or Taft-Hartley Act) (1947) was a response to public outcries against a wide variety of strikes in the years after World War II; its basic purpose was to curtail and limit union practices.

A closed shop refers to a workplace in which only workers who are already union members may be hired by the employer.

A union shop agreement includes various types of union security agreements in addition to a requirement that a nonunion member can be hired, although he or she must join the union within a specified time to keep his or her job.

The Landrum-Griffin Act (officially called the Labor Management Reporting and Disclosure Act) focused on eliminating various unethical, illegal, and undemocratic union practices.

EXHIBIT 11.2 The Basic Structure of a Union

National or international union

Local union — Local union — Local union — Local union — Local union

Shop steward — Shop steward — Shop steward — Shop steward — Shop steward

Source: Ricky Griffin and Ronald Ebert, *Business,* 3rd, ed. Copyright © 2000. Reprinted by permission of Prentice-Hall, Inc., Upper Saddle River, NJ.

It also requires unions to file annual financial statements with the Department of Labor. Finally, the Landrum-Griffin Act stipulates that unions provide certain information regarding their internal management and finances to all members.

> The Landrum-Griffin Act (officially called the Labor Management Reporting and Disclosure Act) focused on the elimination of various unethical, illegal, and undemocratic practices within unions.

Union Structures

All organizations have their own unique structure, and so do large labor unions. But most unions have some basic structural characteristics in common. Exhibit 11.2 shows the most common basic structure. The cornerstone of most labor unions, regardless of their size, is the local union, more frequently referred to as a *local*. **Locals** are unions organized at the level of a single company, plant, or small geographic region. Each local has an important elected position called the **shop steward**, who is a regular employee who functions as a liaison between union members and supervisors.

Local unions are usually clustered by geographic region and coordinated by a regional officer. These regional officers in turn

Locals *are unions organized at the level of a single company, plant, or small geographic region.*

The **shop steward,** *an elected position in a local union, is a regular employee who functions as a liaison between union members and supervisors.*

report to and are part of a national governing board of the labor union, which then may be involved with some umbrella group such as the AFL-CIO. The national affairs of a large union are generally governed by an executive board and a president. These individuals are usually elected by members of the union themselves. This election takes place at an annual national convention that all union members are invited to and encouraged to attend.

The president is almost always a full-time union employee and may earn as much money as the senior manager of a business. The executive board functions much more like a board of directors and is generally composed of individuals who serve on the board in addition to their normal duties as employees of an organization. Just as large businesses have various auxiliary departments (such as a public relations and a legal department), so do large national unions. These auxiliary departments may handle issues such as the legal affairs of the union. They may oversee collective-bargaining issues and may provide assistance and services to the local unions as requested and needed.

LEARNING OBJECTIVE 2

TRENDS IN UNIONIZATION

While understanding the historical, legal, and structural context of labor unions is important, so too is an appreciation of other trends regarding union membership, union-management relations, and bargaining perspectives. These topics are each discussed in the sections that follow.

Trends in Union Membership

Since the mid-1950s, labor unions in the United States have experienced increasing difficulty in attracting new members. Although millions of U.S. workers still belong to labor unions, union membership as a percentage of the total workforce has continued to decline at a steady rate. For example, in 1977, more than 26 percent of U.S. wage and salary employees belonged to labor unions. Today, that figure is about 12.4 percent of those workers. If government employees are excluded from consideration, then less than 10 percent of all wage and salary employees in private industry currently belong to labor unions. Note, however, that membership figures essentially remained steady from 2004 to 2005. Moreover, union membership has actually increased a bit in recent years. For instance, membership increased from 15,359,000 in 2006 to 15,670,000 in 2007; after a small decline from 2007 to 2008, membership jumped to 16,098,000 in 2009. Hence, the current trend seems to be small fluctuations from year to year. And the economic uncertainties facing workers in 2009 probably played a role in more people choosing to join unions. These membership trends are shown in Exhibit 11.3.

Although unionization in the service sector of the economy has increased by substantial numbers, this trend has been somewhat offset in the rest of the economy. Will unions ever disappear? Probably not, but they may look different in the years ahead than they have in the past. For example, some experts suggest that a basic transformation in unionism and the relationship between unions and management is already taking place. Nowhere is this more evident than in the U.S. automobile industry.

One major reason often cited for the lack of global competitiveness by U.S. automakers is high labor costs. Over a period of decades, companies such as Ford and General Motors (GM) routinely agreed to higher wages and more lucrative benefits to avoid costly strikes. But because foreign competitors—especially those in Asia—have maintained lower labor costs, they can make automobiles for $2,000 to $4,000 cheaper than their American

EXHIBIT 11.3 Trends in Union Membership

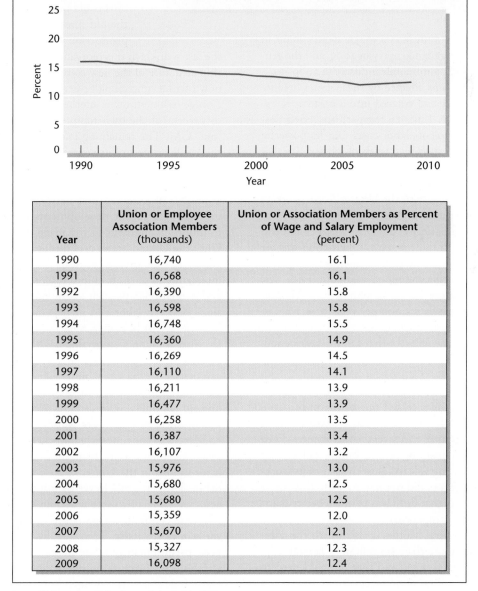

Year	Union or Employee Association Members (thousands)	Union or Association Members as Percent of Wage and Salary Employment (percent)
1990	16,740	16.1
1991	16,568	16.1
1992	16,390	15.8
1993	16,598	15.8
1994	16,748	15.5
1995	16,360	14.9
1996	16,269	14.5
1997	16,110	14.1
1998	16,211	13.9
1999	16,477	13.9
2000	16,258	13.5
2001	16,387	13.4
2002	16,107	13.2
2003	15,976	13.0
2004	15,680	12.5
2005	15,680	12.5
2006	15,359	12.0
2007	15,670	12.1
2008	15,327	12.3
2009	16,098	12.4

Sources: U.S. Department of Labor, Bureau of Labor Statistics, 2010.

Labor relations in the U.S. auto industry continue to involve compromises and concessions by both sides.

competitors. This certainly was a major determinant in GM's decision to declare bankruptcy in 2009, and the general decline of the U.S. automobile industry in 2009–10.

Ford has not been as affected by these issues because earlier in the decade it had entered into a creative agreement with its unions[5]. Like its competitors, Ford desperately needed to lower its labor costs, but its powerful unions had negotiated such high levels of job security that Ford found it difficult to either lower wage and benefits costs or reduce the size of its workforce. In response, Ford, working in concert with the United Auto Workers (UAW) and its other unions, devised eight different plans under which it could basically "buy out" workers and end their employment with the company. One option was for workers to accept a one-time cash payment ranging from $35,000 to $140,000 (depending on years of service, age, and how close the employee was to retirement). Another option offered as much as $15,000 per year for 4 years to be applied to college tuition and expenses, plus half of the employee's salary and benefits for that same 4-year period. Yet another included tuition and 70 percent of salary for 2 years.

During the enrollment period that lasted throughout 2006, 38,000 employees accepted one of the packages—about 46 percent of Ford's unionized workforce. This reduction in force, in turn, had several consequences. Ford incurred short-term costs of several billion dollars but gained flexibility in being able to adjust the size of its workforce that its competitors did not have. Again, this surely contributed to the fact that Ford was in much better shape in 2010 than its U.S. competitors.

The story at General Motors is also worth considering. After receiving more than $19 billion in federal help, the iconic U.S. automaker realized that it would need to declare bankruptcy.[6] The announcement in June 2009 stunned many Americans who believed that GM was simply too large to fail. But only a few weeks later, in July 2009, GM announced that it was about to emerge from bankruptcy and would repay $50 billion in federal loans faster than required. How did this happen? First of all, General Motors shed several brands, including Saab, Hummer, Saturn, and Pontiac. The company closed 6,000 dealerships (costing approximately 100,000 additional job losses) and announced the closure of a dozen production facilities around the country. But all of this required the cooperation (or at least nonresistance) of the United Auto Workers. In part, the union had no choice but to go along with these changes or else everyone employed at GM could be unemployed, and many of the old master contracts that drove up production costs were abrogated. But the last wrinkle in this reorganization relates to the ownership structure of the new company. The U.S. government now owns a controlling 61-percent interest, and the Canadian government owns another 12 percent. Approximately 10 percent of the ownership went to bondholders of the "old" GM. The remaining 17.5 percent, however, went to the UAW as part of its retiree health-care trust.[7]

Although the UAW held a seat on Chrysler's board of directors for many years, and although there have been a number of joint ventures between automakers and the union, these recent developments open a new chapter in union involvement in the management of a company. Until the United States gets through the financial crisis of 2009–10, similar types of deals may take place. It will be interesting to see how unions react to these new challenges and if relationships such as the one at GM reduces tensions between labor and management—as labor actually becomes a part of management.

Just as union membership has been generally declining, so also has the percentage of successful union-organizing campaigns. In the years immediately after World War II and continuing through the mid-1960s, for instance, most unions routinely won certification elections. In recent years, however, unions are winning certification less than 50 percent of the times when workers are called on to vote. From most indications then, the power and significance of labor unions in the United States, while still quite formidable, is significantly lower than it was just a few decades ago. Several factors explain declining membership.

One common reason is the changing composition of the workforce itself. Traditionally, union members have been predominantly white males in blue-collar jobs, but today's workforce is increasingly composed of women and ethnic minorities. These groups have a much weaker tradition of union affiliation, so their members are less likely to join unions when they enter the workforce. A corollary to these trends has to do with the fact that much of the workforce has shifted toward geographic areas in the South and toward occupations in the service sector that have also been less heavily unionized.

A second reason for the decline in union membership in the United States is more aggressive antiunionization strategies undertaken by businesses.[8] The National Labor Relations Act and other forms of legislation specify strict management practices vis-à-vis labor unions; nevertheless, companies are still free to pursue certain strategies intended to eliminate or minimize unionization. For example, both Motorola and Procter & Gamble now offer no-layoff guarantees for their employees and have created formal grievance systems for all workers. These arrangements were once available only through unions, but because these firms offer them without any union contract, employees are likely to see less benefit from joining a union.

Some companies have also tried to create a much more employee-friendly work environment and are striving to treat all employees with respect and dignity. One goal of this approach has been to minimize the attractiveness of labor unions for employees. Many Japanese manufacturers that have set up shop in the United States have successfully avoided unionization efforts by the UAW by providing job security, better wages, and a work environment in which employees are allowed to participate in the management of the facilities.

Trends in Union–Management Relations

The gradual decline in unionization in the United States has been accompanied by significant trends in union–management relations. In some sectors of the U.S. economy, perhaps most notably the automobile and steel industries, labor unions still remain strong. In these areas, unions have a large membership and considerable power vis-à-vis the organizations in which their members work. The United Auto Workers, for example, is still one of the strongest unions in the United States today.

In most sectors of the economy, however, labor unions are clearly in a weakened position. As a result, many have had to take more conciliatory stances

in their relations with managers and organizations.[9] This contrasts sharply with the more adversarial relationship that once dominated labor relations in this country. For instance, unions recognize that they do not have as much power as they once held and that it is in their best interests, as well as the best interests of the workers they represent, to work with rather than work against management. Hence, union–management relations are in many ways better today than they have been in years. Although this improvement is attributable in large part to the weakened power of unions, most experts would agree that union–management relations have still improved.[10]

None of this means that unions are dead or that unions and management do not still struggle with more basic issues as well as newer issues. In August 2003, for example, Verizon Communications faced a strike by the Communication Workers of America (CWA) and several other unions representing 85,000 employees. The issues were an interesting mix of traditional union concerns and some of the more recent concerns discussed earlier. For example, telephone operators and customer-service representatives complained that they were forced to work overtime and that the lack of sufficient break time had led to undue stress on the job. This "stress in the workplace" issue is surely typical of the more recent union issues. There were also problems with pay raises, and the fact that the company was shifting jobs to lower-paying regions of the country.

One additional issue at stake never made it to the bargaining table. The CWA, which represents about 75,000 Verizon employees, has been trying to unionize Verizon Wireless as well. The wireless communications sector has thus far resisted unionization, and because that sector is extremely competitive, Verizon has been fighting hard to keep it that way.

The CWA's strike lasted 15 days. Verizon found that it was difficult to replace the striking high-tech workers and that it needed to get workers back on the job. As a result, the union won on most issues, including a 12-percent wage increase and a 14-percent pension increase over the 3-year contract. The company also granted stock options to every union employee for the first time in the company's history. The company won some freedom to move around employees in return

© Sergey Lazarev/Shutterstock

for some job-security promises, and service reps were guaranteed "close time" when they could shut down their station to relieve stress. But the unspoken issue remains unresolved as the CWA continues to try to unionize the Wireless employees. The strike, and the way it was settled, illustrates that the world of labor–management relations is indeed changing even though basic issues can still lead to labor problems. It also illustrates that there may be cases where union power is not as low as had been reported. Specifically, in a competitive industry with a strong demand for well-trained, well-educated workers, the American union movement may find it has more leverage than it has had for many years

Trends in Bargaining Perspectives

Building on the trends in membership and union–management relationships, bargaining perspectives have also altered in recent years. For example, previous union–management bargaining situations were usually characterized by union demands for dramatic increases in wages and salaries. A secondary issue was usually increased benefits for union members. But now unions often bargain for different goals such as job security. Of special interest in this area is the trend toward moving jobs to other countries to take advantage of lower labor costs. Thus, unions might want to restrict job movement, and companies might want to maximize their flexibility by moving jobs to other countries.[11]

As a result of organization downsizing and several years of relatively low inflation in this country, many unions today opt to fight against wage cuts rather than strive for wage increases. Similarly, organizations might be prone to argue

> "History is a great teacher. Now everyone knows that the labor movement did not diminish the strength of the nation but enlarged it. By raising the living standards of millions, labor miraculously created a market for industry and lifted the whole nation to undreamed of levels of production. Those who attack labor forget these simple truths, but history remembers them."
>
> —MARTIN LUTHER KING, JR.

for less health care and other benefits for workers, and a common union strategy today is simply preserving what workers currently have. Unions also place greater emphasis on improved job security for their members. This has become an even more serious issue since the financial crisis of 2009. In fact, as discussed earlier, both Ford and General Motors have been working to reduce their workforces, a real challenge in a heavily unionized environment. An issue that has become especially important in recent years needed improving pension programs for employees. The restructuring of General Motors, however, required retirees to take cuts in pension and health-care benefits, and it will be interesting to see if this becomes a trend in the next few years.

THE UNIONIZATION PROCESS

The laws discussed earlier, as well as various associated regulations, prescribe a specific set of steps that employees must follow if they want to establish a union. These laws and regulations also dictate what management can and cannot do during an effort by employees to form a union.

Why Employees Unionize

Why do employees choose to join labor unions? In the simplest of terms, the answer seems straightforward: They believe they will somehow be better off as a result of joining a union.[12] More precisely, employees are more likely to unionize when they are dissatisfied with some aspect of their job, they believe that a union can help make this aspect of the job better, and they are not philosophically opposed to unions or collective action.[13]

The real answer is more complex. In the early days of labor unions, people joined them because their working

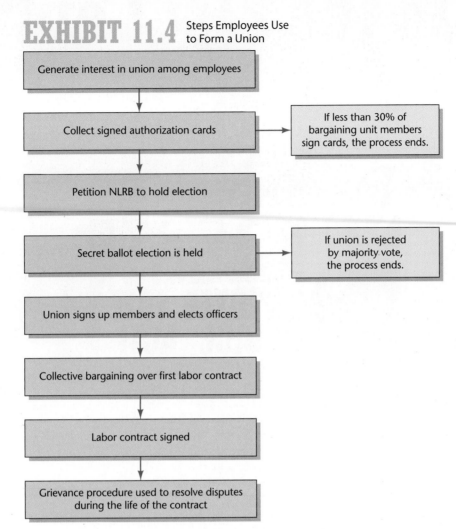

EXHIBIT 11.4 Steps Employees Use to Form a Union

Generate interest in union among employees

↓

Collect signed authorization cards → If less than 30% of bargaining unit members sign cards, the process ends.

↓

Petition NLRB to hold election

↓

Secret ballot election is held → If union is rejected by majority vote, the process ends.

↓

Union signs up members and elects officers

↓

Collective bargaining over first labor contract

↓

Labor contract signed

↓

Grievance procedure used to resolve disputes during the life of the contract

Source: Ricky Griffin, *Management*, 10th ed. (Cincinnati: Cengage, 2011), p. 458. Reprinted with permission.

conditions were unpleasant in many cases. In the eighteenth and nineteenth centuries, in their quest to earn ever-greater profits, some business owners treated their workers with no respect. They often forced their employees to work long hours, and minimum-wage laws and safety standards did not exist. As a result, many employees worked 12-, 15-, or 18-hour days and sometimes were forced to work 7 days a week. The pay was sometimes just pennies a day, and employees received no vacation time or other benefits. They worked entirely at the whim of their employers; if they complained about working conditions, they were dismissed. So people initially chose to join labor unions because of the strength that lay in the numbers associated with the large-scale labor unions.

In many parts of the United States and in many industries, these early pressures for unionization became an ingrained part of life. Union values and union membership expectations were passed down from generation to generation. This trend typified many industrialized northern cities such as Pittsburgh, Cleveland, and Detroit. In general, parents' attitudes toward unions are still an important determinant for whether or not an employee elects to join a union.[14] As noted earlier, strong unionization pressures

still exist in some industries today such as the automobile industry, the steel industry, and other economic sectors relying on heavy manufacturing.

Steps in Unionization

Several prescribed steps must be followed if employees are to form and join a labor union. These general steps are shown in Exhibit 11.4 and are described in more detail below.

1. First, employees must exhibit some interest in joining a union. In some cases, this interest may arise from current employees who are dissatisfied with some aspects of the employment relationship. In other instances, existing labor unions may send professional union organizers to nonunionized plants or facilities to generate interest in unionization.[15]

2. If interest in forming a union exists, the National Labor Relations Board is asked to define the **bargaining unit**, or the specifically defined group of employees

The bargaining unit refers to the specifically defined group of employees who are eligible for representation by the union.

HR in the 21st Century

As we discussed in Chapter 2, a proposal for a new law would change the process of union certification. The Employee Free Choice Act (or Union Relief Act of 2009) is really an amendment to the Taft-Hartley Act that deals with union certification among other things. The law also guarantees workers a right to a contract once a union is formed. Specifically, the law states that when an employer and a newly formed union are unable to bargain a first contract within 90 days, either party can request mediation by the Federal Mediation and Conciliation Service; if no agreement has been reached after 30 days of mediation, then the dispute is referred to binding arbitration. In addition, the law imposes tougher penalties on management if there is an attempt to interfere with the process during either the certification phase or contract negotiations.

The most controversial part of the proposed legislation relates to the steps in certification. Under the proposed legislation, if a simple majority of the employees in a bargaining unit sign authorization cards, then a union would be certified by the National Labor Relations Board without a secret ballot election. This is important because, even when a union gets the required number of signatures, it often loses the election. Labor leaders believe that this is because management coerces and bribes workers in the time between the card signing and the election, and this new process would eliminate that possibility. Of course, the other side of the argument is that, by eliminating the secret ballot, workers would be more prone to harassment and coercion—not by management, but by the union. The financial challenges facing the Obama administration in 2009–10 have distracted both the president and Congress from doing anything about this bill, but President Obama is said to support the new law.[17]

THINK IT OVER
1. What are the advantages and disadvantages of the proposed new law from the standpoint of both management and labor?
2. Research the current status of this law and determine if it has been passed.

who will be eligible for representation by the union. For example, a bargaining unit might be all non-management employees in an organization or perhaps all clerical workers at a specific site within the organization.

3. Once the bargaining unit has been defined, organizers must then strive to get 30 percent of the eligible workers within the bargaining unit to sign authorization cards requesting a certification election. Signing an authorization card does not necessarily imply that the individual signing the card wants to join a union; it simply indicates the individual's belief that a union election should be held. If organizers cannot get 30 percent of the workers to sign authorization cards, then the process ends.

4. If the required number of signatures is obtained, the organizers petition the NLRB to conduct an election. The NLRB sends one or more representatives, depending on the size of the bargaining unit, to the facility and conducts an election. The election is always conducted via secret ballot. If a simple majority of those voting approve union certification, then the union becomes the official bargaining agent of the eligible employees. But if a majority fails to approve certification,

the process ends. In this instance, organizers cannot attempt to hold another election for at least 1 year.[16] HR in the Twenty-First Century discusses a potential new law that may alter this process in a substantive way.

5. If the union becomes certified, then its organizers create a set of rules and regulations that govern the conduct of the union. They also elect officers, establish a meeting site, and begin to recruit members from the labor force in the bargaining unit to join the union. Thus, the union comes into existence as a representative of the organization's employees who fall within the boundaries of the bargaining unit.

Decertification of Unions

Just because a union becomes certified, however, does not mean it will exist in perpetuity. Under certain conditions, an existing labor union can be decertified. A company's workers, for example, might become disillusioned with the union and may even come to feel that they are being hurt by its presence in their organization. They may believe that the management of the organization is trying to be cooperative and bargain in good faith but that the union itself is refusing to cooperate.

© Lisa DeJong/The Plain Dealer/Landov

For decertification to occur, two conditions must be met.

1. First, no labor contract can currently be in force (that is, the previous agreement must have expired and a new one is awaiting approval).
2. Second, the union must have served as the official bargaining agent for the employees for at least 1 year.

If both these conditions are met, then employees or their representatives can again solicit signatures on decertification cards. As with the certification process, if 30 percent of the eligible employees in the bargaining unit sign the decertification cards, then the NLRB conducts a decertification election. Again, a majority decision determines the outcome. Thus, if a majority of those voting favor decertification, the union is then removed as the official bargaining agent for the unit. Once a union has been decertified, a new election cannot be requested for certification for at least 1 year.

THE COLLECTIVE-BARGAINING PROCESS

When a union has been legally certified, it becomes the official bargaining agent for the workers it represents. Collective bargaining can be thought of as an ongoing process that includes both the drafting and the administration of a labor agreement.

Preparing for Collective Bargaining

By definition, collective bargaining involves two sides: management representing the employing organization and the labor union representing its employees. The goal of the collective-bargaining process is to produce agreement on a binding labor contract that will define various dimensions of the employment relationship for a specified period of time. Thus, it is incumbent on both management and union leaders to be adequately prepared for a bargaining and

© Helder Monteiro/Shutterstock

negotiation period because the outcome of a labor negotiation will have long-term effects on both parties.

Management can take several actions to prepare for collective bargaining. For example, the firm can look closely at its own financial health to work out a realistic picture of what it can and cannot offer in terms of wages and salaries for its employees. Management can also conduct a comparative analysis to see what kinds of labor contracts and agreements exist in similar companies and what this particular labor union has been requesting—and settling for—in the past.

The union can and should undertake several actions to be effectively prepared for collective bargaining. It too should examine the financial health of the company through sources such as public financial records. Like management, the union can also determine what kinds of labor agreements have been reached in other parts of the country and can determine what kinds of contracts other divisions of the company or other businesses owned by the same corporation have negotiated recently.

Setting Parameters for Collective Bargaining

Another part of preparing for collective bargaining is prior agreement about the parameters of the bargaining session. In general, two categories of items may be dealt with during labor contract negotiations.

1. One set of items, as defined by law, consists of **mandatory items**. Mandatory items include wages, working hours, and benefits. If either party expresses a desire to negotiate one or more of these items, then the other party must agree.
2. Almost any other aspect of the employment relationship is also subject to negotiation, provided both sides agree. These items are called **permissive items**. For example, if the union expresses an interest in having veto power over the promotion of certain managers to higher-level positions and if, for some reason, the company were willing to agree to this demand as a point of negotiation, it would be permissible to enter this point into the negotiations. Many years ago, when one of the authors was a graduate student, a supermarket in Chicago signed a contract with the butchers' union stating that once the butchers went home (around 6 p.m.), the store could not sell any more meat. The store remained open until midnight but covered all its meat cases after 6. When the company complained to the NLRB that this was unfair and unfavorably affected its business, the NLRB

Mandatory items, including wages, working hours, and benefits, must be included as part of collective bargaining if either party expresses a desire to negotiate one or more of them.

Permissive items may be included in collective bargaining if both parties agree.

essentially responded that it understood the concern but that because the supermarket had been foolish enough to agree to those terms, it had to live with them. The first issue on the table when the contract was to be renewed was a removal of that provision, and the company managed to get the rule changed 2 years later. The point is that almost anything is negotiable if the parties agree to discuss it.

Some items are not permissible for negotiation under any circumstances. For example, in a perfect world, management might want to include a clause in the labor contract specifying that the union promises not to strike. However, legal barriers prohibit such clauses from being written into labor contracts, and therefore this item would not be permissible.

NEGOTIATING LABOR AGREEMENTS

After appropriate preparation by both parties, the negotiation process itself begins. Of course, barriers may also arise during this phase, and bargaining impasses may result in strikes or other actions.

The Negotiation Process

Generally speaking, the negotiation process involves representatives from management and the labor union meeting at agreed-on times and at agreed-on locations and working together to attempt to reach a mutually acceptable labor agreement. In some instances, the negotiation process itself might be relatively brief and cordial. In other instances, it might be lengthy, spanning weeks or perhaps even months, and it might also be quite acrimonious. For example, the labor agreement reached between the team owners and the union representing baseball players that was settled in late 1996 took several years to negotiate and was interrupted by a strike by the baseball players.

A useful framework for understanding the negotiation process refers to the bargaining zone, which is illustrated in Exhibit 11.5.[18] During preparations for negotiation, both sides are likely to attempt to define three critical points. For the organization, the bargaining zone and its three intermediate points include the employer's (1) maximum limit, (2) expectation, and (3) desired result on items being negotiated. For example, the organization might have a zero increase in wages and benefits as a desired result (also known as management's *target point*). But it also recognizes that this desired result is unlikely and that it expects to have to provide a modest increase in wages and benefits totaling perhaps 4 percent to 5 percent. If preparations are done thoroughly, however, managers also know the maximum amount they are willing to pay, which might be as high as 7 percent or 8 percent (management's *resistance point*). Note that management in this example would rather suffer through a strike than pay more than an 8-percent pay increase.

On the other side of the table, the labor union also defines a bargaining zone for itself that includes three points: (1) the union's minimum acceptable limit on what it will take from management (the union resistance point may be the settlement level below which the union will strike), (2) its own expectations about what management is likely to agree to, and (3) the most it can reasonably expect to get from management (the union target point). For instance, the labor union might feel that it has to provide a minimum increase of 2 percent to 3 percent in wages and benefits to its members. It expects a settlement of around 5 percent but would like to get 9 percent or 10 percent. In the spirit of bargaining, it may make an opening demand to management of as high as 12 percent.

Hence, during the opening negotiation session, labor might inform management that it demands a 12-percent wage and benefit increase. And the employer might begin by stating emphatically that no increases should be expected. Assuming, however, that some overlap exists between the organization's and the union's demands and expectations in the bargaining zone (a positive settlement zone), and also assuming that both sides are willing to compromise and work hard at reaching an agreement, then an agreement probably will be attained. Where exactly within that range the final agreement falls depends on the relative bargaining power of the two parties. This power is a function of many

EXHIBIT 11.5 The Bargaining Zone

Source: Ricky Griffin and Ronald Ebert, *Business,* 6th ed. Reprinted with permission of Prentice-Hall, Inc., Upper Saddle River, NJ.

factors such as negotiating skills, data on other settlements, and the financial resources needed by the union to call for a strike or by management to survive one.

Much of the actual negotiating revolves around each party trying to discover the other's resistance point without revealing its own. Because this point represents the least favorable settlement the party is willing to accept, the opponent who discovers that point then makes a "final" offer exactly at the resistance point. For example, if the union discovers that management is willing to go as high as 8 percent before breaking off negotiations and facing a strike, the union would then make an offer at 8 percent and indicate that this was its final offer. Management would rather pay 8 percent than have a strike, so it should settle at 8 percent, which is actually the most favorable contract the union could have possibly won. Incidentally, once a party makes a true final offer, it cannot back away from that position without losing face in the negotiations. Parties usually leave themselves some room for further negotiations and use statements such as the following: "I cannot imagine our members accepting anything less than an 8-percent raise, and I'm sure they would walk out on strike if we came back with less."

The resulting agreement is not necessarily the end of the bargaining process. First, the new contract agreement must be ratified by the union membership. If the union membership votes to reject the contract (which typically reflects internal union politics more than anything else), the parties must return to the bargaining table. But even before the union membership votes, a final step in the bargaining process must be followed. As soon as an agreement is reached, both parties begin to make public statements about how tough a negotiator the other party was. Both acknowledge that they really wanted a lot more and that they hope they can live with this agreement, but that the other party was such a good negotiator that this agreement was the best they could come up with. This posturing helps both parties "sell" the agreement to their constituencies and also allows both parties to maintain their image as strong negotiators no matter how one-sided the final agreement might be. Once ratified, this agreement then forms the basis for a new labor contract.

Barriers to Effective Negotiation

The foremost barrier to effective negotiation between management and labor is the lack of an overlap for the bargaining zones of the respective sides (i.e., there is a negative settlement zone). In other words, if management's upper limit for a wage increase is 3.5 percent and the union's minimum limit for what it is willing to accept is 5 percent, then no overlap exists in the bargaining zones and the two sides

will almost certainly be unable to reach an agreement. Beyond such differences in bargaining zones, however, other barriers to effective negotiation can also come into play.

For example, sometimes a long history of acrimonious relationships between management and labor makes it difficult for the two sides to negotiate in good faith. If, for example, the labor union believes that the management of the firm has a history of withholding or distorting information and that management approaches negotiations from the standpoint of distrust and manipulation, then the union will be suspicious of any proposal made by management and may, in fact, be unwilling to accept almost any suggestion made by management. Of course, the same pattern can occur for the other side, with management exhibiting extreme distrust of the labor union.

Negotiations can also be complicated by inept negotiators and poor communication between negotiators. Effective negotiation is a critical skill and one that not everyone possesses. Thus, if managers select as a representative someone who does not understand the negotiation process, then difficulties are likely to arise.

As a result of diligent negotiation, however, management and labor should be able to agree on a mutually acceptable labor contract. If, however, management and labor cannot agree on a new contract or one to replace an existing contract after a series of bargaining sessions, then either side or both sides might declare that they have reached an impasse. An **impasse** is simply a situation in which at least one party believes that reaching an agreement is not imminent.

RESOLVING IMPASSES

If labor and management have reached an impasse, several actions can be taken by either side or both sides in an attempt to break the impasse. The basic objective of most of these tactics is to force the other side to alter or redefine its

*An **impasse** is a situation in which one or both parties believe that reaching an agreement is not imminent.*

bargaining zone so that an accord can be reached.

The most potent weapon that the union holds is the potential for a strike. A **strike** occurs when employees walk off their jobs and refuse to work. In the United States, most strikes are called *economic strikes* because they are triggered by impasses over mandatory bargaining items such as salaries and wages. During a strike, workers represented by the union frequently march at the entrance to the employer's facility with signs explaining their reasons for striking. This action is called **picketing** and is intended to elicit sympathy for the union and intimidate management.

Strikes are costly to both parties. Although the company can try to hire strikebreakers, they are likely to lose some if not all their business during a strike—especially when picketers are present at their place of business. Clients and customers then have to look elsewhere for goods and services, and there is no guarantee that they will return once the strike is settled. The union must deal with the fact that members, while out on strike, receive no pay. Unions often pay picketers for their time, and there are often other payments that the union makes to workers while they are out on strike. But these represent true financial costs to the union. In addition, members may become dissatisfied with the union if they believe that the strike could have been averted except for union decisions. Unless the union is clearly triumphant, it usually loses members after a strike.

Strike costs are so important for the process that one of the tactics involved in labor negotiations is directly tied to strike costs. Both parties recognize that each side will suffer costs if there is a strike, so the union, for example, will try to convince management that the union's strike costs are relatively low (because they have built a cash reserve to pay striking workers or

because they have a unanimous vote in favor of a strike) and that management's strike costs are higher than they realize (because of the misunderstood effect of the picket line or because of information about low inventories of goods). Management, on the other hand, will try to convince the union that management's strike costs are low (because of stockpiled inventory, for example) and that the union's strike costs are high (because replacement workers are readily available). In the vast majority of cases, however, neither party wants a strike.

Two less extreme tactics that unions sometimes use are boycotts and slowdowns.

1. A **boycott** occurs when union members agree not to buy the products of a targeted employer.
2. A **slowdown** occurs when workers perform their jobs but at a much slower pace than normal. A variation on the slowdown occurs when union members agree, sometimes informally, to call in sick in large numbers on certain days, an action called a *sickout*. Pilots at American Airlines engaged in a massive sickout in early 1999, causing the airline to cancel thousands of flights before a judge ordered the pilots back to work.

Some kinds of strikes and labor actions are illegal. Foremost among these illegal actions is the **wildcat strike**, which occurs during the course of a labor contract and is usually undertaken in response to a perceived injustice on the part of management. Because strikes are not legal during the course of a binding labor agreement, a wildcat strike is also unauthorized, at least theoretically, by the strikers' union.

Management also has certain tactics that it may employ in its efforts to break an impasse. One possibility is called a **lockout**, and it occurs when the employer denies employees access to the workplace. Managers must be careful when they use lockouts, however, because the practice is closely regulated by the government. A firm cannot lock out its employees simply to deprive them of wages or to gain power during the labor negotiations. Suppose, however, that the employer can meet a legitimate business need by locking out its employees. If this business need can be carefully documented, then a lockout might be legal. For example, in 1998 ABC Television locked out its off-camera employees

*A **strike** occurs when employees walk off their jobs and refuse to work.*

***Picketing** occurs when workers representing the union march at the entrance to the employer's facility with signs explaining their reasons for striking.*

*A **boycott** occurs when union members agree not to buy the products of a targeted employer.*

*A **slowdown** occurs when workers perform their jobs at a much slower pace than normal.*

*A **wildcat strike** occurs during the course of a labor contract and is usually undertaken in response to a perceived injustice on the part of management.*

*A **lockout** occurs when an employer denies employees access to the workplace.*

because they staged an unannounced one-day strike during a critical broadcasting period.[19] Almost half of the 1998–99 NBA season was lost when team owners locked out their players over contract issues.[20] Management occasionally uses temporary workers or replacements for strikers. These individuals are called *strikebreakers* (and sometimes *scabs* by striking workers). Conflict sometimes erupts between strikebreakers attempting to enter an employer's workplace and picketers representing the interests of the union at the employer's gates.

Sometimes the various tactics described above are successful in resolving the impasse. For instance, after workers have gone out on strike, the organization may change its position and indeed modify its bargaining zone to accommodate potentially larger increases in pay. After management experiences a strike, it sometimes realizes that the costs of failing to settle are greater than previously believed, and so managers are willing to give more to avoid a longer strike (i.e., their resistance point has shifted). In many situations, other alternatives for resolving an impasse are also available. Common alternatives include the use of mediation and arbitration.

In **mediation**, a neutral third party called the *mediator* listens to and reviews the information presented by both sides. The mediator then makes an informed recommendation and provides advice to both parties about what she or he believes should be done. For example, suppose the impasse concerns wage increases, with the union demanding 8 percent and the company willing to pay only 5 percent. The mediator listens to both sides and reviews all the evidence and may subsequently conclude that because of the financial profile of the company and other labor negotiations in other industries, 5 percent is both fair and all the organization can afford to pay. This advice is then provided to both sides. The union does not have to accept this information, however, and can continue its efforts to exact a higher wage increase from the employer. In many cases, dispute mediation is done through the offices of the Federal Mediation and Conciliation Service. In fact, it is not uncommon for contracts to require mandatory mediation when there is an impasse.

Another alternative to resolving impasses is **arbitration**, or the process in which both sides agree in advance that they will accept the recommendations made by an independent third-party arbitrator. Like a mediator, the arbitrator listens to both sides of the dispute and presents and reviews all the evidence. In arbitration, however, the information that results is placed in the form of a proposed settlement agreement that the parties have agreed in advance to accept. Thus, a settlement is imposed on the parties and the impasse is ended. But some critics believe that arbitrators tend to impose settlements that "split the difference." If both parties believe that the arbitrator has proposed such a settlement, then they have an incentive to stick to their original positions and not move toward a settlement because such a move shifts the middle further away from their target points.[21] As such, the threat of arbitration may "chill" the negotiation process and actually make a negotiated settlement less likely. It is becoming more common for contracts to include some form of required arbitration when there is an impasse because both sides in negotiations are beginning to recognize just how costly a strike really is.

An alternative form of arbitration has therefore been proposed that should induce the parties, it is argued, to negotiate a settlement by potentially imposing strikelike costs on both parties.[22] Under **final-offer arbitration**, the parties bargain until impasse. At that point, the two parties' final offers are submitted to the arbitrator. Under traditional arbitration, the arbitrator is then free to impose a settlement at any point he or she wishes. But under final-offer arbitration, the arbitrator has only two choices for the imposed settlement—the two parties' final offers—and the arbitrator must select either one *as the imposed settlement*. Thus, the party that does not bargain in good faith may get everything it wants in the arbitrator's decision but may just as easily lose everything. Under such a system, the parties are more willing to try to reach a settlement on their own rather than go to the arbitrator. Professional baseball uses final-offer arbitration to resolve contract disputes between individual players and owners.

Administering Labor Agreements

Another key clause in the labor contracts negotiated between management and labor defines how the labor agreement will be enforced. In some cases, enforcement is clear. If the two sides agree that the company will increase the wages it pays to its employees by 2 percent a year over the next 3 years according

© Aspen/Shutterstock

In **mediation**, a neutral third party called the mediator listens to and reviews the information presented by both sides and then makes an informed recommendation and provides advice to both parties about what she or he believes should be done.

In **arbitration**, both sides agree in advance that they will accept the recommendations made by an independent third-party arbitrator.

Under **final-offer arbitration**, the parties bargain until impasse and then the two parties' final offers are submitted to the arbitrator.

to a prescribed increase schedule, then there is little opportunity for disagreement. Wage increases can be calculated mathematically, and union members will see the effects in their paychecks. Other provisions of many labor contracts, however, are more subjective in nature and thus more prone to misinterpretation and different perceptions.

For example, suppose a labor contract specifies how overtime assignments are to be allocated in the organization. Such allocation strategies are often relatively complex and suggest that the company may have to take into account various factors such as seniority, previous overtime allocations, and the hours or days in which the overtime work is needed. Now suppose that a supervisor in the factory is attempting to follow the labor contract and offers overtime to a certain employee. This employee, however, indicates that before he or she can accept, he or she must check with a spouse or partner to learn more about previous obligations and commitments. The supervisor may feel a time crunch and be unable to wait as long as the employee would like. As a result, the supervisor gives the overtime opportunity to a second employee. The first employee may feel aggrieved by this course of action and elect to protest.

When such differences of opinion occur, the individual labor union member takes the complaint to her or his shop steward, the union officer described earlier in this chapter, who listens to the complaint and forms an initial impression. The shop steward has the option of advising the employee that the supervisor handled the matter appropriately. But other appeal mechanisms are also available so that the employee, even if denied by the shop steward, still has channels for appeal.

Of course, if the shop steward agrees with the employee, she or he may also follow prescribed methods for dealing with the situation. The prescribed methods might include starting with the supervisor to listen to his or her side of the story and then continuing along the lines of appeal up the hierarchy of both the labor union and the company. In some cases, mediation and arbitration may be started to resolve the disagreement. For example, some of the potential resolutions to the grievance described earlier would be to reassign the overtime opportunity to the employee who was asked first. Or the overtime opportunity may stay with the second employee but the first employee would also receive overtime pay.

LABOR UNIONS IN THE TWENTY-FIRST CENTURY

Earlier in this chapter, we discussed the historical roots of the U.S. labor movement. We noted that the labor movement in this country focused on bread-and-butter issues such as wages and hours of work, unlike the labor movements in many European countries. Early American unionists were less concerned with social issues and, partly as a result, a labor party in the United States never drew much interest. Unions and union members supported political candidates who favored their goals, and unions have spoken out on any number of political issues. But for the most part, the issues in which U.S. labor unions became involved were pretty close to the basic issues facing U.S. labor. This situation is clearly changing, however.

U.S. labor unions have become quite vocal in several areas where they have traditionally been silent, speaking out against child labor in Third World countries and the general exportation of jobs to lower-paying countries. Union positions on these issues reflect their self-interests to some extent; moving manufacturing jobs to Mexico, for example, means that U.S. unions will lose members. But there is more to this issue than obvious self-interest. These public positions have changed the way many people think about unions. Although union membership has declined over the past several decades, these changes can enhance the power of labor unions and thus affect the relationship between unions and management. A wide array of issues has attracted the involvement of the U.S. labor movement, but we will focus on only a few. Note, however, that these issues are simply meant to be illustrative of the new scope of union interests in this country.

"Replacement" Sources of Labor

We discussed the trends to export jobs overseas in Chapter 3. The U.S. labor movement has become quite interested in these trends and has generally argued that these trends lead to job losses in the United States. But overseas labor markets are only one source of "replacement" laborers. Labor unions in the United States have also voiced concern over the use of other such sources.

For example, in 2005, roughly 1 million people were serving time in federal, state, and local prisons and jails (we discussed concerns associated with this in Chapter 8). Although many of these inmates work in paid jobs, they are paid much less than the minimum wage, meaning the goods they produce can be sold for less, causing serious problems for unskilled workers in the general population. Furthermore, many critics of the U.S. prison system argue that these prison jobs do not prepare prison inmates for outside jobs once they are released and thus do not lessen the rate of subsequent arrest and incarceration. The U.S. labor movement and its advocates argue that this system needs reform to provide more rights to prison laborers and to ensure that prison labor does not take away civilian population jobs, which in the long run can lead to increased crime.

Unions also have become more involved in social issues over the past few years, including the use of prison labor. Eighty-five inmates at the Central California Women's Facility, near Fresno, for example, are now working on electronics components for Joint Venture Electronics, which actually pays them the minimum wage. The only other job available to the inmates, working in the state-sponsored denture lab, pays just $0.33 an hour. Of course, assemblers of circuit boards on the outside would earn several times the minimum wage, so relying on convict labor reduces company costs. But it also reduces the number of jobs available to noninmates, which could lead to more crime.

Contingent Workers

Another source of "replacement labor" is the pool of contingent workers, which was discussed in Chapter 6. Perhaps it is no surprise that U.S. unions have taken a stand on the topic of contingent workers. Under U.S. labor laws, contingent workers are considered independent contractors or self-employed laborers, and in 1998 these self-employed workers numbered about 10.3 million—or approximately 8 percent of the workforce.[19] As independent contractors, these workers are not covered by most employment and labor laws. In fact, to be covered by almost any legislation related to employment, a person must have some type of employment relationship with an entity, which is not the case for most contingent workers. This problem will become more serious as more organizations turn to contingent workers as a way to manage their demand for labor.

Clearly, organized labor has a vested interest in opposing the reliance on these groups of potential "replacement" laborers. Although the representatives of the unions focus on the social implications of these practices, and probably are concerned about these social costs, clearly labor unions have more to lose in these cases than do others. Nonetheless, U.S. labor unions have been able to form coalitions with other community groups who oppose the use of prison labor or are concerned about exporting jobs overseas, and they have become very vocal in this movement. As a result, labor unions have gained a great deal of credibility as guardians of middle-class jobs.

Unions and the Electronic Age

The Internet also presents many interesting challenges for U.S. labor unions. The most obvious one stems from the fact that computers and new technology often mean that work can be done by fewer employees. As noted earlier, companies have been trying to move more production sites to foreign countries where labor costs are lower and U.S. unions have no input. Thus, unions would lose members. At the same time, the introduction of technology is also reducing the number of workers and the number of union members. Although unions must oppose some of these technological advances for the sake of their members' jobs if nothing else, they cannot simply reject these advances wholesale. Clearly, in many cases the firms involved will lose business and perhaps even be forced out of business if they cannot keep pace with the technology (and cost controls) of their competitors. Such outcomes are not desirable from the unions' perspective either, and so the U.S. labor movement is in a difficult position.

Changes in technology have also posed a much different set of challenges for unions and for the management of firms with unionized employees. For example, many firms who fear unionization efforts have no-solicitation rules at work. These rules simply mean that no employee can solicit other employees on company time for any cause except United Way campaigns; that is, under such rules, employees cannot sell candy for a high school band, raffle tickets for a new car, or even tickets for a church dinner. An important aspect of these rules is that they also outlaw any attempts by union organizers to solicit employees to sign cards appointing the union as sole bargaining agent. Organizations are usually vigilant about no-solicitation rules because they stop union-organizing efforts at work.

The Internet presents a challenge to these no-solicitation rules. Monitoring solicitation on the Internet is much more difficult, and some of this solicitation may even come from outside the firm. If the company fails to stop these forms of solicitation, then can it still legally stop union solicitation at work? Can unions use the Internet to solicit union membership if they do so from outside the company? Recent NLRB rulings and opinions have not clarified the answers to these questions.

© Franck Boston/Shutterstock

For example, if the organization allows employees to use the Internet (even if the computers are company owned) to post thank-you notes, it may be forced to allow union solicitation as well. The NLRB will have to deal with these issues in the coming years, but the key seems to be non-discrimination. In other words, companies cannot (apparently) forbid employees from using the Internet for union solicitation if companies allow employees to use the Internet for other nonbusiness-related purposes.[20] In any case, the Internet has complicated the problem of solicitation—by any party—on the job.

It seems, however, that unions have generally seen Internet solicitation as a useful tool in a different setting. In many high-tech firms, it is common to outsource work and for people to work at home. In these situations, employees rarely meet face to face. How can a union hope to organize these workers? A recent article has pointed out that unions in the Silicon Valley area have been successful in using the Internet for union-organizing campaigns.[21] They have been active in trying to organize a wide variety of contingent workers in the area, and they successfully organized janitorial workers across firms in the Silicon Valley through Internet solicitation. This approach has enabled union organizers to reach workers they could not meet personally, and it plays on the fact that many workers at all levels in this area have easy access to computers. Unions in the Silicon Valley area have also used Internet-based campaigns to mount successful boycotts against some firms.

Finally, unions have found that the Internet has significant effects on the way they conduct their own internal business. Unions in this country can now communicate immediately with union leaders and members from around the world, making unions more democratic in their internal policies. It has also enabled unions to mobilize international resources to deal with issues that all union members face wherever they work such as the lower wages and looser labor regulations associated with agreements under the World Trade Organization.

It remains to be seen how unions will be able to use and be challenged by computers and the electronic age in the coming years. It is already clear, however, that new electronic technology has been a mixed blessing for the U.S. labor movement. Although technology continues to threaten jobs, it also allows unions to reach workers in ways that were never possible before. It is not yet clear that computers will be able to revitalize the union movement in the United States, but they certainly seem capable of breathing new life into that movement.

CLOSING CASE

"GIVE AND TAKE"

The general view of management and labor unions is that they are antagonists: When one wins, the other loses—and vice versa. In reality, of course, they are many situations where businesses and unions coexist quite peacefully. And there are other situations where businesses and unions find they have little choice but to work together in order for both to survive. During the economic recession of 2009, for example, unions agreed to help out the businesses that employed their members in several cases.

One notable example came from Harley-Davidson, the big motorcycle manufacturer. One of Harley's biggest factories is in York, Pennsylvania. The York plant, one of Harley's oldest, employed about 2,000 nonmanagerial workers. The recession caused a dramatic drop in revenue for Harley and the firm desperately needed to cut costs. Company officials determined that Harley needed to reduce its overall costs by $120 million to $150 million to remain competitive.

"These were changes that had to be made to keep [Harley-Davidson] viable.

—**Sharon Zackfia, investment banker**

The York factory was a key site for cost reduction. For one thing, the factory was in dire need of modernization. For another, the labor contract governing York workers called for wages well above the industry average; moreover, the factory had more than sixty different job classifications, and the union contract made it nearly impossible to move workers across classifications.

One of the first options Harley considered was simply closing the York plant and moving its jobs to the firm's newest factory in Kentucky. That plant had a more flexible union contract and the newest technology. The International Association of Machinists and Aerospace Workers, however, persuaded the company to negotiate a new arrangement that would allow some of the union's workers to retain their jobs.

Under terms of the new agreement, which took effect in February 2010, about half of the plant's 2,000 jobs would be eliminated. The number of job classifications would also be cut from

60 to five, and Harley would have considerable flexibility to move workers from one to another. Moreover, any new employees hired after February 2010 would start at an hourly rate of $19.28, about 20 percent less than the previous starting rate of $24.10. Finally, the 1,000 or so workers who retained their jobs would be divided into two groups. About 750 "first-tier" production workers would retain their full-time jobs with current wages and benefits. The other 250 or so would be classified as "casual" workers; these workers would take a wage cut of about 30 percent and would only work on an as-needed basis.

For its part, Harley agreed to invest $90 million to modernize the plant with the goal of allowing the York factory to be the first one to create new jobs when demand for motorcycles begins to increase. The state of Pennsylvania also agreed to chip in $15 million to support both plant upgrades and new training programs for workers. Finally, Harley also agreed that the 750 first-tier production workers would have their jobs guaranteed for the duration of the 7-year deal.

Many observers saw this new contract as one-sided in favor of Harley-Davidson. One expert, Professor Gary Chaison at Clark University, commented, "This is tying the hands of the union for a long time." In contrast to similar renegotiations, the union does appear to have given up a lot. For instance, the UAW renegotiated its labor contract with General Motors during the automaker's recent financial problems. Under terms of the new agreement, GM would be allowed to eliminate one-third of its jobs and reduce its retiree health-care obligations by funding a portion of its obligations with stock rather than cash. In exchange, the UAW received job guarantees for two-thirds of the GM workforce, a large equity stake in GM, and a seat on GM's board of directors.[23]

THINK IT OVER

1. Do you think the Harley deal was too one-sided? Why or why not?

2. If you were a Harley or GM employee and union member, would you have voted for the new deal? Why or why not?

3. Do you think it is appropriate for a government entity (such as the state of Pennsylvania) to take an active role in union–management negotiations? Why or why not?

STUDY TOOLS

■ **Rip out the chapter review card located at the end of the book.**

■ **Review the valuable study tools located online at www.cengagebrain.com**

  ■ **Review the Key Terms flashcards.**

  ■ **Download audio and visual summaries to review on the go.**

  ■ **Complete practice quizzes to prepare for the test.**

  ■ **Play "Beat the Clock" and "QuizBowl" to master chapter concepts.**

  ■ **Complete "Crossword Puzzle" to review key terms.**

  ■ **Watch the chapter video for a real-life example of key concepts.**

Safety, Health, WELL-BEING, & Security

Fed

SPEED CAN TAKE A TOLL

FedEx provides air-cargo express services, moving everything from an urgent business letter to a human heart for transplant. FedEx employs thousands of aircraft, vehicles, and workers in dozens of countries. At FedEx's Memphis airport hub, the company typically processes more than 5 million packages—per average day—and as many as 7.5 million items per day during holidays. Looking around on a recent, typical night, Reginald Owens, Sr., vice president, admits it may look like controlled chaos, but in reality "is a well-conditioned, well-organized machine."

Clearly, jobs at FedEx can be stressful. For example, FedEx package handlers and couriers must sort, load, and deliver a variety of different kinds of packages under tight deadlines. Moreover, they often work outside, with heavy machinery, on day and night shifts, and they are required to use physical coordination, strength, speed, and attention to detail.

Call-center employees face different sources of stress. They do not lift or sort packages, and they work in a more controlled environment. But they answer a high volume of calls and must do so with accuracy, courtesy, and speed. Employee performance is sometimes evaluated by supervisors who listen in on calls.

Even managers at FedEx experience stress. Executive Vice President T. Michael Glenn explains that performance is critical: "We've got to work our people pretty hard to guarantee that every child gets her Christmas doll on time." Nightly deadlines contribute to the urgency. As managing director for global operations control John G. Dunavant says, "Everything we do, we're managing to a time clock."

LEARNING OBJECTIVES
After studying this chapter, you should be able to:

LO1 Identify and discuss the central elements associated with employee safety and health

LO2 Describe the basic issues involved in the physical work environment

LO3 Discuss stress and stress-management programs in organizations

LO4 Identify and describe the most important HR-related security issues in organizations

In addition, the business environment is characterized by its intense competition with UPS and DHL, its high need for security, and unpredictable weather. Each element further adds to stress. High stress can cause mental and physical problems and reduce motivation. These consequences, in turn, can lead to increased absenteeism and turnover, burnout, and loss of productivity. FedEx competes in a customer-oriented service industry, where these consequences could be devastating.

FedEx uses two strategies to effectively address employee stress. First, it tries to reduce the stress inherent in its jobs to the extent that is possible. For example, the company conducts time-and-motion studies to identify less-tiring ways of completing tasks. Employees are then trained in the proper techniques. Employee suggestions are also used to redesign jobs to make them less stressful. Automated tools such as bar-code scanners and computerized package-tracking systems handle some of the repetitive tasks.

FedEx's second strategy is to help employees more effectively cope with stress. Job duties can be modified if an employee needs a temporary break. Company benefits include paid sick time and leave, as well as assistance with stressful life events such as birth, adoption, and death. An employee-assistance program also provides counseling and help for legal, financial, mental health, relationship, child-care, and elder-care problems.

Although stress seems inevitable at FedEx, the company's strategies do seem to at least partly offset this stress. As one indicator of how well the company helps its employees, for example, FedEx has been named as one of the best companies for workers by *Fortune*, *ComputerWorld*, *The Wall Street Journal*, and *Business Ethics*.[1]

THINK IT OVER

1. Would you like to work for FedEx? Why or why not?
2. How do you think jobs at FedEx compare to those at the United States Postal Service? What accounts for the differences?

Most people do not think a great deal about their safety or health when they go to work. They assume that their employer has done whatever is possible to make the workplace as safe and as healthy as it can be. Although many people routinely experience stress, many workers do not see it as something they can really control. In addition, ever since September 11, 2001, some American workers have experienced more concern about their physical security at work, as well as at home.

The truth is that many accidents do occur in the workplace and that many workplaces are actually not healthy. This chapter is about ways in which organizations and human resource (HR) managers can make the workplace environment safe and healthy. As we shall see, some legal pressures (recall the Occupational Safety and Health Act of 1970 we described in Chapter 2) operate to make workplaces safe, and there are also some practical issues that lead HR managers to keep workplaces healthy and secure.

EMPLOYEE SAFETY AND HEALTH

An organization tries to create and maintain a safe and healthy workplace for many reasons. For one thing, it is simply an ethical and socially responsible position; no responsible employer would argue that it is acceptable for employees to get hurt or become ill because of their working conditions. But there are also many other very specific reasons. First, recall from our discussion in Chapter 9 that mandated workers' compensation provides insurance coverage for employees who are hurt or who become ill on the job. The insurance premium an organization pays for this coverage is determined by several factors, including the value of the claims paid out to employees of the firm. Firms that have fewer accidents and workers' compensation claims actually pay lower premiums. In addition, the Occupational Safety and Health Administration (OSHA) can impose fines against organizations that have unsafe workplaces. Finally, lost time from accidents and illness can cost an organization a great deal of money, so it is simply good business to maintain a safe and healthy workplace. An important step in this process is to identify and eliminate safety and health hazards on the job.

Safety hazards are those conditions in the work environment that have the potential to cause harm to an employee. **Health hazards**, on the other hand, are elements of the work environment that more slowly and systematically, and perhaps cumulatively, result in damage to an employee's health. A safety hazard might be a poorly connected string of wiring that might result in electrical shock to an employee; a continuous and ongoing exposure to chemicals that may increase the risk of cancer represents a health hazard.

These risks do not seem to be equally likely in all types of businesses or occupations. In fact, some types of work are much more likely to experience injuries than others. Table 12.1 lists several of the most dangerous occupations in the United States. For example, in 2008 there were 969 reported fatalities among construction workers; the most frequent cause of these fatalities was falling from construction sites (buildings, bridges, etc.). This figure represented 19 percent of all work-related fatalities that year. Likewise, 304 U.S. workers died while engaged in crop production.

> **Safety hazards** *are conditions in the work environment that have the potential to cause harm to an employee.*
>
> **Health hazards** *are characteristics of the work environment that more slowly and systematically, and perhaps cumulatively, result in damage to an employee's health.*

Common Workplace Hazards and Threats

In this section, we address some of the more frequent causes of accidents and then describe some of the more pervasive health hazards. One major category of factors that can cause accidents in the workplace is the characteristics of the physical environment. At a general level, of course, accidents can happen anywhere. People can slip on wet flooring or a loose piece of carpeting, or they can drop something heavy on a foot in almost any setting. But in

congested storage areas can result in accidents. Of course, hazards are not restricted to manufacturing settings. They can occur in almost any work setting; home-office safety, for example, must be a concern for businesses that allow telecommuting.[2]

Some personal actions of individual employees also present common workplace hazards. Among the more frequently described and identified personal actions that lead to accidents are taking unnecessary risks, failing to

> **The Occupational Safety and Health Act of 1970 (or OSHA) grants the federal government the power to establish and enforce occupational safety and health standards for all places of employment that directly affect interstate commerce.**

manufacturing settings, several specific conditions of the work environment might prove to be potentially dangerous. Among the more common are unguarded or improperly guarded machines. In this instance, "guarding" refers to a shield or other piece of equipment that keeps body parts from contacting moving machine parts such as gears and conveyor belts.

Defective equipment and tools can cause accidents. Poor lighting and poor or improper ventilation can also be dangerous. Improper dress poses a hazard; loose clothing presents the risk of getting caught in the moving parts of a machine. Sharp edges around machinery can be a hazard. Finally, poor housekeeping that results in dirty or wet floors, improperly stacked materials, and

wear protective equipment such as goggles or gloves, using improper tools and equipment for specific jobs, taking unsafe shortcuts, and simply engaging in foolish horseplay. Any of these actions has the potential to harm or injure people in the workplace quickly and without warning. These kinds of actions caused an excessive number of injuries for years at Georgia-Pacific, as detailed later in this chapter's closing case. Fatigue can also be a major contributor to workplace hazards. Even without hazardous conditions, a tired employee can still fall or become overly careless.

A separate set of workplace factors may produce negative health effects that appear more gradually. Chemicals, toxic fumes, and similar workplace elements may fall into this category. Secondary smoke may also

TABLE 12.1 Most Dangerous Occupations in the United States, 2008

Industry	Number of Fatalities	Percentage of Total Fatalities	Most Frequent Cause
Construction	969	19	Falls
Natural resources and mining	826	16	Struck by object
Transportation and warehousing	762	15	Highways
Forestry, fishing, and hunting	651	13	Struck by object
Specialty trade contractors	586	11	Falls
Truck transportation	469	9	Highways
Professional and business services	389	8	Highways
Manufacturing	404	8	Highways and falls
Administrative and waste services	321	6	Highways
Crop production	304	6	Struck by object

Source: www.bls.gov/news.release/cfoi.t02.htm,

be a factor. Some buildings themselves have relatively unsafe characteristics, including asbestos insulation and carpeting that has been treated with improper combinations of chemicals and dyes. In many cases, health hazards are occupational. For example, people who work in coal mines and pesticide plants may be especially prone to exposure to potential health hazards. The U.S. Department of Labor has identified seven major categories of occupational illnesses:

1. occupational skin diseases or disorders,
2. dust diseases of the lungs,
3. respiratory conditions because of toxic agents,
4. poisoning,
5. disorders resulting from physical agents,
6. disorders associated with repeated trauma, and
7. other categories of occupational illness.

As discussed later in this chapter, stress is another type of long-term health and safety hazard.

Organizations and OSHA

Widespread concern about employee safety and health led to the passage in 1970 of the most comprehensive law regarding worker safety. This act is technically known as the Occupational Safety and Health Act of 1970 but is most frequently referred to simply by its initials: OSHA. At the time OSHA was passed, approximately 15,000 work-related deaths occurred in the United States every year.

OSHA authorized the U.S. government to create and enforce various standards regarding occupational safety and health. The responsibility for enforcing the provisions of OSHA was assigned to the Department of Labor. This enforcement group today is called the Occupational Safety and Health Administration but still operates within the Department of Labor. Somewhat confusingly, then, the acronym "OSHA" can refer to either the original act passed in 1970 or the enforcement group itself.

In concert with the Department of Labor, the Department of Health was also given the task of sponsoring research to establish the criteria for various tasks

OSHA is both the act that authorized the U.S. government to create various standards regarding occupational safety and health and the administrative agency that enforces those standards.

and occupations and for training employees to comply with the act. Most of this work is conducted by an agency within the Department of Health called the National Institute for Occupational Safety and Health (NIOSH); that is, NIOSH conducts research to help establish appropriate safety and health criteria. These criteria are then communicated to OSHA in the Department of Labor for administration and enforcement. A sample of the guidelines developed from this work is shown in Table 12.2.

Through research and analysis of workplace statistics, OSHA has created various safety standards. These standards are defined as "practices, means, operations, or processes, reasonably necessary to provide safe . . . employment." The various standards that OSHA creates are regularly published and disseminated to employers across the country. Organizations are responsible for keeping current on OSHA standards, which can be difficult because of the length and volume of the various sets of regulations and standards. Each year, new standards, revisions of old standards, or extensions or reinterpretations of various existing standards **are published by** OSHA in volumes that total hundreds of pages in length. Thus, managers frequently feel that OSHA represents unnecessary regulation of their activities.

To ensure compliance with OSHA, inspectors from the U.S. Department of Labor visit places of employment either randomly or by invitation from an employer, an employee, or a union. If an employee requests an OSHA inspection, then her or his identity is kept confidential. If the OSHA inspector determines that the employer is guilty of major violations, significant penalties can result. An employer can be fined $10,000 per violation for willful or repeated major violations. In addition, company officials may be personally fined for failure to comply with OSHA regulations and can conceivably be sentenced to jail time.

OSHA also requires that employers keep highly specific and standardized records of illnesses and injuries that occur in the workplace. These records must be produced and shown to any OSHA compliance officer who requests them. In addition to routine record keeping, employers must also report immediately and directly to OSHA all accidents and illnesses that result in deaths in the workplace or that pose serious health hazards to all employees in the organization. Employers have avenues for appeal; if they disagree with the recommendations of an OSHA

TABLE 12.2 Sample General Industry Safety and Health Regulations from OSHA

For drinking water . . .

- Potable water shall be provided in all places of employment.

- The nozzle of a drinking fountain shall be set at such an angle that the jet of water will not splash back down the nozzle; and the end of the nozzle shall be protected by a guard to prevent a person's mouth or nose from coming in contact with the nozzle.

- Portable drinking water dispensers shall be designed and serviced to ensure sanitary conditions, shall be capable of being closed, and shall have a tap. Unused disposable cups shall be kept in a sanitary container, and a receptacle shall be provided for used cups. The "common drinking cup" is prohibited.

For fire protection . . .

- Portable fire extinguishers, suitable to the conditions and hazards involved, shall be provided and maintained in effective operating condition.

- Portable fire extinguishers shall be given maintenance service at least once a year. A durable tag must be securely attached to show the maintenance or recharge date.

- In storage areas, clearance between sprinkler systems deflectors and the top of storage varies with the type of storage. For combustible material, stored over 15 feet, but not more than 21 feet high, in solid piles, or over 12 feet, but not more than 21 feet, in piles that contain horizontal channels, the minimum clearance shall be 36 inches. The minimum clearance for smaller piles, or for noncombustible materials, shall be 18 inches.

For portable ladders . . .

- The maximum length for portable wooden ladders shall be as follows: step, 20 feet; single straight ladders, 30 feet; sectional ladders, 60 feet; trestle ladders, 20 feet; platform stepladders, 20 feet; painter's stepladders, 12 feet; mason's ladders, 40 feet.

- Non-self-supporting ladders shall be erected on a sound base at a 4 to 1 pitch, and placed to prevent slippage.

- The top of a ladder used to gain access to a roof should extend at least 3 feet above the point of contact.

Source: *General Industry Standards and Interpretations*, U.S. Department of Labor, OSHA (Vol. 1, Revised 2008, Part 1914).

compliance officer, they can turn to the Occupational Safety and Health Review Commission. They can also pursue their claims through the federal courts.

Many experts believe that OSHA has not been terribly effective. They argue, for example, that its standards are too comprehensive, too technical, and often too arbitrary. Critics also point out that enforcement of OSHA standards is still relatively uneven. Even in terms of actual measurable effects, OSHA has been less than successful. Although awareness of safety issues has undoubtedly increased, the number of occupational accidents and occupational illnesses has not been significantly diminished.[3]

Controlling Accidents at Work

Regardless of whether OSHA is involved or not, an organization can take several precautions in its effort to create a safer work environment, especially regarding accidents at work. One important approach is to design more safety into the workplace through a process called *safety engineering*. **Safety engineers** are experts who carefully study the workplace, try to identify and isolate particularly dangerous situations, and recommend solutions for dealing with those situations.

In addition, organizations can sometimes help control workplace accidents by providing protective clothing and safety devices to employees. Among the more common kinds are various types of head protection, eye goggles and face shields, hearing protection for excessively noisy environments, gloves for hand protection, safety shoes for foot protection, waist support belts for people lifting heavy objects, and belts and lifelines for employees who work in high places. In today's technology-driven workplaces, safety equipment also includes wrist and elbow supports and screen filters for people who keyboard several hours a day, as well as properly designed chairs and desk surfaces for people who sit for most of their workday.

In addition, employee training is an important ingredient in controlling accidents at work. Employees should be taught the safest work procedures that the organization can identify, and they should be taught to follow safe work procedures and report unsafe conditions to managers. Finally, providing safety incentives and behavior modification training to employees has also been found effective in reducing the number of accidents on the job.[4]

An organization can try to make the workplace safer in one of two ways. First, it can emphasize a reduction in the number of accidents or in the number of workdays lost to accidents.

Safety engineers *are experts who carefully study the workplace, try to identify and isolate particularly dangerous situations, and recommend solutions for dealing with those situations.*

© KOUNADEAS IOANNHS/Shutterstock

You may have seen a construction site or facility that has a sign indicating the number of days, weeks, or months since someone missed work because of an accident. Accidents and lost workdays can be counted and so can easily be used to justify whatever measures the organization takes. Second, the organization also can focus on safe behaviors—that is, making the workplace safer—rather than on accidents themselves. An example of an emphasis on safe behavior would be training and rewards for people who engage in safe behaviors (e.g., wearing their hardhats), with the assumption that this behavior will lead to a decrease in the number of accidents. Although safe behavior is a step removed from reduced numbers of accidents, increasing safe behaviors is clearly a necessary step in reducing accidents. Both approaches can work, but they operate in much different ways.

The kinds of interventions described above can also be part of a larger safety culture. One of the authors recently observed a group of managers from several companies going down a flight of stairs for lunch during an executive development training session. In one group, all managers held the railing as they went down the stairs, whereas most people just walked down without holding anything. The mangers holding the railing were all employees at various DuPont plants, an organization that has a strong norm for safe behavior.

This idea has been formalized as a construct called *safety climate*. The safety climate of an organization is usually considered to be the perception of the importance and priority an organization gives to safety.[5] Basically, the safety climate should influence employees' behavior because they perceive a relationship between their safety behavior and the rewards and punishments meted out by the company. A company with a positive safety climate is one in which employees recognize that they will be rewarded for their safe behaviors and punished for their unsafe behaviors. There is, however, only mixed research support for a relationship between safety climate and accidents at work.[6]

Controlling Occupational Diseases

Controlling occupational diseases is a bit more complex. The effects of occupational diseases are often observable only after extended periods of time, so it may be difficult for the organization to know if its disease-prevention efforts are effective. For example, several years ago it was determined that a disproportionate number of workers at an Amoco research facility had contracted brain cancer. Experts studied the problem for more than 10 years. Some observers theorized that chemicals at the work site were

responsible, but neither independent researchers nor the company itself were able to pinpoint the problem or to establish conclusively that the work site was to blame.[7]

Nonetheless, certain precautions can be taken. For example, the organization should be thoroughly familiar with all hazardous conditions in the work environment that might cause occupational diseases. If these hazards can be eliminated or minimized, then the organization should attempt to do so. If the hazardous environment is unavoidable, then the organization can still take precautions. For example, all employees should be clearly informed of the various risks and hazards associated with their jobs. This information should enable them to take a larger role in maintaining their own health. Again, in many cases, proper equipment might be helpful. Respiratory shields for breathing, pressurized or rubberized bodysuits, and appropriate safety materials and equipment such as gloves and masks might be helpful.

THE PHYSICAL ENVIRONMENT

The actual physical environment in which an employee works is also extremely important and obviously can affect safety, health, and well-being. In addition, the physical environment can affect how pleasant or unpleasant a work setting is. Although many aspects of the physical environment may affect an employee's attitudes and behavior on the job, we will focus on just a few.

Hours of Work

In Chapter 14, we will discuss some trends toward nontraditional workweeks as techniques to enhance performance; we note here, however, that the hours worked and how they are distributed can also affect employee safety and well-being. For example, 4 days on, 3 days off a week may be attractive to some people, but not to others. This work schedule can create problems, too. For example, one study found that young males were much more receptive to compressed workweeks than were any other group.[8] Preferences aside, studies of compressed work schedules have also found that construction accidents are more likely to occur later in the day (which would be 10 hours long) because of fatigue on construction jobs, and generally mixed results were found for productivity in jobs with compressed work schedules.[9]

In many industries, the problems of shift work present another challenge to managing the work environment effectively. All human beings are subject to **circadian rhythms**, which tell our bodies when to eat and sleep. When employees work a night shift, their bodies must adapt to sleeping during the day and staying awake at night. Although this change is disruptive, the body adapts and learns to switch day and night. But employees who must work on rotating shifts are never able to establish a new rhythm. As a result, they are more likely to have ulcers than other employees because their bodies struggle to find equilibrium.[10] Nonetheless, other research has indicated that some workers, especially older, more experienced employees, may actually like the variety and can cope with the changes in biological rhythms.[11]

Illumination, Temperature, Office and Work Space Design

One phase of the Hawthorne studies conducted in 1924 in a Western Electric plant outside Chicago was concerned with the effects of illumination on productivity. The results indicated that changes in the level of illumination were not responsible for the changes in productivity observed. This failure discouraged scholars from examining the effects of lighting on workplace behavior for quite some time. Considerable evidence, however, shows that extremes of temperature (in either direction) can affect both attitudes and decision making on the job.[12] It has even been suggested that ambient temperature helps explain national differences in stress on the job.[13] Research has also shown that different tasks require different levels of optimal lighting and that employees who perceive their work environments as dark are generally less satisfied with their jobs.[14]

Other aspects of the physical work environment that have received attention over the years include the use of music in the workplace. These studies, many of them going back more than 50 years, have indicated that almost any type of background music can improve employee attitudes and performance on the job.[15] A recent study found that the use of personal stereos on the job improved both attitudes and performance, especially on relatively simple jobs.[16] The physical layout of office space and the use of dividers and cubicles also have been found to influence attitudes and behavior at work.[17] The HR in the Twenty-First Century feature explores some modern twists on workplace design.

Although many of these studies found that changes in the physical environment affect performance, the physical environment seems to have the strongest effect on attitudes. Even when light, temperature, or office layout did not influence performance, these factors were associated with differences in how employees felt about their jobs and where they worked. Clearly, however, some aspects of the environment can influence employee safety and health, a topic we turn to next.

STRESS AND STRESS MANAGEMENT AT WORK

Organizations today are also increasingly becoming involved in stress-management and wellness programs for their employees.[18] To see how such programs can be effective, we must first understand the causes and consequences of stress at work. Exhibit 12.1 notes the major causes and consequences.

Causes of Stress at Work

Stress is a person's adaptive response to a stimulus that places excessive psychological or physical demands on him or her. The stimuli that cause stress are called *stressors*. Organizational stressors are various factors in the workplace that can cause stress. We mentioned this topic briefly in Chapter 6 when we discussed the importance of job satisfaction at work. Four general sets of organizational stressors are task demands, physical demands, role demands, and interpersonal demands.

Task demands are stressors associated with the specific job a person performs. By nature, some occupations are more stressful than others. The jobs of surgeon, air traffic controller, and professional football coach obviously are more stressful than those of a general practitioner, an airlines baggage loader, and a football team equipment manager, respectively. Beyond specific task-related pressures, other task demands may pose physical threats to a person's health. Such conditions exist in occupations such as coal mining, toxic-waste handling, and so forth. Security is another task demand that can cause stress. Someone in a relatively secure job is not likely to worry too much about losing that position. On the other hand, if job security is threatened, stress can increase dramatically. For example, stress generally increases throughout an organization during a period of layoffs or immediately following a merger with another firm. Such a phenomenon has been observed at several organizations including AT&T, Safeway, and Digital Equipment.

Overload is another task demand stressor. It occurs when a person simply has more work to do than he or she can handle. The overload can be either quantitative (the individual has too many tasks to perform or too little time in which to perform them) or qualitative (the person may believe she or he lacks the ability to do the job). More managers report going to their office on weekends to get their jobs done, a direct result of overload.[19]

Advances in information technology may make this problem even worse for some managers. Certainly, new information

Circadian rhythms *are natural cycles that indicate when a body needs to eat or sleep.*

Stress *is a person's adaptive response to a stimulus that places excessive psychological or physical demands on him or her.*

HR in the 21st Century

Building the Perfect Work Environment

One of the more interesting changes sweeping corporate America today involves architecture. Specifically, many companies are seeking new and innovative designs for the workplace to make it more interesting and appealing to workers and to promote interaction and spontaneity. Traditionally, offices were arrayed down long corridors; the further a manager moved up the hierarchy, the bigger the office until the ultimate prize was obtained—the corner office.

> ### "Before, we were in a typical office. Nothing stood out about the space. We wanted atmosphere that was comfortable, untraditional, and more open."
>
> —Debbie Shecterle, director of human resources, Doane Pet Care Company

The next major trend was the installation of cubicles. These modular constructions afforded only a modicum of privacy but still defined specific work space for each employee. Workplace arrangements could be dismantled or rearranged with minimal difficulty. But cubicles also reduce individuality and interaction, which is partly why they became the object of derision in Dilbert and other cartoons. Today, many firms are moving in new and nontraditional ways as they seek to redefine their physical environments.

Several characteristics generally are reflected in how companies structure their space today. A popular movement now is large, well-lit, open spaces where people can gather, talk, and interact. Designers often hope that such features promote greater interaction among employees. Workplaces used to be straight lines, squares, and rectangles, but today they are more likely to feature curves, circles, and other oblique lines and spaces. Right

angles are avoided whenever possible, ceilings rise and fall, and bright colors intermix with more somber wood tones.

Of course, such designs have problems as well. Furniture may not fit into a round office as well as in a square one. If a design is too idiosyncratic, landlords may worry that it may be difficult to find a new tenant if the current one leaves. Still, many companies are attracted to the benefits of this new model. Doane Pet Care, for example, eliminated all of its cubicles and redesigned its work space with curved walls, few interior walls, and gold, brown, and green colors. First Bank Systems in Minneapolis, The Gap, and Sears, Roebuck & Co. are also adopting this new approach.

THINK IT OVER

1. What physical characteristics would you most like to have in your own office? What characteristics would you least want in your office?
2. As a customer or visitor to an office complex, how much individuality would you be comfortable with? Do you think it would better if all offices were uniformly designed and decorated or if each office was unique?

Sources: "A Place of Their Own," *USA Today* (Jan. 13, 2006): 1B, 2B; "Designers Work to Create New Kinds of Work Space," *Wall Street Journal* (Mar. 27, 2006): B3; "New Trends in Office Design," *Design Today* (Jan. 2010): 46–48; Dominic Bencivenga, "A Humanistic Approach to Space," *HR Magazine* (Mar. 1998): 68–74; "Curves Ahead," *Wall Street Journal* (Mar. 10, 1999): B1, B10.

technology has enabled many human resource managers to make decisions better and faster than ever before. And it also promotes more frequent communication among people, resulting in improved coordination and enhanced organizational flexibility and response times. Managers can keep in constant touch with others, and a manager's boss, colleagues, and subordinates can get in touch anytime. But some trouble also crops up. For example, information

technology makes it easier than ever before for HR managers to suffer information overload. Some estimates suggest that managers send or receive more than 400 messages each day. The forms of these messages run the gamut from e-mail to text messages to Post-it Notes. And many HR managers fall into the trap of thinking that because they can always be in touch, they must always be in touch, so they check their e-mail constantly, carry their cell phones

EXHIBIT 12.1
The Causes and Consequences of Stress in Organizations

Source: Reprinted from James C. Quick and Jonathan D. Quick, *Organizational Stress and Preventive Management*, McGraw-Hill, 1984, pp. 19, 44, and 76. Copyright © 1984 by The McGraw-Hill Companies. Reprinted with the permission of James C. Quick.

on vacation or to the golf course, and keep a BlackBerry or iPhone handy at all times.

We should also note that the opposite of overload may also be undesirable—low task demands can result in boredom and apathy just as overload can cause tension and anxiety. Thus, a moderate degree of workload-related stress is optimal because it leads to high levels of energy and motivation.

Physical demands relate to the job setting. Many of the physical aspects of the work environment that we discussed earlier, such as working in extreme temperatures, have been associated with stress on the job. Also, office design can be related to stress if its end result is isolation or boredom or too much interaction with co-workers. Strenuous labor such as loading heavy cargo or lifting packages can also lead to stress, as can poor lighting and inadequate work surfaces.

Role demands can cause stress, too. A role is a set of expected behaviors associated with a position in a group or organization. Stress can result from either role ambiguity or role conflict that people experience in groups. For example, an employee who is feeling pressure from her boss to work longer hours and from her family for more time at home will almost certainly experience stress. A new employee experiencing role

ambiguity because of poor orientation and training practices by the organization will also suffer from stress.

Another set of organizational stressors consists of three *interpersonal demands*.

1. Group pressures include pressure to restrict output, pressure to conform to the group's norms, and so forth. For instance, it is quite common for a work group to arrive at an informal agreement about how much each member will produce. Individuals who produce much more or much less than this level may be pressured by the group to get back in line. An individual who feels a strong need to vary from the group's expectations (perhaps to get a pay raise or promotion) will experience a great deal of stress, especially if acceptance by the group is also important to him or her.

2. Leadership style can cause stress. Suppose an employee needs a great deal of social support from his leader. The leader, however, is quite brusque and shows no concern or compassion for the employee. This employee will likely feel stressed. Similarly, assume that an employee feels a strong need to participate in decision making and to be active in all aspects of management. Her boss is autocratic and refuses to consult subordinates about anything. Once again, stress is likely to result.

© Kutlaev Dmitry/Shutterstock

TABLE 12.3 Most and Least Stressful Jobs

Most Stressful Jobs	Least Stressful Jobs
1. Surgeon	1. Actuary
2. Commercial airline pilot	2. Dietitian
3. Photojournalist	3. Computer systems analyst
4. Advertising account executive	4. Statistician
5. Real estate agent	5. Astronomer
6. Physician (general practice)	6. Mathematician
7. Reporter (newspaper)	7. Historian
8. Physician assistant	8. Software engineer

Source: www.careercast.com/jobs/content/StressfulJobs_page1, accessed Mar. 5, 2010.

3. Conflicting personalities and behaviors may cause stress. Conflict can occur when two or more people must work together even though their personalities, attitudes, and behaviors differ. For example, a person with an internal locus of control—that is, who always wants to control events—might get frustrated working with an external person who likes to wait and see what happens.

Table 12.3 provides a subjective list of the most and least stressful jobs. Other relatively high-stress jobs include inner-city teacher, police officer, miner, and stockbroker. Other relatively low-stress jobs include toolmaker, yoga instructor, and civil engineer. Finally, it is important that all of the stressors noted above exist against a background of general life events that can also cause stress.

The Type A personality is characterized by being highly competitive and highly focused on work with few interests outside of work.

The Type B personality is characterized as being less aggressive, more patient, and more easygoing. In general, individuals with Type B personalities experience less stress and are less likely to suffer some type of illness because of stress than Type A personalities.

Hardiness is an individual difference that allows some individuals to experience less stress when dealing with stressful events, and that makes them more effective in dealing with the stress they do experience.

Differences in How One Experiences Stress

Regardless of the stressors present on any job, different individuals will experience that stress differently. Some individuals respond positively to many types of stress, while others react negatively to any type of stress, so it is important to note some of the factors that influence how one experiences stress.

One factor that is important is personality.

Some years ago, a group of medical researchers noticed that patients with certain personality characteristics were more likely to suffer early heart attacks.[20]

1. They identified these patients as having a **Type A personality**. They are highly competitive, highly focused on their work, and have few interests outside of work.
2. These individuals are often contrasted with the **Type B personality**. They tend to be less aggressive, more patient, and more easygoing. In general, Type A personalities experience more stress and are more likely to suffer some type of illness due to stress than are Type B personalities.[21]
3. Another personality variable that appears to be related to how people experience stress is called **hardiness**. A high degree of hardiness actually reduces the experienced stress associated with stressful events, and so hardy personalities experience less stress overall and are more effective in dealing with the stress they do experience.[22]
4. Individuals high in self-esteem are also less susceptible to the problems associated with stress. They tend to have a more positive outlook on life and are better able to cope with any stress they encounter.[23]
5. Finally, gender appears to be an important factor in determining how one experiences stress. Specifically, women are more likely to experience stress at work, and they are more likely to be absent because of stress-related problems, although these differences may reflect true differences in the stressors that men and women are exposed to at work.[24]

Consequences of Stress at Work

Stress can lead to several positive and negative consequences. If the stress is positive, then the result may be more energy, enthusiasm, and motivation. Of more concern, of course, are the negative consequences of stress. Three sets of consequences that can result from stress are individual consequences, organizational consequences, and burnout.[25] Individual consequences are as follow:

1. Behavioral consequences of stress are responses that may harm the person under stress or others. One such behavior is smoking. Research has clearly documented that people who smoke tend to smoke more when they experience stress. Other possible behavioral consequences are accident tendencies, violence, and appetite disorders.
2. Psychological consequences of stress relate to an individual's mental health and well-being. When people experience too much stress at work, they may become depressed or find themselves sleeping too much or not enough. Stress may also lead to family problems and sexual difficulties.

People often bring their work-related problems home with them. A partner and friends, for example, can help people cope better with stress, keep things in perspective, and take their minds off work, as also shown in this cartoon.

3. The medical consequences of stress affect a person's physical well-being. Heart disease and stroke, among other illnesses, have been linked to stress. Other common medical problems resulting from too much stress include headaches, backaches, ulcers and related stomach and intestinal disorders, and skin conditions such as acne and hives.

Clearly, any of the individual consequences just discussed can also affect the organization, but other consequences of stress have even more direct consequences for organizations.

1. One clear organizational consequence of too much stress is a decline in performance. For operating workers, such a decline can translate into poor-quality work or a drop in productivity. For managers, it can mean faulty decision making or disruptions in working relationships as people become irritable and hard to get along with. As discussed in Chapter 6, withdrawal behaviors such as absenteeism and turnover can result from stress on the job.

2. Another direct organizational consequence of employee stress relates to attitudes. As noted, job satisfaction, morale, and organizational commitment can all suffer, along with motivation to perform at high levels. As a result, people may be more prone to complain about trivialities, do only enough work to get by, and so forth. There has been a trend in the United States over the past 20 years that suggests a gradual decline in job satisfaction. Moreover, a major source of the problem seems to be stress-related aspects of the job. Specifically, respondents in a poll conducted by the Conference Board indicated that less than 36 percent of employees expressed contentment with their workload, work–life balance, or communication channels.[26]

Finally, **burnout**, another consequence of stress, has clear implications for both employees and organizations. It is a general feeling of exhaustion that develops when an individual simultaneously experiences too much pressure and too few sources of satisfaction.

Other consequences of stress include various dysfunctional behaviors that detract from, rather than contribute to, organizational performance. Two of the more common are absenteeism and turnover. Some incidents of absenteeism, of course, have legitimate causes, including illness, jury duty, and death and illness in the family. At other times, the employee may feign a legitimate cause as an excuse to stay home. When an employee is absent, legitimately or not, her or his work does not get done at all or a substitute must be hired to do it. In either case, the quantity or quality of actual output is likely to suffer. Obviously, some absenteeism is expected, but organizations strive to eliminate feigned absenteeism and reduce legitimate absences as much as possible.

Turnover occurs when people quit their jobs. An organization usually incurs costs when replacing workers who have quit; if turnover involves especially productive people, it is even more costly. It seems to result from several factors, including aspects of the job, the organization, the individual, and the labor market and family influences. In general, a poor person–job fit is also a likely cause of turnover. People may also be prone to leave an organization if its inflexibility makes it difficult to manage family and other personal matters; they may be more likely to stay if an organization provides sufficient flexibility to make it easier to balance work and nonwork considerations.

Other forms of **dysfunctional behavior** may be even more costly for an organization. Theft and sabotage, for example, result in direct financial costs for an organization. Sexual and racial harassment are also costly to an organization, both indirectly (by lowering morale, producing fear, and driving off valuable employees) and

Burnout *is a general feeling of exhaustion that develops when an individual simultaneously experiences too much pressure and too few sources of satisfaction.*

Turnover *refers to people leaving their jobs, whether voluntarily or involuntarily (i.e., through firings).*

Dysfunctional behavior *refers to any behavior at work that is counterproductive. These behaviors may include theft and sabotage, as well as sexual and racial harassment.*

directly (through financial liability if the organization responds inappropriately).

Workplace violence and aggression are also growing concerns in many organizations. People who are having problems coping with stress may vent their difficulties by yelling at or harassing their colleagues. They may also engage in other destructive behaviors such as damaging company property or physically assaulting bosses or co-workers. Violence by disgruntled workers or former workers results in dozens of deaths and injuries each year.[27]

It is also possible that stress has some positive effects on behavior at work. Several studies[28] have suggested that not all stress is the same and that some sources of stress can actually lead to positive outcomes at work.[29] Also, it has been argued that without some stress, employees can become bored.

Wellness Programs in Organizations

Two basic organizational strategies for helping employees manage stress are institutional programs and collateral stress programs. Institutional programs for managing stress are undertaken through established organizational mechanisms. For example, properly designed jobs and work schedules, as discussed earlier, can help ease stress. Shift work, in particular, can cause major problems for employees because they have to adjust their sleep and relaxation patterns constantly. Thus, the design of work and work schedules should be a focus of organizational efforts to reduce stress.

The organization's culture can also be used to help manage stress. Some organizational cultures, for example, have a strong norm against taking time off or going on vacation. In the long run, such norms can cause major stress. To avoid this, the organization should strive to foster a culture that reinforces a healthy mix of work and non-work activities. Supervision can play an important institutional role in managing stress. A supervisor is a potential major source of overload. Those who are made aware of their potential for assigning stressful amounts of work can do a better job by keeping workloads reasonable.

Institutional programs *for managing stress are undertaken through established organizational mechanisms.*

Collateral stress programs *are organizational programs created specifically to help employees deal with stress.*

In addition to their institutional efforts aimed at reducing stress, many organizations are turning to **collateral stress programs**, or programs created specifically to help employees deal with stress. Organizations have adopted stress-management programs, health-promotion programs, and other kinds of programs for this purpose. More and more companies are developing their own programs or adopting existing programs of this type. For example, Lockheed Martin offers screening programs for its employees to detect signs of hypertension, and Hospital Corporation of America offers its employees four cents a mile for cycling, sixteen cents a mile for walking or jogging, and sixty-four cents a mile for swimming.

Many firms today also have employee-fitness programs. These kinds of programs attack stress indirectly by encouraging employees to exercise, which in turn is presumed to reduce stress. On the negative side, this kind of effort costs considerably more than stress-management programs because the firm must invest in exercise facilities. Still, more and more companies are exploring this option. Both Tenneco and L. L. Bean, for example, have state-of-the-art fitness centers available for their employees' use.

Organizations try to help employees cope with stress through other kinds of programs. For example, existing career-development programs like that at General Electric are used for this purpose. Other companies use programs promoting everything from humor to massage as antidotes for stress. Of course, little or no research supports some of the claims made by advocates of these programs, so managers must take steps to ensure that any organizational effort to help employees cope with stress is at least reasonably effective.

Given the widespread adoption of wellness and stress-reduction programs, it is important to understand how effective these programs are. Much of the "evidence" supporting their effectiveness is anecdotal, with employees reporting how much better they feel when they are allowed to participate in wellness programs. Such data, although encouraging, cannot substitute for more rigorous evaluations of these programs. Unfortunately, a recent report from the Society for Human Resource Management (SHRM) suggests that many of the programs being established may not be as effective as they could be.[30]

The problem appears to be that many companies, especially smaller firms with more limited resources, do not have comprehensive wellness programs. Instead, they focus on one or two health risks (such as high blood pressure), do not continue the programs over the long run, and tend to focus on salaried employees who are already generally healthier than other employees. The report also suggests that top leadership in the organization must support these programs and develop a culture in which employees feel valued if these programs are to be effective. Finally, the report cites several examples of successful programs (for example, at 3M and at General Mills) where the corporation has partnered with a health-care organization (such as the Mayo Clinic) to ensure that employees have access to good assessment tools, have programs that can help them deal with specific health problems, and have adequate follow-up. Although it may not be easy for every organization to implement all of these features, it would seem that these are the keys to more effective wellness programs.

Other Interventions

In 2009, while unemployment inched closer to 10 percent and major banks disappeared from existence (both causing significant stress), Americans began concerning themselves with a new threat to their well-being. A new and virulent strain of influenza was spreading across the country. Originally and unfortunately called *swine flu*, the H1N1 influenza reached pandemic proportions in 2009, indicating that it had spread across significant areas of the country (technically, a pandemic indicates a disease prevalent throughout an entire country, continent, or the whole world). In fact, by January 2010, the World Health Organization reported confirmed cases of the H1N1 virus in more than 209 countries, including at least 14,142 deaths.[31]

OSHA began issuing statements and testifying before Congress on the ways to deal with the H1N1 virus at work.[32] Here the interventions went far beyond making medical facilities available. OSHA guidelines called for ordering respirators, fitting employees for these respirators, and training employees in the use of respirators and gloves, as well as programs urging employees to regularly wash their hands and providing sufficient stores of vaccine. Although this set of events is not typical, it does help illustrate that concerns over safety and health extend beyond the normal threats that occur in work settings.

One last type of threat to safety and health at work also warrants discussion. For the past 20 years or so, acquired immune deficiency syndrome (AIDS) has become a major problem in the world in general—and at work. AIDS is relevant to employers for several reasons. An employee with AIDS must cope with a life-threatening medical issue, but it is also important to that individual's co-workers. Unfortunately, there is no clear-cut solution for dealing with this issue. Individuals who publicly disclose their condition increase the potential for retaliation from co-workers: Many people fear the disease and may shun those who have it. And the organization faces various privacy-related issues.

An organization that wants to deal with this issue must start by developing and implementing a comprehensive AIDS policy. As a premise for developing a policy, however, all employers must keep in mind certain points. First, it is illegal to ask an applicant if she or he has AIDS. Some but not all states allow organizations to require applicants to take an AIDS test. Regardless of the test outcome, an employee can be denied employment only if it is determined that the applicant cannot perform the job. As long as the individual who is already hired is capable of performing the job, then he or she cannot be terminated or placed on leave. All medical information regarding the individual and her or his condition must be kept absolutely confidential.

In general, organizations can adopt three strategies in trying to deal with AIDS from a management perspective. One strategy is to categorize AIDS under a comprehensive life-threatening illness policy. In this instance, AIDS is treated like terminal cancer or any other life-threatening illness. The organization can then apply the same sorts of insurance coverage provisions, early-retirement and leave provisions, and so forth.

Another strategy is to form an AIDS-specific policy. This action is completely legal for an organization to contemplate as long as neither the intent nor the implementation of the policy results in discrimination against people on the basis of an AIDS condition. In general, most companies that form an AIDS-specific policy do so in an affirmative way. The essence of such a policy is to affirm the organization's stance that employees with AIDS are still entitled to work, receive benefits, and be treated comparably to all other employees.

The third approach that some companies take is to have no policy at all, an approach taken by far too many companies. The organization either does not want to confront the necessity for having an AIDS policy, is afraid to confront the need for such a policy, or does not know how to approach such a policy.

WAR ON GERMS

HAND TO HAND COMBAT

© robert mobley/Shutterstock

In any of these events, managerial ignorance can potentially result in serious problems for both the employer and the employees.

WORKPLACE SECURITY

The need to live in a safe and secure environment is a basic driver of human behavior (as will be discussed in Chapter 13). But security can be threatened (or guaranteed) in many different ways at work. For example, individuals working in organizations with low accident rates are more likely to feel secure about their safety on the job. Even individuals working on relatively dangerous jobs, however, can feel more secure if the organization (or someone else) is concerned about their safety. Thus, employees working at nuclear power facilities may feel quite secure because the organization, as well as the federal government, constantly monitors their environment for any threats.

On the other hand, announcements about impending or actual layoffs are likely to increase feelings of insecurity concerning employment.[33] Once layoffs have been announced, many employees will remain feeling insecure for some time as they wonder when the next series of cutbacks will be announced. Potential cuts can lead to increased stress, with all the outcomes that **are** associated with stress. During times of high unemployment (such as 2010), very few employees for any employer feel truly secure about their jobs.

In addition, some organizations are active in allaying employees' fears about an uncertain future in other ways. The whole idea behind private pension plans to provide employees with some assurance that they will have enough money to live on when they retire. Recall from Chapter 9 that, in the United States, just about every employee is covered by Social Security but that the retirement benefits from this program are not enough for many people to survive on and so serve more as a safety net to make sure they have *some* pension. Instead, employers set up and contribute to private pension plans to make sure that retired employers can live productive lives after they stop working.

Finally, insurance programs are also designed to provide security in various forms. Health insurance (discussed in Chapter 9) is designed to make sure that an employee can afford the medical services he or she may require. Disability insurance is designed to provide some income for employees who are temporarily unable to work. In fact, there are many programs within the human resource management (HRM) function that are designed to provide some type of security for employees at work.

A different type of security issue has become much more salient to employees in the United States since September 11, 2001. The threat of bombings or kidnappings is not new to the world, but Americans have traditionally felt these concerns only when they were traveling abroad, not when they were at their jobs. During the 1970s, there were many kidnappings of executives visiting Latin America and even in some European countries. Organizations began training drivers in evasion tactics, and firms such as GTE bought executives inexpensive plastic briefcases to take when they traveled, outside the United States, based on the belief that terrorists would target individuals wearing expensive clothes or carrying expensive briefcases. In countries such as Israel, an everyday commute on the bus is far from relaxing because terrorists have repeatedly bombed these buses. In London, for many years, riders on the underground (subway) were often searched in an attempt to stop IRA bombings. Such threats, however, were foreign to U.S. workers.

Of course, there had been an earlier terrorist attack in the United States. On the morning of April 19, 1995, a bomb in a van parked outside the facility exploded at the Alfred P. Murrah Federal Building in downtown Oklahoma City. The explosion killed 168 people in what was then termed the worst terrorist attack on U.S. soil. But that incident did not threaten the basic security of the U.S. population. The bombing could be blamed on one or two irrational men who were certainly not declaring war on the United States. Even the first attack on the World Trade Center in 1993, which killed 6 people, was not really taken seriously.

The 2001 attack on the World Trade Center, however, changed all that. One reaction to these attacks was to pass various pieces of legislation that fall under the heading of homeland security. How secure have these laws and actions made the United States? It is difficult to tell because no one knows how many attacks there would have been without these measures in place. Furthermore, debates over the trade-offs between privacy and security continue. The discussion in Chapter 6 of Google's decisions on how to deal with China's apparent violation of the privacy of Google users in the name if national security is a good example of the problem.

© Palto/Shutterstock

Also, over the years, additional attempts at terrorism have brought on more and more restrictive measures. When someone concealed flammable materials in his shoes, we demanded that all airline passengers remove their shoes for security clearance. When someone carried explosives suspended in a liquid onto a plane, we lost our ability to carry most liquids on board. Still, on Christmas Day 2009, a man whose name was on most terrorist watch lists boarded a plane in Amsterdam bound for Detroit and tried to ignite an explosive device as the plane was getting ready to land.

Thus, despite the many measures that have been taken, Americans may still feel insecure about their safety relative to potential terrorism. It is not surprising, then, that these continuing concerns over security from terrorism have also affected the HRM functions in many organizations. One simple way in which this has occurred is in restricting the labor pool available to U.S. employers. Traditionally, most U.S. firms have been willing to hire non–U.S. citizens for certain types of jobs and to help those new employees attain the proper status with immigration officials. In fact, non–U.S. residents have been an important source for skilled labor especially in some technical fields. That has now changed. Many U.S. companies are now less willing to hire foreigners, especially those from the Middle East. In fact, many American universities have also become less willing to recruit students from certain parts of the world, and the U.S. government has made it more difficult for any potential students and employees to obtain visas. The issue with foreign students has become especially serious because several of the attackers at the World Trade Center were in this country on student visas. To the extent that these concerns and practices eliminate potentially qualified employees and students from consideration, they hurt the ability of businesses to recruit the best-qualified people available.

Concerns over security have also made many Americans less willing to travel abroad—especially to areas that are potentially dangerous. Although these concerns have been present for quite some time, the new feelings of vulnerability have resulted in U.S. business leaders being even less willing to travel to certain parts of the world on business. This, in turn, has necessitated an increased reliance on teleconferencing and other substitutes for face-to-face meetings. But the reluctance to travel abroad also makes it more difficult to manage overseas operations and more difficult to give managers expatriate assignments.

In addition, most U.S. firms are now engaging in high-level emergency preparedness planning. The World Trade Center attacks wiped out the entire financial records of some firms. In addition, although not a completely human-made disaster, Hurricane Katrina also destroyed the employee records for many firms in the Gulf Coast area. Many companies have often followed the practice of backing up important records, but those backup files were not always put in safe locations, which made them vulnerable as well. Today, heightened security concerns have led organizations to develop multiple backup systems as well as information technology systems that are not tied to a single location.

Perhaps the greatest impact of September 11 has been on the general sense of well-being of many Americans. Americans are now subject to constant reminders of threat levels (color coded for ease of interpretation), and there are repeated warnings of potential threats and the message that Americans must be more vigilant. Because there are really no specific instructions given as to what should be the target of that vigilance, such warnings mainly serve to increase the stress levels of everyone involved. It is interesting to note that concerns over security from terrorist attacks are relevant for people all over the world. What makes the situation in the United States so interesting is that Americans traditionally felt themselves isolated and insulated from such attacks. The United States has now really joined the global community in the sense that Americans now realize they are vulnerable and so share the same security concerns as most of the rest of the world's population.

In August 2005, Hurricane Katrina struck the Gulf Coast of the United States, breached the levees in New Orleans, and resulted in a large portion of New Orleans being underwater for weeks. In the immediate months following Katrina, surveys of stress in the city of New Orleans indicated that self-reported stress, as well as the incidence of psychosomatic symptoms, had increased dramatically, and security had become a major concern for many New Orleanians. In late 2009, however, the Centers for Disease Control and Prevention published the results of a study conducted on "happiness." Basically, the study involved asking people questions about how satisfied they were with their lives. The results showed that residents of Louisiana were the happiest in the United States.[34] Whatever the explanation, these results seem to suggest that although there is a great deal of stress in the lives of people today, it is possible to be resilient and happy, even in the face of adversity. As more Americans lose their jobs and their homes, perhaps there is something that can be learned from the people of Louisiana that will help us through the recent hard times.

© Terry Chan/Shutterstock

Indeed, despite the increased sources of stress in the world, there are always people who can handle stress better than others. For these people, stress is a problem but not a debilitating one. It is not clear why some people are more resilient than others when they deal with stress and physical threats. In January 2010, a major earthquake struck Haiti. Perhaps a quarter of a million people died, but as soon as they could, survivors began rebuilding and getting back to their "normal" lives. Perhaps there is something about the psychological makeup of human beings, not just the Haitian people, that allows us to handle stress and security threats more easily.

CLOSING CASE

SAFETY COMES TO GEORGIA-PACIFIC

Georgia-Pacific Corporation is the world's largest distributor of building products (including wood panels, lumber, and gypsum products) and one of the five largest manufacturers of packaging materials, correspondence paper (such as office printing products and stationery), wood pulp, and tissue paper. The firm is based in Atlanta, Georgia, and has more than 100 distribution centers scattered across North America. It controls more than 6 million acres of timberland in the United States and Canada. Its annual revenues generally run about $20 billion.

Forest-products businesses have never been known for their safe, pleasant, and comfortable work environments. Paper mills, sawmills, and plywood factories, for example, are generally characterized by constant, deafening noise; huge, razor-toothed blades, shredders, and grinders; long chutes loaded with rumbling tons of lumber; and giant vats full of boiling water and caustic chemicals. The products they make are awkward in size, heavy, and often full of painful splinters, and the machinery used to make them requires frequent maintenance and close contact with sharp edges and dangerous moving parts.

Throughout much of its history, Georgia-Pacific had an unenviable accident record, even for what experts see as a highly dangerous and hazardous industry. For example, between 1986 and 1990, the firm averaged 9 serious injuries per year per 100 employees, and 26 workers lost their lives on the job. Two factors contributing to these statistics were unrelenting pressure to keep productivity high and a macho organization culture that promoted risk taking and bravado.

For example, top management continually reinforced the importance of keeping production lines moving, no matter what. As a result, workers would often attempt to perform routine maintenance or repair broken equipment parts without shutting down the line. And if they did not have a pair of safety gloves handy, they would carry around heavy—and sharp— saw blades with their bare hands rather than "waste" an extra few minutes to take appropriate safety precautions. Indeed, one observer noted that you were not considered a real Georgia-Pacific "mill guy" unless you were missing a finger or two!

This situation started to change a few years ago when a new top management team came in. The new managers were appalled by the firm's poor safety record and vowed to make it a source of pride rather than a source of embarrassment. The starting point was creating a task force charged with learning more about operating practices that contributed to accidents and then figuring out how to change those practices. The next step was altering the firm's basic culture so that it reinforced safe rather than risky practices and behaviors. Finally, Georgia-Pacific implemented an array of new rules and regulations that explicitly promoted safe work and punished those responsible for unnecessarily hazardous or dangerous actions.

The results were impressive. Accident rates have dropped consistently for each of the past 20 years, for instance, and workplace fatalities at Georgia-Pacific have become rare. At one of the firm's most hazardous plants, injuries run about only 0.7 per 100 workers annually. OSHA indicates that this ratio is about one-third the injury rate at the average bank. The company also has realized that being more cautious and following safer work procedures has boosted its productivity rather than lowering it. Stopping a production line to correct a problem usually takes only a few minutes, whereas stopping it because of an accident or injury might shut down production for hours or even days.

Injury rates now play a major role in the performance evaluation and compensation for all supervisors and managers at Georgia-Pacific. Safety equipment is an absolute requirement. One top manager, for example, proudly tells the story of how he was chewed out by an hourly worker while visiting a sawmill because he carelessly stepped too close to a dangerous piece of equipment. All employees in the mills have to wear earplugs, hardhats, goggles, gloves, and steel-toed shoes at all times. Failure to follow these regulations can result in immediate dismissal. Georgia-Pacific is now so proud of its achievements in safety that it is working to extend the same principles used to make these changes to other areas of its business, including quality and customer service.[35]

THINK IT OVER

1. Why do you think Georgia-Pacific has been so successful in reducing its accident and injury rates?
2. What other industries and businesses might benefit from the same kind of approach?
3. Research Georgia-Pacific's most recent safety statistics and see if the firm is still doing as well.

STUDY TOOLS

■ Rip out the chapter review card located at the end of the book.

■ Review the valuable study tools located online at www.cengagebrain.com

　■ Review the Key Terms flashcards.

　■ Download audio and visual summaries to review on the go.

　■ Complete practice quizzes to prepare for the test.

　■ Play "Beat the Clock" and "QuizBowl" to master chapter concepts.

　■ Complete "Crossword Puzzle" to review key terms.

　■ Watch the chapter video for a real-life example of key concepts.

CHAPTER 12

Motivation AT WORK

The U.S. government and citizens give generously, donating billions of dollars to troubled regions of the world desperate for aid and assistance. For instance, donations from the United States to Haiti exceeded $350 million in the first month after the 2010 earthquake that destroyed much of that country's infrastructure and killed more than 200,000 citizens. Yet one of the biggest contributions from Americans is not money: it's time. Each year, more than 65 million Americans volunteer, collectively investing 3.65 billion hours. In the case of Haiti, hundreds of volunteers and aid workers willingly gave time to help restore basic human services, distribute food and other provisions, and treat the injured. These volunteers derive satisfaction from their efforts. In addition, corporations that support volunteers are very effective in recruiting and retaining workers, making profitable business connections, and promoting excellent corporate public relations.

Corporate-sponsored volunteers work within the United States and abroad. For example, at drug manufacturer Pfizer, workers volunteered to provide services to low-income communities from the Philippines to the Bronx. Cisco Systems, a networking provider, sent an executive to Southeast Asia for a year. He set up wireless networks to coordinate aid workers throughout the region. Microsoft employee Frank Schott visited a refugee camp in Kosovo and came away convinced that his company needed to help. Schott says, "It's very hard to go on a mission to a refugee camp and go out of there without thinking, 'Gosh, we've got to do something.'" Microsoft built a software system to register refugees,

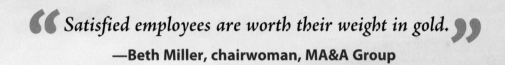

❝ *Satisfied employees are worth their weight in gold.* **❞**
—Beth Miller, chairwoman, MA&A Group

LEARNING OBJECTIVES
After studying this chapter, you should be able to:

LO1 *Describe the basic model of performance*

LO2 *Discuss motivation and human needs*

LO3 *Identify the basic process models of motivation and describe an integrative model of motivation*

LO4 *Describe other related theories and perspectives on motivation*

© Norm Betts/Bloomberg via Getty Images

making it easier for families to reunite, and then sent 400 employees to Kosovo to implement it.

Robert Nardelli, former Home Depot chief executive officer, participated personally in building schools and playgrounds and launched a program in which Home Depot employees volunteer 250,000 hours a year. He noted at the time that IBM, Target, UPS, and Avon, among other firms, have strong corporate volunteering programs. "Each corporation should play to its strength. The specific tactics should be tied to the specific skills of the corporation," says Nardelli. "For us . . . it's about building things."

Beth Miller runs a consulting firm that formerly provided information consulting services. When the company could not recruit enough skilled programmers in a tight job market, it began a corporate-sponsored volunteering program. The program was so successful that it became a full-time concern for Miller, whose company now helps corporations form philanthropic partnerships with not-for-profit organizations. Miller found that the volunteering program made recruiting easier, reduced turnover, and enabled employees to develop in skills and leadership, leading her to believe that volunteering increases worker satisfaction.

"Satisfied employees are worth their weight in gold," according to Miller. "[A volunteering] program would be especially appealing to Generation Y—those socially conscious workers now in their twenties who grew up doing community service."

Volunteering can motivate workers by increasing their sense of self-esteem, fulfilling their need for achievement, and satisfying other higher-level needs. Workers whose companies support volunteering feel pride in their employer, too. And corporations clearly benefit, as do communities in need. When asked about whether companies that support corporate volunteering are promoting a cause or their own self-interest, Nardelli says, "They're inseparably linked. Not only does a corporation have to provide financial value, it also has to build itself on values."[1]

THINK IT OVER

1. How motivated are you to donate your time and talent to help others? Will this likely increase, decrease, or remain the same over the next several years?
2. Do businesses face any risks or pitfalls if they encourage their employees to donate time to social programs and causes? If so, what are they?

Why do some people choose to volunteer their time for important causes and others do not? Even more germane, if two people are equally capable of performing the same task, why might one consistently outperform the other? We might say that one tries harder, or exerts more effort, but what we really mean is that one person is more motivated than the other to perform well. **Motivation** determines how a person will exert his or her effort. More specifically, it represents the forces operating on the person to exert effort, as well as the direction in which that effort will be exerted. One person might work hard at academics while another person might work hard at sports. Both are motivated, but the direction of their motivations are quite different and will produce much different outcomes.

Motivation at work is a critical determinant of what will occur on the job. An effective manager not only must motivate employees to exert *some* effort but also must make sure the effort is exerted in a way that produces organizationally valued outcomes. The human resource (HR) manager must design systems that make it more likely that employees will exert effort in these desirable ways. The key is to understand how we can motivate people to engage in behaviors we desire. As we shall discuss, several models or theories of motivation have been proposed as a way to accomplish this. We will review some of these theories and discuss some of their strengths and weaknesses. No one model of motivation, however, is guaranteed to work in all situations for all people. Instead, several models of motivation provide us with insights into how to motivate people; by taking them together, we can formulate a set of clear suggestions about how HR managers could develop systems that improve work motivation, lead to improved performance, and help develop competitive advantage for a firm.

> "True motivation comes from achievement, personal development, job satisfaction, and recognition."
>
> —FREDERICK HERZBERG (1923–2000), American psychologist

> **Motivation** *determines how a person will exert his or her effort. It represents the forces operating on the person to exert effort, as well as the direction in which that effort will be exerted.*

LEARNING OBJECTIVE 1

A BASIC MODEL OF PERFORMANCE

For most of us, the possibility of playing basketball like LeBron James, hitting a tennis ball like Venus Williams, or singing like the most recent winner on *American Idol* has little to do with motivation. We simply lack the necessary talent to perform at those levels (and few people do). Hence, it should be clear that any level of performance on any task is not solely a function of motivation—it is a joint function of ability, motivation, and context. The HR manager must play a critical role in determining two of these critical elements: the ability and the motivation sides of performance. (The third element, context, refers to such things as equipment and materials. Although Venus Williams can certainly hit a tennis ball and might be motivated to do so at any given time, if her racket is improperly strung or there is a defect in her shoes that causes pain when she runs, then she will still not be able to play well. Context, however, is usually not the purview of human resources.)

Specifically, the human resource management decisions we discussed in Part Two of this book dealt with the determinants of ability on the job. If the HR manager collected the right information about the job requirements, recruited qualified people, selected the best among these recruits, and then trained them on exactly what they were required to do, it is quite likely that all the employees in the firm would be capable of performing their jobs at a reasonably high level of proficiency. The difference between employees who performed at a mediocre level and those who performed at a higher level, would then be a function of motivation alone.

Of course, no human resource manager does a perfect job of recruiting, selecting, or training, and so not everyone may be capable of performing at the level the organization desires. For some of these employees, though, they may still be able to reach desired performance levels by exerting an extraordinary level of effort. In other words, high levels of motivation can compensate for lower levels of ability—up to a point. Similarly, if an employee was extremely talented (or able), then she or he might be able to perform at a desired level while exerting little effort. So either ability or motivation can compensate for the other up to a point. But to maximize performance, we need a workforce that is fully capable of doing its various jobs and a system that motivates its workers to exert their highest levels of effort. For the remainder of this chapter, we will assume that the HR manager has staffed the organization with capable people and that the only issue is how to motivate them to do their best work.

© Pling/Shutterstock

MOTIVATION AND NEEDS

Everyone has needs they attempt to satisfy. For most of us on a day-to-day basis, these needs are pretty simple and relatively easy to satisfy. We stop at a drinking fountain when we are thirsty or get a candy bar or piece of fruit when we are hungry. But what about more serious needs that might truly be capable of determining behavior? For example, what if you found yourself abandoned on a desert island (like Tom Hanks in the movie *Castaway*)? Probably the first thing you would do, once you figured out that you could not get off the island, would be to search for food and water. Hunger and thirst, at this level, are critical and basic needs that must be satisfied in order to survive. Once you located food and water, you would probably begin working on finding or making a shelter and only then might you begin searching to see if there was anyone else on the island (or you might begin talking to a volleyball as Tom Hanks did). Through all of this, you would probably not worry much about how you looked or how others might view your behavior if they could see you. All your behavior would be aimed at satisfying basic needs in life, and only after these were satisfied would you begin thinking about other, less critical needs. This view includes several **need-based theories** of motivation.

Some readers will recognize that the discussion above is similar to Abraham Maslow's **hierarchy of needs**. Maslow proposed this well-known theory of motivation almost 70 years ago,[2] and it has been quite popular ever since. The basic hierarchy model is presented in Exhibit 13.1 and illustrates the five categories of needs arranged from the most basic needs at the bottom to the more complex needs at the top. The lowest level of needs, labeled *physiological needs*, includes such things as the need for food or water. The next level of needs, *security needs*, includes anything involving a safe and secure environment. This is followed by *social needs*, which

Need-based theories *are theories of motivation that focus on what motivates a person, rather than on how that motivation occurs.*

Probably the best known of the need-based theories, the **hierarchy of needs** *model proposed by Abraham Maslow specifies five levels of needs that are capable of motivating behavior: physiological, security, social, esteem, and self-actualization.*

EXHIBIT 13.3 Reinforcement and Behavior

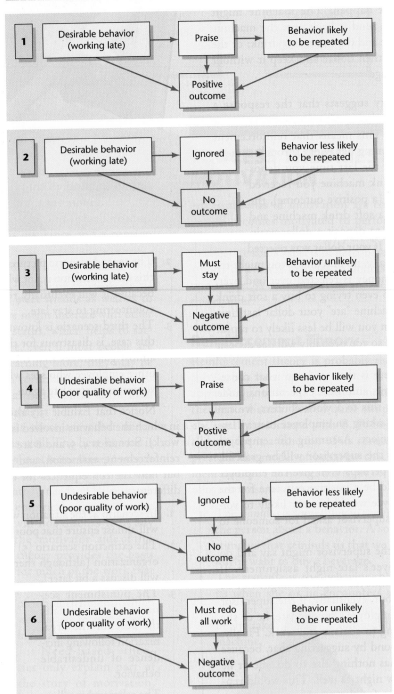

make sure that there are consequences for all behaviors and that desired behaviors are followed by positive consequences and undesired behaviors are followed by negative consequences (or perhaps no consequences). The stronger the links between the behavior and the consequences perceived

Behavior modification is the combination of positive reinforcement with either punishment or extinction that replaces an undesired behavior with a desired behavior.

by the employee, the more likely will the supervisor get the behavior that he or she desires. When a supervisor works to simultaneously eliminate undesired behavior (through punishment or extinction) and reward desired behavior, it is known as **behavior modification**. However, some critics question the ethics of behavior modification. You may wonder why anyone would possibly reward undesired behavior, and yet it happens all the time—although presumably unintentionally. In the preceding examples, a supervisor would probably not actually praise an employee for poor quality, but the supervisor could reward that behavior in other ways. Perhaps the supervisor would respond to poor-quality work by losing faith in the employee's ability to perform good-quality work and ask someone else (presumably more trustworthy) to redo the work. Alternatively, the supervisor may simply assign his job to someone else in the future, and if the job is one that is not really desirable, this would be a reward to the employee who performs poorly.

We also need to say a bit more about the relative merits of extinction versus punishment as a means of eliminating undesirable behavior. Punishment is quite effective because, when done properly, it establishes a strong link between a behavior and a negative outcome. We learn not to touch exposed wires because we get a shock when we do; we learn to avoid hot surfaces because we get burned when we touch them.

But we do not always need to punish someone in order to get a behavior to disappear. For example, some children act out in school because their classmates laugh and so reward them. If we can remove the laughter (the reward), the behavior will eventually be extinguished (i.e., it will disappear). So extinction is a more benign means to remove undesired behavior, although it takes a bit longer to work. It also will not work with certain types of behavior. Smoking is a good example of the problem. If we want a loved one to stop smoking (because we believe it to be unhealthy), then ignoring the behavior will not result in the person quitting smoking. Why not? Because smoking is itself rewarding to those who choose to smoke; the person is not smoking because she or he expects to get rewarded by others (surely not in today's environment) but because nicotine is addictive and smoking satisfies the craving for nicotine. If we ignore the smoking, the person is actually being rewarded because he or she is getting the craved drug. We can only stop someone from smoking by punishing them for it or by finding a substitute source of nicotine that is less harmful (e.g., a nicotine patch).

Note also that punishment (and positive reinforcement) work best when there is a strong link between behavior and consequences. *Every* time the undesired behavior is exhibited, it is punished. But that is quite difficult to manage and requires a great deal of monitoring. Furthermore, if someone realizes that undesired behavior is only punished when it is "caught," then the person is motivated to not get caught rather than to cease the behavior. This is how we explain the fact that motorists often speed until they see a police officer. As a result it is easier, and more pleasant, if we can change behavior by focusing on positive reinforcement rather than on punishment. Employees are drawn to supervisors who reward them but hide from supervisors who punish them—and it is difficult to supervise employees who are hiding!

Finally, although rewards and punishment are most effective when they are administered following every behavior (also referred to as *continuous reinforcement*), they can still work if they are administered some times but not others—that is, by **partial reinforcement** (it can be applied to punishment as well, but the reward case is simpler). Specifically, the rewards are administered on some schedule that dictates when the reward is and is not administered. These schedules can vary on two dimensions, so that there are four different schedules of reinforcement that can be used as illustrated in Table 13.1.

First, there are interval schedules versus ratio schedules. **Interval schedules** reinforce behavior as a function

TABLE 13.1 Effects of Different Partial Reinforcement Schedules

Schedule	Time to Learn	Resistance to Extinction	Productivity[a]
Continuous	Shortest	Least resistant	Average
Fixed interval	Longer	Resistant	Lowest
Variable interval	Longest	Most resistant	Next lowest
Fixed ratio	Longer	Resistant	Next highest
Variable ratio	Longest	Most resistant	Highest

[a]Productivity refers to the number of desired responses or behavior exhibited.

Partial reinforcement *means rewarding a behavior only part of the time rather than all the time (it can be applied to punishment as well, but the reward case is simpler).*

Interval schedules *are partial reinforcement schedules in which behavior is reinforced as a function of the passage of time—for example, rewarding someone every 10 minutes as long as they were exhibiting desired behavior.*

© Miguel Angel Salinas Salinas/Shutterstock

of the passage of time. A schedule in which someone is rewarded every 10 minutes as long as they exhibit a desired behavior would be an interval schedule. A **ratio schedule** reinforces behavior as a function of how many times it occurs. For example, rewarding someone every fifth time a desired behavior occurs would be an example of a ratio schedule. But in addition, the ratio or the interval can either be fixed or variable; the number times

Managers need to ensure that the expectations they have of their employees are clear and in line with the reward and incentive systems of the organization.

Ratio schedules *are partial reinforcement schedules in which behavior is reinforced as a function of how many times the behavior occurs— for example, rewarding someone every fifth time a desired behavior occurs.*

Fixed interval schedules *are interval schedules in which the amount of time that must pass before a reward is given is constant over time.*

Variable interval schedules *are interval schedules in which the amount of time that must pass before a reward is given can change from one reward period to another.*

Fixed ratio schedules *are ratio schedules in which the number of times a behavior must occur before it is rewarded remains constant over time.*

Variable ratio schedules *are ratio schedules in which the number of times a behavior must occur before it is rewarded changes over time.*

Expectancy theory (or VIE theory) *is a fairly complex process theory of motivation that casts the employee in the role of decision maker. Basically, an employee decides whether or not to exert effort, depending on the outcomes he or she anticipates receiving for those efforts as based on calculations concerning expectancies, instrumentalities, valences, and the links among these three components.*

the behavior must be displayed or the amount of time that must pass before a reward is given can be constant over time or it can change. Examples include the following.

1. With a **fixed interval schedule**, employees are paid once every 2 weeks as long as they continue to do their jobs.
2. With a **variable interval schedule**, employees are promoted as a function of time with the firm, but the amount of time between promotions can vary substantially.
3. With a **fixed ratio schedule**, an employee is paid on a piece rate such as one dollar for every ten units produced.
4. With a **variable ratio schedule**, a bonus system is based on performance, with the number of units that must be produced to obtain a bonus varying over time.

From the perspective of the HR manager, or even the general manager, there are a few things about these partial reinforcement schedules that are worth noting. First, if we are trying to shape an employee's behavior through reinforcement, it will take longer for the employee to "learn" the correct behavior under any partial reinforcement schedule as compared to a continuous reinforcement schedule, and it will take even longer for the employee to learn a behavior under any variable schedule. On the other hand, we might also be concerned about a learned behavior disappearing because we fail to reinforce it for a while. Here we are interested in how resistant any learned behavior might be to extinction. Any partial reinforcement schedule is more resistant to extinction than a continuous reinforcement schedule, and furthermore, any variable schedule (i.e., variable ratio or variable interval) is more resistant to extinction than any fixed schedule. Finally, ratio schedules, because they reward individual responses, result in higher levels of behavior (such as higher productivity) than do interval schedules, and variable ratio schedules produce more consistent levels of behavior (e.g., output) than do fixed ratio schedules because employees will slow down right after receiving a reinforcement and speed up again as they anticipate the next reinforcement.[8] All of this is summarized in Table 13.1.

Expectancy Theory

Expectancy theory, sometimes referred to as **VIE theory**,[9] is a fairly complex theory from a cognitive perspective, because it casts the employee in the role of decision maker. It developed from early work in psychology,[10] as well as basic economic theory, which assumes that people work to maximize their personal (positive) outcomes. Expectancy theory is concerned with three components and

EXHIBIT 13.4 The Expectancy Theory of Motivation

the links among them. The components are termed *effort*, *performance*, and *outcomes* and are used in the usual ways. The links among these three, however, are more central to the theory.

The first link is between effort and performance, and it is sometimes referred to as the *expectancy* term. Specifically, the **effort-to-performance expectancy** is a person's perception of the probability that an increase in effort will result in an increase in performance. This can range from 0 to 1.0. Expectancy is zero when the employee believes that increasing effort will definitely not increase performance, and this could be the result of a task that is too easy ("I can perform at the highest level with no effort") or a task that is too difficult ("No matter how hard I try, I cannot do any better"). Clearly, ability plays a role in determining this expectancy term because a lack of ability (from poor selection or poor training) will always result in a low level of expectancy.

The second link is between performance and outcomes and is sometimes referred to as the *instrumentality* term. Specifically, the **performance-to-outcomes expectancy (instrumentality)** is the person's perception of the probability that improved performance will lead to certain outcomes. Operationally, this is viewed as a correlation coefficient, indicating that as performance improves, the chances of gaining outcomes can either go up (a positive correlation), remain unchanged (a zero correlation), or go down (a negative correlation). As such, the values can range from +1.0, through 0, to −1.0. We will explain how this works as soon as we discuss the final link in the model.

The final piece of the model is not really a link between two other components but an extra component. **Valence** refers to how attractive or unattractive an outcome looks to a person. Thus, as noted above, many outcomes might be associated with work, and some of these might be quite attractive, whereas others may be rather unattractive. For example, good performance might be associated with receiving a raise, which would be attractive to most people. But poor performance might be associated with being fired, which would presumably be unattractive. Another way of stating this would be to suggest that improving performance *increases* the chances of receiving

a raise (thus a positive correlation or instrumentality) but *decreases* the chances of being fired (thus a negative correlation or instrumentality), and it has no effect on the chances of winning the lottery (thus, a zero correlation or instrumentality). Valences can thus be positive, negative, or neutral, and it is possible to specify that some outcomes are more positive (or negative) than others.

Note that all the terms in expectancy theory are based on a person's perceptions. In other words, we are less interested in whether, in fact, a person's efforts will result in increased performance and more interested in whether the person believes that to be the case. Of course, if individuals' perceptions are incorrect, then they will learn this over time and adjust their perceptions, but it is essential to remember that we are dealing with perceived links here, not the actual relationships between the components in the model.

Exhibit 13.4 illustrates the way the model works and indicates that the model is used to estimate the "force" operating on the employee to increase her or his effort. Note that in the example, the expectancy is set at 1.0, suggesting that there is a certainty that increased effort will lead to improved performance. There are also three outcomes in the example: two positive (pay raise and winning the lottery) and one negative (getting fired). Winning the lottery is more attractive than getting a pay raise. The key here, though, is the instrumentality term. Although winning the lottery is attractive, improved performance is not associated with increased chances of winning the lottery, and so this drops from consideration (zero times three is zero), suggesting that

Effort-to-performance expectancy *(or expectancy) is a person's perception of the probability that an increase in effort will result in an increase in performance. This can range from 0 to 1.0.*

Performance-to-outcomes expectancy *(or instrumentality) is a person's perception of the probability that improved performance will lead to certain outcomes. Operationally seen as a correlation coefficient indicating that as performance improves, the chances of gaining outcomes can either go up (a positive correlation), remain unchanged (a zero correlation), or go down (a negative correlation).*

Valence *refers to how attractive or unattractive an outcome is for a person.*

winning the lottery does not play a role in an employee's decision to increase effort at work. Notice, too, that getting fired is a negative outcome, but that increased performance decreases the chances of getting fired, producing a negative instrumentality. When we multiply two negatives we get a positive, suggesting here that increasing performance makes it less likely that an employee will be fired, which is really a benefit of improved performance.

In the example, the force is calculated to be positive, which suggests that the employee should increase effort on the job. We could imagine a situation in which the force would be negative (suggesting there would be no chance of improving effort because it would result in bad things only) or a situation in which the force would be less positive, and so it would be less likely, but still somewhat likely, that the employee would increase effort. If any term in this model goes to zero, the resulting force goes to zero. This also makes sense because there would be no reason for an employee to increase effort if (1) performance was unlikely to improve as a result of that effort, (2) there were no outcomes associated with any improved performance, or (3) increased performance would result in some good outcomes but be canceled out by negative outcomes.

Research on expectancy theory supports the general logic of the theory, but not many of the specific mechanisms, and it suggests that the theory is much more rational and calculating than are most employees.[11] Several variations on expectancy theory also have been proposed,[12] the most comprehensive of which was put forth by Naylor, Pritchard, and Ilgen,[13] and which we discuss later in the context of performance-enhancement interventions. In any case, expectancy theory has important lessons for the HR manager. First, this theory underscores the importance of selecting the right employees for the job and then training them so that they can perform their jobs effectively. The theory also suggests that it is important for the organization to have as many desirable outcomes associated with improved performance as possible. Finally, the theory suggests that organizations can best influence performance by establishing clear links between increased performance and rewards. This will be the basis for our discussion of incentive pay plans in Chapter 14.

Equity theory *is concerned with a person's perceived inputs to a (work) setting and the outcomes received from that setting. The theory suggests that everyone calculates the ratio of inputs to outcomes, similar to considering a return on any investment.*

Equity Theory

J. Stacey Adams developed another somewhat narrow but useful process theory called **equity theory**.[14] This theory is most concerned with a person's perceived inputs to a (work) setting and the outcomes he or she receives from that setting. The theory suggests that everyone calculates the ratio of inputs to outcomes, almost the way one would consider a return on any investment. But once individuals calculate this ratio for themselves, they then must determine if their ratio (or rate of return) is "fair." They try to determine this by comparing their ratio to the perceived ratio of some other comparison person. The target for this comparison could be anyone an employee chooses to use—a co-worker, a supervisor, a friend, or even an ideal that does not really exist. The employee then compares his or her input–outcome ratio to the ratio of this other person to determine whether the employee's ratio is fair. Employees will be most likely to be motivated when they believe they are being treated fairly, which in the case of this theory is defined as *equitably*.

Exhibit 13.5 illustrates the comparison process and also shows the three potential results of the comparison process. Numbers are provided simply as a matter of clarification because there are really no "scores" for inputs and outcomes. In the first case, the two ratios are the same. Neither the actual inputs nor the actual outcomes need to be the same for the person to perceive equity; instead, it is simply the ratio or rate of return on investment. So an employee may perceive that a co-worker is earning more money but still perceive equity if the employee believes that the co-worker is making greater inputs to the work setting. These additional inputs could take the form of longer hours worked, greater effort on the job, or additional education or experience. As long as the ratios are the same, however, the employee should perceive equity and exert effort on the job.

In the second case in Exhibit 13.5, the employee's ratio is less favorable than that of the comparison person. Again, this could be the case even if the employee perceived her- or himself as being paid more, if the employee thought the comparison person was making fewer inputs (such as working much less, or having much less education or experience). As long as the ratio, or rate of return, was less for the employee, then he or she would be said to perceive underpayment inequity. Not only is an employee not likely to exert effort at work when underpayment inequity is perceived (because the employee feels that any effort will not be "fairly" rewarded) but also the employee will work to restore

© Daniel Yordanov/Shutterstock

EXHIBIT 13.5 The Equity Comparison Process

COMPARISON OF SELF WITH OTHER

$$\frac{\text{Outcomes (self)}}{\text{Inputs (self)}} = \frac{\text{Outcomes (other)}}{\text{Inputs (other)}}$$

Inequity

Equity

Motivation to reduce inequity:
1. Change inputs
2. Change outcomes
3. Alter perceptions of self
4. Alter perceptions of other
5. Change comparisons
6. Leave situation

Motivation to maintain current situation

equity: The employee will try to either reduce his or her inputs (e.g., exert *less* effort), increase his or her outcomes (e.g., ask for a raise), or try to influence the comparison person to either reduce outcomes or increase inputs (unlikely to be successful). Thus, perceived underpayment inequity can present a real problem for a manager trying to enhance performance. Also, we must note again that this is all based on perceived inequity; in reality, the employee in question might be treated quite fairly, but the fact that the employee does not perceive that to be the case will present problems.

The final example illustrated in Exhibit 13.5 is a case in which the employee's input–outcome ratio is more favorable than that of the comparison person. The situation is known as *overpayment inequity*. There is some debate about whether anyone really perceives overpayment inequity because it would be easy to justify the overpayment as actually being deserved ("I guess I do work a lot harder"), and research support for overpayment inequity is mixed at best.[15] According to the theory, however, an employee facing overpayment inequity should also seek to restore equity, which would be easiest to do by increasing her or his inputs in the situation.

Equity theory can be quite useful to the human resource manager because it makes it clear that any rewards associated with effort or performance will be evaluated, in part, for their fairness as well as their innate attractiveness. In other words, giving someone a raise for a job well done may not be particularly motivating if another employee received a larger raise for a similar job. Whether or not overpayment inequity really exists, the HR manager needs to be aware of this potential problem with underpayment inequity. Also, if the employee perceiving underpayment inequity were a woman (or a member of any protected class), and the comparison person were a white male, then she would also be likely to sue under the Equal Pay Act (see Chapter 2)—even though she is being paid fairly relative to the male employee. You may recall that equity theory is also the basis for much of the discussion of justice and fairness in Chapter 2, suggesting that this is indeed a useful theory to keep in mind.

Before leaving our discussion of equity theory, however, consider one important point. Our discussion here, as in Chapter 2, revolved around the definition of "fair." In both cases, we are assuming that most people consider equity a good rule for determining fairness; that is, most people would assume that the person who contributes more should receive more. But this is really an assumption based on our Western cultural values. There is evidence to suggest that other cultures are more likely to judge fairness using a rule of equality,[16] which would suggest that everyone shares equally in any outcomes regardless of their contributions. Still others have suggested that, in some settings, individuals prefer a rule of need; that is, individuals should share in outcomes according to what they need.[17] We are not suggesting that any one rule is better than the others, but it is important for the HR manager to realize that not everyone judges what is fair in the same way.

An Integrative Model of Motivation

Although we will discuss a few more models of motivation, need-based models, reinforcement theory, expectancy theory, and equity theory collectively deal with most of the issues facing a human resource manager. In each case, we have presented the major aspects of the theory and have commented on the empirical support each has received, but we have said nothing about which theory is better. That is because each has something to offer, and each has weaknesses as well. But we can integrate the useful information provided by each theory to develop a single, integrative model that will make it easier to discuss what the HR manager should understand about motivation.

First, we should note that few of these theories actually conflict with each other. They tend to deal with different aspects of the motivational process, and it is rare that two theories would make different predictions about a situation that could not be easily resolved.[18]

Next we note that the five categories of needs from Maslow can be easily mapped onto the three categories used in ERG theory, so the only issue is how many categories of needs we wish to consider. Finally, although expectancy theory is much more complex than reinforcement theory, both theories would lead us to make the same basic recommendations: that we strengthen the links between performance and gaining valued outcomes. With these comments in mind, Exhibit 13.6 presents a possible integration of the various motivational theories we have discussed thus far.

The basic notion here is that an employee will exert effort on the job *only if* that effort will lead to improved performance, that performance will lead to rewards (which depends on whether or not the improved performance will help the organization meet its goals), and those rewards are considered to be fair *and* satisfy important needs of the employee.

From the perspective of the human resource manager, this model suggests that there is a lot to be done to enhance employee motivation. The process really begins with recruitment and selection activities. Organizations must attract and keep the "best" employees. The *best* in this context means employees who desire to work at the organization *and* who can perform the job effectively. If the selection process yields employees who cannot perform effectively, then they will not be able to enjoy the rewards associated with high performance and will actually lose motivation, or leave the organization, or both.

Once a person is working at the firm, it is critical that the human resource manager apply a compensation system that can recognize good performers. This means creating and using a system that is perceived as fair so that everyone will feel they are being rewarded for their efforts. In addition, this requires a formal appraisal system that fits the culture of the organization and is also perceived as being fair. These two pieces are also combined in setting the tone for incentive pay plans. We will discuss these further in the next chapter,

*First proposed by Ed Locke, **goal theory** is a fairly simple model of motivation based on the premise that people with goals work harder than people without goals. Beyond that, the theory suggests that not all goals are created equal, and that goals that are difficult and yet specific and concrete will motivate employees best.*

but for now we can simply state that incentive plans must be designed to reward the "right" behaviors—that is, those that can lead to organizational effectiveness and firm profitability. Finally, that incentive system must include rewards that are truly valued by the employee. If a person is capable of doing a job, believes that she or he is fairly compensated for doing that job, feels that he or she is being evaluated fairly, *and* if those evaluations are closely tied to valued outcomes (such as money or recognition or promotion), then there is every reason to believe that the employee will exert effort on behalf of the organization.

RELATED THEORIES AND PERSPECTIVES ON MOTIVATION

In addition to the various theories described in the previous section, four other important theories and related perspectives warrant discussion.

Goal Theory

One of these is **goal theory**, first proposed by Ed Locke.[19] Goal theory is fairly simple because it based on the premise that people with goals work harder than people without goals. Beyond that, the theory suggests that not all goals are created equal, and that goals that are difficult and yet specific and concrete will motivate employees the best. So, for example, a goal to "work harder" is not specific or concrete and would not be likely to motivate effort. Goals such as "reducing waste by 10 percent" or "increasing sales by 15 percent," on the other hand, are quite specific and should lead to increased effort because employees will know exactly how to exert effort and exactly what direction that effort should take, and they will also be able to monitor their own progress toward meeting those goals. Difficult goals are also preferable to easy goals because an employee does not need to exert much effort to meet an easy goal. Impossible goals, on the other hand, are not good because eventually the employee will realize that he or she cannot ever attain the goal and will stop trying.

The empirical evidence is rather supportive of goal theory across a wide variety of settings.[20] Goal theory has been used as the basis for some performance-appraisal systems (see Chapter 10), and is very useful as part of a performance management system (which we will discuss in Chapter 14). For goals to be effective, though, the employee must accept the goal as his or her own. This has led some theorists to suggest that goal setting should be done jointly

© justaa/Shutterstock

EXHIBIT 13.6 An Integrative Model of Motivation

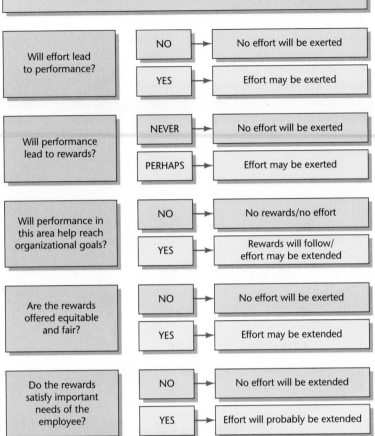

The goal of any attempt to motivate employees is assumed to be to convince them to exert effort on some aspect of the job.

| Will effort lead to performance? | NO → No effort will be exerted |
| | YES → Effort may be exerted |

| Will performance lead to rewards? | NEVER → No effort will be exerted |
| | PERHAPS → Effort may be exerted |

| Will performance in this area help reach organizational goals? | NO → No rewards/no effort |
| | YES → Rewards will follow/ effort may be extended |

| Are the rewards offered equitable and fair? | NO → No effort will be exerted |
| | YES → Effort may be extended |

| Do the rewards satisfy important needs of the employee? | NO → No effort will be extended |
| | YES → Effort will probably be extended |

by managers and their subordinates,[21] although others have argued that joint goal setting is helpful but not essential as long as the employee can be convinced to accept the goal and internalize it.[22] We will discuss other issues associated with the type of goals set in Chapter 14 when we discuss the use of theory in performance-management systems.

Agency Theory

Another interesting model of motivation is based almost entirely in economics and is known as **agency theory**.[23] This theory is also important for the incentive pay plans we will discuss in Chapter 14, but it is especially useful in the design of incentive plans for executives. Agency theory addresses potential conflicts of interests among different groups of stakeholders in an organization. The name of the theory, and some of its basic principles, is derived from the fact that the individuals who own most modern organizations do not actually run them on a day-to-day basis. Thus, we can think about the owners (including the stockholders) as being the principals for a firm and the management as being their agents. The theory is concerned with the conflicts that arise from this division, and the fact that what is in the best interests of the principals is not always in the best interests of the managers. Yet when an owner hires a manager, the

owner really does assume that the manager will act as his or her agent and work for the best interest of the owner.

In fact, principals and agents differ on several important issues. Agents are less likely than principals to take risks when they make decisions because their livelihood tends to depend on the business being successful; agents are also more likely than principals to focus on a short time horizon because it is usually easier to affect firm performance in the short run, and the agents may not be working for the firm in the long run. Yet it is not easy for the principals to monitor all the decisions made by the agents, and the agents often have more information about the day-to-day business than do the principals.

Empirical research on agency theory is less concerned with supporting the theory, but research has demonstrated that agents do often behave in ways that are inconsistent with the goals of the owners, which

Agency theory *addresses potential conflicts of interests among different groups of stakeholders in an organization. The name of the theory, and some of its basic principles, is derived from the fact that, in most modern organizations, the individuals who own a firm do not actually run it on a daily basis. Problems arise when the interests of the owners (the principals) are in conflict with the interests of the managers (agents).*

is consistent with the theory.[24] As noted, executive compensation and executive incentive plans are the areas in which agency theory is most often applied, but the HR manager can learn more from agency theory than just how to structure executive compensation plans. The basic logic underlying agency theory can be applied to a wide variety of settings where different groups of individuals may have conflicting interests. Managers versus union representatives, supervisors versus hourly employees, and research and development scientists versus accountants are all instances in which we might find groups within an organization that have conflicting goals. Agency theory can provide guidance on how to change some parameters of any such situation so that we can align the interest of the groups involved. This is often done with incentives or even with appraisal systems. However the problem is approached, agency theory provides HR managers with a useful framework for trying to deal with conflicts of interest so that everyone works toward the common organizational goals.

Intrinsic Motivation

Most models and theories of motivation are concerned primarily with extrinsic motivation, which requires an external agent to administer a reward that is separate from the actual task or job being performed. This is in contrast to **intrinsic motivation**. As others have stated it, "Intrinsic motivation is the motivation to do work because it is interesting, engaging, or possibly challenging."[25] The factors usually associated with high levels of intrinsic motivation at work include a sense of self-determination at work (i.e., "I am doing the work because I want to rather than because someone else is rewarding me"), feelings that one's skills are being utilized, and generally positive feelings about the work.[26]

Thus, performing work that is interesting and challenging can be its own reward, and this is the basis for much of the work on job enrichment that is discussed in the next chapter. We can easily think of examples of individuals expending a great deal of time and effort at tasks for which they receive no reward other than the satisfaction of doing something interesting. Typically, we think of these as hobbies or leisure activities, but there are also jobs that people would probably be willing to perform for free if they simply had the opportunity to perform the job.

But what if we added extrinsic rewards, such as contingent pay, to jobs that were already challenging and interesting? At first glance, this would seem to represent a great opportunity to improve productivity. It would seem reasonable that, if the extrinsic rewards are administered properly (consistent with the theories discussed earlier), this would improve extrinsic motivation, which would then work with the intrinsic motivation that came from the challenging job, and the organization would have a highly motivated employee. Evidence suggests this would not be the case, however. In fact, the results from a series of studies[27] suggest that the introduction of extrinsic rewards actually destroys intrinsic motivation. Although there is still room to question this outcome,[28] it is quite clear that intrinsic and extrinsic motivation do not simply interact or add together to form a higher level of motivation.

It is also clear that some types of motivation do not require any intervention on the part of a manager. There are certain types of tasks and jobs for which performing the job is its own reward. This type of motivation does not fit neatly into any of the theories we have discussed, but it will play an important part in the next chapter as we discuss other ways to enhance performance.

Creativity

At first glance, it might seem that the topic of creativity is misplaced here. After all, only a few highly gifted people are truly creative, and there are very few jobs where one can really be creative on the job. Yet creativity has been suggested as one of the outcomes of intrinsic motivation. Furthermore, and more critically, scholars have begun using a broader definition of creativity at work that encompasses many more employees than we would initially expect.

The most commonly used definition of **creative behavior** at work involves doing things that are innovative and provide some value for the organization.[29] In general, experts characterize creativity as the process of generating new and useful ideas concerning new products, services, manufacturing methods, and administrative processes.[30] Given this broad definition, almost any employee at

Intrinsic motivation *is the motivation to do work because it is interesting, engaging, or possibly challenging rather than because someone is rewarding us to do the work.*

Creative behavior *involves doing things at work that are innovative and provide some value for the organization.*

almost any job could be creative at work.

In line with this broader view, a great deal of attention has been focused on how to motivate employees to be more creative at work. As noted above, one factor that has been linked to creativity at work is intrinsic motivation; that is, if we can design jobs to be more challenging and interesting, it is more likely that employees will engage in creative behaviors at work. Interestingly, Amabile has argued that extrinsic motivating factors that serve primarily as information for the employee can also lead to creative behavior at work, as long as they do not threaten the employee's feelings of competency.[31]

Thus, the HR manager can do things to enhance the creativity of any employee. As noted earlier, we will discuss the topic of job enrichment in some detail in the next chapter, but some other factors have been found to be related to creativity at work that can also be affected by human resource management policies. For example, informative and constructive feedback has been found to be related to high levels of creativity at work,[32] while another study found that structuring jobs in ways that are consistent with the creativity requirements of those jobs (e.g., allowing more autonomy for jobs requiring more creativity) led to increased satisfaction on the job.[33] Also, in an interesting development, Zhou and George reported that job dissatisfaction was related to creativity

© NREY/Shutterstock

at work under the right circumstances.[34] Specifically, they found that dissatisfied employees, who were also committed to remain with the organization, were more likely to engage in creative behavior at work when they received useful feedback from co-workers and when perceived organizational support for creativity was high.

Clearly, a human resource manager can do things to encourage creative behavior from all employees. But before leaving the topic, we need to make one additional point. The definition of creative behavior introduced earlier suggests that ideas or behaviors should be both innovative and useful to the organization. It would seem reasonable, however, that employees might generate a number of ideas that are innovative but not really useful to the organization. It is critical that the organization react to such ideas in a positive way. An employee puts him- or herself at a certain amount of risk when he or she proposes an innovative approach to a problem. If the management reacts badly and belittles the employee for an idea that is not very useful, the employee is not likely to come forward with new ideas in the future, and overall creativity is likely to be suppressed. Therefore, it is critical that the organization maintain a climate of openness and make an employee feel comfortable to suggest even a "useless" idea. Only when employees feel safe in this way will they be willing to propose the kinds of creative solutions that the organization needs.[35]

CLOSING CASE

MOTIVATIONAL SILOS

Experienced managers sometimes refer to the *silo effect* in which various departments within an organization or across organizations act as if each were a stand-alone unit, ignoring important shared resources and interactions. One silo effect area of constant concern for many corporations is the tense, even hostile relationship that often exists between workers in sales and marketing departments.

To an outsider, sales and marketing may appear to be compatible and harmonious complements—both, after all, are bridges between the organization and its customers. Yet in many, if not most, organizations, salespeople claim that marketers are too abstract, too academic, too focused on creativity, and not focused enough on outcomes. But most of all, they claim that marketing staff do not understand sales

© Sue Smith/Shutterstock

because they never have to interact directly with a customer. On the other side, marketers claim that salespeople are too egotistical and too focused on making the sale at any cost, and they do not understand the organization's strategy.

According to Christopher Kenton, president of the marketing firm Cymbic, neither marketers nor salespeople understand the relationship that should exist between them. Kenton explains the ideal relationship as similar to that between professional sports coaches and their players. "Every year [coaches] get fired while flashy players get fame and million-dollar contracts. Marketers are coaches and salespeople are players. Whatever role you choose, you need to understand that it's meaningless without your partner. If you fail to recognize you're joined at the hip, your team will lose."

How then can organizations inspire marketers and salespeople so that employees in each department are motivated, satisfied, and productive? CollabNet, a unique software company, provides a great answer. Marketing and sales departments cooperate. This requires marketing to start viewing the sales department, not the buyer, as their customer. "[Sales] is our customer. They're the ones who will be in front of the client," says Bernie Mills, CollabNet's marketing vice president. "And treating sales as a customer means understanding their requirements." Rather than resenting the other department, each unit is encouraged to see the different yet equitable treatment they both receive.

Managers in both units realize that the probability of success and rewards is greater when both take on tasks that will benefit the other department. Marketing staff, for example, go on sales calls with salespeople. They meet customers, watch negotiations, and begin to understand how to build relationships with customers. When CollabNet's marketing department created a sales kit for a new product launch, salespeople were involved in every aspect of the process. Mills says, "We showed up at the launch with a sales kit already [approved] by sales." These techniques ensure that the resources provided by marketing are helpful and needed by the salespeople.

Sales is also doing more to support marketing. As part of a sales call, salespeople now ask questions about competing products and customer expenditures to gain useful market research for the marketing department. With constant customer contact, salespeople hear bits of market intelligence that might be useful to marketing staff, and now the relationship between the two units ensures that the intelligence is passed on.

The sales and marketing personnel seem very satisfied with the new way of conducting business. "I love our marketing department," says CollabNet salesperson Bart Tilly. "They're great." Tilly lists more participation and collaboration in sales calls, meetings, and strategy formulation as some of the ways that marketing provides support to sales. Marketing vice president Mills describes himself as "thrilled" by the developments and gives the credit for the initial collaborative efforts to his counterpart in sales.

According to Mills, both departments have a lot to gain through collaboration and shared goal setting. "Sales is selling one-to-one. Marketing is selling one-to-many. For sales, that means selling deal-to-deal, quarter-to-quarter, while marketing needs to focus on the longer-term picture," Mills asserts. "We need to understand and respect that difference." Mills still sees marketing as responsible for the big picture, but adds, "Marketing needs to lead with a listening ear. Marketing doesn't need to have all the good ideas, they just need to recognize them." Sounds like CollabNet has already recognized the best idea of all—collaboration.[36]

THINK IT OVER

1. Describe the jobs of salesperson and marketer at a typical firm in terms of the employee needs that are being met. Then describe the jobs of salesperson and marketer at CollabNet in terms of met needs. What are the differences?

2. Use equity theory to compare inputs and outcomes for a salesperson and a marketer at CollabNet. In your opinion, does equity exist? Why or why not?

3. Based on what you read in the case, does worker satisfaction seem to lead to higher performance at CollabNet? Or does higher performance lead to satisfaction? Explain.

STUDY TOOLS

- Rip out the chapter review card located at the end of the book.

- Review the valuable study tools located online at www.cengagebrain.com

  - Review the Key Terms flashcards.

  - Download audio and visual summaries to review on the go.

  - Complete practice quizzes to prepare for the test.

  - Play "Beat the Clock" and "QuizBowl" to master chapter concepts.

  - Complete "Crossword Puzzle" to review key terms.

  - Watch the chapter video for a real-life example of key concepts.

SPEAK UP!

HR was built on a simple principle: to create a new teaching and learning solution that reflects the way today's faculty and students teach and learn. Through conversations, focus groups, surveys, and interviews, we collected data that drove the creation of the version of **HR** that you are using today.

But it doesn't stop there – in order to make **HR** an even better learning experience, we'd like you to SPEAK UP and tell us how **HR** works for you. What do you like about it? What would you change? Do you have additional ideas that would help us build a better product for next year's Human Resource Management students?

Speak Up! **Go to CourseMate for HR. Access at login.cengagebrain.com.**

Managing
& Enhancing
Performance:
THE BIG PICTURE

" As the parent of a toddler, it's exciting to have the coolest job at preschool. "

—Robert Sunday, associate marketing manager, General Mills

PULL

Cheerios.
Toasted Whole Grain Oat Cereal

Cheerios Can Re

os.

Cheerios Can

NET WT 1.3 OZ (3? g)

Three grams of soluble fiber daily from whole grain oat foods, like Cheerios® in a diet low in saturated fat and cholesterol, may reduce the risk of heart disease. Cheerios® has 1 gram per container.

daily from wh
diet low in

Nutrition Fac
Serving Size 1 container
Amount Per Servin
Calories
Calori

BUILDING ENTHUSIASM

Myriad articles, books, and television shows suggest that many Americans are unhappy at work. And even if they are not truly unhappy, neither are they excited and engaged with their jobs. Increased competition, longer hours, an uncertain economy, technology that allows workers to work continuously—all of these have been blamed for the trend. Employees of videogame maker Electronic Arts, for example, claim they routinely work between 65 and 85 hours a week without overtime pay, which has led to some unhappy workers and at least one lawsuit. The consequences for businesses in terms of increased turnover, lost efficiency, low morale, and so on is high, and the consequences for workers are even worse. Although statistics are inconclusive, observers report that white-collar injuries, illnesses, and even suicides related to work have risen recently. One study found that 23 percent of male stockbrokers were clinically depressed, three times the national average for U.S. men.

There are also many people who are motivated by and fully engaged with their work. Another study describes 40 percent of American workers as excited about their jobs, eager to begin work on Monday mornings, and loving what they do. In many cases, happy workers have jobs that are easy to love. Sandor Zombori was working as an engineer but always longed to cook. He walked away from his job, invested his savings in a restaurant, and 20 years later is the owner and chef at an award-winning restaurant. "All the time, I am soaking it up, like a sponge, trying to learn as much as I can," Zombori explains. Artists, game inventors, knitters, designers, and architects have a passion to express themselves and to learn, which often leads to career happiness.

Net WT 1.8 OZ (52g)

Honey Nut Cheerios
Sweetened Whole Grain Oat Cereal with Real Honey & Natural Almond Flavor

General Mills
with Whole Grain Guaranteed

© Rob Kim/Landov

LEARNING OBJECTIVES

After studying this chapter, you should be able to:

LO1 Describe the relationships among performance measured at different levels within an organization and discuss how training, development, and job redesign can help improve performance

LO2 Discuss the role of alternate work arrangements in motivating and enhancing performance

LO3 Describe the role of incentive pay and identify different programs for individual-based and team-based incentive plans

LO4 Discuss the best ways to deliver performance feedback and the issues involved with feedback and describe the basic operation of the ProMES system

LO5 Discuss how organizations evaluate performance-enhancement programs

For others, more traditional careers also hold substantial rewards. Robert Sunday, associate marketing manager of Cheerios brand at General Mills, says about his job, "I truly love it! As the parent of a toddler, it's exciting to have the coolest job at preschool." For college professors, nurses, bank loan officers, research scientists, and executive assistants, job happiness comes from satisfying intellectual curiosity, helping others, giving back to their communities, and feeling needed. Sometimes the job can even be designed to increase satisfaction. Richard Karlgaard is the publisher of *Forbes* magazine. He enjoys acting as an editor at large and writing about technology while leaving most of the financial reporting to others.

Still, there are individuals who do not find their jobs rewarding and who cannot change the jobs themselves. In these cases, looking elsewhere may be the best option. Mary Lou Quinlan was the chief executive officer (CEO) of a New York City advertising agency and at the pinnacle of her profession, but she chose to quit and start a small consulting business. The pay is less, but she is happier. "Finally, I'm doing something I can picture doing for a long, long time," Quinlan says. Harvard University lecturer Laura Nash agrees that individuals can be happier in their personal and professional lives if they separate notions of success and money. If you cannot be a star ballerina, Nash recommends, "you can start a ballet company or design a new ballet shoe, or even supply shoes to the dancers."[1]

THINK IT OVER
1. What seems to distinguish rewarding and exciting jobs from those that are less rewarding and satisfying?
2. If you were to find yourself "stuck" in an unrewarding and unsatisfying job, what would you do?

The last chapter discussed theories of motivation and, in general terms, things human resource (HR) managers could do to enhance motivation in organizations. Chapter 12 discussed safety and health, noting how stress could interfere with performance on the job. In Chapter 11, we pointed out how some organizations resisted unionization because they believed that it hurt productivity. Chapter 10 outlined procedures for evaluating performance but stated that the ultimate purpose of any performance-appraisal system was to improve performance. In Chapter 9, we discussed how effective compensation systems could attract good employees and how competitive benefit programs could help organizations attract and retain the best employees. Much of our discussion of diversity in Chapter 8 focused on why effectively managing diverse employees could enhance productivity and firm performance, and the major focus of recruitment and selection, as discussed in Chapter 7, was the attraction and retention of employees who could perform well. In fact, an important legal issue in the selection process was to be able to demonstrate how scores on selection techniques were associated with performance on the job.

By now it should be clear that every decision and activity engaged in by the human resource manager is supposed to help improve performance in some way. Of course, employee satisfaction is also important—but important partly because it is related to attrition, and organizations need to retain valued employees. The responsible and professional HR manager does all of this in an ethical way and does not violate the law or anyone's rights, but the ultimate goal of the human resource function is to enhance performance. More specifically, we can assert that the ultimate goal of the HR activities and programs we have described is to enhance *organizational* performance.

This last distinction is important because we are suggesting an ultimate goal of organizational performance rather than simply individual or even group performance. Yet many of the techniques available for performance enhancement that we discuss in this chapter focus on improving the performance of the individual or group; the assumption here is that if the performance of all the individuals working in a firm improves, then so will firm performance Unfortunately, this is not always the case. Therefore, we will begin by discussing some issues associated with the relationship between individual-level and firm-level performance, and this will serve as a background for our discussion of specific performance-enhancement techniques, including different kinds of work arrangements, incentive and performance-based pay, and performance management and rewards. We conclude with a discussion of how managers can best evaluate their performance-enhancement programs.

LEARNING OBJECTIVE 1

ENHANCING PERFORMANCE AT DIFFERENT LEVELS

Performance in any organization exists at multiple levels. The most basic level of performance is that of the individual employee, and this is the level that most people find easiest to conceptualize. In fact, in Chapter 10, we discussed primarily measures and models of individual-level performance; that is, most appraisal techniques are concerned with determining how many products a person assembles or how many units *individual contributors* sell. We can usually aggregate this up to the group or department level by simply combining sales or productivity data for individuals, but when we move up to the organizational level, things become more complicated. Of course, we can still talk about how many products are produced by the firm, or what a company's total sales are for a quarter, but this is often not very meaningful data.

For example, sales representatives might sell a lot of a product, but they may need to lower their prices so much that the firm is not profitable. Also, not all product lines are equally profitable, so that one person can sell less and actually generate more profit for a firm than another person who sells more. But it makes little sense to talk about profitability at the level of the individual because profits depend largely on costs that can often be computed only at the firm level. As a result, a performance management or enhancement intervention designed to improve sales might not actually improve firm performance. There is no simple answer to the question of how to translate individual-level performance to organizational-level performance, but the key seems to be adopting a systems approach: The firm can focus on individual-level performance but in a systematic way that recognizes the interrelationships among individuals and the need to coordinate across individuals.[2]

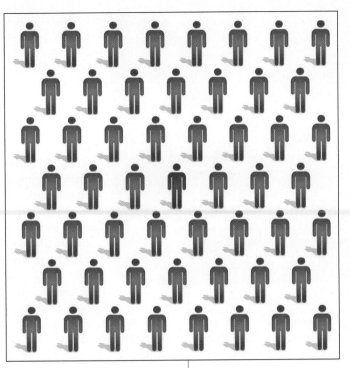

It is critical that these performance-enhancement interventions ultimately improve **firm-level performance**. This is the level that determines the long-term survival of the firm, generates profits for potential profit sharing, and determines the company's stock price. As you read through the rest of this chapter, keep this in mind: Regardless of the level of performance targeted by a specific intervention, these interventions are effective only as long as they also improve organizational performance. With this as background, we can now review several techniques that have been shown to improve performance at some level within the organization.

Training and Development

Training and development activities within an organization are a very basic type of performance-enhancement intervention. Training and development represent a fundamental investment in the employees who work for an organization, with the overall goal of improving their ability to make contributions to the firm's effectiveness.

1. Employee **training** can be defined as a planned attempt by an organization to facilitate employee learning of job-related knowledge, skills, and behaviors.
2. **Development** usually refers to teaching managers and professionals the skills needed for both current and future jobs. Thus, each has a slightly different orientation.[3]

Training usually involves teaching operational or technical employees how to do their jobs more effectively, or more efficiently, or both. Teaching telephone operators to help customers more efficiently, showing machinists the proper way to handle certain kinds of tools, and demonstrating to short-order cooks how to prepare food orders systematically are all part of training, and all these activities are aimed at helping the organization function more effectively.

For example, suppose that a small manufacturing company has a workforce of machinists and other operating employees who are currently capable of working at 85 percent of plant capacity. The space, equipment, and technology in the plant may actually be capable of producing, say, 100,000 units of output per day, but the existing workforce can turn out only 85,000 units per day. Because of anticipated growth in product demand, managers want to be prepared to meet this demand when it occurs by boosting the plant's level of potential performance. They want their workforce to be able to produce more without having to hire new employees or invest in new equipment or technology. As a first step, the organization might want to work toward achieving 95 percent of capacity—or 95,000 units per day—using existing employees and facilities. Thus, these existing employees will need to be trained in more efficient work methods with the ultimate goal of making them more productive. Such an approach should work as long as the workers have the ability they need to perform at this higher level of productivity. UPS invests heavily in training its drivers and other parcel handlers in the proper techniques for lifting and moving packages. Their goals include minimizing injuries and improving efficiency.[4]

Whereas training focuses on specific job-related skills, development is aimed at helping managers improve more general skills such as time management, motivating employees, and solving problems.

Firm-level performance *is an indication of a firm's chances of long-term survival. Performance at this level generates profits for potential profit sharing and determines the company's stock price.*

Training *can be defined as a planned attempt by an organization to facilitate employee learning of job-related knowledge, skills, and behaviors.*

Development *usually refers to teaching managers and professionals the skills needed for both current and future jobs.*

IBM's Basic Blue training program helps all of its new first-line managers better understand how to perform their jobs.

IBM helps develop its new first-line managers with an extensive 9-month training program called Basic Blue that covers such topics as people management, HR policies, and leadership development. Program participants complete 6 months of online e-learning before traveling to IBM's learning center next door to its headquarters in Armonk, New York, to continue the program. Almost 20,000 IBM managers worldwide have attended the program since its inception more than 10 years ago. Similarly, Halliburton provides 6 weeks of development annually for its top executives under a program it calls the Presidential Leadership Seminar.[5]

Rather than focusing on specific job-related skills, development is more generally aimed at helping managers better understand and solve problems, make decisions, and capitalize on opportunities.[6] For example, managers need to understand how to manage their time effectively. Some management-development programs thus have components that deal with time management. Other management-development programs may help managers better understand how to motivate employees (for example, to get the employees discussed above to exert extra effort). Thus, managers do not necessarily return from development programs with a specific new operational method for doing their job more effectively. Instead, they may return with new skills that may be of relevance to them in a general sense at some point in the future. They may have a better understanding of how to work more effectively, how

to motivate their employees better, and how to make better decisions, and they may possess a more complete understanding of how the overall organization functions and their role within it. Development is often considered a human resource function in most organizations, but because of its strategic nature and importance, one or more senior executives are usually given specific responsibility to ensure that management development is approached systematically and comprehensively.

There are several basic steps in the design of any training or development intervention, and these are illustrated in Exhibit 14.1. The process should begin with a needs analysis: HR managers responsible for training and development must determine the organization's true needs vis-à-vis training. This analysis generally focuses on two issues: the organization's job-related needs and the capabilities of the current workforce. The organization's needs are determined by the nature of the work that the organization needs to have performed. In other words, what knowledge, skills, and abilities does the organization's workforce need to have if it is to perform the organization's work most effectively?

As part of this analysis, the manager must carefully assess the company's strategy, the resources it has available for training, and its general philosophy regarding employee training and development. By "philosophy," we mean the extent to which the organization views training as a true investment in human resources or simply as a necessity to alter or change a specific outcome or criterion measure. Workforce analysis involves carefully assessing the current workforce's capabilities, strengths, and weaknesses. In other words, it is important to understand the extent to which the organization's workforce is skilled or unskilled, motivated or unmotivated, committed to the organization or not, and so forth. Furthermore, it is important for the organization to decide that it wishes to train employees for the present or to be more proactive and train the employees for what is expected to come in the future.

Once these needs are assessed, whether through direct observation or some type of survey or interview process, the organization must then determine its goals for training and development. Unless a manager knows what to expect from the training, it is difficult (if not impossible) to

EXHIBIT 14.1 Assessing Training and Development Needs

Needs analysis		Setting training and development goals		Determining approach
• Organization's job-related needs • Capabilities of existing workforce	→		→	• In-house programs • Outsourced programs

determine how effective any training or development activity has been. For example, consider the case of an insurance claims office. Assume that claims adjusters are processing insurance claims at an average rate of 6 business days per claim. Responses and feedback from customers suggest that some customers are becoming unhappy because they would like to have their claims processed more quickly. Using this information and other relevant data, the HR manager—working in conjunction with operating managers—might decide that an appropriate and reasonable goal would be to cut the average processing time from 6 days down to 4 days. Thus, a "4-day processing average" becomes the goal of this particular training endeavor.

The next step in the process is to decide between in-house versus outsourced training. Many larger organizations, such as Texas Instruments and Exxon Mobil, have large training staffs, and so the organization itself assumes the responsibility for training and developing its employees, thus ensuring that the content of its training and development efforts are precisely and specifically tailored to fit the organization's needs. Alternatively, outsourcing training activities enables a firm to draw on expertise not available inside to maximize training effectiveness. But outsourced programs tend to be more general and even generic, and thus they have less applicability and direct relevance to the organization's needs.

Finally, once the organization has decided on whether to conduct training and development in-house or through outsourcing, it must decide on the specific techniques to be used. For some situations, organizations might prefer to rely on various work-based programs.

1. *Work-based programs* tie the training and development activities directly to performance of the tasks. The most common method of work-based training is *on-the-job training*. This approach to training can help an organization achieve a return on the labor cost of the employee almost immediately, assuming that the individual is capable of performing at a minimal level of competency. Also, direct training costs may be lower because the organization may not need to hire dedicated trainers or send employees to training programs.[7] Two other types of work-based training are apprenticeship programs and vestibule training. *Apprenticeships* involve a combination of on-the-job training and classroom instruction, and *vestibule training* involves a work-simulation situation in which the job is performed under a condition that closely simulates the real work environment.

2. *Instructional-based programs* are also quite common, especially the *lecture or discussion approach*. In these situations, a trainer presents the material to those attending the program in a lecture format; although lectures continue to play a role in most training programs, there is evidence that their use has been declining, and they are being replaced with training outside the classroom, primarily using electronic technologies.[8]

3. Another instructional-based program for training and development is *Web-based instruction*. In this situation, a trainee sits at a personal computer and operates software that has been developed specifically to impart certain material to the individual. The major advantage of this method is that it allows self-paced learning, and immediate feedback can be given to the trainee.[9]

4. Another method that involves basic instruction as a training device is *programmed instruction*. In recent years, these activities have become computerized but remain self-paced and include self-assessment. Also, in recent years, all of these approaches have been affected by changes in training technology. Video teleconferencing allows a trainer in a centralized location to deliver material live via satellite hookup to remote sites in different locations; the training can thus be delivered effectively but without the travel costs of transporting people to a common training site. Interactive videos involve presenting information on a monitor from a central serving mechanism, on a DVD, or via the Web. The trainee interacts with the system with a mouse, keyboard, or touch screen. Feedback can be provided when inadequate responses or improper answers are given, and the trainee can skip material that has already been learned.

Job Redesign

A much different approach to enhancing organizational performance is through the redesign of jobs. Specifically, this technique involves changing—redesigning—jobs so that the work itself will motivate employees to exert greater effort. This motivation is stimulated by making the job more interesting or more challenging. We will discuss five motivational approaches to the redesign of work: job rotation, job enlargement, job enrichment, the job characteristics approach, and work teams. As we shall see, the use of work teams is a bit different in its intent. Although a driving consideration is still to motivate employees to work harder, this approach is also concerned with designing more effective ways of doing a job, and it has a great deal of applicability in today's organizations.

Job rotation involves systematically moving employees from one job to another. A worker in a warehouse might unload trucks on Monday, carry incoming inventory to storage on Tuesday, verify invoices on Wednesday, pull outgoing inventory from storage on Thursday, and load trucks on Friday. Thus, the jobs do not change; instead, workers move from job to job. For this very reason, however, job rotation has not been very successful in enhancing employee motivation or satisfaction. Jobs that are amenable to rotation tend to be relatively standard and routine. Workers who are rotated to a "new" job may be more satisfied at first, but the novelty soon wanes. Although many companies (among them DuPont, Nucor Steel, Ford, Prudential Insurance, Maytag, and Western Electric) have tried job rotation, it is most often used today as a training device to improve worker skills and flexibility.

Based on the assumption that doing the same basic task over and over is the primary cause of worker dissatisfaction, **job enlargement** was developed to increase the total number of tasks that workers perform. As a result, all workers perform a wide variety of tasks, presumably reducing the level of job dissatisfaction. Many organizations have used job enlargement, including IBM, Detroit Edison, AT&T, the U.S. Civil Service, and Maytag. At Maytag, for example, the assembly line for producing washing-machine water pumps was systematically changed so that work originally performed by six workers who passed the work sequentially from one person to another was now performed by four workers, each of whom assembled a complete pump. Although job enlargement does have some positive consequences, they are often offset by several disadvantages: (1) training costs usually rise, (2) unions argue that pay should increase because the worker is doing more tasks, and (3) the work often remains boring and routine even after job enlargement.

A more comprehensive approach, **job enrichment**, assumes that increasing the range and variety of tasks alone is not sufficient to improve employee motivation.[10] Thus, job enrichment attempts to increase both the number of tasks a worker does and the control the worker has over the job. To accomplish this objective, managers remove some controls from the job, delegate more authority to employees, and structure the work in complete, natural units. These changes increase the subordinates' sense of responsibility. Another part of job enrichment is to assign new and challenging tasks continually, thereby increasing the employees' opportunity for growth and advancement.

AT&T was one of the first companies to try job enrichment. In one experiment, eight typists in a service unit prepared customer-service orders. Faced with low output and high turnover, management determined that the typists felt little responsibility to clients and received little feedback. The unit was changed to create a typing team. Typists were matched with designated service representatives, the task was changed from ten specific steps to three more general steps, and job titles were upgraded. As a result, the number of orders delivered on time increased from 27 percent to 90 percent, the need for messenger service was eliminated, accuracy improved, and turnover became practically nil.[11] Other organizations that have tried job enrichment include Texas Instruments, IBM, and General Foods. Problems have been found with this approach, however. For example, analysis of work systems before enrichment is needed but seldom performed, and managers rarely deal with employee preferences when enriching jobs.

The **job characteristics approach** is an alternative to job specialization in that it does take into account the work system and employee preferences.[12] It is also one of the most widely used and widely studied approaches to job design. As illustrated in Exhibit 14.2, the job characteristics approach suggests that jobs should be examined and improved along the following five core dimensions.

1. *Skill variety* is the number of tasks a person does in a job.
2. *Task identity* is the extent to which the worker does a complete or identifiable portion of the total job.
3. *Task significance* is the perceived importance of the task.
4. *Autonomy* is the degree of control the worker has over how the work is performed.
5. *Feedback* is the extent to which the worker knows how well the job is being performed.

The higher a job rates on these five dimensions, the more employees will experience various psychological states. Experiencing these states, in turn, presumably leads to high motivation, high-quality performance, high satisfaction, and low absenteeism and turnover. Finally, a variable called *growth-need strength* is presumed to affect how the model works for different people. People with a strong

> ## "It is better to have one person working with you than to have three persons working."
> —Dwight D. Eisenhower

Job rotation *involves systematically moving employees from one job to another.*

Job enlargement *was developed to increase the total number of tasks workers perform based on the assumption that doing the same basic task over and over is the primary cause of worker dissatisfaction.*

Job enrichment *attempts to increase both the number of tasks a worker does and the control the worker has over the job.*

The job characteristics approach *is an alternative to job specialization that takes into account the work system and employee preferences; it suggests that jobs should be diagnosed and improved along five core dimensions.*

EXHIBIT 14.2 The Job Characteristics Model of Job Design

Source: J. R. Hackman and G. R. Oldham, "Motivation Through the Design of Work: Test of a Theory," from *Organizational Behavior and Human Performance*, Vol. 16, 1976, pp. 250–279. Reprinted with permission from Elsevier.

desire to grow, develop, and expand their capabilities (indicative of high growth-need strength) are expected to respond strongly to the presence or absence of the basic job characteristics; individuals with low growth-need strength are expected not to respond as strongly or consistently.

Several studies have been conducted to test the usefulness of the job characteristics approach. The southwestern division of Prudential Insurance, for example, used this approach in its claims division. Results included moderate declines in turnover and a small but measurable improvement in work quality. Other research findings have not supported this approach as strongly. Thus, although the job characteristics approach is one of the most promising alternatives to job specialization, it is probably not the final answer.

Work teams represent a much different way of approaching job design. Under this arrangement, a group is given responsibility for designing the work system to be used in performing an interrelated set of jobs. These groups are sometimes referred to as *self-directed work teams* or *autonomous work teams*, and they are permanent parts of the organizational architecture. In these teams, the group itself decides how jobs will be allocated. For example, the work team assigns specific tasks to members, monitors and controls its own performance, and exercises autonomy over work scheduling.

The original impetus for the reliance on work teams comes from a famous series of studies conducted in England by the Tavistock Institute and dealing with the coal-mining industry.[13] The researchers determined that it was important for miners to have social interaction, and so they suggested that the miners work in teams. The researchers also identified and suggested several changes in the actual coal-mining jobs themselves. As it turned out, the job changes were also conducive to team settings in that they increased the need for coordination. After the jobs were changed and the workers formed into teams, performance in the mines improved considerably, and the miners reported more satisfaction and increased motivation. Hence, in some settings, teams make a great deal of sense. But work teams are not without problems, and they certainly are not the answer in all cases.

For example, if work is designed to be done by teams, then all rewards must be based on team performance; that is, we cannot reward individuals in true teamwork settings. This may decrease the motivation of some employees, especially those who might exert exceptional effort only to see less effort exerted by fellow team members. Finally, in situations where we cannot identify the work product of any single individual, there is greater likelihood of "shirking," or simply not exerting effort with the assumption that someone else will get the work done. These problems may not argue against teamwork, but they do underscore the importance of making sure that the situation really calls for teamwork.

LEARNING OBJECTIVE 2

ALTERNATIVE WORK ARRANGEMENTS

Another approach to performance enhancement allows employees more flexibility in their working arrangements. The assumption is that

A work team is an arrangement in which a group is given responsibility for designing the work system to be used in performing an interrelated set of jobs.

EXHIBIT 14.3 Flexible Work Schedules

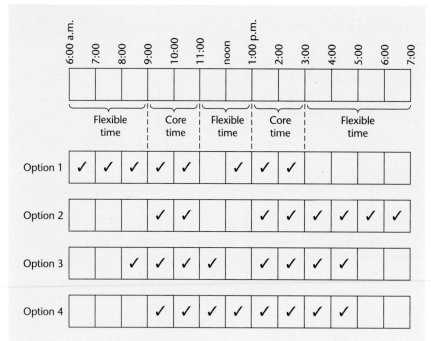

if employees can work in ways that better suit their lifestyles, then they will be less distracted and more likely to be productive. But these interventions are also designed to affect organizational-level performance by simply reducing costs and increasing efficiency. Traditionally, employees came to a specific workplace and were expected to be physically present at work 5 days a week, 8 hours a day, unless the employee was required to spend time on the road. In modern organizations, however, it is becoming increasingly common for people to work on a schedule other than 5 days 40 hours per week or to work at a place other than the office or place of business.

Alternate Work Schedules

The two most common alternatives to the traditional workweek are programs known as *flexible work hours* and *compressed workweeks*. Employees working under **flexible work hour plans** usually must still work a full 40 hours per week and, typically, 5 days a week. The employees have control, however, over the starting and ending times for work on each day. In almost every case, there is a core time each day when every employee must be at work. During these hours, the organization can schedule meetings or other activities that require coordination among employees. The remaining hours (flextime) can be made up in any way that the employee prefers. For example, if a company's core time is 10 A.M. until 2 P.M., then everyone is expected to be at work during those

Flexible work hour plans *are plans in which employees usually must still work 40 hours per week and typically 5 days a week but in which they have control over the starting and ending times for work on each day.*

hours. But starting times might be anywhere between 7 A.M. and 10 A.M., and quitting times might be anywhere between 2 P.M. and 7 P.M. Under such a plan, the core time represents 20 hours a week, and the employee is free to work the remaining 20 hours in any fashion within the stated constraints.

Exhibit 14.3 illustrates how an organization might function with one type of flexible work schedule. This organization has defined 6 A.M.–9 A.M., 11 A.M.–1 P.M., and 3 P.M.–7 P.M. as flexible time, and 9 A.M.–11 A.M. and 1 P.M.–3 P.M. as core time. A worker choosing option 1 (i.e., the early riser) comes to work at 6 A.M., takes an hour for lunch, and is finished for the day at 3 P.M. Option 2, perhaps more attractive for those not considered to be morning people, involves starting work at 9 A.M., taking 2 hours for lunch, and working until 7 P.M. Option 3 is closest to a standard workday, starting at 8 A.M., taking an hour at lunch, and leaving at 5 P.M. Finally, option 4 involves starting at 9 A.M., taking no lunch, and finishing at 5 P.M. In every case, however, each employee works during the core time periods.

These plans are believed to reduce stress because the employee does not have to travel during peak commuting times and can have more control over the commute.[14] They are also believed to increase job satisfaction because the employee is given more control over the work environment and a stronger feeling that he or she is trusted by the organization.[15] They are not as feasible in organizations that place a strong emphasis on teams; otherwise, no serious problems associated with their use are reported. HR in the Twenty-First Century provides additional perspectives on flexible work schedules.

HR in the 21st Century

Creating Humane Work Schedules

Sixty-hour workweeks used to be the norm in the United States; now 80 hours is not uncommon. But working longer hours does not always increase productivity. One recent study showed that U.S. workers were less productive per hour worked than those from countries with shorter workweeks, including France and Germany. Experts hypothesize that overworked employees become tired, stressed, and less motivated. Lowell Bryan, a McKinsey & Company partner, claims, "We've created jobs that are literally impossible. The human cost is profound, and the opportunity cost is also great in terms of organizational effectiveness." Problems made worse by overwork are costly

> ## "We've created jobs that are literally impossible. The human cost is profound, and the opportunity cost is also great in terms of organizational effectiveness."
>
> —Lowell Bryan, McKinsey & Company partner[16]

and can include injuries, mistakes, rework, workplace violence, stress-related diseases, absenteeism, and high turnover. The 2009 recession only made things worse as businesses cut jobs but then expected those who were still employed to pick up the slack.

Some companies are now actively seeking ways to offer a more reasonable work–life balance. Fox News, for example, split the job of one senior executive between two individuals who both work full-time and share responsibilities equally. The editorship of the *Los Angeles Times* was once held by one person, but now three workers do the job. Part-time work is another increasingly popular option. JetBlue allows key managers to work part-time schedules in exchange for reduced compensation. In many cases, it is not hard to implement these new working arrangements. Law associates can handle fewer cases, and auditors can work with fewer clients by putting in less time and receiving lower compensation.

It is accepted wisdom that willing workers are plentiful, no matter how demanding the schedule, but most companies note that there is often a shortage of qualified managers. Increasingly, people want time off and are willing to give up money and career advancement to get it. Both men and women now talk freely in many companies about wanting to "have it all," referring to a career and a rewarding life outside of work. As these conversations become more widespread and more intense, perhaps U.S. companies will respond. Alternate, flexible work arrangements are more acceptable to workers, and they can also create a more motivated, productive, and loyal workforce.

THINK IT OVER

1. Do you think working hours will get longer or shorter in the future? Why?
2. Would you be willing to trade off scheduling flexibility and balance for slightly reduced compensation? What factors would be important to you in such an arrangement?

Sources: "Doing More With Less," *Business Week* (Dec. 17, 2009): 35–38; "Nice Work If You Can Get It," *Business Week* (Jan. 9, 2006): 56–57; Jody Miller and Matt Miller, "Get a Life!" *Fortune* (Nov. 28, 2005): 109–124; Danielle Sacks, "Scenes from the Culture Clash," *Fast Company* (Jan. 2009): 28–31.

Compressed workweeks are arrangements in which the employee works the required number of hours (typically 40) but does so in fewer than 5 days. For example, a 4-day, 10-hour-a-day work schedule is fairly common, and schedules that involve 4 days with 12 hours a day, followed by 4 days off, are also fairly common. The employee gains the flexibility of 3 days off a week, presumably making it less likely that he or she will lose work time to deal with personal business. These schedules are also well suited for employees who work at sites that are difficult to get to such as offshore drilling rigs. These schedules are not for everyone, however, and longer workdays are related to increased accidents in some settings.[17] Nonetheless, compressed workweeks are extremely popular with some employees.

Both of these alternative schedule plans are growing in popularity, and few problems seem to be associated with them (except as noted). These alternative schedules present some unique challenges to the HR manager, however. As noted above, flexible schedules are often not feasible in organizations that rely heavily on teams. In fact, whenever one employee's work depends on input from another employee, these schedules may be a problem. Even when they are not a problem, flexible schedules reduce the amount of time that employees interact

> **Compressed workweeks** *are arrangements in which the employee works the required number of hours (typically 40) but does so in fewer than 5 days. For example, a 4-day, 10-hour-a-day work schedule is fairly common.*

with their co-workers, which makes it more difficult to develop a strong culture or even a strong esprit de corps.

Although employees are at work the same number of hours as before and have the opportunity to interact with co-workers, compressed workweeks present similar challenges because the stress of longer hours may make social interaction less likely, and the greater number of days off may also affect some social aspects of the job. The HR manager must try to find ways to replace socializing activities with other experiences so that employees, especially new employees, can learn more about their co-workers and become more fully socialized into the organization.

Alternate Work Sites

In addition to employees working on alternate schedules, employees performing their work at a location other than the place of business, most likely at home, is a growing trend. Home work and telecommuting are two popular variations on this theme. Table 14.1 shows the number and distribution of people currently working under an alternative work arrangement. *Home work programs* include

TABLE 14.1 Employed Workers with Alternative Work Arrangements by Occupation and Industry (Percentage Distribution for 2009)

Characteristic	Workers with Alternative Arrangements (%)			
	Independent Contractors	On-Call Workers	Temporary Agency Workers	Workers Provided by Contract Firms
Total, 16+ years of age (1,000s)	10,342	2,454	1,217	813
Management, professional, and related occupations	39.9	35.6	20.3	39.6
Service occupations	13.7	22.1	15.6	26.2
Sales and office occupations	20.5	12.6	26.9	7.2
Natural resources, construction, and maintenance occupations	19.7	16.9	7.1	21.8
Production, transportation, and material-moving occupations	6.1	12.7	30.1	5.2
Agriculture and related industries	2.6	0.6	—	0.2
Mining	0.1	1.0	0.5	0.2
Construction	22.0	12.2	3.4	16.5
Manufacturing	3.2	4.8	28.4	14.1
Transportation and utilities	3.9	8.4	3.1	4.0
Wholesale trade	2.1	2.1	5.4	3.4
Retail trade	8.9	5.6	2.1	3.1
Information	2.0	1.8	1.8	4.0
Financial activities	10.4	3.4	4.1	6.8
Professional and business services	2.0	1.8	1.8	4.0
Education and health services	8.7	33.8	11.1	15.7
Leisure and hospitality	4.5	10.4	1.8	4.5
Other services	9.9	3.8	2.9	0.3
Public administration	0.3	4.4	2.8	16.6

Source: U.S. Department of Labor, Bureau of Labor Statistics.

arrangements that are often referred to as *cottage industries*. In the earliest days of the Industrial Revolution, before many factories were built, employees would take parts back home to their cottages and manufacture them, then return them to a central point where they could be assembled. Similar types of cottage industries still exist for the manufacturing of small and not very complex items.

It is more common, however, to operate in what can be called an *electronic cottage*. Employees take office work home with them and complete it on home computers. They can then return to the office to collect more work. They are connected to that office via a modem, fax machine, and e-mail. These arrangements can even result in a virtual office and are becoming especially popular with people who want (or need) to work but do not wish to work full-time or who have other responsibilities such as child care or elder care.[18]

Telecommuting is simply the logical extension of the electronic cottage. Under this arrangement, employees may do almost all of their work at home and may even receive assignments electronically. This arrangement provides employees with the ultimate in flexibility because they can choose the hours they work and even the location. A growing body of evidence suggests that this arrangement increases job satisfaction and even productivity, and it also allows organizations to use the services of individuals who may not be able to work at a given site.[19] For example, an employee can live many hours from his or her office if he or she performs most of the work via telecommuting. Finally, larger organizations can save considerable amounts of money if they do not need large (or any) real office space. Cisco Systems, a pioneer in telecommuting, estimates that, by allowing employees to work at home, it has boosted productivity by 25 percent, lowered its own overhead by $1 million, and retained key knowledge workers who might have left for other jobs without the flexibility provided by the firm's telecommuting options.[20]

Alternative work sites present a more serious challenge to the HR manager. In the past, the AFL-CIO has complained that home work arrangements allow management to impose unfair working conditions on employees, and it also makes it more difficult for unions to organize workers. So unions continue to oppose these arrangements. As with alternative work schedules, communication among employees is difficult under these arrangements, and it is extremely difficult for a new employee to become socialized. In fact, little socialization may be possible if many

of the employees are working under nontraditional work arrangements and many are working at home.

In addition, some individuals may simply lack the self-discipline to get the work done in a completely unconstrained environment, although the available evidence suggests that this outcome is not much of a problem. What does seem to be a problem is that these alternative work sites are likely to increase employees' sense of alienation at work.[21] They have no social connections and no support from co-workers, and so loyalty or commitment to the organization is unlikely to develop. Companies are trying, however, to overcome these problems. For example, Merrill Lynch allows potential telecommuters a 2-week dry run to see how they like the arrangement. Aetna assigns each of its telecommuters an office buddy to help those working at home stay in touch with the office. And America West even arranges monthly potluck dinners to maintain social interaction among employees who work at home.[22]

INCENTIVES AND PERFORMANCE-BASED REWARDS

Yet another approach to enhancing performance is by explicitly tying rewards, especially pay, to performance—that is, organizations try to reinforce certain types of behaviors and outcomes (recall our discussion in Chapter 13) by tying compensation directly to measures of performance or productivity. Many plans allow this to be done.

The most basic form of incentive compensation is **merit pay**, which generally refers to pay awarded to employees on the basis of the relative value of their contributions to the organization. Employees who make greater contributions are given higher pay than those who make lesser contributions. **Merit-pay plans**, then, are formal compensation plans that base at least some meaningful portion of compensation on merit.

The most general form of the merit-pay plan is to provide annual salary increases to individuals in the organization based on their relative merit. Merit, in turn, is usually determined or defined based on

Merit pay *is pay awarded to employees on the basis of the relative value of their contributions to the organization.*

Merit-pay plans *are compensation plans that formally base at least some meaningful portion of compensation on merit.*

© juliengrondin/Shutterstock

the individual's performance and overall contributions to the organization. Recall that in Chapter 10 we discussed various methods for evaluating employee performance. We noted, as well, that performance appraisal had the most meaning to employees if it was subsequently connected with a reward such as a salary increase. However, it is important for the organization to have valid and reliable measures for merit. Merit generally refers to performance, but for the plan to have motivation and performance effects, people throughout the organization must clearly understand what the firm means by the term *merit*. Otherwise, the plan not only will not be effective in improving performance but also may cause problems with employees' perceptions of justice.

Another basic approach is based on systems of *skill-* and *knowledge-based pay*. Recall from Chapter 9 that, under these systems, instead of rewarding employees for increased performance they are rewarded for acquiring more skills or knowledge. But these skills or this knowledge is related to what the organization believes it will need in the future. Thus, in effect, the organization is rewarding the employee for increasing his or her capacity to perform well in the future, while more traditional merit-pay systems reward employees for achieving some level of performance, but this performance is defined by what the organization needs (or wants) right now. Although problems are associated with these systems and their administration, they offer an alternative to more traditional merit-pay systems and provide a more strategic long-term focus for the organization.[23] In addition, they allow the organization to move employees toward focusing on more than just basic productivity.[24]

Incentive compensation systems are among the oldest forms of performance-based rewards. For example, as noted earlier, some companies used individual piece-rate incentive plans more than 100 years ago.[25] Under a piece-rate incentive plan, the organization pays an employee a certain amount of money for every unit she or he produces. For example, an employee might be paid $1 for every dozen units of product that she or he completed successfully. But such simplistic systems fail to account for factors such as minimum-wage levels, and they rely heavily on the assumptions that performance is under an individual's complete control and that the individual employee does a single task continuously throughout his or her work time. Thus,

most organizations that try to use incentive compensation systems today use more sophisticated methods, and we will now discuss some of these.

Individual Incentive Pay Plans

Generally speaking, **individual incentive plans** reward individual performance on a real-time basis. Rather than increasing a person's **base salary** at the end of the year, an individual instead receives some level of salary increase or financial reward in conjunction with demonstrated outstanding performance in close proximity to when that performance occurred. Individual incentive systems are most likely to be used in cases where performance can be objectively assessed in terms of number of units of output or similar measures rather than on a subjective assessment of performance by a superior.

Some variations on a piece-rate system are still fairly popular. Although many of these systems still resemble the early plans in most ways, a well-known piece-rate system at Lincoln Electric illustrates how an organization can adapt the traditional model to achieve better results. For years Lincoln's employees were paid individual incentive payments based on their performance. However, the amount of money shared (or the incentive pool) was based on the company's profitability. A well-organized system allowed employees to make suggestions for increasing productivity. Motivation was provided in the form of a reward equaling one-third of the profits (another third went to the stockholders, and the last third was retained for improvements and seed money). Thus, the pool for incentive payments was determined by profitability, and an employee's share of this pool was a function of his or her base pay and rated performance based on the piece-rate system.

Lincoln Electric was most famous, however, because of the stories (which were apparently typical) of production workers receiving a year-end bonus payment that equaled their yearly base pay.[26] In recent years, Lincoln has partially abandoned its famous system for business reasons, but it still serves as a benchmark for other companies seeking innovative piece-rate pay systems.

Perhaps the most common form of individual incentive is the **sales commission** that is paid to salespeople. For example, sales representatives for consumer products firms and retail sales agents may be compensated under this type of commission system. In general, the person might receive a percentage of the total volume of attained sales as her or his commission for a period of time. Some sales jobs are based entirely on commission, while others use a combination of base minimum salary with additional commission as an incentive. Notice that these plans put a considerable amount of the salesperson's earnings at risk. Although organizations often have drawing accounts to allow the salesperson to live during lean periods (the person then "owes" this money to the organization), if he or she does not perform well, then he or she will not be paid much. The portion of salary based on commission is simply not guaranteed and is paid only if the employee's sales reach some target level.

Finally, organizations occasionally may use other forms of incentives to motivate employees. For example, a nonmonetary incentive such as additional time off or a special perk might be a useful incentive. A company might establish a sales contest in which the sales group that attains the highest level of sales increase over a specified period of time receives an extra week of paid vacation, perhaps even at an arranged place such as a tropical resort or a ski lodge.[27]

As with merit systems, incentive compensation systems have some shortcomings and weaknesses. One major shortcoming is that they are practical only when performance can be measured easily and objectively. Most managerial work does not fit this pattern and, in fact, is often characterized by ambiguous performance indicators that are difficult to assess. Thus, it may be much more difficult to provide valid and appropriate incentives for these individuals. Individual incentives are also likely to focus attention on only a narrow range of behaviors, perhaps at the expense of other behaviors. Consider, for example, a sales representative in a department store. This sales representative may be able to maximize his or her pay by greeting all customers aggressively, trying continually to sell them items that they may or may not need, and overlooking deficiencies or shortcomings in the product offered for sale. In such cases, sales representatives sometimes make grandiose claims that have no basis in reality and may stretch the truth to the point of creating totally inaccurate expectations. Thus, the individual sales representative may maximize her or his income in the short term—but at the cost of poor morale among other less aggressive salespeople and increasingly dissatisfied customers.

Team and Group Incentive Plans

In addition to incentive plans designed to improve individual performance, there are plans that focus on group or team performance. These programs are particularly important for managers to understand today because they focus attention on higher levels of performance, and because of the widespread trends toward team- and group-based methods of work and organization.[28]

A fairly common type of group incentive system is an approach called **gainsharing**. Gainsharing programs are designed to share the cost savings from productivity improvements with employees. The underlying assumption of gainsharing is that employees and the employer have the same goals and thus should share in incremental economic gains,[29] consistent with our discussion of agency theory in Chapter 13.

In general, organizations that use gainsharing start by measuring team- or group-level productivity. It is important that this measure is valid and reliable and that it truly reflects current levels of performance by the team or group. The team or work group itself is charged with attempting to lower costs and otherwise improve productivity through any measures that its members develop and that its manager approves. Resulting cost savings or productivity gains that the team or group is able to achieve are then quantified and translated into dollar values. A predetermined formula is used to allocate these dollar savings between the employer and the employees themselves. A typical formula for distributing gainsharing savings is to provide 25 percent of the dollar savings to the employees and 75 percent to the company.

One specific type of gainsharing plan is an approach called the **Scanlon plan**. This approach was developed by Joseph Scanlon in 1927. The Scanlon plan has the same basic strategy as gainsharing plans because teams or groups of employees are encouraged to suggest strategies for reducing cost. However, the distribution of these gains is usually tilted much more heavily toward employees, with employees usually receiving between two-thirds and three-fourths of the total cost savings that the plan achieves. The cost savings resulting from the plan are not given just to the team or group that suggested and developed the ideas but are instead distributed to the entire organization.

In addition to gainsharing and Scanlon plans, other systems are also used by some organizations. Some companies, for example, have begun to use true incentives at the team or group level. As with individual incentives, team or group incentives tie rewards directly to performance. And like individual incentives, team or group incentives are paid as they are

Gainsharing *is a team- and group-based incentive system designed to share the cost savings from productivity improvements with employees.*

Scanlon plans *are gainsharing plans in which teams or groups of employees are encouraged to suggest strategies for reducing costs; gains are distributed according to who suggested the cost-reduction strategy.*

earned rather than being added to employees' base salaries. The incentives are distributed at the team or group level, however, rather than at the individual level. In some cases, the distribution may be based on the existing salary of each employee, with incentive bonuses being given on a proportionate basis. In other settings, each team or group member receives the same incentive pay.

Some companies also use nonmonetary rewards at the team or group level. These rewards come most commonly in the form of prizes and awards. For example, a company might designate the particular team in a plant or subunit of the company that achieves the highest level of productivity increase, the highest level of reported customer satisfaction, or a similar index of performance. The reward itself might take the form of additional time off (as described earlier in this chapter) or a tangible award such as a trophy or a plaque. In any event, however, the reward is given to the entire team and serves as recognition of exemplary performance by the entire team.

Other kinds of team- or group-level incentives go beyond the contributions of a specific work group. These incentives are generally organizationwide. One long-standing method for this approach is **profit sharing**, in which some portion of the company's profits is paid at the end of the year into a shared pool that is distributed to all employees. This amount is either distributed at the end of the year or put into an escrow account, and payment is deferred until the employee retires.

The basic rationale behind profit-sharing systems is that everyone in the organization can expect to benefit when the company does well. During bad economic times, however, when the company is perhaps achieving low or no profits, no profit sharing is paid out. This situation sometimes results in negative reactions from employees who come to feel that the profit sharing is really part of their annual compensation.

Various types of *stock-based incentives* are also ways to tie incentives to the performance of the firm, although these are more typically used with executive employees rather than hourly employees, as discussed in Chapter 9. For example, in many companies, executives may be given a certain number of *stock options*, which enable them to purchase shares of the company's stock at a fixed price. Thus, under a **stock-option plan** an executive may be given 1,000 options to purchase the firm's stock at $5 per share (the current trading price) for as long as 1 year. If the stock price rises to $6 a share (presumably because of something the executive did), the employee can exercise his or her option: buy the shares at $5, sell them at $6, and make a $1,000 profit.

Alternatively, some firms offer **stock-purchase plans**, which are typically offered to all the employees of a firm rather than just the executives. Many start-up firms, especially in high-tech sectors, also offer restricted stock plans, which are really used as a retention tool rather than as a performance incentive. Under these plans, employees are entitled to the stock only if they remain with the company for a specified period of time. If they leave before that time, they have no rights to the shares of stock.

Employee stock ownership plans (ESOPs) represent another group-level reward system that some companies use. Under the ESOP, employees are gradually given a major stake in the ownership of a corporation. The typical form of this plan involves the company taking out a loan, which is then used to buy a portion of the company's own stock in the open market. Over time, company profits are then used to pay off this loan. Employees, in turn, receive a claim on ownership of some portion of the stock held by the company based on their seniority and perhaps their performance. Eventually, each individual becomes an owner of the company.

Although group reward systems can be effective in some situations, they are also subject to difficulties. For example, not every member of a group may contribute equally to the group's performance. But if the group-incentive system distributes rewards equally to group members, then people may feel that some factors beyond individual performance dictate the distribution of rewards. Also, for incentive plans based on firm profitability, employees may

Profit sharing *is an incentive system in which, at the end of the year, some portion of the company's profits is paid into a profit-sharing pool, which is then distributed to all employees.*

A stock-option plan *is an incentive plan established to give senior managers the option to buy company stock in the future at a predetermined fixed price.*

A stock-purchase plan *is typically offered to all the employees of a firm rather than just the executives to serve more as a retention tool. Under these plans, employees are entitled to the stock only if they remain with the company for a specified period of time. If they leave before that time, they have no rights to the shares of stock.*

Employee stock ownership plans (ESOPs) *are group-level reward systems in which employees are gradually given a major stake in the ownership of a corporation.*

not see how their efforts lead to increased profits (often referred to as a *line-of-sight problem*). In fact, many factors that are beyond the employees' control can affect profitability. Thus, the links among effort, performance, and outcomes, as specified by expectancy theory, are often quite weak, resulting in little motivation. In addition, a limitation noted earlier in our discussion on profit sharing is that employees may come to view the group-level incentive as a normal part of their compensation and consequently be unhappy or dissatisfied if that reward is withheld 1 year.

Stock-based programs have special problems, since the employees' incentives are tied to the price of the stock. An employee, especially an executive, may therefore make decisions or take actions that might result in a short-term increase in the stock price, while causing long-term problems for firm performance. Also, stock programs are effective only so long as the price of the stock is rising—or at least not falling. In the example given earlier, if the employee has the option to buy the stock at $5.00 per share, and price of the stock goes down to $4.00 a share, there is no incentive value and no reason for the employee to exercise the option. In such cases, the stock options are said to be "below water."

Finally, a recent scandal illustrates how organizations can manipulate stock options.[30] A high-tech company, Brocade Systems, Inc., granted employees stock options when they joined the company in 1999. This was a start-up company, and the initial offering price was $2.37, which was also the option price for employees at that time. The stock quickly rose (to more than $133 a share), making those options quite valuable. But then the high-tech bubble burst in 2002, and the share price plummeted. Employees who joined the firm later were also offered options, but at the sell- ing price in effect when they were hired. As the stock price continued to drop, these later options became eventually worthless (i.e., underwater). The management at Brocade then asked employees to change their employment date to make it later than it actually was—at a time when the stock's price was low—so that the employees would qualify for option prices that were low enough for the options to still have some value. The article reporting the scandal noted that similar (but less egregious) practices were carried out by many high-tech firms, but a follow-up piece indicated that the former CEO and several others who were involved were being charged with both civil and criminal securities fraud.[31]

PERFORMANCE MANAGEMENT AND FEEDBACK

There are also a series of programs and interventions that are referred to as *performance-management techniques* that are somewhat more specific than the programs we have discussed thus far. We discuss two of these that were introduced in Chapter 13—behavior modification and goal setting—and we will also discuss some issues associated with feedback, which is a key component of many of these performance-management interventions.

Performance-Management Techniques

Recall our discussion of reinforcement theory in Chapter 13. The basic notion underlying this theory is that all behavior is a function of its consequences—whether actual or anticipated—and so we can shape behavior by arranging for the "right" set of consequences. We also noted that positive reinforcement was designed to reward desirable behaviors that we wanted to see repeated, whereas punishment and extinction were techniques to discourage behaviors that were less desirable. *Behavior modification*, as discussed in the preceding chapter, is the systematic and simultaneous application of positive reinforcement and either punishment or extinction (or both). The basic notion is that it is not enough to eliminate undesirable behaviors unless we can also provide the person with a new set of desirable behaviors.

For example, perhaps an organization is concerned that employees are spending too much time standing around a coffee vending machine. Productivity is suffering because employees are talking and socializing rather than working. The company could begin by taking out the coffee machine (removing an incentive for congregating) and perhaps even install a loud piece of equipment in the space to make it uncomfortable for employees to remain there for long. At the same time, the firm could provide free coffee, delivered to workstations on a cart, but only to people actually working. The idea here would be to discourage congregating and socializing *and* to encourage people to remain at their workstations.

One key to any successful behavior-modification plan is to make sure that the employee can see strong links between his or her behavior and the consequences that can follow. The other, more critical component, however, is to make absolutely sure that desirable behaviors are never punished and that undesirable behaviors are never rewarded. Too often, supervisors reward the wrong behaviors and punish the behaviors they should be rewarding. One of the authors of this text recently had to put together a faculty committee for a task that no one really wanted carried out. When he suggested a certain faculty member, he was told that it was unwise to assign that faculty member to any committees because the person did not usually show up for meetings. Instead, it was suggested, he should assign a different faculty member who always showed up for meetings. This apparently had been a long-standing practice and yet no one could understand why it was so difficult to get the first faculty member to perform any service activities. The author, of course, assigned the first faculty member to the committee and actually released the second faculty member from one or two committee assignments.

We also discussed *goal theory* in the previous chapter and indicated that this theory was very useful for managing performance as well as simply motivating it. Recall that goal theory suggests that employees will exert the greatest effort when they have specific, difficult goals to work toward. Thus, from a performance-management perspective, managers should provide employees with difficult, specific goals, and then reward them when those goals are achieved. The earlier discussion also included consideration of some issues in choosing the "right" goal, but, for the current discussion, it is extremely important that all parties can agree on what is the "right" goal.

Quite often, when employees (and managers) are asked to think about goals, they tend to focus on things that can be readily counted. That is not necessarily bad, because such goals are often concrete and specific, but they can simply be wrong. We can think about a police officer who is told by her supervisor that she should set goals for her job and so decides to set a goal of ten arrests per week. This goal is concrete, specific, and presumably difficult, but what purpose would be served if the officer spent her time trying to arrest as many people as she could? Would that reduce crime or increase public perceptions of safety? Probably not, unless she was arresting truly dangerous criminals. But it would be easier to arrest people for petty crimes or even arrest people who could never be convicted. Thus, the officer could meet her goal every week and still perform her job poorly in a more objective sense. Note that we would not want the goal to be a reduction of crimes either, or the officer would have no incentive to accurately report (or even respond to) all the crimes committed.

In the case of police officers, perhaps goals should be stated in terms of public perceptions, but there are many other examples of goal setting that reflect this problem. Think about a customer-service representative whose goal might be to respond to fifty customers a day (and therefore have no incentive to really deal with any of their problems), a repair person whose goal is to respond to fifty calls a day, or even a teacher whose goal is to have the highest percentage of students passing a course (and therefore has no incentive to fail anyone regardless of how little they have learned). The key here is that any goal chosen as part of a performance-management system must be aligned with the higher-level, strategic goals of the organization. Ideally, one can think about these goals as "cascading down" so that at each level in the organization the performance goals that are set will influence the goals at the next lower level. In terms of goal accomplishment, we can think about the goals cascading upward so that goals met at one level help the next level to meet its goals and so on up to the strategic level.

Performance feedback plays an important role in both behavior modification and goal setting, and it is also seen as useful tool in its own right for performance management. But many managers do a poor job in this area, in part because they do not understand how to provide feedback properly and in part because they do not enjoy it. Almost by definition, performance appraisal in many organizations tends to focus on negatives; as a result, managers may have a tendency to avoid giving feedback because they know an employee who hears negative feedback may be angry, hurt, discouraged, or argumentative. But clearly, if employees are not told about their shortcomings, they have no reason to try to improve and have no guidance concerning how to improve. Therefore, it is critical that a rater provide feedback, so he or she must understand how it might be done better.

One method of improving performance feedback is to provide feedback on a regular basis via feedback interviews. Instead of providing feedback annually, in tandem with the annual performance-appraisal interview, it might be more appropriate for managers to provide feedback on an ongoing basis. Feedback might be provided on a daily or weekly basis, depending on the nature of the job, and it should focus on various characteristics of performance, including both effective and ineffective performance.[32] In fact, if managers remember that the goal of performance management is changing employee behavior, then they should also recognize that they clearly are more likely to effect change with more frequent feedback, and this approach is consistent with both behavior modification and goal setting.

Another useful method for improving performance feedback is to have the individual appraise his or her own performance in advance of an appraisal interview. This method involves having employees think about their own performance over the rating period, which helps sensitize them to areas where they have done good and ineffective jobs. This method also lends efficiency to the process because the manager and the subordinate may be able to focus most of their time and effort in a performance-appraisal interview on those areas of performance assessment where they disagree. That is, if the manager and the subordinate both agree that certain elements of the subordinate's performance are very good and that certain other elements need improvement, it may be possible to spend little time discussing those elements and to focus more energy on the performance areas that are in disagreement.

It is also important during a performance feedback interview to encourage participation and two-way communication. Some managers are prone to lecture a subordinate on the outcome of the performance-appraisal interview. The basic nature of the meeting, then, involves the manager telling the subordinate how he or she has been evaluated and then concluding the interview. As a result, the subordinate may feel threatened and that she or he had no voice in the process. Participation and two-way dialogue, however, allow the individual to express her or his own feelings and opinions about job performance and to provide other kinds of feedback as appropriate.[33]

It is also important for the manager to try to balance positive and negative feedback. As already noted, many managers tend to focus on the negative. In reality, however, employees are likely to have many positive characteristics related to performance as well. Thus, even though the manager must clearly address the negative performance characteristics noted in the appraisal, these negative attributes should be balanced against praise and recognition of the positive aspects of the employee's performance.

Also, throughout the interview and the performance-management process, it is essential that the manager take a developmental and problem-solving orientation to the process. In other words, it is important not to focus on the individual as a person by saying things such as "You are a bad employee." Instead, the focus should be on providing developmental feedback targeted at behavior, not on the individual him- or herself. A simple distinction between saying things like "You are a poor performer" versus "Your performance is not acceptable" can help keep the focus on behavior and not on the individual.

The performance-appraisal interview should conclude with a future-oriented discussion of what will happen next. This discussion often includes topics such as setting goals for correcting performance deficiencies and discussing the possibility of pay raises, promotion prospects, and similar kinds of awards. Of course, if performance is judged to be deficient, the feedback interview may

focus on topics such as the establishment of a probationary period (after which employment may be terminated), the development of a training strategy for improving performance, and so forth. Regardless of the level of current performance, this interview setting should provide a time when the rater and the employee discuss future performance goals for the employee. If the organization uses a goal-based appraisal system, this discussion may be automatic. Even if a different type of appraisal model is used, it is helpful for the employee to have clear and specific goals for improving future performance. These goals, along with continued and regular feedback, should constitute the critical part of any performance-management program.

Even with these recommendations, however, feedback is not always as effective as we would like to believe. Many of today's recommendations and practices are based on the assumption that, if done properly, they will provide employees with feedback about their job performance. Several years ago, however, a study reviewed the research on the effectiveness of feedback interventions, beginning with early studies from the nineteenth century.[34] This study found that, although feedback was effective in almost two-thirds of the cases, it was not effective in the rest. In fact, in a large number of cases, providing feedback to employees actually lowered subsequent performance. This result was independent of the nature of the feedback (i.e., whether it was positive or negative), which suggests that any feedback can, under certain conditions, have a negative effect on subsequent performance.

The study found that feedback was more likely to have a negative effect when the employee was new to a job, the job was extremely complex, ways to improve performance were not discussed, or goals for the future were not considered. The study also reported that feedback must focus the employee's attention on the task at hand. When feedback is provided so that the employee can take it personally, the feedback is much more likely to interfere with rather than enhance subsequent performance. Thus, the recommendations above will help ensure that feedback has the desired effect.

ProMES

Some of the techniques and interventions we have described are best suited for enhancing individual performance (which hopefully will result in ultimate improvements in firm performance), and others could be used with groups as well. Furthermore, we have been discussing these techniques relative to how they can improve some type of performance, but it is also possible to establish systems that can reduce turnover or absenteeism. These outcomes might also well be related to firm performance, but

EXHIBIT 14.4 A Sample ProMES Curve

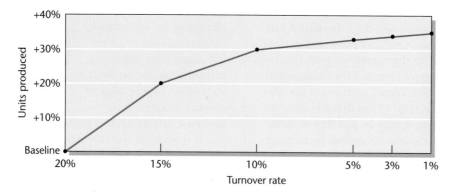

it is critical that such a link be established. In fact, if any performance-enhancement technique is doing what it was designed to do, the organization as a whole should perform better. One such technique allows for the consideration of a wide range of outcomes and is concerned directly with team or organizational performance.

The **productivity measurement and evaluation system (ProMES)** incorporates ideas from goal setting to feedback, and it includes incentives for improvement.[35] More important, it includes a method for tying performance at the individual and group levels to organizational productivity. Specifically, team members work with outside experts to literally map the relationship between a given outcome and productivity. For example, assume that a group is focusing on reducing turnover. In most cases, reducing turnover will lower costs and boost productivity (as discussed in Chapter 6). In most cases, too, the incremental value of reducing turnover will be greatest when turnover is high; similarly, when turnover is low, further reductions will likely have a smaller impact. This pattern of diminishing returns is shown in the sample ProMES curve in Exhibit 14.4.

In this hypothetical example, the curve shows that the group has a current annual turnover rate of 20 percent and that there is a known baseline level of units currently being produced (it does not matter what this baseline is, only that it is known). The team has also calculated that if turnover can be reduced from 20 percent to 15 percent, then the number of units produced will increase by 20 percent. An additional reduction in turnover from 15 percent to 10 percent will achieve another 10-percent increase in units produced (a 30-percent increase in total). However, another 5-percent turnover reduction from 10 percent to 5 percent increases the number of units produced by only an additional 3 percent (33 percent total). Further reductions in turnover from 5 percent to 3 percent and 1 percent yields a unit increase of only 1 percent each.

The **productivity measurement and evaluation system (ProMES)** *is a program developed to improve group- or firm-level productivity. This approach incorporates ideas from goal setting, with incentives for improvement, and is based on a model of motivation similar to expectancy theory.*

Now, understand that reducing turnover is likely to have costs associated with it such as paying higher wages, paying bonuses for longevity, and so forth. The initial costs of reducing turnover from 20 percent to 15 percent will almost certainly be outweighed by the increased unit production of 20 percent. The additional costs for reducing turnover from 15 percent to 10 percent for an additional 10-percent increase in production may or may not be a cost-effective decision. But almost certainly the cost for reducing turnover from, say, 5 percent to 1 percent for only a 2-percent increase in unit production will end up costing more money than is gained. Of course, the point along the diminishing returns curve where costs begin to outweigh benefits must be calculated for each individual work setting.

The other important part of the ProMES process involves the various "connections" among the components. The procedure is based on a model of motivation[36] that is similar to the expectancy model discussed in the previous chapter. Thus, these connections are concerned with the relationship between effort and performance and between performance and attaining outcomes, as well as the link between obtaining outcomes and satisfying needs. The model and the technique are also based on the assumption that individuals and group have a pool of resources (and effort) that they can assign to different activities, and the technique is designed to help them understand which activities they should focus on to increase firm productivity. The system has been widely adopted (especially in Europe)[37] and has been quite successful, and it is one of the few performance-enhancement techniques that focuses on performance above the level of the individual.

LEARNING OBJECTIVE 5

EVALUATING PERFORMANCE-ENHANCEMENT PROGRAMS

Any discussion of how a firm evaluates the effectiveness of these performance-enhancement techniques must really become a discussion of how one measures firm performance. When we think about individual performance, we can think about units produced, or total sales, or some index of waste, but measuring organizational-level performance is much more difficult. First, any true measure of organizational success must tie back to the organization's strategic goals. Thus, the simplest way to assess firm performance is to determine whether or not those strategic goals were met. For example, if a firm's goal is to expand into six new countries, then success is determined by whether those businesses have been established. In addition, several more general indexes of firm-level performance could be used to help evaluate the effectiveness of these interventions.

The first set of indexes can be considered human resource indicators. These would include measures such as turnover rates, absenteeism, accident rates, and even general labor costs. Each of these indicators speaks to how well the organization is managing its human resources, and, given a steady rate of production or sales, changes in these indicators in the desired direction (i.e., lowering them) would also translate into higher profitability. In addition, there are measures of profitability, productivity, and controllable costs. These measures actually are related, with specific measures making more sense in some businesses than in others. For example, food service companies often focus on controllable costs as the major indicator of success, whereas manufacturing firms often focus on some measure of productivity that includes output as well as the cost of production.

Finally, organizations also use a set of financial and accounting indicators. One of these is the stock price, which presumably reflects the market's view of a firm's success, although there are surely other factors that could affect stock price as well. Market share is another similar indicator of success, with the assumption that market share translates into market power and so some ability to influence prices or costs. Indexes such as "return on investment" or "return on assets" are more explicit financial indicators that speak to the rate of return on either corporate investment.

There is no clear rationale for why one of these indexes should be favored over the others, and each provides useful information for a firm trying to measure its success. Therefore, when an organization is interested in gauging the effectiveness of a performance-enhancement technique, it makes sense to examine multiple indicators. One could even think of these as forming a type of hierarchy: If the intervention is working, then individual performance should increase, one or more corporate human resource measures should improve, and these should translate into higher rates of return and higher stock prices. An important caveat, however, is to note that many of these indicators can be affected by a wide variety of factors so that changes in any one index may not be a good measure of how effective the intervention has really been.

CLOSING CASE

ENHANCING PERFORMANCE AT HP

Imagine an organization that must attract and retain a skilled workforce to stay at the forefront of technological innovation. Imagine further that highly qualified workers are scarce, expensive, and switch employers readily. What can this organization do to motivate its employees?

Hewlett Packard (HP), a provider of computer products and services, knows. "Being known as a great place to work makes it easier to attract top talent," reads HP's Web site. "For us, being a great place to work is good business." The challenge is great. HP employs more than 140,000 workers worldwide in every function. Alternative work arrangements are one effective way to motivate such a diverse group of employees.

HP provides a "flexible, supportive environment to manage work and personal life demands, including flexible time,

telecommuting, and job-sharing," according to its Web site. Vice president of diversity and work/life Sid Reed acknowledges that motivation can result from alternative work arrangements. "We very definitely see that employees feel empowered when they are able to work in a schedule and a location that suits their needs. They have some flexibility to really integrate in a positive way their personal life and their work life," Reed asserts.

One motivated employee is Kristy Ward, a marketing manager. With more than two decades at HP, she has experienced several types of alternative work arrangements and is currently job sharing. "Much of what I've been able to do seems uncommon in the rest of the industry," Ward relates. "I talk to my friends that work at other companies. They don't have the same alternatives. . . . That has really added to my loyalty to the company."

CLOSING CASE

Ward explains that HP determines each individual's optimal work environment based on the employee's and the company's needs: "Some have the 2-minute commute, downstairs in the house. Others still drive to be able to be in a work environment with other employees. There's a lot of personal preference." HP engineer Cheryl Marks says, "One of the reasons I stay with HP is because [it allows] me to telework. I get burned out if I can't be as productive as I want to be." Nikki Cheatham telecommutes and estimates it takes her roughly half as much time to absorb complex information at home as in her office cubicle. For just $3,500, HP set up a telework arrangement for a systems engineer with a physical handicap to work at home. The company helped this valuable worker keep his job and saved the cost of finding a replacement.

Among the significant benefits to employees are shorter or nonexistent commuting times, the ability to control their level of interaction with others, and support for family or personal needs. Yet the benefits to the organization are just as great or greater. In addition to support for recruiting and retention, alternative work arrangements can help increase diversity by encouraging employees with various needs. According to Reed, "It's a part of the overall inclusion and diversity strategy. . . . We support employees so that they can contribute to their full potential." Other advantages are the lowered costs for office and parking space, the ability to hire the best talent regardless of location, ease in forming virtual teams, and the capacity to better manage emergencies such as storms or power failures.

Yet surely the greatest benefit to the organization is the increased motivation experienced by workers when they feel supported by their employer. *ComputerWorld* magazine recently surveyed 17,000 high-tech professionals and found that access to leading technology, training, and flexible workplaces were the top three issues of concern. HP employees show that flexibility is becoming more popular at the firm: Telecommuting has grown from 10 percent in 1999 to virtually 100 percent today. Many are also trying other alternatives such as job sharing and part-time work.

Tom Johnson, an HP human resources manager, says, "We have enough hard data and anecdotal evidence to suggest telework can increase productivity, [but] most important is fit." Another HR manager, Darryl Roberts, characterizes telework as an "employee-driven business decision," a win–win agreement between HP and employees. Ward would certainly agree, as she states with evident satisfaction, "The nice thing about HP is you can do what suits your work style."[38]

THINK IT OVER

1. What types of employees are likely to be motivated by alternative work arrangements? Why?
2. Consider HP's use of flextime, job sharing, and telecommuting. What are some of the potential drawbacks or limitations of these approaches? What can HP do to prepare for, reduce, or eliminate these negative outcomes?
3. In your "job" as a student, do you think you would be more or less effective if you had the opportunity to telecommute (or do more telecommuting if you already use distance learning)? Explain your answer.

STUDY TOOLS

- Rip out the chapter review card located at the end of the book.
- Review the valuable study tools located online at www.cengagebrain.com
  - Review the Key Terms flashcards.
  - Download audio and visual summaries to review on the go.
  - Complete practice quizzes to prepare for the test.
  - Play "Beat the Clock" and "QuizBowl" to master chapter concepts.
  - Complete "Crossword Puzzle" to review key terms.
  - Watch the chapter video for a real-life example of key concepts.

CHAPTER 14

Chapter 1

1 "Employees First!" *Time* (July 7, 2008): 45

2 *Hoover's Handbook of American Business 2009* (Austin: Hoover's Business Press, 2010): 389–390, 760–761, 895–896; "Employees First!"

3 Robert M. Grant, "Toward a Knowledge-Based View of the Firm," *Strategic Management Journal* (1996), 17: 109–122.

4 Jeffrey Pfeffer, "Producing Sustainable Competitive Advantage Through the Effective Management of People," *Academy of Management Executive* (Feb. 1995): 55–69; Peter Cappelli and Anne Crocker-Hefter, "Distinctive Human Resources Are Firms' Core Competencies," *Organizational Dynamics* (Winter 1996): 7–22.

5 See Charles R. Greer, *Strategy and Human Resources* (Englewood Cliffs, NJ: Prentice-Hall, 1995), for an overview of the strategic importance of human resources.

6 Aaron Bernstein, "Too Many Workers? Not for Long," *Business Week* (May 20, 2002): 78.

7 Robert R. Blake, "Memories of HRD," *Training & Development* (Mar. 1995): 22–28.

8 Randall S. Schuler, "Repositioning the Human Resource Function: Transformation or Demise?" *Academy of Management Executive* (Aug. 1990): 49–60.

9 Pamela Babcock, "America's Newest Export: White-Collar Jobs," *HR Magazine* (Apr. 2005): 50–57.

10 For an excellent review of some of the problems involved in selecting employees in the context of high-security settings, see Paul R. Sackett, Neal Schmitt, Jill E. Ellingson, and Melissa Kabin, "High-Stakes Testing in Employment, Credentialing, and Higher Education," *American Psychologist* (Apr. 2001): 302–418.

11 "Life Goes On," *HR Magazine* (Sept. 2002): 42–49.

12 Daniel Wren, *The Evolution of Management Thought*, 5th ed. (New York: Wiley, 2005).

13 Thomas A. Mahoney, "Evolution of Concept and Practice in Personnel Administration Human Resource Management (PAHRM)," *Journal of Management* (1986), 12 (2): 223–241.

14 Frederick W. Taylor, *Principles of Scientific Management* (New York: Harper, 1911).

15 Oliver E. Allen, "This Great Mental Revolution," *Audacity* (Summer 1996): 52–61.

16 J. M. Fenster, "How General Motors Beat Ford," *Audacity* (Fall 1992): 50–62.

17 Wren, *The Evolution of Management Thought*.

18 Elton Mayo, *The Human Problems of an Industrial Civilization* (New York: Macmillan, 1933).

19 Abraham Maslow, "A Theory of Human Motivation," *Psychological Review* (July 1943): 370–396.

20 Douglas McGregor, *The Human Side of Enterprise* (New York: McGraw-Hill, 1960).

21 James H. Dulebohn, Gerald R. Ferris, and James T. Stodd, "The History and Evolution of Human Resource Management," in Gerald R. Ferris, Sherman D. Rosen, and Harold T. Barnum (Eds.), *Handbook of Human Resource Management* (Cambridge, MA: Blackwell, 1995): 18–41.

22 Dave Ulrich, "A New Mandate for Human Resources," *Harvard Business Review* (Jan.–Feb. 1998): 124–133.

23 Brian Becker and Barry Gerhart, "The Impact of Human Resource Management on Organizational Performance: Progress and Prospects," *Academy of Management Journal* (Aug. 1996): 779–801; Russell A. Eisenstat, "What Corporate Human Resources Brings to the Picnic: Four Models for Functional Management," *Organizational Dynamics* (Autumn 1996): 7–22.

24 John W. Kendrick, *Understanding Productivity: An Introduction to the Dynamics of Productivity Change* (Baltimore: Johns Hopkins University Press, 1977).

25 Ross Johnson and William O. Winchell, *Management and Quality* (Milwaukee: American Society for Quality Control, 1989).

26 "Bonus Limits Not as Bad as They Look," *Wall Street Journal* (Feb. 14, 2009): A1, A14.

27 Rudy M. Yandrick, "Help Employees Reach for the Stars," *HR Magazine* (Jan. 1997): 96–100.

28 Michelle Martinez, "Prepared for the Future," *HR Magazine* (Apr. 1997): 80–87.

29 For an interesting contrast between large and small firms and HRM activities, see Allison E. Barber, Michael J. Wesson, Quinetta M. Roberson, and M. Susan Taylor, "A Tale of Two Job Markets: Comparing the Hiring Practices of Large and Small Organizations," *Personnel Psychology* (1999), 52: 841–861.

30 For an excellent review, see John W. Boudreau, "Utility Analysis for Decisions in Human Resource Management," in Marvin D. Dunnette and Leatta M. Hough (Eds.), *Handbook of Industrial and Organizational Psychology*, vol. 2, 2nd ed. (Palo Alto, CA: Consulting Psychologists Press, 1991): 621–745.

31 See, for example, Mark A. Huselid, "The Impact of Human Resource Management Practices on Turnover, Productivity, and Corporate Financial Reporting," *Academy of Management Journal* (1996), 39: 779–801.

32 Lotte Bailyn, "Patterned Chaos in Human Resource Management," *Sloan Management Review* (Winter 1993): 77–89.

33 Martha Finney, "Degrees That Make a Difference," *HR Magazine* (November 1996): 74–82; Bruce Kaufman, "What Companies Want from HR Graduates," *HR Magazine* (Sept. 1994): 84–90.

34 Steve Bates, "Facing the Future," *HR Magazine* (July 2002): 26–32.

35 Brian D. Steffy and Steven D. Maurer, "Conceptualizing and Measuring the Economic Effectiveness of Human Resource Activities," *Academy of Management Review* (1988), 13(2): 271–286.

36 *Hoover's Handbook of Private Companies 2009* (Austin: Hoover's Business Press, 2010): 174–175; Brian O'Reilly, "The Rent-A-Car Jocks Who Made Enterprise #1," *Fortune* (Oct. 28, 1996): 125–128; "Enterprise Takes Idea of Dressed for Success to a New Extreme," *Wall Street Journal* (Nov. 20, 2002): B1.

Chapter 2

1 *Hoover's Handbook of American Business 2009* (Austin: Hoover's Business Press, 2010): 688–689; "Workers File Suit Over Long Hours," Associated Press news story, *Bryan-College Station Eagle* (TX) (Aug. 3, 2002): B1, B7.

2 David Israel, "Learn to Manage the Legal Process," *HR Magazine* (July 1993): 83–87.

3 "HR and the Government," *HR Magazine* (May 1994): 43–48. See also J. Ledvinka, *Federal Regulation of Personnel and Human Resource Management* (Boston: Kent, 1982).

4 Jon M. Werner and Mark C. Bolino, "Explaining U.S. Court of Appeals Decisions Involving Performance Appraisal: Accuracy, Fairness, and Validation," *Personnel Psychology* (Spring 1997): 1–24.

5 See Philip E. Varca and Patricia Pattison, "Evidentiary Standards in Employment Discrimination: A View Toward the Future," *Personnel Psychology* (Summer 1993): 239–250.

6 *Diaz v. Pan American World Airways, Inc.*, 442 F. 2d 385 (5th Cir. 1971).

7 James E. Jones, William P. Murphy, and Robert Belton, *Discrimination in Employment*, 5th ed. (American Casebook Series) (St. Paul, MN: West, 1987): 381.

8 *Griggs v. Duke Power Company*, 401 U.S. 424 (1971).

9   Technically, neither guilt nor innocence is determined in civil cases. Instead, the defendant is judged to be either liable or not liable for discrimination. We will use the terms *guilty* and *innocent* occasionally, however, because readers are more comfortable with these terms.

10 *Wards Cove Packing Co., Inc. v. Antonio*, U.S. Sup. Ct. 1387 (June 5, 1989).

11 *McDonnell-Douglas Corporation v. Green*, 411 U.S. 792 (1973).

12 "Culture of Racial Bias at Shoney's Underlines Chairman's Departure," *Wall Street Journal* (Dec. 21, 1992): A1.

13 "When Quotas Replace Merit, Everybody Suffers," *Forbes* (Feb. 15, 1993): 80–102.

14 *Bakke v. The Regents of the University of California at Davis*, 438 U.S. 265 (1978).

15 *United Steelworkers of America, AFL-CIO v. Weber*, Sup. Ct. (1979); 443 U.S. 193; 99 S. Ct. 2721; 61 L. Ed. 2d 480.

16 *Wygant v. Jackson Board of Education*, Sup. Ct. (1986); 106 S. Ct. 1842; 90 L. Ed. 2d 260.

17 *Local 93 of the International Association of Firefighters, AFL-CIO, C.L.C. v. City of Cleveland*, Sup. Ct. (1986); 106 S. Ct. 3063, 92 L. Ed. 2d 405.

18 *U.S. v. Paradise*, Sup. Ct.; 478 US 1019; 106 S. Ct. 3331, 92 L. Ed. 2d737 (1986).

19 *Einsley Branch, NAACP v. Seibels*, 60 F. 3d 717 (11th Cir. 1994).

20 *Hopwood v. State of Texas*, 78 F. 3d 932 (5th Cir. 1996).

21 Jonathan A. Segal, "Sexual Harassment: Where Are We Now?" *HR Magazine* (Oct. 1996): 68–73; Gerald D. Block, "Avoiding Liability for Sexual Harassment," *HR Magazine* (Apr. 1995): 91–94.

22 *Meritor Savings Bank, FSB v. Vinson et al.*, Sup. Ct.; 477 U.S. 57 (1986).

23 *Harris v. Forklift Systems* 510 U.S. 17 (1993).

24 Jonathan A. Segal, "Proceed Carefully, Objectively to Investigate Sexual Harassment Claims," *HR Magazine* (Oct. 1993): 91–95.

25 *Scott v. Sears Roebuck*, 798 F. 2d 210 (7th cir. 1986).

26 *Oncale v. Sundowner Offshore Servs.*, 96 Sup. Ct. 568, 523 U.S. 75; S. Ct. 998; 140 L. Ed. 2d 201 (1998).

27 "Justices' Ruling Further Defines Sexual Harassment," *Wall Street Journal* (Mar. 5, 1998): B1.

28 "How to Shrink the Pay Gap," *Business Week* (June 24, 2002): 151.

29 *Johnson v. Mayor and City Council of Baltimore*, Sup. Ct. 105; S. Ct. 2727; 86 l. Ed. 2d 286 (1985).

30 Allen Smith, *EEOC Stats Show Spike in Age Discrimination Charges*. SHRM Report (Nov. 2009).

31 "Recent Suits Make Pregnancy Issues Workplace Priorities," *Wall Street Journal* (Jan. 14, 1998): B1.

32 The most noteworthy of these are the Wards Cove (1989) case discussed earlier, *Patterson v. McLean Credit Union* [109 S. Ct. 2363 (1989)] and *Pricewaterhouse v. Hopkins* [109 S. Ct. 1775 (1989)].

33 Most of these issues were decided in *EEOC v. Arabian American Oil Co.*, 89 Sup. Ct. 1838, 1845; 498 U.S. 808; 111 S. Ct. 40; 112 L. Ed. 2d 17 (1990).

34 Francine S. Hall and Elizabeth L. Hall, "The ADA: Going Beyond the Law," *Academy of Management Executive* (Feb. 1994): 17–26.

35 Albert S. King, "Doing the Right Thing for Employees with Disabilities," *Training & Development* (Sept. 1993): 44–46.

36 "Disabilities Act Abused?" *USA Today* (Sept. 25, 1998): 1B, 2B.

37 Michael Barrier, "A Line in the Sand," *HR Magazine* (July 2002): 35–43.

38 For a review and a discussion of the determinants of this problem, see Adrienne Colella, "Coworker Distributive Fairness Judgments of the Workplace Accommodation of Employees with Disabilities," *Academy of Management Review* (2001), 26(1): 100–116.

39 David Stamps, "Just How Scary Is the ADA?" *Training* (1995), 32: 93–101.

40 "Court Narrows Disability Act," *USA Today* (June 23, 1999): 1A.

41 Michelle Neely Martinez, "FMLA—Headache or Opportunity?" *HR Magazine* (Feb. 1994): 42–45.

42 Jonathan A. Segal, "Traps to Avoid in FMLA Compliance," *HR Magazine* (Feb. 1994): 97–100. See also Timothy Bland, "The Supreme Court Reins in the FMLA (Slightly)," *HR Magazine* (July 2002): 44–48.

43 John Montoya, "New Priorities for the '90s," *HR Magazine* (Apr. 1997): 118–122.

44 David Israel, "Check EEOC Position Statements for Accuracy," *HR Magazine* (Sept. 1993): 106–109.

45 Allen Smith, *EEOC's Proposed ADA Rule Would List Presumptive Disabilities*. SHRM Report (Sept. 2009).

46 David C. Ankeny and David Israel, "Completing an On-Site OFCCP Audit," *HR Magazine* (Mar. 1993): 89–94.

47 Labor Law Center, *Federal Minimum Wage Increases for 2007, 2008, and 2009*. Labor Law Center Report (Nov. 2009).

48 "Maryland First to OK 'Wal-Mart Bill,'" *USA Today* (Jan. 13, 2006): 1B; "SEC to Propose Overhaul of Rules On Executive Pay," *Wall Street Journal* (Jan. 10, 2006): A1.

49 "Health Care Reform." SHRM Government Affairs News Update (Nov. 2009).

50 *Electromation v. NLRB*, US Court of Appeals for the 35 F. 3d 1148 (7th Cir. 1994).

51 *E.I. Du Pont de Nemours and Company v. NLRB*, 12 F. 3d 209 (5th Cir. 1993).

52 HRhero.com, "Employee Free Choice Act—EFCA" (Sept. 2009).

53 "Fewer Employers Are Currently Conducting Psych and Drug Tests," *HR Focus* (Oct. 2000): 78.

54 Stephanie Overman, "Splitting Hairs," *HR Magazine* (Aug. 1999): 42–48.

55 "Laws, Juries Shift Protection to Terminated Employees," *USA Today* (Apr. 2, 1998): 1B, 2B.

56 Sources: "The *Seinfeld* Firing," *Wall Street Journal* (May 11, 1998): A20; "Ex-Miller Executive Wins Award in '*Seinfeld*' Case," *Wall Street Journal* (July 16, 1997): B13.

Chapter 3

1   "Managing the Global Workforce," *BusinessWeek* (Jan. 28, 2008): 34.

2   "Managing the Global Workforce"; *Hoover's Handbook of World Business 2009* (Austin: Hoover's Business Press, 2010); Ricky W. Griffin and Michael W. Pustay, *International Business—A Managerial Perspective*, 6th ed. (Upper Saddle River, NJ: Prentice-Hall, 2010); Thomas L. Friedman, *The World Is Flat* (New York: Farrar, Straus, and Giroux, 2005); "Firms in China Think Globally, Hire Locally," *Wall Street Journal* (Feb. 27, 2006): B1, B3.

3   Martha I. Finney, "Global Success Rides on Keeping Top Talent," *HR Magazine* (Apr. 1996): 68–74.

4   Gregory D. Chowanec and Charles N. Newstrom, "The Strategic Management of International Human Resources," *Business Quarterly* (Autumn 1991): 65–70.

5   Griffin and Pustay, *International Business*.

6   Richard M. Steers, "The Cultural Imperative in HRM Research," in Albert Nedd, Gerald R. Ferris, and Kendrith M. Rowland (Eds.), *Research in Personnel and Human Resources Management* (Supplement 1: International Human Resources Management) (Greenwich, CT: JAI Press, 1989): 23–32.

7   Geert Hofstede, *Culture's Consequences: International Differences in Work-Related Values* (Beverly Hills, CA: Sage Publishers, 1980).

8   Nakiye Boyacigiller, "The Role of Expatriates in the Management of Interdependence, Complexity, and Risk in Multinational Corporations," *Journal of International Business Studies*, 21(3): 357–382.

9   See Richard Posthuma, Mark Roehling, and Michael Campion, "Applying U.S. Employment Discrimination Law to International Employers: Advice for Scientists and Practitioners," *Personnel Psychology* (Fall 2006): 705–739.

10 "U.S. Child-Labor Law Sparks a Trade Debate Over Brazilian Oranges," *Wall Street Journal* (Sept. 9, 1998): A9.

11 Sakhawat Hossain and Herbert J. Davis, "Some Thoughts on International Personnel Management as an Emerging Field," in Nedd, Ferris, and Rowland (Eds.), *Research in Personnel and Human Resources Management*, 121–136.

12 Griffin and Pustay, *International Business*.

13 Ibid.

14 "The High Cost of Expatriation," *Management Review* (July 1990): 40–41.

15 Cynthia Fetterolf, "Hiring Local Managers and Employees Overseas," *The International Executive* (May–June 1990): 22–26.

16 "Bringing Back the Beetle," *Forbes* (Apr. 7, 1997): 42–44.

17 "What We Earn . . ." *Time* (Nov. 2, 2006): 86.

18 Carla Johnson, "Save Thousands per Expatriate," *HR Magazine* (July 2002): 73–77.

19 Winfred Arthur, Jr., and Winston Bennett, Jr., "The International Assignee: The Relative Importance of Factors Perceived to Contribute to Success," *Personnel Psychology* (Fall 1995): 99–113.

20 Anil Gupta and Venkat Govindarajan, "Knowledge Flows within Multinational Organizations," *Strategic Management Journal* (2000), 21: 473–496.

21 Michael Jensen and William Meckling, "Theory of the Firm: Managerial Behavior, Agency Costs and Ownership Structure," *Journal of Financial Economics* (1976), 3: 305–360.

22 C. A. Bartlett and Sumatra Ghosal, *Managing Across Borders: The Trasnational Solution*, 2nd ed. (Boston: Harvard Business School Press, 1998).

23 For more on the role of knowledge contracts and expatriate managers, see Brian Connelly, Micahel Hitt, Angelo DeNisi, and R. Duane Ireland, "Expatriates and Corporate-Level International Strategy: Governing with the Knowledge Contract," *Management Decision* (2007), 45: 564–581.

24 J. Stewart Black, Hal B. Gregersen, and Mark E. Mendenhall, *Global Assignments* (San Francisco: Jossey-Bass, 1992).

25 See, for example, Ian Torbion, "Operative and Strategic Use of Expatriates in New Organizations and Market Structures," *International Studies of Management and Organization* (1994), 24: 5–17.

26 "Global Managers Need Boundless Sensitivity, Rugged Constitutions," *Wall Street Journal* (Oct. 13, 1998): B1.

27 "Firms in Europe Try to Find Executives Who Can Cross Borders in a Single Bound," *Wall Street Journal* (Jan. 25, 1991): B1.

28 "Younger Managers Learn Global Skills," *Wall Street Journal* (Mar. 31, 1992): B1.

29 "As Costs of Overseas Assignments Climb, Firms Select Expatriates More Carefully," *Wall Street Journal* (Jan. 9, 1992): B1, B6.

30 J. Stewart Black and Hal B. Gregersen, "The Right Way to Manage Expats," *Harvard Business Review* (Mar.–Apr. 1999): 52–62; see also Johnson, "Save Thousands per Expatriate."

31 For example, see Paula Caligiuiri, MaryAnne Hyland, Aparna Joshi, and Allon Bross, "Testing a Theoretical Model for Examining the Relationship Between Family Adjustment and Expatriate Work Adjustment," *Journal of Applied Psychology* (1998), 83: 598–614.

32 Margaret Shaffer and David Harrison, "Expatriates' Psychological Withdrawal from International Assignments: Work, Nonwork, and Family Influences," *Personnel Psychology* (1998), 51: 87–96.

33 See review by Denis Ones and Chockalingam Viswesvaran, "Personality Determinants in the Prediction of Expatriate Job Success," in D. Saunders and Z. Aycan (Eds.), *New Approaches to Employee Management* (1994), 4: 63–92; and the study by Paula Caligiuri, "The Big Five Personality Characteristics as Predictors of Expatriate's Desire to Terminate the Assignment and Supervisor-Rated Performance," *Personnel Psychology* (2000), 53: 67–88.

34 See G. W. Florkowski and D. S. Fogel, "Expatriate Adjustment and Commitment: The Role of Host-Unit Treatment," *International Journal of Human Resource Management* (1999), 10: 783–807.

35 For a more complete discussion of this potential problem, see Soo Min Toh and Angelo DeNisi, "Host Country National Reactions to Expatriate Pay Policies: A Proposed Model and Some Implications," *Academy of Management Review* (2003), 28: 606–621.

36 "Companies Use Cross-Cultural Training to Help Their Employees Adjust Abroad," *Wall Street Journal* (Aug. 9, 1992): B1, B6.

37 Paul Vanderbroeck, "Long-Term Human Resource Development in Multinational Organizations," *Sloan Management Review* (Fall 1992): 95–99; see also Carl Fey, Antonina Pavlovskaya, and Ningyu Tang, "A Comparison of Human Resource Management in Russia, China, and Finland," *Organizational Dynamics* (2004), 33(1): 79–97.

38 Kathryn Tyler, "Targeted Language Training is Best Bargain," *HR Magazine* (Jan. 1998): 61–68.

39 Frank Jossi, "Successful Handoff," *HR Magazine* (Oct. 2002): 48–52.

40 K. Cushner and Richard Brislin, *International Interactions: A Practical Guide* (Thousand Oaks, CA: Sage, 2000).

41 Simca Ronen, "Training the International Assignee," in I. L. Goldstein and Associates, *Training and Development in Organizations* (New York: Jossey-Bass, 1989): 418.

42 Richard M. Hodgetts and Fred Luthans, "U.S. Multinationals' Compensation Strategies," *Compensation & Benefits Review* (Jan.–Feb. 1993): 57–62.

43 Michael J. Bishko, "Compensating Your Overseas Executives, Part I: Strategies for the 1990s," *Compensation & Benefits Review* (May–June 1990): 33–43.

44 "For Executives Around the Globe, Pay Packages Aren't Worlds Apart," *Wall Street Journal* (Oct. 12, 1992): B1, B5.

45 Stephanie Overman, "In Sync," *HR Magazine* (Mar. 2000): 86–92.

46 See Johnson, "Save Thousands per Expatriate."

47 Robert O'Connor, "Plug the Expat Knowledge Drain," *HR Magazine* (Oct. 2002): 101–107.

48 Andrea Poe, "Welcome Back," *HR Magazine* (Mar. 2000): 94–105.

49 National Foreign Trade Council report, cited in Johnson, "Save Thousands per Expatriate."

50 "In France, Boss Can Become Hostage," *Wall Street Journal* (Apr. 3, 2009): B1, B5.

51 *Hoover's Handbook of World Business 2009* (Austin: Hoover's Business Press, 2010): 77–78, 110–111; "Gentlemen, Start Your Engines," *Fortune* (June 8, 1998): 138–146; James Aley and Matt Siegel, "The Fallout from Merger Mania," *Fortune* (Mar. 2, 1998): 26–56; "Labor Holds a Key to Fate of Daimler-Chrysler Merger," *Wall Street Journal* (May 7, 1998): B1, B18; "Oil Companies Pump Out $50 Billion Merger Deal," *USA Today* (Aug. 12, 1998): 1B, 2B; "BP Restructuring Starts Bearing Fruit," *Wall Street Journal* (Oct. 28, 2009): B1.

Chapter 4

1 Jennifer Reese, "Starbucks—Inside the Coffee Cult," *Fortune* (Dec. 9, 1996): 196.

2 "The Starbucks Strategy," *Washington Post* (Sept. 1, 2002): E1, E6; "Brewing a British Coup," *USA Today* (Sept. 16, 1998): 1D, 2D; Reese, "Starbucks—Inside the Coffee Cult," *Fortune* (Dec. 9, 1996): 190–200; *Hoover's Handbook of American Business 2009* (Austin: Hoover's Business Press, 2010): 770–771.

3 Charles R. Greer, *Strategy and Human Resources* (Englewood Cliffs, NJ: Prentice-Hall, 1995).

4 The points in the debate are best explained in Brian Becker and Barry Gerhart, "The Impact of Human Resource Management on Organizational Performance: Progress and Prospects," *Academy of Management Journal* (Aug. 1996): 779–801. The different sides are represented in Mark A. Huselid, "The Impact of Human Resource Management Practices on Turnover, Productivity, and Corporate Financial Reporting," *Academy of Management Journal* (1995), 38: 635–672;

John Delery and D. Harold Doty, "Modes of Theorizing in Strategic Human Resource Management: Tests of Universalistic, Contingency, and Configurational Performance Predictions," *Academy of Management Journal* (1995), 38: 802–835; and Patrick Wright, Dennis Smart, and Gary McMahan, "Matches Between Human Resources and Strategy Among NCAA Basketball Teams," *Academy of Management Journal* (1995), 38(5): 1052–1074.

5 To read more about this model, see Jay Barney, "Firm Resources and Sustained Competitive Advantage," *Journal of Management* (1991), 17: 99–120; and Jay Barney, "Is the Resource-based 'View' a Useful Perspective for Strategic Management Research? Yes," *Academy of Management Review* (2001), 26: 41–56.

6 See Charles W. L. Hill and Gareth R. Jones, *Strategic Management: An Integrated Approach*, 9th ed. (Stamford, CT: Cengage Learning, 2010).

7 Janine Nahapiet and Sumantra Ghoshal, "Social Capital, Intellectual Capital, and the Organizational Advantage," *Academy of Management Review* (1998), 23: 242–266.

8 Catherine M. Daily and Charles Schwenk, "Chief Operating Officers, Top Management Teams, and Boards of Directors: Congruent or Countervailing Forces?" *Journal of Management* (1996), 22(2): 185–208.

9 S. A. Kirkpatrick and Edwin A. Locke, "Direct and Indirect Effects of Three Core Charismatic Leadership Components on Performance and Attitudes," *Journal of Applied Psychology* (1996), 81: 36–51; see also Harry G. Barkema and Luis R. Gomez-Mejia, "Managerial Compensation and Firm Performance: A General Research Framework," *Academy of Management Journal* (1998), 41: 135–145.

10 See, for example, Donald C. Hambrick and Sidney Finkelstein, "Managerial Discretion: A Bridge Between Polar Views on Organizations," in L. L. Cummings and B. Staw (Eds.), *Research in Organizational Behavior*, Vol. 9 (Greenwich, CT: JAI Press, 1987): 369–406; or Sidney Finkelstein and Donald Hambrick, "Top Management Team Tenure and Organizational Outcomes: The Moderating Role of Managerial Discretion," *Administration Science Quarterly* (1990), 35: 484–503.

11 Eugene F. Fama and Michael C. Jensen, "Separation of Ownership and Control." *Journal of Law and Economics* (1983), 2: 301–325.

12 See, for example, Idalene Kessner and Richard Johnson, "An Investigation of the Relationship Between Board Composition and Stockholder Suits," *Strategic Management Journal* (1990), 15: 327–336; see also Jay Barney, *Gaining and Sustaining Competitive Advantage*, 2nd ed. (Upper Saddle River, NJ: Prentice Hall, 2002): 452–456, for an overview of the role of boards of directors.

13 Lynn Sweet, "Obama Will Move to Block AIG Bonus Payments. Said It Is 'Hard To Understand' Why AIG Traders Deserve Money," *Chicago Sun Times Media* (Mar. 16, 2009).

14 Hill and Jones, *Strategic Management: An Analytical Approach*.

15 Brian Becker and Barry Gerhart, "The Impact of Human Resource Management on Organizational Performance: Progress and Prospects," *Academy of Management Journal* (Aug. 1996), 39(4): 779–801.

16 Donald Laurie, Yves Doz, and Claude Sheer, "Creating New Growth Platforms," *Harvard Business Review* (May 2006): 80–92.

17 David M. Schweiger and James P. Walsh, "Mergers and Acquisitions: An Interdisciplinary View," in Kenneth Rowland and Gerald Ferris (Eds.), *Research in Personnel and Human Resource Management*, Vol. 8 (Greenwich, CT: JAI Press, 1990): 41–107.

18 David M. Schweiger and Angelo DeNisi, "Communications with Employees Following a Merger: A Longitudinal Field Study," *Academy of Management Journal* (1991), 34: 110–135.

19 Hill and Jones, *Strategic Management: An Analytical Approach*.

20 Jay Barney and Ricky W. Griffin, *The Management of Organizations* (Boston: Houghton Mifflin, 1992).

21 Russell A. Eisenstat, "What Corporate Human Resources Brings to the Picnic: Four Models for Functional Management," *Organizational Dynamics* (Autumn 1996): 7–21.

22 John O. Whitney, "Strategic Renewal for Business Units," *Harvard Business Review* (July–Aug. 1996): 84–98.

23 Raymond E. Miles and Charles C. Snow, *Organizational Strategy, Structure, and Process* (New York: McGraw-Hill, 1978).

24 Michael Porter, *Competitive Strategy* (New York: Free Press, 1980).

25 Robert L. Cardy and Gregory H. Dobbins, "Human Resource Management in a Total Quality Organizational Environment: Shifting from a Traditional to a TQHRM Approach," *Journal of Quality Management* (1996), 1(1): 5–20.

26 Henry Mintzberg, "Patterns in Strategy Formulation," *Management Science* (Oct. 1978): 934–948.

27 David Fiedler, "Know When to Hold 'Em," *HR Magazine* (Aug. 2002): 89–94.

28 Edilberto F. Montemayor, "Congruence Between Pay Policy and Competitive Strategy in High-Performing Firms," *Journal of Management* (1996), 22(6): 889–912.

29 David Lepak and Scott Snell, "The Human Resource Architecture: Toward a Theory of Human Capital Allocation and Development," *Academy of Management Journal*, 24(1): 31–48; David Lepak and Scott Snell, "Examining the Human

Resource Architecture: The Relationships Among Human Capital, Employment, and Human Resource Configuration," *Journal of Management* (2002), 28(4): 517–544; David Lepak and Scott Snell, "Managing the Human Resource Architecture for Knowledge-Based Competition," in Susan Jackson, Michael Hitt, and Angelo DeNisi (Eds.), *Managing Knowledge for Sustained Competitive Advantage: Designing Strategies for Effective Human Resource Management* (San Francisco: Jossey-Bass, 2003).

30 Peter Bamberger and Avi Fiegenbaum, "The Role of Strategic Reference Points in Explaining the Nature and Consequences of Human Resource Strategy," *Academy of Management Review* (Oct. 1996): 926–958.

31 Richard L. Daft, *Organization Theory and Design*, 10th ed. (Stamford, CT: Cengage Learning, 20107).

32 John Purcell and Bruce Ahlstrand, *Human Resource Management in the Multi-Divisional Company* (Oxford, UK: Oxford University Press, 1994).

33 Terrence E. Deal and Allan A. Kennedy, *Corporate Cultures: The Rights and Rituals of Corporate Life* (Reading, MA: Addison-Wesley, 1982).

34 Jay Barney, "Organizational Culture: Can It Be a Source of Sustained Competitive Advantage?" *Academy of Management Review* (July 1986): 656–665.

35 See, for example, David Jemison and Sim Sitkin, "Corporate Acquisitions: A Process Perspective," *Academy of Management Review* (1986), 11(1): 145–163; or Nancy Napier, "Mergers and Acquisitions, Human Resource Issues and Outcomes: A Review and Suggested Typology," *Journal of Management Studies* (1989), 26(3): 271–289.

36 See discussion of this strategy in Bruce Nissen, "The 'Social Movement' Dynamics of Living Wage Campaigns," in Paula Voos (Ed.), *Proceedings of the 53rd Annual Meeting of the Industrial Relations Research Association* (Washington, DC: Industrial Relations Research Association, Jan. 2001): 232–240.

37 Lawrence Hrebiniak, "Obstacles to Effective Strategy Implementation," *Organizational Dynamics* (Fall 2006): 12–31.

38 Gary Johns, "The Essential Impact of Context on Organizational Behavior," *Academy of Management Review* (2006), 31(2): 386–408.

39 Denise Rousseau, "Changing the Deal While Keeping the People," *Academy of Management Executive* (Feb. 1996): 50–61.

40 Elizabeth Wolfe Morrison and Sandra L. Robinson, "When Employees Feel Betrayed: A Model of How Psychological Contract Violation Develops," *Academy of Management Review* (Jan. 1997): 226–256; Sandra Robinson, Matthew Kraatz, and Denise Rousseau, "Changing Obligations and the Psychological Contract," *Academy of Management Journal* (1994): 37(1): 137–152.

41 Murray Barrick and Michael Mount, "The Big Five Personality Dimensions and Job Performance: A Meta-Analysis," *Personnel Psychology* (1991), 44(1): 1–26.

42 Leslie DeChurch and Michelle Marks, "Leadership In Multiteam Systems," *Journal of Applied Psychology* (2006), 91(2): 311–329; Brian Grow, "Renovating Home Depot," *BusinessWeek* (Mar. 6, 2006): 50–58; Jennifer Reingold, "Bob Nardelli Is Watching," *Fast Company* (Dec. 2005): 58–60; George Stalk, Rob Lachenauer, and John Butman, *Hardball: Are You Playing to Play or Playing to Win?* (Cambridge, MA: Harvard Business School Press, 2004).

43 Several critical measurement issues are raised in Barry Gerhart, Patrick Wright, Gary McMahan, and Scott Snell, "Measurement Error in Research on Human Resources and Firm Performance: How Much Error Is There and How Does It Influence Size Estimates?" *Personnel Psychology* (2000), 53(4): 803–834.

44 See, for example, Mark A. Huselid, "The Impact of Human Resource Management Practices on Turnover, Productivity, and Corporate Financial Reporting," *Academy of Management Journal* (1995), 38: 635–672; or Rajiv Banker, Joy Field, Roger Schroeder, and Kingshuk Sinha, "Impact of Work Teams on Manufacturing Performance: A Longitudinal Study," *Academy of Management Journal* (1996), 39(4): 867–890.

45 *Hoover's Handbook of American Business 2009* (Austin: Hoover's Business Press, 2010): 36–37; "Activision's Unlikely Hero," *Forbes* (Feb. 12, 2009): 45–47; "A Company Looks to Its Creative Side to Regain What It Had Lost," *New York Times* (Feb. 19, 2008): B6.

Chapter 5

1 "While Hiring at Most Firms Chills, Wal-Mart's Heats Up," from *USA Today* (Aug. 26, 2002): 3B.

2 *Hoover's Handbook of American Business 2009* (Austin: Hoover's Business Press, 2010): 874–875; "While Hiring at Most Firms Chills, Wal-Mart's Heats Up."

3 Lee Dyer, "Human Resource Planning," in K. Rowland and G. Ferris (Eds.), *Personnel Management* (Boston: Allyn & Bacon, 1982): 52–77.

4 R. G. Murdick and F. Schuster, "Computerized Information Support for the Human Resource Function," *Human Resource Planning* (1983), 6(1): 25–35.

5 Taylor H. Cox and Stacy Blake, "Managing Cultural Diversity: Implications for Organizational Competitiveness," *Academy of Management Executive* (Aug. 1991): 45–56.

6 "The Geography of Work," *Time* (June 22, 1998): 98–102.

7 Carla Johnson, "Developing a Strong Bench," *HR Magazine* (Jan. 1998): 92–97.

8 "P&G Will Make Jager CEO Ahead of Schedule," *Wall Street Journal* (Sept. 10, 1998): B1, B8; *Hoover's Handbook of American Business 2006* (Austin: Hoover's Business Press, 2006): 706–708.

9 "Firms Plan to Keep Hiring, Spending," *USA Today* (Jan. 26, 1995): B1.

10 "Firms Find Ways to Grow Without Expanding Staffs," *Wall Street Journal* (Mar. 18, 1993): B1, B2.

11 Donald Laurie, Yves Doz, and Claude Sheer, "Creating New Growth Platforms," *Harvard Business Review* (May 2006): 80–92.

12 "When UPS Demanded Workers, Louisville Did the Delivering," *Wall Street Journal* (Apr. 24, 1998): A1, A10; *Hoover's Handbook of American Business 2006* (Austin: Hoover's Business Press, 2006): 873–874

13 "Layoffs on Wall Street Will Bruise Big Apple," *USA Today* (Oct. 15, 1998): 1B; "Its Share Shrinking, Levi Strauss Lays Off 6,395," *Wall Street Journal* (Nov. 4, 1997): B1, B8.

14 See especially Roger Griffeth, Peter Hom, and Stefan Gaertner, "A Meta-Analysis of Antecedents and Correlates of Employee Turnover: Update, Moderator Tests, and Research Implications for the Next Millennium," *Journal of Management* (2000), 26: 463–488; and Charlie Trevor, "Interactions Among Actual Ease of Movement Determinants and Job Satisfaction in the Prediction of Voluntary Turnover," *Academy of Management Journal* (2001), 44: 621–638.

15 For a more detailed discussion of this phenomenon applied to human resource management, see Edward Lazear, *Personnel Economics for Managers* (New York: Wiley, 1998).

16 E. J. McCormick, *Job Analysis: Methods and Applications* (New York: American Management Association, 1979).

17 Charles R. Greer, *Strategy and Human Resources* (Englewood Cliffs, NJ: Prentice Hall, 1995).

18 A. S. DeNisi, "The Implications of Job Clustering for Training Programmes," *Journal of Occupational Psychology*, 49: 105–113.

19 K. Pearlman, "Job Families: A Review and Discussion of Their Implications for Personnel Selection," *Psychological Bulletin*, 87: 1–27.

20 McCormick, *Job Analysis: Methods and Applications*.

21 U.S. Department of Labor, Employment, and Training Administration, *The Revised Handbook for Analyzing Jobs* (Washington, DC: U.S. Government Printing Office, 1991).

22 Frank Landy and Joseph Vasey, "Job Analysis: The Composition of SME Samples," *Personnel Psychology* (1991), 44(1): 27–50.

23 Ibid.

24 Norman Peterson, Michael Mumford, Walter Borman, P. Richard Jeanneret, Edwin Fleishman, Kerry Levin, Michael Campion, Melinda Mayfield, Frederick Morgeson, Kenneth Pearlman, Marilyn Gowing, Anita Lancaster, Marilyn Silver, and Donna Dye, "Understanding Work Using the Occupational Information Network (O*NET): Implications for Practice and Research," *Personnel Psychology* (2001), 54: 451–492.

25 U.S. Department of Labor, Employment, and Training Administration, *The Revised Handbook for Analyzing Jobs*.

26 E. A. Fleishman, *Manual for the Ability Requirements Scale* (MARS, revised) (Palo Alto, CA: Consulting Psychologists Press, 1991).

27 For example, see J. E. Morsh, *Job Types Identified with an Inventory Constructed by Electronics Engineers* (Lackland Air Force Base, San Antonio, TX: U.S. Air Force Personnel Research Laboratory, 1966).

28 S. A. Fine and W. W. Wiley, *An Introduction to Functional Job Analysis* (Kalamazoo, MI: W. E. Upjohn Institute for Employment Research, 1971).

29 E. J. McCormick, P. R. Jeanneret, and R. C. Mecham, "A Study of Job Characteristics and Job Dimensions as Based on the Position Analysis Questionnaire (PAQ), *Journal of Applied Psychology* (1972), 56: 347–368.

30 McCormick, *Job Analysis: Methods and Applications*.

31 See, for example, McCormick, Jeanneret, and Mecham, " A Study of Job Characteristics and Job Dimensions," or E. J. McCormick, A. S. DeNisi, and J. B. Shaw, "The Use of the Position Analysis Questionnaire (PAQ) for Establishing the Job Component Validity of Tests," *Journal of Applied Psychology* (1978), 64: 51–56.

32 A. S. DeNisi, E. T. Cornelius, and A. G. Blencoe, "A Further Investigation of Common Knowledge Effects on Job Analysis Ratings: On the Applicability of the PAQ for All Jobs," *Journal of Applied Psychology* (1987), 72: 262–268.

33 Walter Tornow and Patrick Pinto, "The Development of a Managerial Job Taxonomy: A System for Describing, Classifying, and Evaluating Executive Positions," *Journal of Applied Psychology* (1976), 61: 410–418.

34 J. C. Flanagan, "The Critical Incident Technique," *Psychological Bulletin*, 51: 327–358.

35 Milan Moravec and Robert Tucker, "Job Descriptions for the 21st Century," *Personnel Journal* (June 1992): 37–40.

36 Karen Cook and Patricia Bernthal, *Job/Role Competency Practices Survey Report* (Bridgeville, PA: Development Dimensions Inc., 1998).

37 For an excellent review of the various issues associated with competency modeling, the reader is referred to Jeffrey Shippman, Ronald Ash, Mariangela Battista, Linda Carr, Lorraine Eyde, Beryl Hesketh, Jerry Kehoe, Kenneth Pearlman, Erich Prien, and Juan Sanchez, "The Practice of Competency Modeling," *Personnel Psychology* (2000), 53: 703–740.

38 See also Adrienne Fox, "At Work in 2020," *HR Magazine* (Jan. 2010): 18–23.

39 *Albermarle Paper Co. v. Moody*, Sup. Ct. of the U.S., 1975, 422 U.S. 405, 95 S. Ct. 2362, L. Ed. 2d. 280.

40 For a complete discussion of these sources of inaccuracy, see Frederick Morgeson and Michael Campion, "Social and Cognitive Sources of Potential Inaccuracy in Job Analysis," *Journal of Applied Psychology* (1998), 82: 627–655.

41 Richard Arvey, "Sex Bias in Job Evaluation Procedures," *Personnel Psychology* (1986), 39: 315–335.

42 *Electromation Inc. v. National Labor Relations Board*, 1992.

43 "These Six Growth Jobs Are Dull, Dead-End, Sometimes Dangerous," *Wall Street Journal* (Dec. 1, 1994): A1, A8; *Hoover's Handbook of American Business 2006* (Austin: Hoover's Business Press, 2006). See also the continuing television series *Dirty Jobs*.

Chapter 6

1 "Cutting Costs Without Cutting Jobs," *Business Week* (Mar. 2009): 55; "Chopping Hours, Not Heads," *Business Week* (Jan. 5, 2009): 85; "Do Pay Cuts Pay Off?" *Time* (Apr. 27, 2009): 47; "Cutbacks: Don't Neglect the Survivors," *Business Week* (Jan. 11, 2010): 68.

2 "What to Do with Bad News," *HR Magazine* (July 2002): 58–63.

3 Snapshots, *USA Today* (Dec. 3, 2001): B-1.

4 "Cuomo Demands Bonus Data from Eight Big Banks," *New York Times* (Jan. 11, 2010): B1.

5 Araiana Cha and Ellen Nakashima, "Google China Cyberattack Part of Vast Espionage Campaign, Experts Say," *Washington Post* online (Jan. 14, 2010).

6 Anne T. Lawrence, "Google, Inc.: Figuring out how to deal with China", in Emmanuel Raufflet and Albert Mills (Eds.), *The Dark Side: Critical Cases on the Downside of Business* (London: Greenleaf, 2009): 257–278.

7 Data are from Transparency International's Corruption Perceptions Index carried out in 2005 (www.transparency.org).

8 Gilbert Nicholson, "Get Your Benefit Ducks in a Row," *Workforce* (Sept. 2000): 78–84.

9 Lee Phillion and John Brugger, "Encore! Retirees Give Top Performance as Temporaries," *HR Magazine* (Oct. 1994): 74–78.

10 See, especially, David Lepak and Scott Snell, "The Human Resource Architecture: Toward a Theory of Human Capital Allocation and Development," *Academy of Management Review* (1999), 24: 31–48.

11 See Sylvia Roch and Linda Shanock, "Organizational Justice in an Exchange Framework: Clarifying Organizational Justice Distinctions," *Journal of Management* (Apr. 2006): 299–322.

12 J. Stacy Adams, "Inequity in Social Exchange," in L. Berkowitz (Ed.), *Advances in Experimental Social Psychology*, Vol. 2 (New York: Academic Press, 1965): 267–299.

13 Gerald Leventhal, "The Distribution of Rewards and Resources in Groups and Organizations," in L. Berkowitz and W. Walster (Eds.), *Advances in Experimental Social Psychology*, Vol. 9 (New York: Academic Press, 1976): 91–131.

14 Joel Brockner and Batia Wiesenfeld, "An Integrative Framework for Explaining Reactions to Decisions: Integrative Effects of Outcomes and Procedures," *Psychological Bulletin* (1996), 120: 189–298.

15 Robert Bies and Joseph Moag, "Interactional Justice: Communication Criteria of Fairness," in R. Lewicki, B. Sheppard, and M. Bazerman (Eds.), *Research on Negotiations in Organizations*, Vol. 1 (Greenwich, CT: JAI Press, 1986): 43–55.

16 Jerald Greenberg, "The Social Side of Fairness: Interpersonal and Informational Classes of Organizational Justice," in R. Cropanzano (Ed.), *Justice in the Workplace: Approaching Fairness in Human Resource Management* (Hillsdale, NJ: Erlbaum, 1993): 79–103.

17 "USA's New Money-Saving Export: White-Collar Jobs," *USA Today* (Aug. 5, 2003): 1B.

18 Wayne Cascio, Clifford Young, and James Morris, "Financial Consequences of Employment Change Decisions in Major U.S. Corporations," *Academy of Management Journal* (1997), 40: 1175–1189.

19 For example, see Dan Worrell, Wallace Davidson, and Varinder Sharma, "Layoff Announcements and Stockholder Wealth," *Academy of Management Journal* (1991), 34: 662–678.

20 Joel Brockner, "The Effects of Work Layoffs on Survivors: Research, Theory and Practice," in B. Staw and L. Cummings (Eds.), *Research in Organizational Behavior*, Vol. 10 (Greenwich, CT: JAI Press, 1988): 213–215.

21 American Management Association, *Corporate Job Creation, Job Elimination, and Downsizing: Summary of Key Findings* (New York: American Management Association, 1997).

22 Fay Hansen, "Employee Assistance Programs (EAPs) Grow and Expand their Reach," *Compensation and Benefits Review* (Mar.–Apr. 2000): 13.

23 See, for example, Meg Bryant, "Testing EAPs for Coordination," *Business and Health* (Aug. 1991): 20–24; or Barbara Pflaum, "Seeking Sane Solutions: Managing Mental Health and Chemical Dependency Costs," *Employee Benefits Journal* (1992), 16: 31–35.

24 James Smith, "EAPs Evolve to Health Plan Gatekeepers," *Employee Benefit Plan Review* (1992), 46: 18–19.

25 M. R. Buckley and W. Weitzel, "Employment at Will," *Personnel Administrator* (1988), 33: 78–80.

26 This approach was pioneered by Union Carbide. See A. B. Chimezie, Osigweh Yg, and William Hutchinson, "To Punish or Not to Punish: Managing Human Resources Through Positive Discipline," *Employee Relations* (Mar. 1990): 27–32. For a more complete picture, see Dick Grove, *Discipline Without Punishment* (New York: American Management Association, 1996).

27 See, for example, Michael Abelson and Barry Baysinger, "Optimal and Dysfunctional Turnover: Toward an Organizational Level Model," *Academy of Management Review* (1984), 9: 331–341.

28 On the positive side, job satisfaction has been defined as the positive feeling that "results from the perception that one's job fulfills . . . one's important job values." See Edwin Locke, "The Nature and Causes of Job Dissatisfaction," in M. Dunnette (Ed.), *Handbook of Industrial and Organizational Psychology* (Chicago: Rand McNally, 1976): 901–969.

29 For an excellent review of this literature, see Charles Hulin, Mary Roznowski, and Dan Hachiya, "Alternative Opportunities and Withdrawal Decisions," *Psychological Bulletin* (1985), 97: 233–250.

30 The original model was presented in William Mobley, "Intermediate Linkages in the Relationship Between Job Satisfaction and Employee Turnover," *Journal of Applied Psychology* (1977), 62: 237–240. A refined model was later presented in Peter Hom and Roger Griffeth, "A Structural Equations Modeling Test of a Turnover Theory: Cross Sectional and Longitudinal Analysis," *Journal of Applied Psychology* (1991), 76: 350–366.

31 John Sheridan and Michael Abelson, "Cusp-Catastrophe Model of Employee Turnover," *Academy of Management Journal* (1983), 26: 418–436.

32 Thomas Lee and Terrence Mitchell, "An Alternative Approach: The Unfolding Model of Voluntary Employee Turnover," *Academy of Management Review* (1994), 19: 51–89.

33 Terrence Mitchell, Brooks Holtom, Thomas Lee, Christopher Sablynski, and Miriam Erez, "Why People Stay: Using Job Embeddedness to Predict Voluntary Turnover," *Academy of Management Journal* (2001), 44: 1102–1121.

34 Richard Arvey, Thomas Bouchard, Neal Segal, and Len Abraham, "Job Satisfaction: Genetic and Environmental Components," *Journal of Applied Psychology* (1989), 74: 187–193.

35 See, for example, Barry Staw, Nancy Bell, and J. Clausen, "The Dispositional Approach to Job Attitudes: A Lifetime Attitudinal Test," *Administrative Science Quarterly* (1986), 31: 56–78; and Timothy Judge, "Does Affective Disposition Moderate the Relationship Between Job Satisfaction and Affective Turnover?" *Journal of Applied Psychology* (1993), 78: 395–401.

36 Barry Gerhart, "How Important Are Dispositional Factors as Determinants of Job Satisfaction? Implications for Job Design and Other Personnel Programs," *Journal of Applied Psychology* (1987), 72: 493–502.

37 See Locke, "The Nature and Causes of Job Dissatisfaction," for a review of the literature on these determinants of job satisfaction.

38 Bruce Meglino, Elizabeth Ravlin, and Cheryl Adkins, "A Work Values Approach to Corporate Culture: A Field Test of the Value Congruence Process and Its Relationship to Individual Outcomes," *Journal of Applied Psychology* (1989), 74: 424–433.

39 For an excellent review of the relationship between leader behavior and employees' reactions, such as satisfaction, see Victor Vroom, "Leadership," in M. Dunnette (Ed.), *Handbook of Industrial and Organizational Psychology* (Chicago: Rand McNally, 1986): 560–663.

40 Rick Hackett and Robert Guion, "A Re-evaluation of the Job Satisfaction-Absenteeism Relation," *Organizational Behavior and Human Decision Processes* (1985), 35: 340–381.

41 Richard Mowday, Richard Steers, and Lyman Porter, "The Measurement of Organizational Commitment," *Journal of Vocational Behavior* (1979), 14: 224–247.

42 See, for example, Chester Schriesheim, "Job Satisfaction, Attitudes Towards Unions, and Voting in a Union Representation Election," *Journal of Applied Psychology* (1978), 63: 548–553. For a somewhat more complex model that still focuses on job dissatisfaction, see Stuart Youngblood, Angelo DeNisi, Julie Molleston, and William Mobley, "The Impact of Worker Attachment, Instrumentality Beliefs, Perceived Labor Union Image, and Subjective Norms on Voting Intentions and Union Membership," *Academy of Management Journal* (1994), 15: 576–590.

43 The original research is summarized in Dennis Organ, *Organizational Citizenship Behavior: The Good Soldier Syndrome* (Lexington, MA: Heath, 1988).

44 See Walter Borman, "Job Behavior, Performance and Effectiveness," in M. Dunnette and L. Hough (Eds.), *Handbook of Industrial and Organizational Psychology*, Vol. 1, 2nd ed. (Palo Alto, CA: Consulting Psychologists Press, 1991): 271–326.

45 See the discussion in Susan Jackson, Donald Schwab, and Randall Schuler, "Toward an Understanding of the Burnout Phenomenon," *Journal of Applied Psychology* (1986), 71: 630–640. For an update and a more complex model, see Evangelia Demerouti, Arnold Bakker, Friedhelm Nachreiner, and Wilmar Schaufei, "The Job Demands-Resources Model of Burnout," *Journal of Applied Psychology* (2001), 86: 499–512.

46 See Locke, "The Nature and Causes of Job Dissatisfaction," for a review.

47 Patricia Smith, Lorne Kendall, and Charles Hulin, *The Measurement of Satisfaction in Work and Retirement* (Chicago: Rand McNally, 1969).

48 Theodore Kunin, "The Construction of a New Type of Attitude Measure," *Personnel Psychology* (1955), 8: 65–78.

49 See review by Gunter Stahl, Mark Mendenhall, Amy Pablo, and Mansour Javidan, "Sociocultural Integration in Mergers and Acquisitions," in Gunter Stahl and Mark Mendenhall (Eds.), *Mergers and Acquisitions: Managing the Culture and Human Resources* (Palo Alto, CA: Stanford University Press, 2005): 3–16.

50 See discussion of various reasons for success and failure of mergers and acquisitions in A. T. Kearney, *White Paper on Post Merger Integration*, KPMG Report, 1998.

51 Tim Arango, "In Retrospect: How the AOL-Time Warner Merger Went So Wrong," *New York Times* (Jan. 11, 2010): B-1.

52 For further discussion of these processes, see H. Tajfel and J. C. Turner, "An Integrative Theory of Intergroup Conflict," in W. Austin and S. Worchel (Eds.), *The Social Psychology of Intergroup Psychology* (Monterey, CA: Brooks-Cole, 1979): 33–47.

53 *New York Times* (Jan. 10, 2010); available online at www.nytimes.com/2010/01/11/business/media/11merger.html?pagewanted=1.

54 David Schweiger and Angelo DeNisi, "The Effects of Communication with Employees Following a Merger: A Longitudinal Field Experiment," *Academy of Management Journal* (1991), 34: 110–135.

55 For more detail and further discussion of these processes in the context of a merger or acquisition, see Angelo DeNisi and Shung Jae Shin, "Psychological Communication Interventions in Mergers and Acquisitions," in Gunter Stahl and Mark Mendenhall (Eds.), *Mergers and Acquisitions: Managing the Culture and Human Resources* (Stanford, CA: Stanford University Press, 2005): 228–249.

56 Andrea Poe, "Keeping Hotel Workers," *HR Magazine* (Feb. 2003): 91–93; "The 100 Best Companies to Work For!" *Fortune* (Feb. 8, 2010): 56–88.

Chapter 7

1 "Airport Screening Hits Barrier: No Staff," Associated Press wire story, *Bryan-College Station Eagle* [TX] (July 29, 2002): A3.

2 "Screener Shortage Causes Long Wait at Airport," *Palm Beach Post* (Apr. 18, 2006): A1; "9.11.02," *Business Week* (Sept. 16, 2002): 34–38; "Airport Screening Hits Barrier: No Staff"; "Feds Take Over Airport Screening," *USA Today* (Nov. 18, 2002): 1A, 2A.

3 James A. Breaugh, *Recruitment: Science and Practice* (Boston: PWS-Kent, 1992).

4 Robert Bretz, Jr., and Timothy Judge, "The Role of Human Resource Systems in Job Applicant Decision Processes," *Journal of Management* (1994), 20(3): 531–551.

5 Allison Barber, Christina Daly, Cristina Giannantonio, and Jean Phillips, "Job Search Activities: An Examination of Changes Over Time," *Personnel Psychology* (1994), 47: 739–750.

6 Timothy Judge and Robert Bretz, "Effects of Work Values on Job Choice Decisions," *Journal of Applied Psychology*, 77(3): 261–271.

7 "Right Here in Dubuque," *Forbes* (Mar. 29, 1993): 86–88.

8 Andy Bargerstock and Hank Engel, "Six Ways to Boost Employee Referral Programs," *HR Magazine* (Dec. 1994): 72–77.

9 "Software Firm Tests College Job Hopefuls," *USA Today* (Apr. 8, 1993): B1, B2.

10 Beth McConnell, "Companies Lure Job Seekers in New Ways," *HR News* (Apr. 2002): 1–5.

11 Peter Cappelli, "Making the Most of Online Recruiting," *Harvard Business Review* (Mar. 2001): 139–146.

12 Bill Leonard, "Online and Overwhelmed," *HR Magazine* (Aug. 2000): 37–42.

13 Candee Wilde, "Recruiters Discover Diverse Value in Websites," *Informationweek* (Feb. 7, 2000): 144.

14 Peter Kuhn and Mikal Skuiterud, "Job Search Methods: Internet Versus Traditional," *Monthly Labor Review* (Oct. 2000): 3–11.

15 Cappelli, "Making the Most of Online Recruiting."

16 www.depts.ttu.edu/careercenter/webpage/Internships/Internship%20Quotes.htm

17 J. P. Wanous and A. Colella, "Organizational Entry Research: Current Status and Future Directions," in K. Rowland and G. Ferris (Eds.), *Research in Personnel and Human Resource Management* (Greenwich, CT: JAI Press, 1989).

18 "It's Not Easy Making Pixie Dust," *Business Week* (Sept. 18, 1995): 134.

19 B. M. Meglino and A. S. DeNisi, "Realistic Job Previews: Some Thoughts on Their More Effective Use in Managing the Flow of Human Resources," *Human Resource Planning* (1987), 10: 157–167.

20 Jean Phillips, "Effects of Realistic Job Previews on Multiple Organizational Outcomes: A Meta-Analysis," *Academy of Management Journal* (1998), 41: 673–690.

21 R. A. Dean and J. P. Wanous, "Effects of Realistic Job Previews on Hiring Bank Tellers," *Journal of Applied Psychology* (1984), 69: 61–68.

22 B. M. Meglino, A. S. DeNisi, S. A. Youngblood, and K. J. Williams, "Effects of Realistic Job Previews: A Comparison Using Enhancement and Reduction Previews," *Journal of Applied Psychology* (1988), 73: 259–266.

23 B. M. Meglino, A. S. DeNisi, and E. C. Ravlin, "The Effects of Previous Job Exposure and Subsequent Job Status on the Functioning of Realistic Job Previews," *Personnel Psychology* (1993), 46: 803–822.

24 See Neal Schmitt and Ivan Robertson, "Personnel Selection," *Annual Review of Psychology*, 1990, Vol. 41, pp. 289–319.

25 Michael Stevens and Michael Campion, "The Knowledge, Skill, and Ability Requirements for Teamwork: Implications for Human Resource Management," *Journal of Management*, 1994, Vol. 20, No. 2, pp. 503–530.

26 M. R. Barrick and M. K. Mount, "The Big Five Personality Dimensions and Job Performance: A Meta-Analysis," *Personnel Psychology*, 1991, Vol. 44, pp. 1–26.

27 It is not always clear that recruiters and interviewers can effectively distinguish between the two types of fit. See, for example, Amy Kristof-Brown, "Perceived Applicant Fit: Distinguishing Between Recruiters' Perceptions of Person-Job and Person-Organization Fit," *Personnel Psychology*, 2000, Vol. 53, pp. 643–672.

28 Orlando Behling, "Employee Selection: Will Intelligence and Conscientiousness Do the Job?" *Academy of Management Executive* (Feb. 1998): 77–86.

29 J. E. Hunter and R. F. Hunter, "Validity and Utility of Alternative Predictors of Job Performance," *Psychological Bulletin* (Spring 1984): 72–98.

30 C. J. Russell, J. Mattdson, S. E. Devlin, and D. Atwater, "Predictive Validity of Biodata Items Generated from Retrospective Life Experience Essays," *Journal of Applied Psychology* (1990): 75: 569–580.

31 See "Can You Tell Applesauce from Pickles?" *Forbes* (Oct. 9, 1995): 106–108 for several examples.

32 J. E. Hunter, "Cognitive Ability, Cognitive Aptitudes, Job Knowledge, and Job Performance," *Journal of Vocational Behavior* (1986), 29: 340–362.

33 A. R. Jensen, *Bias in Mental Testing* (New York: Free Press, 1980).

34 M. K. Mount and M. R. Barrick, *Manual for the Personal Characteristics Inventory* (Iowa City, IA: 1995).

35 Daniel P. O'Meara, "Personality Tests Raise Questions of Legality and Effectiveness," *HR Magazine* (Jan. 1994): 97–104.

36 See L. M. Hough, "The Big Five Personality Variables–Construct Confusion: Description Versus Prediction," *Human Performance* (1992), 5: 139–155. For an opposing view, see J. E. Hunter and R. F. Hunter, "Validity and Utility of Alternative Predictors of Job Performance," *Psychological Bulletin* (1984), 96: 72–98.

37 "Employers Score New Hires," *USA Today* (July 9, 1997): 1B, 2B.

38 P. R. Sackett, "Integrity Testing for Personnel Selection," *Current Directions in Psychological Science* (1994), 3: 73–76.

39 R. C. Hollinger and J. P. Clark, *Theft by Employees* (Lexington, MA: Lexington Books, 1983).

40 U.S. Congress, Office of Technology Assessment, *The Use of Integrity Tests for Pre-Employment Screening* (Washington, DC: U.S. Government Printing Office, 1990); S. W. Gilliland, "Fairness from the Applicant's Perspective: Reactions to Employee Selection Procedures," *International Journal of Selection and Assessment* (1995): 3: 11–19.

41 Michael McDaniel, Deborah Whetzel, Frank Schmidt, and Steven Maurer, "The Validity of Employment Interviews: A Comprehensive Review and Meta-Analysis," *Journal of Applied Psychology* (1994), 79(4): 599–616.

42 "Think Fast!" *Forbes* (Mar. 24, 1997): 146–151.

43 Elaine Pulakos and Neal Schmitt, "Experience-Based and Situational Interview Questions: Studies of Validity," *Personnel Psychology* (1995), 48: 289–308.

44 M. A. McDaniel, D. L. Whetzel, F. L. Schmidt, and S. D. Maurer, "The Validity of Employment Interviews: A Comprehensive Review and Meta-Analysis," *Journal of Applied Psychology* (1994), 79: 599–616.

45 *Watson v. Fort Worth Bank and Trust*, 108 Sup. Ct. 2791 (1988).

46 See Thomas Dougherty, Daniel Turban, and John Callender, "Confirming First Impressions in the Employment Interview: A Field Study of Interviewer Behavior," *Journal of Applied Psychology* (1994), 79(5): 659–665.

47 Paul Falcone, "Getting Employers to Open Up on a Reference Check," *HR Magazine* (July 1995): 58–63.

48 "Think Fast!" *Forbes* (Mar. 24, 1997): 146–151.

49 Annette C. Spychalski, Miguel A. Quinones, Barbara B. Gaugler, and Katja Pohley, "A Survey of Assessment Center Practices in Organizations in the United States," *Personnel Psychology* (Spring 1997): 71–82.

50 Justin Martin, "So, You Want to Work for the Best . . . ," *Fortune* (Jan. 12, 1998): 77–85.

51 See especially *Washington v. Davis*, Sup. Ct.; 426 U.S. 229; S. Ct. 2040, L. Ed. 2d 597 (1976).

52 See, for example, *Albermarle Paper Company v. Moody*, Sup. Ct.; 422 U.S. 405; 95 S. Ct. 2362, 45 L. Ed. 2d 280 (1975); *Connecticut v. Teal*, Sup. Ct.; 457 U.S. 440; 102 S. Ct. 2525; L. Ed. 2d 190 (1982); and *Watson v. Fort Worth Bank and Trust*, Sup. Ct.; 487 U.S. 977; 108 S. Ct. 2777; L. Ed. 2d 827 (1988).

53 "Job-Test Ruling Cheers Employers," *Wall Street Journal* (July 1, 2009): B1, B2.

54 C. R. Williams, C. E. Labig, and T. Stone, "Recruitment Sources and Posthire Outcomes for Job Applications and New Hires," *Journal of Applied Psychology* (1993), 78: 163–172.

55 "Extreme HR: Pushing the Limits of Risk," *Boston Globe* (July 5, 2005): B1; "Worker Shortage Forces Small Businesses into Creative Hiring," *USA Today* Oct. 30, 1998): 1B, 2B; "Making Risky Hires into Valued Workers," *Wall Street Journal* (June 19, 1997): B1, B2.

Chapter 8

1 "How One Hotel Manages Staff Diversity," *Wall Street Journal* (Nov. 20, 1996): B1, B11

2 "The 40 Best Companies for Diversity," *Black Enterprise* (June 12, 2006): 18–22; "How One Hotel Manages Staff Diversity"; *Hoover's Handbook of American Business 2009* (Austin: Hoover's Business Press, 2010): 538–539; "In a Factory Schedule, Where Does Religion Fit In?" *Wall Street Journal* (Mar. 4, 1999): B1, B12; Roy Johnson, "The 50 Best Companies for Blacks & Hispanics," *Fortune* (Aug. 3, 1998): 94–106.

3 David A. Thomas and Robin J. Ely, "Making Differences Matter: A New Paradigm for Managing Diversity," *Harvard Business Review* (Sept.–Oct. 1996): 79–90.

4 Dora C. Lau and J. Keith Murnighan, "Demographic Diversity and Faultlines: The Compositional Dynamics of Organizational Groups," *Academy of Management Review* (1998), 23(2): 325–340.

5 Frances J. Milliken and Luis L. Martins, "Searching for Common Threads: Understanding the Multiple Effects of Diversity in Organizational Groups," *Academy of Management Review* (1996), 21(2): 402–433.

6 "In a Factory Schedule, Where Does Religion Fit In?"

7 Adrienne Colella, "The Work Group Perspective: Co-Worker Responses to Group Member Accommodations," in D. Harrison (Chair), "Implementing What Matters Most: Multiple Stakeholders in Accommodating People with Disabilities at Work. All-Academy Symposium," presented at annual meeting of Academy of Management, San Diego, CA, August 1998.

8 Barbara L. Hassell and Pamela L. Perrewe, "An Examination of Beliefs about Older Workers: Do Stereotypes Still Exist?" *Journal of Organizational Behavior* (1995), 16: 457–468.

9 For a more complete discussion of these dimensions, see Diane L. Stone and Adrienne Colella, " A Model of Factors Affecting the Treatment of Disabled Individuals in Organizations," *Academy of Management Review* (1996), 21: 352–401.

10 *Faith Communities Today: Mosque in America: A National Portrait* (April 2001). Hartford Seminary's *Hartford Institute for Religious Research*. Quoted in the *Demographic Facts* report by the U.S. Department of State, *International Information Programs*, at http://usinfo.state.gov/products/pubs/.

11 Based on Taylor H. Cox and Stacy Blake, "Managing Cultural Diversity: Implications for Organizational Competitiveness," *Academy of Management Executive* (Aug. 1991): 45–56; see also Gail Robinson and Kathleen Dechant, "Building a Business Case for Diversity," *Academy of Management Executive* (Aug. 1997): 21–30.

12 C. Marlene Fiol, "Consensus, Diversity, and Learning in Organizations," *Organization Science* (Aug. 1994): 403–415.

13 Douglas Hall and Victoria Parker, "The Role of Workplace Flexibility in Managing Diversity," *Organizational Dynamics* (Summer 1993): 5–14.

14 Janice R. W. Joplin and Catherine S. Daus, "Challenges of Leading a Diverse Workforce," *Academy of Management Executive* (Aug. 1997): 32–44.

15 "As Population Ages, Older Workers Clash with Younger Bosses," *Wall Street Journal* (June 13, 1994): A1, A8

16 "Pursuit of Diversity Stirs Racial Tension at an FAA Center," *Wall Street Journal* (Dec. 3, 1998): A1, A8.

17 www.usatoday.com/money/industries/retail/2004-06-24-walmart-workers_x.htm

18 "Generational Warfare," *Forbes* (Mar. 22, 1999): 62–66.

19 For a review of these results, see Milliken and Martins, "Searching for Common Threads: Understanding the Multiple Effects of Diversity in Organizational Groups," *Academy of Management Review* (1996), 21: 402–433; or Belle Rose Ragins and Jorge Gonzalez, "Understanding Diversity in Organizations: Getting a Grip on a Slippery Construct," in J. Greenberg (Ed.), *Organizational Behavior: The State of the Science* (Mahwah, NJ: Erlbaum, 2003).

20 See for example, Christopher Earley and Elaine Mosakowski, "Creating Hybrid Team Cultures: An Empirical Test of Transnational Team Functioning," *Academy of Management Journal* (2000), 43: 26–49.

21 Ibid.; Orlando Richard, Tim Barnett, Sean Dwyer, and Ken Chadwick, "Cultural Diversity in Management, Firm Performance, and the Moderating Role of Entrepreneurial Orientation Dimensions," *Academy of Management Journal* (2004), 47: 255–266.

22 Karen Hildebrand, "Use Leadership Training to Increase Diversity," *HR Magazine* (Aug. 1996): 53–57.

23 "Do Diversity Programs Make a Difference?" *Wall Street Journal* (Dec. 4, 1996): B1.

24 Patricia L. Nemetz and Sandra L. Christensen, "The Challenge of Cultural Diversity: Harnessing a Diversity of Views to Understand Multiculturalism," *Academy of Management Review* (1996), 21(2): 434–462.

25 This discussion derives heavily from Taylor H. Cox, "The Multicultural Organization," *Academy of Management Executive* (May 1991): 34–47.

26 The relationship between individual and organizational learning is discussed in much more detail in Lois Tetrick and Nancy Da Silva, "Assessing the Culture and Climate for Organizational Learning," in Susan Jackson, Michael Hitt, and Angelo DeNisi (Eds.), *Managing Knowledge for Sustained Competitive Advantage* (San Francisco: Jossey-Bass, 2003): 333–360.

27 See, for example, Michael Hitt, Barbara Keats, and Sam DeMarie, "Navigating in the New Competitive Landscape: Building Strategic Flexibility and Competitive Advantage in the 21st Century," *Academy of Management Executive* (1998), 12: 22–42; and Angelo DeNisi, Michael Hitt and Susan Jackson, "The Knowledge-Based Approach to Sustainable Competitive Advantage," in Jackson, Hitt, and DeNisi (Eds.), *Managing Knowledge for Sustained Competitive Advantage*, pp. 3–36.

28 For more on the pressures and challenges facing these firms, see Matthew Jaffe and Scott Mayerowitz, "Unapologetic CEOs: What Did the Bank Do with Your Case?" *ABC News Online* (Feb. 11, 2009).

29 Max Boisot, *Knowledge Assets* (Oxford, UK: Oxford University Press, 1998).

30 M. L. Tushman and C. A. O'Reilly, *Winning Through Innovation* (Cambridge, MA: Harvard Business School Press, 1996).

31 M. A. Von Glinow, *The New Professionals* (Cambridge, MA: Ballinger, 1988).

32 T. W. Lee and S. D. Maurer, "The Retention of Knowledge Workers with the Unfolding Model of Voluntary Turnover," *Human Resource Management Review* (1997), 7: 247–276.

33 J. C. Kail, "Compensating Scientists and Engineers," in D. B. Balkin and L. R. Gomez-Mejia (Eds.), *New Perspectives on Compensation* (Englewood Cliffs, NJ: Prentice-Hall, 1987): 278–281.

34 G. T. Milkovich, "Compensation Systems in High-Technology Companies," in A. Klingartner and C. Anderson (Eds.), *High Technology Management* (Lexington, MA: Lexington Books, 1987).

35 Thomas Stewart, "In Search of Elusive Tech Workers," *Fortune* (Feb. 16, 1998): 171–172.

36 See, for example, the various discussions in the edited volume by Jackson, Hitt, and DeNisi, *Managing Knowledge for Sustained Competitive Advantage*.

37 Beth McConnell, "HR Implements Corporate Social Responsibility Globally," *HR News* (Nov. 28, 2006): 1-2..

38 Angelo DeNisi and Carrie Belsito, "Strategic Aesthetics: Wisdom and HRM" in Eric H. Kessler and James R. Bailey (Eds.), *Handbook of Organizational and Managerial Wisdom* (Thousand Oaks, CA: Sage Publications, 2007).

39 Lynn Gibson, "Implications of the FLSA for Inmates, Correctional Institutions, Private Industry and Labor." Statement before the U.S. Senate Hearings of the Committee on Labor and Human Resources, Oct. 18, 1993.

40 For a more in-depth discussion of these issues, see Ray Marshall, "Industrial Relations and Inmate Labor," *Proceedings of the 53rd Annual Meeting of the Industrial Relations Research Association*, New Orleans (2001), pp. 339–348.

41 Jeffrey Kling and Alan Krueger, "Costs, Benefits, and Distributional Consequences of Inmate Labor," *Proceedings of the 53rd Annual Meeting of the Industrial Relations Research Association*, New Orleans (2001), pp. 349–358.

42 See for example, Sandra Waddock, "Building a New Institutional Infrastructure for Corporate Responsibility," *Academy of Management Perspectives* (2008), 22: 87–108.

43 For a more detailed history, see Sandra Waddock, "Parallel Universes: Companies, Academics, and the Progress of Corporate Citizenship," *Business and Society Review* (Mar. 2004), 109: 5–42.

44 Stefan Ambec and Paul Lanoie, "Does It Pay to Be Green? A Systematic Overview," *Academy of Management Perspectives* (2008), 22: 45–62.

45 See www.wholefoodsmarket.com/company/corevalues.php#caring

46 John Mackey, "The CEO's Blog," Whole Foods Online (Dec. 24, 2009).

47 "Alpha Females," *Fortune* (Nov. 14, 2005): 125–170; "If Women Ran the World, It Would Look a Lot Like Avon," *Fortune* (July 21, 1997): 74–79; *Hoover's Handbook of American Business 2009* (Austin: Hoover's Business Press, 2010): 150–151.

Chapter 9

1 "The Art of Motivation," *Business Week* (May 1, 2006): 57–62.

2 "About Us," Nucor Web site (www.nucor.com), Feb. 22, 2010; "The Art of Motivation"; Gretchen Morgenson, "Companies Not Behaving Badly," New York Times (Oct. 9, 2005): B3; "Reinventing the Mill," *New York Times* (Oct. 22, 2005): B5.

3 Kathryn Tyler, "Compensation Strategies Can Foster Lateral Moves and Growing in Place," *HR Magazine* (Apr. 1998): 64–69.

4 Emily Pavlovic, "Choosing the Best Salary Surveys," *HR Magazine* (Apr. 1994): 44–48.

5 "Web Transforms Art of Negotiating Raises," *Wall Street Journal* (Sept. 22, 1998): B1, B16.

6 J. Stacey Adams, "Inequity in Social Exchange," in L. Berkowitz (Ed.), *Advances in Experimental Social Psychology* (New York: Academic Press, 1965): 267–299.

7 Jeffrey Pfeiffer, "Six Dangerous Myths About Pay," *Harvard Business Review* (May–June 1998): 109–119.

8 See "Is Minimum Wage Minimum Life?" Associated Press news story (Jan. 23 1995), as published in the *Bryan-College Station Eagle* [TX], p. B1.

9 Brian S. Klaas and John A. McClendon, "To Lead, Lag, or March: Estimating the Financial Impact of Pay Level Policies," *Personnel Psychology* (1996), 49(1): 88–98.

10 Edward E. Lawler III, "The New Pay: A Strategic Approach," *Compensation & Benefits Review* (July–Aug. 1995): 145–154.

11 Sandra O'Neal, "Aligning Pay with Business Strategy," *HR Magazine* (Aug. 1993): 76–80.

12 Charles Greer, *Strategy and Human Resources* (Englewood Cliffs, NJ: Prentice-Hall, 1995).

13 "Many Companies Lower Pay Raises," *USA Today* (Apr. 4, 2002): 1B.

14 Judith Collins and Paul Muchinsky, "An Assessment of the Construct Validity of Three Job Evaluation Methods: A Field Experiment," *Academy of Management Journal* (1993), 36(4): 895–904.

15 Ibid.

16 G. D. Jenkins and N. Gupta, "The Payoffs of Paying for Knowledge," *National Productivity Review* (1985), 4: 121–130.

17 Adrienne Colella, Ramona Paetzold, Asghar Zardkoohi, and Michael Wesson, "Exposing Pay Secrecy," *Academy of Management Review* (2007), 32: 35–56.

18 Bureau of National Affairs, U.S. Chamber of Commerce data (Sept. 1, 2006).

19 "Detroit Meets a 'Worker Paradise,'" *Wall Street Journal* (Mar. 3, 1999): B1, B4.

20 For a recent discussion of these issues, see Maureen Minehan, "Islam's Growth Affects Workplace Policies," *HR Magazine* (Nov. 1998): 216.

21 Mina Westman and Dov Eden, "Effects of Respite from Work on Burnout: Vacation Relief and Fade-Out," *Journal of Applied Psychology* (Aug. 1997): 516–527.

22 Richard Wolfe and Donald Parker, "Employee Health Management: Challenges and Opportunities," *Academy of Management Executive* (1994), 8(2): 22–31.

23 Tamara Lytle, "Six Critical Health Care Reform Issues" *AARP Bulletin Today* (May 13, 2009).

24 "Health Care Reform," *HR Issues Update* (SHRM) (Jan. 12, 2010).

25 "Employer Benefit Surveys Target Unhealthy Habits," *USA Today* (May 28, 1998): 1B.

26 S. Caudron, "The Wellness Pay Off," *Personnel Journal* (July 1990): 55–60.

27 Shirley Hand and Robert Zawacki, "Family-Friendly Benefits: More Than a Frill," *HR Magazine* (Oct. 1994): 74–79.

28 E. E. Kossek and V. Nichol, "The Effects of On-Site Child Care on Employee Attitudes and Performance," *Personnel Psychology* (1992), 45: 485–509.

29 Rudy Yandrick, "The EAP Struggle: Counselors or Referrers?" *HR Magazine* (Aug. 1998): 90–91.

30 W. J. Sonnenstuhl and H. M. Trice, *Strategies for Employee Assistance Programs: The Crucial Balance* (Ithaca, NY: Cornell University ILR Press, 1990).

31 Melissa Barringer and George Milkovich, "A Theoretical Exploration of the Adoption and Design of Flexible Benefit Plans: A Case of Human Resource Innovation," *Academy of Management Review* (Apr. 1998): 305–324.

32 A. E. Barber, R. B. Dunham, and R. A. Formisano, "The Impact of Flexible Benefits on Employee Satisfaction: A Field Study," *Personnel Psychology* (1992), 45: 55–57.

33 "Gay Employees Win Benefits for Partners at More Corporations," *Wall Street Journal* (Mar. 18, 1994): A1.

34 Louise Story, "Goldman Sachs Considers Charity Requirement," *New York Times* (July 11, 2009), business section: 1.

35 Ibid.

36 DealBook, *New York Times* (July 30, 2009).

37 T. A. Steward, "The Trouble with Stock Options," *Fortune* (Jan. 1, 1990): 93–95.

38 Harry Barkema and Luis Gomez-Mejia, "Managerial Compensation and Firm Performance: A General Research Framework," *Academy of Management Journal* (1998), 41(2): 135–145.

39 Rajiv D. Banker, Seok-Young Lee, Gordon Potter, and Dhinu Srinivasan, "Contextual Analysis of Performance Impacts of Outcome-Based Incentive Compensation," *Academy of Management Journal* (1996), 39(4): 920–948.

40 J. Pfeffer and N. Langton, "The Effects of Wage Dispersion on Satisfaction, Productivity and Working Collaboratively: Evidence from College and University Faculty," *Administrative Science Quarterly* (1993), 38: 382–407.

41 R. G. Ehrenberg and M. L. Bognanno, "The Incentive Effects of Tournaments Revisited: Evidence from the European PGA Tour," *Industrial and Labor Relations Review* (1990), 43: 74–88.

42 For a more in-depth discussion of the requirements and advantages of qualification, see Michael Sarli, "Nondiscrimination Rules for Qualified Plans: The General Test," *Compensation and Benefits Review* (Sept. 1991): 56–67.

43 H. W. Hennessey, P. L. Perrewe, and W. A. Hochwarter, "Impact of Benefit Awareness on Employee and Organizational Outcomes: A Longitudinal Field Experiment," *Benefits Quarterly* (1992), 8(2): 90–96.

44 M. Wilson, G. B. Northcraft, and M. A. Neale, "The Perceived Value of Fringe Benefits," *Personnel Psychology* (1985), 38: 309–320.

45 Michael Orey, "Wage Wars," *Business Week* (Oct. 1, 2007): 50–60 (quote); Steven Greenhouse, "Restaurants Must Rehire Deliverymen, Judge Rules," *New York Times* (Feb. 21, 2008) (www.nytimes.com, Mar. 23, 2008); "The Clock and the Paycheck," *Business Week* (Oct. 15, 2007) (www.businessweek.com, March 23, 2008).

Chapter 10

1 "Goodyear to Stop Labeling 10% of Its Workers as Worst," *USA Today* (Sept. 11, 2002): B1, B2; "Goodyear Backs Down," *Beacon Journal* (Sept. 12, 2002): A15; Cathleen Flahardy, "Companies Should Get Their Policies in Order to Avoid Potential Age Discrimination Lawsuits," InsideCounsel.com (Nov. 18, 2006); "Using the ABC Method to Boost Performance," *HR Magazine* (Nov. 2008): 36.

2 See Chapter 8 in Charles R. Greer, *Strategy and Human Resources* (Englewood Cliffs, NJ: Prentice-Hall, 1995), for a review of the strategic importance of performance management in organizations.

3 W. Timothy Weaver, "Linking Performance Reviews to Productivity and Quality," *HR Magazine* (Nov. 1996): 93–98.

4 A. S. DeNisi, *Cognitive Approach to Performance Appraisal: A Program of Research* (London: Routledge, 1996).

5 For several excellent reviews of these "cognitive" decision-making processes on the part of the rater, see A. S. DeNisi, T. P. Cafferty, and B. Meglino, "A Cognitive Model of the Performance Appraisal Process," *Organizational Behavior and Human Decision Processes* (1984), 33: 360–396; and D. R. Ilgen and J. M. Feldman, "Performance Appraisal: A Process Focus," in B. Staw and L. Cummings (Eds.), *Research in Organizational Behavior*, Vol. 5 (Greenwich, CT: JAI Press, 1983).

6 Arup Varma, Angelo S. DeNisi, and Lawrence H. Peters, "Interpersonal Affect and Performance Appraisal: A Field Study," *Personnel Psychology* (Summer 1996): 341–360.

7 K. Kraiger and K. Ford, "A Meta-Analysis of Ratee Race Effects in Performance Rating," *Journal of Applied Psychology* (1985), 70: 56–65.

8 See, for example, J. N. Cleveland, R. M. Festa, and L. Montgomery, "Applicant Pool Composition and Job Perceptions: Impact on Decisions Regarding an Older Applicant," *Journal of Vocational Behavior* (1988), 32: 112–125.

9 For example, see the review by V. F. Nieva and B. Gutek, "Sex Effects in Evaluations," *Academy of Management Review* (1980), 5: 267–276.

10 A. Colella, A. S. DeNisi, and A. Varma, "A Model of the Impact of Disability on Performance Evaluations," *Human Resource Management Review* (1997), 7: 27–53.

11 For example, see Kevin R. Murphy and Jeanette N. Cleveland, *Understanding Performance Appraisal: Social, Organizational, and Goal-Based Perspectives* (Thousand Oaks, CA: Sage Publications, 1995).

12 Forest J. Jourden and Chip Heath, "The Evaluation Gap in Performance Perceptions: Illusory Perceptions of Groups and Individuals," *Journal of Applied Psychology* (1988), 81(4): 369–379.

13 Angelo S. DeNisi, W. Alan Randolph, and Allyn G. Blencoe, "Potential Problems with Peer Ratings," *Academy of Management Journal* (1983), 26: 457–467.

14 Leanne Atwater, Paul Roush, and Allison Fischtal, "The Influence of Upward Feedback on Self- and Follower Ratings of Leadership," *Personnel Psychology* (Spring 1995): 35–59.

15 See, for example, Alan Walker and James Smither, "A Five-Year Study of Upward Feedback: What Managers Do with Their Results Matters," *Personnel Psychology* (1999), 52: 393–423.

16 For a good review of the work in this area, see David Waldman and Leanne Atwater, *The Power of 360-Degree Feedback: How to Leverage Performance Evaluations for Top Productivity* (Houston: Gulf Publishing, 2000).

17 James M. Conway, "Analysis and Design of Multitrait-Multirater Performance Appraisal Studies," *Journal of Management*, 22(1): 139–162.

18 For an in-depth discussion of these problems, see Susan Haworth, "The Dark Side of Multi-Rater Assessments," *HR Magazine* (May 1998): 106–112; or Angelo DeNisi and Avraham Kluger, "Feedback Effectiveness: Can 360-Degree Appraisals Be Improved?" *Academy of Management Executive*, 14: 129–139.

19 See discussions of these processes in Walter Borman, "Exploring the Upper Limits of Reliability and Validity in Job Performance Ratings," *Journal of Applied Psychology* (1978), 63: 135–144; and DeNisi, Cafferty, and Meglino, "A Cognitive Model of the Performance Appraisal Process."

20 See, for example, H. John Bernardin and C. S. Walter, "Effects of Rater and Training and Diary Keeping on Psychometric Errors in Ratings," *Journal of Applied Psychology* (1977), 62: 64–69; or Angelo DeNisi, Tina Robbins, and Thomas Cafferty, "The Organization of Information Used for Performance Appraisals: The Role of Diary Keeping," *Journal of Applied Psychology* (1989), 74: 124–129.

21 For an excellent review of some relevant court cases, see Jon Werner and Mark Bolino, "Explaining U.S. Courts of Appeals Decisions Involving Performance Appraisal: Accuracy, Fairness, and Validation," *Personnel Psychology* (1997), 50: 1–24.

22 Andrew Likierman, The Five Traps of Performance Measurement," *Harvard Business Review* (Oct. 2009): 96–105.

23 For a more complete discussion of the proper focus for appraisals in different settings, see Angelo DeNisi, "Performance Appraisal and Control Systems: A Multilevel Approach," in K. Klein and S. Kozlowski (Eds.), *Multilevel Theory, Research, and Methods in Organizations*, SIOP Frontiers Series (San Francisco: Jossey-Bass, 2000): 121–156.

24 E. D. Sisson, "Forced Choice: The New Army Rating," *Personnel Psychology* (1948), 1: 365–381.

25 J. C. Flanagan, "The Critical Incident Technique," *Psychological Bulletin* (1954), 51: 327–358.

26 J. C. Flanagan and R. K. Burns, "The Employee Performance Record: A New Appraisal and Development Tool," *Harvard Business Review* (Sept.–Oct. 1955): 95–102.

27 P. C. Smith and L. M. Kendall, "Retranslation of Expectations: An Approach to the Construction of Unambiguous Anchors for Rating Scales," *Journal of Applied Psychology* (1963), 47: 149–155.

28 H. J. Barnardin, M. B. LaShells, P. C. Smith, and K. M. Alvares, "Behavioral Expectation Scales: Effects of Development Procedures and Formats," *Journal of Applied Psychology* (1976), 61: 75–79.

29 G. P. Latham, C. H. Fay, and L. M. Saari, "The Development of Behavioral Observation Scales for Appraising the Performance of Foremen," *Personnel Psychology* (1979), 33: 815–821.

30 For an excellent review of the variations on these methods, see Chapter 4 in H. J. Bernardin and R. W. Beatty, *Performance Appraisal: Assessing Human Behavior at Work* (Boston: PWS-Kent, 1984).

31 See, for example, Joseph Mishra and Susan Crampton, "Employee Monitoring: Privacy in the Workplace?" *SAM Advanced Management Journal* (1998), 53: 4.

32 See Elizabeth Douthitt and John R. Aiello, "The Role of Participation and Control in the Effects of Computer Monitoring on Fairness Perceptions, Task Satisfaction, and Performance," *Journal of Applied Psychology* (2001), 86: 867–874.

33 American Management Association, *Workplace Monitoring and Surveillance: A 1999 AMA Survey* (New York: American Management Association, 2000).

34 See, for example, reviews by Frank Landy and James Farr, "Performance Rating," *Psychological Bulletin* (1980), 87: 72–102; or Angelo DeNisi, *A Cognitive Approach to Performance Appraisal* (London: Routledge, 1996): 1–20.

35 Jeffrey S. Kane, H. John Bernardin, Peter Villanova, and Joseph Peyrefitte, "Stability of Rater Leniency: Three Studies," *Academy of Management Journal* (1995), 38(4): 1036–1051.

36 Walter C. Borman, Leonard A. White, and David W. Dorsey, "Effects of Ratee Task Performance and Interpersonal Factors on Supervisor and Peer Performance Ratings," *Journal of Applied Psychology* (1995), 80(1): 168–177.

37 Juan I. Sanchez and Phillip De La Torre, "A Second Look at the Relationship Between Rating and Behavioral Accuracy in Performance Appraisal," *Journal of Applied Psychology* (1996), 81(1): 3–10.

38 See also Michael Hammer, "The 7 Deadly Sins of Performance Measurement (And How to Avoid Them)," *MIT Sloan Management Review* (Spring 2009): 36–45.

39 W. C. Borman, "Job Behavior, Performance, and Effectiveness," in M. D. Dunnette and L. Hough (Eds.), *Handbook of Industrial and Organizational Psychology*, Vol. 2, 2nd ed. (Palo Alto, CA: Consulting Psychologists Press, 1991); W. C. Borman and S. J. Motowidlo, "Expanding the Criterion Domain to Include Elements of Contextual Performance," in N. Schmitt and W. Borman (Eds.), *Personnel Selection in Organizations* (San Francisco: Jossey-Bass, 1993).

40 D. W. Organ and K. Ryan, "A Meta-Analytic Review of Attitudinal and Dispositional Predictors of Organizational Citizenship Behavior," *Personnel Psychology* (1995), 48: 775–802.

41 J. M. Werner, "Dimensions That Make a Difference: Examining the Impact of In-Role and Extrarole Behaviors on Supervisory Ratings," *Journal of Applied Psychology* (1994), 79: 98–107.

42 Maria Rotundo and Paul Sackett, "The Relative Importance of Task, Citizenship, and Counterproductive Performance to Global Ratings of Job Performance: A Policy-Capturing Study," *Journal of Applied Psychology* (2002), 87: 66–80.

43 *Brito v. Zia Company*, 478 F. 2d 1200 (10th Cir. 1973).

44 Manuel London, "Redeployment and Continuous Learning in the 21st Century: Hard Lessons and Positive Examples from the Downsizing Era," *Academy of Management Executive* (Nov. 1996): 67–79.

45 Adrianne H. Geiger-DuMond and Susan K. Boyle, "Mentoring: A Practitioner's Guide," *Training & Development* (Mar. 1995): 51–55.

46 Douglas T. Hall, "Protean Careers of the 21st Century," *Academy of Management Executive* (Nov. 1996): 8–16.

47 Ibid.

48 For a discussion of a wide variety of issues at every stage in one's career, see Daniel Feldman (Ed.), *Work Careers: A Developmental Perspective* (San Francisco: Jossey-Bass, 2002).

49 See Boris Groysberg and Robin Abrahams, "Five Ways to Bungle a Job Change," *Harvard Business Review* (Jan.–Feb. 2010): 137–140.

50 Bruce Avolio and David Waldman, "Variations in Cognitive, Perceptual, and Psychomotor Abilities Across the Working Life Span: Examining the Effects of Race, Sex, Experience, Education, and Occupational Type," *Psychology and Aging* (1994), 9: 430–442.

51 See for example, reviews by Glen McEvoy and Wayne Cascio, "Cumulative Evidence of the Relationship Between Employee Age and Job Performance," *Journal of Applied Psychology* (1989), 74(1): 11–17; and Susan Rhoades, "Age-Related Differences in Work Attitudes and Behavior: A Review and Conceptual Analysis," *Psychological Bulletin*, 93: 328–367.

52 Terry Beehr, "The Process of Retirement: A Review and Recommendations," *Personnel Psychology* (1986), 39(1): 31–55.

53 "The 100 Best Companies to Work For," *Fortune* (Feb. 8, 2010): 75–88.

54 Gregory K. Stephens, "Crossing Internal Career Boundaries: The State of Research on Subjective Career Transitions," *Journal of Management* (1994), 20(2): 479–501.

55 Suzyn Ornstein and Lynn A. Isabella, "Making Sense of Careers: A Review 1989–1992," *Journal of Management* (1993), 19(2): 243–267.

56 Kenneth R. Brousseau, Michael J. Driver, Kristina Eneroth, and Rikard Larsson, "Career Pandemonium: Realigning Organizations and Individuals," *Academy of Management Executive* (Nov. 1996): 52–66.

57 M. Ferber, B. O'Farrell, and L. Allen, *Work and Family: Policies for a Changing Workforce* (Washington, DC: National Academy Press, 1994).

58 H. Morgan and K. Tucker, *Companies That Care: The Most Family-Friendly Companies in America, What They Offer, and How They Got That Way* (New York: Simon & Schuster, 1991).

59 S. Zedeck and K. L. Mosier, "Work in Family and Employing Organizations," *American Psychologist* (1990), 45: 240–251.

60 V. J. Doby and R. D. Caplan, "Organizational Stress as Threat to Reputation: Effects on Anxiety at Work and at Home," *Academy of Management Journal* (1995), 38: 1105–1123.

61 P. B. Doeringer, "Economic Security, Labor Market Flexibility, and Bridges to Retirement," in P. B. Doeringer (Ed.), *Bridges to Retirement* (Ithaca, NY: Cornell University ILR Press, 1990): 3–22.

62 "The Midyear Review's Sudden Impact," *Business Week* (July 6, 2009): 50–52; "Early Performance Reviews: Taking the Bad With the Good," *Wall Street Journal* (Mar. 3, 2006): B6; "Getting a Jump Start with an Early Review," *USA Today* (Nov. 13, 2005): 1B; "New Hires Win Fast Raises in Accelerated Job Reviews," *Wall Street Journal* (Oct. 6, 1998): B1, B16.

Chapter 11

1 "Dividing Line is Drawn," *USA Today* (Mar. 3, 2010): 1C, 2C; "MLS: No Talks, No Posturing," *USA Today* (Mar. 5, 2010): 2C; *Hoover's Handbook of Private Companies 2009* (Austin: Hoover's Business Press, 2010): 28.

2 David Lipsky and Clifford Donn, *Collective Bargaining in American Industry* (Lexington, MA: Lexington Books, 1981).

3 "Two Rebel Unions Split From AFL-CIO," *USA Today* (July 26, 2005): 1B, 2B.

4 Alabama, Arkansas, Florida, Georgia, Iowa, Kansas, Kentucky, Louisiana, Mississippi, Nebraska, Nevada, North Carolina, North Dakota, South Carolina, South Dakota, Tennessee, Texas, Utah, Virginia, and Wyoming are right-to-work states, although a state can change its status on this issue at any time.

5   "Ford Says 38,000 Have Taken Buyouts," *Wall Street Journal* (Nov. 29, 2006): B1, B14; "38,000 Ford Workers Take Buyout Offers," *USA Today* (Nov. 29, 2006): 1B, 2B.

6   Chris Isidore, "GM Bankruptcy: End of an Ara," CNN Money.com (June 2, 2009).

7   "GM Emerges from Bankruptcy," Associated Press (reported in *New York Post*) (July 10, 2009).

8   "Companies Counter Unions," *USA Today* (Sept. 1997): 1B, 2B.

9   Edward E. Lawler III and Susan A. Mohrman, "Unions and the New Management," *Academy of Management Executive* (1987), 1(3): 65–75.

10 "Reinventing the Union," *Wall Street Journal* (July 27, 2006): B1, B2.

11 "Why Mexico Scares the UAW," *Business Week* (Aug. 3, 1998): 37–38.

12 Clive Fullagar, Paul Clark, Daniel Gallagher, and Michael E. Gordon, "A Model of the Antecedents of the Early Union Commitment: The Role of Socialization Experiences and Steward Characteristics," *Journal of Organizational Behavior* (1994), 15: 517–533.

13 Stuart Youngblood, Angelo DeNisi, Julie Molleston, and William Mobley, "The Impact of Worker Attachment, Instrumentality Beliefs, Perceived Labor Union Image, and Subjective Norms on Voting Intentions and Union Membership," *Academy of Management Journal* (1984), 27: 576–590.

14 J. Barling, E. K. Kelloway, and E. H. Bremermann, "Pre-Employment Predictors of Union Attitudes: The Role of Family Socialization and Work Beliefs," *Journal of Applied Psychology* (1991), 75: 725–731.

15 "Some Unions Step Up Organizing Campaigns and Get New Members," *Wall Street Journal* (Sept. 1, 1995): A1, A2.

16 See Jeanette A. Davy and Frank Shipper, "Voter Behavior in Union Certification Elections: A Longitudinal Study," *Academy of Management Journal* (1993), 36(1): 187–199, for a discussion of some of the determinants of individual voting behavior in union elections.

17 HRhero.com, "Employee Free Choice Act—EFCA" (Sept. 2009).

18 Adapted from R. E. Walton and R. B. McKersie, *A Behavioral Theory of Labor Negotiations* (New York: McGraw-Hill, 1965). Note that we have used the terminology used by those authors, which is adapted from game theory. The reader might encounter different terms in other treatments of bargaining, but the concepts are the same as those described here.

19 "ABC Locks Out Striking Employees," *USA Today* (Nov. 3, 1998): B1.

20 Phil Taylor, "To the Victor Belong the Spoils," *Sports Illustrated* (Jan. 18, 1999): 48–52.

21 H. S. Farber and H. C. Katz, "Interest Arbitration, Outcomes, and the Incentive to Bargain," *Industrial and Labor Relations Review* (1979), 33: 55–63.

22 P. Feuille, "Final Offer Arbitration and the Chilling Effect," *Industrial Relations* (1975), 14: 302–310.

23 See Kevin Banks, "Contingent and Informal Workers in North America: Workplace Human Rights," *Proceedings of the 53rd Annual Meeting of the Industrial Relations Research Association*, New Orleans (2001): 90–98.

24 For a complete discussion of the issues and the rulings in this area, see Camille Olson and Michael Rybick, "Spotlight on Union Organizing: 'No Solicitation No Distribution' and Related Rules in the Age of E-mail and the Internet," *Legal Report* (published by Society of Human Resource Managers) (May–June 2002): 5–7.

25 Nathan Newman, "Union and Community Mobilization in the Information Age," *Perspectives on Work* (2002), 6(2): 9–11.

26 Sources: "What's Really Behind GM's Strike? A Battle Over a Hot New Truck," *Wall Street Journal* (July 28, 1998): A1, A5; "What Price Peace?" *Business Week* (Aug. 10, 1998): 24–25; "GM Might Stop Benefits for Workers," *USA Today* (June 26, 1998): B1; "Rivals Make Strides After Nasty Strike," *USA Today* (Dec. 16, 1998): B1, B2.

27 "Harley Union Makes Concessions," *Wall Street Journal* (Dec. 3, 2009): B3; "GM, UAW Reach Crucial Cost-Cutting Pact," *Wall Street Journal* (May 22, 2009): B1.

Chapter 12

1   *Hoover's Handbook of American Business 2009* (Austin: Hoover's Business Press, 2010): 340–341; "FedEx Philosophy," "Team Member Benefits," FedEx Web site (www.fedex.com), Mar. 3, 2010; "HR's Push for Productivity," *Employee InfoLink* (Aug. 23, 2002): 19–26; Claudia H. Deutsch, "Planes, Trucks and 7.5 Million Packages: FedEx's Big Night," *New York Times* (Dec. 21, 2003): BU; Shu Shin Luh, "Asian Employers Give Workers Training, Respect and Merit Pay," *Asian Wall Street Journal* (Mar. 14, 2005): 25.

2   "Working at Home Raises Job Site Safety Issues," *USA Today* (Jan. 29, 1998): 1A.

3   "Labor Secretary's Bid to Push Plant Safety Runs into Skepticism," *Wall Street Journal* (Aug. 19, 1994): A1, A5.

4   R. S. Haynes, R. C. Pine, and H. G. Fitch, "Reducing Accident Rates with Organizational Behavior Modification," *Academy of Management Journal* (1988), 25: 407–416.

5   Dov Zohar, "Safety Climate in Industrial Organizations: Theoretical and Applied Implications," *Journal of Applied Psychology* (1980), 65: 96–102.

6   See, for example, Andrew Wills, Barry Watson, and Herbert Biggs, "An Exploratory Investigation into Safety Climate and Work-Related Driving," *Work: A Journal of Prevention, Assessment, and Rehabilitation*, 32: 81–94.

7   "In an Amoco Lab, Researchers Hunt for Colleagues' Killer," *USA Today* (Apr. 13, 1999): 8D.

8   Myron D. Fottler, "Employee Acceptance of a Four Day Work Week," *Academy of Management Journal* (1977), 20: 656–668.

9   S. Ronen and S. B. Primpts, "The Compressed Work Week as Organizational Change: Behavioral and Attitudinal Outcomes," *Academy of Management Review* (1981), 6: 61–74.

10 A. Purach, "Biological Rhythm Effects of Night Work and Shift Changes on the Health of Workers," *Acta Medica Scandinavia* (1973), 152: 302–307.

11 S. Zedeck, S. E. Jackson, and E. S. Marca, "Shift Work Schedules and Their Relationship to Health, Adaptation, Satisfaction, and Turnover Intentions," *Academy of Management Journal* (1983), 26: 297–310.

12 G. B. Meese, M. I. Lewis, D. P. Wyon, and R. Kok, "A Laboratory Study of the Effects of Thermal Stress on the Performance of Factory Workers," *Ergonomics* (1982), 27: 19–43.

13 E. Van de Vliert and N. W. Van Yperen, "Why Cross National Differences in Role Overload? Don't Overlook Ambient Temperature," *Academy of Management Journal* (1996), 39: 986–1004.

14 D. G. Hayward, "Psychological Factors in the Use of Light and Lighting in Buildings," in J. Lang, C. Burnette, W. Moleski, and D. Vachon (Eds.), *Designing for Human Behavior: Architecture and the Behavioral Sciences* (Stroudsburg, PA: Dowden, Hutchinson, & Ross, 1974): 120–129.

15 R. I. Newman, D. L. Hunt, and F. Rhodes, "Effects of Music on Employee Attitude and Productivity in a Skateboard Factory," *Journal of Applied Psychology* (1956), 50: 493–496.

16 G. R. Oldham, A. Cummings, L. J. Mischel, J. M. Scmidtke, and J. Zhou, "Listen While You Work? Quasi-Experimental Relations Between Personal Stereo Headset Use and Employee Work Responses," *Journal of Applied Psychology* (1995), 80: 547–564.

17 G. R. Oldham, "Effects of Changes in Workspace Partitions and Spatial Density on Employee Reactions: A Quasi-Experiment," *Journal of Applied Psychology* (1988), 73: 253–258.

18 Karen Danna and Ricky W. Griffin, "Health and Well-Being in the Workplace," *Journal of Management* (1999), 19: 125–146.

19 "Workplace Demands Taking up More Weekends," *USA Today* (Apr. 24, 1998): 1B.

20 Myron Friedman and Robert Rosenman, *Type A Personality and Your Heart* (New York: Knopf, 1974).

21 James C. Quick and Jonathan D. Quick, *Organizational Stress and Preventive Management* (New York: McGraw-Hill, 1984).

22 David Turnipseed, "An Exploratory Study of the Hardy Personality at Work in the Health Care Industry," *Psychological Reports* (1999), 85: 1199–1218.

23 Daniel Ganster and John Schaubroeck, "Work Stress and Employee Health," *Journal of Management* (1991), 17: 235–271.

24 Debra Nelson and James Quick, "Professional Women: Are Distress and Disease Inevitable?" *Academy of Management Review* (1985), 10: 206–213.

25 Richard S. DeFrank and John M. Ivancevich, "Stress on the Job: An Executive Update," *Academy of Management Executive* (1998), 12(3): 55–67.

26 "U.S Job Satisfaction Declines," *The Conference Board Reports* (**Feb. 23, 2007**).

27 See Anne O'Leary-Kelly, Ricky W. Griffin, and David J. Glew, "Organization-Motivated Aggression: A Research Framework," *Academy of Management Review* (Jan. 1996): 225–253.

28 See, for example, Wendy Boswell, Julie Olson-Buchanan, and Marcie Cavanaugh, "Investigation of the Relationship Between Work-Related Stress and Work Outcomes: The Role of Felt Challenge, Psychological Strain, and Job Control," paper presented at the Academy of Management meetings, Toronto, Ontario (2000); and Marcie Cavanaugh, Wendy Boswell, Mark Roehling, and John Boudreau, "An Empirical Examination of Self-Reported Work Stress Among U.S. Managers," *Journal of Applied Psychology* (2000), 85: 65–74.

29 See, for example, Cynthia McCauley, Marian Ruderman, Patricia Ohlott, and Jane Morrow, "Assessing the Developmental Components of Managerial Jobs," *Journal of Applied Psychology* (1994), 79: 544–560.

30 Kathy Gerchiek, "Report Cites Barriers to Wellness Programs' Effectiveness," *HR News* (June 27, 2006).

31 World Health Organization, Global Alert and Response, H1N1 Alert 84 (Jan. 22, 2010).

32 For example, see "Ensuring Preparedness Against the H1N1 Flu Virus at School and Work," U.S. Department of Labor, Occupational Safety and health Administration Bulletin (May 7, 2009).

33 Joel Brockner, Stephen Grover, Thomas Reed, and Rocki DeWitt, "Layoffs, Job Insecurity and Survivors' Work Effort: Evidence of an Inverted-U Relationship," *Academy of Management Journal* (1996), 35: 413–435.

34 Randolph Schmid, "Study Ranks States with the Happiest People: Louisiana Ranks First and New York Ranks Last," *Chicago Times Archive* (Dec. 18, 2009).

35 Anne Fisher, "Danger Zone," *Fortune* (Sept. 8, 1997): 165–167; *Hoover's Handbook of American Business 2009* (Austin: Hoover's Business Press, 2010): 402–403.

Chapter 13

1 "Caring for Community," Pfizer Web site (www.pfizer.com) (Mar. 4, 2010); "Volunteers by Annual Hours," Bureau of Labor Statistics Web site (www.bls.gov) (Sept. 2009); "A Corporate Peace Corps Catches On," *Business Week* (Jan. 31, 2005): 56–58; William J. Holstein, "The Snowball Effect of Volunteer Work," *New York Times* (Nov. 21, 2004): BU12; "Tsunami Relief Aid at $6.28 Billion—U.N." *Washington Post* (Feb. 25, 2005): 1.

2 Abraham H. Maslow, "A Theory of Human Motivation," *Psychological Review* (1943), 50: 370–396; Abraham H. Maslow, *Motivation and Personality* (New York: Harper & Row, 1954).

3 Mahmond A. Wahba and Lawrence G. Bridwell, "Maslow Reconsidered: A Review of Research on the Need Hierarchy Theory," *Organizational Behavior and Human Performance* (Apr. 1976): 212–240.

4 Frederick Herzberg, Bernard Mausner, and Barbara Synderman, *The Motivation to Work* (New York: John Wiley & Sons, 1959); Frederick Herzberg, "One More Time: How Do You Motivate Employees?" *Harvard Business Review* (Jan.–Feb. 1968): 53–62.

5 Marvin Dunnette, John Campbell, and Milton Hakel, "Factors Contributing to Job Satisfaction and Job Dissatisfaction in Six Occupational Groups," *Organizational Behavior and Human Performance* (May 1967): 143–174; Charles L. Hulin and Patricia Smith, "An Empirical Investigation of Two Implications of the Two-Factor Theory of Job Satisfaction," *Journal of Applied Psychology* (Oct. 1967): 396–402.

6 B. F. Skinner, *Science and Human Behavior* (New York: Macmillian, 1953) and *Beyond Freedom and Dignity* (New York: Knopf, 1972).

7 Alexander D. Stajkovic, "A Meta-Analysis of the Effects of Organizational Behavior Modification on Task Performance, 1975–95," *Academy of Management Journal* (1997): 40(5): 1122–1149.

8 Fred Luthans and Robert Kreitner, *Organizational Behavior Modification and Beyond* (Glenview, IL: Scott, Foresman, 1985).

9 Victor Vroom, *Work and Motivation* (New York: John Wiley & Sons, 1964).

10 Craig Pinder, *Work Motivation in Organizational Behavior* (Upper Saddle River, NJ: Prentice Hall, 1998).

11 See Terence R. Mitchell, "Expectancy Models of Job Satisfaction, Occupational Preference, and Effort: A Theoretical, Methodological, and Empirical Appraisal," *Psychological Bulletin* (1974), 81: 1096–1112; and John P. Campbell and Robert D. Pritchard, "Motivation Theory in Industrial and Organizational Psychology," in Marvin D. Dunnette (Ed.), *Handbook of Industrial and Organizational Psychology* (Chicago: Rand McNally, 1976): 63–130 for reviews.

12 Lyman W. Porter and Edward E. Lawler, *Managerial Attitudes and Performance* (Homewood, IL: Dorsey Press, 1968).

13 James C. Naylor, Robert D. Pritchard, and Daniel R. Ilgen, *A Theory of Behavior in Organizations* (New York: Academic Press, 1980).

14 J. Stacy Adams, "Inequity in Social Exchange," in L. Berkowitz (Ed.), *Advances in Experimental Social Psychology*, Vol. 2 (New York: Academic Press, 1965): 267–299.

15 Craig Pinder, *Work Motivation in Organizational Behavior* (Upper Saddle River, NJ: Prentice Hall, 1998).

16 See Nancy Adler, *International Dimensions of Organizational Behavior*, 3rd ed. (Boston: PWS-Kent, 1997).

17 Priti Pradham Shah, "Who Are Employees' Social Referents? Using a Network Perspective to Determine Referent Others," *Academy of Management Journal* (1998), 41(3): 249–268.

18 Reinforcement theory and expectancy theory would seem to be in conflict in some instances, mostly in cases of partial reinforcement schedules. A discussion or attempted resolution of these differences is far beyond the scope of the current discussion.

19 See Edwin A. Locke, "Toward a Theory of Task Performance and Incentives," *Organizational Behavior and Human Performance* (1968), 3: 157–189.

20 Gary P. Latham and Gary Yukl, "A Review of Research on the Application of Goal Setting in Organizations," *Academy of Management Journal* (1975), 18: 824–845.

21 Gary P. Latham and J. J. Baldes, "The Practical Significance of Locke's Theory of Goal Setting," *Journal of Applied Psychology* (1975), 60: 187–191.

22 Gary P. Latham, "The Importance of Understanding and Changing Employee Outcome Expectancies for Gaining Commitment to an Organizational Goal," *Personnel Psychology* (2001), 54: 707–720.

23 See Michael Jensen and William Meckling, "Theory of the Firm: Managerial Behavior, Agency Costs, and Ownership Structure," *Journal of Financial Economics* (1976), 11: 305–360; Eugene Fama, "Agency Problems and the Theory of the Firm," *Journal of Political Economy* (1980), 88: 288–307; and Eugene Fama and Michael Jensen, "Separation of Ownership and Control," *Journal of Law and Economics* (1983), 26: 301–325.

24 See, for example, Richard Johnson, Robert Hoskisson, and Michael Hitt, "Board of Director Involvement in Restructuring: The effects of Board Versus Managerial Controls and Characteristics," *Strategic Management Journal* (1993), 14: 33–50; Rita Kosnik, "Effects of Board Demography and Directors' Incentives on Corporate Greenmail Decisions," *Academy of Management Journal* (1990), 33: 129–150; or Edward Zajac and James Westphal, "The Costs and Benefits of Managerial Incentives and Monitoring in Large U.S. Corporations: When Is More Not Better?" *Strategic Management Journal* (1994), 15: 121–142.

25 Teresa Amabile, "Stimulate Creativity by Fueling Passion," in E. A. Locke (Ed.), *Handbook of Principles of Organizational Behavior* (Oxford, UK: Blackwell Publishing, 2000): 331.

26 For more information, see Edward Deci and Robert Ryan, *Intrinsic Motivation and Self-Determination in Human Behavior* (New York: Plenum, 1985).

27 For a review of this work, see Teresa Amabile, "Stimulate Creativity by Fueling Passion," in E. A. Locke (Ed.), *Handbook of Principles of Organizational Behavior*, pp. 331–341.

28 For example, see the review by James Cameron and William Pierce, "Reinforcement, Reward, and Intrinsic Motivation: A Meta-Analysis," *Review of Educational Research* (1994), 64: 363–423.

29 Greg Oldham and Anne Cummings, "Employee Creativity: Personal and Contextual Factors at Work," *Academy of Management Journal* (1996), 39: 607–634.

30 Jing Zhou and Jennifer George, "When Job Dissatisfaction Leads to Creativity: Encouraging the Expression of Voice," *Academy of Management Journal* (2001), 44: 682–696.

31 Teresa Amabile, "Motivational Synergy: Toward New Conceptualizations of Intrinsic and Extrinsic Motivation in the Workplace," *Human Resource Management Review* (1993), 3: 185–201.

32 Teresa Amabile and S. Gryskiewicz, "Creativity in the R&D Laboratory," *Technical Report No. 30* (Greensboro, NC: Center for Creative Leadership, 1987).

33 Christina Shalley, Lucy Gilson, and Terry Blum, "Matching Creativity Requirements and the Work Environment: Effects on Satisfaction and the Intent to Leave," *Academy of Management Journal* (2000), 43: 215–233.

34 Zhou and George, "When Job Dissatisfaction Leads to Creativity: Encouraging the Expression of Voice."

35 For more information see Todd Dewett, *Differentiating Outcomes in Employee Creativity: Understanding the Role of Risk in Creative Performance* (2002). PhD dissertation submitted to the faculty of the Department of Management, Texas A&M University, College Station, TX.

36 "Services," CollabNet Web site (www.collab.net) (Mar. 3, 2010); "Reps and Marketers: Across the Great Divide," *Business Week*, May 26, 2004, p. 28; "When Sales Meets Marketing: Part I, II, and III," *Business Week* (www.businessweek.com) (Feb. 19, 2005); "The Collaborator," *Forbes* (Mar. 14, 2005): 55.

Chapter 14

1 Daniel Akst, "White-Collar Stress? Stop the Whining," *New York Times* (Sept. 19, 2004): BU6; Lisa Belkin, "Take This Job and Hug It," *New York Times* (Feb. 13, 2005): W1 (quotation); Claudia H. Deutsch, "Grab the Brass Ring, or Just Enjoy the Ride?" *New York Times* (June 27, 2004): BU7; Claudia H. Deutsch, "She Didn't Stop the World, but She Slowed It Down," *New York Times* (Feb. 13, 2005): BU6; Claudia H. Deutsch, "Yes, You Can Follow Your Bliss to Anytown, U.S.A." *New York Times* (Oct. 31, 2004): BU7; Keith Dunnavant, "Cooking Up a New Life," *Business Week Small Biz* (Fall 2004): 53–55; Randall Stross, "When Long Hours at a Video Game Stop Being Fun," *New York Times* (Nov. 21, 2004): BU3; Landon Thomas Jr., "Depression, A Frequent Visitor to Wall St.," *New York Times* (Sept. 12, 2004): BU1, 9.

2 See, for example, Paul Goodman, F. Javier Lerch, and T. Mukhopadhyay, "Individual and Organizational Productivity: Linkages and Processes," in D. H. Harris (Ed.), *Organizational Linkages: Understanding the Productivity Paradox* (Washington, DC: National Academy Press, 1994): 55–80; Steve Kozlowski, Stan Gully, E. Nason, and E. Smith, "Developing Adaptive Teams: A Theory of Compilation and Performance Across Levels and Time," in Dan Ilgen and Elane Pulakos (Eds.), *The Changing Nature of Work and Performance: Implications for Staffing, Personnel Actions and Development* (San Francisco: Jossey-Bass, 1999): 240–292.

3 See Chapter 1 in Charles R. Greer, *Strategy and Human Resources* (Englewood Cliffs, NJ: Prentice-Hall, 1995), for an overview of the importance of training and development.

4 "The making of a UPS Driver," *Fortune* (Nov. 12, 2009): 118–129.

5 "Despite Cutbacks, Firms Invest in Developing Leaders," *Wall Street Journal* (Feb. 9, 2009): B4.

6 Paul Chaddock, "Building Value with Training," *Training & Development* (July 1995): 22–25.

7 Jack Stack, "The Training Myth," *Inc.* (Aug. 1998): 41–42.

8 "Training Takes Front Seat at Offices," *USA Today* (Jan. 19, 1999): 6B.

9 Jane Webster and Joseph J. Martocchio, "The Differential Effects of Software Training Previews on Training Outcomes," *Journal of Management* (1995), 21(4): 757–787.

10 Frederick Herzberg, *Work and the Nature of Man* (Cleveland: World Press, 1966).

11 Robert Ford, "Job Enrichment Lessons from AT&T," *Harvard Business Review* (Jan.–Feb. 1973): 96–106.

12 J. Richard Hackman and Greg R. Oldham, *Work Re-design* (Reading, MA: Addison-Wesley, 1980).

13 Eric Trist and Kenneth Bamforth, "Some Social and Psychological Consequences of the Longwall Method of Coal-Getting," *Human Relations* (1965), 4: 3–38.

14 A. N. Kluger, "Commute Variability and Strain," *Journal of Organizational Behavior* (1998), 19: 147–166.

15 D. Denton, "Using Flextime to Create a Competitive Workforce," *Industrial Management* (Jan.–Feb. 1993): 29–31.

16 Jody Miller and Matt Miller, "Get a Life!" *Fortune* (Nov. 28, 2005): 109–124.

17 J. Pearce and R. Dunham, "The 12-Hour Work Day: A Forty-Eight-Hour, Eight-Day Week," *Academy of Management Journal* (1992), 35: 1086–1098.

18 S. Greengard, "Making the Virtual Office a Reality," *Personnel Journal* (Sept. 1994): 66–79.

19 S. Cauderon, "Working at Home Pays Off," *Personnel Journal* (Nov. 1992): 40–49.

20 "Making Stay-at-Homes Feel Welcome," *Business Week* (Oct. 12, 1998): 155–156.

21 S. D. Atchison, "The Care and Feeding of 'Lone Eagles'," *Business Week* (Nov. 15, 1993): 58.

22 "Saying Adios to the Office," *Business Week* (Oct. 12, 1998): 152–153.

23 G. D. Jenkins, G. E. Ledford, N. Gupta, and D. H. Doty, *Skill-Based Pay* (Scottsdale, AZ: American Compensation Association, 1992).

24 John L. Morris, "Lessons Learned in Skill-Based Pay," *HR Magazine* (June 1996): 136–142.

25 Daniel Wren, *The Evolution of Management Theory*, 4th ed. (New York: Wiley, 1994).

26 C. Wiley, "Incentive Plan Pushes Production," *Personnel Journal* (Aug. 1993): 91.

27 "When Money Isn't Enough," *Forbes* (Nov. 18, 1996): 164–169.

28 Jacquelyn DeMatteo, Lillian Eby, and Eric Sundstrom, "Team-Based Rewards: Current Empirical Evidence and Directions for Future Research," in L. L. Cummings and Barry Staw (Eds.), *Research in Organizational Behavior*, Vol. 20 (Greenwich, CT: JAI Press, 1998): 141–183.

29 Theresa M. Welbourne and Luis R. Gomez-Mejia, "Gain-Sharing: A Critical Review and a Future Research Agenda," *Journal of Management* (1995), 21(3): 559–609.

30 Steve Secklow, "How One Tech Company Played with Timing of Stock Options," *Wall Street Journal* (July 20, 2006): A1, A10.

31 Charles Forelle, James Bandler, and Steve Stecklow, "Brocade Ex-CEO, Two Others Charged in Options Probe," *Wall Street Journal* (July 21, 2006): A1, A8.

32 Kate Ludeman, "To Fill the Feedback Void," *Training & Development* (Aug. 1995): 38–43.

33 Allan H. Church, "First-Rate Multirater Feedback," *Training & Development* (Aug. 1995): 42+.

34 Avraham Kluger and Angelo DeNisi, "Feedback Interventions: An Historical Review, and Meta-Analysis and a Proposed New Model," *Psychological Bulletin* (1996), 119: 254–284.

35 For a full description of the model and its effectiveness, see Robert Pritchard, Steven Jones, Phillip Roth, Karla Stuebing, and Steven Ekeberg, "Effects of Group Feedback, Goal-Setting, and Incentives on Organizational Productivity," *Journal of Applied Psychology* (Monograph) (1988), 73: 337–358; and Robert Pritchard, Steven Jones, Phillip Roth, Karla Steubing, and Steven Ekeberg, "The Evaluation of an Integrated Approach to Measuring Organizational Productivity," *Personnel Psychology* (1989), 42: 69–115.

36 James C. Naylor, Robert D. Pritchard, and Daniel R. Ilgen, *A Theory of Behavior in Organizations* (New York: Academic Press, 1980).

37 For a description of various ProMES projects, see Robert D. Pritchard, H. Holling, F. Lemming, and Barbara Clark (Eds.), *Improving Organizational Performance with the Productivity Measurement and Enhancement System: An International Collaboration* (Huntington, NY: Nova Science, 2002).

38 "About Us," "Awards and Recognitions," "Jobs at HP," and "Work/Life Navigation," Hewlett Packard Company Web site (www.hp.com) (Mar. 8, 2010); "Alternative Work Arrangements at Hewlett Packard," video case (quotation); "Case Study: Hewlett Packard Company," Commuter Challenge Web site (1999) (www.commuter.challenge.org), Oct. 5, 2006; Mary Brandel, "Overview: 100 Best Places to Work in IT," *ComputerWorld* (www.computerworld.com) (June 14, 2004); *Hoover's Handbook of American Business 2009* (Austin: Hoover's Business Press, 2010): 419–420.

INDEX

Index INDEX

Note: Locators with a *t* refer to tables, with an *ex* refer to examples.

Work
Life
Balance

Learn

27.35
27.34

Content correlation for DeNisi/Griffin, HR, 1e

The responsibilities and knowledge required for an effective HR professional are listed below. They are also called the "PHR/SPHR Body of Knowledge."

HR subject matter experts create the PHR/SPHR Body of Knowledge. Their work is guided by research and validated by other HR professionals.

The PHR/SPHR Body of Knowledge is updated regularly to make sure that it represents current practices in the HR profession. The percentages that follow each functional area heading are the PHR and SPHR percentages, respectively.

FUNCTIONAL AREA

01 Strategic Management (12%, 29%)

Developing, contributing to and supporting the organization's mission, vision, values, strategic goals and objectives; formulating policies; guiding and leading the change process; and evaluating HR's contributions to organizational effectiveness.

Responsibilities:

01 Interpret information related to the organization's operations from internal sources, including financial/accounting, business development, marketing, sales, operations and information technology, in order to contribute to the development of the organization's strategic plan.

02 Interpret information from external sources related to the general business environment, industry practices and developments, technological developments, economic environment, labor pool and legal and regulatory environment, in order to contribute to the development of the organization's strategic plan.

03 Participate as a contributing partner in the organization's strategic planning process.

04 Establish strategic relationships with key individuals in the organization to influence organizational decision-making.

05 Establish relationships/alliances with key individuals and organizations in the community to assist in achieving the organization's strategic goals and objectives.

06 Develop and use metrics to evaluate HR's contributions to the achievement of the organization's strategic goals and objectives.

07 Develop and execute strategies for managing organizational change that balance the expectations and needs of the organization, its employees and all other stakeholders.

08 Develop and align the organization's human capital management plan with its strategic plan.

09 Facilitate the development and communication of the organization's core values and ethical behaviors.

10 Reinforce the organization's core values and behavioral expectations through modeling, communication and coaching.

11 Develop and manage the HR budget in a manner consistent with the organization's strategic goals, objectives and values.

12 Provide information for the development and monitoring of the organization's overall budget.

13 Monitor the legislative and regulatory environment for proposed changes and their potential effect on the organization, taking appropriate proactive steps to support, modify or oppose the proposed changes.

14 Develop policies and procedures to support corporate governance initiatives (for example, board of directors training, whistleblower protection, code of conduct).

15 Participate in enterprise risk management by examining HR policies to evaluate their potential risks to the organization.

16 Identify and evaluate alternatives and recommend strategies for vendor selection and/or outsourcing (for example, HRIS, benefits, payroll).

17 Participate in strategic decision-making and due diligence activities related to organizational structure and design (for example, corporate restructuring, mergers and acquisitions [M&A], off shoring, divestitures). **SPHR ONLY.**

18 Determine strategic application of integrated technical tools and systems (for example, HRIS, performance management tools, applicant tracking, compensation tools, employee self-service technologies).

Knowledge of:

01 The organization's mission, vision, values, business goals, objectives, plans and processes. (chpt 4, pp 79-80)

02 Legislative and regulatory processes. (chpt 2, pp 22-49)

03 Strategic planning process and implementation. (chpt 5, pp 101-104)

04 Management functions, including planning, organizing, directing and controlling. (chpt 4, pp 80-81)

05 Techniques to promote creativity and innovation. (chpt 13, pp 296-297)

06 Corporate governance procedures and compliance (for example, Sarbanes-Oxley Act). (cpht 4, pp 81-82)

07 Transition techniques for corporate restructuring, M&A, offshoring and divestitures. **SPHR ONLY.** (chpt 6, pp 122-128, 136-138; chpt 1, pp 6-7)

FUNCTIONAL AREA

02 Workforce Planning and Employment (26%, 17%)

Developing, implementing and evaluating sourcing, recruitment, hiring, orientation, succession planning, retention and organizational exit programs necessary to ensure the workforce's ability to achieve the organization's goals and objectives.

Responsibilities:

01 Ensure that workforce planning and employment activities are compliant with applicable federal, state and local laws and regulations.

02 Identify workforce requirements to achieve the organization's short-and long-term goals and objectives (for example, corporate restructuring, M&A activity, workforce expansion or reduction).

03 Conduct job analyses to create job descriptions and identify job competencies.

04 Identify and document essential job functions for positions.

05 Establish hiring criteria based on job descriptions and required competencies.

06 Analyze labor market for trends that affect the ability to meet workforce requirements (for example, SWOT analysis, environmental scan, demographic scan). **SPHR ONLY.**

07 Assess skill sets of internal workforce and external labor market to determine the availability of qualified candidates, using third party vendors or agencies as appropriate.

08 Identify internal and external recruitment sources (for example, employee referrals, online job boards, resume banks) and implement selected recruitment methods.

09 Evaluate recruitment methods and sources for effectiveness (for example, return on investment [ROI], cost per hire, time to fill).

10 Develop strategies to brand/market the organization to potential qualified applicants.

11 Develop and implement selection procedures, including applicant tracking, interviewing, testing, reference and background checking and drug screening.

12 Develop and extend employment offers and conduct negotiations as necessary.

13 Administer post-offer employment activities (for example, execute employment agreements, complete I-9 verification forms, coordinate relocations, schedule physical exams).

14 Implement and/or administer the process for non-U.S. citizens to legally work in the United States.

15 Develop, implement and evaluate orientation processes for new hires, rehires and transfers.

16 Develop, implement and evaluate retention strategies and practices.

17 Develop, implement and evaluate succession planning process.

18 Develop and implement the organizational exit process for both voluntary and involuntary terminations, including planning for reductions in force (RIF).

19 Develop, implement and evaluate an Affirmative Action Plan (AAP), as required.

Knowledge of:

08 Federal/state/local employment-related laws and regulations related to workforce planning and employment (for example, Title VII, ADA, ADEA, USERRA, EEOC, Uniform Guidelines on Employee Selection Procedures, Immigration Reform and Control Act, Internal Revenue Code, Executive Order 11246). (chpt 2, pp 24-48)

09 Quantitative analyses required to assess past and future staffing effectiveness (for example, cost-benefit analysis, costs per hire, selection ratios, adverse impact). (chpt 7, p 164)

10 Recruitment sources (for example, Internet, agencies, employee referral) for targeting passive, semi-active and active candidates. (chpt 7, pp 143-148)

11 Recruitment strategies. (chpt 7, pp 141-148)

12 Staffing alternatives (for example, temporary and contract, outsourcing, job sharing, part-time). (chpt 6, pp 122-124)

13 Planning techniques (for example, succession planning, forecasting). (chpt 5, pp 98-101)

14 Reliability and validity of selection tests/tools/methods. (chpt 7, pp 161-163)

15 Use and interpretation of selection tests (for example, psychological/personality, cognitive, motor/physical assessments, performance, assessment center). (chpt 7, pp 150-159)

16　Interviewing techniques (for example, behavioral, situational, panel). (chpt 7, pp 157-158)

17　Relocation practices. (chpt 3, pp 51-52; pp 65-71)

18　Impact of total rewards on recruitment and retention. (chpt 6, p 136)

19　International HR and implications of global workforce for workforce planning and employment. **SPHR ONLY.** (chpt3, pp 54-65)

20　Voluntary and involuntary terminations, downsizing, restructuring and outplacement strategies and practices. (chpt 6, pp 122-136)

21　Internal workforce assessment techniques (for example, skills testing, skills inventory, workforce demographic analysis) and employment policies, practices and procedures (for example, orientation and retention). (chpt 7, pp 154-159)

22　Employer marketing and branding techniques. (chpt 7, p 145)

23　Negotiation skills and techniques. (chpt 11, pp 254-255)

FUNCTIONAL AREA

03 Human Resource Development (17%, 17%)

Developing, implementing and evaluating activities and programs that address employee training and development, performance appraisal, talent and performance management, and the unique needs of employees, to ensure that the knowledge, skills, abilities and performance of the workforce meet current and future organizational and individual needs.

Responsibilities:

01　Ensure that HR development programs are compliant with all applicable federal, state, and local laws and regulations.

02　Conduct a needs assessment to identify and establish priorities regarding HR development activities. **SPHR ONLY.**

03　Develop/select and implement employee training programs (for example, leadership skills, harassment prevention, computer skills) to increase individual and organizational effectiveness. Note that this includes training design and methods for obtaining feedback from training (e.g., surveys, pre and post-testing).

04　Evaluate effectiveness of employee training programs through the use of metrics (for example, data obtained from participant surveys, pre and post-testing). **SPHR ONLY.**

05　Develop, implement, and evaluate talent management programs that include assessing talent, developing talent and placing high-potential employees. **SPHR ONLY.**

06　Develop/select and evaluate performance appraisal process (for example, instruments, ranking and rating scales, relationship to compensation, frequency).

07　Implement training programs for performance evaluators. **PHR ONLY.**

08　Develop, implement and evaluate performance management programs and procedures (for example, goal setting, job rotations, promotions).

09　Develop/select, implement and evaluate programs (for example, flexible work arrangements, diversity initiatives, cultural awareness, repatriation) to meet the unique needs of employees. **SPHR ONLY.**

Knowledge of:

24　Applicable federal, state and local laws and regulations related to HR development activities (for example, Title VII, ADA, ADEA, USERRA, EEOC Uniform Guidelines on Employee Selection Procedures). (chpt 2, pp 24-48)

25　Career development and leadership development theories and applications. (chpt 10, pp 234-238)

26　OD theories and applications. (chpt 4, pp 89-90)

27　Training program development techniques to create general and specialized training programs. (chpt 14, pp 303-305)

28　Training methods, facilitation techniques, instructional methods and program delivery mechanisms. (chpt 14, p 305)

29　Task/process analysis. (chpt 14, pp305-307)

30　Performance appraisal methods (for example, instruments, ranking and rating scales). (chpt 10, pp 218-231)

31　Performance management methods (for example, goal setting, job rotations, promotions). (chpt 13, pp 294-297; chpt 14, pp 315-318)

32　Applicable global issues (for example, international law, culture, local management approaches/practices, societal norms). **SPHR ONLY.** (chpt3, pp 54-71)

33　Techniques to assess training program effectiveness, including use of applicable metrics (for example, participant surveys, pre-and post-testing). (chpt 14, pp 318-319)

34　E-learning. (chpt 14, p 305)

35　Mentoring and executive coaching. (chpt 10, p 232)

FUNCTIONAL AREA

04 Total Rewards (16%, 12%)

Developing/selecting, implementing/administering and evaluating compensation and benefits programs for all employee groups that support the organization's strategic goals, objectives and values.

Responsibilities:

01 Ensure that compensation and benefits programs are compliant with applicable federal, state and local laws and regulations.

02 Develop, implement and evaluate compensation policies/programs (including incentive programs) and pay structures based upon internal equity and external market conditions that support the organization's strategic goals, objectives and values.

03 Administer payroll functions (for example, new hires, deductions, adjustments, terminations).

04 Conduct benefits programs needs assessments (for example, benchmarking, employee survey).

05 Develop/select, implement/administer, and evaluate benefit programs that support the organization's strategic goals, objectives and values (for example, health and welfare, retirement, stock purchase, wellness, employee assistance programs [EAP], time-off).

06 Communicate and train the workforce in the compensation and benefits programs and policies (for example, self-service technologies).

07 Develop/select, implement/administer and evaluate executive compensation programs (for example, stock options, bonus, supplemental retirement plans). **SPHR ONLY.**

08 Develop, implement/administer and evaluate expatriate and foreign national compensation and benefits programs. **SPHR ONLY.**

Knowledge of:

36 Federal, state and local compensation, benefits and tax laws (for example, FLSA, ERISA, COBRA, HIPAA, FMLA, FICA). (chpt 2, pp 24-48)

37 Total rewards stategies (for example, compensation, benefits, wellness, rewards, recognition, employee assistance). (chpt 9, pp 194-200)

38 Budgeting and accounting practices related to compensation and benefits.

39 Job evaluation methods. (chpt 9, pp 200-203)

40 Job pricing and pay structures. (chpt 9, pp 200-204; chpt 5, 106-108)

41 External labor markets and/or economic factors. (chpt 5, 104-108)

42 Pay programs (for example, incentive, variable, merit). (chpt 14, pp 311-315)

43 Executive compensation methods. **SPHR ONLY.** (chpt 9, p- 210-213)

44 Non-cash compensation methods (for example, stock options, ESOPs). **SPHR ONLY.** (chpt 14, pp 311-315)

45 Benefits programs (for example, health and welfare, retirement, wellness, EAP, time-off). (chpt 9, pp 204-210)

46 International compensation laws and practices (for example, expatriate compensation, entitlements, choice of law codes). **SPHR ONLY.** (chpt 3, pp 65-71)

47 Fiduciary responsibility related to total rewards management. **SPHR ONLY.** (chpt 9, pp 199-200)

FUNCTIONAL AREA
05 Employee and Labor Relations (22%, 18%)

Analyzing, developing, implementing/administering and evaluating the workplace relationship between employer and employee, in order to maintain relationships and working conditions that balance employer and employee needs and rights in support of the organization's strategic goals, objectives, and values.

Responsibilities:

01 Ensure that employee and labor relations activities are compliant with applicable federal, state, and local laws and regulations.

02 Assess organizational climate by obtaining employee input (for example, focus groups, employee surveys, staff meetings).

03 Implement organizational change activities as appropriate in response to employee feedback.

04 Develop employee relations programs (for example, awards, recognition, discounts, special events) that promote a positive organizational culture.

05 Implement employee relations programs that promote a positive organizational culture.

06 Evaluate effectiveness of employee relations programs through the use of metrics (for example, exit interviews, employee surveys).

07 Establish and communicate workplace policies and procedures (for example, dress code, attendance, computer use) and monitor their application and enforcement to ensure consistency.

08 Develop, administer and evaluate grievance/dispute resolution and performance improvement policies and procedures.

09 Resolve employee complaints filed with federal, state and local agencies involving employment practices, using professional resources as necessary (for example, legal counsel, mediation/arbitration specialists and investigators).

10 Develop and direct proactive employee relations strategies for remaining union-free in non-organized locations.

11 Participate in collective bargaining activities, including contract negotiation and administration. **SPHR ONLY.**

Knowledge of:

48 Applicable federal, state and local laws affecting employment in union and nonunion environments such as antidiscrimination laws, sexual harassment, labor relations and privacy (for example, WARN Act, Title VII, NLRA). (chpt 2, pp 24-48; chpt 11, pp 244-246)

49 Techniques for facilitating positive employee relations (for example, employee surveys, focus groups, dispute resolution, labor/management cooperative strategies and programs).

50 Employee involvement strategies (for example, employee management committees, self-directed work teams, staff meetings).

51 Individual employment rights issues and practices (for example, employment at will, negligent hiring, defamation, employees' rights to bargain collectively). (chpt 11, pp 250-252)

52 Workplace behavior issues/practices (for example, absenteeism and performance improvement). Ch. 6, p. 130; Ch. 14, pp. 315-317.

53 Unfair labor practices (for example, employee communication strategies and management training).

54 The collective bargaining process, strategies and concepts (for example, contract negotiation and administration). **SPHR ONLY.** (chpt 11, pp 253-258)

55 Positive employee relations strategies and non-monetary rewards. (chpt 14, pp 311-315)

FUNCTIONAL AREA
06 Risk Management (7%, 7%)

Developing, implementing/administering and evaluating programs, plans and policies that provide a safe and secure working environment and to protect the organization from liability.

Responsibilities:

01 Ensure that workplace health, safety, security and privacy activities are compliant with applicable federal, state and local laws and regulations.

02 Identify the organization's safety program needs.

03 Develop/select and implement/administer occupational injury and illness prevention, safety incentives and training programs. **PHR ONLY.**

04 Develop/select, implement and evaluate plans and policies to protect employees and other individuals, and to minimize the organization's loss and liability (for example, emergency response, evacuation, workplace violence, substance abuse, return-to-work policies).

05 Communicate and train the workforce on plans and policies to protect employees and other individuals, and to minimize the organization's loss and liability.

06 Develop and monitor business continuity and disaster recovery plans.

07 Communicate and train the workforce on the business continuity and disaster recovery plans.

08 Develop internal and external privacy policies (for example, identity theft, data protection, HIPAA compliance, workplace monitoring).

09 Administer internal and external privacy policies.

Knowledge of:

56 Federal, state and local workplace health, safety, security and privacy laws and regulations (for example, OSHA, Drug-Free Workplace Act, ADA, HIPAA, Sarbanes-Oxley). (chpt 2, pp 24-48; chpt 12, pp 264-268)

57 Occupational injury and illness compensation and programs. (chpt 12, pp 264-268)

58 Occupational injury and illness prevention programs. (chpt 12, pp 264-268)

59 Investigation procedures of workplace safety, health and security enforcement agencies (for example, OSHA, National Institute for Occupational Safety and Health [NIOSH]). (chpt 12, pp 264-268)

60 Workplace safety risks. (chpt 12, pp 264-268)

61 Workplace security risks (for example, theft, corporate espionage, asset and data protection, sabotage). (chpt 12, pp 276-278)

62 Potential violent behavior and workplace violence conditions. (chpt 12, pp 269-274)

63 General health and safety practices (for example, evacuation, hazard communication, ergonomic evaluations).Ch. 12, p. 264

64 Incident and emergency response plans.

65 Internal investigation, monitoring and surveillance techniques.

66 Issues related to substance abuse and dependency (for example, identification of symptoms, substance-abuse testing, discipline). (CHAPTER 2, p. 45

67 Business continuity and disaster recovery plans (for example, data storage and backup, alternative work locations and procedures).CH. 12, pp. 276-278

68 Data integrity techniques and technology (for example, data sharing, firewalls)

Core Knowledge Required by HR Professionals

69 Needs assessment and analysis. (chpt 5, pp 96-116)

70 Third-party contract negotiation and management, including development of requests for proposals (RFPs). (chpt 11, pp 254-258)

71 Communication skills and strategies (for example, presentation, collaboration, influencing, diplomacy, sensitivity).

72 Organizational documentation requirements to meet federal and state requirements. (chpt 2,pp 24-48)

73 Adult learning processes. (chpt 14, pp 303-305)

74 Motivation concepts and applications. (chpt 13, pp 282-297)

75 Training techniques (for example, computer based, classroom, on-the-job). (chpt 14, pp 303-305)

76 Leadership concepts and applications. (chpt 4, pp 76-82)

77 Project management concepts and applications.

78 Diversity concepts and applications. (chpt 8, pp 168-182)

79 Human relations concepts and applications (for example, interpersonal and organizational behavior). (chpt 4, pp 91-93)

80 HR ethics and professional standards. (chpt 2, pp 24-48; chpt 6, pp 120-122)

81 Technology to support HR activities (for example, HRIS, employee self-service, e-learning, ATS). (chpt 1, pp 10-11; chpt 5, pp 108-110; chpt 7, pp 146-147))

82 Qualitative and quantitative methods and tools for analysis, interpretation and decision-making purposes (for example, metrics and measurements, cost/benefit analysis, financial statement analysis). (chpt 5, pp 98-117, chpt 7, p 164)

83 Change management methods. (chpt 6, pp 122-128, 136-138)

84 Job analysis and job description methods. (chpt 5, pp 106-115)

85 Employee records management (for example, electronic/paper, retention, disposal).

86 The interrelationships among HR activities and programs across functional areas. (chpt 1, pp 15-19)

87 Types of organizational structures (for example, matrix, hierarchy). (chpt 4, pp 89-90)

88 Environmental scanning concepts and applications.

89 Methods for assessing employee attitudes, opinions and satisfaction (for example, opinion surveys, attitude surveys, focus groups/panels) Ch. 6, pp. 132-135.

90 Basic budgeting and accounting concepts.

91 Risk management techniques. (chpt 12, pp 264-278)

CHAPTER SUMMARY

Human resource management (HRM) is a relatively new functional area in many organizations. As today's large organizations began to emerge a little more than a century ago, they found it necessary to establish specialized units to handle the hiring and administration of current employees. These units were usually called *personnel departments* and were headed by personnel managers. Contemporary HRM deals with different complex and strategic issues.

Human resource management generally has four basic goals to pursue: facilitating organizational competitiveness, enhancing productivity and quality, complying with legal and social obligations, and promoting individual growth and development. Each goal is an important ingredient in organizational effectiveness.

Line (or operating) managers and staff managers (or specialized human resource managers) typically share the responsibility for effective human resource management. Both sets of managers must work to deal with the conflict that often occurs. The owner or general manager still often handles HRM in smaller firms, but as organizations grow, they usually establish separate human resource (HR) departments. Managers should also adopt a systems perspective on the HR function.

Today's human resource managers are becoming increasingly professional in both their training and orientation toward their work. A variety of career paths are also available for people who want to work in the HR function.

LEARNING OBJECTIVES

LO1 *Describe contemporary human resource perspectives.*

LO2 *Trace the evolution of the human resource function in organizations.*

LO3 *Identify and discuss the goals of human resource management.*

LO4 *Discuss the setting for human resource management.*

LO5 *Describe the job of human resource managers from the perspectives of professionalism and careers.*

KEY TERMS

A psychological contract *is the overall set of expectations held by the employee with regard to what he or she will contribute to the organization and that are held by the organization with regard to what it will provide to the individual in return.*

Human resources (HR) *are the people that an organization employs to carry out various jobs, tasks, and functions in exchange for wages, salaries, and other rewards.*

Human resource management (HRM) *is the comprehensive set of managerial activities and tasks concerned with developing and maintaining a qualified workforce— human resources—in ways that contribute to organizational effectiveness.*

Abraham Maslow's **hierarchy of human needs** *was developed during the human relations era.*

A **human resource management system** *is an integrated and interrelated approach to managing human resources that fully recognizes the interdependence among the various tasks and functions that must be performed.*

The **human relations era** *supplanted scientific management as the dominant approach to management during the 1930s.*

The human relations era was instigated by the **Hawthorne studies**.

Knowledge workers *are employees whose jobs are primarily concerned with the acquisition and application of knowledge, and they contribute to an organization through what they know and how they can apply what they know.*

Line managers *are those directly responsible for creating goods and services.*

Outsourcing *is the process of hiring outside firms to handle basic HRM functions, presumably more efficiently than the organization.*

Personnel departments, *specialized organizational units for hiring and administering human resources, became popular during the 1930s and 1940s.*

Personnel management, *a new type of management function, grew from the recognition that human resources needed to be managed.*

Productivity *is an economic measure of efficiency that summarizes and reflects the value of the outputs created by an individual, organization, industry, or economic system relative to the value of the inputs used to create them.*

The manager who ran the personnel department was called the **personnel manager**.

Quality *is the total set of features and characteristics of a product or service that bears on its ability to satisfy stated or implied needs.*

Scientific management, *one of the earliest approaches to management, was concerned with structuring individual jobs to maximize efficiency and productivity.*

Staff managers *are those responsible for an indirect or support function that would have costs but whose bottom-line contributions were less direct.*

Douglas McGregor's **Theory X** *and* **Theory Y** *framework grew from the human relations movement.*

Utility analysis *is the attempt to measure, in more objective terms, the impact and effectiveness of HRM practices in terms of such metrics as a firm's financial performance.*

KEY LEGISLATION

Title VII of the Civil Rights Act of 1964 *prohibits discrimination on the basis of an individual's race, color, religious beliefs, sex, or national origin.*

KEY POINTS FOR FUTURE MANAGERS

- The effective management of a firm's human resources is probably the most important source of sustained competitive advantage for a modern organization.
- The changing legal environment has made it critical that an organization be aware of the legal requirements involved in all HRM practices. Failure to do so can be quite costly.
- Effective human management practices support corporate strategic goals.
- Everyone who deals with people has a need to understand some basic notions of human resource management.

To see Key Points for Future HR Professionals, please visit 4ltrpress.cengage.com.

CHAPTER SUMMARY

The legal context of human resource management (HRM) is shaped by various forces. The first step in this process is the actual creation of new regulation. The second step is the enforcement of those regulations. The third step is the actual practice and implementation of those regulations in organizations. Regulations exist in almost every aspect of the employment relationship.

The basic goal of all equal employment opportunity regulation is to protect people from unfair or inappropriate discrimination in the workplace. Illegal discrimination results from behaviors or actions by an organization or managers within an organization that cause members of a protected class to be unfairly differentiated from others. Four basic kinds of discrimination are disparate treatment, disparate impact, pattern or practice discrimination, and retaliation. Depending on the specific law, a protected class consists of all individuals who share one or more common characteristic as indicated by that law.

The major laws and related regulations that affect equal employment opportunity include Title VII of the Civil Rights Act of 1964, Executive Order 11246, Executive Order 11478, the Equal Pay Act of 1963, the Age Discrimination and Employment Act (ADEA), the Vocational Rehabilitation Act of 1973, the Vietnam Era Veterans' Readjustment Act of 1974, the Pregnancy Discrimination Act of 1979, the Civil Rights Act of 1991, the Americans with Disabilities Act of 1990 (ADA), the Americans with Disabilities Amendments Act (2008), and the Family and Medical Leave Act of 1993. The enforcement of equal opportunity legislation generally

LEARNING OBJECTIVES

LO1 *Describe the legal context of human resource management.*

LO2 *Identify key laws that prohibit discrimination in the workplace and discuss equal employment opportunity.*

LO3 *Discuss legal issues in compensation, labor relations, and other areas in human resource management.*

LO4 *Discuss the importance to an organization of evaluating its legal compliance.*

KEY TERMS

Affirmative action *represents a set of steps, taken by an organization, to actively seek qualified applicants from groups underrepresented in the workforce.*

A **bona fide occupational qualification (BFOQ)** *states that a condition like race, sex, or other personal characteristic legitimately affects a person's ability to perform the job, and therefore can be used as a legal requirement for selection.*

A **business necessity** *is a practice that is important for the safe and efficient operation of the business.*

Disparate impact *discrimination occurs when an apparently neutral employment practice disproportionately excludes a protected group from employment opportunities.*

Disparate treatment *discrimination exists when individuals in similar situations are treated differently based on the individual's race, color, religion, sex, national origin, age, or disability status.*

The **four-fifths rule** *suggests that disparate impact exists if a selection criterion (such as a test score) results in a selection rate for a protected class that is less than four-fifths (80 percent) of that for the majority group.*

Geographical comparisons *involve comparing the characteristics of the potential pool of qualified applicants for a job (focusing on characteristics such as race, ethnicity, and gender) with those same characteristics of the present employees in the job.*

A **hostile work environment** *is one that produces sexual harassment because of a climate or culture that is punitive toward people of a different gender.*

Illegal discrimination *results from behaviors or actions by an organization or managers within an organization that cause members of a protected class to be unfairly differentiated from others.*

The **McDonnell-Douglas test** *is used as the basis for establishing a prima facie case of disparate impact discrimination.*

Pattern or practice discrimination *is similar to disparate treatment but occurs on a classwide basis.*

A **protected class** *consists of all individuals who share one or more common characteristic as indicated by that law.*

Quid pro quo harassment *is sexual harassment in which the harasser offers to exchange something of value for sexual favors.*

A **utilization analysis** *is a comparison of the racial, sex, and ethnic composition of the employer's workforce compared to that of the available labor supply.*

KEY LEGISLATION

The ADA Amendments Act (or ADAAA) of 2008 *broadens the protection offered to persons with disabilities at work by defining certain disabilities as "presumptive," thus negating several court cases that had ruled certain persons having disabilities as not qualifying for coverage under the ADA.*

The Age Discrimination and Employment Act (or ADEA) *prohibits discrimination against employees age forty and older.*

The Americans with Disabilities Act of 1990 (or ADA) *prohibits discrimination based on disability and all aspects of the employment relationship such as job application procedures, hiring, firing, promotion, compensation, and training, as well as other employment activities such as advertising, recruiting, tenure, layoffs, and leave and fringe benefits.*

The Civil Rights Act of 1991 *makes it easier for individuals who feel they have been discriminated against to take legal action against organizations and provides for the payment of compensatory and punitive damages in cases of discrimination under Title VII.*

The Drug-Free Workplace Act of 1988 *was passed to reduce the use of illegal drugs in the workplace.*

Executive Order 11478 *requires the federal government to base all of its own employment policies on merit and fitness and specifies that race, color, sex, religion, and national origin should not be considered.*

Executive Order 11246 *prohibits discrimination based on race, color, religion, sex, or national origin for organizations that are federal contractors and subcontractors.*

The Employee Free Choice Act (EFCA) *would make it easier for unions to be recognized as sole bargaining agents, eliminating the need for secret ballot elections.*

The Employee Retirement Income Security Act of 1974 (ERISA) *guarantees a basic minimum benefit that employees could expect to be paid at retirement.*

SUMMARY (Continued)

is handled by the Equal Employment Opportunity Commission (EEOC) and the Office of Federal Contract Compliance Procedures (OFCCP).

The most far-reaching law dealing with total compensation is the Fair Labor Standards Act, which was passed in 1938. This law established a minimum hourly wage for jobs. Another important piece of legislation that affects compensation is the Employee Retirement Income Security Act of 1974 (ERISA).

The National Labor Relations Act, or Wagner Act, was passed in 1935 in an effort to control and legislate collective bargaining between organizations and labor unions. Congress subsequently passed the Taft-Hartley Act in 1947 and the Landrum-Griffin Act in 1959 to regulate union actions and their internal affairs.

Several related areas of HRM are affected by laws and associated legal issues. These related areas include employee safety and health (especially as related to the Occupational Safety and Health Act, or OSHA), various emerging areas of discrimination law (especially sexual harassment), and ethics.

The Equal Pay Act of 1963 *requires that organizations provide men and women who are doing equal work the same pay.*

The Family and Medical Leave Act of 1993 *requires employers having more than fifty employees to provide as many as 12 weeks unpaid leave for employees after the birth or adoption of a child; to care for a seriously ill child, spouse, or parent; or if the employee is seriously ill.*

The Genetic Information Nondiscrimination Act (GINA) of 2009 *prohibits employers from obtaining genetic information about employees.*

The Labor Management Relations Act (or Taft-Hartley Act) *curtailed and limited union powers and regulates union actions and their internal affairs in a way that puts them on equal footing with management and organizations.*

The Landrum-Griffin Act *focused on eliminating various unethical, illegal, and undemocratic practices within unions themselves.*

The National Labor Relations Act (or Wagner Act) *was passed in an effort to control and legislate collective bargaining between organizations and labor unions, to grant power to labor unions, and to put unions on a more equal footing with managers in terms of the rights of employees.*

The Occupational Safety and Health Act of 1970 (or OSHA) *grants the federal government the power to establish and enforce occupational safety and health standards for all places of employment directly affecting interstate commerce.*

The Patriot Act *expanded the rights of the government or law enforcement agencies to collect information about and pursue potential terrorists.*

The Pregnancy Discrimination Act of 1979 *protects pregnant women from discrimination in the workplace.*

The Privacy Act of 1974 *allows federal employees to review their personnel files periodically to ensure that the information contained in them is accurate.*

The Reconstruction Civil Rights Acts of 1866 and 1871 *further extended protection offered to people under the Thirteenth and Fourteenth Amendments.*

The Vietnam Era Veterans' Readjustment Act of 1974 *requires that federal contractors and subcontractors take affirmative action toward employing Vietnam-era veterans.*

The Vocational Rehabilitation Act of 1973 *requires that executive agencies and subcontractors and contractors of the federal government receiving more than $2,500 a year from the government engage in affirmative action for disabled individuals.*

The Worker Adjustment and Retraining Notification (WARN) Act of 1988 *stipulates that an organization employing at least 100 employees must provide notice at least 60 days in advance of plans to close a facility or lay off 50 or more employees.*

KEY POINTS FOR FUTURE MANAGERS

- The law represents a major constraint on corporate HR practices.

- The Civil Rights Act is probably the single most important piece of legislation that addresses which HR practices are allowed under the law.

- Under the Civil Rights Act, policies that are applied equally to all employees but have a different (and adverse) effect on employees based on race, gender, religion, color, or national origin are potentially illegal.

- Sexual harassment is outlawed under the Civil Rights Act, and the scope of activities covered here is quite broad.

- Laws also outlaw discrimination on the basis of disability and age.

- Still other laws regulate how people are paid, how organizations deal with unions (or attempts to unionize), and worker safety and privacy.

- No human resource decision should be made without consulting someone knowledgeable about the legal implications of the action. These consultations should include a professional HR manager as well as a lawyer.

To see Key Points for Future HR Professionals, please visit 4ltrpress.cengage.com.

in review

CHAPTER SUMMARY

Various global issues in international human resource management (HRM) must be addressed by any international firm. One issue is the development of an international HRM strategy. Another is developing an understanding of the cultural environment of human resource management. A third is developing an understanding of the political and legal environment of international business.

The international human resource (HR) function must deal with several fundamental management challenges in international business. The first major set of challenges relates to differences that may exist in culture, levels of economic development, and legal systems that typify the countries where the firm operates. A second fundamental HR challenge in international business is the determination of the most appropriate source of employees: the host country, the home country, or a third country. Third, international businesses must also deal with different complex training and development challenges. Yet another important international HRM question relates to working conditions, compensation, and the cost of living.

Organizations can adopt a wide variety of strategies for competing in the international environment. One strategy is exporting, which is the process of making a product in the firm's domestic marketplace and then selling it in another country. In licensing, a company grants its permission to another company in a foreign country to manufacture or market its products in the foreign country's local market. Direct investment occurs when a firm headquartered in one country builds or purchases operating facilities or subsidiaries in a foreign

LEARNING OBJECTIVES

LO1 *Describe the growth of international business.*

LO2 *Identify and discuss global issues in international human resource management.*

LO3 *Discuss the human resource management function in international business.*

LO4 *Identify and discuss domestic issues in international human resource management.*

LO5 *Describe the issues involved in managing international transfers and assignments.*

LO6 *Summarize the issues in international labor relations.*

KEY TERMS

Culture *refers to the set of values that helps an organization's members understand what it stands for, how it does things, and what it considers important.*

Direct foreign investment *occurs when a firm headquartered in one country builds or purchases operating facilities or subsidiaries in a foreign country.*

The **ethnocentric staffing model** *primarily uses parent-country nationals to staff higher-level foreign positions.*

Expatriates *are employees who are sent by a firm to work in another country; they may be either parent-country or third-country nationals.*

Exporting *is the process of making a product in the firm's domestic marketplace and then selling it in another country. Exporting can involve both goods and services.*

The **geocentric staffing model** *puts parent-country, host-country, and third-country nationals all in the same category, with the firm attempting to always hire the best person available for a position.*

A **hardship premium** *(also called a* **foreign service premium***) is an additional financial incentive offered to individuals to entice them to accept a "less than attractive" international assignment.*

In a **joint venture (strategic alliance),** *two or more firms cooperate in the ownership or management of an operation on an equity basis.*

Licensing *involves one company granting its permission to another company in a foreign country to manufacture or market its products in its local market.*

The **polycentric staffing model** *calls for the dominant use of host-country nationals throughout the organization.*

KEY LEGISLATION

The North American Free Trade Agreement (NAFTA) *reduced trade barriers between Canada, the United States, and Mexico. NAFTA also includes separate labor agreements among the three countries.*

KEY POINTS FOR FUTURE MANAGERS

- It is critical that a firm develop an international HRM strategy for dealing with overseas business.

- An important part of this strategy is to determine the appropriate mix of HCNs, expatriates, and third-country nationals who will staff operations in a given country.

- It is critical for an organization to understand the cultural, political, and legal environments in a country where it is considering doing business.

- It is critical that a firm develop an international business strategy that includes consideration of the relative importance of exporting, licensing, direct investment, and joint ventures for doing business in a given country or region.

- Policies for recruiting, selecting, training, and compensating expatriate managers must consider the impact these practices have on host-country nationals because these HCNs must help the expatriate adjust to his or her new environment, and they may be less likely to do so if they feel resentment toward the expatriate manager.

- A strategic approach to expatriation must include a strategy for repatriation.

To see Key Points for Future HR Professionals, please visit 4ltrpress.cengage.com.

SUMMARY (Continued)

country. In a joint venture or strategic alliance, two or more firms cooperate in the ownership or management of an operation, often on an equity basis.

All firms dealing in foreign markets must also confront three sets of domestic issues in the management of their human resources. These domestic issues are local recruiting and selection, local training, and local compensation. International HRM must also pay close attention to the various issues involved in the effective management of expatriate employees. Key areas of importance include selecting, training, and compensating expatriates.

Labor relations are the processes of dealing with employees who are organized into labor unions. In the United States, membership in labor unions has steadily declined in recent years, and labor relations are heavily regulated by laws. Different situations exist, however, in other countries.

CHAPTER 4

in review

CHAPTER SUMMARY

The strategic context of human resource management (HRM) plays an important role in determining the effectiveness of not only the human resource (HR) function but the entire organization as well. Understanding the organization's purpose and its mission guides HR managers as they formulate their strategy. They must also recognize the role of the top management team.

Corporate strategy involves decisions about which markets or businesses the firm intends to address, whereas business strategy deals with competitive issues within a particular market or business. The firm's HR strategy itself is an important functional strategy that must be integrated with marketing, finance, operations, and other relevant functional strategies.

The actual process of formulating human resource strategy results in separate but consistent strategies for staffing, employee development, and compensation. To enact HR strategy effectively, it must be closely coordinated with the particular form of organization design the firm uses, the culture it creates, and the impact of unionization and collective bargaining.

The implementation of human resource strategy requires an understanding of fundamental individual and interpersonal behavioral processes. Individual processes include psychological contracts, individual personality traits, employee attitudes, motivation, and stress. Interpersonal processes include group behavior, leadership, and communication.

Managers should attempt to evaluate the effectiveness of the human resource function and its role in helping the

LEARNING OBJECTIVES

LO1 *Describe the strategic context of human resource management.*

LO2 *Identify three types of strategies and relate each to human resource management.*

LO3 *Discuss human resource strategy formulation and relevant organizational factors.*

LO4 *Discuss the processes through which human resource strategy is implemented.*

LO5 *Discuss how the human resource function in organizations can be evaluated.*

KEY TERMS

The **adaptation model** *is one popular approach to business strategy where a business seeks ways to adapt to its environment.*

Business strategy *deals with how the firm will compete in each market where it conducts business.*

Corporate strategy *deals with determining what businesses the corporation will operate.*

A **cost leadership strategy** *is one that focuses on minimizing the costs as much as possible.*

An organization's **culture** *refers to the set of values that helps its members understand what the organization stands for, how it accomplishes what it wants to accomplish, and what it considers important.*

A company that uses a **differentiation strategy** *attempts to develop an image or reputation for its product or service that sets the company apart from its competitors.*

A **diversification strategy** *is used by companies that are adding new products, product lines, or businesses to their existing core products, product lines, or businesses.*

The **focus strategy** *is undertaken when an organization tries to target a specific segment of the marketplace for its products or services.*

Functional strategy *deals with how the firm will manage each of its major functions such as marketing, finance, and human resources.*

Growth strategy *focuses on growing and expanding the business. It can be pursued internally by opening additional locations or externally through mergers, joint ventures, or the acquisition of other businesses.*

An organization's **mission** *is a statement of how it intends to fulfill its purpose.*

Motivation *is the set of forces that causes people to behave in certain ways. Individual motivation is also a major determinant of individual performance, but motivation is at the heart of what causes an employee to choose to expend the effort that will support any organizational activity.*

Organization design *refers to the framework of jobs, positions, clusters of positions, and reporting relationships among positions that are used to construct an organization.*

Personality *is the relatively stable set of psychological attributes or traits that distinguish one person from another. Some organizations believe that one or more particular personality traits may relate to how well an employee can perform a certain job or type of job.*

*A **psychological contract** is the overall set of expectations held by an individual with respect to what he or she will contribute to the organization and what the organization will provide the individual in return.*

*An organization's **purpose** is its basic reason for existence.*

Related diversification *is used when a corporation believes it can achieve synergy among the various businesses that it owns.*

*A **retrenchment** or **turnaround strategy** occurs when an organization finds that its current operations are not effective, and major changes are usually needed to rectify the problem. In most cases, this strategy involves rightsizing the organization by closing operations, shutting down factories, and terminating employees in order to get back on the right track.*

Stability strategy *essentially calls for maintaining the status quo. A company that adopts a stability strategy plans to stay in its current businesses and intends to manage them as they are already being managed. The organization's goal is to protect itself from environmental threats. A stability strategy is frequently used after a period of retrenchment or after a period of rapid growth.*

Stress *is a person's adaptive response to a stimulus that places excessive psychological or physical demands on that person. It is important for HR managers to include an understanding of the causes of stress, the processes by which stress affects individuals, and how organizations and individuals can cope better with stress in organizational settings.*

*The **top management team** of an organization refers to the group of senior executives responsible for the overall strategic operation of the firm.*

Unrelated diversification *is used when a firm attempts to operate several unique businesses in different, unrelated markets. The basic logic behind unrelated diversification is that a company can shield itself from the adverse effects of business cycles, unexpected competition, and other economic fluctuations.*

KEY POINTS FOR FUTURE MANAGERS

- Corporate and business strategies define how an organization will operate and compete in the market.
- Common strategies at the corporate level include a growth strategy, a retrenchment (or turnaround) strategy, and a stability strategy.
- A diversification strategy is one in which an organization decides to operate different related or unrelated businesses.
- The adaptation model of strategy suggests that organizations should match their strategy to the environment. The model includes defender, prospector, analyzer, and reactor strategies.
- Major competitive strategies include differentiation, cost leadership, and focus strategies (i.e., targeting a specific segment of the market).
- Human resource management strategy is determined by organizational-level strategy as well as by organizational design, culture, technology, and the workforce.
- Certain specific HR practices may be capable of providing a competitive advantage to organizations.

To see Key Points for Future HR Professionals, please visit 4ltrpress.cengage.com..

SUMMARY (Continued)

organization attain its strategic goals. This evaluation usually focuses on specific HR practices. However, recent evidence suggests that bundles of so-called best practices may be a viable alternative approach.

CHAPTER SUMMARY

Human resource (HR) executives rely on many sources of information to make decisions and to manage human capital. HR planning, for example, draws from forecasts of the supply of human resources, labor force trends and issues, and forecasts of the demand for human resources.

The organization's strategy is also a critical information source. Growth, stability, and reduction strategies, for example, each carry substantially different implications for human resource managers. Another important source of information comes from various economic conditions. Unemployment rates, market wage rates, and human capital investments each provide useful information to HR executives.

Job analysis is one of the building blocks of the human resource planning process and is also a fundamental source of information for that same planning process. Job analysis involves the gathering and organizing of detailed information about various jobs within the organization so that managers can better understand the processes through which jobs are most effectively performed. Job analysis provides input to the HR planning process by helping planners better understand exactly what kinds of work must be performed.

Job analysis itself generally follows a three-step process: determining information needs, determining methods for obtaining information, and determining who will collect information. The responsibility of analysis is jointly shared by line managers, the human resource group or department, and job analysts.

© Christine Balderas/Getty Images

LEARNING OBJECTIVES

LO1 *Describe human resource planning as a source of information for decision making.*

LO2 *Discuss strategy as a source of information for making human resource decisions.*

LO3 *Discuss economic conditions as a source of information for making human resource decisions.*

LO4 *Describe job analysis as a source of information for making human resource decisions.*

LO5 *Discuss the job-analysis process and identify and summarize common job-analysis methods.*

KEY TERMS

The **critical incidents approach** to job analysis focuses on critical behaviors that distinguish effective from ineffective performers.

Executive succession involves systematically planning for future promotions into top management positions.

The **Fleishman job-analysis system** is a job-analysis procedure that defines abilities as the enduring attributes of individuals that account for differences in performance; it relies on the taxonomy of abilities that presumably represents all the dimensions relevant to work.

Human capital investments are investments people make in themselves to increase their value in the workplace. These investments might take the form of additional education or training.

A **human resource information system** is an integrated and increasingly automated system for maintaining a database regarding the employees in an organization.

Human resource planning is the process of forecasting the supply and demand for human resources within an organization and developing action plans for aligning the two.

Job analysis is the process of gathering and organizing detailed information about various jobs within an organization so that managers can better understand the processes through which they are performed most effectively.

Job analysts are individuals who perform job analysis in an organization.

A **job description** lists the tasks, duties, and responsibilities for a particular job. It specifies the major job elements, provides examples of job tasks, and provides some indication of their relative importance in the effective conduct of the job.

A **job specification** focuses on the individual who will perform the job and indicates the knowledge, abilities, skills, and other characteristics that an individual must have to be able to perform the job.

Knowledge, skills, and abilities (KSA) are the fundamental requirements necessary to perform a job.

Management Position Description Questionnaire (MPDQ) *is a standardized job-analysis instrument, similar in approach to the PAQ, that also contains 197 items. The MPDQ's focus, however, is on managerial jobs, and the analysis is done in terms of 13 essential components of all managerial jobs.*

The **market wage rate** *is the prevailing wage rate for a given job in a given labor market.*

Occupational Information Network (O*NET) *is technically not a job-analysis procedure but a database that provides both basic and advanced job-analysis information; as such, IT can be viewed as an alternative to conducting job analysis.*

The **Position Analysis Questionnaire (PAQ)** *is a standardized job-analysis instrument consisting of 194 items that reflect work behavior, working conditions, and job characteristics that are assumed to be generalizable across a wide variety of jobs.*

The **rate of unemployment** *is calculated by the Bureau of Labor Statistics as the percentage of individuals looking for and available for work who are not currently employed.*

A **subject matter expert (SME)** *is an individual presumed to be highly knowledgeable about particular job and who provides data for job analysis. A SME may be an existing job incumbent, a supervisor, or another knowledgeable employee.*

The **task-analysis inventory** *is a family of job-analysis methods, each with unique characteristics; each focuses on analyzing all the tasks performed in the focal job.*

KEY LEGISLATION

The Americans with Disabilities Act *prohibits discrimination based on disability and all aspects of the employment relationship such as job application procedures, hiring, firing, promotion, compensation, and training, as well as other employment activities such as advertising, recruiting, tenure, layoffs, and leave and fringe benefits.*

KEY POINTS FOR FUTURE MANAGERS

- Planning is as important for human resource management as for any other function in an organization.

- Human resource management should be an integral part of the organization's strategy.

- Job analysis is and should be the basic cornerstone for all other human resource management functions.

- It is essential to understand the strengths and weaknesses of different job analysis approaches because one is not better than the others.

- Competency modeling is concerned with identifying broader sets of requirements that may cut across individual jobs within an organization.

To see Key Points for Future HR Professionals, please visit 4ltrpress.cengage.com.

SUMMARY (Continued)

Commonly used methods of job analysis include the narrative approach, Fleishman job-analysis system, task-analysis inventory, functional job analysis, Position Analysis Questionnaire, Management Position Description Questionnaire, and critical incidents approach. The Occupational Information Network (O*NET), while not technically a job-analysis procedure, provides advanced job-analysis information.

Job analysis results in a job description and a job specification. The changing nature of work and of jobs must also be understood and appreciated by managers. Finally, there are also important legal implications related to job analysis.

CHAPTER SUMMARY

Organizations strive to maintain the right number of employees. Options for such rightsizing include hiring new employees when there is a long-term need for more employees (discussed in the next chapter), responding to temporary demands for additional employees using various methods, and reducing the size of the organization's workforce. When organizations have temporary or short-term needs for additional employees, managers can generally use overtime, temporary workers, leased employees, or part-time employees instead of hiring permanent workers.

Organizations that need to reduce the number of employees can achieve these reductions through early retirement and plans to encourage early retirement or through layoffs. Layoffs can bring legal problems (especially concerning potential age discrimination), and the survivors of layoffs often experience guilt. Furthermore, evidence suggests that downsizing is not an effective strategy. A final way to reduce the size of the labor force is through termination—that is, some people can be fired. Although employment at will is the law, there are enough exceptions to this doctrine that organizations are often sued for wrongful termination.

Even as organizations seek to eliminate some employees, they must also strive to retain valued employees. This process involves reducing voluntary turnover and requires an understanding of the causes of voluntary turnover. The major determinant of voluntary turnover is usually job dissatisfaction, or being unhappy in one's job.

Several models of the voluntary turnover process exist, but these models usually focus on helping us understand

LEARNING OBJECTIVES

LO1 *Discuss the role of ethics in human resource decision making.*

LO2 *Describe the concept of rightsizing and identify organizational strategies for rightsizing.*

LO3 *Describe how to manage termination and retention.*

LO4 *Describe the elements of voluntary turnover.*

LO5 *Discuss the key human resource issues during mergers and acquisitions.*

KEY TERMS

Discipline *refers to the system of rules and procedures for how and when punishment is administered and how severe the punishment should be.*

Distributive justice *refers to perceptions that the outcomes a person faces are fair when compared to the outcomes faced by others.*

Employee leasing *involves an organization paying a fee to a leasing company that provides a pool of employees who are available on a temporary basis. This pool of employees usually constitutes a group or crew intended to handle all or most of the organization's work needs in a particular area.*

Employment at will *states that an employer can terminate any employee, at any time, for any reason (good or bad), or for no reason at all.*

Ethics *refers to an individual's beliefs about what is right and wrong and what is good and bad. Ethics are formed by the societal context in which people and organizations function.*

Interactional justice *refers to the quality of the interpersonal treatment people receive when a decision is implemented.*

Involuntary turnover *is terminating employees whose services are no longer desired.*

Job dissatisfaction *is the feeling of being unhappy with one's job. It is a major cause of voluntary turnover.*

Job embeddedness *refers to the fact that some people stay on their jobs, even when they decide they are unhappy and should leave. Other ties in the community or obligations keep the employee on the job.*

Organizational citizenship behaviors (OCBs) *include employee behaviors that are beneficial to the organization but are not formally required as part of an employee's job.*

Organizational commitment *is the degree to which an employee identifies with an organization and is willing to exert effort on behalf of the organization.*

Overtime *refers to hours worked above the normal 40 hour workweek, for which there is usually a pay premium.*

Part-time workers *refers to individuals who are regularly expected to work less than 40 hours a week. They typically do not receive benefits and afford the organization a great deal of flexibility in staffing.*

Procedural justice *refers to perceptions that the process used to determine the outcomes were fair.*

Progressive disciplinary plans *are organizational disciplinary programs where the severity of the punishment increases over time or across the problem.*

Punishment *simply refers to following unacceptable behavior with some type of negative consequences.*

Realistic job previews (RJPs) *are pre-employment previews that provide accurate and realistic information to the job applicant. They can also be used with new employees as a means of socializing them in their new job roles, and they are effective in reducing turnover.*

As part of a progressive disciplinary program, a **suspension** *is a temporary layoff, usually with pay, when there is an ongoing investigation.*

Stock options *are rights given to employees to purchase a certain number of shares of stock at a given price.*

As part of progressive disciplinary program, **termination** *is an act by the organization to end the employment relationship.*

Rightsizing *is the process of monitoring and adjusting the composition of the organization's workforce to its optimal size.*

Verbal warnings—*the first step in most progressive disciplinary programs*—*are cautions conveyed orally to the employee.*

Written warnings—*the second step in most progressive disciplinary programs*—*are more formal warnings. They are given to the employee in writing and become part of the employee's permanent record.*

KEY LEGISLATION

The Fair Labor Standards Act *stipulates that hourly workers must be compensated at a rate of one and a half times their normal hourly rate for work in excess hours of 40 hours per week.*

The Worker Adjustment and Retraining Notification (WARN) Act *requires at least sixty days' notice for a facility closure or a mass layoff.*

KEY POINTS FOR FUTURE MANAGERS

- Rightsizing of the workforce may involve hiring new permanent employees, temporarily increasing the size of the workforce, or downsizing (reducing the workforce).

- Temporary needs for additional employees can be achieved through overtime, the use of temporary or leased employees, or the use of part-time workers.

- When possible, reductions should be made by relying on natural attrition and early retirement rather than on layoffs because layoffs can lead to legal problems and have been shown to be relatively ineffective at reducing costs.

- Although employment at will is the common-law rule, it is not acceptable to terminate employees without cause. The various exceptions to employment at will can result in serious legal problems.

- While trying to reduce the workforce, it is also necessary to retain valued employees. The best way to retain valued employees is to monitor and improve job satisfaction.

- Job satisfaction is related to absenteeism and turnover, but it is also related to organizational commitment.

- Job satisfaction is also related to organizational citizenship behaviors. These behaviors are not the responsibility of employees; if someone does not carry them out, however, the organization suffers.

- It is very important that general managers actively involve their human resource colleagues during a merger or acquisition.

To see Key Points for Future HR Professionals, please visit 4ltrpress.cengage.com.

SUMMARY (Continued)

how job dissatisfaction results in turnover. One model, however, focuses on job embeddedness and helps us understand why some dissatisfied employees choose to remain on their jobs.

In addition to relating to turnover, job satisfaction can lead to other outcomes, and it is therefore a major concern for organizations that seek to monitor levels of employee satisfaction and dissatisfaction. For example, higher levels of employee satisfaction are related to higher levels of employee commitment and a greater frequency of behaviors known as *organizational citizenship behaviors* (OCBs). OCBs are behaviors that are not required of an employee but are important for the functioning of the organization.

Finally, it is important that managers understand the role and importance of human resources during and after a merger or an acquisition. A failure to do so will greatly increase the chances that the merger or acquisition will fail to meet its intended goals or, worse, result in outright failure.

in review

© Ramin Talaie/Corbis

CHAPTER SUMMARY

Recruiting is the process of developing a pool of qualified applicants who are interested in working for the organization and from which the organization might reasonably select the best individual or individuals to hire for employment. Organizational goals in recruiting are to optimize, in various ways, the size of the pool of qualified applicants and to offer an honest and candid assessment to prospective applicants of what kinds of jobs and what kinds of opportunities the organization can potentially make available to them.

Internal recruiting is the process of looking inside the organization for existing qualified employees who might be promoted to higher-level positions. The two most common methods used for internal recruiting are job posting and supervisory recommendations. External recruiting involves looking to sources outside the organization for prospective employees. Different methods are likely to be used by an organization engaged in external recruiting. These include the general labor pool, direct applicants, referrals, advertisements, employment agencies, and colleges and universities.

Many organizations today are finding that it is increasingly important to provide prospective employees with what is called a *realistic job preview*. Realistic job previews might involve providing job applicants with an opportunity to actually observe others performing the work.

The selection process involves three clear, distinct steps: gathering information about the members of the pool of qualified recruits, evaluating the qualifications of each applicant from among the recruiting pool, and making

LEARNING OBJECTIVES

LO1 *Describe the relationships among planning, recruiting, and selection.*

LO2 *Identify and discuss the basic sources for recruiting; discuss realistic job previews and their role in effective recruiting.*

LO3 *Describe the steps in the selection process and identify and summarize basic selection criteria that organizations use in hiring new employees.*

LO4 *Discuss popular selection techniques that organizations use to hire new employees.*

LO5 *Discuss the selection decision itself.*

LO6 *Describe reliability and validity and their importance in employee selection.*

LO7 *Identify and summarize the basic legal issues in selection and discuss the importance of evaluating recruiting and selection activities.*

KEY TERMS

The **big five personality traits**—neuroticism, extraversion, openness to experience, agreeableness, *and* conscientiousness—*tend to be more behavioral than cognitive or emotional and are likely to be more important for job performance than more traditional personality traits.*

Biodata application blanks *focus on the same type of information that is found in a regular application but go into more complex and detailed assessments about that background.*

Cognitive ability tests *measure mental skills.*

A **contrast error** *occurs when the interviewer is unduly influenced by other people who have been interviewed. For example, suppose an interviewer meets with one candidate who is extremely good or extremely bad. The next person interviewed may suffer or benefit by the contrast with this person.*

Criterion-related validity *is the extent to which a selection technique accurately predicts elements of performance. It is most typically demonstrated by establishing a correlation between a test or measured performance in a simulated work environment and measures of actual on-the-job performance.*

Education *refers to the formal classroom training an individual has received in public or private schools and in a college, university, or technical school.*

An **employment application** *asks individuals for various bits of information pertaining to their personal background.*

An **employment test** *is a device for measuring the characteristics of an individual such as personality, intelligence, and aptitude.*

Experience *is the amount of time the individual has spent working in either a general capacity or a particular field of study.*

External recruiting *is the process of looking to sources outside the organization for prospective employees.*

False negatives *are applicants who are predicted to fail and are not hired, but if they had been hired, they would have been successful.*

False positives *are applicants who are predicted to be successful and are hired but who ultimately fail.*

A **first-impression error** *occurs when an interviewer makes a decision too early in the interview process. This error may significantly affect a decision even when subsequent information indicates the first impression may have been wrong.*

A **headhunter** *is an individual working for an executive search firm who seeks out qualified individuals for higher-level positions.*

In-basket exercises *are special forms of work simulations for prospective managers. They consist of collections of hypothetical memos, letters, and notes that require responses.*

Integrity tests *attempt to assess an applicant's moral character and honesty.*

Internal recruiting *is the process of looking inside the organization for existing qualified employees who might be promoted to higher-level positions.*

Job posting *is a mechanism for internal recruiting in which vacancies in the organization are publicized through various media such as company newsletters, bulletin boards, internal memos, and the firm's intranet.*

Nonrelevancy *is a type of error that occurs when an interviewer really does not know enough about the job for which he or she is interviewing candidates. As a result, the interviewer bases an assessment of the individual's abilities to perform the job on incomplete or inaccurate assessments of the nature of that job.*

Personality tests *measure traits, or tendencies to act, that are relatively unchanging in a person.*

The **projective technique** *involves showing an individual an ambiguous stimulus, such as an ink blot or a fuzzy picture, and then asking what he or she "sees."*

Psychomotor ability tests *measure physical abilities such as strength, eye–hand coordination, and manual dexterity.*

A **realistic job preview (RJP)** *is an effective technique for ensuring that job seekers understand the actual nature of the jobs available to them.*

Recruiting *is the process of developing a pool of qualified applicants who are interested in working for the organization and from which the organization might reasonably select the best individual or individuals to hire for employment.*

Reliability *is the consistency of a particular selection device—that is, it measures whatever it is supposed to measure without random error; not the same as accuracy.*

Selection *is concerned with identifying the best candidate or candidates for jobs from among the pool of qualified applicants developed during the recruiting process.*

A **self-report inventory** *is a paper-and-pencil measure in which an applicant responds to a series of statements that might or might not apply to him or her.*

A **semistructured employment interview** *is a type of interview that involves advance preparation of major or key questions to be asked so that all applicants will be asked essentially the same questions. However, the interviewer is also given the prerogative to ask additional follow-up questions to probe specific answers that the interviewee provides.*

A **similarity error** *occurs when the interviewer is unduly influenced by the fact that the interviewee is similar to the interviewer in one or more important ways. As a result of the perception of similarity, the interviewer may be more favorably disposed toward the candidate than the candidate's credentials warrant.*

Situational interview *is a type of interview, growing in popularity, in which the interviewer asks the applicant questions about a specific situation to see how the applicant would react.*

SUMMARY (Continued)

the actual decision about which candidate or candidates will be offered employment with the organization. The basic selection criteria that most organizations use in deciding whom to hire are education and experience, skills and abilities, and personal characteristics. Firms must also decide whether to focus on fit or skills.

Organizations use various techniques for gathering information about job candidates. The most common are employment applications and background checks, employment tests, work simulations, and employment interviews. Each technique has its unique strengths and weaknesses but also can play an important role in selection.

After subjecting the pool of qualified applicants to the organization's selection process, it is then necessary to make a final selection decision. Most organizations choose to rely on several selection techniques and, in fact, may use all or most of the selection techniques discussed in this chapter. Managers also strive to avoid various selection errors.

It is important that the organization understand the legal context in which it can recruit and select new employees and that it evaluate its selection and placement activities periodically.

Structured employment interview *is a type of interview where the interviewer either prepares or receives from others a list of standard questions to be asked during the interview. All interviewers ask the same questions of each candidate to achieve consistency across interviews.*

Using **supervisory recommendations**, *a mechanism for internal recruiting, a manager simply solicits nominations or recommendations for a position that needs to be filled from supervisors in the organization.*

An **unstructured employment interview** *involves relatively little advance preparation. The interviewer may have a general idea about what she or he wants to learn about the job applicant but has few or no advance questions that are formally constructed and ready to be asked.*

Utility analysis *is an attempt to determine the extent to which a selection system provides real benefit to the organization.*

Validity *refers to whether an assessment tool measures what it is supposed to measure. Usually, in selection settings, this is determined empirically by means of criterion-related validity, and it is critical to defending against charges of discrimination in hiring.*

A **weighted application blank** *relies on the determination of numerical indexes to indicate the relative importance of various personal factors for predicting a person's ability to perform a job effectively.*

In **word-of-mouth recruiting**, *the organization simply informs current employees that positions are available and encourages them to refer friends, family members, or neighbors for those jobs.*

Work simulations *(or* **work samples***) involve asking the prospective employee to perform tasks or job-related activities that simulate or represent the actual work for which the person is being considered.*

KEY POINTS FOR FUTURE MANAGERS

- The goal of recruiting is to generate qualified applicants for jobs.
- Recruiting can be either internal or external, and each has advantages and disadvantages.
- Decisions about the best methods for external (or internal) recruiting should be based on the kind of applicants the firm wants to attract.
- Electronic recruiting is revolutionizing the recruiting field. It is cost-effective and allows the firm to reach a broad range of applicants, but it can increase administrative costs.
- Realistic job previews involve telling applicants both the positive and negative aspects of the job. Some applicants may be frightened by this information, but these are people who would not have been successful anyway. The use of realistic job previews has been linked to more positive attitudes about the job, higher performance, and lower turnover rates for a wide variety of jobs.
- Applicants decide which jobs to apply for and to accept based on the extent to which they feel they will fit with the company (in addition to considering basic issues such as compensation, benefits, and terms of employment).
- Selection is one of the most important functions carried out by the HR department.
- No selection system is perfect, and decisions have to be made about which types of errors are the most and the least costly.
- Selection systems should be based on careful job-analysis information.

- Decisions must be made about the basis for selection decisions. It is especially important to decide the extent to which people should be selected on the basis of their fit with the organization.

- Many techniques are available for selecting individuals. Each has advantages and drawbacks. An ideal system would combine several of these techniques into a single system, but there is no one best way to select people, and when any technique is used for making a selection decision, including interviews, it is treated as a "test" for legal purposes and must be validated.

- Using tests that are not valid (and not reliable) is irrational and can lead to serious legal problems.

- Methods are available, all falling under the general category of utility analysis, that can allow an assessment of whether the costs of a selection system are justified by increased productivity or decreased costs.

To see Key Points for Future HR Professionals, please visit 4ltrpress.cengage.com.

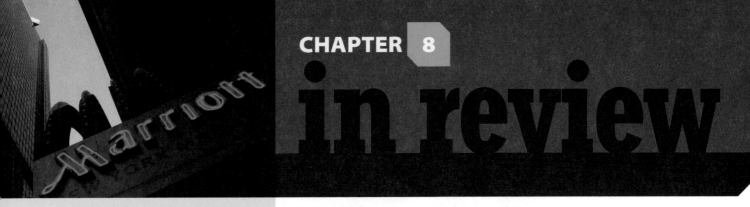

CHAPTER SUMMARY

Diversity exists in a group or organization when its members differ from one another along one or more important dimensions. Diversity is increasing in organizations today because of changing demographics, the desire by organizations to improve their workforces, legal pressures, and increased globalization.

Diversity management and equal employment opportunity may appear to be the same, but they are actually quite different. Equal employment opportunity is intended to eliminate discrimination in the workplace; management diversity focuses on recognizing and accommodating differences among people.

Diversity involves several key dimensions. Four of the more common are age, gender, ethnicity, and disability. The overall age of the workforce is increasing. More women are also entering the workplace, although a glass ceiling still exists in many settings. In the United States, more Hispanics are entering the workplace as the percentage of whites in the general population gradually declines.

Diversity affects organizations in many different ways. It also serves as a force for social change. Many organizations are realizing that diversity can be a major force for competitive advantage. Finally, diversity can also be a significant source of conflict. More recent views of this potential trade-off seem to suggest that further increases in diversity might lead to more positive outcomes and fewer problems with conflict.

Managing diversity in organizations can be done by both individuals and the organization itself. Individual approaches

LEARNING OBJECTIVES

LO1 *Discuss the nature of diversity and distinguish between diversity management and equal employment opportunity.*

LO2 *Identify and describe the major dimensions of diversity in organizations.*

LO3 *Discuss the primary impact of diversity on organizations.*

LO4 *Describe individual and organizational strategies and approaches to coping with diversity and discuss the multicultural organization.*

LO5 *Discuss the basic issues in managing the knowledge function in organizations.*

LO6 *Relate human resource management to social issues.*

KEY TERMS

Diversity *exists in a group or organization when its members differ from one another along one or more important dimensions.*

Diversity management *places a much heavier emphasis on recognizing and appreciating differences among people at work and attempting to provide accommodations for those differences to the extent that is feasible and possible.*

Diversity training *is specifically designed to enable members of an organization to function better in a diverse workplace.*

Equal employment opportunity *means treating people fairly and equitably and taking actions that do not discriminate against people in protected classes on the basis of some illegal criterion.*

Ethnicity *refers to the ethnic composition of a group or organization.*

The **glass ceiling** *describes a barrier that keeps many females from advancing to top management positions in many organizations.*

Knowledge workers *are employees who add value simply because of what they know.*

The **multicultural organization** *is one that has achieved high levels of diversity, can capitalize fully on the advantages of the diversity, and has few diversity-related problems.*

Organizational learning *is the process by which an organization "learns" from past mistakes and adapts to its environment.*

Organizational memory *is the collective, institutional record of past events.*

KEY POINTS FOR FUTURE MANAGERS

- Managing diversity is critical for the company that wants to remain competitive in the new century. Extremely effective diversity management can lead to a strong competitive advantage as a firm becomes more attractive to a broader set of applicants, has easier access to a broader set of markets, and increases creativity within the firm.

- Effective diversity management is a full-time job and requires strong and consistent support from top management.

- Although managing the knowledge function is an organizationwide imperative, human resource managers need to be included in specific issues associated with knowledge workers.

To see Key Points for Future HR Professionals, please visit 4ltrpress.cengage.com.

SUMMARY (Continued)

to dealing with diversity include understanding, empathy, tolerance, and communication. Major organizational approaches are through policies, practices, diversity training, and culture.

Few, if any, organizations have become truly multicultural. The key dimensions that characterize organizations as they eventually achieve this state are pluralism, full structural integration, full integration of the informal network, an absence of prejudice and discrimination, no gap in organizational identification based on a cultural identity group, and low levels of intergroup conflict attributable to diversity. Ultimately, the people of any country with a diverse population such as the United States must decide if a model of pluralism will also work on the national level.

Managers are increasingly recognize that they need to address the knowledge function in their organizations in order to be successful. The knowledge function starts with an understanding of both organizational learning and organizational memory. HR managers may play an especially important role in managing knowledge workers.

Human resource management is also becoming increasingly linked to social issues. Key examples include prison labor, a living wage, immigration, and social responsibility and social entrepreneurship.

CHAPTER SUMMARY

Compensation and benefit programs have several fundamental purposes and objectives. One purpose is to provide an adequate and appropriate reward system for employees so that they feel valued and worthwhile as organizational members and representatives. Firms can adopt one of three basic compensation strategies to help achieve this goal: Pay above-market compensation rates, market compensation rates, or below-market compensation rates. Several different factors contribute to the compensation strategy that a firm develops. The critical source of information that many organizations use in developing compensation strategies is pay surveys.

Once an overall strategy has been chosen, human resource managers must determine what each job should be paid. The starting point here is job evaluation, a method for determining the relative value of a job to the organization so that individuals who perform that job can be compensated adequately and appropriately. Several job-evaluation techniques have been established, although alternative approaches to compensation such as pay for knowledge and skill-based pay are increasingly popular. Continued administration of the wage and salary structure in an organization requires consideration of how to deal with such things as pay secrecy and salary compression.

Benefits take up an ever-larger portion of employers' total compensation costs. Organizations sustain these costs because they believe that competitive benefits packages attract better applicants and help the company retain employees. Although benefits costs are high in the United States, levels of mandated benefits are much higher in Europe

LEARNING OBJECTIVES

LO1 *Describe the basic issues involved in developing a compensation strategy.*

LO2 *Discuss how organizations develop a wage and salary structure.*

LO3 *Identify and describe the basic issues of wage and salary administration.*

LO4 *Discuss the basic considerations in understanding benefit programs.*

LO5 *Identify and describe mandated benefits.*

LO6 *Identify and describe nonmandated benefits.*

LO7 *Discuss contemporary issues in compensation and benefits.*

KEY TERMS

Benefits *generally refer to various rewards, incentives, and other things of value that an organization provides to its employees beyond their wages, salaries, and other forms of direct financial compensation.*

Cafeteria-style benefits plans *allow employees to choose the benefits they really want.*

The **classification system** *for job evaluation attempts to group sets of jobs together into clusters, which are often called grades.*

Compensation *is the set of rewards that organizations provide to individuals in return for their willingness to perform various jobs and tasks within the organization.*

Defined benefit plans *are private pension plans in which the size of the benefit is precisely known and is usually based on a simple formula using input such as years of service.*

Defined contribution plans *are private pension plans in which the size of the benefit depends on how much money is contributed to the plan.*

External equity *in compensation refers to comparisons made by employees to others employed by different organizations performing similar jobs.*

The **factor-comparison method** *for job evaluation assesses jobs, on a factor-by-factor basis, using a factor-comparison scale as a benchmark.*

Internal equity *in compensation refers to comparisons made by employees to other employees within the same organization.*

Job evaluation *is a method for determining the relative value or worth of a job to the organization so that individuals who perform that job can be compensated adequately and appropriately.*

A **maturity curve** *is a schedule specifying the annual increase a person will receive.*

Pay compression *occurs when individuals with substantially different levels of experience, or performance abilities, or both are paid wages or salaries that are relatively equal.*

Pay for knowledge *involves compensating employees for learning specific information.*

In **pay inversion**, *the external market changes so rapidly that new employees are actually paid more than experienced employees.*

Pay secrecy *refers to the extent to which the compensation of any individual in an organization is secret or the extent to which information on compensation is formally made available to other individuals.*

Pay surveys *are surveys of compensation paid to employees by other employers in a particular geographic area, industry, or occupational group.*

The **point manual**, *used to implement the point system of job evaluation, carefully and specifically defines the degrees of points from first to fifth.*

The **point system** *for job evaluation requires managers to quantify, in objective terms, the value of the various elements of specific jobs.*

Private pension plans *are prearranged plans administered by the organization that provide income to employees at their retirement.*

Salary *is income paid to an individual on the basis of performance, not on the basis of time.*

Skill-based pay *rewards employees for acquiring new skills.*

Social security *(officially the* **Old Age Survivors and Disability Insurance Program***) was originally designed to provide limited income to retired individuals to supplement their personal savings, private pensions, part-time work, and so forth.*

Unemployment insurance, *a mandated protection plan, is intended to provide a basic subsistence payment to employees who are between jobs.*

Vesting rights *are guaranteed rights to receive pension benefits.*

Wage and salary administration *is the ongoing process of managing a wage and salary structure.*

Wages *generally refer to hourly compensation paid to operating employees; the basis for wages is time.*

Wellness programs *are special benefits programs that concentrate on keeping employees from becoming sick rather than simply paying expenses when they do become sick.*

Workers' compensation, *another mandated protection program, is insurance that covers individuals who suffer a job-related illness or accident.*

KEY LEGISLATION

The Employee Retirement Income Security Act of 1974 *guarantees a basic minimum payment that employees could expect to be paid upon retirement.*

The Equal Pay Act 1962 *states that men and women who perform essentially the same job must be paid the same.*

The Fair Labor Standards Act *established a minimum hourly wage for jobs; further stipulated that wages for hourly workers must be paid at a rate of one and a half times the normal rate for work in excess of 40 hours per week.*

The Social Security Act of 1935, *among other things, provides social welfare and social insurance coverage for retired workers.*

KEY POINTS FOR FUTURE MANAGERS

- Critical strategic decisions relate to determining what should be paid to employees and what that rate should be relative to market rates.
- The decision concerning what to pay employees for is probably the most critical, and new pay systems such as pay for knowledge and skill-based pay advocate paying employees for what they know rather than what they do.
- All decisions to pay wages and salaries at rates below, above, or at the going market rate should be made with full knowledge of the implications of each decision.
- Indirect compensation and benefits represent a large portion of total compensation costs. Many of the benefits are required by law; others (such as vacations and medical insurance) have become such a strong part of employee expectations that they cannot easily be eliminated.
- Cafeteria-style benefits plans may allow the company to spend its benefits dollars so that the plan has the greatest impact on employee satisfaction, although these plans have some disadvantages.
- Executive compensation and the legal context of compensation and benefits are important issues that affect businesses.
- Communication is a key part of the indirect compensation strategy, but the link between indirect compensation and organizational-level outcomes is unclear.

To see Key Points for Future HR Professionals, please visit 4ltrpress.cengage.com.

SUMMARY (Continued)

and elsewhere. The kinds of benefits that are attractive or appropriate to employees around the world differ considerably. Several laws provide guidelines for how benefits plans should be administered.

Additional laws mandate that all employees must have certain benefits such as Social Security, unemployment insurance, and workers' compensation. In addition, many organizations offer optional protection plans such as health and dental insurance coverage and private pension plans.

Paid time off is another important benefit. The most common forms are vacation time, holidays, religious days, sick leave, and personal time. This benefit, in particular, varies widely from country to country. Organizations are becoming more likely to offer benefits in wellness programs, child care, elder care, and employee assistance programs. Finally, some benefits are services and perks that the employee would otherwise have to pay for.

Because needs and preferences differ, some organizations offer cafeteria-style benefits plans in which the employee gets to choose the benefits desired. Though expensive to run, these programs result in employees getting exactly what they want, which makes the program more cost-effective.

Executive compensation issues have attracted considerable attention in recent years. This attention increased when executives in the financial sector received substantial bonuses even after their firms received large infusions of government bail-out funds in 2009. There are numerous ongoing legal issues that confront managers as they manage their organizations' compensation and benefits programs. Given the enormous cost of compensation and benefits packages, it is important that managers carefully assess the advantages of those packages to the organization to ensure that organizational and employee interests are optimized.

CHAPTER SUMMARY

Performance appraisal and career management are two tools used by organizations to start performance improvement. Performance appraisal is the specific and formal evaluation of an employee. Careers are the set of experiences that one has through his or her work life. The management of that career is critical for employee development.

Performance appraisals are important because they ensure that recruiting and selection processes are adequate. They play an important role in training, helping to link performance with rewards demonstrating that important employment-related decisions are based on performance. They also promote employee motivation and development, providing valuable information to the organization's human resource (HR) planning process.

The organization, primarily through the work of HR, develops the general performance-appraisal process for its managers and employees. The organization is also responsible for ensuring that clear and specific performance standards are available.

Both the rater and the ratee have specific responsibilities. Raters can include the supervisor, peers, colleagues, co-workers, subordinates, the individual him- or herself, and customers and clients. When all of these raters are used, the appraisal is called *360-degree feedback*.

Several methods can be used to assess performance, ranging from ranking systems to rating systems employing behaviorally anchored rating scales (BARS), behavioral observation scales (BOS), and goal-based or management-by-objectives systems. Regardless of the approach used, once the appraisal is completed, the next major activity is the provision of feedback to the employee with the goal of improving performance and guiding the employee's self-development.

LEARNING OBJECTIVES

LO1 *Describe the purposes of performance appraisal in organizations.*

LO2 *Summarize the performance-appraisal process in organizations.*

LO3 *Identify and describe the most common methods that managers use for performance appraisal.*

LO4 *Discuss other general issues involving performance appraisal in organizations.*

LO5 *Describe the nature of careers in organizations.*

LO6 *Discuss human resource management and career management.*

LO7 *Identify and discuss basic career-development issues and challenges.*

KEY TERMS

A **behaviorally anchored rating scale (BARS)** *is an appraisal system that represents a combination of the graphic rating scale and the critical incident method.*

A **behavioral observation scale (BOS)** *is developed from critical incidents like a BARS but uses substantially more critical incidents to define specifically all the measures necessary for effective performance.*

A **career** *is the set of experiences and activities that people engage in related to their job and livelihood over the course of their working life.*

Career counseling *involves interaction between an individual employee or manager in the organization and either a line manager or a human resource manager.*

Contextual performance *refers to tasks an employee does on the job that are not required as part of the job but that still benefit the organization in some way.*

Contrast error *occurs when we compare people against one another instead of against an objective standard.*

The **critical incident method** *relies on instances of especially good or poor performance on the part of the employee.*

The fourth traditional career stage, **disengagement**, *involves the individual gradually beginning to pull away from work in the organization. Priorities change, and work may become less important.*

A **distributional error** *occurs when the rater tends to use only one part of the rating scale.*

The **establishment** *stage of the traditional career model involves creating a meaningful and relevant role in the organization.*

Exploration *is the first traditional career stage and involves identifying interests and opportunities.*

The **forced-distribution method** *involves grouping employees into predefined frequencies of performance ratings.*

A **goal-based** *or* **management-by-objectives (MBO)** *system is based largely on the extent to which individuals meet their personal performance objectives.*

A **graphic rating scale** *consists of a statement or question about some aspect of an individual's job performance.*

A **halo error** *occurs when one positive performance characteristic causes the manager to rate all other aspects of performance positively.*

A **horns error** *occurs when the manager downgrades other aspects of an employee's performance because of a single performance dimension.*

The **individual assessment phase** *of career planning requires that individuals analyze carefully what they perceive to be their own abilities, competencies, skills, and goals.*

The **maintenance** *stage involves optimizing talents or capabilities.*

In the **paired-comparison method** *of performance appraisal, each individual employee is compared with every other individual employee, two at a time.*

A **performance appraisal** *is the specific and formal evaluation of an employee to determine the degree to which the employee is performing his or her job effectively.*

Performance management *is the general set of activities carried out by the organization to change (improve) employee performance.*

The **simple ranking method** *involves having the manager rank-order each member of a particular work group or department from top to bottom or from best to worst.*

In a **360-degree appraisal**, *performance information is gathered from people on all sides of the manager: above, beside, below, and so forth.*

KEY LEGISLATION

The Age Discrimination in Employment Act (or ADEA) *prohibits discrimination against employees over the age of forty.*

KEY POINTS FOR FUTURE MANAGERS

- Appraisal systems should always be designed so that they have the greatest likelihood of improving individual and organizational performance.

- Raters must be convinced that it is in their best interests to be fair and accurate in appraisals. No type of system can replace rater motivation to do a good job.

- Although 360-degree appraisals are popular, evidence does not support their effectiveness relative to other, less-expensive methods, and it is problematic to use 360-degree appraisals for decision making.

- In team settings, decisions must be made about whether appraisals and feedback should focus on the whole team or on individual members.

- Contextual performance refers to those behaviors that we do not evaluate formally but that must occur for the organization to function effectively. Decisions have to be made about how to treat contextual performance.

- Clear evidence shows that one appraisal system is not more effective than any other type of appraisal system, although there is some reason to believe that goal-based systems may offer some advantages over the alternatives.

- Feedback does not always have the desired effect on performance. Sometimes providing feedback can hurt subsequent performance.

- Although the traditional career may be dead, it is still critical to think through and plan an employee's entire career and help the employee to manage that career.

To see Key Points for Future HR Professionals, please visit 4ltrpress.cengage.com.

SUMMARY (Continued)

A career is the set of experiences and activities that people engage in related to their job and livelihood over the course of their working life. Career stages include exploration, establishment, maintenance, and disengagement. A more recent perspective refocuses career stages on career age and acknowledges the likelihood of multiple careers, and it recognizes retirement as a part of career progression.

Career planning requires coordination between individual employees and the organization. Even though career planning is important and beneficial to both organizations and individuals, career planning also has limitations and potential pitfalls.

In many ways, the early career stages are the most tumultuous because new entrants into an organization always feel a certain degree of uncertainty and apprehension about a new employer. An important starting point for HR managers is understanding some of the early career problems that employees often encounter.

After an individual completes the first few years of a job successfully, many of the early career problems may have been addressed. But some problems, such as *midcareer plateau*, still loom for these individuals once they reach the midcareer stage.

In the latter stages of a person's career, it is perhaps even more important for the organization to provide career-management services, such as retirement planning, for the problems people face in the later career stages.

Career-counseling programs are important to an organization interested in career development. Such programs usually address a wide variety of career-related issues, such as dual-career and work-family issues, and are readily accessible to employees.

The success of career management activities can only be judged according to success at any one point in time. If an employee is satisfied with his or her career at one point, then career management must be judged successful up to that point.

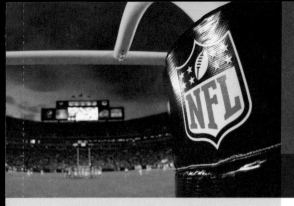

CHAPTER SUMMARY

Labor relations is the process of dealing with employees who are represented by a union. A labor union is a legally constituted group of individuals working together to achieve shared job-related goals. Collective bargaining is the process by which managers and union leaders negotiate acceptable terms and conditions of employment for those workers represented by the unions. The historical formation of U.S. labor unions closely parallels the history of the United States itself. Many laws and other regulations have been passed, some of which are intended to promote unionization and union activities; others are intended to limit or curtail union activities. Like any large organization, labor unions also have structures that facilitate their work.

Since the mid-1950s, labor unions in the United States have experienced increasing difficulty in attracting new members. Indeed, while millions of U.S. workers still belong to labor unions, union membership as a percentage of the total workforce has continued to decline at a steady rate. Unions recognize that they don't have as much power as they once held and that it is in their best interests, as well as the best interests of the workers they represent, to work with management as opposed to working against management. Bargaining perspectives have also altered in recent years.

Employees must follow a specific set of steps if they want to establish a union. First, employees must express some interest in joining a union. If interest exists in forming a union, then the National Labor Relations Board (NLRB) is asked to define the bargaining unit. Once the bargaining unit has been defined,

© Tim Steadman/Icon SMI/Corbis

LEARNING OBJECTIVES

LO1 Describe the role of labor unions in organizations.

LO2 Identify and summarize trends in unionization.

LO3 Discuss the unionization process.

LO4 Describe the collective-bargaining process.

LO5 Discuss how labor agreements are negotiated.

LO6 Describe how impasses get resolved and agreements are administered.

LO7 Discuss emerging labor union issues in the twenty-first century.

KEY TERMS

The **American Federation of Labor (AF of L)** *was another early union; it focused its efforts on improved working conditions and better employment contracts rather than getting involved in legislative and political activities.*

In **arbitration**, *both sides agree in advance that they will accept the recommendations made by an independent third-party arbitrator.*

The **bargaining unit** *refers to the specifically defined group of employees who are eligible for representation by the union.*

A **boycott** *occurs when union members agree not to buy the products of a targeted employer.*

A **closed shop** *refers to a workplace in which only workers who are already union members may be hired by the employer.*

Collective bargaining *is the process by which managers and union leaders negotiate acceptable terms and conditions of employment for those workers represented by the unions.*

Another important early union was the **Congress of Industrial Organizations (CIO)**, *which focused on organizing employees by industry, regardless of their craft, skills, or occupation.*

Under **final-offer arbitration**, *the parties bargain until impasse and then the two parties' final offers are submitted to the arbitrator.*

An **impasse** *is a situation in which one or both parties believe that reaching an agreement is not imminent.*

The **Knights of Labor** *was an important early union that expanded its goals and its membership to include workers in numerous fields rather than a single industry.*

The **Labor Management Relations Act (or Taft-Hartley Act)** *(1947) was a response to public outcries against a wide variety of strikes in the years after World War II; its basic purpose was to curtail and limit union practices.*

Labor relations *is the process of dealing with employees who are represented by a union.*

A **labor union** *is a legally constituted group of individuals working together to achieve shared, job-related goals, including higher pay and shorter working hours.*

The **Landrum-Griffin Act** *(officially called the **Labor Management Reporting and Disclosure Act**) focused on eliminating various unethical, illegal, and undemocratic union practices.*

Locals *are unions organized at the level of a single company, plant, or small geographic region.*

A **lockout** *occurs when an employer denies employees access to the workplace.*

Mandatory items, *including wages, working hours, and benefits, must be included as part of collective bargaining if either party expresses a desire to negotiate one or more of them.*

In **mediation,** *a neutral third party called the mediator listens to and reviews the information presented by both sides and then makes an informed recommendation and provides advice to both parties about what she or he believes should be done.*

The **National Labor Relations Act** *(or* **Wagner Act***) administers most labor law in the United States.*

The **National Labor Relations Board (NLRB)** *administers most labor law in the United States.*

Permissive items *may be included in collective bargaining if both parties agree.*

Picketing *occurs when workers representing the union march at the entrance to the employer's facility with signs explaining their reasons for striking.*

The **shop steward,** *an elected position in a local union, is a regular employee who functions as a liaison between union members and supervisors.*

A **slowdown** *occurs when workers perform their jobs at a much slower pace than normal.*

A **strike** *occurs when employees walk off their jobs and refuse to work.*

A **union shop agreement** *includes various types of union security agreements in addition to a requirement that a nonunion member can be hired, although he or she must join the union within a specified time to keep his or her job.*

A **wildcat strike** *occurs during the course of a labor contract and is usually undertaken in response to a perceived injustice on the part of management.*

KEY LEGISLATION

The Labor Management Relations Act (or Taft-Hartley Act) *curtailed and limited union powers and regulates union actions and their internal affairs in a way that puts them on equal footing with management and organizations.*

The Landrum-Griffin Act (officially called the Labor Management Reporting and Disclosure Act) *focused on the elimination of various unethical, illegal, and/or undemocratic practices within unions themselves.*

The National Labor Relations Act (or Wagner Act) *passed in an effort to control and legislate collective bargaining between organizations and labor unions, to grant power to labor unions, and to put unions on a more equal footing with managers in terms of the rights of employees.*

KEY POINTS FOR FUTURE MANAGERS

- Unions have traditionally played an important role in improving working conditions for U.S. workers, and many workers still view unions in this light. Therefore, if a firm has a union, it may be difficult to vote it out; if a firm does not have a union, it may be more difficult than some managers believe to keep a union out.

- Some firms have found unions to be helpful partners as they explore new ways to organize work, while others have found unions to be tenacious opponents to any change. It is important to think seriously about the kind of relationship management wants to have with unions.

- A well-developed legal framework is in place to guide management in dealing with unions, and enforcement of these laws has been fairly consistent over the years.

- Unions have become effective at calling for social reform, and such actions have increased their popularity in the media.

To see Key Points for Future HR Professionals, please visit 4ltrpress.cengage.com.

SUMMARY (Continued)

organizers must then strive to get 30 percent of the eligible workers within the bargaining unit to sign authorization cards requesting a certification election. If organizers cannot get 30 percent of the workers to sign authorization cards, the unionization process ends. But if the required number of signatures is obtained, then organizers petition the NLRB to conduct an election. If the union becomes certified, its organizers create a set of rules and regulations that will govern the conduct of the union. Under certain conditions, an existing labor union may be decertified.

Collective bargaining involves management representing the employing organization and the labor union representing its employees. The collective-bargaining process is aimed at agreement on a binding labor contract that will define various dimensions of the employment relationship for a specified period of time. One important part of preparing for collective bargaining is prior agreement on the parameters of the bargaining session.

Generally speaking, the negotiation process involves representatives from management and the labor union meeting at agreed-on times and locations and working together to attempt to reach a mutually acceptable labor agreement. A useful framework for understanding the negotiation process is the bargaining zone. Of course, numerous barriers to effective negotiation exist, and several methods are available for both management and labor to use in their attempts to overcome an impasse.

A key clause in the labor contracts negotiated between management and labor defines how the labor agreement will be enforced. Although some enforcement issues are relatively straightforward, others may rely heavily on a formal grievance procedure.

in review

CHAPTER SUMMARY

There are many reasons why modern organizations are more concerned about employee safety and health issues than ever before. Lost work time and increased insurance costs are among the most important of these reasons, but organizations also are very interested in ways of keeping employees safe, healthy, and secure.

As such, organizations are interested in managing the work environment to make it safer. Basic issues involve actions that the organization can and should take to control or eliminate safety hazards and health hazards. Safety hazards refer to those conditions in the work environment that have the potential to cause harm to an employee. Health hazards are those characteristics of the work environment that more slowly and systematically, and perhaps cumulatively, result in damage to an employee's health. OSHA authorized the U.S. government to create and enforce various standards regarding occupational safety and health.

In addition, the actual physical environment in which an employee works is also extremely important. Many aspects of the physical environment may affect an employee's attitudes and behavior on the job and can affect employee health and well-being. Work hours reflect one such aspect. Illumination, temperature, and office and work-space design are also important.

Stress is a person's adaptive response to a stimulus that places excessive psychological or physical demands on him or her. The stimuli that cause stress are called *stressors*. Organizational stressors are various factors in the workplace

Justin Sullivan/Getty Images

LEARNING OBJECTIVES

LO1 *Identify and discuss the central elements associated with employee safety and health.*

LO2 *Describe the basic issues involved in the physical work environment.*

LO3 *Discuss stress and stress-management programs in organizations.*

LO4 *Identify and describe the most important HR-related security issues in organizations.*

KEY TERMS

Burnout *is a general feeling of exhaustion that develops when an individual simultaneously experiences too much pressure and too few sources of satisfaction.*

Circadian rhythms *are natural cycles that indicate when a body needs to eat or sleep.*

Collateral stress programs *are organizational programs created specifically to help employees deal with stress.*

Dysfunctional behavior *refers to any behavior at work that is counterproductive. These behaviors may include theft and sabotage, as well as sexual and racial harassment.*

Hardiness *is an individual difference that allows some individuals to experience less stress when dealing with stressful events, and that makes them more effective in dealing with the stress they do experience.*

Health hazards *are characteristics of the work environment that more slowly and systematically, and perhaps cumulatively, result in damage to an employee's health.*

Institutional programs *for managing stress are undertaken through established organizational mechanisms.*

OSHA *is both the act that authorized the U.S. government to create various standards regarding occupational safety and health and the administrative agency that enforces those standards.*

Safety engineers *are experts who carefully study the workplace, try to identify and isolate particularly dangerous situations, and recommend solutions for dealing with those situations.*

Safety hazards *are conditions in the work environment that have the potential to cause harm to an employee.*

Stress *is a person's adaptive response to a stimulus that places excessive psychological or physical demands on him or her.*

Turnover *refers to people leaving their jobs, whether voluntarily or involuntarily (i.e., through firings).*

The **Type A personality** *is characterized by being highly competitive and highly focused on work with few interests outside of work.*

The **Type B personality** *is characterized as being less aggressive, more patient, and more easygoing. In general, individuals with Type B personalities experience less stress and are less likely to suffer some type of illness because of stress than Type A personalities.*

KEY LEGISLATION

The Occupational Safety and Health Act of 1970 (or OSHA) *grants the federal government the power to establish and enforce occupational safety and health standards for all places of employment directly affecting interstate commerce.*

KEY POINTS FOR FUTURE MANAGERS

- Employee safety is not only a matter of the law but also good business because it reduces costs and increases productivity.

- The physical work environment is critical for productivity, health, safety, and employee attitudes.

- Stress on the job could be the result of job demands, physical demands, role demands, and interpersonal demands.

- Stress can have many negative effects, although there are individual differences in how people experience stress.

- Security concerns at work have become much more important, especially in the United States.

To see Key Points for Future HR Professionals, please visit 4ltrpress.cengage.com.

SUMMARY (Continued)

that can cause stress. Four general sets of organizational stressors are task demands, physical demands, role demands, and interpersonal demands. If the stress is positive, the result may be more energy, enthusiasm, and motivation. Three other sets of consequences that can result from stress are individual consequences, organizational consequences, and burnout. But it is important to note that not everyone experiences stress in the same way, and there are also individual differences in the effects that stress has on employees. Two basic organizational strategies for helping employees manage stress are institutional programs and collateral stress programs. In addition, organizations develop programs to reduce the threat of various diseases at work, including AIDS.

Finally, security concerns have emerged as a real issue for employees. The United States has probably seen the greatest change in stress due to security concerns because such concerns were not salient to Americans in the past. But, especially since the September 11 attacks, U.S. firms have become much more security conscious, as have most Americans.

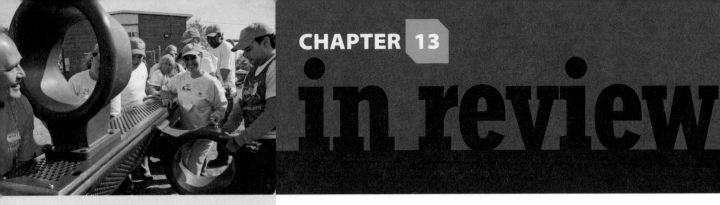

in review

CHAPTER SUMMARY

Motivation refers to the efforts employees exert at work. Individuals' performance is a function of both their ability to perform a task and their motivation to exert effort on that task. Thus, it is critical that human resource managers understand how they might motivate employees to exert effort toward reaching an organization's strategic goals.

There are a number of models or theories of motivation that can provide some help. Need-based theories are more concerned with *what* motivates people, and Maslow's hierarchy of needs is the best known of these theories. The most important lesson a human resource manager can learn from these need theories is that, at any one time, different employees may be motivated by different things as they try to satisfy different needs.

Process theories of motivation are more concerned with *how* people become motivated. Reinforcement theory, expectancy theory, and equity theory are three process theories that can be useful to human resource managers. The insights from these three theories plus the insights from need-based theories can be combined to form a more integrative view of motivation at work. In this view, employees will be motivated to exert effort on their jobs when they believe their effort can lead to improved performance, and that improved performance will be rewarded with outcomes that are fair and that can satisfy basic needs.

Goal theory and agency theory are two other theories of motivation that can be useful to the human resource manager. Finally, it is important to realize that

LEARNING OBJECTIVES

LO1 **Describe the basic model of performance.**

LO2 **Discuss motivation and human needs.**

LO3 **Identify the basic process models of motivation and describe an integrative model of motivation.**

LO4 **Describe other related theories and perspectives on motivation.**

KEY TERMS

Agency theory *addresses potential conflicts of interests among different groups of stakeholders in an organization. The name of the theory, and some of its basic principles, is derived from the fact that, in most modern organizations, the individuals who own a firm do not actually run it on a daily basis. Problems arise when the interests of the owners (the principals) are in conflict with the interests of the managers (agents).*

Behavior modification *is the combination of positive reinforcement with either punishment or extinction that replaces an undesired behavior with a desired behavior.*

Creative behavior *involves doing things at work that are innovative and provide some value for the organization.*

A need-based theory proposed by Frederick Herzberg, **dual factor theory** *identifies motivators and hygiene factors as two sets of conditions at work that can satisfy needs. Research into this theory, however, has provided little empirical support for its model.*

Effort-to-performance expectancy *(or expectancy) is a person's perception of the probability that an increase in effort will result in an increase in performance. This can range from 0 to 1.0.*

A need-based theory of motivation proposed by Clayton Alderfer, **ERG theory** *involves three rather than two levels of needs, and also allows for someone to regress from a higher-level need to a lower-level need.*

Equity theory *is concerned with a person's perceived inputs to a (work) setting and the outcomes received from that setting. The theory suggests that everyone calculates the ratio of inputs to outcomes, similar to considering a return on any investment.*

Expectancy theory *(or VIE theory) is a fairly complex process theory of motivation that casts the employee in the role of decision maker. Basically, an employee decides whether or not to exert effort, depending on the outcomes he or she anticipates receiving for those efforts as based on calculations concerning expectancies, instrumentalities, valences, and the links among these three components.*

Also a term from reinforcement theory, **extinction** *refers to the situation in which a behavior is followed by no consequences and eventually disappears.*

Fixed interval schedules *are interval schedules in which the amount of time that must pass before a reward is given is constant over time.*

Fixed ratio schedules *are ratio schedules in which the number of times a behavior must occur before it is rewarded remains constant over time.*

First proposed by Ed Locke, **goal theory** *is a fairly simple model of motivation based on the premise that people with goals work harder than people without goals. Beyond that, the theory suggests that not all goals are created equal, and that goals that are difficult and yet specific and concrete will motivate employees best.*

Probably the best known of the need-based theories, the **hierarchy of needs** *model proposed by Abraham Maslow specifies five levels of needs that are capable of motivating behavior: physiological, security, social, esteem, and self-actualization.*

Interval schedules *are partial reinforcement schedules in which behavior is reinforced as a function of the passage of time—for example, rewarding someone every 10 minutes as long as they were exhibiting desired behavior.*

Intrinsic motivation *is the motivation to do work because it is interesting, engaging, or possibly challenging rather than because someone is rewarding us to do the work.*

Motivation *determines how a person will exert his or her effort. It represents the forces operating on the person to exert effort, as well as the direction in which that effort will be exerted.*

Need-based theories *are theories of motivation that focus on what motivates a person, rather than on how that motivation occurs.*

Partial reinforcement *means rewarding a behavior only part of the time rather than all the time (it can be applied to punishment as well, but the reward case is simpler).*

Performance-to-outcomes expectancy (or instrumentality) *is a person's perception of the probability that improved performance will lead to certain outcomes. Operationally seen as a correlation coefficient indicating that as performance improves, the chances of gaining outcomes can either go up (a positive correlation), remain unchanged (a zero correlation), or go down (a negative correlation).*

A term from reinforcement theory, **positive reinforcement** *refers to the situation in which a behavior is followed by positive consequences and thus is likely to be repeated.*

According to Maslow's theory, **prepotent** *needs are those specific needs (of the five levels in the model) that are capable of motivating behavior at any given point in time.*

Process theories *are motivation theories that focus on how people become motivated and what they are motivated to do rather than on what motivates them.*

Yet another term from reinforcement theory, **punishment** *refers to a situation in which a behavior is followed by negative consequences and so is not repeated.*

Ratio schedules *are partial reinforcement schedules in which behavior is reinforced as a function of how many times the behavior occurs—for example, rewarding someone every fifth time a desired behavior occurs.*

Reinforcement theory *is a process theory, usually associated with B. F. Skinner, that proposes that all behavior is a function of its consequences.*

Valence *refers to how attractive or unattractive an outcome is for a person.*

Variable interval schedules *are interval schedules in which the amount of time that must pass before a reward is given can change from one reward period to another.*

Variable ratio schedules *are ratio schedules in which the number of times a behavior must occur before it is rewarded changes over time.*

KEY POINTS FOR FUTURE MANAGERS

- Employee motivation is essential for organizational success.
- Reward systems must be designed to motivate the behaviors that the organization really desires.
- Managing employee behavior is easiest when there is a strong link between desired behaviors and outcomes that are important to the employee.
- It *is* possible to motivate employees by increasing intrinsic motivation.
- It *is* possible to increase creativity at work.

To see Key Points for Future HR Professionals, please visit 4ltrpress.cengage.com.

SUMMARY (Continued)

all motivation at work does not follow from the introduction of some type of reward. Intrinsic motivation is an important source of motivation at work, and this motivation is derived from having people work on jobs that are challenging and interesting.

Intrinsic motivation is also related to creative behavior at work, which can be exhibited by almost any employee. Creativity also depends on informative feedback and a climate where it is safe for people to make mistakes.

The most important application of all these theories comes with attempts to enhance performance. The next and final chapter is devoted to discussing various techniques for performance enhancement, and we will discuss and critique each of them from the framework of the various theories of motivation discussed in this chapter.